1948

The First Arab-Israeli War

GENESIS 1948

The First Arab-Israeli War

Dan Kurzman

DA CAPO PRESS • NEW YORK

Library of Congress Cataloging in Publication Data

Kurzman, Dan.
  Genesis 1948 : The first Arab-Israeli war / Dan Kurzman. —
Da Capo ed.
     p.   cm.
  Includes bibliographical references and index.
  ISBN 0-306-80473-5
  1. Israel-Arab War, 1948-1949. I. Title.
DS126.6.K87   1992   91-44131
956.9405'9405'2 — dc20   CIP

First Da Capo Press edition 1992

This Da Capo Press paperback edition of *Genesis 1948* is an
unabridged republication of the edition published in
New York in 1970, with the addition of a new introduction
by Yitzhak Rabin. It is reprinted by arrangement
with Dan Kurzman.

Published by Da Capo Press, Inc.
A Subsidiary of Plenum Publishing Corporation
233 Spring Street, New York, N.Y. 10013

Introduction to the Da Capo Edition

The timing of the new edition of Dan Kurzman's book, *Genesis 1948: The First Arab-Israeli War,* is most appropriate. At this time, when new conditions have arisen and present a genuine opportunity to resolve the Arab-Israeli dispute once and for all, it is necessary to observe and study the roots of the War of Independence, which fostered a new reality in the Middle East.

The State of Israel's War of Independence in 1948-49 was the first declared war in the Arab-Israeli conflict, as well as the most significant war in the history of that conflict. Mr. Kurzman has done a thorough job of research and taken an in-depth look at both the Israeli and Arab sides, enabling him to accurately express the war's true meaning. He has explored both the political-military aspects and the human side of the events that occurred before and during the war.

During 2000 years of exile, Jews prayed for and dreamed of a return to Zion, to the Land of Israel, where they would re-establish an independent Jewish State as a solution to the central problem of the Jewish people, the phenomenon of the wandering Jew with no real roots anywhere in the world.

After the great tragedy of the Jewish people, the systematic annihilation of six million during the Second World War, the urgent need to help the Jews create a state of their own was recognized by some of the most important world leaders, including those of the two superpowers that had triumphed over German Nazism, Italian Fascism, and Japanese imperialism.

Thus, with the British Mandate in Palestine about to end, the United States and the Soviet Union, in what was then a rare display of agreement,

i

jointly backed a United Nations plan to partition the area into two states—Jewish and Arab. Even so, there was an intense struggle within the international community over the question of whether a Jewish State should, in fact, be created.

The Arab world was neither willing nor ready to accept the principle that the Jewish people have a right to a place of their own, let alone a state. And the support of most other countries for the establishment of such a state proved less important than the Arab decision to oppose its birth by force.

If the *Yishuv,* the organized Jewish community in Palestine, had not been able to withstand the Arab violence that began the moment the U.N. partition resolution was passed on November 29, 1947, that decision for a Jewish State would have been meaningless. Most of the world's leaders did not believe that the *Yishuv,* which comprised only 600,000 people, could, standing alone, resist the power of the combined forces of the Arab countries, which threatened to drive the Jews into the sea.

In the first stage of the War of Independence, before the British Mandate ended, the Palestinian Arabs alone launched a struggle against the Jewish community. This was a difficult and painful period in which the Arabs had full freedom to sabotage all transit routes crossing the coastal plains between Tel Aviv and Haifa, and running through the Negev, Jerusalem, and western and northern Galilee.

The main battles in this stage of the war took place in the cities populated by both Jews and Arabs, such as Jerusalem, Haifa, and Tel Aviv-Jaffa, and along the vital arteries where the aim was to isolate Jewish areas from one another. Only in the months of April and May 1948 did the Haganah, which would later become the Israel Defense forces (IDF), make significant gains—though only in Haifa and Tel Aviv-Jaffa. The defenders were less successful in other areas, especially in Jerusalem and the Negev.

The Arab countries did not wait long to act after the end of the British Mandate and the departure of British forces from Palestine on May 15, 1948. The armies of five Arab countries invaded the new State of Israel, hoping to win control of most of former Palestine.

The Egyptian army advanced along two invasion routes. The main one stretched along the coastal road from the Egyptian-Israeli border through Gaza, continuing through Ashkelon and Ashdod to Yavneh, 20 kilometers from Tel Aviv. The second column advanced towards Beersheba in the direction of Hebron and reached southern Jerusalem, including Kibbutz Ramat-Rachel.

After The Jordanian and Iraqi armies gained control over what was later called the "West Bank," the Jordanians sought to conquer Jerusalem and Tel Aviv as well. They succeeded in capturing Lod Airport, which today is Israel's main airport, and advanced to a point only 10 kilometers from Tel Aviv.

Meanwhile, the Iraqi army attacked in the area north of the Jordanian battle zone, planning to sever the Haifa-Tel Aviv road and reach the sea, but this drive failed. The Syrian army invaded Israel just south of the Sea of Galilee, advancing to the gates of Kibbutz Degania, where it, too, was stopped. And the Lebanese army, together with an independent Arab force under Fawzi el-Kaoukji, took over the center of western Galilee, including the city of Nazareth.

The counterattack against the invading Arab armies was hard and bitter. Many Jewish settlements fell to the Egyptian army along the invasion route leading to Yavneh, while others, northeast and south of Jerusalem, were overrun by the Jordanians. Only with the cease-fire of June 11, 1948, did the Arab armies halt their advance.

After a month's lull, however, the IDF went on the attack. And during ten days of battle, it succeeded in liberating Lod and Ramle and in securing the roads connecting the coastal region to besieged Jersualem. It also liberated western Galilee in a swift military operation that forced the Lebanese and independent Arab forces to retreat into Lebanon. Latrun, however, remained in Jordanian hands.

After a second cease-fire that ended in October 1948, the IDF launched a general attack on the Egyptian forces, liberating Beersheba and lifting the siege of the Negev. At the end of December, the Israelis carried out an additional campaign against the Egyptians that removed them from all of Israel, though some remained in the Gaza Strip. This retreat and the trapping of a third of the Egyptian army without any possibility of rescue induced the Egyptian government to seek an end to the war.

And so Egypt agreed to negotiate a final cease-fire accord with Israel under the auspices of the U.N., the first Arab state to do so. Israel's decision to concentrate its main effort in the last stages of the war against Egypt, the leading country in the Arab world, thus bore fruit. Before signing the accord, however, Israel launched one last military operation that ensured its control over the whole Negev, including Eilat. It then signed. Shortly, all of Israel's other Arab neighbors — Jordan, Syria, and Lebanon — also signed such agreements.

The War of Independence was the most important Jewish war since the destruction of the Second Temple. It was also the longest and most agonizing war in Israel's history. Six thousand Jewish civilians and soldiers were killed in the fighting, constituting one percent of the entire Jewish community in Israel at the time.

If the purpose of the War of Independence was to establish a Jewish State in the Middle East that would coexist in peace and security with its neighbors, then that war has not yet ended. The roots of this endless conflict are to be found in the unwillingness of the Arab world to recognize the State of Israel, or even to accept its existence as a sovereign Jewish State.

The peace treaty with Egypt, though not producing peace in the full sense of the word, was a milestone and a turning point in the attitude toward Israel of at least one country in the Arab world. Let us hope that the rulers of other Arab countries and the leaders of the Palestinian Arabs living in the occupied territories will follow in the footsteps of Egypt. Only then will Israel's War of Independence finally draw to a close.

—Yitzhak Rabin
Jerusalem
November 1992

To Bunny and Sol

Contents

List of Maps

Preface

This book tells for the first time the full epic story of the initial Arab-Israeli war and the events leading up to it. Lasting from November, 1947, to March, 1949, that conflict gave birth not only to the State of Israel after 2,000 years of Jewish dispersion, but to one of the most explosive international problems since World War II. Today, more than four decades later, the Arabs and Israelis are still locked in mortal combat—fighting the war that started in 1947.

The Suez War of 1956, the Six Day War of 1967, and the Yom Kippur War of 1973 were massive eruptions of that encounter; the Arab terrorism and uprising and the Israeli retaliatory strikes have been simmering manifestations of it. This war without end escalated into a major threat of confrontation between the Soviet Union, which supported the Arabs, and the United States, which is committed to Israel's survival. Recent events in the Soviet Union eliminated that threat, but the blood continues to flow, with only Egypt at peace with Israel.

Today's headlines are thus rooted in the original struggle of a nation in the throes of violent rebirth, as are the policies of many current Middle Eastern leaders who participated in that struggle. The events explored in this book, therefore, shed a revealing light on the character of the present continuing crisis, and may hint of the future.

The unusually dramatic nature of these events can be attributed largely to the amateur conduct of the initial war. During the first period of fighting from November, 1947, to the invasion of Palestine by regular Arab armies in May, 1948, civilian villagers faced each other armed with little more than rifles, grenades, and homemade Stens. Teen-aged Jewish girls, and even children of ten and eleven, fought side by side with the men; and Arab peasants with hardly a day's military training blindly stormed Jewish settlements.

Even after the invasion, neither side showed any degree of military professionalism—with the exception of Jordan's British-commanded Arab Legion. The invaders came with artillery, tanks, and planes, but for the most part did not know how to use them effectively. And the Israelis, who received substantial arms shipments from abroad only in the midst of battle, owed many of their victories more to an unyielding spirit than to military equipment or proficiency.

The result was a tragi-comic war in which thousands died needlessly in ill-conceived attacks; in which prisoners were commonly killed after capture; in which field commanders deliberately disobeyed the orders of their superiors; in which battles were won because a Molotov cocktail luckily struck a leading tank, or lost because fighters on the same side did not understand each other's language.

The cost of this war of blunders and raw courage was exorbitant. The Israeli dead numbered from 7,000 to 10,000, more than one out of every hundred Jews living in Israel at that time. And the Arab toll was even higher. By contrast, the Israelis lost only about 800 dead out of a population of 2.5 million in the Six Day War, which revealed the once amateur Israeli army to have become perhaps the greatest, man for man, in the world.

Odd as it may seem, considering its historical significance and dramatic character, little has been written about the first war. It has been difficult indeed to obtain detailed information about it. The Arabs have understandably been reluctant to publicize the story of their defeat. And the Israelis, having created an illegal underground army during the British mandate, are traditionally hypersensitive to the publication of material related to their military tactics and thinking. Both sides, moreover, have been less than anxious to stress the internal political factionalism that so greatly weakened them, a disunity that constitutes a major thread running throughout this book.

I am grateful for having won far greater cooperation from the belligerent governments than a writer on this subject can normally expect. Even so, I owe much of my success in learning the facts to the willingness of many individuals to tell me their personal stories and furnish me with diaries and other valuable documents. On the Israeli side, a large proportion of official documents from the first war remain in the hands of individual commanders and politicians, since the newborn state did not have an organized message-filing system.

I was particularly fortunate to have completed my research in the Arab States just before the Six Day War—I conducted my last interview in Beirut the day before it began—since restrictions on information and contacts with officers were severely tightened following that conflict. (I put my book aside temporarily to cover the Six Day War for *The Washington Post*.)

In order to grasp the full scope of the original struggle, during almost three years spent on this book I interviewed nearly 1,000 people in the Arab States, Israel, the United States, Great Britain, France, and Italy; and read over 300 books—including many that had to be translated from Arabic and Hebrew—as well as innumerable diaries, newspapers, magazines, and pamphlets, in addition to official documents.

I have checked every fact to the extent possible, and discarded any questionable information that could not be verified. In the case of conflicting and irreconcilable accounts of events, I generally present them all with their sources. Quotations and reflections are taken from documentary material or personal interviews.

Using the techniques of the novelist and biographer, without resort to fictionalization, I have tried to bring history alive. To an important degree, history is the story of people; and this book describes their role in one of the most poignant and important stories of our time.

DAN KURZMAN

Acknowledgments

In preparing this book, I was especially fortunate to have the assistance of Florence Knopf (later my wife), a brilliant young editor whose imaginative suggestions on the handling of research material proved invaluable. Miss Knopf also helped in the massive research task. It would be difficult to express fully the depth of my gratitude to her.

I also wish to thank Jack Bresler and Malka Gruenberg for their expert translations of Hebrew works into English (Jack helped greatly with the research as well); Victor Saka and Shoukri Alawy for their excellent translations of Arabic works; Ligia Chavez, Judy Crillo, and Katharine Penson for their generous and warm-hearted editorial assistance; Richard Deane Taylor, one of America's finest artists, for agreeing to draw the maps in this book; and Ruth Aley, my agent, for her constant encouragement and wise counsel.

Others to whom I am indebted for facilitating my research include: Helmy Allam, United Arab Republic Information Department; Yehia Abu Bakr, Arab League Information Department; Lt. Colonel Eli Bar-Lev, Israeli Defense Ministry Information Department; Colonel Rafael Effrat, chief, Israeli Defense Ministry Information Department; Nabil Elleissy, United Arab Republic Information Department; Avahim Ezzidim, chief, Jordan Information Department; Dan Garcia, press attaché, American Embassy, Cairo; Mohammed Habib, press attaché, United Arab Republic Embassy, Washington, D. C.; Dr. Abraham Laufer, son of the hospital director in the Old City Jewish Quarter; Salim Odeh, Jordan Information Department; Dan Pattir, press attaché, Israeli Embassy, Washington, D. C.; Victor

Perry, Israeli newspaper and public relations writer; Colonel Gershon Rivlin, editor of the Israeli military publication, *Maarachot;* Charles Rizik, director-general, Lebanese Information Ministry; David Roberts, press attaché, American Embassy, Beirut; Richard Ross, United States Information Service, Jerusalem; Ghazi Saudi, Jordan Information Department; Lt. Colonel Zrubaval Shalev, Israeli Defense Ministry Information Department; Mattatyahu Sharon, press attaché, Israeli Embassy, London; Harlie Smith, American Embassy, Beirut.

Among the persons who were kind enough to grant me personal interviews (identified by the positions they held during the war) were:

MOHAMMED ABUFARA—*Arab resident of Surif in Hebron hills;* HAJ MOUSSA ABU GHOSH—*an elder in Arab village of Abu Ghosh near Jerusalem;* BENJAMIN ADIN—*driver for Hadassah Hospital;* YIGAL ALLON— *Palmach commander;* MOHAMMED ABDEL AREF—*Egyptian soldier;* SAMUEL ARIEL—*Irgun official in Paris;* REUBEN ARONOVICH—*Haganah official and captain of the* Exodus; MAJID ASLAN—*Lebanese Minister of Defense;* SONYA ASTRAKAN—*Hadassah Hospital nurse;* SHIMON AVIDAN— *Givati Brigade commander;* URI AVNERI—*Israeli soldier and journalist;* EHUD AVRIEL—*Israeli arms procurer in Europe;* BENJAMIN AVRUNIN— *member of Kibbutz Mishmar Ha'emek;* ABDUL RAHMAN AZZAM PASHA— *secretary-general of Arab League;* OTHMAN BADRAN—*Palestinian Arab fighter;* HARDING F. BANCROFT—*State Department official;* ABDEL BARI— *mukhtar of southern Jaffa;* NAOMI BARKAY—*member of Kibbutz Mishmar Ha'emek;* CHAIM BASOK—*Israeli soldier;* BERNARD BECKHOEFFER—*State Department legal adviser;* MOSHE BEGINSKY—*Palmach soldier;* MENACHEM BEGIN—*commander, Irgun Zvai Leumi;* CHANAN BELKIND—*commander, Kibbutz Degania A;* MICHAEL BEN-AMI—*Irgun official;* LEA BENDOR—*a* Palestine Post *editor;* MICHAEL BEN-GAL—*Tel Aviv commander;* DAVID BEN-GURION—*Prime Minister of Israel;* PAULA BEN-GURION—*the Prime Minister's wife;* ISAAC BEN-OVADIA—*Haganah agent and son of Abed and Mathilda Muhtaseb;* NETIVA BEN-YEHUDA—*Palmach soldier;* LEONARD BERNSTEIN—*American conductor and composer who entertained Israeli troops;* NAHUM BERNSTEIN—*American lawyer working for Haganah;* COLONEL H. C. BLACKDEN—*British officer in Arab Legion;* PHILIP BOCK—*American Haganah soldier;* RACHEL BRADA—*Palmach soldier;* MUNIO BRANDWEIN—*field commander, Kibbutz Yad Mordechai;* MOSHE BRODETSKY—*American Irgun soldier;* ALEXANDER BROIDA— *Haganah officer (aide to Colonel Marcus);* CAPTAIN NIGEL BROMAGE— *British officer in Arab Legion;* WILLIAM BURDETT—*State Department official;* MOSHE CARMEL—*Israeli commander, northern front;* ISRAEL CARMI —*Negev Brigade officer;* EMANUEL CELLER—*congressman from New York;* AMOS CHOREV—*Harel Brigade officer;* CLARK CLIFFORD—*adviser* to President Truman; BENJAMIN COHEN—*adviser to State Department and American delegate to United Nations;* JOSHUA COHEN—*Stern Group officer in Jerusalem;* MULAH COHEN—*Yiftach Brigade commander;* YERO-HAM COHEN—*Palmach officer (aide to Allon);* HERBERT J. CUMMINGS—*American diplomat in Israel;* SIR ALAN CUNNINGHAM—*British High Commissioner in Palestine;* Captain D.—*Israeli officer;* EZRA DANIN—*Israeli specialist in Arab affairs;* AISHA DARWISH—*resident of Deir Yassin near Jerusalem;* AHARON DAVIDI—*Negev Brigade communications officer;* MOSHE DAYAN—*Israeli commander in Jerusalem (who would not discuss his own experiences but referred me to excellent sources);* CARTER DAVIDSON—*Associated Press correspondent in Jerusalem;* EDUARD DEPREUSE—*French Minister of the Interior;* KHALIL DIAB—*Arab resident of Tiberias;* RAUL DIEZ DE MEDINA—*Bolivian member of United Nations Palestine Commission;* YAACOV DORI—*chief of staff, Army of Israel;* ABBA EBAN—*Israeli delegate to United Nations;* YAACOV EDELSTEIN—*member of Kibbutz Kfar Etzion;* MENASHE EICHLER—*Orthodox member of Stern Group;* ELIAHU ELATH—*Israeli representative in Washington;* EZRA EL-NAKAM—*member of Stern Group;* DAN EVEN—*commander, Alexandroni Brigade;* ENRIQUE RODRIGUEZ FABREGAT—*Uruguayan delegate to United Nations;* MUNIR ABU FADIL—*Palestine Arab commander;* AMIHAI FAG-LIN—*chief of operations, Irgun Zvai Leumi;* MONROE FEIN—*American captain of the* Altalena; ALIZA FEUCHTWANGER (BEGINSKY)—*Palmach radio operator, Kfar Etzion;* MICHAEL FLANAGAN—*Irish sergeant who fought with Israelis;* SHIMON FORSCHER—*commander, Kibbutz Beeirot Yitzhak;* NATHAN FRIEDMAN-YELLIN (later YELLIN-MOR)—*commander, Stern Group;* SHLOMO FREIDRICH—*French supporter of Haganah operations;* ISRAEL GALILI—*Haganah commander;* LIEUTENANT SAAD EL-GAMMAL—*Egyptian officer;* SIMON GARFEH—*Greek Orthodox Archimandrite of Lydda;* MORDECHAI GAZIT—*Etzioni Brigade officer;* BAHJAT GHARBIEH—*Palestine Arab officer;* GRETA GHARBIEH—*wife of Mohammed Gharbieh;* MOHAMMED GHARBIEH—*Palestine Arab officer;* EMILE AL-GHOURI—*assistant to Grand Mufti of Jerusalem;* ZVI GILAT—*battalion commander, Israeli 7th Brigade;* YOEL GISES—*member of Kibbutz Negba;* GIRSHON GIVONI—*member of Kibbutz Yad Mordechai;* MIRA GIVONI—*wife of Girshon;* SIR JOHN BAGOT GLUBB PASHA—*commander, Arab Legion;* STANLEY GOLDFOOT—*Stern Group officer;* COLONEL DES-MOND GOLDIE—*British officer in Arab Legion;* NAHUM GOLDMANN—*member of Jewish Agency Executive;* DAVID GOTTLIEB—*Stern Group officer;* ERNEST GROSS—*State Department adviser;* YITZHAK GRUEN-BAUM—*Israeli Minister of the Interior;* ABRAHAM HALPERIN—*commander of Old City Jewish Quarter;* GOTTFRIED HAMMER—*American Jewish Agency official;* YOUSIF HANNA—*Palestine Arab journalist;* RAMZI HARARAH—*Arab resident of Haifa;* RAYMOND HARE—*member of United*

States delegation to United Nations; LEE HARRIS—*American adviser to
Prime Minister Ben-Gurion;* LOY HENDERSON—*State Department official;*
CHAIM HERZOG—*Israeli chief of intelligence;* ISMAIL HIJAZI—*Palestine
Arab official;* ISSAHAR HIRSCHLER—*member of Kibbutz Nitzanim;* HAMDI
HIRZALLAH—*assistant postmaster in Beersheba;* SHABA'AN HISSI—*Arab
resident of Jaffa;* SHALOM HOCKBAUM—*member of Kibbutz Degania A;*
ARTHUR HOLZMAN—*Columbia Broadcasting System correspondent in
Israel;* SHEIKH MOHAMMED ALI JABARY—*Mayor of Hebron;* SHEIKH
KHALIL JABER—*resident of Deir Yassin;* AMINEH SALIM KNABEH JABER
—*Sheikh Jaber's wife;* IBRAHIM JADALLAH—*Palestine Arab fighter;*
MOHAMMED JADALLAH—*Palestine Arab fighter;* MALKA (TOPSY) JAFFET
Irgun nurse and later Captain Fein's wife; JUDITH JAHARAN—*Israeli
fighter in Old City Jewish Quarter;* SIR BARNETT JANNER—*British mem-
ber of Parliament;* JULIUS JARCHO—*director of American underground
military procurement;* JOSEPH JOHNSON—*adviser to State Department;*
BRIGADIER SIR CHARLES JONES—*British commander in Jerusalem;*
GEORGE LEWIS JONES—*American diplomat in London;* DOV JOSEPH—
military governor, New City of Jerusalem; FAWZI EL-KAOUKJI—*com-
mander, Arab Liberation Army;* HAMED KASHASH—*businessman in
Ramle;* MOHAMMED KASSIM—*resident of Deir Yassin;* SHMUEL KATZ—
Irgun official; JOSHUA KATZIR—*member of Kibbutz Yad Mordechai;*
MOSHE KELMAN—*battalion commander, Yiftach Brigade;* CAPTAIN
MOHAMMED KHAFAGY—*Egyptian artillery officer;* SIR ALEC KIRKBRIDE
—*British Minister to Jordan;* CHAVA KIRSHENBAUM (LAPIDOT)—*nurse
and assistant to Commander Rousnak in Old City Jewish Quarter;* ELIAS
KOUSSA—*Arab notable in Haifa;* ABBA KOVNER—*educational officer,
Givati Brigade;* LOLA KRAMARSKY—*American Zionist leader;* ZVI KRAU-
SHAR—*American Irgun soldier;* HAFEZ ABU KUWAIK—*mukhtar of north-
ern Lydda;* YEHUDA LAPIDOT—*Irgun officer;* CHAIM LASKOV—*battalion
commander, Israeli 7th Brigade;* MARLIN LEVIN—*American reporter on
Palestine Post;* ELIEZER LINSKI—*Palmach soldier charged with accidental
killing of Colonel Marcus;* JOSEPH LINTON—*assistant to Chaim Weiz-
mann;* SIDNEY LURIA—*American Jewish Agency adviser;* TED LURIE—
editor, Palestine Post; ROBERT MACATEE—*American Consul in Jeru-
salem;* LT. COLONEL HABIS MAJALIS—*regimental commander, Arab
Legion;* MORDECHAI MAKLEFF—*commander, Carmeli Brigade;* SIR JOHN
MARTIN—*British Colonial Office official;* ROBERT McCLINTOCK—*State
Department official;* GENERAL SIR GORDON McMILLAN—*commander,
British forces in Palestine;* GOLDA MEIR—*Israeli political leader;* MEIR
MAIVAR—*commander, local Jewish forces in Safed;* RIKA MENACHE—
Haganah soldier in Old City Jewish Quarter; YAACOV MERIDOR—*deputy
commander, Irgun Zvai Leumi;* SAMUEL MERLIN—*Irgun official;* YOHA-
NAN MEROY—*Israeli official;* GRISHA MIRHOV—*commander, Kibbutz Yad*

Mordechai; SAID MUFTI—*aide to King Abdullah;* CAPTAIN ZAKARAYA MUHIEDDIN—*Egyptian officer (and fellow conspirator with Gamal Abdel Nasser);* MATHILDA MUHTASEB—*Jewish wife of Arab nationalist;* MAJOR HAYDAR MUSTAFA—*Arab Legion officer;* UZI NARKIS—*Harel Brigade officer;* ROBERT NATHAN—*American legal adviser to Jewish Agency;* ISSAR NATHANSON—*Irgun commander in Old City Jewish Quarter;* ABDULLAH OMARI—*aide to Palestine Arab commander Abd el-Kader el-Husseini;* GABRIEL PADON—*Israeli official;* YOSHUA PALMON—*Israeli specialist in Arab affairs;* ESTHER PASSMAN-EPSTEIN—*Hadassah Hospital nurse;* AKIBA PELED—*member of Kibbutz Nitzanim;* MATTITYAHU PELED—*Givati Brigade officer;* MOSHE PELEG—*Palmach soldier who fought at Nitzanim;* MICHA PERI—*Palmach officer;* YAACOV PRULOV—*battalion commander, Givati Brigade;* YITZHAK RABIN—*deputy to Allon;* AHMAD RADWAN—*resident of Deir Yassin;* AZIZA RADWAN—*mother of Ahmad Radwan;* NAZEEHA RADWAN—*resident of Deir Yassin;* SHULAMITH RAM—*member of Kibbutz Nirim;* MORDECHAI RAANAN—*Irgun commander in Jerusalem;* KASIM AL-RIMAWY—*Palestine Arab leader;* JOHN ROSS—*member of American delegation to United Nations;* BEN ROTTENSTEIN—*American Irgun soldier;* CAPTAIN MAHMOUD AL-ROUSAN—*Arab Legion officer;* MOSHE ROUSNAK—*Haganah commander in Old City Jewish Quarter;* DESMOND RUTLEDGE (later ZVI RIMER)—*British sergeant who fought with Israelis;* MIRIAM RUTLEDGE—*Desmond's Israeli wife;* GENERAL FUAD SADEK—*supreme commander, Egyptian forces in Palestine;* IRENE SAK—*resident of New City of Jerusalem;* NAHUM SARIG—*commander, Negev Brigade;* ELIAHU SASSON—*Israeli specialist in Arab affairs;* YESHURIN SCHIFF—*Etzioni Brigade officer;* ARON SCHNEIDER—*member of Kibbutz Negba;* AL SCHWIMMER—*American procurer of aircraft for Israel;* ADA SERENI—*chief Haganah agent in Italy;* DAVID SHALTIEL—*commander, Etzioni Brigade in Jerusalem;* SHLOMO SHAMIR—*commander, Israeli 7th Brigade;* AHMAD SHANNAK—*Arab fighter in village of Surif;* MOSHE SHAPIRO—*Israeli cabinet member;* YAACOV S. SHAPIRO—*Israeli lawyer and Attorney General;* GENERAL SHUQUAR SHAWKAT—*commander-in-chief, Syrian army;* ISRAEL SHEIB—*ideological chief, Stern Group;* ADINA SHIRION (ARGAMAN)—*nurse in Old City Jewish Quarter;* HASSAN SHUBLAQ—*Palestine Arab fighter;* NAYEF SHUBLAQ—*Palestine Arab fighter;* AHMED SHUKAIRY—*Palestine Arab official;* PAUL SHULMAN—*American commander of Israeli navy;* MOSHE SNEH—*Haganah commander (preceding Galili);* RUDOLF SONNENBORN—*American industrialist and organizer of underground aid for Israel;* WELLES STABLER—*American Consul-General in Amman;* MAJ. GENERAL SIR HUGH STOCKWELL—*British commander of northern Palestine;* YOSEF TABENKIN—*commander, Harel Brigade;* HIND AZMI TAHA—*daughter of Abed and Mathilda Muhtaseb;* AVRAHAM TAMIR—*Palmach officer;* YAACOV TANGY—*Haganah soldier in*

Old City Jewish Quarter; SHAUL TAWIL—*Haganah officer in Old City Jewish Quarter;* COLONEL ABDULLAH TEL—*commander and then Military Governor of Old City;* WASFI TEL—*Arab Legion officer;* MUSTAFA SAID TURK—*Arab policeman in Haifa;* HAMADA HASSAN USROF—*Arab resident of Jaffa;* LT. COLONEL ROBERT W. VAN DE VELDE—*military attaché, American Mission in Israel;* BERTHA SPAFFORD VESTER—*American sponsor of orphanage in Old City;* MASHA WEINGARTEN (KAPLAN) —*daughter of Rabbi Weingarten of Old City Jewish Quarter;* RIVCA WEINGARTEN (DAGANI)—*daughter of Rabbi Weingarten;* YEHUDIT WEINGARTEN (KAMMAR)—*daughter of Rabbi Weingarten;* DAVID WHITING— *American businessman in Old City;* YIGAL YADIN—*acting chief of staff, Army of Israel;* YAACOV YANNAI—*commander, Israeli Signal Corps;* FANNI YASSKY—*wife of Hadassah Hospital director Chaim Yassky;* YEHUDA YEVZORI—*commander, Kibbutz Mishmar Ha'emek;* YITZHAK YIZERNITZKY—*Stern Group leader;* RECHAVAM ZE'EVY (GANDHI)—*Palmach officer;* YEHOSHUA ZETLER—*commander of Stern Group in Jerusalem;* and ALEXANDER ZVILLI—*linotype operator,* Palestine Post.

Some years before I decided to write this book, I interviewed Haj Amin el-Husseini, the Grand Mufti of Jerusalem and Palestine Arab leader; Moshe Sharett, the Israeli Foreign Minister (and later Prime Minister); and Colonel Adib Shishekly, the Syrian commander in the Arab Liberation Army (and later President of Syria). Although these interviews did not principally concern the 1948 war, they provided information that has been incorporated into this work.

A considerable number of persons missing from the above acknowledgments deserve to be listed, but either they requested anonymity or I felt that their identification might be harmful to them. To these individuals, and to all others who contributed to this book but are not mentioned here, I express my deepest appreciation.

PART I

THE CIVIL WAR

Prologue

WHAT'S the matter with you? Can't you see they're burning and pillaging? Why don't you do something?"

Richard Graves, British Mayor of Jerusalem, was remonstrating furiously with British policemen in the midst of a swirling crowd of rioters in Allenby Square, the center of Jerusalem's New City. But in vain.

"I'm sorry, sir," one of them replied, "but we have orders not to interfere until we are reinforced."

Graves looked at him in shocked disbelief. What had started out on that crisp morning of December 2, 1947, as a peaceful Arab demonstration —to mark the start of a three-day protest strike against a United Nations decision to partition Palestine—had turned into a frenzied orgy of destruction.

Howling Arab mobs were breaking into Jewish shops and setting them on fire; already the sky was black with ash. The people had gone mad, thought Graves, as he watched his shoemaker's shop disappear in a fountain of flame. And the British police were just standing around refusing to interfere, though the mobs, he felt, could be dispersed with a "swish of canes." He could understand the bitterness of the British forces toward Jewish terrorists who had killed and maimed so many of their number. But it was shameful to permit these young hooligans to destroy whole areas senselessly at a time of such shortage.

In nearby Government House, Lieutenant General Sir Alan Cunningham, High Commissioner for Palestine, was equally shocked when he received reports that British police were permitting the destruction. He or-

3

dered an immediate crackdown on the mobs. He also called the leaders of the Arab Higher Committee, which represented the Arab community, and demanded that they intervene; but a spokesman answered that the Arabs were not responsible for the disorders, since they had been provoked by Jewish outbursts of jubilance after the United Nations partition vote.

There was something to that, thought Cunningham, a pink-cheeked English gentleman who had spent much of his time since coming to Palestine in 1946 pleading with both Arab and Jew not to provoke each other— while receiving almost no help from London. Now he rose from his desk to walk to a window overlooking the jumble of ancient and modern buildings that was Jerusalem. If only his superiors had listened to him when he had advocated partition a year before. He had warned them then that time was running out. But the only reply had been blistering criticism from Field Marshal Montgomery (the army Chief of Staff) for not cracking down harder on the Jews to snuff out terrorism.

Seven years earlier, Cunningham had been at the pinnacle of his career; his troops had stormed into Addis Ababa, knocking out Mussolini's Central African empire, and had then attacked General Rommel's forces to pave the way for victory at Tobruk. His reward had been Palestine. "You haven't given me any directives," he had complained to the colonial secretary before leaving London. "It's not our custom to give directives on Palestine," was the answer. And this proved to be the most illuminating guidance the General was to receive.

Was this just the beginning, Cunningham wondered as he watched the sky blacken. Was the Holy City, revered source of modern civilization, about to become a great battleground? What an inglorious ending to his regime. . . .

I

The Conception

THE ending had begun on February 18, 1947, when Foreign Secretary Ernest Bevin rose ponderously to the rostrum in the House of Commons and announced with curdled resignation: "We have . . . reached the conclusion that the only course now open to us is to submit the [Palestine] problem to the judgment of the United Nations. . . . We shall then ask the United Nations . . . to recommend a settlement . . ."

Bevin was apparently convinced that the United Nations would only too readily refer so hot a diplomatic issue straight back to Britain—obligingly giving her complete freedom to impose a solution favorable to what he believed were the West's strategic interests. The best solution, in his view, would be to establish a new British trusteeship, or else a unitary Arab State that would be either absorbed or dominated by Transjordan, a British client, with the Jews being given internal autonomy. Fringe zones of Palestine might be thrown to other hungry Arab countries.

The postwar road to Bevin's decision was paved with bitter diplomatic failures. Ironically, the Jewish Agency of Palestine, the shadow Jewish government, had rejoiced when the Labour Party had come to power in Britain in 1945, for this party had traditionally supported Zionism and, during World War II, had actually embarrassed the Jews by demanding that the Arabs leave Palestine to make way for Jewish immigration. Even after the Labour victory, Prime Minister Clement Attlee had expressed the view to Zionist leaders that not only should there be a Jewish "national home" but that it should include Transjordan. But within months, Britain was to consider it more practical for Transjordan to control the Jews.

5

As Harold Beeley, suave *eminence grise* behind Bevin on Middle Eastern policy, explained to Richard H. Crossman, a Labour member of Parliament: "The Palestine issue must be seen in the context of Soviet expansionism. The Russians plan to move into the Middle East. Britain, with American support if possible, must establish a *cordon sanitaire* of Arab States. Palestine, as an Arab State, would be a strong link in this chain"—the other links being Transjordan, Egypt, and Iraq, reinforced by British positions in Libya, Sudan, the Suez Canal Zone, and the Persian Gulf.

But President Truman was not persuaded by this logic, which coincided with that of many top State Department officials. His skepticism was rooted partly in the American Jewish voting potential, but also in other factors. He had not been overly impressed by the strength of the Arab "links" during World War II, when most Arabs were pro-Nazi despite British imposition of immigration restrictions on the Jews. At the same time, he was deeply moved by the plight of the 100,000 Jewish refugees who languished without home or hope in Displaced Persons camps throughout Europe—a sentiment reinforced by the report of an American envoy, Earl Harrison, who had investigated the refugee problem and recommended in September, 1945, that Palestine open her doors to 100,000 of them.

When the President publicly agreed with Harrison's recommendation, Bevin and Prime Minister Attlee were both infuriated. They accused the United States of trying to dictate Palestine policy to Britain while refusing to assume any of the responsibility for this policy or for Middle Eastern security. Bevin then persuaded the United States to join an Anglo-American Commission of Inquiry, certain that this group would support Britain's anti-Zionist policies. But after long hearings in Palestine and the Displaced Persons camps, the commission unanimously called for the immediate entry of the refugees into the Holy Land, among other measures.

Though Bevin had promised to accept any unanimous recommendations, he rejected the refugee proposal and berated Truman for singling out this provision for acceptance while ignoring others that rejected partition and called for a United Nations trusteeship. The President, he charged, had wrecked all chances for an Arab-Jewish agreement by giving the Jews hope that they could get more without such an accord. The President wanted to dispatch the refugees to Palestine, scoffed Bevin at a Labour Party Conference in Bournemouth on June 12, 1946, because "they didn't want too many Jews in New York."

While the diplomatic struggle lingered on, the Jews were taking matters into their own hands. More and more refugees entered Palestine regardless—smashing through the British blockade in crumbling, unseaworthy vessels of the Jewish underground. And more and more British soldiers fell victim to Jewish terrorist bombs and bullets. Gradually, to these pressures on Bevin were added others.

Attlee began to question the validity of Bevin's argument that British interests in the Middle East required an armed presence whatever the cost. And supported by the cabinet, he felt that Britain perhaps should get out of Palestine—whether or not the United States filled the power vacuum. After all, had not Britain decided to abdicate her colonial responsibilities in other territories—India, Burma, Ceylon—and to suspend military and economic aid to Turkey and Greece? And anyway, Britain, faced with severe postwar shortages of manpower, coal, and wheat, had enough domestic problems without the Jewish terrorists on her back.

But Bevin continued to scrape for some agreement that would permit the British to stay in Palestine—or at least to leave her in the hands of trusted Arab friends who would grant Britain base rights. When new Anglo-American talks had failed, he mediated negotiations between Arabs and Jews (who met in separate rooms) at a London conference starting on January 27, 1947.

After endless bickering, he proposed on February 7 what he said would be Britain's final offer: a four-year British trusteeship, followed by independence if both sides could agree on terms. Limited Jewish immigration would be permitted meanwhile. Hardly had he spoken to the Jews than the lights went out for lack of electricity, underscoring Britain's desperate situation. There was no need for candles, jested Bevin, since the Israel*ites* were present. The Jews tensed at what they considered another example of Bevin's crude insensibility. They coldly rejected his proposal—as did the Arabs—and the time had come for the Foreign Secretary to play his last card.

On April 2, 1947, he bowed to the demands of bereaved mothers and blustering parliamentarians, referring the whole problem to a startled, cold war–torn United Nations.

Once again, Bevin pinned his hopes for ultimate victory on an international commission—a United Nations Special Committee on Palestine (UNSCOP). This committee left for Palestine in June, 1947, to make a new study of the Arab-Jewish problem, and, after endless wrangling, finally ironed out differences—with the help of the British. By forcibly preventing the refugee ship *Exodus* from disgorging its pathetic load of passengers in Palestine, the British had dramatized the refugee plight and defeated their purpose. In a historic majority report, UNSCOP recommended on September 3, 1947, that the mandate, which had begun in 1919 after the Turkish Ottoman Empire, defeated in World War I, lost control of the Arab world, be terminated and that Palestine be partitioned into sovereign Arab and Jewish states. Bevin had lost his gamble.

Shortly afterward, White House aide David K. Niles telephoned Jewish officials and asked them to come immediately to his office. When they arrived, Niles, who was staunchly pro-Zionist, greeted them smiling, his eyes moist.

"The President," he cried in Yiddish, "accepts the partition plan! Now there will be a Jewish State! *Mazel tov!* If only my mother could have lived to see this moment...!"

The Jews now sought to win over the Arabs to partition. But all efforts to meet with the Arabs failed. Then one morning in London Jon Kimche, a pro-Zionist British journalist, telephoned David Horowitz of the Jewish Agency and asked if he would like to talk with Abdul Rahman Azzam Pasha.

Horowitz was incredulous. As secretary-general of the Arab League Azzam Pasha, an Egyptian, was one of the most influential Arab leaders.

He had seen Azzam, Kimche explained, and Azzam had agreed to an interview.

The next day, Horowitz, Kimche, and Aubrey (Abba) Eban, another Jewish Agency official, drove to the Savoy Hotel and were courteously received by the tall, lean-faced Arab diplomat in his suite. The visitors realized that Azzam, reputedly a moderate Arab nationalist who clung to his position by taking an extremist stand publicly, had consented to this extraordinary secret interview at no small political risk, considering the explosive Middle Eastern atmosphere. Horowitz opened the conversation by stating his view of the UNSCOP report. Then he went on: "The Jews are a *fait accompli* in the Middle East. Sooner or later the Arabs will have to reconcile themselves to the fact and accept it. You Arabs cannot wipe out over half a million people. We, for our part, are genuinely desirous of an agreement with the Arabs and are prepared to make sacrifices for one...."

Horowitz then proposed a plan embracing a political arrangement, security guarantees, and an economic program for joint development of the Middle East.

Azzam Pasha responded dryly: "The Arab world is not in a compromising mood. It's likely, Mr. Horowitz, that your plan is rational and logical, but the fate of nations is not decided by rational logic. Nations never concede; they fight. You won't get anything by peaceful means or compromise. You can, perhaps, get something, but only by force of arms. We shall try to defeat you. I'm not sure we'll succeed, but we'll try. We were able to drive out the Crusaders, but on the other hand we lost Spain and Persia. It may be that we shall lose Palestine. But it's too late to talk of peaceful solutions."

Eban commented: "The UNSCOP report establishes the possibility of a satisfactory compromise. Why shouldn't we at least make an effort to reach an agreement on those lines? At all events, our proposal is a first draft only and we shall welcome any counterproposal from your side."

"An agreement will only be acceptable on our terms," Azzam calmly retorted. "The Arab world regards you as invaders and is ready to fight you. The conflict of interests among nations is, for the most part, not amenable to anything except an armed clash."

Astonished, Horowitz interrupted, "Then you believe in force of arms alone . . . ?"

"It's in the nature of peoples," replied Azzam, "to aspire to expansion and to fight for what they think is vital. It's possible I don't represent, in the full sense of the word, the new spirit which animates my people. My young son, who yearns to fight, undoubtedly represents it better than I do. He no longer believes in the older generation. When he came back from one of the more violent student demonstrations against the British, I told him that in my opinion the British would evacuate Egypt without the need for his demonstrations. He asked me in surprise: 'But, Father, are you really so pro-British?' "

Smiling briefly, Azzam went on gently: "The forces which motivate peoples are not subject to our control. They're objective forces . . . Nationalism, that's a greater force than any which drives us. We don't need economic development with your assistance. We have only one test, the test of strength. . . ."

Azzam smiled again, sadly. His listeners detected no hatred in his tone; he had referred to the Jews over and over again as "cousins." Not once during the two-hour conversation had he expressed an unkind thought or used a hostile expression about the Jews. But the visitors shivered. For Azzam had confirmed what they viewed as the terrifying character of the majority Arab position, a position founded unashamedly not on logic—not even the logic of rancor—but on a blind fatalism, ungovernable as the wind.*

If most Arab leaders viewed partition as synonymous with war, the more practical British immediately modified their aims and devised new strategies to achieve them. If there was to be a partition, it would be one that favored the Arabs, for the Arabs—at least in Transjordan, which was completely dependent on British subsidies—could be persuaded to grant Britain military base rights.

"Partition is now unavoidable," Harold Beeley conceded to his friendly enemy, Horowitz, when the Jewish Agency representative arrived at Lake Success, New York (then the headquarters of the U.N. Security Council), for the debate on the UNSCOP report. "But so is a conflict. You may find a way open later for peace, and you'll perhaps be left with a narrow coastal

* Condensed from *State in the Making,* by David Horowitz. Copyright 1953 by Alfred A. Knopf, Inc. Reprinted by permission of the publisher.

strip after the Arabs take Galilee and the Negev." (Under the UNSCOP partition plan, the Jewish State was to include the Negev and part of Galilee.)

Beeley, a pragmatist whose anti-Zionism stemmed from an honest if not necessarily infallible assessment of British imperial interests, assured Horowitz that Russia and the United States would never agree on a solution. And without the support of those two countries, he added, no plan would receive the two-thirds majority needed to approve a decision by the United Nations General Assembly.

Beeley—and Bevin—were basing their analysis at least partly on the knowledge that top State Department officials, including Undersecretary of State Robert Lovett, Palestine specialist Loy Henderson, and Assistant Secretary of State Dean Rusk, supported the British position in opposition to the White House. True, President Truman had persuaded Secretary of State George Marshall that the United States, which so firmly backed the United Nations, could not veto a recommendation by a United Nations commission. True, also, Russia favored the partition plan, which seemed the easiest way to oust Britain from the Middle East and to keep out the United States—the central Soviet objectives—while offering the best opportunity for playing the Arabs off against the Jews. Since the Jews favored partition and the Arabs did not, Russia would be siding with the Jews—at least until they proved less willing to serve Soviet aims than the Arabs.

But British leaders were convinced that the United States and Russia would never agree on the details of partition; in the current cold war atmosphere they had not yet agreed upon a single important proposal put before the United Nations.

Then, one day, American U.N. delegate Herschel Johnson and his Soviet counterpart, Semyon Zarapkin, emerged smiling from a committee room and announced to a startled crowd of reporters that they had smoothed out their differences on Palestine.

Beeley was stunned when his friend Horowitz, meeting him in a corridor, revealed the news with pointed casualness.

"It seems you've miscalculated again." Horowitz grinned, patting him gently on the shoulder.

The UNSCOP majority report (supported by eight members) and a minority report (backed by three members, who favored a federation of Jewish and Arab states) then went to a Palestine Ad Hoc Committee. Each of the two reports was considered by a separate subcommittee composed of members favoring the report submitted to it. Though all members in the subgroup dealing with the majority report advocated partition in principle, they debated the boundary problem acrimoniously. How large should each of the two states be?

State Department officials, who had only accepted the majority report under White House orders, now tried, in cooperation with the British, to whittle down the size of the proposed Jewish State. The vast, almost uninhabited southern Negev, including the port of Elath on the Gulf of Aqaba, must go to the Arabs, American delegates insisted. But to the Jews, a Jewish State without that enormous desert area and the port would be little more than an oversized ghetto. They were counting on the Negev for settling new immigrants; many felt they could not accept a partition solution that deprived them of it.

The situation seemed hopeless for the Jews, particularly after Moshe Sharett—head of the Jewish Agency delegation to the United Nations—was invited to meet with Herschel Johnson, the American delegate. Sharett learned in advance from friendly American officials that Johnson intended to inform him that the United States would officially recommend the allocation of the southern Negev to the Arabs. Sharett's appointment with Johnson was scheduled for 3 P.M. on November 19, just before the subcommittee on partition was to meet.

In a desperate last-ditch move, Eliahu Elath, Jewish Agency representative in Washington, decided to enlist the help of Chaim Weizmann . . .

CHAIM WEIZMANN, THE RUSSIAN-BORN SCIENTIST AND ZIONIST statesman, had first helped to shape the Zionist movement in 1903, when he had opposed a British offer of Uganda to the Jews as a national home. He had bitterly fought Theodor Herzl, Austrian journalist and founder of the movement, who favored accepting the proposal as a temporary panacea for Jewish persecution (Herzl had covered the French anti-Semitic trial of Alfred Dreyfus and written a book calling for a Jewish State). The Jews, Weizmann insisted, must accept nothing less than their Biblical homeland. And, in the end, the Uganda project was dropped.

Then, in 1906, Weizmann met British Prime Minister Lord Arthur James Balfour and planted the seeds of Zionism in the British consciousness. Eleven years later, with the Ottoman Empire crumbling, he saw Balfour, now Foreign Secretary, again and the latter agreed to issue a pronouncement supporting Zionism. Weizmann's charm and persistence, as well as his important scientific contributions to the war effort, thus produced the famous Balfour Declaration:

> His Majesty's Government views with favor the establishment in Palestine of a national home for the Jewish people, and will use their best endeavours to facilitate the achievement of this object, it being clearly

understood that nothing shall be done which may prejudice the civil
rights of existing non-Jewish communities in Palestine, or the rights and
political status enjoyed by Jews in any other country.

For years the nature and size of the promised national home
was a subject of controversy, even within Zionist circles. Weizmann
himself, until late in the day, had never argued for the establishment of an independent Jewish State, thus leaving the way open
for a bi-national Arab-Jewish State, a state within a Middle Eastern
federation—or even a permanent British protectorate. He saw no
diplomatic advantage in pushing prematurely for a goal he envisioned only as a vague and possibly unnecessary objective at the
end of a long road of nation building.

But the Balfour Declaration, which was subsequently supported
by President Woodrow Wilson and the League of Nations, had
converted Zionism, whatever form it ultimately took, from a wishful
dream into an international pledge . . .

Now, 30 years later, Weizmann was an old man, partially blind. He
had just arrived in New York from his home in England for the debate
on partition when Elath called on him at the Waldorf-Astoria.

"What can I do?" asked Weizmann, his deeply seamed face, tipped by
a small beard, gaunt and weary.

"You must see President Truman," Elath replied. "He's our only
chance of saving the Negev."

"Of course. If you can arrange an appointment."

Elath then called David Niles, Truman's aide, who set up an appointment with the President for November 19, a few hours before Sharett was
to see Herschel Johnson.

Early on the nineteenth, Chaim Weizmann with his wife's help put on
his best black suit and, accompanied by Elath, climbed into a train bound
for Washington.

Little time was wasted on small talk after President Truman had
greeted him warmly in the Oval Room of the White House. Glancing occasionally at the notes Elath had prepared for him, Weizmann outlined the
plans for Jewish development of the Negev:

". . . Mr. Henry Wallace, recently returned from a visit to the Negev,
says he was particularly struck by a huge plantation of carrots, which
had been preceded on the same soil by a good crop of potatoes, while
nearby there was a plantation of bananas. All this seems fantastic when
one takes into account that there has not been a blade of grass in this part
of the world for thousands of years . . ."

The President listened with a glow in his eyes, as if drawn into the
fresh green world painted by his visitor, the kind of world any man from
rural Missouri could understand.

Then Weizmann rose from his armchair, walked to the President's desk, unfolded a map, and pointed to an encircled dot marked "Aqaba." "Aqaba is indispensable to the Jewish State," he stressed. "It is now a gulf of little advantage to anyone. We shall dredge and deepen it and make it a waterway capable of taking vessels of substantial tonnage. If Aqaba is taken from us, it will remain a desert until who knows when. But if it is given to us, it will become a new communications center for the world, and there may even come a time when it will be the terminus of a canal from a point on the Mediterranean . . . It will be a parallel route to the Suez Canal, which will no doubt be taken over by the Egyptians within a few years . . ."

Weizmann then concluded: "It is essential that the southern Negev be part of the Jewish State."

Truman looked up from the map without saying a word. Weizmann sat down, sighing almost audibly. He felt certain that the silence meant the President was thinking of a delicate way to reject his plea. At last, Truman nodded slightly and said: "Very well, I've heard your case. I'll get in touch with the head of our delegation at Lake Success at once."

Weizmann's hopes rose, but he was not sure precisely what the President had in mind: Would he approve the suggestion or simply consult with the head of his United Nations delegation?

The Zionist leader went to his hotel room and tried to call Jewish Agency headquarters in New York City, but no one was in. As the hours slipped by, Weizmann began to worry. If Herschel Johnson failed to cancel the meeting with Sharett scheduled for that afternoon, he calculated, it would mean that the President had decided not to change the American position after all.

Shortly before 3 P.M., Weizmann finally contacted a Jewish Agency official in New York.

"The meeting with Shertok [Sharett's original name]—is it still on?" he asked excitedly.

"No one has called it off."

Weizmann put down the receiver with a shaky hand and slumped into a chair, awaiting the bitter outcome of the meeting.

With equally heavy heart, Moshe Sharett met Johnson at the appointed time in the Delegates' Lounge at Lake Success and, after a perfunctory handshake, sat down as the American began to explain: "Mr. Shertok, about the question of boundaries . . . I'd like to clarify our position. You see . . ."

But while Sharett listened gloomily, an American official interrupted Johnson: "There's a call for you from Washington, sir."

Johnson looked up irritably: "Tell them to call back! I'm busy now!"

The aide then bent down and whispered a few words in Johnson's ear. Johnson leaped to his feet and blurted out: "Please excuse me, Mr. Shertok. I'll be back immediately."

He rushed to a nearby telephone and talked for several minutes while Sharett remained alone, depressed and nervous. When Johnson emerged from the booth, he ran toward a group of his colleagues who surrounded him, as if in a football huddle.

Finally, the impromptu meeting broke up and Johnson strode uneasily toward Sharett.

"I hope you'll forgive me for having taken up your time," Johnson apologized with a smile. "But could we postpone our meeting until another time?"

"Of course," Sharett replied, in complete bewilderment.

A few minutes later, an American friend revealed to him that President Truman had personally telephoned the American delegation to ensure that the southern Negev be incorporated into the Jewish State.

While the British raged at this American *volte-face,* the "partition" subcommittee finally completed its plan. Palestine, with a population of 1.2 million Arabs and 568,000 Jews, would be divided into two states, linked by an economic union, with a United Nations trusteeship area in Jerusalem. The Jewish State would include 55 per cent of the land and a 58 per cent Jewish population; the Arab State, 45 per cent of the land and a 99 per cent Arab population. A five-member United Nations Palestine Commission would implement partition, gradually taking over the administration of Palestine from Britain, while Arab and Jewish militias kept order.

This plan, together with the one calling for federation, was submitted to the full Ad Hoc Committee, and a violent debate ensued between pro-Arabs and pro-Jews. The arguments boiled down to seven main points of conflict:

1. LEGAL

The Arabs—The Balfour Declaration had no legal basis, conflicted with British pledges of independence previously given the Arabs, and was in any case already fulfilled, since the Jews now had a national home if not a state. Furthermore, no international organization had the legal right to take juridical decisions and define territorial rearrangements.

The Jews—The Balfour Declaration was backed by the League of Nations, which in fact approved the British mandate on the basis of that promise. Prime Minister Lloyd George, moreover, had publicly defined

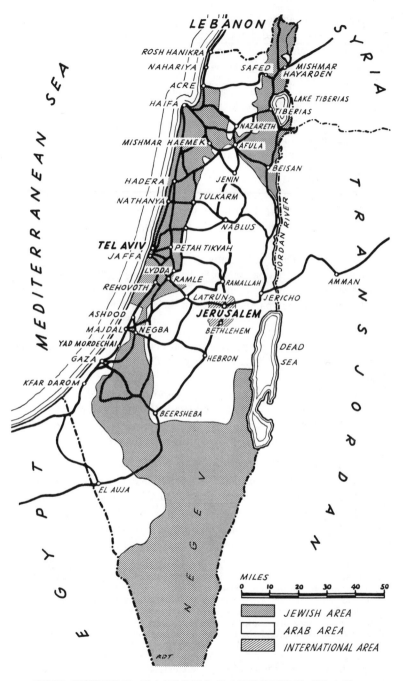

THE UNITED NATIONS PARTITION PLAN

the declaration as calling ultimately for a Jewish State. Also, three international commissions had condemned the British White Paper of 1939, which artificially prevented the Jews from becoming a majority.

2. "DEMOCRATIC"

The Arabs—Since the Arabs constituted a majority of the population, they were entitled to decide the fate of their country.

The Jews—Democracy is not a formal concept of majority and minority alone. Furthermore, in the areas of Palestine earmarked for the Jews, the Jews constituted a majority.

3. HISTORICAL

The Arabs—The Jews were not the descendants of the ancient Hebrews but came from the Khazar tribes of southern Russia who had embraced Judaism, whereas the Arabs had occupied Palestine for the last 1,300 years.*

The Jews—The descendants of the ancient Hebrews had never abandoned Judaism, but had clung to their religious traditions even in the face of pogroms and persecution. And their historic right to Palestine had never lapsed since they had never broken their ties with that country.

4. POLITICAL

The Arabs—The proposed partition boundaries were artificial and absurd and would precipitate a military conflict that could escalate into a wider war.

The Jews—Absurd or no, the proposed partition plan was the only possible compromise and the United Nations could enforce it if it so desired. Only if it failed to do so would war become inevitable, for the Jews would have no alternative but to fight for their survival.

5. NATIONALISTIC

The Arabs—A rejuvenated Arab nationalism should not be expected to permit Jewish intrusion into a land that belonged to the Arabs.

The Jews—Absolute sovereignty of a people over the territory it occupied was no longer possible. The world gave priority to the rehabilitation of the ravaged Jewish people. Moreover, while the Arabs gained

* In the year A.D. 740, a Tartaric warrior people living in the kingdom of Khazar on the western shore of the Caspian Sea, speaking Greek and practicing a blend of Christianity and paganism, were converted to Judaism under their king, Bulan. However, in 969, an army from Kiev defeated the Khazars, incorporated their territory into a new Russian state, and reconverted them to Christianity. In 1500, another incredible episode took place in Russia when two Greek Orthodox priests in Lithuania converted to Judaism, proselytized in the hinterland, and won thousands of other converts, including the daughter-in-law of the Duke of Moscow. The frightened Orthodox Church stamped out the rush to Judaism by drowning 300 Jews as a form of "baptism," and trying—unsuccessfully—to banish the rest from Russian territory.

seven independent states after World War I, the Jews, who had bought all the land they owned—and, in any case, had settled mainly on unused wasteland—were asking for only one per cent of the vast territories in Arab possession.

6. ECONOMIC

The Arabs—Economic union (called for under the partition plan) could not be achieved against the will of the Arabs, and the proposed Arab State could not by itself endure economically.

The Jews—The Jews had already helped to raise Arab living standards in Palestine far above those in other Arab countries, and they could continue to foster prosperity in the Middle East. If the Arabs refused such assistance, they would have only themselves to blame for their economic difficulties.

7. IDEOLOGICAL

The Arabs—Zionism was an artificial creature imposed on Palestine from the outside, without roots in historical, national, cultural, or political reality. It was essentially a European ideology that would corrupt Arab culture and tradition.

The Jews—If Zionism was an artificial creature because it was a product of immigration, what then of a country like the United States, which was strictly the product of large-scale immigration? Nor was modernism necessarily a corrupting influence.

After listening for weeks to this conflict between two appeals for justice, the Ad Hoc Committee approved partition over federation by a simple majority and submitted the plan for approval to the General Assembly, which was to meet in September, 1947. A two-thirds vote of that body would be required for passage—and the Zionists were far from sure they could muster such support.

With the fate of partition thus still uncertain, the Jews and the Arabs hurled themselves into one of the most passionate behind-the-scenes pressure campaigns in United Nations history. The Zionist leaders did reject a proposal by Jewish underworld figures to kidnap anti-partitionist delegates until the vote had been taken! But an American Zionist underground movement nevertheless decided on daring action, viewing such tactics as more than justified by the stakes—survival of the Palestine Jews, in its opinion. It would penetrate the British and Arab delegations to discover *their* tactics.

Nahum Bernstein, a New York lawyer in charge of the operation,

approached the Jewish owner of the car rental service that was leasing a
limousine to the British delegation, and asked him: "Would you do your
bit to create a Jewish State?"

"How?"

Bernstein then explained that all the car rental man had to do was
install a listening device in the British delegation's limousine.

"Connect it to a switch on the dashboard and tell the chauffeur to turn
it on when the British get in."

The eavesdroppers particularly enjoyed one of the first playbacks:

"Who is that bloke? Where did he learn to speak the King's English?"

"He's a bloody don from Cambridge."

The British were obviously worried that Abba Eban had made a favorable impression at the United Nations in his first speech.

Once tuned in on the British, Bernstein sought to give the Arabs equal
time. He contacted the Jewish house detective at the Hotel McAlpin and
came right to the point: "You have an important guest at your hotel—
Faris Bey el-Khouri."

"You mean the Syrian delegate to the Security Council?"

Later that day, a listening device was dangling inside a ventilated steel
column in Khouri's room!

The pro-Zionists soon learned why the female representative of one
small country had voted against partition in the Ad Hoc Committee though
officials in that nation's capital had "assured" them of an affirmative vote.
The strikingly handsome delegate of an Arab contingent had assiduously
courted the lady and won her vote as well as her heart. Unromantic Zionists
with connections in the country immediately spoke with members of the
lady's Foreign Ministry, and a new delegate—male—replaced her in the
General Assembly.

Other nations proved harder to crack and it was not at all evident that
even the strongest Zionist pressure could clear the many obstacles to final
victory. Although most Latin American countries backed partition, a few,
led by Cuba, supported the Arab view, hoping that a working arrangement
between the Latin and Arab nations would strengthen the influence of the
lesser powers in the United Nations. China's sizable Moslem population
demanded a pro-Arab stand, as did France's Moslem North African territories and Holland's Moslem Indonesian protectorate. India did not want
to give Pakistan any new pretext for grievance, or to justify the principle
of partition that had split the Indian subcontinent. Yugoslavia also had
many Moslems and was a federation of peoples based on amalgamation, not
separation. The Belgian Socialists had close links with Bevin's Labour
Party.

At the same time, Arab pressure mounted. And its burden was apparent
in the vitriolic warning of Jamal el-Hasseini, acting president of Palestine's

Arab Higher Committee, to the Ad Hoc Committee: "The partition line will be nothing but a line of fire and blood!"

The main Arab strategy was to work on the Americans—to at least keep them from "twisting arms." For it appeared that if switches to a pro-partition position could be minimized, the Arabs would have enough support to prevent the necessary two-thirds affirmative vote. And the Arabs were convinced that only American pressure on potential anti-partitionists could lose them the game. True, some members of the U.S. delegation, particularly Eleanor Roosevelt and General John Hilldring, were frankly pro-Zionist and would not budge. Hilldring, a tough professional soldier who had formerly served in the American administration in Germany, had been persuaded by his investigation of Nazi atrocities and the plight of Jewish survivors that a Jewish State was necessary, and he made no secret of his view. But most of the other American delegates were by no means overjoyed about partition and listened to the Arabs with sympathy. Sam Kopper and George Wadsworth, passionate Arabophiles with close oil company connections, even assured them that the United States would not press for partition despite her official stand.

Often, the Arabs appealed directly to Washington, and once one group bluntly warned Secretary of State George Marshall that American economic interests, including the oil concessions, would suffer irreparable harm if the United States sanctioned a Jewish State. They worked hand in glove with American oil lobbyists who haunted the State Department corridors.

Finally, with the support of Under Secretary of State Lovett, Loy Henderson, chief of the division of Near Eastern and African Affairs, telephoned Herschel Johnson and ordered: "Remember, Herschel, no pressure tactics. I've given my word to the Arabs."

On November 26, 1947, the General Assembly met at Flushing Meadows to vote on the partition plan. The atmosphere was tense and solemn. As speech followed anti-partition speech, the Zionists stalked out of the hall to consult in the corridor.

"We've got to postpone the vote or we're finished!" said one.

"If we can," agreed another, "we'll have two extra days to work on the delegations. Tomorrow is Thanksgiving Day."

Word was then sent to friendly delegations: filibuster!

And so, in the supercharged atmosphere, speakers drawled out long pamphleteering speeches unheeded until the Assembly president, Oswaldo Aranha, a friend of the Zionists, rapped his gavel and announced that, unfortunately, it was getting late. Voting would be postponed for two days.

The pro-Zionists rushed to the Jewish Agency offices to draw up plans for a flash campaign to turn the tide. Telephones jangled. Cables sped to every corner of the globe. People were dragged from their beds to carry out strange errands. Finally, it appeared that the fate of Zionism lay in the hands of a few small, remote nations; in particular, Liberia, Haiti, the Philippines, and Ethiopia.

Niles and Washington economist Robert Nathan, leaders of the drive, decided to mince no words with the Liberian delegate, Gabriel Dennis, who was believed to oppose partition. After all, former Secretary of State Edward R. Stettinius, who favored partition despite his lukewarm attitude toward Zionism while in office, was president of the highly influential American-Liberian Development Company, which had important business interests in Liberia.

Nathan telephoned Dennis to request a meeting.

"I'm sorry," said the Liberian, "but I have no time right now."

Nathan replied that he might speak with Stettinius about the Palestine question.

Dennis complained to the State Department that he had been "intimidated," but Nathan called Stettinius nonetheless. Stettinius, in turn, telephoned Harvey Firestone, president of the Firestone Tire and Rubber Company, and Firestone asked his representatives in Liberia to exert pressure on the Liberian government.

That took care of the Liberian vote.

Next came Haiti. Before the Ad Hoc Committee vote, the Haitian delegate, Antonio Vieux, had informed his colleagues that his government would vote for partition. But at the last minute, he had received instructions to vote in the negative. A Zionist investigator soon disclosed that Haiti had switched her vote in an effort to pressure the United States into approving a $5 million loan that was being negotiated. The pro-Zionists went to work to persuade the Haitian government that the best way to "influence" the United States was to vote for partition.

The Jews saw their chance to change the Philippine attitude when Carlos Romulo left New York after delivering an anti-Zionist speech. Apparently at the behest of Niles, Supreme Court Justices Frank Murphy and Felix Frankfurter visited the Philippine Ambassador to Washington, Joaquin Elizalde, and pressed the Jewish case. Elizalde then telephoned President Roxas in Manila and said that the Philippines might be jeopardizing the passage of seven bills pending in the U.S. Congress in which the Philippines had a large stake.

"I'll think about it," Roxas replied.

A joint cable urging support of partition drafted by New York's Senator Robert F. Wagner and listing the signatures of 25 other senators then arrived in Manila, as in 12 other capitals, and helped President Roxas to make up his mind. The Philippines switched its stand.

But despite a few such conquests, it appeared that nothing short of arm twisting by American officials could guarantee partition.

With Truman's approval, Niles telephoned Johnson: "Herschel, the President wants the delegation to exert every possible influence on other delegations to support partition."

"But the State Department . . ." Johnson began.

"Never mind the State Department! This is an order from the President!"

Johnson, a sharp-witted, independent-minded diplomat, was not unhappy about the new order. When first assigned to the Palestine question, he had leaned toward the conventional State Department view on partition. But as he delved more deeply into the problem he grew more sympathetic toward Zionism. So now, together with Mrs. Roosevelt and General Hilldring, he moved rapidly from delegation to delegation announcing with a smile: "I have been instructed by the President of the United States to seek your support" for the partition plan . . .

When Arab diplomats complained to Loy Henderson of these tactics, he went red with rage. Picking up the telephone, he called Johnson immediately: "What is this about you pressuring delegates to support partition? Didn't I give you orders . . . ?"

"I'm sorry, Loy," Johnson interrupted quietly. "But I thought you knew. Niles called me and said the President wants me to exert every possible influence."

Henderson slammed down the receiver.

O N NOVEMBER 27, during this last-minute frenzy, a messenger called at the home of Ahmed el-Iman in Haifa with a note. "It's from His Eminence. It's very urgent," he said.

("His Eminence" was the former Grand Mufti, or religious leader, of Jerusalem, Haj Amin el-Husseini, who led the Palestinian Arabs. He was living in exile in Lebanon out of the range of the British dragnet—Britain having accused him of murder and pro-Nazi wartime activities.)*

Iman, the Mufti's emissary in Haifa, ripped open the envelope and removed the message:

> The Mufti requests you to contact Dr. Mordechai Eliash [a leader of the Zionist religious Misrachi Party] and ask him to propose secret talks between the Jewish Agency and the Mufti prior to the final decision of the United Nations General Assembly. These talks are to be conducted without the mediation of any of the Arab countries.

* "Haj" is an honorary title given to Moslems who have visited Mecca. The "Grand" in Grand Mufti has no official meaning, but Haj Amin's followers have used it to distinguish him from other muftis, or religious leaders, less powerful than he.

Iman was to tell Eliash that the Mufti was ready to compromise in seeking a solution to the Palestine dilemma. The negotiations were to be conducted at the Mufti's residence in Lebanon. A reply was requested within 24 hours.

Shocked by this offer—the first time the Mufti had ever indicated he would consider a compromise—Iman rushed to the home of Eliash, who within hours submitted the proposal to an urgent meeting of the Jewish Agency Executive called by Chairman David Ben-Gurion in Jerusalem.

After a long and highly emotional discussion, the group drafted a message stressing that the Agency would negotiate with any Arab leader except the Mufti. Another Mufti emissary, Sharif el-Shanti, transmitted the reply to his master, ending the secret exchange without the Jews ever learning what was in the Mufti's mind.

It is probable, however, that the Mufti was thinking of the Arab nations. For despite the fury of their public anti-Zionist diatribes, most of them showed less enthusiasm for blocking the birth of a Jewish State than for grabbing for themselves choice slices of the Palestinian Arab State envisaged by the partition plan. Only Syria, it seemed, strongly desired an independent Arab Palestine under the Mufti—as a buffer against Transjordan, which wanted to absorb both Palestine and Syria.

Thus, the Mufti viewed with horror the prospect of seeing his lifelong ambition—to rule all Palestine—frustrated by both sides. Not only might the Jews snatch part of Palestine, but his fellow Arabs might split up the remaining part among themselves. A secret agreement with the Jews, however repellent the thought, could save him half a loaf—until he was powerful enough to seize the other half as well.[1]

Such an unholy alliance must have seemed all the more urgent if the Mufti's many spies in Amman had learned (as is likely) that on that very day, November 27, King Abdullah of Transjordan was to meet secretly with Jewish leaders to "settle" the future of Palestine . . .

King Abdullah glanced furtively at the tall, matronly woman with the black hair who was chatting with another Transjordanian at the meeting, which took place at a Jewish rest house in the Jordan River village of Naharayim.

"But Ezra, I thought Mr. Shertok would be leading your delegation," the King whined in a soft, concerned voice.

Ezra Danin, a ponderous Iraqi Jew who had long been a close personal friend of Abdullah, smiled with a casualness that suggested he had expected the question. After all, Abdullah was an Arab king. He didn't fancy dealing with anyone he thought might be of secondary importance—particularly a woman.

"Don't worry, Your Majesty," Danin assured him, "Mrs. Myerson [the original name of Mrs. Golda Meir] is replacing Mr. Shertok and has full authority from the Jewish Agency to talk with you."

The King's tawny, wrinkled face, framed by a neatly wound white turban and a small, frizzly-edged beard, showed guarded skepticism.

When coffee and refreshments had been served in the reception room, Abdullah opened the discussion in Arabic:

"During the last thirty years, you have grown and strengthened yourselves. Your achievements are many. We cannot disregard you and we must compromise with you. There is no quarrel between you and the Arabs. The quarrel is between the Arabs and the British, who brought you to Palestine; and between you and the British, who have not kept their promises to you.

"Now, I am convinced that the British are leaving, and we will be left face to face. Any confrontation between us will be to our own disadvantage. I will agree to a partition that will not shame me before the Arab world. I would like to take this opportunity of suggesting that you consider the possibility of a future independent Hebrew Republic within a Transjordan State that would include both banks of the Jordan, and in which the economy, the military, and the legislature would be divided equally."

The King then emphasized, before Jewish frowns could be translated into a reply, that the "Hebrew Republic" would not be dominated by Transjordan but would simply be part of the Transjordanian monarchy. If the Jews accepted, he said enthusiastically, the kingdom could probably expand to embrace Syria and even Saudi Arabia, which his father, Sherif Hussein, once ruled.*

Mrs. Meir, Russian-born librarian and schoolteacher from Milwaukee who had moved to Palestine in the 1920's, wore a troubled expression that accentuated the severity of her lined face. Finally she retorted: "Your Majesty, our cause is being discussed at present at the United Nations and we are hoping for a resolution that would establish two states—Arab and Hebrew. We wish to speak with you only about an agreement based on such a resolution."

The King then asked: "What would your attitude be to an attempt by Transjordan to take control of the Arab part of Palestine?"

Mrs. Meir looked more at ease. "We would view such action in a favorable light," she said, "especially if Your Majesty undertakes not to inter-

---

* Abdullah had promised Bevin at a meeting in London in February, 1946, that he would not press for the establishment of an Amman-controlled Greater Syria. The Foreign Secretary had extracted this pledge as part of the price for giving Transjordan independence.

fere with our efforts to set up a state and not to foster confrontations between your forces and ours. We would be particularly happy if you declared that such action was taken in order to maintain law and order and keep the peace until the United Nations could set up a government in that area."

It was the King who frowned this time. "But I want to annex the area to my kingdom. I don't want to create another Arab State that would ruin my plans. I want to ride, not to be ridden!"

Mrs. Meir suggested that he hold a referendum in Arab Palestine, which he presumably could control. That would enable him to annex the area without United Nations interference.

Abdullah's intelligent dark eyes narrowed in doubt. Then the subject switched to a possible Arab invasion of Palestine.

"I have notified the Arab powers, including Iraq, that I would not allow their armies to pass through my kingdom," Abdullah said. "I have also given notice that I will not cooperate with any plan not centered in my country and under my jurisdiction. The situation and circumstances neither justify nor require war, but rather compromise."

The Jewish representatives then expressed concern that the Mufti might prevent compromise. They said they had information that the Mufti planned to provoke a confrontation between the Jews and the Arab Legion, as the Transjordanian army was called, by attacking the Jews with his own fighters masquerading in Legion uniforms.

"I appreciate the information," Abdullah said, with an amused smile, "but such a confrontation, or any other, is utterly impossible. You can remove that possibility from your minds. I will give the appropriate orders. As for the Mufti, he is our common enemy. He should be removed to an isolated area . . . I would suggest that he be transferred to Transjordan. We would take care of him!"

When the meeting came to a close, Abdullah escorted the Jewish representatives to the door and urged rather sheepishly that they use their influence on the Jewish press not to "discuss" him so much.

"Don't pay any attention to my public statements," he grinned. "I have to make them, you know."

Novsmber 29th, day of decision, dawned cold and clear. The General Assembly had met the previous day to vote, but French delegate M. Parodi unexpectedly introduced a proposal to adjourn the balloting for 24 hours. Such a move, he explained, would permit a final attempt at conciliation between Arabs and Jews. Assembly approval of the move threw the Zionists into despair. They had thought that their last-minute campaign had lifted them over the summit, but the new postponement, they feared, would give the anti-partitionists time to apply possibly fatal counterpressures.

Tensely they listened as Assembly President Oswaldo Aranha of Brazil, after leaning over to whisper to Trygve Lie, the United Nations Secretary-General, ruled: "We shall now proceed to vote by roll call on the report of the Ad Hoc Committee."

A nervous hush settled over the packed hall as Aranha, silhouetted against a huge painted representation of the globe, rapped his gavel . . .

In his room at the Waldorf-Astoria Hotel, Chaim Weizmann sat alone, sick and exhausted, sobbing uncontrollably as he waited for his wife to return from the meeting with news of the decision . . . In Palestine, where it was about 2 A.M., the streets were deserted. But inside each house, hardly a soul slept as families sat round radios listening to the clear reception from New York, the Jews mumbling prayers and counting delegates, the Arabs playing with their beads, sipping coffee, puffing on hookahs . . .

"No!"
"Yes!"
"No!"
"Yes!"
"Yes!"

The votes rang out with eerie unreality, like ghostly echoes at a convention of resurrected prophets. When the French delegate shouted "Yes," a great cheer rose from the pro-Zionist gallery. When the Chilean delegate, whom the Zionists had regarded as "sure," shouted "No," a thunderous sigh resounded through the hall.

Gradually, the partitionists began to move ahead. But would they harvest two-thirds of the vote? When the Venezuelan delegate, near the end of the alphabetical roll, boomed "Yes," hysteria started to gather momentum as those with pencil and paper realized the significance of that cry. Hardly anyone could hear Aranha by the time he hammered his gavel and announced the final result: 33 votes for, 13 against, with 10 abstentions.

Applause reverberated round the walls, and men and women embraced and kissed each other, shouting: "We've won! We've won!"

In the midst of the pandemonium, Harold Beeley, grim-faced, conferred quietly with his colleagues, while the Arabs sat white with fury.

That evening, at a mass celebration in St. Nicholas Skating Rink, Manhattan, throngs of ecstatic people carried Chaim Weizmann, dazed but beaming with joy, on their shoulders and fought to kiss the hem of his overcoat. And in Palestine, the Jews burst into the streets and danced all night in the euphoria of Biblical fulfillment.

At last, after so many cruel centuries! Peace and protection—at last!

2

Nothing
But the Sword

"**A**TTACK the Jews!" rang the cry through the Arab world.
And nowhere did it echo louder than in the British protectorate
of Aden, where in early December, 1947, thousands of olive-skinned Jews
were gathered together in camps after making the perilous trip across
steaming deserts and icy mountains from the distant reaches of Yemen.
Hardly had news of the United Nations resolution reached Aden than
Arab residents stormed through the Crater, the largest Jewish-inhabited
section, destroying shops, homes, and schools, and leaving scores of dead
behind before British soldiers finally intervened.

"We are better protected here," Salem Jarufi assured his wife Naami
(they had set up a tent in the Aden suburb of Sheikh Othman, where most
Yemenite refugees were quartered). "The British will not let them harm
us."

He stroked his short gray beard, which sprouted from a sunken, finely
chiseled face. Besides, had not enough of his people died already on the
road to Jerusalem? God would certainly take that into account. . . .

FOR AS LONG AS HE COULD REMEMBER, SALEM HAD DREAMED OF
going to Jerusalem. He would proudly ride the streets on a donkey
and live in a house that towered into the sky. In Yemen, Jews were
forbidden to mount animals or live in houses as high as those inhabited by Moslems.*

* In the 6th century, one Yemenite dynasty embraced Judaism and converted
many Arab subjects. The last Jewish king, Zorah Yussuf Dhu-Nowas, embittered by

26

But the time was never propitious and the vision of Jerusalem had gradually receded in his mind. Then, one memorable night, when Salem was almost an old man, he caught one of his six sons—ten-year-old Yihyeh—trying to sneak out of the house.

"Forgive me, Father," the boy (who was blind with trachoma) explained nervously. "But I am going to Jerusalem with some neighbors. I cannot wait any longer. In Jerusalem I shall see again, for God will no longer fear that I shall look upon misery and ugliness."

Salem felt a thrill of exultation. Within a few weeks, he had sold all his heavier possessions for a trifling sum, and—shorn of a lifetime's accumulation of wealth earned from his silver work—set out with his family and friends for Aden, en route for the Holy Land.

After days of trekking through rugged, snow-covered mountains, they reached the great desert plain that separated them from Aden. Removing their heavy goatskin jackets and the extra blankets they had wrapped around them, they were soon dripping with sweat in the intense heat.

As they trudged along, their thirst intensifying at every step, they saw what at first they took for a mirage—high white walls reaching into the clear sky.

"That's Kataba!" shouted Salem. "Water at last!"

The travelers stumbled toward the village but halted abruptly when guards standing on the walls started to throw down rocks at them.

"We want no more Jews here!" one of them cried.

"Please let us enter," Salem pleaded. "We have traveled far and we have no water. We will pay you well."

This the Jews did, giving up almost half the money they had brought with them. But when they entered, they found themselves trapped. Many Jews had arrived here before them on their way to Aden, but none was permitted to continue his journey and most had died from beatings, disease, starvation, or thirst. Salem, as he roamed the village, saw Jews of all ages lying unconscious or dead in the filthy alleys.

Byzantine persecution of his adopted people, killed some Christians in retaliation and tried to convert others forcibly. His army was finally crushed by invading Ethiopian Christians, and in the following centuries the fortunes of the Jews depended on the mood of rulers who sometimes favored and sometimes suppressed them.

It should be understood that in more advanced Arab territories the Arabs generally treated the Jews with tolerance and respect until the advent of political Zionism. Indeed, in the heyday of the great, enlightened Mohammedan Empire from the 8th to the 11th centuries, the Jews experienced a Golden Age of prosperity and cultural development. The subsequent decline of their fortunes paralleled that of the Arabs themselves under the even-handed exploitative policies of foreign conquerors. Before Zionism, what anti-Jewish policies existed in the Arab areas, including Yemen, were based strictly on religious grounds, and any Jew converting to Islam was accepted as a social equal.

He then offered the guards an additional bribe, if they would let the group leave that night, and the guards agreed.

After midnight, the Jews stealthily made their way out of the village and into the vast desert. But when they had marched about 10 miles and sat down to rest, Salem, looking back, saw a dustcloud forming.

"They're coming after us!" he shouted.

Some started to run, but Salem called them back.

"What is the use?" he said. "They are armed and mounted. We are weaponless and on foot. Let us wait here. God will decide our fate."

And he ran to fetch a strange hornlike instrument, the ceremonial ram's horn or *shofar,* which Jews were forbidden to use in Yemen. He had planned to blow it in Jerusalem. But he would do it right now—in the very face of the pursuers.

As the Jews wailed their homage to God, Salem put the *shofar* to his parched lips and blew. Twice, three times, the blast echoed through the desert. Then, miraculously, the dust rolling toward them began to settle. The Arabs had halted about 30 yards away and huddled together for a talk. Once more, Salem blew the ram's horn, and he heard a cry in Arabic: "They're calling for the Devil's help!"

Within minutes, the Arab band had disappeared in a receding trail of dust.

It was about six weeks after starting on their trek that the party, depleted by more than a third, finally faltered half alive into Aden . . .

Now, after several weeks in Aden, the Arabs were terrorizing the Jews again to prevent their reaching Jerusalem. Salem picked up a bucket and left his tent to fetch water from a nearby well. He had almost reached it when he heard a noise in the distance: the familiar sound of rage and revenge.

He ran back swiftly past crazed men wielding long knives, past dying men, with their throats slashed. At the tent he paused for a moment, afraid to open the flap. Then he entered. In a corner, the body of his wife Naami lay curled. He went to her side and wept . . .

A shadow fell across the bar of light flooding through the open tent flap. Salem gazed up into the face of an Arab gripping a long knife. The Jew looked around frantically at the crude furnishings, boxes, and clothing that lay scattered over the earthen floor—a pistol! He dived for it, pointed it at the man in the doorway, and pulled the trigger blindly. The knife dropped from the attacker's clenched fist and, as he slumped to the earth, Salem struck his head with the butt of his pistol until blood drenched the man's *khaffiya.*

British troops arrived eventually and the orgy of killing ended. But Salem grieved, not only for his wife, but for all his people. For he had discovered a new and bitterly paradoxical justice—one that he had read about in the Bible, but had never imagined applying to his own world. The Jews must kill to fulfill the will of God.

IN his house on the Mount of Olives (in Arab Jerusalem), Mohammed Gharbieh sat munching an after-midnight snack as he listened to the radio.

"Stop worrying!" Greta his tall, blond German wife said gently as she rose from her chair. "We'll win. You'll see. I'll be right back with the fruit."

Mohammed did not reply. His wife was perpetually optimistic, at least she appeared to be. Ever since they had met as students in Cairo, she had been saying that things could be worse—no matter what the Jews did. She was always trying to calm him and keep him from fighting. How could he remain calm at a time like this—when the fate of the Palestine Arabs was at stake, when the Jews were trying to steal their homeland?

The voting at the United Nations had already begun, and he was jotting down figures with one hand while manipulating his fork with the other. Finally, the voting ended, and as he nervously began totting up the totals, the announcement came: a two-thirds majority of the General Assembly had supported partition and the establishment of a Jewish State.

Mohammed slammed his fist on the table, almost knocking the dishes off. He sprang to his feet, his slightly protruding dark eyes wild and agonized.

"What happened?" cried Greta, as she rushed back with the bowl of fruit.

"What do you think happened?" roared Gharbieh. "The Jews—they've won! It's time for action!"

He reached for the telephone and called up members of his small unit of fighters, ordering them to meet immediately at his brother's house. Then he dashed out to a waiting taxi. As the driver, a member of his group, sped through the night, Mohammed quietly raged to himself. Yes, action . . .

He would fight . . . He had always been a fighter . . . ever since that day in 1933, when, at the age of ten, he had watched Musa Kasim Pasha el-Husseini, the Mufti's uncle, lead a demonstration through the streets of Jerusalem demanding an end to British occupation and Jewish immigration.

Stirred by nationalist fervor, he had gone directly from the demonstration to buy a sword, and within weeks was an accomplished swordsman. He was ready to fight the Jews. And when an Arab revolt against the British and Jews broke out in 1936, he fought them relentlessly. That Jewish public works official—what was his name, Cohen? Well, Cohen would never forget him, Mohammed was sure. Cohen had discriminated against Arab workers, punishing or firing them, scolding them insolently. Someone had to deal with him.

While four men covered the building from outside, Mohammed had walked to the second floor of an apartment house in Jerusalem's Mea Shearim District and rung Cohen's doorbell. Cohen wasn't home, but within minutes his Arab servant and two British visitors who were waiting for him were locked into a room. Mohammed then went onto the veranda, waited, and as Cohen passed beneath to enter the building, leaped on him, and shot him four times. Later, he learned that his victim would recover from his wounds. Still, Mohammed had struck a powerful blow for the Arab cause.

And now it was time to seek out more Cohens . . .

"Your Eminence," a servant announced, "a call from Jerusalem."

The Mufti was a white-bearded, blue-eyed man, Spartan in black robes and a white, flat-topped turban. He took the telephone and snapped impatiently: "Is that you, Emile? What's happening in Jerusalem?"

Emile al-Ghouri, head of the political department of the Mufti's Arab Higher Committee, shouted back: "Everybody is furious at the news."

"Well, what do you think we should do?"

"We suggest a general strike."

"I don't agree. There might be violence and we're not ready for that yet. The Arab States should take the first step to forestall partition."

"But we can't hold back the people. We have no choice."

"Well, do as you see fit."[1]

The Mufti was alarmed. The Jews had ignored his suggestion for negotiations and, he was sure, had made a deal with King Abdullah that would permit him to occupy the Arab part of Palestine as defined by the partition plan. The Palestinian Arabs would thus have to crush the Jews before the British left in order to keep Transjordan out. But the irony was that while his own fighters were not yet ready and needed arms from the other Arab States, these states, it appeared, would rather send volunteer soldiers of their own to make sure they shared the spoils with Abdullah.

IT WAS INDEED IRONIC THAT ARABS NOW THREATENED TO SNUFF out the dream that a Jew, of all people, had helped so auspiciously to promote. Who could have guessed that Sir Herbert Samuel would prove so generous when he arrived in Palestine in July, 1920, as the first British High Commissioner for the territory? Only the April before, Haj Amin had been forced to flee the country when a British military court had charged him with incitement to violence after an Arab riot (in which 5 Jews and 4 Arabs were killed, and 211

Jews and 21 Arabs wounded), the first real Arab response to the
Balfour Declaration.

But then Sir Herbert, perhaps to "prove" his fairness despite
his Jewish background, had said magnanimously to a group of local
Arab notables: "Let Haj Amin come to Jerusalem. He will not be
molested; we have pardoned him."

And to the amazement of the British, Haj Amin sprang out of
nowhere, to be lifted to the shoulders of an adoring Arab crowd!

But that was just the beginning. Only a few months later, in
February, 1921, the reigning Mufti of Jerusalem died, and the
British administration invited the Ulema, composed of Moslem
notables, to hold elections and submit the names of the three men
receiving the most votes. The law called for an appointment to be
made from one of these three men. Haj Amin el-Husseini came
fourth in the election and so was ineligible—but oddly enough the
top man decided to withdraw his candidacy, so Haj Amin was on
the list after all.

Sir Herbert, still hoping to win over the Arabs with a show of
benevolence, then did what a Christian High Commissioner might
never have done. He chose Haj Amin as Mufti of Jerusalem over the
heads of the two men with higher votes. Thus Haj Amin achieved
a position of real power at last. His ancestors would be proud of
him. After all, the main branch of his family, the Aswads, had
not even been Palestinian but had originated in Yemen. A member
of the clan had then married into the family of Sheikh Abu
Ghosh, a clan that owned much land near Jerusalem; and later
a male member of the Asward family married the daughter of a
Moslem notable named Husseini, who claimed descent from
Hussein, son of the Caliph Ali, and Fatima, only daughter of the
Prophet Mohammed. The Aswads took the prestigious name
of Husseini and thereafter became one of the most prominent
families in Palestinian society.

The Mufti, born in 1893, had decided at an early age to convert
this social prominence into political power. But his dream was
rooted in more than personal ambition. He was determined to
preserve Moslem traditions in a Palestinian society gradually bending before the winds of westernization. And the biggest threat
came from the Jews, who had begun to immigrate from Eastern
Europe in small but increasing numbers. Arab youth in particular, he
felt, was being morally shattered. His generation was the first no
longer to live in the desert. Now suddenly the town sprang out of the
earth, with all its vanities and distractions, and Jewish girls walked
the streets in shorts brazenly enticing young men who were not
prepared to distinguish between good and evil. Even Haj Amin himself had not been immune. As a young man, he had cut a dashing
figure with his perfume, jewels, and rather gaudy Western dress.

While serving as a functionary for the Turkish-controlled Jeru-

salem government, Haj Amin casually told a Jewish acquaintance
who worked with him: "Remember, Abbady, this was and will
remain an Arab land. We do not mind you [Jewish] natives of the
country, but those alien invaders, the Zionists, will be massacred to
the last man. We want no progress, no prosperity. Nothing but the
sword will decide the future of this country."[2]

With his appointment as Mufti, Haj Amin el-Husseini found
himself again the beneficiary of Sir Herbert Samuel's good-will
policy when the High Commissioner transferred the administration of Moslem affairs from the government to Moslem leaders like
the Mufti. Haj Amin became president of a newly formed Supreme
Moslem Council. Thus, he was now in a position to fight Zionists—
and Arabs who didn't support him—the only way, he felt, that
they could effectively be fought: by terror. In 1929, he provoked
bloody anti-Jewish riots across the country. And in 1936, he
sparked the full-scale Arab revolt against the British and their
"Jewish protégés," demanding that London cut off Jewish immigration, which Hitler's policies were encouraging; although, in this
effort, ironically, his fighters killed more Arab than Jewish foes. The
following year he was forced to flee Palestine again, but it had been
made clear to the world that most Palestine Arabs would never accept Zionism—or any other leader than the Mufti.

And the Mufti had plans to keep the Palestine pot boiling—with
the help of Adolf Hitler. The Führer despised the Jews for economic
and ideological reasons; the Mufti, for political and social reasons.
Hitler wanted to weaken Britain's worldwide imperialist system;
Haj Amin, to oust her from the Middle East. The two men had a
good deal in common.

But Hitler at that time was not ready for a major conflict with
Britain. And he had been persuaded that Britain was determined
to partition Palestine and to create a Jewish State, as proposed by
the British Peel Commission which investigated the Palestine problem after the 1936 Arab revolt had broken out.[3]

Nor was Germany yet prepared to meet the Mufti's demand that
she end Jewish emigration from the Reich to Palestine. Hitler at
that time wanted the Jews to leave Europe; and since most of the
world's doors were closed to them, he did not wish to prevent the
flow to Palestine, whatever the Arab attitude.

But when the British government did not accept the Peel Commission proposal, Germany's attitude gradually changed. And with
the outbreak of World War II, Hitler and the Mufti found themselves bedfellows. In 1941, with German backing, the Mufti insti-
gated a *coup d'état* in Iraq which brought to power a pro-Axis
government. Before the Germans could pour into the country,
however, Allied troops overthrew the pro-Nazi regime—with the
help of King Abdullah's Arab Legion.

But the Mufti, on the run again, was not discouraged. Hitler would still win the war, he was certain. And so he fled to Germany. There he began to organize Moslem troops for an invasion of the Middle East and, in radio talks, to exhort his followers in Palestine to frustrate Allied designs. And there, he met Hitler in person . . .

"My Führer, may I present Haj Amin el-Husseini, the Grand Mufti of Jerusalem," said the interpreter.

The Mufti smiled through his beard as he shuffled forward to meet Adolf Hitler, his hand extended.

But Hitler stood rigid, his arms at his side, and the Mufti, awkwardly drawing his hand back and putting it over his heart in Arabic fashion, sat down. Hitler, also seating himself, said stiffly: "Tell him that I welcome him here, and I am glad that the free people recognize that Germany has their interests at heart."

When this had been translated, the Mufti nodded, and Hitler continued: "And now I will tell him my ideas of Pan-Arabism . . ."

But the translator interrupted: "My Führer, you have forgotten the coffee . . . This is the Mufti of Jerusalem . . . Even with minor dignitaries in Arabic countries, it is usual to start with coffee. It is the custom. We must not talk before coffee."

Hitler stared at the translator, his eyes blazing, and shouted: "I do not drink coffee!"

Then he sprang to his feet and headed for the door, screaming: "I will not have anyone—anyone, do you hear?—drinking coffee in these headquarters!"

He went out, slamming the door behind him.

Five minutes later, he marched back in, glancing irritably at his guest as he again sat down. Then an SS man entered with a tray and, laying it on the table between the two men, set a glass of lemon barley water in front of each. As the white-faced Mufti began to sip his, Hitler continued his lecture on Pan-Arabism . . .

"We will reach the southern Caucasus . . . then the hour of the liberation of the Arabs will have arrived . . . The hour will strike when you will be the lord of the supreme word, and not only the conveyor of our declarations. You will be the man to direct the Arab force, and at that moment I cannot imagine what would happen to the Western peoples . . ."[4]

As the war progressed, the Nazis not only supplied the Mufti with ample funds to carry on his propaganda activities, but heeded many of his requests—particularly his complaints about deals for the migration of some Jews to Palestine from Nazi territory. On May 13, 1943, he submitted a note to Foreign Minister von Ribbentrop protesting against a plan for the emigration of 4,000 Jewish children:

It has come to my attention from reliable sources that the English and American Governments asked their representatives in the Balkans (especially in Bulgaria) to intervene with the governments and request that they be given permission to allow Jews to emigrate to Palestine. . . . The Arabs see in this emigration a great danger to their lives and existence. The Arab peoples put themselves at the disposal of the Axis without any hesitation in the fight against communism and international Jewry. The Jews will take out with them from the Balkans many military secrets and will give them to Allied agents who are awaiting their arrival at the port. I request Your Excellency to act with all possible effort to avoid this plan of the international Jewry and Anglo-Americans without delay. This service will never be forgotten by the Arab people.[5]

Immediately, Horst Wagner (of Abteilung II in the German Foreign Office) sent a telegram to the German Ambassador in Sofia instructing him to draw the attention of the Bulgarian government to common German-Arab interests in cancelling the emigration plan.

In some cases, the Mufti suggested to the pro-Nazi governments how to deal with their Jews, if the problem was simply to remove them from a particular country. On July 28, 1944, he wrote the Hungarian Foreign Minister that "if there are reasons which make their [the Jews'] removal necessary, it would be indispensable and infinitely preferable to send them to other countries where they would find themselves under active control, as for example Poland, thus avoiding danger and preventing damage."[6]

- After the war, the Jews claimed that this suggestion was tantamount to requesting the extermination of the deportees, since all Jews in Poland were being herded into the gas chambers there. But, replied the Mufti, was he to blame for what the Nazis did or didn't do? Was it, indeed, his concern? His only objective was to keep the Jews out of Palestine, to serve the cause of Arab nationalism.

Then came the new catastrophe. Hitler lost the war.

As the Allies closed in, the Mufti fled to Switzerland, but the Swiss handed him over to the French. To his relief, the French, instead of throwing him into prison as a war criminal, kept him under surveillance in a villa outside Paris. And the British, although they had long been after him for murder and other charges, did not request his extradition. The Mufti was still popular in the Middle East, and the British wanted bases, not political troubles, in the Arab world.

The French, however, competing with the British for influence in the Middle East, preferred political troubles for Britain. So the Mufti, his beard shaved off, had little trouble fleeing from France to Cairo in 1946. He would soon be back in Palestine, he promised his cheering followers—when the British had been driven out . . .

Now the British were leaving at last; but would he be going back, with the Jews and his fellow Arabs conspiring to squeeze him out? After all the sacrifices, the dashed hopes, the hairbreadth escapes, would his dream finally die in the ashes of Arab betrayal?

It was clear that his people would have to fight the Jews alone—with the guns supplied by the Arab States. The general plan had already been formulated at a meeting of his Arab Higher Committee in Alli, Lebanon, in October, 1947. Local national committees, responsible to the central committee and embracing all the Arab towns and some 275 villages, would be set up to train and arm guerrilla forces and a home guard. His fighters would have to be knitted into a powerful irregular army before they entered battle. Too bad he could not direct the operation personally from Jerusalem; but the British would certainly arrest him if he returned to Palestine, and then how could he lead his people? He would have to depend on his advisers and lieutenants in Palestine to carry out his orders.

One of them was Abed Muhtaseb.

"The strike will begin soon," said Abed Muhtaseb, staring anxiously from the window of his large stone house within sight of an Arab quarter in Jerusalem. "If there's trouble it may be too dangerous to stay here."

His plump Jewish wife, Mathilda, preparing lunch in the kitchen, sighed audibly.

THEY HAD MET IN 1918—SHE WAS ONLY SIXTEEN—AMID THE throng of people who crowded Jerusalem's Jaffa Road every Saturday for their Sabbath stroll in the sun. It was hard to avoid the Moslem men, who, unable to approach veiled Arab women, avidly sought Jewish female companionship. What would her Orthodox mother say if she knew that Arab men smiled at her daughter—men with brown wavy hair, sensitive dark eyes, and a gracious manner?

But Abed Muhtaseb was persistent, and so for months the two met secretly. Finally, he proposed to her.

"I can never marry you," Mathilda replied. "You are a Moslem."

"I shall convert to Judaism. I shall put it in writing right now."

"No, I will not marry you."

"Then I shall kidnap you and marry you by force."

And, true to his word, Muhtaseb broke into her home one night, with a group of armed friends, confronted her in bed, and said: "If you don't marry me, we'll kill your whole family!"

Pulling the blankets over her, Mathilda, white-faced, agreed. Then she smiled.

So they were married—by a rabbi who did not know that the young man, a journalist for Hebrew-language newspapers, was an Arab.

During the early years of their marriage, the young couple observed Jewish customs and ran a Jewish household in a Jewish sector of Jerusalem. Their guests were invariably Jewish and their children attended Jewish schools. Even Arab visitors were not permitted to smoke on Friday night, the Jewish Sabbath eve. But gradually these visitors increased in number, and Muhtaseb's nostalgia for Moslem traditions grew. Soon the family was celebrating Moslem as well as Jewish festivals.

Then came the first great trial—the 1936 Arab revolt, accelerating Arab-Jewish hostility, which exploded into killings and counter-killings. Any Arab who befriended—or was married to—a Jew was suspected of treason by the Mufti and his followers. In 1937, when Britain sent the Peel Commission to investigate the causes of the Arab revolt and recommend a solution to the Arab-Jewish problem, the Mufti asked Muhtaseb to translate from Hebrew into Arabic certain documents to be submitted to the commission. When Muhtaseb agreed, Mathilda protested: "A good husband you are! Helping the Arabs destroy the Jews—including your wife and children!"

"Don't worry," he reassured her. "I'm cooperating more with the Jews than with the Arabs. Besides, we've been living in terror. The Arabs call me a traitor and threaten to kill me. If I help Haj Amin, he will protect us."

Unable to refute this, she agreed reluctantly, and even let her husband hang a picture of the Mufti on the wall for the benefit of Arab guests. Soon the children were going to a British school, and Muhtaseb was publishing a daily newspaper sponsored by the Mufti.

In 1939, when the Mufti had fled Palestine and the revolt had ended, Mathilda demanded that her husband cut his ties with the Arab nationalists and that the children resume their Jewish education. But in vain. Her husband had become a true Arab nationalist. They continued to live together, but in different worlds, often viciously vying for the sympathies of their ten children, five of whom eventually embraced Judaism, the other five Islam . . .

"We could go to live with Isaac," Mathilda suggested now, referring to their second eldest son. "We'd be safe there."

"Safe!" exclaimed Muhtaseb, scowling. "The Arabs would consider me a traitor. They would kill me and maybe the whole family. No, if there's trouble, we must go to Hebron. I am an Arab, not a Jew!"

He waited expectantly for the reply, which came in a bitter outburst: "And I am a Jew!"

After almost 30 years of love and hate and hurt, their marriage, Mathilda knew, was headed for final ruin. Palestine would be partitioned; the family divided. It was inevitable, she sensed with both pain and relief.

As she served lunch, she glanced at her husband and could still see his anguish and frustration. Despite all his entreaties, their eldest son, David, had just married a Jewish girl. Isaac had earlier taken a Jewish wife, as had a third son.

And now the partition resolution had all but completely split the family.

He looked up at her once more, pleading: "Mathilda, come to Hebron with me . . . please."

Late in the afternoon of December 2, Bahjat Gharbieh, a slender, mild-mannered kinsman of Mohammed Gharbieh, the fiery activist, returned to Jerusalem from the nearby hills, where he had been training a group of Arabs in guerrilla tactics. He was shocked to find himself in the midst of rioting mobs that had turned part of the New City into a blazing inferno.

"My God," he gasped, "they're playing the enemy game!"

The Arabs, he was convinced, were not ready for battle. About the only ones with experience were men like himself who had fought the British and Jews in the 1936–39 rebellion. And the Jews were well-armed and well-trained. They were no longer Jews like the little old watchmaker for whom he had worked during his vacations in his student days. How had they become so strong? Ironically, Hitler was at fault.

Like most Arabs, Bahjat had deeply sympathized with the Nazis during World War II—until they started to lose in Russia. His father had warned him about Germany: "I know the Germans from World War I. They acted as if they were gods and treated the Arabs and Turks like servants. They were cruel. What can we expect if they return as governors?"

Bahjat had shrugged: "Never mind, father. They are the enemies of the British and Jews, our enemies."

But now, he felt, it was the Nazis who were mainly responsible for the Zionist threat. They had permitted thousands of Jews to migrate from Europe to Palestine before World War II. More important, Jewish militancy nurtured by the Nazi atrocities had exploded not in Germany, but in Palestine. Yes, the Germans had lit the Zionist flame. And now the British were dumping fuel on it.

As Bahjat mingled with the surging, screaming crowds, he was certain that some of the "Arabs" he saw, oddly fair-faced, were actually Britons in disguise; in British-accented Arabic, they were aggressively encouraging the mobs to set Jewish shops afire. That, he concluded, accounted for the violence in the face of rigid warnings by Arab leaders not to provoke fighting that might force the Arabs into war prematurely. A typical British trick! The British wanted a premature war so that the Jews, who were prepared for one, could enforce partition.

Bahjat was bitter as he saw his restless raw recruits straining at the leash to join in the rioting. His people, it seemed, were bent on suicide. The war had started—as the British had planned.

*

Isaac Ben Ovadia—"Ovadia," his adopted name, was the Hebrew equivalent of the first name of his Moslem father, Abed Muhtaseb—looked worried as he chatted after dinner at his brother David's home. That evening—December 11—the news was gloomy. Since the first riots in Jerusalem, the Arabs had begun to attack Jews throughout the country, their immediate objective apparently being to sever communication lines, isolate outlying villages, and disrupt urban life. They wanted to show the world that partition could not be imposed on Palestine, and they seemed to be succeeding.

"Maybe it's too dangerous to make the trip tomorrow," Isaac warned his brother. "There are rumors the Arabs may be waiting for you."

David had just been appointed manager of the British Overseas Airways Corporation in Jerusalem and was due to move his office from Lydda to that city the following day. He was aware that some of his Arab employees, who had been working for the company far longer than he, deeply resented his promotion. And he knew, too, that the Arabs considered him a "traitor" for marrying a Jewish girl at a time of such conflict.

"Do you think the Arabs might stop our car?" David asked his accountant.

"I don't know," the accountant replied. "If they do, they might kill me as a Jew. But you would be safe. All you'd have to say is that you're the son of Abed Muhtaseb."

David smiled. "If they want to shoot you," he said, "I'll insist that they shoot me first."

Son of Abed Muhtaseb! thought Isaac. The son of a Moslem, of a man who worked with a "Nazi-loving murderer" like the Grand Mufti. He remembered the Mufti's smile. The impenetrable blue, half-moon eyes . . . And the soft-spoken words. Yes, he remembered listening to his father and the Mufti on those frequent childhood visits to His Eminence—remembered listening to them plot the death of Jews. He wondered what his father would say if he knew that his son Isaac was working as an intelligence agent for Haganah, the underground Jewish army; that he was plotting against the Arabs.

"It's no joking matter," said Isaac. "Maybe you should wait for a convoy."

But the next morning, David drove from his Jerusalem home to Lydda to gather up his papers and other possessions, which he and his fellow BOAC employees piled into a small airline bus for the return trip to the Holy City. With the bus loaded, the employees—10 Arabs and 3 Jews, including David—crowded aboard, and set off for Jerusalem. At Bab el-Wad the bus ran into a roadblock and was forced to halt. David realized in horror that the joke had become a reality; an Arab opened the door and jumped in.

"No one move or talk!" he shouted in Arabic, aiming a rifle at the passengers.

Several other Arabs then entered the bus, and one of them drove it to a nearby field. The leader ordered the passengers off, pointing with his rifle: "All Jews stand over here! All Arabs over there!"

When David joined the larger Arab group, the leader barked at him: "You! You're no Arab! Get over there with the Jews!"

"I am an Arab," David nervously protested. "I am the son of Abed Muhtaseb."

The Arab leader smiled sourly. "You are no Arab."

David then recited several lines from the Koran. "You see," he insisted. "Only a Moslem would know the Koran."

"We know you," the Arab said, still smiling. "You are a Jew! Get over there with the Jews!"

David haltingly joined the three Jews, including his accountant. A burst of fire echoed through the green countryside, and the four men fell dead.

Abed Muhtaseb gently caressed his wife's shoulder as she sat with her head buried in her hands, sobbing softly. She looked up, her damp eyes afire, and cried: "Get away from me! I don't want to talk with you again! I don't want to see you! Your people killed my son!"

"If the killers are bad," Muhtaseb groaned, "does that mean I should hate all my people? Come with me to Hebron. We will be safe there."

"I will never live with the Arabs! Get away from me!"

His pained brown eyes darted to Isaac, his second son. Both men had been threatened immediately after David's slaying. The father had found a note in his mailbox demanding that he divorce his Jewish wife or die, and the son had been warned to write a newspaper article declaring that he was a Moslem and that his brother's death was justified because he was a Jew.

"Then I shall go alone with the girls," Muhtaseb said. "Come with us, Isaac. If you come to Hebron, the Arabs will trust you. You won't be in danger."

Isaac, his face drawn, his eyes narrow with contempt, said softly: "You want me to live with the Arabs after they killed my brother? But I hate the Arabs! I hate *you!*"

A few weeks later, Muhtaseb, accompanied by four daughters, left for Hebron where he became active in the Arab guerrilla movement. And Mathilda moved in with Isaac and his wife. But the Arabs continued to

threaten Isaac, and finally demanded that he prove his good faith to
the Arab cause by blowing up Jewish installations.

"I'll do anything you want," Isaac told one Arab agent.

"Then blow up the house of Eliahu Sasson" (head of the Jewish
Agency's Arabic section).

Isaac immediately informed the Haganah of his assignment.

"Stall them off as long as possible," he was ordered, "and find out as
much as you can about their plans. We'll give you as much protection as
possible."

The Arabs, however, soon began to suspect him. One day, several
British policemen who were collaborating with them tried to kidnap him
off the street. But Haganah agents who had been following dashed up and
whisked him away in time. In February, 1948, he moved with his wife and
mother to Tel Aviv, where he continued his intelligence work.

Mathilda heard nothing more of her husband until about a year later,
when he was killed in an automobile accident. In his wallet was a lock
of her hair.

WITH violence spreading throughout Palestine, Moshe Rousnak brooded in the small room he rented in the New City. It was now two
months since he had been appointed an officer in the Haganah and he had
not been called up for active duty yet. As he lay in bed listening to the
radio, he silently fumed each time he heard a battle report. What was he
doing while other Jews were getting killed? Working as a clerk in a Jerusalem bank! He could wait no longer.

The next day, December 11, 1947, Rousnak went to the Haganah
secret headquarters in Jerusalem and stood defiantly beside a young officer's battered desk. "How long is my leave going to last?" he asked. "Can't
you find something for me to do?"

The commander looked up from a report and said sympathetically:
"I know how you feel, but we'll call you when we want you."

Rousnak had turned to leave, more depressed than ever, when the
commander called him back. "Since you're here," he said, "how would you
like to go to the Old City?"

A tentative smile came to Rousnak's face. "When do I leave?" he asked.

"In the morning. You'll be going in an ambulance in the British convoy.
They agreed to let us take a doctor in. You're the doctor."

"What do you want me to do there?"

"As you probably know, the British are moving into position today between the Jewish and Arab quarters. So things should be quieter. We'll have an opportunity to dig defense positions of our own behind the British positions, so that when they leave we'll have an adequate defense line. Your job will be to supervise the establishment of those positions."

Rousnak was delighted. He realized that the Jewish Quarter of the Old City was the most vulnerable of all Jewish-occupied areas in Jerusalem, being a tiny ghetto squeezed between the Moroccan Arab Mugrab Quarter to the east, the Armenian Quarter to the west, and the Moslem Quarter to the north; only along a small stretch of wall between the Zion and Dung gates was it close to the New City. Here lived about 1,700 Jews, including only 150 fighters, surrounded by more than 20,000 Arabs who were determined to destroy this potential stepping stone to the Jewish conquest of the entire Old City.

Barely a week before, the Arabs had just missed breaking into the Warsaw Synagogue. But the British had intervened and, fired on heavily by the Arabs, had taken cover inside the Haganah defenses in the houses around the synagogue, saving the Jews just in time. However, the Haganah had been required to evacuate the buildings. Since then, two Jews had been stabbed to death, and sniping had forced the closing of shops and schools and even the suspension of sanitary services.

The British, it was true, were now sealing off the Jewish Quarter from the Arab areas, but at heavy Jewish expense, since they were only doing so after having promised the Arabs that they would prevent the entry into the Old City of any Jewish reinforcements in manpower or military equipment. All too clearly this meant possible wholesale slaughter of the Jewish inhabitants as soon as the British left.

"How long do you want me to stay?" Rousnak asked.

"Oh, I'd say it should take you about a week to finish your job. I don't think we'll need you there longer than that."

While Rousnak went to bed that night in an exhilarated mood, Judith Jaharan, as she stood guard on a shadowy street corner in the New City, gripped her Sten fiercely. She had asked her commander day after day for a short leave so that she could go to the Old City to see her sick mother, but the answer was always "maybe tomorrow."

Now the British had cracked down, and the Haganah would attempt to smuggle in only essential personnel. She might never get home, she mused bitterly as a bright half-moon cast a soft glow over her round dark face.

Daughter of a Yemenite father and a Moroccan mother, Judith had joined the Haganah two years before, at the age of fourteen, saying she was sixteen. In fact her plumpish figure was fully developed, and her brooding brown eyes and quiet manner reflected the thoughtfulness of a woman who had long since outgrown the frivolities of adolescence.

Yet there were times when she felt like a child, and this was one of them. As she stood gripping her Sten, she thought only of going home and running into her mother's arms.

Moshe Rousnak soon found that he would very likely be around to test the defense system he was helping to build in the Jewish Quarter. It had become clear that considerably more than a week would be required to complete his job. Nor did it seem logical to the Haganah command to bring him out when the difficulty of smuggling replacements in was growing. Toward the end of December, the Arabs set up roadblocks and stopped all traffic into the Jewish Quarter. And the British, hoping that the Jews would move to the New City to reduce the areas of conflict, offered the Arabs little argument. During the first five days of January, no food at all entered and even children were deprived of milk. Kerosene was in extremely short supply, and the dead who were to be transferred out of the Old City went unburied.

The British began to relent slightly under Jewish pressure, and permitted "essential" people to enter. The Haganah then decided to send in a "male nurse" in the person of Abraham Halperin, a highly experienced and capable officer and administrator. With morale gradually breaking down in the Jewish Quarter, Haganah officials were dissatisfied with the efforts made so far to organize the community for siege and war. Nor, they felt, was Rabbi A. Mordechai Weingarten, known as the "mukhtar" of the quarter (the Arab word for village leader), doing much to stir up popular resistance to British pressure and Arab assault. Halperin, they felt, was just the man to save the Old City Jews from their enemies and themselves.

Shortly after Halperin arrived, Rabbi Weingarten called on him at his headquarters. The new commander was a tall, thin man with a black beard that partially hid a strong, ascetic face. He had been waiting for this moment, if not with happy anticipation. Halperin had known Weingarten since 1940, when he had been based in Jerusalem, and had often been invited to dine with him, his wife, and his three eldest daughters. The mukhtar was a valuable man to work through, since he got along well with the British and could obtain many favors from them. The trouble was, in Halperin's view, that Weingarten was a little too friendly with them, considering they were clearly the enemy; even at this late date they arrested

Jews they found with arms, but usually looked the other way when Arabs attacked Jews. Of course, it was good to have someone who could influence the British, but where did influence end and collaboration begin . . . ?

"It's been many years," the rabbi said, after the two men had shaken hands.

"It has indeed," Halperin agreed. "How are your wife and daughters?"

"They're fine, fine. Always complain that I'm working too hard."

"Well, maybe you are, mukhtar. Maybe you should give up some of your duties."

Weingarten ignored this. "I haven't received the £5,000 the Jewish authorities usually give me each month for civic expenses. Do you know anything about it?" he asked abruptly.

Halperin was silent for a long moment. "Yes. It was given to me. You understand, mukhtar, that in wartime conditions the military must assume the heaviest share of responsibility in community affairs."

"But you have no right to take that money," Weingarten said. "It is my job to administer the quarter."

"I'm sorry," Halperin replied. "I simply take orders. You'll have to speak with the Jewish authorities if you wish to complain."

Weingarten's round, bearded face paled, and his bespectacled blue eyes reflected shock. He rose from his chair and grumbled: "It isn't right, it isn't right." And he tramped out.

Halperin suddenly felt sorry for him. After all, the mukhtar had done a lot for the Jewish Quarter, and his pride, which many people took for vanity, was not altogether unjustified. He and his family seemed almost as much a part of the Old City as some of its most ancient monuments. But monuments could be roadblocks in wartime.

Weingarten moved slowly up the narrow, walled-in street leading to his house about two blocks from the edge of the Jewish Quarter. As he walked along, he was not thinking of the danger. He had absolute faith that his Arab friends would not harm him. He had something in common with them, he thought, that the young troublemakers who were taking over his territory could never understand. His family and the Arabs had lived side by side for years, had participated in each other's religious festivals, shared the comfort of living in the hallowed birthplace of three great religions, in the midst of holiness and brotherhood. The Arabs had not touched his house, whatever damage they had done to other Jewish property.

As long as he was mukhtar there was a chance that the Jewish Quarter could survive, for both the British and the Arabs trusted him and respected his family. But now the impetuous young Halperin had come along and taken over, eliminating any chance of peace and reconciliation.

He shook his head sadly as he came to his house, its massive stone front broken here and there by tiny square windows that resembled the lookout holes of a fort. He walked up the unevenly carved stairway into 200 years of history. He was always comforted when he returned to this rabbit warren of rooms, passages, and courts where he and his ancestors had entertained high commissioners, patriarchs, sheikhs, and visiting dignitaries from all over the world. His greatest joy was to browse through his library, which contained rare books in many languages and manuscripts dating back hundreds of years; and to show visitors his collections of stamps, silver, and the heirlooms of six generations.

Weingarten took off his crumpled brown hat and went up to the roof to survey his Old City in the gray light of dusk. He scanned the scene stretched magnificently before him: golden domes, soaring minarets and church steeples, small stone houses connected haphazardly across narrow, winding streets by vaulted roofs and subterranean cellars . . .

THE SAME GLORIOUS SCENE THAT HIS WIFE'S GREAT-GRANDFATHER had gazed upon when he had arrived in 1740 from Lithuania—the first Ashkenazic Jew to settle in the Old City since the dispersion. Weingarten's own family had moved to the Old City in 1813. Not even when the first large Jewish migrations from Europe began to build the New City in the late 19th century did the two families consider moving to the more modern, safer Jewish quarters springing up. Nor did they follow the lead of other Jews who left the Old City after the Arab pogroms of 1921 and 1929, and during the Arab revolt of 1936–39. The Jewish population decreased from 28,000 in 1895, to 5,000 in 1939, to 1,700 in 1948; but they stayed on.

Since Weingarten had been chosen in the mid-1930's by the Jewish elders as head of a Jewish Council to represent the Jewish Quarter in dealings with the British and the Arabs, he had done everything in his power to improve living conditions and encourage Jews to settle there. He had persuaded the British to provide a water system and electricity, and to start a bus service (with special coaches that could move down the narrow streets). He had spent his own money to build a free polyclinic for residents of all races. He had set up a free kitchen for the poor, and established other services.

It was unfair of the Haganah people to complain of his unwillingness to cooperate with them. He had allowed them to store arms in his house, had used his influence with the British to permit the smuggling in of soldiers and guns. Halperin himself could never have entered if Weingarten had not vouched for his identity as a "male nurse." He was risking his good relations with the British and the Arabs, and indeed, the lives of his family, to help in the cause. And now he was being brutally discarded, deprived of dignity and influence, by a group of immature, arrogant boys who would certainly lead the whole Jewish community to slaughter.

Halperin began reorganizing the life of the quarter. He realized it would not be an easy job. He would have to steel for war a quarter that had no taste for violence and little understanding of the Zionism for which it would have to fight and die. Few young Jews lived in the quarter; most of the inhabitants were old, ill, and mystically religious, their lives revolving almost entirely around ancient synagogues and rabbinical schools, or *yeshivoth*.

They lived mainly in crumbling, centuries-old stone houses built around tiny inner courtyards in which raggedly dressed women and children lingered most of the day in the grimy air. Halperin wondered how they could breathe at all in the crowded, domed rooms at the top of the narrow staircases leading from the courts, or at the foot of others leading underground. Even the jerry-built concrete apartment blocks that had sprung up failed to relieve the congestion. While lacking the esthetic grace of the old buildings, with their heavily latticed, iron-screened windows, they had become beehive slum dwellings.

Halperin studied the pale, bearded faces of frail old men under their broad-brimmed black hats as they moved through the dirty, twisting alleys that smelled of urine and garbage and, in the market areas, of fresh meat, stale leather, Oriental spices, and musty furniture. Some of the men were members of the ultra-Orthodox Neturei Karta sect, which regarded the very concept of a Jewish State as blasphemy since the Bible said it would not be resurrected until the Messiah came. In general, the inhabitants were determined to stay in the Old City, even at great risk, but for reasons having nothing to do with Zionism. Now he would undertake to reinforce this determination by giving them a stake in the coming state even before it was born.

Halperin took a census and gave everyone a food ration card, selling convoy supplies rather than giving them away as before. He also put people to work building defense works, cleaning the streets, and manufacturing trinkets, brushes, and brooms; opened two bakeries; reopened two rabbinical academies and paid people for studying the Torah; established schools, children's clubs, and social welfare agencies for the sick and aged, paying people for reciting psalms four hours a day. Everybody had to do something, and beggars suddenly disappeared from the newly swept alleys.

Simultaneously Halperin, aided by Moshe Rousnak, formulated battle plans and set up an intricate defense system. He split the quarter into two sectors, A and B, dividing each into blocks, every block autonomously commanded so that it could continue fighting whatever the fate of the others. He also established a civilian guard to keep public order, which he put under the command of Emmanuel Meidav, a brilliant Old City native whose magnetic personality, broad smile, and blond good looks endeared him to his besieged colleagues, not least the women—though he was committed to Rika Menache, whom he had not seen in months.

Hardly had Halperin's various programs got under way than the British halted the supply convoys again. This time they said they would restart them only if the Jewish authorities agreed to let Weingarten handle the supplies as well as the money intended for civic purposes. On receiving word of this from his superiors in the New City, Halperin replied angrily: "I, for one, refuse to be blackmailed. We'll hold out whatever the difficulties."

When the British finally backed down, Weingarten came to see Halperin and said he was glad the convoys had started again. "I hope you understand," he added, "that I had nothing to do with their suspension."

But the mukhtar was not so sure that Halperin did understand, and he worried about this. Eventually he became obsessed with the idea that the Haganah wanted to kill him, and he challenged Halperin to a "trial" in accordance with the Torah, at which Israel Zief Mintzberg, an eighty-six-year-old rabbi, would judge his accusation in the presence of the accused.

Halperin accepted the challenge and met with Weingarten at Mintzberg's home. As they sat down, Weingarten removed a gun from his belt and laid it on the table, saying: "It is customary for gentlemen to put their weapons on the table when they participate in a trial."

When Halperin made no move to follow suit, Weingarten asked: "Is it possible that the Haganah commander bears no weapon?"

Halperin replied quietly: "A pistol is effective only at short range. It can't help against attack from a distance. At close range, who have I got to be afraid of? I sit among my people. Would a Jew harm me? There is no such fear in my heart."

Weingarten then outlined his claim that the Haganah was planning to kill him.

Halperin immediately responded: "I am responsible for security here, and I can therefore assure you that you have no reason to fear for your life."

Rabbi Mintzberg, a smile brightening his sallow face, then said: "I suggest that we all drink a toast and go back to our jobs."

So Mintzberg served some wine, and the trial was over.

That was not to be the last meeting between Weingarten and Halperin, however. On March 3, 1948, Halperin went to see the mukhtar at his house to ask him to use his influence with the British to increase the number of convoys allowed into the Old City.

Over coffee, he chatted with Weingarten in an atmosphere as congenial as when he had visited the family during his previous assignment in Jerusalem. Perhaps even more pleasant, for Weingarten's three elder daughters, Rivca, who was about to be married, Masha, and Yehudit—all in their early twenties now and considered among the prettiest girls in Jerusalem, either side of the wall—were also present. (The rabbi also had two younger girls.)

When this very amiable meeting had ended, Halperin walked outside and was greeted by two British soldiers. "Our commander would like to speak with you," one of them said politely.

In a few minutes, Halperin was at Zion Gate. While he stalled for time, Rousnak and other Haganah leaders who had been informed of his arrest and imminent expulsion from the Old City came running up to him. The British commander, Captain Faulkner, agreed to let Halperin speak to them and the Haganah leader promised that he would do his best to get back. Then, looking at Rousnak, he said quietly: "Meanwhile, Moshe, you take command. Follow our plans and you won't have any trouble."

Rousnak ran his hand across his forehead while he tried to digest the news. He had wanted a simple soldier's job. Now suddenly he was being given ultimate responsibility for the future of the Jewish community in the spiritual center of Judaism. He stared at Halperin, hiding his inner turbulence.

"Don't worry," he said firmly.

While being interrogated by a British intelligence sergeant in the New City, Halperin asked a question of his own: "Would you be interested in making a little money?"

The sergeant smiled, and soon it was agreed that he would return Halperin to the Old City for reasonable compensation.

On April 2, about a month after his expulsion, the sergeant drove him through Jaffa Gate in an open command car. As they headed toward the Jewish Quarter, a British officer shouted for the car to stop and confronted Halperin.

"So happy to see you, Captain Faulkner," Halperin said with a faint smile. "I had forgotten my toothbrush and was just coming back to get it."

THE Arabs launched their first big operation against the Jews on January 14, when about 1,000 Arab villagers shouting *"Jihad! Jihad!"* ("Holy War! Holy War!") stormed the Etzion Bloc of settlements perched atop the rolling Hebron hills. Wave upon wave, they surged up the rocky gray slopes seeking the first great Arab victory of the war. Yaacov Edelstein, watching from a dugout with his machine-gun team, thought Arabs were emerging from behind every bush and rock on every hillside around the Etzion Bloc. But he was calm as he held his fire. . . .

ALMOST SINCE ABRAHAM, ISAAC, AND JACOB ROAMED THESE HILLS with their flocks and herds, conquering armies had crossed swords for every knoll and ravine. For each was a stepping stone to Jerusalem, just to the north. Jewish settlement in the region was liquidated by the Crusaders in 1100, but was resumed in the early thirteenth century to continue uninterrupted for over 700 years. Then, in 1929, an Arab massacre of Jews in Hebron ended all Jewish settlement in the area once more—for six years. In 1935, a group of about 40 Jews bought some land in the hills six miles north of Hebron and formed a settlement called Kfar Etzion. In the following year, this patch of Judaism was washed away in the flood of Arab revolt. Finally, in 1943, another group of settlers revived Kfar Etzion, and three other settlements—Ein Tsurim, Massuot Yitzhak, and Revadim—blossomed on neighboring hills.

The Jews had returned, but so had the curse. For these isolated settlements, overlooking the road from Hebron to Jerusalem, constituted uniquely strategic fortresses that the Arabs could hardly ignore. Indeed, since these strongholds were surrounded by Arab villages and completely cut off from the Jewish heartland, they were encouraged to attack them. Recently, the Arabs had encountered two Jewish convoys trying to crack the blockade and had killed a number of men. Now, in the spirit of their forefathers, they were determined to root out the enemy in their midst once and for all.

But more agonizing to Yaacov than the prospect of annihilation was the probability that in the end he and his comrades would have to give up the land they so loved. For under the United Nations partition resolution, the area occupied by the Etzion Bloc was to be part of the new Arab State. Yet they would fight to the last settler to keep the Arabs from obtaining the land prematurely. That was what the Jewish national leaders—and the settlers—wanted. Despite the dissent of some who, using sound military logic, opposed defending "undefendable" outposts.

To Yaacov and others, it was precisely because the Etzion Bloc had become so vulnerable that it had to be defended at all cost. For if the bloc could survive, what settlement could not? Jewish military strategy was simple: don't attack the Arabs (except in special hit-and-run cases to boost Jewish morale and discourage the enemy), but defend *every* settlement, however isolated—until, the Jews hoped, the United Nations sent troops to enforce partition. . . .

Sprawled now in his dugout at the outer edge of Kfar Etzion, Yaacov started firing at the specks in the distance as the ancient, hallowed hills erupted into a monstrous echo of long-vanished worlds. But the specks grew larger and larger, until they reached the peripheries of Kfar Etzion and Revadim. And in the shade of orange trees far to the rear, other Arabs stood peeling ripe fruit while they watched the show, awaiting the moment when they could safely enter the conquered settlements to loot and plunder.

But the Jews counterattacked and the watchers paused, then vanished. Soon the surrounding valleys were silent as a cemetery—speckled only by lifeless Arabs, more than 150.

None too soon, either, thought Yaacov. The defenders—less than 30 after light casualties—were almost out of ammunition. Another attack might finish them, unless the Haganah in Jerusalem could slip supplies through the Arab lines.

The following evening, January 15, a detachment of 40 fighters, most of them Hebrew University students, piled into armored cars with heavy packs of arms and ammunition, headed from their base near Jerusalem for Hartuv. From there, they would continue on foot to the Etzion Bloc. Accompanied by two girlfriends, who were to stay in Hartuv, the unit arrived at 9:30 P.M. and was advised by the local commander to postpone the march until the following night. Not only would they be starting out very late, he told Dani Mass, the leader, but they would have to travel about five miles farther than originally planned in order to bypass a police station manned by British police constables and a unit of the Arab Legion.

"Even if you meet no obstacles and do three miles an hour," he argued, "you couldn't reach your objective before daylight."

"But I have orders," Dani replied. "Headquarters in Jerusalem promised that if for any reason we had to delay our departure a plane would signal us over Hartuv. And there has been no signal."

"Even so, try to contact Jerusalem and explain the situation."

Dani then tried to radio Jerusalem, but could not get through.

"It's no use," he said. "We've got to go."

He order two weaponless soldiers to stay behind, then departed with his 38 remaining men and a group of the local commander's troops, who accompanied the detachment through a wadi leading into the open hills before turning back. Shortly thereafter, one of Dani's men stumbled over a stone and sprained his ankle. Groaning at this ill fortune, Dani ordered two other men to accompany the injured boy back to Hartuv.

The detachment, now reduced to 35, hurried on over unfamiliar terrain into the Hebron hills—unaware that a plane, apparently flashing a signal, was then circling over Hartuv.

The morning of January 16 dawned drowsily in the Arab village of Surif, nestled in a gentle hollow about five miles west of the Hebron-Jerusalem road. A sleepy-eyed villager emerged from a stone hut, his *khaffiya* askew, and shuffled into the rocky fields to find his cows. He rounded them up and led them to a well some distance away. As he struck their bony haunches with his stick, his eyes swept the undulating, misty green landscape around him. Suddenly he halted. Then, abandoning his cows, he dashed into the village and barged into the home of Ahmad Shannak.

"Ahmad! Ahmad!" the peasant cried. "I've seen them! In the hills!"

"You've seen what?" growled Shannak, a slim man with a thin, hollow-cheeked face, who was sitting munching *pita* bread.

"The Jews! I've seen them! Only a few hundred yards away! About fifty of them! And they have guns!"

Shannak was silent for a moment, incredulous. Then he sprang to his feet and raced out of the house to see Ibrahim Abu Daya, the military leader of the region, who was equally startled when his deputy told him the news. His eyes flashing with excitement, he ordered: "Call a meeting of all the men in the village in the square near the mosque! After the meeting, distribute the weapons while I drive to the other villages for help!"

What luck! Right into the lion's den! He put on his *khaffiya* and his bandolier, grabbed a rifle, and strode briskly to the square, where an excited crowd was already waiting for him.

"Now is our chance," Abu Daya told them. "A group of about fifty Jews have been seen in the hills, apparently heading toward the Etzion settlements. Now we can avenge our losses. Go get your rifles!"

The men shouted gleefully as they ran to a nearby house where the village arms were stored.

Abu Daya then raced off in a jeep with several men to sound the alarm in Jaba and other villages, while Shannak led his armed men on foot into the hills to track down the Jews.

"There they are!" the cry soon sounded.

The first shots cracked out in the crisp morning air, echoing from hill to hill.

The surprised detachment of Jews fired back and began to run toward a forest that crowned the peak of a hill in the distance. But as the shooting intensified, they stopped abruptly. Shannak soon realized why. Abu Daya and fighters from other villages had swung around behind the Jews to cut them off. Wherever the Jews turned, Arab fighters blocked their path. They were trapped atop a barren hill.

As the Arabs closed in from all sides, the cry "Kill the Jews!" nearly drowned out the sputter of gunfire. But now heavy fire was coming from the Jews as well, and the thousands of villagers momentarily halted. Ahmad Shannak lay on the crest of a neighboring hill and squinted across a swooping, jagged chasm at the enemy's lair, about 200 yards away. He could see Jews hiding behind rocks and shrubbery. Cupping his hands to his mouth, he yelled: "Throw down your weapons and put up your hands and we will not harm you!"

The order resounded through the valleys like the rumble of an angry demon and a strange silence settled over the area. Then a voice thundered back in perfect Arabic: "We refuse! Go back or we shall kill you!"

And the Jews began to fire more heavily than ever.

Shannak could not help admiring their courage, but courage, he knew, would not be enough to save them. He took aim with his rifle, panning in search of a target. After observing that several Jews were carrying wounded men to what appeared to be the entrance of a cave, his sight came to rest on an unlikely figure: a girl! She was partially hidden behind a rock, apparently with a radio on her back. Perhaps she was communicating with other enemy forces. Shannak pulled the trigger but missed her. The Arabs had to move closer.

Suddenly one of his men, Jamal Hamaid, dashed down the Arab-held hill toward the foot of the Jewish-controlled height. He slumped to earth with a bullet in his head, the first Arab to die in the battle. Shannak then signaled with his arm and the rest of his men began edging down the hill, scrambling for cover behind rocks and isolated trees. Another Arab was killed at the bottom of the hill, then Shannak himself fell gasping with a bullet wound in his neck, and was carried to safety by his men. But Abu Daya was by now in full command of the Arab forces.[7]

In the early afternoon, the fighting raged as the chain slowly tightened around the Jews. By about 3 P.M., Jewish firing had greatly slackened, and the Arabs could see only a handful of figures still moving on the hill. Apparently not more than eight Jews remained to fight. One tall, dark

Jew suddenly dashed down the eastern slope in a desperate effort to snap a link in the Arab chain, throwing grenades as he ran. But he was mowed down in flight, and was later found with a stone in his hand.

By sunset, the attackers had crept almost to the crest of the enemy-held hill. Several could make out three figures standing huddled together in the dusk. The stony earth trembled under the force of an explosion and the three figures collapsed in a heap of ripped flesh. The last-known Jewish survivors had destroyed themselves with a grenade.

Thousands of joyous Arabs converged on the silenced hilltop. In the cave, according to the Arab fighters, lay three bodies—two bandaged men and the girl, who had apparently been treating the men's wounds. But the Arabs are vague about how the three in the cave died. Had they committed suicide, too? Or were they killed on discovery?

Two nights later, on January 18, three trucks covered with canvas tarpaulins were escorted into Kfar Etzion by British half-tracks and a military guard. A British police inspector stepped out and spoke gravely to the waiting settlers: "Would all the women please go indoors."

When they had gone, several settlers removed the tarpaulins and gasped in horror. Chunks of mutilated flesh—testicles stuffed into eye sockets, penises into mouths—lay piled in the truck in a pool of blood. Some of the men turned away at the sight, unable to help in carrying the bodies.

"Dim your lights, will you!" shouted someone to the British drivers. Then the settlers proceeded to remove the cadavers in the dark and wrap them carefully.

The British had had great difficulty in finding the bodies. On receiving a report of the battle, a British officer had gone to Surif to interrogate the village leaders, but they claimed they knew nothing about the matter. He returned again with orders from his superiors to find the bodies, accompanied this time by a platoon of British troops. When the villagers still denied knowledge of the deaths, the officer, using other tactics, said: "What you have done to the Jews has been well done, for they were your enemies. But remember that the souls belong to Allah and you must give up the bodies so that they can be buried."

After a short pause, an Arab youth burst out: "Come! I will show you where the bodies lie."

He then led the British to the hill where the mutilated bodies lay scattered. When the villagers refused to carry them on their camels to the army trucks, the British soldiers brought stretchers and performed the grisly task themselves.

They apparently did not find the body of the "girl." And therein lies a mystery that may never be solved. The Israelis vigorously deny that a girl had accompanied the ill-fated unit—and the list of 35 victims does not reveal one. Yet many Arab participants in the battle insist that a girl was indeed among the dead. And Arab informers working for the Jews said the same thing in their first reports of the fighting. The Arabs had no clear motive for lying. They have always stressed, justifiably or not, their traditional respect for women, including Jewish fightingwomen.* The killing, and perhaps mutilation and violation, of a girl—especially if occurring after her capture—would by no means have added luster to the Arab military record. It is thus not inconceivable that the Arabs might have hidden such a body. Had one of the two "girlfriends" who went with the detachment to Hartuv continued on with the group?

The Haganah would obviously not have wished to publicize this if so, being already concerned about whispered criticism of the mission as foolishly suicidal: So concerned, in fact, that a month later, on February 14, it raided the Arab village of Sasa deep in Arab-controlled territory near the Lebanese border principally for the purpose, according to a report by commander Moshe Kelman (who quotes his superior, Yigal Allon), of proving to the Jewish public—though also to the Haganah itself and to the enemy—that such attacks were not necessarily suicidal. Kelman's men blew up over 35 houses and killed more than 60 Arabs in Sasa and, after a harrowing retreat through swampland, returned to base safely, thereby silencing critics of the earlier failure.

The mystery of the girl is relevant in the context of the legend that has blossomed around *The Thirty-five*. The immediate result of their fall, celebrated by the Arabs as a tremendous victory and mourned by the Jews as a glorious martyrdom, was to set the ruthless tone of the subsequent fighting, in which few prisoners on either side survived beyond interrogation—though the war became more "civilized" when the relatively disciplined regular Arab armies invaded Palestine in mid-May. Since the war, the Israelis have come to regard the event as comparable in heroic sacrifice to the famous mass suicide of a group of Jewish zealots who were about to be overrun by the Romans at Masada in A.D. 70.†

But unanswered is the question whether the new legend should honor, among those who died, a nameless Israeli Joan of Arc.

---

* The Egyptian press reported during the war that six women prisoners captured by Egyptian forces in the Negev had stripped naked before their captors in order to "embarrass" them. The Egyptian guards—simple, religious peasants—covered their eyes with one hand while hastily wrapping the women in sheets. Israeli officers discounted these reports as "ridiculous." Although Israeli women enjoyed sex, they would not risk inviting rape, these officers said.

† Masada was the last Jewish fortress held by the Jewish zealots against the Romans following the fall of the Second Temple in A.D. 70. After three years of siege, the remaining defenders and their families agreed to permit several of the number to cut their throats, after which the executioners cut each other's. The last surviving executioner then committed suicide.

THE Haganah is sitting back while the Arabs kill Jews. It's up to us and Etzel to strike back.* But we need guns. How do we get them? The British have guns. We've got to relieve every British soldier we see in the streets of his gun."

Yehoshua Zetler spoke slowly, emphasizing every word; he wanted the urgency of his message to sink in. He had just arrived from Tel Aviv to take command of the Jerusalem contingent of the Stern Group, a more extreme if much smaller nationalist organization than the Irgun Zvai Leumi. The bristling manner, the cold fire in deep-set eyes, the controlled movement of thin, tight lips under a thick mustache blended into a portrait of steely determination.

"Are we to kill the British?" asked Ezra Elnakam, a young, rabidly dedicated Sternist.

"Only if they resist."

Before the United Nations resolution, the Sternists had killed the British indiscriminately in an attempt to terrorize the occupation forces into leaving Palestine. But since they were now getting ready to leave, this was no longer necessary. The main enemy, Zetler thought, would now be the Arabs. His men would throw bombs into marketplaces, blow up their headquarters and homes. They would retaliate for every Jewish death. To hell with the Haganah, which was waiting for the United Nations to impose partition, afraid to strike back for fear of antagonizing world opinion. The United Nations would never enforce partition. Nor should the Jews let it do so. For the partition plan not only gave the Arabs a part of the traditional Jewish homeland but called for the internationalization of Jerusalem, and he and his men would never stop fighting until, at the least, the whole sacred city was Jewish.

Zetler despised Nathan Friedman-Yellin (later Yellin Mor), the top Sternist leader, who wanted the Stern Group to dissolve as an activist organization and convert itself into a political party. Immediately after the partition resolution had been passed, he and Friedman-Yellin had had a bitter falling out. "Our role as a fighting group is over," Friedman-Yellin had insisted. "We have beaten the British imperialists. If the Arabs now resist partition by force, we should join with the Haganah to fight them. We are not prepared for open warfare on our own."

* *Etzel* is the popular Hebrew name for the Irgun Zvai Leumi, or National Military Organization, based on the letters I.Z.L. *Lehi* is the popular Hebrew name for the Lehame Herut Israel, or Fighters for the Freedom of Israel (Stern Group), based on the letters L.H.I.

Zetler had argued back that the Haganah would not fight the Arabs, and that, anyway, the Sternists had to frustrate the plan to internationalize Jerusalem. And he had the support of Israel Sheib (later Eldad), the ideological leader of the Stern Group and one of the three members of its executive committee. (The third member, Yitzhak Yizernitzky—later Shamir—had been exiled by the British to a detention camp in Eritrea.) As a student of the Bible, Sheib could quote any number of divine phrases to justify the use of violence and terrorism to achieve a Jewish State. A thin-faced, wizened little man with a fluffy graying thatch of hair, Sheib had never committed a violent act himself. Once when his men, posing as hospital attendants, were helping him to escape from a British prison hospital, one of them handed him a gun.

"What am I supposed to do with this?" he exclaimed, horrified by the prospect of having to pull the trigger.[8]

But his ideas, rooted in a literal interpretation of the Bible, gave other men the strength to kill enemies of the Jewish State without a trace of reluctance or regret. With Sheib thus backing Zetler, Friedman-Yellin had finally given in to the activist view, after the Arabs had attacked relentlessly and the Haganah, as expected, had not responded forcefully. But as far as Zetler was concerned, Friedman-Yellin was a traitor.

Zetler had come to Jerusalem and taken personal control of the operation there—but he had no intention of asking Friedman-Yellin to approve anything. He would make his own decisions, in consultation with Sheib.

THE VIRTUAL SPLIT IN THE STERN GROUP WAS THE DISTILLATION OF a process that had started in 1930, when some members of the Haganah formed their own independent group calling for a more militant attitude toward the British. When the Arabs revolted against the British and attacked the Jews in 1936, a large number of the dissidents returned to the Haganah fold and helped the British resist the Arabs. But a hard core, belonging to a Zionist political splinter group, the Revisionists, remained independent. It organized a revolutionary armed group called the National Military Organization, or Irgun Zvai Leumi (IZL), with the immediate dual purpose of retaliating with terrorist attacks against the Arabs and forcing the British to open the doors of Palestine without restriction to Jewish refugees from Nazi Germany.

Vladimir Jabotinsky, the Revisionist leader, even at this time, however, retained a long-held faith in ultimate British good intentions. But unlike his more moderate political foe, Chaim Weizmann, he was ready to use force to urge the British along. And he made it clear, as Weizmann did not, that unrestricted immigration was to be a final step toward the conversion of all Palestine—and Transjordan, which had formerly been a part of Palestine, as well—into a Jewish State.

Then World War II produced a new division among the ultra-nationalists. Jabotinsky favored halting Irgun attacks on British installations—he had always opposed killing British individuals—and cooperating with Britain in the struggle against Hitler. But a small group within the Irgun, led by a brilliant Polish-born poet and nationalist fanatic, Abraham Stern, bitterly objected. Unaware yet of Nazi plans to exterminate the Jews, Stern argued that the British were just as responsible as the Nazis for the Jewish plight in Europe since they would not let the Jews enter Palestine, the only country to which they could flee. The Jews in Palestine, he reasoned, were too few to be effective in the fight against Nazism anyway. But they could be effective in forcing Britain to give them independence as the price of peace in Palestine at a moment when she was so fiercely engaged in Europe.

Stern and his followers thus broke away from the Irgun and struck down British soldiers, as well as some Jewish enemies; and the Irgunists helped the British attack Axis targets in the Middle East—until a new Polish immigrant named Menachem Beigin took over the Irgun in 1942 and ordered attacks on British installations (though, unlike the Sternists, not on individual soldiers).* Finally, in 1941, British police killed Stern in a Tel Aviv hideout.[9]

One of Stern's most fervent disciples was Yehoshua Zetler, who had been the Irgun's chief of operations. After Stern's death, he found himself a hunted, powerless man, reduced to sleeping on park benches. He was finally arrested, but escaped, only to be captured again after he had robbed a bank to obtain funds for new operations. Imprisoned in Jerusalem, he was charged with leading Jewish inmates in bloody riots against Arab prisoners, and was sent to Acre Fortress, a maximum security prison.

His fellow prisoners at Acre were glad to see him. While in the Jerusalem prison, he had spent over two years planning a mass escape of Jewish prisoners. Indeed, he succeeded in digging a tunnel, but when Irgun and Sternist fighters attacked the prison from outside to provide a diversion for the escape, the British beat them back, foiling the plot. However, Zetler had meanwhile become an expert in escape techniques, and his knowledge helped to set the stage for one of the most sensational prison breaks in history—the mass breakout from Acre Fortress. In May, 1947, some 60 Irgunists and Sternists, divided into three groups, raced from the stronghold after sappers had blown down prison doors with explosives smuggled into prison in the false bottoms of jam jars and other receptacles. Zetler led the third and last group, which leaped into waiting jeeps and drove away with fewer casualties than were suffered by the other two groups.[10]

*Beigin succeeded David Raziel, who was killed in 1941 by a strafing Axis plane while in Iraq on a secret mission for the British. Raziel had planned, as a side operation, to assassinate the Mufti, who was in Iraq helping to guide the pro-Axis forces that had come to power. Beigin's name would later be spelled "Begin."

After five years of prison, Zetler was free again—free to strike new terror into Zion's enemies. And now it was time to kill Arabs—with British guns.

Ezra Elnakam was seething with excitement as he and three other Sternists roamed the streets of Jerusalem searching for British prey. Each carried a pistol, a hand grenade, a noise grenade, and a burlap sack (to be filled with confiscated British arms). Ezra, short, slight, intense, had not felt as exhilarated since that day some months earlier when he had lain in a field waiting to detonate a mine under the car of General Sir Gordon McMillan, commander of the British forces in Palestine—though the plot ultimately failed.

As the four men strolled casually through the main commerical area, it was Ezra who shouted: "Look! Two British policemen with Stens!"

They followed the policemen, and when they were within a few yards of them, two of the pursuers darted out to one side. At that moment, the British saw the strangers and, realizing what was about to happen, began to run down the street. Ezra and a companion then jumped on one and wrestled him to the ground, trying to grab his Sten. The weapon went off in the struggle, and Ezra reached for the pistol in his pocket. The policeman broke away, but Ezra aimed his pistol shakily and fired. As the man slumped to the street, Ezra ran over to examine him. A bullet in the head had killed him instantly.

Ezra grabbed the dead man's gun, deposited it in his sack, and began to run. But he found himself limping unsteadily. He had been hit. He stumbled into the Orion Cinema helped by a theater employee and fell into a seat. After watching cowboys shoot at each other for an hour, he made his way to a clinic for treatment, then home.

"What happened to you?" his mother exclaimed, seeing the bandaged leg.

"Nothing. Just scratched myself."

Ezra had never told his mother about his Sternist affiliations. He had offered every kind of excuse for leaving the house at all hours of the night; his membership must be kept secret from everybody, even his parents. Besides, he knew that they, like most Jews less imbued than himself with the righteous fury of God, regarded the Sternists as little more than gangsters.

He turned on the radio, and, with satisfaction, learned that the second British policeman had also been killed. During the struggle, the announcer said, one of the killers was believed to have been wounded.

Ezra's mother stared at him in silent shock, and quietly wept.

O<small>N</small> December 17, 1947, King Abdullah sat in his study in Amman's Shuneh Palace reading a report from Cairo, where the Arab Prime Ministers had been meeting in urgent session for five days. The Arab States were to decide at this crucial conference what to do about the partition plan. Abdullah had instructed his representatives to oppose the arming of the Mufti's Palestinian supporters and to urge intervention by the regular Arab armies upon the withdrawal of British troops. Since his Arab Legion was the only modernized, well-trained regular Arab force, such a decision, he felt, would give him the opportunity to occupy without opposition the area allocated by the United Nations to the Arabs in accordance with his secret proposal to the Jews.

But the hardening lines on his face as he read the report showed that all had not gone well. After endless bickering, the premiers had agreed to "do all in their power to frustrate the partition plan." To this end, they had also agreed to collect 10,000 rifles and other light arms for distribution to the Palestine Arabs, to recruit about 3,000 volunteers, and to establish a military committee attached to the Arab League which would train and organize the volunteers.

This program, he was sure, would have little practical effect, for the Jews could easily deal with such an army. That was the danger, in fact. Guerrilla attacks by the Mufti's men and other volunteers would simply serve to provoke the Jews to counterattack and give them a pretext to take territory not allocated to the projected Jewish State.

Yet how could he have held out against all the other Arab States? The Mufti, of course, pressed for the decisions, and so did the Syrians and Egyptians, all of whom feared that the Arab Legion would otherwise occupy Arab Palestine. Saudi Arabia opposed arming the Palestinians, but also the dispatch of regular armies.* Even Iraq, whose rulers were

---

* Saudi Arabia has never been as opposed to Zionism as most other Arab states. Harry St. John Philby, a British adviser to King Ibn Saud, writes[11] that he suggested to Weizmann a plan whereby all Palestine would go to the Jews, who would furnish Saud with £20 million to resettle the Palestine Arabs.

Referring to this plan, Weizmann says[12] that Winston Churchill favored such a solution, under which Saud would become "lord of the Middle East." According to Philby, Saud waited for Churchill and Roosevelt to make the first move, but they did not. Then, apparently fearing the reaction in other Arab countries if the plan leaked out, Saud showed an uncompromising attitude toward Zionism in conversations with Roosevelt aboard a U.S. cruiser in the Mediterranean following the Yalta Conference.

Roosevelt, who, according to Harry Hopkins, his confidant,[13] had been "overly impressed" by Saud's arguments, wrote the King a few weeks later that he "would take no action . . . which might prove hostile to the Arab people." When Truman came into office, the State Department constantly reminded him of this "commitment."[14]

Hashemites like Abdullah, would not cooperate with Transjordan, for the Iraqis were currently negotiating a defense agreement with Britain and wanted to counter resultant protests at home that the government was soft on imperialism and Zionism. So the premiers decided to implement the secret decisions of the Bludan Conference . . .

It was at Bludan, Syria, in June, 1946, that the Arab States had plunged into the political quicksands of Palestine. Until then, most had done little more than pay lip service to anti-Zionism, being too involved in their own domestic problems even to consider serious moves against the Jews. But the Anglo-American Commission recommendation that 100,000 Jewish refugees be permitted to enter Palestine immediately and the consequent conflict between President Truman and the British offered too good an opportunity to miss. Encouraged by the British, who wanted "evidence" that immigration would lead to widespread bloodshed in the Middle East, the Arabs called a conference of the Arab League Political Committee in Bludan. They rejected the Anglo-American proposals and secretly decided that if Zionist efforts forced the Palestinian Arabs into war, the Arab States would not be able to prevent their citizens from coming to the aid of their brethren with money, arms and volunteers.

Abdullah, however, had not been happy with the decision then any more than he was now, almost two years later. It would, of course, be best if the Jews agreed to autonomy within his kingdom; but since it was clear they would not, peaceful partition seemed the next best solution. He could live with the Jews. They might even help him to attain his ends. After all, his father Sherif Hussein had supported Zionism, though he may not have calculated that it would lead to a completely independent Jewish State; and his elder brother Faisal had promised Chaim Weizmann his support in 1918, when Weizmann had visited him in his desert camp.*

*

* Hussein, ruler of the Hedjaz area that later constituted Saudi Arabia, assured a British representative, D. G. Hogarth, in 1918 that he would support the Balfour Declaration—if it did not mean the establishment of an independent Jewish State.

Emir Faisal, his son, told Weizmann a few months later at a desert meeting that he would also back the Declaration, but did not mention conditions. Having an exaggerated notion of international Jewish influence, Faisal felt that the Jews could help him achieve his coveted goal: world sanction for an independent Greater Syria, which he would head.

Unlike many other Arabs, Faisal did not consider the Balfour Declaration to be a British repudiation of earlier promises to support the establishment of an independent Arab world in the Middle East once the Ottoman Empire had crumbled, in return for an Arab military uprising against the Turks. The question of whether these promises—made in vague terms by the British High Commissioner in Egypt, Sir Henry MacMahon, in correspondence with Hussein—applied to Palestine is still a source of controversy.

Voices echoed excitedly through the spacious halls of Shuneh Palace on the evening of January 9, 1948, approximately three weeks after the Cairo conference. Several units of the new Arab Liberation Army (ALA) of volunteers—including Palestinians, Syrians, Iraqis, Lebanese, and Egyptians trained and armed in Syria—had arrived without notice at the Transjordanian border. The commander demanded that they be permitted to cross Transjordanian territory, and thence over Allenby Bridge into Palestine. The local Arab Legion commander radioed Amman asking whether he should allow this.

The British Arab Legion commander, General John Bagot Glubb—usually called Glubb Pasha, after being honored with that high Arab title—was enraged by the volunteers' demand.* Like Abdullah, he had strongly opposed the formation of the Arab Liberation Army in the first place, for both political and professional reasons. He feared, like the King, that such irregular forces would provoke the Jews into grabbing areas allocated to the Arabs under the partition plan without enjoying any military success. He particularly abhorred the ALA commander, Fawzi el-Kaoukji, who was still in Damascus waiting to see if his first units would get through. He regarded Fawzi, a boastful soldier of fortune, as incompetent, and a willing tool of Transjordan's enemies in the Arab League. And Glubb, though appearing on the surface rather mild and meek—in part because of a sharply receding chin shot away in World War I—could hate his enemies as passionately as he loved his own soldiers.

On hearing of the volunteers' arrival, Glubb rushed to see the British minister, Sir Alec Kirkbride, who agreed that they should not be allowed to cross Transjordan, mainly on the grounds that the British administration was responsible for security in Palestine and would be ridiculed if foreign troops freely entered that country. Technically, at least, Britain was "neutral" in the Arab-Jewish conflict.

Indeed, that very day, in another test of British intentions, about 200 volunteers had crossed the Syrian border to attack two Jewish settlements, Dan and Kfar Szold. General Sir Gordon McMillan, commander of the British forces in Palestine, had met the challenge by dispatching a troop of armored cars to each kibbutz to help the defenders, and after a short but concentrated fire fight they had sent the attackers fleeing. The British Ambassador to Damascus had then officially protested to the Syrian government. How, therefore, could the British representatives in Amman now permit volunteers to cross into Palestine from Transjordan?

When Kirkbride and Glubb put this question to Abdullah, the King nodded. He understood the logic and was opposed to the crossing himself.

---

* Glubb's top officers were given the title "Bey," a rank just below Pasha.

"But what shall I tell the other Arab leaders?" he asked in despair. The Englishmen had no answer. Abdullah would certainly be accused of selling out to the British and Jews. Had Transjordan not agreed, if reluctantly, to the establishment of a volunteer force? In fact, Bevin himself had approved the idea.

Finally, Kirkbride and Glubb agreed to let the volunteers pass on three conditions:

1. The troops would move secretly, after midnight, so that it could be said that they had infiltrated into Palestine without official Transjordanian or British knowledge.

2. They would move as a group, with Arab Legion guards marching to the front and the rear, until they crossed into Palestine.

3. They would not stay in Jerusalem, but would march directly to the Nablus area in central Palestine.

A few hours later, the first foreign Arab troops crossed Allenby Bridge into Palestine and made their way stealthily to villages in the Nablus region.

McMillan says he was shocked when an aide informed him early on the morning of January 10 that ALA troops had arrived in Palestine from Transjordan. No one had consulted him, he claims, about permitting their entry. From his residence, he radioed the British Middle East commander in the Suez Canal Zone, General Sir John Crocker, and asked what he should do.

"Drive them out!" was Crocker's reply, according to McMillan.

The latter maintains that this is exactly what he wanted to do. As the battles at Dan and Kfar Szold indicated, he did not want to suffer the indignity of hosting foreign troops in a British-administered area. Apparently before he could act, however, he received an urgent directive from London, signed by Minister for War Emmanuel Shinwell, ordering him not to get involved in any military encounter with either Arabs or Jews unless their actions disturbed the withdrawal of British troops, which had already started.

As if to emphasize this casual attitude toward the arrival of Arab volunteers in Palestine, Britain concluded an agreement with Iraq on that same day promising immediate large-scale military assistance, and two days later confirmed that Britain would continue to supply arms to Egypt, Iraq, and Transjordan under her treaties of alliance with these countries.* Then, on January 21, 20 trucks with Syrian license plates, containing over 700 men of the Arab Liberation Army under Safr Bek, a Syrian officer, sped across the border into Palestine.

---

* The British-Iraqi arms agreement was cancelled shortly after it had been concluded when mobs rioted in Baghdad in protest against British "imperialism."

When the British still did not react, commander Fawzi el-Kaoukji decided that it was time to make his own entry. On January 25, Kaoukji passed through Amman and crossed the border into Palestine, unshaven, dressed in Bedouin robes. Thus, the British Colonial Secretary was able to tell the House of Commons that Kaoukji had "slipped through the border guards."[15]

"You don't have to worry about us," Kaoukji said with a grin as he welcomed his guest into his headquarters tent in the village of Tubas near Nablus. "We will not attack the Jews until the mandate is over."

District Commissioner Pollack, sent by General McMillan to Tubas to determine Kaoukji's intentions, was skeptical. Yet this promise at least gave the British a semblance of an excuse for not forcibly ousting Kaoukji's units from Palestine. As it was, the order from London forbidding such use of force had deeply embarrassed McMillan. Many people would find hard to swallow the Foreign Office argument that the British army in Palestine, though still 40,000 strong, could not take action that might slow up its withdrawal from the country. But if the Arab invaders quietly bided their time, perhaps the world might not notice their presence in British-controlled territory.

"We shall expect you to live up to that pledge," Pollack replied firmly.

Kaoukji, resplendent now in shiny black boots and suede jacket, with a sheepskin overcoat draped around his shoulders, stood up to exchange salutes as the British visitor departed. He smiled, his fair face alight. His plan could not have worked more smoothly; the British had agreed to let his forces remain in Palestine. They were on his side. They had apparently forgotten how during the 1936–39 Arab revolt he had humiliated them. Although the Mufti had tried to take credit for the great Arab victories, it was he, Fawzi el-Kaoukji, who had mobilized every Arab village and proved a master of guerrilla warfare. (The British point out that in the end, the revolt petered out and Kaoukji fled the country.)

Perhaps that was why the British were now so kind to him, he thought. They didn't want another round with him.

Understandably. For he had a strong army behind him: about 4,000 men, divided into four regiments. Most were ex-members of regular Arab armies and police forces, and many had fought under him in the various Arab rebellions against Western domination since World War I. A number of the senior officers and noncommissioned officers were still on the Syrian army's active list and, in theory, on indefinite leave of absence. Of course, some of his men were raw recruits; but they had been given basic training for several weeks in a Syrian army camp.

In such a pick-up army, however efficient, it was only natural, he reasoned, that some men should turn out to be shady characters seeking to profit from the "liberation" venture. He had, in fact, discovered four spies among his men—three Arabs and an Oriental Jew. He had ordered the Arabs hanged as traitors and the Jew, whom he felt was at least serving his country, shot honorably by a firing squad. There were other men who were thieves and looters, but he would crack down hard on them too. He would have a disciplined army, one honored by history. After all, when he had defeated the Jews he would be the military commander of Palestine: the national leader.

Yes, everything would work out well—if only he could keep his more impatient followers from forcing the British to crack down before the mandate ended. He would have to watch carefully for indications of British permissiveness.

"Sir, we've just received a message . . . Arab forces are attacking the Jewish settlement of Tirat Zvi."

Hardly had the British radio operator spoken on the dawn of February 16 than the commander at the British base in Beisan, in the Jordan Valley, dispatched a platoon with 3-inch mortars and machine guns to the kibbutz, a few miles to the south.

When General McMillan learned of the Arab attack, he was furious. On February 4, an Arab Liberation Army unit had ambushed a force of Irish Guards near Tiberias, mistaking them for Jews. The Arabs had been forced to retreat and some of them had been captured—first-class Syrian soldiers who apologized smilingly for the error. They had meant to attack only Jews, they said. But had not Kaoukji promised not to attack the Jews while the British remained in Palestine?

Now, with this latest assault, the British forces would look all the more ridiculous; they would be pictured as permitting the slaughter of Jews in territory under British control. McMillan had cooperated, if reluctantly, with Kaoukji. Why couldn't Kaoukji cooperate with him? Why was he taking advantage of Britain's liberal attitude toward the Arabs? Had not Britain just refused to allow the formation of a legal Jewish militia—in defiance of the United Nations? Had he no gratitude?

"Why is there so much banging?" a child asked pitifully.

"Just some exercises," replied Esther as she fed the little girl, one of many taking refuge on the second floor of a concrete house in Tirat Zvi.

Because of its sturdiness, the house had been turned into a temporary fortress.

"Why do they have to make their exercises next to our house?" the child insisted. "Let them go out into the fields."

Esther smiled grimly. For the Arabs were in the rainswept fields, in the orchards and vineyards, firing ceaselessly as they crept over the mud toward the kibbutz. They were now about 200 yards away, and there were only a handful of men to shoot back—including her husband Naftali. What would become of Naftali—and their new baby? If the Arabs captured the kibbutz, they would slaughter everyone; they were in the mood for vengeance.

Esther hated the wounded Arab who had just been taken prisoner and carried into the house. She could sympathize with the nurse who had not wanted to care for him; yet she could also understand the commander's order to treat him as she would any other patient. And so a man who would have killed them all now lay bandaged with a vase of flowers beside his bed . . .

At that moment three men appeared at the top of the staircase. One of them, Naftali, rushed over to his wife and embraced her.

"We're going up to the roof with the machine gun," he said.

She wanted to tell him not to try to be a hero. But she knew everyone had to be a hero if anyone was to survive.

"Don't worry, we'll stop them," Naftali said rather doubtfully.

At the Arab village of As Samariya, three miles west of the besieged settlement, a British column marched into Arab headquarters for the attack.

"You must withdraw your forces immediately," Major R. Steele, the British commander, ordered his Syrian counterpart.

A tense moment followed. Steele knew that this order would be very difficult to enforce; he did not know that Kaoukji had issued strict orders that the Arab force should under no conditions fight the British. On the other hand, the Arab commander wanted to end what had become a massacre of his own men—but he was afraid of losing face.

"We shall withdraw on one condition," the Syrian finally replied. "Your column must simulate a battle."

"What do you mean?"

"Put down a concentration of mortar and machine-gun fire to one flank."

Steele reflected briefly. It was a harmless enough request. Shortly afterward, his men laid down a barrage while the badly mauled Arabs began their retreat.

In a few hours, the kibbutz was as quiet as a graveyard—with about 40 Arab bodies sprawled in the mud. Only one Jew had been killed—Naftali. He had been shot in the head while firing the machine gun that killed many of the Arabs. Kaoukji was horrified when he learned the results of the attack. But he had never lost a battle—by his standards—and he was determined not to lose this one. Before the day was out, Arabs throughout the land were rejoicing over reports that the Arab Liberation Army had killed 300 Jews while scoring a glorious victory!

Netiva Ben-Yehuda was delighted when she learned of her battalion's new mission. The battalion was a unit of the Palmach (meaning "striking force"), which was the elite, autonomously led spearhead of the Haganah. A high officer in Kaoukji's Arab Liberation Army, with some of his men, was expected to cross the Lebanese frontier into Palestine within a few days by bus. The battalion was to ambush the bus and kill everyone inside. As demolitions officer, Netiva would press the button to blow it up. About time, she thought, that the Jews began retaliating against the Arabs. In any case, this might be her last chance for a combat operation, since women were being transferred to rear echelon jobs.

Her male superiors, particularly battalion commander Moshe Kelman, had unfortunately been influenced by several recent incidents. The Arabs had captured a girl fighter in the Negev, then violated and killed her, and mutilated the body. There was also the operation at the village of Khissas, near the Syrian frontier. In the Palmach's first retaliatory raid against an Arab community, undertaken on December 18, a girl had been accused of messing things up; her battalion was assigned to attack and destroy the hamlet, and she was leading a platoon that was to toss grenades into windows to divert attention from the main attack. But the girl heard a baby crying and failed to order the grenade assault. In any event, the operation, though killing ten Arabs and wounding five, largely failed and Moshe Kelman was enraged.

"I've had enough of you women," he had told Netiva. "You can't fight a war like this with kindness. You can be our cooks and service people."

But Netiva was grateful that Kelman and the other Palmach leaders had not cracked down too hard yet. It was ridiculous that all her training should go to waste. She was as good a soldier as any man. Of course, she was unusually strong; wiry and muscular, though small of frame, she had been an expert shot-putter and would have entered the Olympic Games if war had not broken out. But many other girls also made excellent soldiers —how else could they have passed the training course? Every trainee, man and woman, had to carry 45 pounds on his back for 50-mile hikes, without food or water. Everyone, as part of the training, had to run four miles before breakfast, and slide from a steep cliff down a sharply angled rope.

Usually, fewer women than men fell out on the hikes. They were better snipers, too, and better prepared psychologically to endure pain and hardship. It was insane to make cooks and servants out of fightingwomen. And she would prove it!

Early on the morning of the mission, Netiva's platoon marched in a steady rain to a hairpin curve on the road from Lebanon. The soldiers placed explosives on the inner shoulder of the curve so that the blast would blow the vehicle off the outer edge over a steep embankment. When the charge had been set, Netiva hid in some bushes within the U of the curve beside the detonator, while other Jews waited in the fields close by, ready to fire at the bus on receiving a whistle signal from the girl.

Netiva's heart pounded as the bus came into view. This was like a game, and she was about to win. She placed her finger lightly on the detonator button. Then, as the bus passed within a few yards of her toward the curve of the hairpin, she heard a high, shrill voice—a woman's voice. In panic, she raised her finger. Could she knowingly kill women, maybe young girls? No, this was not her game, after all. Then the image of a mutilated girl's body on the scorched Negev sands consumed her. It was not her game —but it was theirs.

Netiva blew her whistle, then pressed her finger on the button. But the rain had dampened the explosives, and they failed to go off. A Jewish Bren gunner shot the driver, and the vehicle lurched to a halt. The doors opened and screaming passengers emerged to dash in Netiva's direction, out of the line of fire of the other ambushers. Facing the Arabs alone, the girl, still under cover behind a rock, brushed her long blond hair out of her eyes and began firing her Sten. But it jammed. As the Arabs returned the fire on the run, she grabbed a rifle and fired at each man individually as he approached, pulling the bolt and re-aiming after every shot. But the more she fired, the more, it seemed, there were to fire at. On they came, bellowing in fright and fury, no longer fleeing for their lives but hurling themselves hysterically at the devil behind the rock—a devil with long blond hair. One by one they fell crying in agony, and finally the last lurched into a bush hardly two yards away.

Shaking and gasping, Netiva rose unsteadily with her smoking rifle. Suddenly she saw a figure dash from behind the bus toward the embankment, apparently intending to leap into the shallow canyon below. But as the man, dressed in the neat, olive-drab uniform of a high officer, jumped onto the fence rimming the curve, he hesitated for a moment. Netiva took aim and fired, and the figure toppled over the embankment.

Seven minutes after the first shot had been fired, Netiva, her blue eyes fixed in horror behind thick, round lenses, counted the bodies. With her long, sensitive trigger finger, the Blond Devil, as the Arabs were to call her, had killed 16 men, including Kaoukji's high ranking officer.

Kaoukji sat mournfully in his headquarters at Tubas, stunned by his crushing defeat at Tirat Zvi and further successful Jewish exploits—such as the ambush of his commander's bus. Remembering the unaggressive attitude of the Jews in years past, he realized that he had misjudged their military capabilities. It appeared they would be more difficult to knock out than he had anticipated. Word was getting around in the Arab villages that Tirat Zvi had been a disastrous defeat rather than a glorious victory, and he must do something about that. He would have to score a triumph somewhere else to bolster his sagging prestige. But was it really feasible to plan all-out war on the Jews? It would be much simpler if he could make a deal with them instead.

Maybe they would agree to accept him as leader of Palestine, with full autonomy for themselves within a federal state. After all, he and the Jews had something in common—they both hated the Mufti. If the Jews thought that the Mufti might win control of Palestine, they could very well choose to back Kaoukji as a preferable alternative.

"Would you care to meet General Kaoukji?" asked General Madlul Abbas Bek, commander of the Iraqi contingent of the Arab Liberation Army.

Yoshua Palmon, a Jewish Agency official, grinned; exactly what he wanted! He might well be able to exploit the hostility between Kaoukji and the Mufti. In fact, he had been working toward just such a meeting at each secret talk he had had with Abbas Bek.

"I would be glad to," he replied now with restraint.

A few days later, in late March, 1948, Palmon drove his own car to Tulkarm, where he switched to an Arab-owned automobile that sped him to Kaoukji's headquarters. A guard of honor stood at attention and saluted as he entered the small house. Kaoukji and his aides welcomed him warmly, and the men sat round a table sipping coffee, exchanging pleasantries. Then Palmon spoke frankly of Zionist aspirations, assuring his hosts that the future Jewish State would prove beneficial to the Arab world.

"There's no reason for any of us to quarrel," he said with a smile. "When the British leave, we can find a way to live peacefully. I could arrange for us to negotiate all our differences."

Kaoukji put down his coffee and, glancing at his aides, replied: "This man speaks our language, understands our ways, and risked his life to come to us in the cause of peace. I personally do not see why we should not be able to arrive at an understanding with the Jews in the Middle East. We have inherited the sword from our fathers, and the Jews are the inheritors of the book and a knowledge of commerce. We are cousins, who can live together and complement each other."

Palmon did not miss the proud suggestion that Arabs were natural fighters while Jews knew little of war. In a way, Kaoukji was like a small boy playing at war—a rather likable small boy. Palmon decided to throw in his ace.

"We have been driven to the present situation," he said, "not because we do not want peace but because the man who now stands at the head of Palestine's Arabs, Haj Amin, has proved to be a person no one can trust, a treacherous hypocrite, an intriguer, and a layer of snares."

Palmon reminded Kaoukji of the Mufti's intrigues against him, and accused Haj Amin of having killed both Jews and Arabs wantonly in the past.

"It's only natural," he concluded, "that to defend our lives and our honor we have had to take up arms and fight."

Kaoukji seemed impressed by this argument, and in turn scathingly detailed the Mufti's intrigues against him. True, he had supported a pro-Axis government in Iraq during World War II because of his anti-British sentiments. But he had refused a Nazi request that he command a Moslem army in Europe—and had suffered dearly for it. The Germans murdered his son.* Then they threw him in prison—after the Mufti, fearing Kaoukji would replace him in German eyes as the true leader of the Arabs, had accused him of spying for the British.

As for the Mufti's officers, Kaoukji scoffed, they were "corrupt commanders and bandits, not worthy to be called soldiers."

Palmon then suggested that the Jews and the Arab Liberation Army should refrain from attacking each other in the future and negotiate when the British departed. Kaoukji agreed, though he made it clear that in future negotiations he would propose a federal state, with the Jews enjoying internal autonomy under his own general rule—the dream, too, of King Abdullah.

---

* Kaoukji told me that in 1941 the Nazis had asked him to lead a European Moslem army against the Allies. When the Germans would not guarantee, in return, that the Arabs would receive full independence after World War II, Kaoukji rejected the request. Thereupon a German officer snapped threateningly: "Don't forget that you are a Semite like the Jews!" Kaoukji (who was in a German hospital recovering from wounds sustained in Iraq) says he replied: "True, I am a cousin of the Jews. But I can prove that Arab blood has not been mixed with Jewish blood for hundreds of years. Could some Germans do the same?" According to Kaoukji, the Nazis, infuriated by this allusion to the uncertain identity of Hitler's father, then poisoned his son "by mistake" while the latter was also undergoing treatment, and invited the father to the funeral. Kaoukji claims he replied: "Let those who murdered him go."

But Kaoukji posed a condition. He would refrain from attacking the Jews—*after* he had scored one single face-saving victory to make up for the "mistake" at Tirat Zvi. He must redeem himself in the eyes of his people. Palmon was aghast. "It would be very difficult for us," he said diplomatically, "to ask our people to lose a battle. If you insist on attacking, we shall have no choice but to fight back. But in any case, after that battle I hope our agreement will come into force."

"Don't worry," Kaoukji assured him with a grin. "We'll attack once more in the Jezreel Valley. Then we won't attack you again even if you attack Haj Amin's forces."

Palmon took his leave feeling rather like a character in a comic opera.

IN THE name of God, I don't understand Haj Amin," said Syrian President Kuwatly irritably. "If the people of Palestine want him to run the war, I shall abdicate all responsibility for trying to save the country!"

Kuwatly had just read two letters sent to the Arab League Military Committee, which had agreed to organize the Arab Liberation Army under Fawzi el-Kaoukji's command and to supply it with weapons to be contributed by all member nations.

In the first letter, the Mufti demanded that all these weapons be turned over to him for distribution, and that, in any case, no action should be taken without his knowledge. In the second letter, he requested large sums of money to finance his own guerrilla operations.

Since Syria had, almost alone among the Arab nations, supported the Mufti's ambitions in the hope of frustrating King Abdullah's plans for an Amman-dominated Greater Syria, Kuwatly's annoyance underscored the intensity of the three-way Arab struggle for power in Palestine. With both Abdullah and Kaoukji maneuvering for control of a large slice of Palestine, the Mufti (with whom the Jews would not deal) was fighting fiercely to frustrate their designs before it was too late.

At this point early in 1948, Kaoukji, the Mufti's old enemy, posed the greatest danger to him. For the Arab Liberation Army had entrenched itself in Palestine with the full support of all Arab League members except Transjordan. And Syria was the ALA's strongest supporter despite her willingness to cooperate with the Mufti, being more interested in blocking Abdullah by any means than in promoting the fortunes of a particular individual.

The Mufti fought back with threat and stealth. His Palestinian guerrilla army would not cooperate with the ALA, he warned, unless he exercised effective control over all forces in Palestine and their activities. When the

Arab League Military Committee shrugged off his demands, he played one
Arab nation against the other. Early in 1948, he audaciously swept into
Cairo, where he managed to convince King Farouk and his government that
Syria and Iraq sought to dominate Palestine. Egypt took the bait and en-
trusted him, rather than the Military Committee, with most of the rifles
in the Egyptian quota for the ALA. At the same time, when local League
officials in Haifa permitted the Mufti's men to distribute rifles sent by the
Military Committee, many of the guns disappeared, and charges were rife
that the Mufti had sold them to the highest bidder.

Equally bitter was the struggle over the right to choose commanders.
General Ismail Safwat Pasha, an Iraqi appointed by the League as commander-in-chief of all Arab forces in Palestine, finally agreed to a compromise whereby northern Palestine was put under Kaoukji's command
and central Palestine under the command of the Mufti's men—the leaders
being Abd el-Kader el-Husseini in the Jerusalem sector, and Sheikh Hassan
Salame in the Jaffa-Ramle-Lydda region.

The Mufti was satisfied—for the present. The Arab Liberation Army,
he was sure, would soon disintegrate, being composed mostly of foreign
Arabs who would not fight very hard for Palestine. On the other hand, Abd
el-Kader el-Husseini, a cousin of his, would lead the struggle for Jerusalem,
the most important part of Palestine. The people worshiped Abd el-Kader
and would gladly die for him. Eventually, Abd el-Kader would take over
all of Palestine and hand it to his elder cousin as a gift from Allah.

Abd el-Kader el-Husseini was addressing his men at Palestinian Arab
headquarters in Beir Zeit, a village near Ramallah. His piercing eyes held
each of his lieutenants in turn as he spoke with suppressed passion: "We
must carry out a series of dramatic actions that will shake the Jews irrevoca-
bly and let the world know that partition can never be implemented."

He paused, then added: "Besides, Arab morale has been damaged by
Jewish terrorists. We must show our people that we are capable of striking
even greater blows than they."

Abd el-Kader was referring to a number of Jewish terrorist actions,
including the bombing of Damascus Gate by the Irgun, and of Arab buildings in Jaffa by the Stern Group.

Abd el-Kader's listeners, among them Bahjat and Mohammed Gharbieh, agreed with him heartily. Now that their revered commander had
returned to Palestine in late January, 1948, the Arab forces would prove
irresistible. Abd el-Kader had only recently arrived from Cairo where, together with the Mufti, he had sought desperately to acquire arms and am-

munition for the struggle ahead, since the Arab League was distributing most government arms contributions to Kaoukji. But, aside from some direct donations from the Egyptian government, he had managed to obtain few weapons—and those mostly defective World War II rifles found in the Libyan sands by Bedouins, who sold them at outrageous prices. Yet Abd el-Kader would easily make up for the shortage of arms by his almost hypnotic hold on the people, his officers felt. The Palestinians would fight with their bare hands if he ordered them to do so. And Jewish documents and publications made it clear that the Jews, too, respected him for his courage and military capability—however much they feared and hated him.

THE JEWS—AND THE BRITISH—HAD LEARNED OF ABD EL-KADER el-Husseini many years earlier. The son of Musa Kasim Pasha el-Husseini, Arab Palestine's first great nationalist leader, Abd el-Kader had been nourished on Arab nationalism from childhood. Etched in the Arab mind was that glorious moment in 1932 when, at the age of twenty-four, he received his diploma from the American University in Cairo: he had launched angrily into a long speech denouncing the institution as a hotbed of Western imperialism and demanding that Egypt close it down. Then, in a dramatic gesture, he tore his diploma to bits.

As a journalist for Arab newspapers, Abd el-Kader pursued a career of skillfully inflaming Arab passions against both Britain and Zionism. He then went to work for the British—who were delighted with the opportunity to "control" his actions—as an official in the Land Distribution Department, a job in which he was, in fact, able to help control the sale of Arab lands to Jews. When the Arab revolt broke out in 1936, he organized Arab rebels in the villages, often in competition with the overall military leader, Fawzi el-Kaoukji.

In one bloody fight, Abd el-Kader was severely wounded and captured by the British, but he escaped from his hospital bed and soon returned to battle, only to be wounded again, this time almost fatally. Once more he recovered; when World War II broke out, he fled to Iraq, where he helped the Mufti to plot the pro-Axis *coup d'état* and led a Palestinian contingent in the subsequent fighting with the British. When the British finally crushed the pro-Axis forces, they arrested Abd el-Kader and imprisoned him for three years. After World War II, he set to work organizing the "Sacred Fighters" as the military arm of the Mufti's Arab Higher Committee.

Currently, his principal aim was to harass and cut main Jewish lines of communication, isolating the various settlements. But such tactics could not yield swift or dramatic results, and he needed several spectacular successes to feed the enthusiasm of his people. He had therefore decided to embark on a massive campaign of terrorism.

"I think we should start by blowing up the *Palestine Post*," he proposed (referring to Jewish Jerusalem's influential English-language newspaper). Mohammed Gharbieh immediately volunteered for the job, but Abd el-Kader replied with a smile: "You look too much like an Arab. We need people who look English so that we can bluff our way through the British roadblocks. In fact, we need Englishmen!"

Abd el-Kader then selected Abdel Nur Khalil Janho, one of his top deputies, to lead the operation. With him would go two well-paid—and savagely anti-Jewish—British deserters, including one named Eddie Brown whose brother had been killed by Jewish terrorists.

Shortly after 10 P.M. on February 1, two British vehicles—a car with two British soldiers followed by a 5-ton canvas-topped truck driven by a man in police uniform—halted at the Nablus Gate, Jerusalem. The British showed the guards their identity cards and the two vehicles were ushered into the Jewish-inhabited New City.

"We'll be back soon," shouted one of the Englishmen in the car.

With equal ease, the travelers passed through a Haganah checkpoint. Then the two vehicles separated. The truck headed directly for Hassolel Street, where the *Palestine Post* was located; the car moved slowly through the city en route to a point near the newspaper building. The driver of the truck drove carefully; it was carrying two barrels of TNT.

Marlin Levin, an immigrant from Harrisburg, Pennsylvania, raised his eyes from his typewriter to glance at the clock on the wall of the *Palestine Post* newsroom. It was 10:58 P.M. Only two minutes to deadline, and he hadn't finished his story. It was fortunate that the day had been relatively quiet. Only three or four incidents to report in his roundup of the fighting in Jerusalem.

"Let's get that copy in," urged Mike Eskolsky, only recently arrived from Wilkes-Barre, Pennsylvania.

Levin muttered to himself. So let them move back the deadline. No lousy, half-assed story would appear under his byline . . .

In the composing room on the ground floor, the *Post*'s editor, Ted Lurie, another American, was giving last-minute instructions to his stone hand, Nathan Rabinovitz, when his wife came in. She had been visiting with friends and dropped in to accompany her husband on a coffee break to Atara Café, about two blocks away.

As the Luries walked down Hassolel Street toward Jaffa Road—the main thoroughfare of downtown Jewish Jerusalem—the streets were completely deserted. Suddenly, a British army truck swerved toward them from Jaffa Road. Lurie stared at it. The British seldom drove up Hassolel Street, which was little more than an alley. What were they up to now, he wondered . . .

Alexander Zvilli, a linotype operator, watched the Luries morosely as they left the composing room. As usual, he was flooded with copy at deadline time. And his girl Dana wouldn't even bring him a sandwich. He had telephoned her just a couple of hours before and asked her, begged her, to marry him. But it was the same old story. She was engaged to someone else and had to have time to make up her mind.

"Well, at least bring me a sandwich at work," he had urged.

"No," she had replied coldly. "I don't want to see you for a month or two, until I've had time to think things out."

Zvilli broke off work for a moment and started to light a cigarette; suddenly everything turned red, then black. In a few seconds, he woke from what seemed like a nightmare to find himself on the floor. He heard screams and moans and saw great gusts of fire reaching toward him. Then he realized that the building had been bombed . . .

Abdel Nur Janho had parked his truck on Hassolel Street just outside the *Palestine Post,* facing the ground floor area where the composing room was located. He had lit a long fuse attached to the explosives in the back, and walked swiftly to a nearby street where the two British deserters were waiting for him with the car. They sped toward the Nablus Gate, through which they had entered a short time before. First the Haganah border guards and then the British waved them past into Arab territory, still unsuspecting, while flames rose to the skies a few blocks away.

The tremendous blast killed the linotype operator sitting closest to the TNT-loaded truck, and wounded more than 20 other people, mostly in the composing room. Ted Lurie, who heard the explosion as he was about to enter the Atara Café with his wife, ran back to the burning building and saw, among the victims being carried out, Nathan Rabinovitz. His face had been lacerated beyond recognition, and his eyes were dripping blood.

Upstairs, people found themselves cut off from the stairway, which was in flames. They leaped from balconies or climbed down drains, many with the help of Fitzhugh Turner of the New York *Herald Tribune,* who arrived shortly after the explosion. John Donovan of the National Broadcasting Company dashed into the smoke and fire consuming the pressroom to pull out the last wounded.

Alexander Zvilli, though he was dazed and bleeding from facial cuts, also helped in the rescue work. Then he stumbled down the street toward Dana's apartment and found her trying desperately to break through a police line that had formed halfway up the block. He ran to her and they clung to one another.

"Are you all right?" the girl cried, seeing the blood from cuts in his face.

"Just scratched."

"Well, I've thought things out," she sobbed. "Will you marry me?"

A few hours later, an abbreviated edition of the *Palestine Post* was published at a nearby printshop. In a front-page editorial, Roy Elston, a non-Jewish British contributor to the newspaper, wrote: "The truth is louder than TNT and burns brighter than the flames of arson."

But Abd el-Kader el-Husseini saw in the flames of arson, which partially destroyed the *Palestine Post* and two other neighboring buildings, an enticing vision of Arab victory. The Arabs had proved that they could be just as daring as Jewish terrorists. The morale of his people had skyrocketed as sharply as, he was sure, Jewish morale had fallen. One great feat, however, was not enough. He must hit the Jews again and again. Soon even the United Nations would realize that partition was impossible. He decided to strike even more sensationally. He would knock out a whole block of buildings on Ben Yehuda Street, in the heart of the downtown area.

At about 6:10 A.M. on February 22, exactly three weeks after the *Palestine Post* bombing, a convoy of three British army trucks led by a police armored car approached Jerusalem from the direction of Bab el-Wad, west of the city, and halted at a roadblock. Two Haganah guards walked over to the armored car and spoke to the policeman in its turret, a blond young man dressed in the usual greatcoat and blue cap.

"We're just on a routine supply mission," the policeman explained.

"We'd better check the trucks," one guard said to the other.

"They're okay," said the policeman. "They're with me."

The guards looked into the first truck anyway and, seeing nothing suspicious, waved the convoy forward.

The vehicles turned into Ben Yehuda Street and stopped in front of the Atlantic Hotel. The "policeman" then yelled instructions to the men in the trucks—two in each cab—and they jumped to the street and lit several fuses in each vehicle. One of the soldiers dropped a pistol, which went off, and the night watchman in the adjacent Palestine Discount Bank ran out to see what was happening. Another shot rang out and he fell dead.

They all leaped into the armored car, battening down the hatch behind them. The car then tore down Ben Yehuda Street and into Jaffa Road the way it had come. One soldier leveled a Bren at the startled Haganah men guarding the exit roadblock, and the vehicle raced past into the Judaean hills.

On Ben Yehuda Street, early morning strollers saw smoke rising from the three abandoned trucks and shouted the alarm. People ran in all directions and a Hebrew University student in charge of a Haganah patrol ordered his men to throw themselves to the ground behind a wall . . .

In an apartment building overlooking the three trucks, Shmuel Sak had just awakened. He was washing in the bathroom when he heard shots nearby. He ran into the bedroom, where his three-year-old daughter, Esther, was crying: "Daddy, Daddy, shooting again!"

He lifted her from her crib and put her on his bed, then went to the window. His wife, Irene, just waking in her own bed, was irritated as she gradually realized what was happening. How many times had she pleaded with her husband not to stand by the window when there was shooting outside?

Suddenly, a flash of light lit up the room, and the walls and door simply collapsed in the middle. Much of the debris fell on Esther's vacated crib, but she remained uninjured on her father's bed. The Saks' nine-year-old son Michael was saved when the door and window frame formed a rooflike cover, protecting him from the falling walls. But Shmuel lay on a pile of debris in the center of the room, his face bloody and his breathing heavy. He died of his wounds later.

Forty-six other people died, too, and about 130 were wounded. The stone façade of the six-story Vilenchik Building bulged outward and disintegrated spectacularly into a pile of jagged rubble, and other buildings also crumbled either completely or partially. Within minutes, the block had been converted into a massive jungle of twisted girders, shattered timber, and broken frames, a smoking wasteland in which weeping parents and children, many still in their pajamas, searched through the ruins for their loved ones.

The British offered to help, but were chased off with rocks and curses. Too many people had seen and heard the men who had set off the explosion. And indeed, in addition to two Western-looking Arabs four Englishmen had taken part in the action—four deserters, including the two who had helped to blow up the *Palestine Post*.

A few days after the Ben Yehuda Street bombing, a Christian Arab from Bethlehem called on Abd el-Kader el-Husseini at his headquarters and announced that he had a plan for a third sensational blow against the Jews. As chauffeur of the United States Consulate-General in Jerusalem, he could gain entry to the Jewish Agency grounds and blow up the Agency building. Of course, the Arabs would have to protect him and make such a risk worth his while.

Abd el-Kader was delighted. Such a strike could be even more spectacular than the Ben Yehuda Street operation, especially if the explosion killed some of the top Jewish leaders, who all had offices in the Jewish Agency building. In any event, what would the world think of the chances for successful partition when the very seat of Jewish power proved within reach of Arab bombs? Abd el-Kader offered the chauffeur a considerable sum of money and agreed to send him to Costa Rica afterwards, where there was a sizable community of Christian Arabs.

The Arab—who called himself Abu Yussef, though his real name was Daoud—then said he would undertake the job. "But you must leave it to me to choose the time. I can only get the car when I'm sent on an errand."

"Never mind," Abd el-Kader replied. "We'll have explosive materials ready for you to pick up whenever the opportunity arises."

It came on the morning of March 12. American Consulate officials sent Daoud on an errand, and he sped into the Old City nearby and stopped in front of a store by St. Stephen's Gate. Several men quickly put metal ammunition boxes into the trunk of the car and told the chauffeur how to detonate the explosives inside.

Daoud then drove to the Jewish Agency headquarters, and the guards, who were used to seeing him at the wheel of the green Ford with the Stars and Stripes fluttering from its bonnet, greeted him as usual.

"I'm delivering a message for the Consul," Daoud said.

The guards opened the gate, and Daoud parked the Ford in front of the entrance of the building, just below the offices of the political department, where Ben-Gurion and other Jewish leaders had their offices. He then lit a fuse that extended from the trunk to the front seat, and stepped casually out of the car. He went into the building—and immediately disappeared out the back door.

Meanwhile a Jewish guard, seeing that the car was blocking the entrance to the building, jumped in and took it to the left wing, outside the offices of the Jewish Foundation Fund. As he was emerging, a tremendous explosion shattered the car and blasted a great hole in that wing. The guard and 13 Foundation Fund officials were killed, and 40 other people in the building wounded. Not one of the Jewish national leaders was harmed, owing to the guard's impulsive decision to move the car.

A BD EL-KADER EL-HUSSEINI cursed this bad luck, but still rejoiced over the stimulating effect his latest exploit had on Arab morale— especially after his earlier successes. Then, about two weeks later, on March 27, came his chance to translate the spreading Arab optimism into a great military success. He answered the telephone at his headquarters that morning and heard an excited voice.

"Abd el-Kader, we've just received a report that a huge Jewish convoy is on its way from Jerusalem to the Etzion settlements. It will probably be returning as soon as it unloads. Can we stop it on the way back?"

Abd el-Kader smiled as he listened to the caller—a high official of the Mufti-led Arab Higher Committee, to which his guerrilla army was responsible.

"Don't worry," he replied, "we'll stop it."

Rika Menache grabbed the first soldier she saw and embraced him, her eyes shining with joy.

"You've come!" she cried. "We knew you would!"

"No trouble at all," grinned the soldier, returning the hug. "Not a single Arab fired at us. They just ran when they saw us."

Rika was among the scores of Jews turning out at Kfar Etzion to welcome the largest convoy yet assembled since the war in Palestine had started. For more than a month the Etzion Bloc had been completely isolated, and supplies were running out. Finally, the Haganah had decided to smash through the Arab blockade whatever the cost.

The convoy of 19 armored cars and 33 armored trucks and buses, crammed with food, fuel, guns, ammunition, and some 200 soldiers and drivers, had apparently taken the Arabs completely by surprise, and an Arab guard at the entrance of Bethlehem even opened the roadblock for the convoy before fleeing for his life.

And so, at 9:30 A.M. on March 27, the long line of vehicles wound its way slowly up a steep grade along the narrow road from the highway to Kfar Etzion.

Rika Menache, a pretty brunette soldier, had been stationed in Kfar Etzion for some weeks. And although she was proud to have taken part in the defense of the bloc, she could not conceal her delight that she would be returning to Jerusalem with the convoy. Partly because she needed a rest from the tremendous tension under which she had been living, but mostly because she would at last be seeing Emmanuel Meidav again. It had been months since they had parted; he to Cyprus to train refugees detained in camps by the British, and she to see her family in the Congo, her birthplace. She had heard that he was now based in Jerusalem (although she did not know that he was with the isolated Jewish community in the Old City). In a few hours she would be in his arms again.

After embracing the unknown soldier, Rika darted off to greet other people in the convoy. Then she joined one of the chains formed to unload the bulging trucks and stack the equipment. As soon as the vehicles were empty, she helped reload them with empty oil drums, crates, and farm animals that the bloc could no longer feed adequately.

"Hurry!" a Palmach officer urged, as some settlers desperately tried to coax Zimri, a reluctant bull, into one of the trucks. "The longer we take, the more dangerous it'll be."

By 11:30 A.M., Rika Menache and her comrades, mostly soldiers and students, were climbing into the vehicles for the trip to Jerusalem. They waved to those left behind and began joking and laughing like carefree youngsters on holiday.

Only Zimri the bull seemed unhappy, snorting and stomping in a rear truck.

As the convoy moved laboriously along—a scout car, followed by a roadblock buster, the armored cars, the empty trucks, and the buses—the world seemed deserted. Not an Arab car could be seen on the road, not a peasant in the fields. Four miles out of Kfar Etzion, the "buster" smashed through the first roadblock, piles of stones, and then through two others. One of the rear trucks overturned at this point, however, and the hills suddenly resounded with the crackle of gunfire.

An armored car extricated the fallen driver and his assistant, and the convoy, under Arab fire, negotiated three more roadblocks, some of the vehicles on bullet-punctured tires. Finally, the "buster" came to the seventh and biggest barrier, made up of huge rocks, and was forced to halt. Zerubavel Horowitz, in charge of the "buster," helped the crane man to demolish the block. But when the road was almost clear, the "buster" trembled under the impact of the rocks and slid into a roadside ditch.

"Get it up on the road!" Horowitz yelled.

But the vehicle would not move. Then a machine gunner was wounded in the head. Horowitz peered out of the rear window and gasped as he saw the entire convoy stalled about 200 yards behind, waiting for him to clear the road, while bullets peppered each vehicle relentlessly.

With hordes of Arabs descending the slopes on either side of the road and already approaching to within 300 yards of the Jews, the convoy commander, Tsvika, decided that the only possible escape was to the rear. He drove his command car from vehicle to vehicle ordering the drivers to head back to the bloc. Some of the vehicles, including the command car, managed to turn around on the narrow road and smash through the roadblocks the Arabs had quickly constructed behind the convoy. But most had already been knocked out or could not maneuver the turn.

Aryei T., second in command, was now in charge. He passed word down for everyone to gather in an abandoned Arab building, known as Nebi Daniel, on the side of the road. All vehicles that could still operate were then concentrated around the house in a semicircle, and their occupants, under cover of this armored wall, crawled in turn to the building over a period of several hours.

The Arabs, meanwhile, took up positions on a ridge to the south, and in fortified buildings and other strongholds to the east, west, and north. They began firing machine guns and mortar shells from a building only 170 yards away.

"Our position is serious," the acting convoy commander laconically radioed Jerusalem.

"Hold on," headquarters replied. "We're contacting the highest British authorities."

Chief Rabbi Isaac Herzog and other influential Jewish figures pleaded with British officials and Dr. Jacques de Reynier, the Red Cross representative in Jerusalem, to save the beleaguered Jews.

"Two hundred are being murdered at this very hour," Herzog told Sir Henry Gurney, the High Commissioner's anti-Zionist deputy. "In God's name, please help to rescue them!"

"Our attitude, I can assure you," replied Gurney formally, "is in no way influenced by the deliberate Jewish disregard of all our directions. Everything possible is being done. But at this late stage, very little can be done."

By sunset, almost all of the men in the "buster" lay wounded in the rear of the stifling vehicle. Earlier, Zerubavel Horowitz, who was still unwounded, had raised their hopes by assuring them that the armored cars to the rear would come to their rescue. But when several cars failed to negotiate the 200 yards separating them from the "buster," some being overturned in the effort, a sense of despair came over the men. More and more bullets were penetrating the walls, hitting those few still able to stand at the loopholes and fire at the Arabs. And with each Arab volley, the voices of the attackers grew louder.

At 6:30 P.M., two Molotov cocktails struck the vehicle, which began to burn slowly.

"We're on fire!" Horowitz shouted. "All men who can, make a dash for it!"

Three men, all suffering only slight wounds, prepared to crawl out of the smoking vehicle.

"What about you?" one of them, Ya'akov Ai, asked Horowitz.

"I can't leave the wounded," he said.

The three men leaped out and raced to safety under cover of darkness.

Then the earth trembled beneath them as a huge explosion lit up the sky, revealing a shattered hunk of metal where the roadblock buster had been.

Early the next morning, Major Allen, commanding a British relief force, reported to Jerusalem headquarters while negotiating with Arab leaders near the scene of battle:

"The Jews seem to be running short of ammunition. The Arabs are continuing to attack and the Jews will not be able to hold out much longer. Why can't we get them out of here?"

The reply came swiftly. "These are the Brigadier's [Jerusalem commander Charles Jones] orders. He does not want the troops to clash with the Arabs."

Finally, after more lengthy talks, the Arab commanders consented to British evacuation of the Jews, on condition that the Jews were disarmed and that all vehicles—representing almost the whole fleet of Jewish armored trucks plying the Jerusalem–Tel Aviv road—were turned over to the Arabs.

About two hours later, a British lieutenant drove up to Nebi Daniel in an armored car and took Jewish commander Aryei T. and an aide to the rear. There a British lieutenant colonel told them: "You must leave everything you have on the spot—in return, we'll take you to Jerusalem."

"You can evacuate our wounded, but the rest of us want to stay and fight," was Aryei's reply.

When the British officer scoffed, the Jewish commander reminded him of recent episodes in which the British had undertaken to "save" Jews, and had then released them without arms in Arab-held territory. In one such case, Arabs had killed and mutilated four Jews left defenseless in the Old City. Aryei then said he would accept the British terms if the officer would pledge in writing to transport the Jews to a Jewish-held area.

"Isn't the word of a British officer sufficient for you?" the Lieutenant Colonel asked testily.

Aryei finally accepted the terms after Dr. Jacques de Reynier, the Red Cross representative who was also present, had agreed to assume responsibility for the evacuation.

A few minutes later, with 12 Jews and 135 Arabs dead, all firing ceased, and the Arabs advanced toward Nebi Daniel as a British army convoy crawled to the scene. Jewish fighters then slowly filed out of the house, Rika Menache among them. Her cheeks were sunken, her lips parched. Like the others, she had not eaten or drunk since the battle had started. She had dismantled her rifle and scattered the parts, although only a few of her comrades had had time to do this in the brief period after learning the evacuation terms.

Within an hour she was in Jewish Jerusalem, which welcomed her and her comrades as heroes. She was relieved to be alive; to think that she might have died before seeing Emmanuel again!

She collapsed on a bed in her roominghouse and slept for two days, while Jewish leaders, forced into decisive action by the convoy's failure—and an American retreat from partition—drew up emergency plans for changing radically the nature, and course, of the war.

3

The Struggle
in Washington

THE United Nations decision of November 29, 1947, to partition Palestine set the stage for one of the deepest, most dramatic conflicts ever to split the White House and the State Department. President Truman, supported by a world opinion profoundly moved by the plight of Jews who had survived Hitler's gas chambers, had been able to steamroller the State Department in his campaign for the partition resolution. In fact, Secretary of State Marshall himself had cooperated in keeping subordinates under control.

But it was easier to push for a decision than for its enforcement, which could involve American troops in the Palestine struggle and even possibly, in the view of some cold war strategists, in a larger encounter with the Soviet Union. Since the resolution provided no formula for implementation, its opponents took heart. If they could prevent the dispatch of United Nations forces to Palestine and the arming of the Jews, they might yet defeat partition.

President Truman himself nourished a hope in these opponents, however unintentionally, by trying to ease the friction that had developed within his administration over partition. The basic decision had, after all, been made, he felt; partition was inevitable. Therefore, why not let the anti-partitionists enjoy some ineffectual ranting on the issue, and perhaps even certain token concessions on policy?

He was further influenced in this thinking by his own deep resentment of some American Zionist leaders, particularly Rabbi Hillel Silver, who had exerted what he regarded as "indecent" pressure on the White House to support the Jewish cause. Truman believed that Silver, a close supporter of conservative Republican leader Robert Taft, was combining his pressure tactics with efforts to discredit the administration in the interests of the Republican Party. Despite such "unsavory" behavior, Truman had gone all-out in support of partition. But under the circumstances, he was in no mood to be kind to the Zionists now that partition was agreed upon.

At one meeting with State Department and Pentagon officials, Truman admitted that "the United States is limited in what it can do to implement partition since I will not use American forces for that purpose." This was what the anti-partitionists wanted to hear, though they feared that under domestic political pressure Truman might well agree to contribute to an international force if the United Nations called for one.

Still, they managed to get more than talk from Truman. Arguing that the least the United States could do to keep Arab anti-Americanism in check was to treat Arabs and Jews "equally," they wrung from him an important concession—an embargo on arms to the Middle East, announced on December 6. Since Britain still felt free to ship arms to the Arab nations under various agreements, this embargo actually amounted to a ban on arms to the Jews alone.

The anti-partitionists saw this move as critically affecting partition, for the Jews would be unable now to implement the United Nations resolution themselves. The next step was to make sure that the United Nations did not provide the necessary force.

In late December, Sam Kopper, State Department liaison with the Arab States, posed a question to Bernhard Bechhoeffer, a Department legal adviser: "In your opinion, can partition be legally enforced?"

Bechhoeffer had already given the matter much thought and had come to a very definite conclusion.

"No," he replied, "partition cannot legally be enforced." As Kopper smiled, Bechhoeffer continued: "Directly, that is. Indirectly, it can be, for if the Arabs try to prevent enforcement by violent means, action can legally be taken against them under Article 42, Chapter 7, of the U.N. Charter, which deals with breaches of the peace. In other words, the statement in the partition resolution providing for such indirect enforcement is, in my opinion, valid."

Bechhoeffer reached into a drawer to pull out a copy of the resolution. "It states," he said, "that 'the Security Council should determine that any attempt to alter the settlement in Palestine envisaged by this resolution by force is a threat to the peace, breach of the peace, or act of aggression under the U.N. Charter.'"

Bechhoeffer looked up. "So you see, there is a legal basis for enforcing partition."

Kopper's smile had vanished. "That is your opinion," he said. "Perhaps we should have an informal conference of lawyers familiar with U.N. legal matters to decide on this question."

"A good idea," Bechhoeffer said. "But I'm sure they will agree with my conclusion."

Kopper then went to Dean Rusk, Assistant Secretary for Special Political Affairs, including United Nations business, who readily approved the idea of a legal conference. It was decided to submit the enforcement question to a panel of three men: Alger Hiss, a lawyer who had been Rusk's predecessor, and then president of the Carnegie Endowment; Joseph Johnson, new president of the Carnegie Endowment; and Leo Paswolsky, a former State Department official and then an executive of the Brookings Institute.*

The panel met in Rusk's office in early January, 1948. After prolonged discussion, it unanimously reached the same concluson as Bechhoeffer: The United Nations could not legally enforce the partition resolution as such, but it could use force against the Arabs if they tried to sabotage partition by committing a breach of the peace.

When the meeting was over, Bechhoeffer, who had been invited, went to see Robert McClintock, Rusk's assistant. "Well, Mac, the decision has been made," he said. "Should I prepare a telegram for our U.N. mission for guidance?"

"No, never mind," McClintock replied. "I'll take care of it."

McClintock was as good as his word. He wired Ambassador Warren Austin—who headed the United States delegation to the United Nations—instructing him to call for a special session of the United Nations General Assembly to deal with the Palestine problem—on the grounds that partition could *not* be enforced legally.

Simultaneously, Undersecretary of State Lovett briefed reporters. The United States, he said, had reached its decision "after consulting with three leading United Nations lawyers—Alger Hiss, Joseph Johnson, and Leo Paswolsky."

"But, remember," Lovett reminded the newsmen, "all this is off the record."

* In 1950, Alger Hiss was convicted of spying for the Soviet Union and sentenced to prison for five years. Today he works for a private firm and still denies his guilt.

Events played into the hands of the anti-partitionists. The Arabs were attacking the Jews ferociously, and it appeared that any international force that might be sent in would have a full-scale battle to deal with—at a critical moment in the cold war.

Hardly two months after the partition resolution was passed, relations between the United States and the Soviet Union deteriorated seriously as the result primarily of Kremlin efforts to sabotage the Marshall Plan, but also of Communist threats to France and Italy, active Soviet support of leftist rebels in Greece and of Communists in Scandinavia, Iran, China, and Korea, the elimination of constitutional government in the Balkans, and a Russian demand for military ties with Finland.

At a National Security Council meeting on February 17, General Alfred Gruenther, a high staff officer, estimated that from 80,000 to 160,000 troops would be needed to enforce partition. Yet, he said, if the United States employed more than one division in any area, partial mobilization would be necessary.

"There are simply not enough ground troops," he emphasized, "to implement even the existing emergency war plan."

Then a draft of the United States position on Palestine which had been drawn up by State Department and military planners was considered. It stated:

> 1. Any solution of the Palestine problem which invites direct Soviet participation in the administration, policing, or military operations in Palestine is a danger to the security of the United States.
> 2. Any solution of the Palestine problem which results in the continued hostility of the Arab world toward the United States will bring about conditions which endanger the security of the United States.
> 3. The United States should continue support for the partition plan in the United Nations by all measures short of the use of outside armed force to impose the plan upon the people of Palestine. .

When discussion of this draft got under way, the military and the diplomatic members of the Council split on tactics. The military, refusing to support partition, stated flatly in a separate conclusion that the United States should seek another solution.

The State Department felt that this direct approach was too undiplomatic in view of the American commitment to partition, not to mention President Truman's delicate political position. It was better, the Department thought, to push quietly for reconsideration of the problem and then "urge" Britain "to continue to exercise its mandate over Palestine."

Finally, all members agreed that the United States should support the creation of a United Nations trusteeship, a policy pushed by Rusk at the suggestion of McClintock. And despite General Gruenther's earlier remarks on the shortage of available troops to enforce partition, they drew up a paper urging that such a force be sent "to maintain internal order during a transitional period" under trusteeship.*

To bolster the conclusions of the National Security Council for a skeptical White House, the Central Intelligence Agency submitted to President Truman on February 20 its own secret estimate of the Palestine situation. Repeating the standard arguments against support of partition, the CIA called for an Arab-Jewish truce while the International Court of Justice decided on the legality of the partition resolution.

"For the United Nations to admit error and to undertake reconsideration," the report concluded, "would be a momentous step necessitating considerable moral courage, but such procedure would be quite in line with the general practice of tribunals in permitting re-argument where doubt is entertained as to the correctness of the original decision."[2]

A Communist coup in Czechoslovakia that February added to the cold war antagonism and helped further to consolidate the position of the anti-partitionist forces. When, at a White House meeting in early March, State Department and Pentagon officials stated that a war in Palestine now had to be prevented at all costs, Truman did agree that a trusteeship, among other "solutions," was a possible alternative if partition ultimately could not be made to work.

A few days later, as he was traveling in his private train, a State Department official came to sit beside him.

"Here's a first draft of a speech we may make at the United Nations," the official said.

Truman glanced at it casually and noted that it mentioned the possibility of trusteeship as a temporary solution to the Palestine problem. But in its present sketchy form, the draft seemed to offer nothing more than contingency ideas. It was probably enough to appease the anti-partitionists in his administration without seriously threatening partition.

"It looks all right," Truman said, not studying it closely nor intending his comment as any formal approval of a final draft.[3]

White House advisers David Niles and Clark Clifford were deeply distressed by the gradual move away from partition. Niles was emotionally committed to the Zionist cause, while both men felt strongly that partition

* Secretary of the Navy James V. Forrestal, a staunch anti-Zionist, persuaded President Truman to let him seek an understanding between the Democratic and Republican parties to keep Palestine out of politics, but he met with little success in the effort.[1]

was in America's interest—and also in Harry Truman's, considering the proximity of Election Day. Finally Clifford, on March 8, submitted to Truman a detailed memorandum firmly advocating enforcement of partition. Disputing every major contention of the State Department, the Pentagon, and the CIA, the report stated in part:

> The policy of drift and delay urged by opponents of partition makes *absolutely certain* the very military involvements that they profess they want to avoid . . . [since] peace in Palestine depends on firm U.N. action.
>
> Unless the U.N. implements its Palestine decision, Russia may intervene unilaterally in the guise of preserving world peace and defending the U.N. Charter.
>
> The Arab States will continue to sell oil to the United States . . . [since they] need us more than we need them. . . . The Arab leaders would be committing suicide to accept Russian orientation.
>
> Jewish Palestine is strongly oriented to the United States, and away from Russia.
>
> While the British-Moslem alliance is undoubtedly extremely important to Britain, a similar alliance between the United States and the Moslem world is much less important to the United States. . . .
>
> Collapse of a U.N. decision taken at the insistence of the United States would cause serious loss of American prestige and moral leadership all over the world, and damage the U.N. irreparably.

The memorandum then proposed that the United States "call upon the Security Council to invoke economic and diplomatic sanctions against the Arab States as aggressors threatening world peace." It also called for the lifting of the American embargo on arms to the Middle East, for United Nations action to require British cooperation in implementing partition; and for the establishment of an international security force to enforce partition.[4]

On the day that this memorandum was submitted to Truman, George Marshall, acting on a subordinate's report, sent a message to Ambassador Warren Austin informing him that the President had approved a draft statement to be delivered soon before the Security Council—advocating the need for a temporary trusteeship in Palestine.

The anti-partitionists in the Administration were relying in large measure on the results of British policy, for it was the British who were helping to maintain the chaos necessary to support the argument that partition could not be enforced.

Even the pro-British United Nations Palestine Commission, which had been set up to implement partition, began to turn against Britain because of the insignificant role into which it was thrust by British policy.

Indeed, the British refused to allow members to enter Palestine until two weeks before the mandate ended on May 15, arguing that the Arabs might try to kill them. Easy if resentful victims of such intimidation, most of the United Nations Commission members displayed no enthusiasm for the views of Raul Diez de Medina, a Bolivian, and Eduardo Morgan, a Panamanian (the only two pro-Zionists), that the five-man commission should stay if necessary in some neighboring country in order to exert maximum pressure on Britain.

"It is our duty to go at all costs," short, plump Diez de Medina shouted at a meeting in Lake Success. "We cannot let the British make fools of us in defiance of the United Nations."

Per T. Federspiel of Denmark, a sensitive, Oxford-educated man, took issue with what he regarded as empty Latin bombast. "It is foolish to go," he said quietly, "if the British won't let us in. The intelligent thing to do is to wait. Even if we got in, would it help if we were killed?"

Meanwhile, the British, under increasing international pressure, agreed in February to allow an "advance group" representing the commission to enter Palestine. But when it arrived at Lydda on March 2, this group found no one waiting to meet the plane or to see members through customs, courtesies normally accorded official United Nations missions. Eventually British officials arrived, explaining that they had not wanted to make a "big thing" out of the mission's arrival for fear of Arab violence.

Mission members were then piled into a truck and forced to sit on the floor with their heads between their knees as a precaution, they were told, against stray bullets. Their quarters in Jerusalem proved to be a honeycomb of cell-like rooms on the ground floor and in the basement of a house near the King David Hotel. Workers were still whitewashing the dirty, crumbling walls and installing electric lights and toilets.

The worst blow came when a British official arrived one day and announced to the startled visitors—whose food had come from the Old City because of the severe shortage in the Jewish area where they were lodged: "Gentlemen, I'm sorry to say that we have been forced to cut off your food shipments from the Old City. Too much danger of Arab incidents and all that. You understand, of course."

The United Nations officials did not understand. But, doomed to subsist on a Jewish austerity diet, they found themselves the unexpected recipients of meat, sugar, fruit, biscuits, and other tasty products contributed by individual Jews who were quick to capitalize on this opportunity to strengthen relations with the world organization. One elderly woman handed a bottle of strawberry preserves to a mission member, explaining in a motherly tone: "We Jewish people don't have much to eat, but to let the United Nations starve, never!"

Guarded day and night, prohibited from setting foot outside their house without special permission, they received sympathy only from High Commissioner Sir Alan Cunningham, who opposed his own country's policy but was powerless to ease the humiliating plight of his guests—except to take them on rambles through the park where he described with gusto the wild flowers that reminded him of home.

Flowers were certainly not the topic of discussion with Sir Henry Gurney, a vigorous anti-Zionist and perhaps the real strongman of the British administration, who said to the visitors as they sat uncomfortably around his desk: "I hope you enjoy your stay, but of course we could not consider granting any authority to the commission before May 1. That would really stir up things among the Arabs, and the United Nations must understand that it simply hasn't the power to implement partition."

After the delegates had stayed five weeks in Palestine, mainly studying how to implement partition in the confines of their "cells," they returned home to recover.

Shrewdly seizing on such examples of overt disrespect for the commission, Diez de Medina—and the British—helped to turn members into violent critics of Britain.[5] In reports to the Security Council, they indicted Britain for refusing to cooperate with it or to obey United Nations injunctions. Unless the Security Council provided an armed force, the commission announced, it could not "discharge its responsibilities on the termination of the mandate. . . . A dangerous and tragic precedent will have been established, if force, or the threat of the use of force, is to prove an effective deterrent to the will of the United Nations."

The British for their part still hoped for a much smaller Jewish State than that envisaged by the resolution, one which the Jews would presumably accept as the price of protection from massacre.

At the end of February, Bevin discussed this idea at the Foreign Office with Transjordanian Prime Minister Tawfiq Pasha Abdul Huda; Glubb Pasha acted as interpreter. The Jews, Tawfiq said, had already organized a government that would be able to assume power as soon as the mandate ended. And they also had an efficient police force trained in the Palestine Police and, most important of all, an army in the form of the Haganah. The Arabs, on the other hand, had made no preparations to govern themselves and possessed no armed forces and no means of creating an army. Thus, Tawfiq stressed, if the situation were not remedied, either the Jews would try to take the whole of Palestine, or the Mufti, bitter enemy of both Britain and Transjordan, would return and try to rule the Arab part of the country.

Tawfiq continued: In recent weeks he and King Abdullah had received many requests and petitions from Palestine Arab notables asking for the help and protection of the Arab Legion as soon as the British withdrew. Therefore, he proposed sending the Arab Legion across the Jordan when the British mandate ended, to occupy that part of Palestine awarded to the Arabs which was contiguous with the frontier of Transjordan.

Sitting like a giant frog behind the conference table, Bevin gazed through the window and seemed to be contemplating the stark beauty of the bare, black trees in St. James Park across from the Foreign Office. He suddenly turned toward the Prime Minister and said matter-of-factly: "It seems the obvious thing to do."

Glubb then reminded Tawfiq Pasha that the Arab Legion would not be able to occupy peacefully the Gaza area or upper Galilee, which the United Nations had allocated to the Arabs. The Prime Minister agreed.

"It seems the obvious thing to do," Bevin repeated, "but don't go and invade the areas allotted to the Jews."

"We should not have the forces to do that even if we desired," Tawfiq replied.[6]

But Bevin, while apparently reluctant to voice open defiance of the United Nations resolution, had no intention of letting the Jews have the vast, desolate Negev, which he needed for British bases.*

As early as January, 1948, before the idea of trusteeship had been conceived, it was clear to Jewish Agency leaders that Washington was seeking an alternative to partition. So the Jews made up their minds to implement it with or without the help of the United States and the United Nations. Then they began to devise ways of launching a new pro-Zionist drive in Washington, but found themselves handicapped, ironically, by the resentment they had stirred up in their earlier campaign for the partition resolution. David Niles, among other highly placed American friends, told the Zionist leaders frankly that there was no longer any chance of reaching Truman.

---

* At about the time that Bevin threw the Palestine question in the United Nations' lap in early 1947, General McMillan received orders, he told me, to build two permanent bases in the Negev to compensate for the anticipated evacuation of the Suez Canal Zone. Bevin was thus apparently certain that the United Nations would either return Palestine to British control or permit King Abdullah, Britain's dependent ally, to absorb the Negev. McMillan says he received orders to halt work on the bases only after the partition resolution was passed allocating the Negev to the Jewish State. But Bevin did not give up hope of winning it back. Jon Kimche relates[7] that one of Bevin's principal advisers told him that no clear directives had been given to the Arabs or to the British forces in Palestine that the Arabs were to occupy only those areas allotted to the Palestinian Arab State by the United Nations. It was understood by this adviser—and presumably also by King Abdullah—that "some Jewish areas were to be occupied."

After considerable debate, the Jewish Agency Executive in New York decided once again to seek the help of Chaim Weizmann. Some members regarded Weizmann as a "weak reed," out of touch with the new fighting Jewish mentality; but they remembered how he had persuaded Truman to support their demands for the Negev under the partition resolution.

On January 23, Abba Eban, the Agency's representative at the United Nations, cabled Weizmann, then in London and about to leave for Palestine to resume his scientific work at the Weizmann Institute in Rehovoth:

> IN VIEW WORSENING SITUATION ADVISE YOU IF POSSIBLE RECONSIDER DECISION TO GO PALESTINE JANUARY STOP NO CONDITIONS EXIST THERE YOUR CONSTRUCTIVE POLITICAL ACTIVITY EVERYTHING DEPENDING UPON OUTCOME NEGOTIATIONS HERE LAKE SUCCESS AND WASHINGTON STOP MOST CRUCIAL PHASE OF ALL NOW APPROACHES HERE IN WHICH WE SORELY MISS YOUR PRESENCE ADVICE ACTIVITY INFLUENCE AFFECTIONATELY EBAN.

Weizmann did not hesitate over his reply. He would not go. He was ill and deeply hurt by the Jewish Agency's slighting attitude toward him. Anyway, independence was certain to come on May 15. A new effort was then made to persuade him. Dr. Josef Cohn, Weizmann's private secretary, called one evening at the New York hotel room of Joseph Linton, political secretary of the Jewish Agency in London, who had served under Weizmann for years.

"Joe," Cohn said, "we may lose everything if the chief doesn't agree to come. He's our only chance to see the President. We've got to get him here. How about phoning him personally and explaining the situation? He trusts you more than anyone else."

"It's a terrible responsibility—bringing a sick man here in this freezing weather," was Linton's reply. "But I suppose there is no choice." And he put through an urgent call to Weizmann.

"Chief, I hate to bother you," he said, "but we need you. Things are going badly here."

For the first time, Weizmann raised his voice to Linton: "I've wound up everything here and I'm about to leave for Rehovoth to devote the little time I have to the Institute. The *Yishuv* needs me and I intend to go. I'm no longer in the Jewish Agency.* Others have assumed the obligations and it's up to them to deal with the situation."

"But, Chief," Linton insisted, realizing that Weizmann did not want to be blamed for the possible failure of such a mission, "the situation is critical. There's no guarantee even if you do come that things will get better. But I know one thing. If we don't establish the state there will be chaos or worse in Palestine, and you won't even have an Institute."

* *Yishuv* referred to the Jewish community of Palestine.

Linton heard a click. Weizmann had hung up on him. Pounding his fist into his hand, Linton muttered: "Why did I speak to him so abruptly? I'll never forgive myself."

"Well, that's that," Cohn groaned. "It's clear he won't come. I'm terribly sorry for having caused a rift between you and the chief. I know how much he means to you."

After a strained pause, Linton replied: "Never mind. It's not your fault. Wait for me while I get dressed for dinner."

Linton then went into the bedroom, sat down on the bed by the telephone, and picked up the evening newspaper.

As soon as Chaim Weizmann had slammed down the receiver, he turned to his wife, and shouted: "We have just left New York, and the idiots want us to go back!"

"Yes, dear," said Vera Weizmann as she guided him toward a chair. "Sit down and relax and think about it for a while."

What was there to think about? Trying to ruin his plans! Didn't they know he was ill? How could they expect him to face the Atlantic gales and that New York weather? The Jewish Agency hadn't even bothered to send a formal invitation! They needed him but they resented and even mistrusted him. Despite his vital role in pushing through an acceptable partition plan, they suspected that in the end he would cater to British whims—just because he still considered the British a decent, highly cultured people.

Joseph Linton dropped his newspaper abruptly and grabbed the telephone receiver as soon as he heard the first buzz.

"London? One moment, please."

He ran to the door leading to the reception room and shouted to Cohn: "Lift the extension and listen in!"

Then he dashed back to his own phone and heard Weizmann's hoarse, tired voice: "Joe?"

"Yes, Chief, I'm here."

"Well, I've talked it over with Vera and she thinks I should come to New York. But only if I'm officially invited by the Jewish Agency Executive."

"Don't worry, Chief, you'll get the invitation in the morning. I'm looking forward to seeing you and Vera soon."

As Linton put down the telephone, tears in his eyes, Cohn rushed in shouting: "I can't believe it! It's a miracle!"

"No, it's not. I expected him to call."

"You what?"

"Why do you think I asked you to wait for me? I know the chief. I knew he'd call in about half an hour."[8]

Though Weizmann developed a fever on his arrival in New York, he contacted influential friends from his hotel bed, but no one was able to arrange an interview with Truman. The atmosphere in Washington was as arctic as the weather. Then, hearing that the President would be leaving soon on an extended trip, he made a last desperate effort, writing to him on February 10:

> My dear Mr. President,
>
> I was on the eve of leaving for Palestine last week from London when I received an urgent call to return to the United States in view of the crisis which had developed in the affairs of Palestine. It was not easy to postpone my departure for Palestine because I felt that I should be with my people at this critical time. In deciding, however, to return to the United States, I was largely swayed by the hope that it might be possible for me to have an opportunity of meeting with you once more and of trying to be of some help in these difficult and anxious days.
>
> I have heard today that you will shortly be leaving Washington for a trip to the Caribbean. I well understand how heavily occupied you must be in these circumstances, and I would not venture to intrude on you at this moment were not the situation, in my opinion, so serious. Time is of the essence and if the present trend of events is not halted, the crisis might well end in catastrophe not only for my people but for Palestine and indeed the United Nations.
>
> Remembering the kindness and understanding which you showed to me on the last occasion when I was in the United States, I am emboldened to ask you respectfully to receive me during the course of the next few days before your departure and to spare me a few minutes of your precious time . . .

Two days later, Weizmann received a reply from Truman's secretary, Matthew Connelly. The President regretted that he would be unable to receive him, Connelly wrote, as he was going away and his calendar for the coming week was completely filled. Since the reply did not indicate whether it would be worth his while to wait until Truman returned, any chance for an audience seemed to have evaporated.

Weizmann lay back in bed without a word after reading this letter.

Linton, who was sitting by him, had never seen such sorrow in his all but sightless eyes.*

While friends sat mournfully at Weizmann's bedside, as if at a wake, one of them, Frank Goldman, president of B'nai B'rith, said suddenly: "I have an idea. I'm a good friend of Eddie Jacobson, Truman's old pal. Maybe if I telephone him he can do something. He's no Zionist, but I think he's sympathetic."

Goldman put through a call then and there (it was after midnight) to Jacobson in Kansas City, arousing him from his bed.

"I'm sorry to call so late," Goldman said, "but I hope you'll understand why it's so urgent."

Then he told Jacobson that if Weizmann did not see Truman the Jewish State might never come into being.

"The President," Goldman explained, "has turned down all the political leaders in New York City who have been begging him to see Dr. Weizmann. He's even turned down Ed Flynn.† He seems to be very bitter against Zionist leaders for unbecoming conduct and unusual discourtesy."

"What can I do, Frank?" Jacobson—a bald, mild-mannered man who had once owned a haberdashery in partnership with Truman—stood in his pajamas only half awake.

"Well, you could charter a plane and fly to Washington to see the President before he leaves for Key West and beg him to see Dr. Weizmann. I know this is a terrible imposition, Eddie, but Dr. Weizmann came to the United States especially to see the President and you're our last hope."

"It's too late to charter a plane. He's leaving in the morning. But I'll see what I can do."

Jacobson's first action was to send a cable to Matt Connelly urging that the President receive Weizmann, and adding that if the President wished, he would fly to Washington immediately to be present at the meeting.

A reply, by mail, came from the submarine base at Key West a week later. The President expressed regret that he had not had the opportunity

* Weizmann had suffered one of his darkest days in July, 1931, when the 17th Zionist Congress, meeting in Basel, Switzerland, approved a resolution expressing nonconfidence in him as president. The congress regarded him as too "pro-British" and was shocked when he replied to his critics: "Zionism has not the ambition to found an independent Jewish State, be it Kingdom or Republic. . . ."

He was called back to the presidency in 1935; but eleven years later, in the postwar era of terrorism, he was again attacked at a Zionist congress for his moderation and called a "demagogue." Weizmann stormed back: "Somebody has called me a demagogue. I—a demagogue! I who have borne all the ills and travails of this movement. The person who flung that word in my face ought to know that in every house and stable in Nahalal, in every little workshop in Tel Aviv or Haifa, there is a drop of my blood!"

The audience stood up and applauded vigorously—then voted him out of office again.

† Edward J. Flynn was chairman of the Democratic Executive Committee of Bronx County, New York.

to see Weizmann, but said that there was nothing Weizmann could tell him that he did not already know.

"The situation has been a headache to me for two and a half years," the President wrote. "The Jews are so emotional, and the Arabs are so difficult to talk with that it is almost impossible to get anything done. The British, of course, have been exceedingly non-cooperative in arriving at a conclusion. The Zionists have expected a big stick approach on our part, and naturally have been disappointed when we could not do that.

"I hope it will work out all right, but I have about come to the conclusion that the situation is not solvable as presently set up; but I shall continue to try to get the solution outlined in the United Nations resolution."

Jacobson, as he put this letter down, knew the President well enough to realize from his words that he would not easily change his mind. Yet it was worth one more try. When the President had returned to the White House, Jacobson, on March 12, left for Washington, taking his chances on an appointment. On his arrival, Connelly immediately arranged for an audience. "But please don't discuss Palestine with him," he urged. "It's a sore point with him at the moment and he'll only be angry."

"I'm sorry, Matt," Jacobson answered, "but that's what I came to Washington for."

As he entered the President's office, Truman beamed. The two sat down and discussed their families, Jacobson's business, and other personal matters. Then, after a pause, Jacobson said: "There's something I'd like to talk with you about, Harry—Palestine."

Truman's expression immediately changed.

"I don't want to discuss Palestine or the Jews or the Arabs or the British," he snapped. "I've discussed it enough. I'm just going to let the matter run its course in the United Nations."

Jacobson was silent for a moment, shocked by the abrupt, even bitter tone. In all the years of their friendship, Truman had never talked to him like this. For a moment he felt that it was almost impossible for him to continue; after all, Harry *was* the President of the United States. But then he surprised himself by arguing as if they were back in the haberdashery store bickering over a customer's account.

"You should bear in mind," Jacobson said, "that some of the pro-Zionists who have approached you did so only as individuals and did not speak for any responsible leadership. You know how warmly you have always talked about Dr. Weizmann. Why don't you see him?"

"I respect Dr. Weizmann," Truman replied as though regretting his initial abruptness, "but if I saw him, it would only result in more wrong interpretations."

Jacobson felt completely crushed by the President's firm attitude. He was about to concede defeat when he caught sight of a small replica of a

statue of Andrew Jackson, mounted on a horse, which he had hardly
noticed during other visits to the White House.

"Harry," Jacobson found himself saying, "all your life you have had
a hero. You are probably the best-read man in America on the life of
Andrew Jackson. I remember when we had our store together and you
were always reading books and papers and pamphlets on this great American. When you built the new Jackson County Court House in Kansas City,
you put this very statue, lifesize, on the lawn right in front of the new
Court House, where it still stands . . ."

Truman, puzzled, wondered what his friend was leading up to.

"Well, Harry," Jacobson went on, "I too have a hero, a man I have
never met but who is, I think, the greatest Jew who ever lived. I too have
studied his past and I agree with you, as you have often told me, that he is
a gentleman and a great statesman as well. I am talking about Chaim Weizmann. He is a very sick man, almost broken in health, but he traveled
thousands and thousands of miles just to see you and plead the cause of
my people. Now you refuse to see him because you were insulted by some
of our American Jewish leaders, even though you know that Weizmann
had absolutely nothing to do with these insults and would be the last man
to be a party to them. It doesn't sound like you, Harry, because I thought
that you could take this stuff they have been handing out to you. I wouldn't
be here if I didn't know that if you do see him, you will be properly and
accurately informed on the situation as it exists in Palestine; and yet you
refuse to see him."

When Jacobson stopped talking, Truman began drumming on his desk
with his fingers. Then he turned his swivel chair sharply toward the window,
in front of which photographs of his mother, wife, and daughter stood on
a small table. Gazing out at the rose garden, he appeared lost in thought.

Jacobson's heart jumped. He knew the sign. The President was changing his mind. All of a sudden, after what seemed like an eternity, Truman
swiveled back again and, looking Jacobson straight in the eye, spoke the
most endearing words his friend had ever heard.

"You win, you baldheaded son-of-a-bitch! I will see him. Tell Matt to
arrange the meeting as soon as possible after I return from New York."

Jacobson stumbled out of the White House and into the Statler Hotel
bar, where he gulped down two double Bourbons for the first time in his
life.

On Thursday morning, March 18, Chaim Weizmann rose from his sick-
bed in New York and traveled anonymously by train to Washington. He

entered the White House by the East Gate rather than by the front entrance in order to avoid detection by the press, as explicitly instructed by the President.

For the next three-quarters of an hour, the two men discussed the possibilities of development in Palestine, the intended application of Weizmann's scientific work to this end, the need for land to accommodate future immigrants, and the importance of the Negev to the future Jewish State.

Truman explained why he had at first put off seeing him, speaking with the same frankness he had shown in his talk with Eddie Jacobson. He also spoke of his deep interest in the Jewish problem and his desire to see justice done without bloodshed. Then he told Weizmann: "You can be sure that I will work for the establishment and recognition of a Jewish State that will include the Negev."

Truman was not specific about whether he would insist that such a state be created immediately upon the departure of the British, as called for by the United Nations partition resolution. Nor did Weizmann press him on this point. He realized that the President had to move with tactical delicacy in resisting the anti-partition pressures on him, and was persuaded that Truman would do his best to honor the resolution.

"When he left my office," Truman wrote later, "I felt that he had reached a full understanding of my policy and that I knew what it was he wanted."[9]

Less than 24 hours after Truman had committed himself, the permanent members of the Security Council met with United Nations Secretary-General Trygve Lie at Lake Success to discuss the agenda for that day's Council session. To a hushed audience, Ambassador Warren Austin announced that the United States would propose the suspension of the partition plan and the establishment of a temporary trusteeship in Palestine.

There was silence for a moment while listeners absorbed the news.

"But the possibility of trusteeship was raised in UNSCOP by Australia," Lie said, "and it was withdrawn in the realization that the idea would be fought by both sides rather than one. It would require more military force to carry out than partition. As Secretary-General I have to ask whether the great powers, if they adopt your proposal, will accept the responsibility for implementing it."

"The United States," Austin replied, "is ready, of course, to back up a United Nations decision."

Lie was still pale. Yes, he thought; probably as ready as it had been to back up partition.[10]

*

At about 7 o'clock on Saturday morning, March 20, the President of the United States rose from bed, dressed, and sat down at the table for breakfast, scanning the front page of a Washington newspaper as he drank his juice. Astounded, he read the lead story of Austin's speech to the Security Council, in which the senator was quoted as saying:

> . . . There seems to be general agreement that the [partition] plan cannot now be implemented by peaceful means. From what has been said in the Security Council, it is clear that the Security Council is not prepared to go ahead with efforts to implement this plan in the existing situation. . . . My government believes that a temporary trusteeship for Palestine should be established . . . to maintain the peace and to afford the Jews and Arabs of Palestine further opportunity to reach an agreement . . .

The President then read that Austin had asked the Security Council to call a special session of the General Assembly to suspend the partition decision and set up a trusteeship.

Truman rushed to the telephone.

"Clark? Come down right away, will you. There's a story in the papers on Palestine and I don't understand what has happened."

Within half an hour Truman, who had been too busy the previous afternoon to pay much attention to what was going on at Lake Success, was in his office greeting Clark Clifford with as disturbed an expression as Clifford had ever seen on his face.

"How could this have happened?" he demanded, pointing to the article on Austin's speech. "I assured Chaim Weizmann that we were for partition and would stick to it. He must think I am a plain liar. Find out how this could have happened."

Clifford, as angry and baffled as the President, telephoned the State Department, but Marshall was in San Francisco and Lovett in Florida. Loy Henderson, John Hickerson, Assistant Secretary of State for European Affairs, and Charles E. Bohlen, a Department counselor, all said that as far as they knew Lovett had cleared the matter with the White House. McClintock said that this was the basis for a note he had attached to the speech indicating such clearance.

Clifford telephoned Lovett in Florida: "Bob, the President is boiling mad about the Austin speech. It caught him by surprise. How did it happen?"

Lovett said that he was as surprised as Truman about the timing of the speech, but that there had been an understanding that if partition failed, the United States would try trusteeship. Clifford politely pointed out that partition had not yet failed.

After further checking, Clifford learned that Marshall, on Lovett's recommendation, had directed Austin on March 16 to make the speech at the earliest appropriate moment, and that the Secretary of State and his deputy had left no word that the President was to be informed *when* the speech was to be delivered. The text of the speech itself was not submitted to Truman for his approval, though its substance had been contained in the sketchy draft he had earlier seen on the train without realizing or being told of its significance.

Clifford reported the same day what he had learned to the President, who personally telephoned Marshall in San Francisco. With restrained anger, he asked him to issue a statement making it clear that trusteeship had not been proposed as a substitute for partition but had simply been suggested as a temporary measure to fill the political vacuum in Palestine until partition could be effected.

But reaction was violent in the United States and in those countries that had followed Washington's lead in supporting partition in the first place. The non-Zionist *New York Times* said that Austin's speech was "a plain and unmistakable surrender to the threat of force." Special services were held in more than 8,000 synagogues throughout the country in protest against the switch in policy. Mrs. Eleanor Roosevelt threatened to resign from the United States delegation. And a diplomat from a Latin American country summed up the reaction of many of America's friends in a conversation with Sumner Welles, a high State Department official under Roosevelt: "First they convinced us that partition was the only answer. Now they are trying to convince us that partition is insane. It is true that I represent a small nation which cannot stand alone. I am willing to accept United States leadership. But this is treachery. By this latest reversal the United States has forfeited whatever moral justification it once had for leading the small nations."[11]

Or the United Nations, in Trygve Lie's view. The American reversal, Lie later wrote, "was a blow to the United Nations and showed a profoundly disheartening disregard for its effectiveness and standing. I could not help asking myself what the future of the United Nations would be, if this was the measure of support it could expect from the United States."

On the night of the speech, Lie brooded alone at home as, in his own words, he listened to radio reports of "United Nations depression, Arab jubilation, Zionist despair, and British self-righteousness." After lunch the next day, he went to see Austin at his apartment in the Waldorf-Astoria Towers.

He told Austin of his shock and personal grievance. Washington knew well where he stood on the question of implementing partition, Lie said, adding: "Its reversal was a rebuff to the United Nations and to me, because of my direct and deep commitment."

Then he added: "You too are committed. This is an attack on the sincerity of your devotion to the United Nations cause, as well as mine. So I want to propose to you that you and I, that both of us, as a measure of protest against your instructions, and as a means of arousing popular opinion to the realization of the danger in which the whole structure of the United Nations has been placed—I want to propose that we resign."

Austin was startled. What Lie didn't understand, it seemed, was that Austin personally favored the proposal, that he really thought trusteeship had a chance of succeeding. In his talks with the Arabs, they had appeared ready to accept trusteeship for a few months anyway, in order to give the United Nations a chance to arrange a final status for Palestine other than partition. And even some American Jews were interested, the more constructive ones in his view. Leaders of the American Council of Judaism, though of course avowedly anti-Zionist, were openly for trusteeship. And the non-Zionist American Jewish Committee had not replied to queries about its attitude—a good sign. (This group in fact later announced opposition to the proposal.) More important, Austin had the impression from speaking with Moshe Sharett and Nahum Goldmann of the Jewish Agency that it was just possible the Agency might accept it if pressed sufficiently. Trusteeship, in his view, was at least worth a try.

"Trygve," Austin finally said. "I didn't know you were so sensitive!"

He then expressed his understanding of Lie's attitude, but added politely: "I don't think it would be wise for me to resign, and I don't think you should resign either. It's wrong to take Washington's policy in a personal sense."

Lie, still deeply disturbed, went next to see Andrei Gromyko at the Soviet mission, saying: "I feel that I should resign in protest at the American shift of position."

Gromyko's face lit up in sympathy. "Speaking for myself," he said firmly, "I hope you will not resign, and I advise you against it. What good will it do? How will it change American policy? In any case, I would be grateful if you would take no action before I have time to consult my government."

Three days later, on March 23, Gromyko took Lie aside in a corridor at the United Nations and told him that he had cabled Moscow and that the reply was: "No, definitely not."

Being so advised by both the Americans and the Russians, Lie, though continuing to brood, decided not to resign.[12]

*

If much of the adverse response to the American switch was aimed at President Truman personally for permitting it, not all of his supporters had abandoned him. In Kansas City, late in the afternoon of Friday, March 19, Eddie Jacobson was working in his store, happy and rested after having slept late that morning following his return from Washington, when a friend telephoned him.

"Eddie, what do you think of your pal Truman—now that he's betrayed the Jews?"

"What do you mean?" Jacobson demanded.

"You haven't heard?" The friend told him of the news from the United Nations.

Jacobson put down the receiver without speaking. Almost immediately, calls and wires started coming in from all over the country, each declaring that the President was a "traitor" to the Jews.

But despite his shock, Jacobson struck back. "It's not true," he shouted, almost by instinct. "The President couldn't have had anything to do with it. I have complete faith in him and I will not and cannot believe that he knew or had any reason whatever to believe what Austin said before he said it."

Heartsick and confused, Jacobson went home. He stayed in bed throughout Saturday and Sunday pondering what had happened from the time Weizmann had left the White House to the moment when Austin made his speech. On Monday, March 22, he went to the store and the telephone rang. It was Chaim Weizmann.

"Mr. Jacobson," Weizmann said, "don't be disappointed and do not feel badly. I do not believe that President Truman knew what was going to happen in the United Nations on Friday when he talked to me the day before. I am seventy-two years old, and all my life I have had one disappointment after another. This is just another letdown for me. Don't forget for a single moment that Harry S Truman is the most powerful single man in the world. You have a job to do, so keep the White House doors open."

Jacobson was almost in tears. "Thank you, Dr. Weizmann. I can't express my gratitude for your faith in President Truman. Now I know that I'm not alone in believing in him."

4

The Backlash

DAVID BEN-GURION, chairman of the Jewish Agency Executive, sat at the conference table glowering like a bulldog. The more reports he thumbed through as he waited for the High Command meeting to begin that morning, April 1, 1948, the angrier he looked. The loss of the convoy at Nebi Daniel had dramatized the failure of Jewish military policy to date.

And so had two other incidents in the past week. One convoy speeding from Nahariya, north of Acre, to relieve the isolated settlement of Yechiam had run into an ambush that killed all 46 passengers. And only the day before, on March 31, hordes of Arabs had destroyed part of a convoy as it was about to leave Hulda for Bab el-Wad in a new effort to break the Jerusalem blockade. The Arabs had also cut the roads to the Negev in the south and to Galilee in the north.

Throughout March, the Jews had tried to retaliate against Arab communications, blowing up bridges and mining roads; but such operations were limited because most of the Arab roads were far removed from Haganah bases. Jewish casualties were high, while the damage could easily be repaired by the Arabs.

Ben-Gurion recalled the advice of a friendly Norwegian colonel attached to the United Nations mission—that the Jews should rescind their policy of defending every settlement whatever the cost.

"The dispersal of your forces," the Colonel had warned, "might jeopardize the very existence of the Jewish community. Your major task should be to protect the coastal strip."

But Ben-Gurion feared that such tactics would shatter public morale and might result, at best, in the establishment of a small Jewish ghetto state completely cut off from coveted Jerusalem. There was another way—however great a gamble. Strike back remorselessly and capture all areas awarded to the Jews under the partition plan, especially territory overlooking the Tel Aviv-Jerusalem road.

Actually, the High Command had prepared in March a comprehensive Plan D calling for precisely such action. But this plan was to go into effect only when the British mandate terminated in mid-May. Ben-Gurion hoped that the United Nations would send forces to implement partition, and he didn't want to foreclose this possibility with premature all-out Haganah assaults. Moreover, he reasoned, the Haganah was not yet fully mobilized and had hardly enough arms to defend the settlements, much less to launch an offensive; while the British might well side militarily with the Arabs in an effort to crush Jewish forces before they left Palestine—if indeed they really intended to leave.

But Nebi Daniel and the other convoy tragedies, coming on top of the American policy reversal, helped to convince Ben-Gurion that these problems had to be overcome—or at least overlooked. It was necessary to attack immediately in order to defend, or there might be little left to defend. The Jews would have to capture and hold Arab villages, something they had never done before, though Arabs would be permitted to remain if they did not revolt against Jewish military control. Who could have imagined such operations 40 years or so before when, as a new immigrant from Russia, he had first begun his campaign for organized Jewish self-defense? . . .

"WITH THE PLOW HANDLE IN MY LEFT HAND AND THE OX GOAD IN my right, I follow the plow and see black clods of earth turning over and crumbling, while the oxen move slowly, gently and patiently, like helpful friends. Here there are opportunities to think and to plan and to dream . . . "

Soon after Ben-Gurion had written his father this description of life in the new Galilean settlement of Sejera, his plans and dreams were interrupted by gunfire. Local Arabs, fearing the Jewish incursions, were harassing the colony again—burning buildings, stealing cattle, attacking travelers on the road nearby. And where were the Circassians, the hotheaded Arab mercenaries from a neighboring village who were being paid to protect Sejera?

"We can't depend on them," the youthful Ben-Gurion insisted at a hastily summoned settlement meeting. "Jewish land must be guarded by Jewish watchmen!"

"No!" An older Sejera farm manager, backed by other settlement veterans, was adamant. "If we do our own guarding, we will only increase Arab resentment and bring on more attacks. And if we dismissed the Circassians, they would join in the attacks . . . "

"And besides," another settlement member argued, "what do we

Jews know about shooting guns and killing people? We are here as peaceful farmers, not as policemen. The situation could be worse."

Shaking his dark head, Ben-Gurion pointed to the exploits of the romantic Jewish *Shomrim* or "Watchmen," who had provided the first Jewish settlers in the 1870's with their only public security. Their name taken from the Biblical quotation, "Watchman, what of the night?" they had defended their settlements gallantly, riding horseback dressed in Arab headgear, armed with gun, sword, and spear. They had learned Bedouin law and Arab custom, and were highly respected among the Arabs—particularly after one brave Watchman at the first Jewish colony of Petah Tikvah speared an invading Arab sheikh on his lance and then rode to the enemy camp to deliver the corpse.

"It's only when we don't defend ourselves that the Arabs are encouraged to attack us again and again," Ben-Gurion insisted. "And the Circassians are not interested in defending us. Sometimes they even divide the loot with the attackers."

When his eloquent plea failed to move his elders, he decided to prove his point with action.

A few days later, Ben-Gurion and his followers stole the farm manager's favorite mule and hid it, then rushed to the owner.

"Your mule, it's been stolen!"

The manager ran to the stables and, finding the mule had indeed disappeared, shouted for the Circassian watchman. But there was no response. He searched for the guard and found him asleep, while Ben-Gurion stood by smiling.

"All right. Go find my mule," the manager said sullenly.

And in a few minutes, Ben-Gurion and his men obligingly returned with the animal.[1]

From then on, the Jews at Sejera guarded themselves, and neighboring settlements soon followed suit, leading to the establishment of the first country-wide Jewish defense organization, an elite group called *"Hashomer"* (the singular of "Watchmen"). The principle of self-defense had become a fundamental of Jewish colonization.

With the 1917 Balfour Declaration and the resultant jump in immigration, Ben-Gurion supported the conversion of the exclusive Hashomer into the mass-based Haganah, meaning "Defense," despite British refusal to recognize a Jewish armed force. The time had come for an underground army embracing the entire Jewish population, an army that would inspire each settler with the pioneering spirit. Arab attacks in 1920 and 1921 underscored the need for such an organization, since the British were unable to prevent the widespread killing of Jews. Sometimes quietly supported by the British, sometimes persecuted by them, depending on the political climate, Haganah soon established itself in almost every Jewish settlement, complete with secretly trained officers and hidden arms caches.

Bloody Arab attacks in 1929 accelerated the process, but the Arab revolt of 1936 gave Haganah its greatest boost. Under heavy attack from Kaoukji's guerrillas, the British sought support where they could find it—even from the illegal Haganah. By the end of 1936, thousands of Haganah men and women had enrolled as supernumerary police with the task of defending the far-flung isolated settlements.

"But remember," the Haganah leaders told them proudly, "your job is only to defend, to provide security for creative work. You are not to kill the innocent with the guilty. You must be guided by one word: '*Havlagah*.' "

What a beautiful word, thought David Ben-Gurion now as he sat at the conference table about to demand, in ironic contradiction, an all-out war on the Arabs. *Havlagah*—"self-restraint." No Jew was to let the smell of blood go to his head. The Jew was to be the purest fighter in the world. And he was—until a young British intelligence officer smashed the dream . . .

CAPTAIN ORDE WINGATE WAS NO ZIONIST WHEN HE FIRST WALKED down the gangplank into Haifa one day in 1937 to be greeted by silent people who glanced at him with furtive, distrustful eyes. He believed, as did many Englishmen, despite the anti-British Arab revolt, that only Britain stood between these "exploiting" Jews and the "backward, unprotected" Arabs. Yet, within three months, he was to become a mystical Zionist as extreme as any Jew, and far more aggressive than most Jews in asserting Zionist rights.

"When I was at school," he later explained to a friend, "I was looked down on, and made to feel that I was a failure and not wanted in the world. When I came to Palestine I found a whole people who had been treated like that through scores of generations, and yet at the end of it they were undefeated, were a great power in the world, building their country anew. I felt I belong to such people."

A Biblical scholar of ascetic appearance, with deepset, penetrating blue eyes, Wingate had informed Ben-Gurion and other Jewish leaders in impassioned terms that he wanted to devote his life to their cause. "This is the cause of your survival," he said. "I count it as my privilege to help you fight your battle."

And he helped—first of all, by burning the concept of *Havlagah* from the Jewish soldier's consciousness.

"I have seen Jewish youth in the kibbutzim," he wrote his uncle, Sir Reginald Wingate, "and I assure you that the Jews will produce soldiers better than ours."

Soldiers who would attack, not simply "defend." Soldiers who would overcome what he regarded as an inner lack of confidence in their soldierly ability, a complex rooted in *Havlagah*.

In 1938, after an arduous struggle, Wingate finally persuaded his superiors to recruit members of Haganah for Special Night Squads to be used in a counterguerrilla war against the Arabs. Attacking for the first time, Jewish fighters, dressed in blue police shirts, linen trousers, and broad-brimmed Australian army hats, helped to protect the pipeline from Kirkuk to Haifa and to clear Kaoukji's forces from Galilee. In these squads were trained the officers who ten years later were to lead the Jews in the decisive struggle for a Jewish State.

Wingate had wanted to build up and lead a regular Jewish army, but in 1939 the British ordered his transfer because of his close identification with the Jewish cause. In his farewell address at a Haganah camp, he stammered in imperfect Hebrew:

"I am sent away from you and the country I love. I suppose you know why. I am transferred because we are too great friends. They want to hurt me and you. I promise you that I will come back, and if I cannot do it the regular way, I shall return as a refugee. . . ."[2]

Wingate never came back. Instead, early in World War II, he led the British campaign in Burma and was killed. But his spirit remained imbued in Haganah. And it was this spirit, Ben-Gurion knew, that was now, in 1948, to undergo its supreme test.

"We must take decisive action immediately," he admonished the High Command as the April 1 meeting opened. "First, we have to open the road to Jerusalem."

"What is your idea?" a staff officer asked.

"Mobilize an attack force in the next few days."

His commanders then suggested a force of 400 men.

"Nonsense!" Ben-Gurion exclaimed. "We need 1,500 men!"

His listeners were startled. Haganah had never before operated above company level; the proposed force was about three times the size of any previously assembled.

"But where will we get the men and arms? We hardly have enough to go around as it is."

"We'll have to drain the other sectors. We must activate our first brigade. Fortunately, the first shipment of arms from Czechoslovakia is due any time now."

The High Command questioningly agreed to Ben-Gurion's daring plan, naming it Operation Nahshon, after the Jew who, according to legend, was the first to enter the parting waters of the Red Sea during the exodus from Egypt.

That night, Ben-Gurion went to bed with deep misgivings. Reports pouring in indicated that the arms urgently requisitioned for Operation Nahshon from settlements throughout the country were barely able to trickle through vigilant British checkposts. The operation, he felt, might have to be postponed. Then, during the night, he was awakened by a phone call. A plane with the first shipment of arms from Czechoslovakia had just arrived at a secret aerodrome in the south. As the plane had approached the field, operational for one night only, it was lit up for a few minutes by a series of electrical flashes—just long enough for the plane to land and disgorge 200 rifles and 4 heavy machine guns.

Ben-Gurion wanted to shout for joy but restrained himself, remembering his wife Paula, still asleep beside him. The first shipment! At last his efforts had begun to pay dividends. Thank God he had had the foresight to realize what kind of war he must prepare his country for; that he had had the strength and determination to push ahead with preparations despite the opposition of so many colleagues who had refused to believe that the British would abandon the Jews to fate or that this fate might be an invasion by regular Arab armies. . . .

IN SUMMER 1945, BEN-GURION HAD GONE TO THE UNITED STATES and lunched with an old friend, Rudolf Sonnenborn, a wealthy American industrialist.

"Are the Jews prepared to defend themselves?" Sonnenborn asked casually over coffee.

"No," responded Ben-Gurion. "That's why I'm here."

Sonnenborn was shocked; this was the first that he had heard of the postwar danger facing the Palestine Jews. On July 1, the visiting Palestinian met at Sonnenborn's New York home with 17 other rich American Jews—businessmen, bankers, lawyers from all over the country—and shocked them, too, with the grim prophecy of possible disaster.

"Will you help us?" he pleaded.

His listeners pledged their support—even if they had to jeopardize their reputations by committing illegal acts; the secret Sonnenborn Institute was born. A few months later, Ben-Gurion sent word from Palestine that "the time has come," and immediately the machinery began grinding. By 1947, one of the most effective and brilliantly operated underground organizations in history was feeding the Haganah tons of military equipment. . . .

The Sonnenborn Institute formed an arms-gathering group (later called Materials for Israel), and dummy companies and other legal devices permitted purchases from United States government surplus stores and other available sources. A "Land and Labor" organization was created in Palestine—on paper—so that tanks with their gun turrets removed could be addressed to it disguised as tractors, and military uniforms, minus the brass buttons, dispatched as "working clothes."

As the result of secret "Thursday night meetings" held all over the country, Jewish-owned firms contributed everything from sandbags—"for protecting orphanages and old people's homes," the conspirators blandly told customs officials—to classical records for the lifting of Haganah morale; and American-Jewish war veterans left souvenir firearms at "gun drops," usually Jewish-owned stores. A shipping line carried goods without asking questions—including items slipped past customs men through various ruses. Gambling establishments contributed a percentage of each pot to the cause. Even Jews who had died in Hitler's gas chambers contributed; the "underground" purchased from the American army, for less than $1 million, tons of gold teeth collected by the Nazis—gold with which to buy more arms.

Nor were professional gunmen ignored as a possible source of weapons. Once, on a tip from a friend, Julius Jarcho—a former journalist who had become executive director of Materials for Israel—flew from New York to a town in Indiana to contact Mafia representatives. As instructed, he left his hotel at midnight, climbed into a waiting car, lowered the windows on both sides, and placed his hat in his lap. After several minutes, a man gazed in from each side and Jarcho looked straight ahead as ordered, sweating profusely. When the men left, he ran back into the hotel still nervous but hopeful that the odd confrontation would soon produce arms for the Jews. The next day, his friend telephoned that the deal was off.

"Why?" demanded Jarcho.

"I hate to tell you this," replied the friend with obvious embarrassment, "but they said you didn't have an honest face!"[3]

As part of the underground effort, a tough, British-trained Haganah officer, Shlomo Shamir, arrived early in 1947 to recruit American military experts who could shape Haganah into a modern army capable of facing regular Arab forces. One general had agreed to help, but backed down when the United States army could not guarantee that his retirement benefits would remain unaffected. With no generals prepared to accept his offer, Shamir settled for a colonel whom he had earlier considered only as a prospective junior member of the team he wanted—David "Mickey" Marcus.

Marcus, a jovial man with an adventurous spirit, was glad to take the assignment—pension or no pension. And his superior, General Hilldring, who later joined the American United Nations mission, was happy to grant him leave from his Pentagon planning job. At the same time, American intelligence was persuaded that the United States would profit from having one of its own officers in a position to file reports on Zionist military progress.

Shamir also recruited Al Schwimmer, a placid-mannered TWA flight engineer and World War II airforce veteran.

"We need planes to carry refugees from Europe to Palestine," the Haganah officer gravely told Schwimmer in a New York hotel room. "Later, we'll need these aircraft to help us in a war of survival."

"Where will you get the planes?" the young American asked, his green eyes doubtful.

"Where will *you* get them?" Shamir countered with a smile.

Schwimmer—like Marcus, a Jew who had previously shown little interest in Zionism—quit his job to get the planes, and worked together with Nahum Bernstein, the dynamic New York lawyer. With Haganah funds, he soon procured ten C-64's and three Constellations and set up the Schwimmer Aviation Company in Burbank, California, as an operational and maintenance base. Soon after, a second base was opened in Los Angeles—the private airport of Eleanor Rudnick, daughter of a wealthy Jewish cattlebreeder. Crews were trained here with small Stearman-type planes. Then, to establish a legitimate front for Schwimmer's activities, the organization bought up a small private airline in New York called Service Airways, Inc., run by a pilot named Irvin "Swifty" Shindler, who agreed to join the plot.

With the FBI getting too close for comfort, Schwimmer decided he needed another base—outside the United States. The new Tocumen Airport in Panama, he learned, was hungry for customers—and a certain Harvey B. Harvey, a friend of Shindler's, had just signed a contract to use it. A new company called Lineas Aereas de Panama (LAPSA) was thus formed with Harvey's cooperation and Haganah's money. Now all that was necessary was to fly the Haganah-purchased planes to Panama and thence to Palestine. By April, 1948, eight planes had flown to Panama —though only after U.S. agents had tried to prevent the flights. The effort failed for lack of proof where the aircraft were ultimately headed.

At this point Schwimmer received an urgent telephone call from Yehuda Arazi, a Haganah leader who guided the American underground.

"Al," he said, "a Jew from Honolulu, a secondhand dealer, tells me he may be able to get us spare parts for aircraft engines and maybe arms as well. We've got to follow through."

After some further discussion of details, veiled in vague language, Schwimmer agreed to arrange for the "acquisition." But he was skeptical. His men had volunteered to fly immigrants, not to smuggle arms. And the danger of discovery had multiplied after a crate of TNT being loaded aboard a freighter in New York had fallen and broken open—arousing the FBI's interest. Schwimmer called in several friends and colleagues, and all agreed that someone not directly connected with the Schwimmer organization had to direct the operation, just in case things went wrong. Reynold Selk, an old flying buddy, reflected for a moment, then said with a grin: "I know just the man."

"Who?" Schwimmer asked.

"My cousin Hank—Hank Greenspun."

"What does he do?"

"Oh, he's a journalist who dabbles in nightclubs out in Las Vegas."[4]

"Meet my friend Al Schwimmer," Ray Selk said as Greenspun, a powerfully built man with pugilistic features, entered his room at Las Vegas's Last Frontier Hotel. "He's an old war buddy of mine."

As the two men shook hands and sat down, Schwimmer came swiftly to the point, explaining the Jews' desperate need for weapons, including modern planes.

"Arazi asked me to find someone who knows ordnance equipment—guns, cannons, ammunition, tanks. What do you say, Hank? Will you join us?"

Greenspun was on the verge of refusing, though it was true that he knew ground weapons from his experience as an officer in World War II. After all, he had family responsibilities. But he suddenly thought of the Nazi ovens that might someday be rebuilt to burn his children.

"What do you want me to do?"

"We got a hot tip on five hundred acres of war surplus. We want you to go there and check it out."

"Where do I go?"

"Hawaii. According to our information, there's a whole salvage yard full of airplane parts and engines. There's tons of the stuff—the kind of stuff we really need."

"Those furnaces, they remind me of Hitler's ovens," Hank Greenspun remarked to white-haired Nathan Liff, owner of the Universal Airplane Salvage Company, Oahu, as the two men watched a crew of Kanaka laborers melt down mountains of aircraft engines and parts.

They strolled on through a maze of stenciled crates, Greenspun wondering what he was doing there. He didn't even know what engine went with what plane. Then he saw something he did understand—piles of machine guns that had been torn out of the planes. With calculated casualness he inspected several. His excitement increased when he spotted some distance away open crates of new guns still wrapped and coated with grease. Then he saw a figure walk past the crates—a United States Marine with a rifle on his shoulder.

"What's he doing here?" Greenspun asked Liff.

"On that side, it's government property. I own only up to there. The used stuff is mine. All the new equipment on the other side—that belongs to Uncle Sam."

"Can we get it?"

"Some day, please God. Today it's new. Tomorrow it's junk. Junk is my business. That's why I'm here where the junk is."

Greenspun smiled to himself. Who could win a war with airplane engines? But guns, that was a different story. With hardly a moment's reflection, he decided to risk telling Liff, who knew nothing about his true mission, why he had come.

Liff stared at the visitor. "This is God's honest truth, Greenspun?"

"It is, Mr. Liff," Greenspun replied, suddenly fearful that he had committed a terrible, irrevocable error.

"Take what you need," Liff said, spreading his arms wide. "Forget about money. It's all yours."

"Are you out of your mind? Playing cops and robbers with those guns, you'll louse up the whole aircraft deal!"

Greenspun smiled at Willie Sosnow, a rugged Haganah volunteer who had just joined him. He could understand Willie's concern. After all, it was a bit shocking to think that a respectable journalist and businessman was, like a common thief, filching case after case of guns right out of Uncle Sam's lap.

But within weeks, 58 crates—42 loaded with engines and 16 with guns—were ready for shipment to Palestine. To cover shipping expenses, Liff invited a dozen wealthy Hawaiian Jews to his apartment, and within five minutes they had subscribed $5,000. The next day, the shipment, consigned to Schwimmer's firm in Burbank, sailed for Wilmington, California.

"Well, now, where have you been and what have you done?" Barbara Greenspun asked her husband as he embraced her and the children.

"Why, baby doll, I'm going into the airline business with Reynold and a couple of other guys. You know that."

He telephoned Ray Selk to find out the latest.

"The crates just got to Wilmington," Selk reported, "but I'm worried about those guns of yours. This was supposed to be an aircraft deal. And I got a tip that the Feds have been nosing around on Oahu."

"Okay, I'll head for Wilmington right away."

As he put down the phone, Barbara muttered: "I know, the new airline . . ."

Within hours, Greenspun was helping a volunteer crew lift the 16 crates of arms from a warehouse onto a truck for delivery to a new secret storage place. The next day, United States Customs Bureau officials slapped a seizure order on the whole Hawaiian shipment, searching in vain for the missing 16 crates listed on the ship's manifest.

The guns must be smuggled by boat to Acapulco, Mexico, immediately, Greenspun decided. A movie producer, Hank Bellows, introduced him to a young man, Lee Lewis, who owned a 60-foot schooner. Three thousand dollars changed hands, and the *Idalia,* which had once belonged to "Painless Parker," the famous San Francisco dentist, was put at Haganah's service.

While revelry from a Wilmington yacht club party rode the offshore breeze, Greenspun and a crew of amateur stevedores dragged, pushed, and scraped the scores of canvas tarps and wooden cases from a trailer truck to a lumber yard, thence to the pier, and aboard a craft that would carry the freight across the bay to the *Idalia,* moored at the yacht club. Already things had gone wrong. The shipment was to have been loaded directly from the pier onto the *Idalia,* which was to have crossed the bay; but the craft's batteries had gone dead. While they were being recharged, Greenspun and Lee, to save time, had broken into the house of a local boatowner who was too drunk to open the door, taken his keys, and "borrowed" his small landing barge for the transbay trip to the *Idalia.*

The men groaned as they worked, driven by Greenspun's combined curses, threats, and pleas. When the *Idalia's* gangway gave way under the enormous weight, Greenspun set up planking and forced his men on. Finally, only he and an airplane pilot, Leo Gardner, had the strength to remain standing, but even they could no longer lift their arms. Greenspun put the last two canvas bundles on his back and crawled on hands and knees up the gangway.

As he collapsed on deck, Lee Lewis left to return the "borrowed" landing craft to its owner and came back several hours later, grim-faced.

"Where the hell have you been, Lee?" Greenspun shouted, his muscles still aching. "We should have moved out hours ago!"

"I'm not going. Get your stuff off my boat!"

"What are you talking about?"

"The *Idalia* can't take the load. Her portholes are riding at the waterline. She'll be at the bottom before we clear the breakwater. I have no intention of committing suicide."

Greenspun finally persuaded Lewis—for $4,000—to pilot the boat as far as Catalina Island, 30 miles away, where Greenspun promised he would transfer the cargo to another boat.

As the *Idalia* sailed into the open sea with a three-man crew and no provisions (they had arrived at the pier 15 minutes after the boat's departure),

Greenspun turned to Lewis at the helm and said: "I want a word with you, Lee. There's no boat waiting for us at Catalina. The *Idalia* is going all the way to Acapulco and she's taking the guns with her. Now if you'll simply accept that fact and get us there . . ."

"And if I don't?"

Greenspun took a Mauser from his pocket. "I'll blow your brains out and heave you over the side."

Lewis paled.

Greenspun pointed the gun at Lewis's temple. "Will you take us to Acapulco, Lee? You have five seconds to answer. Yes or no?"

Greenspun ticked off the seconds: "One, two, three, four . . ."

The click of his safety hung in the dense air as he stared into the young man's unbelieving dark eyes. Didn't he realize that Hank Greenspun was too far committed to back down now—even if he had to kill?

"Five!"

And as Greenspun reached for the trigger, Lewis gasped: "Yes! YES!"

Greenspun threw up the safety and walked out on deck. He leaned on the railing, swallowing hard.

"We'll have to lighten ship!" Lee Lewis shouted above the storm that struck near the mouth of the Gulf of California. "She'll go down if we don't dump at least half the guns. If we do, we may have a chance to ride it out."

"Forget it!" Greenspun yelled back. "We'll all go overboard before I dump the guns!"

Jake Fouks, the boat's cook, pleaded hysterically: "Lee's right. It's better to get there with half the guns than drown here!"

"How much do you weigh, Jake? Two hundred and fifty? A little more? That means a dozen guns, maybe a baker's dozen . . ."

Fouks dropped to his knees, whimpering.

"Get below, Hank!" Lewis cried, as he gripped the wheel in the lashing wind. "Start heaving those goddamned guns over the side or we'll go to the bottom. I can't hold her!"

"Then you'd better try harder. Those goddamned guns are going one of two places: Palestine or the bottom. Whichever it is, we go with them."

Greenspun listened to the din of the rigging as it strained against the gale. Who would break the news to Barbara . . . ?

Then, as suddenly as it had begun the storm abated and the sun came out.

Shortly, the *Idalia* landed in Acapulco and the guns were shipped overland to Mexico City to await transshipment to Palestine. At last, Greenspun rejoiced, he could go home to baby doll.[5]

WHILE Haganah agents used every means to channel American arms and military equipment to Palestine for the battle of survival ahead, they worked no less feverishly to obtain war material from a source closer to home—the British army. And as the British gradually evacuated the country, the Haganah found growing opportunities for relieving them of their massive burden of lead and steel.

Some British soldiers found the Haganah a most lucrative market for guns and equipment stolen from military warehouses. Others were less interested in making money than in helping the Jewish cause, though only a small minority of British troops favored the Jews over the Arabs, especially in the light of Jewish terrorist acts. None became more involved than those viewing the cause through the eyes of love.

Desmond Rutledge, a handsome, ruddy-cheeked sergeant major, first met Miriam, a beautiful girl of Yemenite parentage, at a party in the sergeants' mess at the Tel Hashomer camp. He had often admired her as she served in the camp canteen; she had dark eyes, full red lips, and long, raven black hair. When his opportunity came, they danced and drank and talked, and he accompanied her home.

After that, they saw each other often, despite the bitter objections of her rigidly Orthodox parents, who had hoped to find a Yemenite Jewish husband for her. The young couple usually met at the popular Simansky Café near the camp, north of Tel Aviv, and, amid a rollicking crowd, sat sipping coffee and discussing the past—and future. Rutledge grew increasingly morose as the time for his evacuation to Britain approached.

"I don't know how I'll go back to my teaching job," he told her finally. "To a bloody humdrum existence. And I know you'd never be happy leaving Palestine."

"Then why go back to a humdrum existence?" Miriam replied casually.

"What do you mean?"

Miriam smiled, left the table, and returned in a few minutes with two young men.

"My friends here," said the girl, "will tell you what I mean."

They proposed that Rutledge stay in Palestine to help the Jews fight the Arabs. Rutledge felt a sense of shock at this suggestion that he should desert, yet he was glad that they had forced him to consider the move. Since meeting Miriam he had come to sympathize with the Jews, anyway. Life would certainly be more interesting fighting for a cause, helping to shape history, than teaching it to a horde of bored children in a gloomy London classroom.

"I'll think about it," Rutledge told the Haganah men cautiously.

The Jews smiled. "Meanwhile," one of them asked, "do you think you could be of any help to us?"

In the days that followed, Rutledge visited the café more frequently, usually driving up in an armored car accompanied by a driver, a sergeant called Tex—after dumping crates of rifles, grenades, and ammunition in a nearby furniture store that served as a Haganah arsenal.

"Have you made up your mind yet?" Miriam asked Rutledge one day as they sat alone at a table. "Will you stay?"

"If I stay and we get married," he replied, "how will I be able to support you? What can I do here after the fighting is over?"

"Don't worry, I'll go to work and look after you if necessary. We Yemenite women are very strong. Anyway, our Haganah friends will see to it that you get a good job."

Rutledge stared into his coffee, oblivious of the buzz of conversation round him.

"All right," he said, looking up at her. "But remember, if I desert, I shall have nothing. Only the clothes on my back."

And he continued to supply Haganah with carload upon carload of arms—planning for the day when he would bring in his final haul.

At about the same time, in the spring of 1948, two other sergeants, Irish Michael Flanagan and Scottish Harry MacDonald, were spending much of their spare time in a café in Haifa where they, too, discussed with distaste the prospect of leaving for home. Flanagan was particularly unhappy; an auto mechanic in Ireland, he found no challenge in his job. He had wanted to attend university, but his parents could not afford to send him.

"Only the rich can get anywhere in Britain," he grumbled to MacDonald. "I'm going to emigrate to Canada or Australia or somewhere. Maybe there'll be more opportunity there."

Both men were quick to grab at opportunities—including the one that presented itself on a warm evening that March. They had stopped at the café, leaving a truckload of jerrycans full of gasoline outside. An officer at their Haifa base had ordered them to "destroy" the gasoline, in line with the official British evacuation policy of keeping items of military value out of both Jewish and Arab hands. As they drank their coffee, the two men discussed ways of destroying the fuel. Then a small, ginger-haired man sitting at a table nearby got up and, approaching the sergeants, smiled and said: "I couldn't help overhearing your conversation. But why destroy the gasoline? I'll buy the whole truckload from you."

Flanagan and MacDonald stared at each other.

"No one said we couldn't," said the Irishman.

"Why not?" remarked the Scotsman. "It'll save us a lot of trouble."

"Here's the key," Flanagan said to the stranger, who seemed dazed by the swiftness of the deal. "Take the whole works, and *mazel tov.*"

The sergeants met the red-haired stranger frequently on subsequent visits to the café, and merely laughed when he kept pestering them for more gasoline—or any other "available" items, such as arms. Finally, the man invited them to accompany him to a "friend's" house for dinner, and they accepted. After finishing a meal of gefülte fish and fried chicken, the four men sat down in the living room for coffee.

"I'll come right to the point," the host, who called himself "Dov," announced gravely. "We need heavy tanks or the Arabs will overrun us. And the only place we can get them is from the British army—with your help."

The two guests were startled. True, both were tank operators, assigned the job of keeping the last four Cromwells still remaining in Haifa in good condition. But it would be dangerous enough smuggling small arms to the Jews—if, indeed, they were to take even that risk. And until this moment, they had not considered providing the Jews with more than the surplus materials they were ordered to destroy anyway. Both men had come to favor the Jews, largely because they were the underdogs. Flanagan even saw the Jews as displaced Irishmen fighting the same Englishmen his people had fought so bitterly in their own underground. But to smuggle arms, and *tanks!* The idea was fantastic. If they were discovered they would certainly be thrown into jail—unless they deserted.

"I don't think it is feasible," Flanagan replied, a remark that convinced the Jews he did not really oppose the idea in principle.

After considerable discussion, Flanagan finally agreed: "Well, maybe we could take two of the tanks."

"No, we want all four," Dov responded firmly.

"But we're only two operators," MacDonald argued. "Who will operate the other two?"

"You could teach some of our truck drivers to operate them."

"And where will we get the tanks to train them with?" Flanagan asked.

"Who needs tanks? Draw some pictures and they can learn right here in this apartment."

The men were aghast. "But tanks, especially the Cromwells, are complicated things," Flanagan said. "How can a man learn to operate one without even having been inside it? You must be dreaming!"

"Well, think it over."

A few evenings later, the two sergeants returned to the apartment. They were exhilarated, having reached a momentous decision.

"All right, we're game," Flanagan announced. "When does school start?"

"Tonight at 7 o'clock."

"Okay," said Flanagan. "We'll have to move your furniture around to give them an idea of what the inside of a tank looks like. But I want you to know I think you chaps are crazy! And we must be, too. This is the most bloody incredible stunt I ever heard of!"

HOWEVER important the illicit operations in the United States and in Palestine itself, Ben-Gurion realized that they could produce but a fraction of the arms needed—particularly if the Jews were to take the offensive. Only legitimate deals with sovereign governments could yield the amount of heavy weapons, including aircraft, necessary to repel an invasion of regular armies. And the governments most likely to cooperate were in Europe.

Actually, most of the arms that Haganah had collected since World War II had come from Europe, but clandestinely. The first shipment was smuggled in late 1945 from the island of Rhodes, disguised as cases of books. Then larger-scale operations were initiated, with the secret help of members of the Palestinian Jewish Brigade that had fought in World War II under British command. While these men "guarded" arms depots in Europe, Haganah agents grabbed a percentage of guns from each, though not enough to arouse British suspicions. When the brigade was finally disbanded, members contributed to the cause whatever arms they could gather up in the dissolution process. Then, with the assistance of Jewish members of the French maquis, the accumulated weapons were hidden in maquis-administered farms and shelters for orphans and refugees.

The French government discovered the conspiracy and cracked down, but the cabinet eventually granted permission for the removal of the arms from France. They were transported to Italy, and then shipped to Palestine as "industrial equipment" after having been dismantled with the parts clearly marked to facilitate reassembly. Each item was packed in a special metal container shaped like a different machine, these containers were then put into wooden cases in such a way that a customs official could look inside and see only as much as was deemed safe.

This daring and intricate European operation, under the direction of Munya Mardor, continued without a hitch—except when the manifests of one shipment were sent to the Arab Chamber of Commerce in Haifa by mistake. All ended well even then, for the Arabs forwarded the manifests to a Haganah post office box address after a request had been sent in the name of an Arab importer. By the end of 1947, clandestine shipments to

Palestine included 200 Bren guns, 1,500 rifles, and 400 submachine guns.[6]

As Ben-Gurion studied these figures in November, 1947, he felt a sense of despair. So much trouble and risk for so little. He called in his military secretary, Nechemia Argov. "I think it's time to send Ehud on another mission. Go to his kibbutz and bring him here, will you?"

"Ehud, leave your mules and come with me."

Ehud Avriel looked around and saw his old friend Nechemia approaching across the fields. Couldn't a man even plow his land in peace? He had been home only a short while after having directed the Paris headquarters of Mosad, the "illegal immigration" branch of Haganah, since the end of World War II. He had lived interminably with the dead and the half-dead. Now, for at least a short while, he wanted to be alone with his mules to enjoy the land.

"Come on," Argov insisted as he caught up with his friend. "Wash up and dress. We're going to Jerusalem."

"Why?"

"B. G. wants to see you. But I can't tell you why."

When Avriel entered Ben-Gurion's office, he was greeted with a solemn smile.

"Ehud," said Ben-Gurion as soon as the visitor had sat down, "if there is partition there will be war. If there is no partition, there will still be war. In any case, we need arms. Not just a trickle as we've been getting, but great shiploads of arms—artillery, tanks, planes, guns of all kinds. I'd like you to go to Europe for six weeks to get those arms."

He then handed Avriel a list, saying: "Those are the items we need."

Avriel, who had long urged such an operation himself, folded the paper and put it carefully in his change pocket.

Then he returned home and packed, not forgetting a folderful of stationery marked with the letterhead of the Ethiopian government. The stationery had been obtained from the Ethiopian Embassy in Washington when his agents had visited it, ostensibly to discuss the employment of Jewish refugees in Ethiopia. The paper—and a "borrowed" visa stamp—had been very useful in getting refugees across borders. Now an "official" document could be prepared, saying that "Mr. Ueberall" was entitled to purchase military equipment for the African nation.

In a few days, Avriel was back in Paris, where his old Mosad co-workers arranged for him to see 17 people in two days in his room at Hotel California—all possible contacts with European governments or firms that might be able to supply the necessary arms. But each interview proved fruitless. Some visitors meant well but could not come up with the desired items. Others were shady characters, who asked exorbitant prices.

"I've hardly arrived and I've failed," Avriel said sadly to an assistant, Yussef Eilan, at the end of the second day. "It looks hopeless."

"I've got a friend I'd like you to see," Eilan suggested.

"No, I'm fed up. I don't want to see anybody else."

"This man is honest. And I think he can help. How about it, Ehud? Let me call him."

"No."

"Look, he gets me tickets for the ballet regularly. He knows you're here, and if he doesn't get to see you he'll never give me another."

"Well," grinned Avriel, "knowing how you like ballet, okay. What's his name?"

"Robert Adam."

"My name is Adam," announced the elegantly dressed, slightly graying visitor as he entered the room, briefcase in hand.

"Sit down," Avriel said, gesturing toward a small table. "Have some oysters and wine. Now, who is it you represent?"

The man silently opened his briefcase and pulled out a catalogue, which he handed to Avriel. The cover was marked: "Czeckoslovenska Sbroyovka-Brno."

Avriel was surprised: the largest arms factory in Czechoslovakia. Adam leaned over as Avriel turned the pages of the catalogue.

"As you can see, we produce the finest rifles. And there's our latest heavy machine gun. And look at the price list. Very reasonable, wouldn't you say?"

"Is this a joke?" Avriel asked suspiciously. "I'm not buying an automobile or women's underwear."

Adam smiled. "I know this seems a bit strange," he said. "Actually, I'm the man Haganah should have sent to obtain arms. But you see, it's my weak character . . . That's why I'm here. I want to ease my conscience."

"What are you talking about?"

"I represented this company in Rumania before the war. In 1942, with the Germans closing in, my wife and I made our way to Palestine. I tried to settle there, but it was just too small and impoverished for me. In Rumania, I owned a mansion and I was used to a better life. I decided that Palestine wasn't for me, and so when Paris was liberated, I left my wife and came here to live. And I'm living very well. But now that the Jews are in trouble, I feel a sense of guilt—as if I'd abandoned my people. So I'd like to help—to put my contacts and experience at your disposal. No man has better connections with the European arms industry."

Before Avriel could reply, Adam removed a small envelope from his briefcase and, holding it up, said to his host: "Here are two plane tickets for Prague. We leave at 9:15 in the morning."

"It's been a long time since we've seen you," declared the managing director of Czeckoslovenska Sbroyovka-Brno.

"Yes," Robert Adam said. "But I've brought you a good customer."

The Czech executive smiled approvingly.

"Wonderful!" he said. Then, turning to Avriel: "What do you need?"

Avriel was pleasantly surprised by his enthusiastic reception. It had not occurred to him before that Czechoslovakia would be willing to sell arms to a private underground army, for this policy directly violated the United Nations arms embargo to the Middle East and jeopardized President Jan Masaryk's effort to strengthen ties with the Anglo-American bloc in the face of a growing domestic Communist threat. He didn't even have to pose as the representative of some sovereign nation. To this firm, business was business.

He reached into his pocket and removed the piece of paper listing the Haganah's needs. Unfolding it, he read slowly: "Well, let's see . . . for a start, 10,000 rifles, 4,500 submachine guns . . . "

When Avriel had read off the entire list, the managing director telephoned a stock official, and within a few moments reported: "Yes, we have everything you have requested."

Then, pensively tapping his pencil on the desk, he added: "Of course, you understand, any transaction is not to be publicized."[7]

While Avriel negotiated for large arms shipments, the Haganah learned that shortly before his arrival in Paris, the Czechoslovakian firm had sold a small arsenal to the Syrians, including 6,000 rifles, 8 million rounds of ammunition, and explosives and hand grenades. The Italian vessel carrying the shipment, the *Lino,* was on its way to Beirut but had been held up in the Yugoslav port of Fiume because of the United Nations embargo. When the Yugoslavs finally agreed to let the boat leave, Haganah agents in Europe plotted its destruction with as much gusto as they sought arms of their own.

At a meeting in Rome on March 28, these agents decided to sink the

Lino in the open sea by bombing it from the air. A C-46 that had flown to Italy from Al Schwimmer's Panama base would fly low over the vessel and crew members would roll the bomb out.

"It's a crazy idea," argued Munya Mardor, representing a minority of dissenters. "We should capture the ship with one of our own and take the arms for ourselves."

But Mardor could not dissuade the others, and as soon as word came that the *Lino* had left Fiume, Jewish planes swept the Adriatic trying to find it, while the "bomber" waited to take off. But the ship seemed to have disappeared, and the Jews grew desperate.

Then Ada Sereni, the attractive Haganah chief in Italy, had an idea. "Maybe the Italian fleet can help us find the boat," she suggested. "I'll call the chief of naval staff."

Her colleagues smiled doubtfully. Yet they did not underestimate her ability to perform miracles.

ADA, BORN IN ROME, HAD MIGRATED TO PALESTINE, THEN RE-turned to Italy immediately after World War II on a journey of hope, seeking word of the fate of her husband, Enzo Sereni, who had dropped as a parachutist behind German lines in Italy and had not been heard from since. When she learned that her husband had died in Dachau, she decided to carry on his Zionist work in Italy. And the Haganah, finding her personal contacts with high Italian officials invaluable to its illegal immigration and arms-gathering program, appointed her in 1947 to replace Yehuda Arazi as head of the Italian mission.

She had scored her greatest coup at an interview with Italian Premier Alcide de Gasperi. After she had pleaded for Italian "cooperation" with the Haganah, de Gasperi had said: "Signora Sereni, what you ask is that we help you win your war in Palestine. What interest has Italy in your victory?"

Two interests, Ada replied. First, a Jewish State would offset future Arab "arrogance" in the Mediterranean area. And second, if the Jews lost the war, a large number would inevitably flee to Italy because of her proximity to Palestine.

"Is a great influx of Jewish refugees in Italy's interest?" she asked pointedly.

After a short silence, de Gasperi asked: "So what kind of help do you want?"

"Mr. Prime Minister," Ada answered, "you should close one eye and, if possible, both eyes to our activities in Italy."

De Gasperi grinned. *"Va bene!"*

Now Ada Sereni would try her charm on another Italian leader.

*

"Admiral," she said to the chief of naval staff, "I have information that an Italian ship with arms is sailing down the Italian coast. It is unclear whether the arms are for use against the Jews in Palestine or against the Italian government."

The Admiral did not doubt the second possibility. With elections coming up in a few weeks, it was very likely that the Communists were planning to overthrow his government.

"Thank you for the information, signora," he answered eagerly. "We'll seize it, don't worry. I'll warn all Italian ports."

The next morning, April 3, the Admiral called back: "Signora, I have good news for you. The ship has entered the port of Mofetta with engine trouble. It has been seized and is being towed to Bari."

The Haganah then decided to sink the *Lino* in port before Italian authorities could determine that the arms were not really intended for the Communists. Mardor, heading the plot, gathered a team of saboteurs. But before they could act, Ada Sereni learned from an Italian official that the vessel was to be freed in a few hours.

"We must have forty-eight hours!" Jussele, the chief saboteur, insisted.

Ada ran to the Italian chief of police, a good friend, and begged him to prevent the departure of the vessel for 48 hours.

"Signora," he replied, "we have no legal pretext to keep the ship here."

"That may be so," said Ada in a quietly persistent voice, "but your decision could mean life—or death—for my people." And she turned her thumbs first up, then down, to emphasize the point.

"I don't understand you," he responded. "Why don't you just sink the ship?"

Ada was startled. The chief of police suggesting what the Haganah was planning to do anyway! In a flash, she decided to gamble and confide in him.

"Your Excellency," she said with a gentle smile, "it's because we plan to do just that that I'm asking for the forty-eight hours."

The police chief reflected silently for a moment. "Signora, to grant your wish I need a good excuse."

"Would you wait here just a few minutes?" she asked.

Ada dashed to her hotel nearby and telephoned certain high-ranking Italian naval officers. Within half an hour, she was back.

"You can't let that ship leave!" she announced gravely. "It's a wooden ship. In Italy, a wooden ship must have a special permit. And this one hasn't."

"Excellent!" the Italian exclaimed.

He then telephoned the police chief in Bari and asked him to delay departure of the *Lino*. As he put down the telephone, he looked morosely at Ada Sereni: "Signora, for your cause I shall be thrown in jail!"

The following night, the saboteurs rowed out toward the *Lino,* but were unable to get near enough because of the close police watch. But the night after that, they tried again and this time managed to attach a mine to the vessel's side and return to shore safely. Leaving hastily in a waiting car before the mine could explode, they did not learn what had happened until they reached Rome. There they met Ada Sereni. One look at her radiant face told them that the *Lino* was at the bottom of Bari Harbor.[8]

In Tel Aviv, David Ben-Gurion was radiant, too. The guns that had been dumped might possibly have been enough to win a war for the Arabs. And this had happened just when other Czech arms were being smuggled into Palestine—some smothered in onions and rotting potatoes that discouraged careful customs inspection by even the most dedicated British bureaucrats—for use in the first large-scale Jewish military offensive in 2,000 years.

W HILE the Jews prepared to smash open the Tel Aviv–Jerusalem road with Operation Nahshon, Fawzi el-Kaoukji, noting that the enemy was fully occupied in the Jerusalem corridor, prepared for an operation of his own against the Jews. As he had politely forewarned Yoshua Palmon of the Jewish Agency in their secret talk, he felt he had to score one great success against the Jews to regain the prestige he had lost after his ignominious defeat at Tirat Zvi. Then he would settle back and quietly watch the Jews tangle with the guerrilla forces of his arch enemy, the Mufti.

On the afternoon of April 4, 1948, Kaoukji stood on a hill overlooking his chosen target—Kibbutz Mishmar Ha'emek. He had made a wise choice, he was sure. The settlement guarded the gateway to Haifa Bay, standing astride the road between Arab-dominated Jenin and divided Haifa. Its capture would end Jewish harassment of Arab transport along this vital link with the outside world, and would permit him, if he decided to continue his offensive, to attack the Haifa–Tel Aviv road to the west or to invade the prosperous Jewish settlements in the Jezreel Valley to the east.

Kaoukji panned the settlement with his binoculars. He had been planning the operation for about two weeks. Now the moment had come. He couldn't conceive of failure this time. He had 1,000 fighters, a dozen 3-inch mortars, several armored cars, and, most important of all, a battery of seven 75mm. and 105mm. guns. He would be using the first artillery yet employed in the war. The Jews would soon discover the true worth of their concrete buildings and fortifications. Perhaps a couple of hours, and they would either flee or surrender. It wouldn't be necessary for mass suicide attacks as at Tirat Zvi.

Kaoukji glanced at his watch. Almost 5 P.M. As he looked through the binoculars again, he saw what he was expecting: The Jews were drifting into the dining hall for afternoon tea. This was the best time to strike, when they were all relaxing together and least prepared for an attack. Also, he noted happily, the cows had been put out to pasture. What fine cows! Little wonder that the Jews seemed to regard their cows as more important than their women. He was glad he wouldn't have to kill the poor things.

While Kaoukji was studying the tranquil dusk-lit scene, Benjamin Avrunin, a small, wiry truck driver, was strolling to the dining hall for tea. He met kibbutz commander Yehuda Yevzori just outside.

"Do you think they'll hit us after dark?" Avrunin asked.

"Well, you can't tell," replied Yevzori, who had learned earlier that day that the kibbutz was surrounded. "Anyway, we're ready."

He spoke with a proud shrug, for under his guidance the kibbutz, consisting of about 300 men, women, and children, had been preparing its defenses for two months—despite the Haganah's feeling that the Arabs would not strike here for fear of interrupting vital Haifa Port traffic to Jenin and Transjordan. The settlers had dug connecting trenches, stolen barbed wire from the British, put away a month's supply of food, and managed to scrounge from local Haganah units a heavy machine gun and a 3-inch mortar to bolster a skimpy arsenal that included only two 2-inch mortars, two light machine guns, and about 50 rifles.

Even so, of course, the situation was critical. The kibbutz had nothing to stop the armor, not even Molotov cocktails, and its radio transmitter had just broken down. Who could judge the effect of the enemy artillery pieces his men had spotted that morning? Well, at least the children would be safe in the concrete baby house.

As the two men were about to enter the dining hall, they heard the high screech of a shell. Instinctively, they threw themselves to the ground just before a loud explosion sent debris flying nearby.

"This is it!" cried Yevzori, as he scrambled to his feet and dashed off to his post.

Within seconds, men and women were pouring out of the dining hall and scattering to their posts. Teatime was over.

*

When the first shell hit, Naomi Barkay—in charge of the baby house—was on the second floor helping the mothers feed their children.

"Lie over the children!" she cried.

As she threw herself over two babies whose mothers had not arrived, a second blast shook the building. Then the third shell struck, hitting the roof and exploding on contact. Shrapnel showered through a gaping hole. Pandemonium broke out, and Naomi felt her leg go numb. A woman ran up to her yelling: "You're bleeding! Let me help you!"

"Never mind," Naomi gasped. "Get the children out of this place—downstairs!"

Then she turned on her side so that two other women could grab the babies from under her, both unhurt but smeared with her blood. Amid screams and sobs, mothers climbed over debris with their children and stumbled through a snow of falling plaster to the staircase. But one young mother lay motionless a few feet away from Naomi, horribly wounded, her dead baby under her. The mother (who died later on the kibbutz operating table in the shower room) and the child were to be the only fatalities in the intensive shelling. Naomi lost her leg.

After two hours and 1,000 shells, the bombardment ceased.

"Get ready to repel an infantry attack," Yehuda Yevzori warned his commanders in the headquarters dugout.

He had never dreamed that artillery could be so destructive. There was hardly a house standing. Thank God for the deep trenches. But he needed reinforcements. If only he could contact Haganah headquarters—the telephone had been cut and his radio transmitter still would not work!

In Afula, some distance away, young Chaim Marcus sat that night watching the lights flashing in the dark—the lights of the small telephone exchange. As he listened to the explosions outside, he clenched his fists in frustration. He would rather be fighting than pushing plugs into sockets. A telephone operator's job was not very exciting at a time when battles were going on all over the country.

He had not had a very busy night, particularly since many of the lines had been cut. At about midnight, he had an idea. Why not try to plug in on an Arab exchange in Nablus or Jenin? He could understand Arabic and perhaps he might hear an interesting conversation. He tried to make contact, but in vain. He sat back waiting in boredom for someone to request a number. Suddenly he smiled . . . maybe it would work. He found a piece of wire, opened up the back of the exchange, and tinkered with the Jenin and Nablus sockets. He pressed the earphone to his ear. Voices speaking Arabic!

Excitedly, Chaim asked in Arabic: "Who is this?"

"Get off the line!" one of the speakers demanded.

But Chaim persisted and an argument developed. Finally, one of the men shouted angrily: "I am Kaoukji!"

"Taib!" ("Good!"), Chaim replied.

But as he continued to eavesdrop, the two men started speaking a strange language he couldn't understand. Chaim immediately called the Haganah regional command and, after explaining the situation to the commanding officer, plugged him into the conversation. The commander was also unable to understand the language, but a friend who happened to be in his office listened in and immediately recognized it as Turkish.

"Mishmar Ha'emek is under attack!" he cried after several moments.

Within minutes, the Haganah was stripping every defense post in the area to gather reinforcements. The first group, after winding its way through the Jezreel Valley, slipped into Mishmar Ha'emek at about 3 A.M. the following morning, April 5.

The Jews were surprised that the unit had been able to get through without a shot being fired. They didn't know that the Arab field commander had received reports of its approach, but had deliberately refrained from blocking its advance.

"I have been informed," he told Arab reporters in his village headquarters, "that trucks carrying a large number of Haganah are approaching the colony. But I will let them enter so that we can trap them all."

The sun rose serenely over the charred ruins of the kibbutz. Before the reinforcements had arrived, Jewish gunfire had chased back Arab infantrymen who had sauntered toward their prey confident of finding not one defender alive. One unit had even reached the surrounding fence before being routed by grenades. The Jews now awaited a full-scale morning attack but, to their surprise, it didn't come.

The reason, unknown to them, lay in an effort by British officers of the 3rd Hussar Regiment, stationed only about two miles away, to end the Arab offensive. Three armored cars had pulled up that morning at Arab field headquarters and a British officer, having found a deputy of Kaoukji, had demanded that he withdraw his troops from the area.

The commander refused, but agreed to a cease-fire, and the British returned to their base, deeply relieved. The mandate troops were in the process of leaving Palestine and could hardly have been used, in the British view, to enforce the withdrawal of so large an Arab force.

When sporadic fighting resumed after a day of relative quiet, the British, on the morning of April 7, again intervened. This time, another officer, Lieutenant Colonel C. A. Peel, emerged from an armored car at a village overlooking the kibbutz and confronted Kaoukji himself.

"The fighting must stop," Peel ordered firmly.

"I have come to Palestine to fight, not to eat," Kaoukji retorted.

He couldn't let the British stop the fighting. But it would be best to humor them and offer conditions for a troop withdrawal that the Jews would never accept. Of course, if the Jews did accept, such a decision could be interpreted as an Arab victory.

"I shall be glad to delay my operations until your mandate ends next month," he continued with a pale smile, "but I have a responsibility to protect the Arabs in the area. The Jews have been attacking our villages. If they would undertake to stop these attacks and stop their sniping on Arab traffic, I would withdraw my troops."

Finding these conditions reasonable, Peel then sped to Mishmar Ha'emek. Yehuda Yevzori, accompanied by Benjamin Avrunin, strolled disinterestedly to the fence.

"Yes?" Yevzori said.

"I wish to speak to the local Haganah commander," Peel stammered in Oxford English.

"What about?"

"I wish to prolong the cease-fire for an indefinite period, or at least for another twenty-four hours."

He then presented Kaoukji's conditions for a withdrawal of his troops.

"We are not authorized to consider such a proposal," Yevzori replied, "but we shall pass on your request and answer it."

"It seems to me that you are not well placed to refuse such a generous proposal."

"Do you know what kind of position we're in?"

The Jews finally agreed to a cease-fire that would permit the evacuation of wounded and children. Kaoukji was delighted when he heard the news, feeling that he could now claim a victory.

The next day, April 8, after the evacuation had been completed, Peel returned to the kibbutz and Yevzori agreed to another 24-hour truce. Peel then overheard one of the men in the Jewish party saying: "This will give us time to bring up reinforcements."

Peel's face reddened. "Under no circumstances," he said firmly, "can you do this. You would be violating the truce."

But the Jews smiled. The Haganah command, they knew, had decided to knock out Kaoukji once and for all.

That night, a large number of reinforcements arrived and a Palmach unit attacked and dislodged Arab forces from a village overlooking the kibbutz. The two sides then fought a seesaw battle for the strategic villages nestled in the surrounding hills, while two Jewish Piper Cubs dropped bombs (composed of irrigation pipes, with a screw top on one end and a match-lit fuse on the other). But by April 12, the Arab superiority in numbers and firepower began to tell. The Palmach positions were near collapse as ammunition ran out and Arab bombardment reached a new peak. It looked as if a final, decisive assault on the Jews, who now comprised about two battalions, was imminent. But instead, the intense shelling turned out to be a cover for the retreat of Kaoukji's troops.

Kaoukji, convinced that *his* force had been on the verge of collapse, desperately cabled the Arab League demanding ammunition and massive reinforcements "because 10,000 Jews have cut Mishmar Ha'emek off and are closing in from all sides."

A little earlier he had cabled the commander of a Druze Battalion, a mercenary formation, at his headquarters in the village of Shfar-Am: " . . . I turn to you, Sons of Maruf. I am in trouble. If you do not help me, my complaint will be to God."

The Druze, a light-skinned people with their own religion—the Moslems sneer that they are idolaters—were frankly mercenary. Their commander had emphasized in an order of the day to his soldiers that their only interest in the war was money. Now it was time to fight for a living. With reckless courage, wave after wave of his men attacked two nearby Jewish-captured Arab villages while their women, as tradition demanded, rushed forward to cover the faces of fallen husbands with a corner of the victim's *abiya*, or mantle, simultaneously shouting and sobbing encouragement to the other fighters. But the villages held out—and not long afterward the Druze decided that it would be more profitable, or at least safer, to fight for the Jews.

With the enemy offering some respite, the Palmach breathed more easily. But on the evening of April 13, Dan Laner, the Palmach commander, radioed Yehuda Yevzori from his mountain headquarters that his forces were exhausted and required two full days of rest.

"During that time," he said, "your kibbutz forces must hold the enemy if he attacks."

The next morning, Yevzori saw that Kaoukji's troops, now reinforced, had again surrounded the settlement, and that a small group was moving into a wooded hillside directly overlooking it.

"Quick!" he ordered a squad of eight men, "get into the forest and fire at them! Move around to make them think you're a big force!"

The squad departed, and immediately the advancing Arab force began to flee in terror, convinced that the Palmach had launched a major assault. Other troops on other hills, seeing their comrades run, also took to their heels. Within minutes, the narrow mountain paths were filled with people, as panicky civilians from the nearby villages joined the soldiers upon whom they had depended for protection against Jewish "vengeance"—though the settlers say they shouted to their neighbors to remain.

"They're all running away!" Yevzori shouted over the radio. "It's unbelievable!"

"I've got the same reports from everywhere," Laner rejoined.

Within half an hour after the eight kibbutzniks attacked, not an Arab remained in the whole region. The battle had ended—and the exodus had begun.

That night the Arab leaders learned the truth, and in an exchange of cables King Abdullah of Transjordan and President Kuwatly of Syria referred to Kaoukji as a "dog," a "thief," and a "traitor." But Arab newspapers treated the routed commander more charitably:

> The forces at Mishmar Ha'emek have surrendered after a week-long battle [announced a Beirut journal]. The mayor and council of elders of the village handed over the village to Kaoukji in the presence of the British commander. They turned over the equipment and the weapons to the Arab Command, which has taken it upon itself to safeguard the lives of the inhabitants and to furnish them with supplies.

At 0330 we shall start around and up Kastel. You all have your instructions. Remember, this objective is a must! Any questions?"

One of the squad leaders standing close to Uzi Narkis, commander of a Palmach unit of over 100 men, asked: "When will the relief come?"

Narkis spat, then scratched his thin, bearded face. A good question, he thought. He had insisted to David Shaltiel, Haganah commander in Jerusalem, that after his Palmach spearhead captured Kastel it be replaced immediately by regular Haganah troops of the Etzioni Brigade based in Jerusalem. He would not waste his spirited, highly trained Palmach unit on "garrison duty" when they were needed to attack elsewhere. But he didn't think it necessary to explain all this to his men at so critical a moment.

"Let me worry about that," he said.

Thus, on April 3, two days after Ben-Gurion had set Operation Nahshon in motion, the Jews were attacking. Narkis' force was part of the Palmach Harel Brigade, which was to assault Kastel from the east, while the Givati Brigade, under the command of Shimon Avidan, who was also in command of the whole operation, attacked the Latrun foothills from the west.

Narkis' squad leaders crawled back to their men, who were standing tensely in a ditch along the side of the road. Finally, the signal was whispered back: "The Brens forward!"

Several men scrambled from the ditch and crawled upward along a circular rocky path. Narkis watched as they advanced up the harsh, barren mountainside bathed in moonlight. It was too dark to see the village perched on the crest of the hill in the shadow of an old Roman fortress. Kastel! After all these centuries, still a monstrous sentinel blocking the way to Jerusalem, dominating the region for miles. Its stony paths led to the flat-topped ridge of Suba about a mile away and to villages as far as Ramallah to the north. How many Jews had already died from bullets and shells fired by men hiding behind its boulders and within its crevices? How many convoys had been wrecked and burned along the road twisting at its foot?

"Follow me!" Narkis whispered to the man behind him, and he started up the hill behind the Bren teams.

Within an hour, the surprised Arabs, after putting up little resistance, were scurrying down the mountainside. The Jews had captured their first Arab village. From Kastel, other attacks could be launched until all the heights overlooking the Tel Aviv–Jerusalem road were in Jewish hands.

"Destroy all the houses and dig in," Narkis advised Mordechai Gazit, who climbed Kastel with about 35 men of the new Etzioni Brigade several hours later to take over from Narkis. The newcomers were simply to hold the hill.

Gazit did fortify Kastel, but then decided that he could effectively defend the hill only by capturing a number of Arab-held heights surrounding it. His men then took three heights, but the Arabs counterattacked in force and the Jews fled back to Kastel where they found themselves virtually under siege and rapidly running out of ammunition and food.

Meanwhile, word of Kastel's fall reached Damascus, where Abd el-Kader el-Husseini had gone several days earlier to plead with Arab League officials for arms to meet the Jewish offensive he knew was about to start. Frustrated in this effort because of the League's deep resentment of the Mufti—the spirit behind his Palestinian force—Abd el-Kader was, in fact, meeting with the League leaders when a messenger burst into the conference room with the report.

"My God!" exclaimed General Ismail Safwat Pasha, the commander-in-chief of the Arab forces in Palestine, "Kastel has fallen to the Jews!"

There was a shocked silence. Then Safwat turned to the Palestinian commander and said: "Abd el-Kader, it's up to you to get it back. If you cannot do it, tell us and we will assign the task to Kaoukji."

Abd el-Kader, who was responsible for the Jerusalem area, turned white with fury as he retorted: "Pasha, the word 'Kastel' is derived from the foreign word 'castle.' And it means a fortress invulnerable to Italian rifles and the little ammunition we have. Give me the arms I've asked for and I'll take it back. My plan was to besiege Jerusalem, the Jewish settlements, and Bab el-Wad . . . However, the Jews now have cannons and planes, as well as trained men, and it is impossible for me to recapture Kastel without cannons. Grant my request and I can assure you victory."

"Abd el-Kader," Safwat snapped, "can't you understand? I have no cannons!"

The Palestinian then rose, picked up a map of Palestine that was spread on the table, and threw it in Safwat's face.

"You are traitors!" he shouted. "Criminals! History will record that you have abandoned Palestine. I'm going to win back Kastel—arms or no arms. I will take it back or die!"

Abd el-Kader returned to Jerusalem on April 6 and breakfasted with some of his commanders, including Bahjat Gharbieh. After ordering Gharbieh to gather what arms and ammunition he could, he went to the headquarters of Ibrahim Abu Daya, who had led the assault on *The Thirty-five* near Kfar Etzion, and said: "Come with me, Ibrahim. You are going to lead an attack on Kastel."

"But we need to prepare . . . "

"Never mind! We attack tonight!"

With some 150 men and several donkeys piled high with packs of ammunition, the two leaders trudged late that day to a hill village near Kastel where Abd el-Kader set up headquarters in an abandoned stone house about two miles from the Jewish positions. When a battle plan had been drawn up, Abu Daya, at about midnight, prepared to continue forward with his men to engage the Jews. Only Abd el-Kader and a few unarmed civilians were to remain behind.

"Don't let him follow us," Abu Daya ordered Abdullah Omari, a civilian aide, well aware of Abd el-Kader's impulsive, daredevil tendencies. "We can't take the chance. We need him too much."

"Don't worry," Abd el-Kader said, without looking up from a map he was examining at the table. "I'll stay here."

The storm broke over Kastel. Abd el-Kader, still sitting at the table poring over the map, seemed to breathe faster but said nothing. As the sounds of war grew louder, he finally sat back and sipped a cup of tea . . .

"I pray that God brings you victory and peace," his wife had written. "Oh, Abd el-Kader, I write to you with tears in my eyes. Because you left us behind. But that is the will of God. You are wrong in being so hard on us, but may God forgive you . . . "

A messenger dashed in.

"Abd el-Kader," he cried, "Ibrahim sent me. He says he is in trouble and needs more help!"

Abd el-Kader grabbed his Sten and announced, his dark eyes burning: "I'm going for a little walk."

"For God's sake, don't go," Omari pleaded.

"I won't go far. I've got to find out what's going on."

Omari, his brother Moussa, and another man then accompanied their commander outside. A mortar shell burst only a few yards away, slightly wounding all but Abdullah Omari.

"Let's get back into the house!" Omari exclaimed. "I'll dress your wounds."

Abd el-Kader laughed as he held a hand to his injured hip.

"A small wound like this? I've had worse."

With a limp, he then continued on toward the front with Moussa, after ordering the other two men to stay behind. When they had climbed some distance, the firing from the Arab side greatly diminished.

"Why have we stopped firing at them?" Abd el-Kader muttered. "Moussa, go and see what's wrong."

"What about you? I don't want to leave you alone."

"Never mind, I'll be all right."

So Moussa moved swiftly ahead.

About an hour later, at 5 A.M., a fighter ran into headquarters crying: "The situation is bad! Ibrahim has been wounded and we're running out of ammunition!"

"Have you seen Abd el-Kader?" Omari asked.

"No."

With a look of desperation, Omari immediately wrote out several messages and ordered them distributed to the surrounding Arab villages. Each note read: "Send help! Abd el-Kader is in danger!"

At about this time, Mordechai Gazit, Haganah commander on Kastel, was entering his headquarters, a stone house jutting from the terraced hillside. He had just visited the Jewish-occupied home of the village mukhtar, located a short distance up the hill in the center of the hamlet. Arab fighters had, to his surprise, reached that vital area and made an abortive attempt to blow up the house with explosives. They had finally retreated down the hill in the face of heavy Jewish fire, but had they been better organized and more used to night fighting, they probably would have overrun Kastel. And they might still do so if they were reinforced. Why didn't the Jewish command send the help he had been urgently requesting for three days? He had only about 60 able men left—one-third of his force had been knocked out. One more attack, and his men would have neither the bullets nor the morale to resist further.

Then Gazit heard his company sergeant shouting outside in Arabic: *"Ta'al ya gama'a!"* ("Come on, fellows!")

The Jewish reinforcements must have arrived! The Jews often used colloquial Arabic expressions.

But a voice answered in English: "Hello, boys."

The Jews did not answer each other in English very often. As Gazit ran to the door, a submachine gun spat into the night. He arrived just as the firing stopped. His sergeant had shot at three men hardly 10 yards away. One lay sprawled on the ground; the other two could be heard fleeing in the darkness.

"When they spoke English," explained the sergeant breathlessly, "I knew they were Arabs."

Gazit decided that the men must have thought this area was in Arab hands and that the sergeant's greeting in accented Arabic had come from friendly British deserters.

The sergeant and several others then examined the body of the heavy-set, mustached Arab victim, and removed from his leather jacket a Koran and some papers that indicated he was a high officer. His name, Abd el-Kader Salim, was inscribed on an Egyptian driving license.

Gazit radioed Jerusalem headquarters: "We have killed a fat fish. The name is Abd el-Kader Salim, repeat Salim . . ." (He sought to emphasize that the man was *not* Abd el-Kader el-Husseini.)

"We've beaten back the enemy," he went on, "but I must stress that this is only a temporary victory. We need help urgently!"

At about 7:30 A.M., Uzi Narkis arrived with three armored trucks loaded with 60,000 rounds of ammunition.

"Well, this is what you wanted," Narkis said as he entered Gazit's headquarters.

He then strolled outside and stared at the Arab corpse, which lay face down.

"Now may I have the papers you found on this Arab?" he asked.

Gazit at first refused, saying he would give them to his own command in Jerusalem, but finally agreed after a heated exchange. Narkis ordered his men to drag the body to his armored car, but when firing started again he decided to leave it where it had fallen. He promised Gazit to send reinforcements by noon, then departed, shuffling through the papers, which included the photographs of four young children and a letter: "I pray that God brings you victory and peace . . ."

*

As the morning crept slowly on, Gazit, his head bandaged (he had been struck by a ricocheting bullet), lay on the floor of his headquarters with several of his men, wracked with pain and almost too exhausted to move, counting the seconds until the reinforcements would arrive. So tired were his soldiers that they distributed the newly arrived ammunition by putting it into fort bags and throwing them to the nearest positions, which in turn, hurled them to others. Then came an amorphous hum, like the sound of locusts in the distance, cries and shouts and the crack of gunfire. An observer yelled: "They're attacking! Thousands of them! From everywhere!"

Gazit pulled himself to his feet and radioed Harel headquarters in the nearby village of Kiryat Anavim: "You said you'd come at noon, but the situation is desperate! Try to come sooner!"

"They're on the way," was the reply.

Half an hour later, as the Arabs closed in, Gazit radioed again: "Where are the reinforcements?"

"We've had some difficulty with the armored car. It's on the way."

His unit was finished, thought Gazit, as the vengeful screams of some 2,000 Arab villagers echoed through the hills.

His men were fighting a last-ditch battle when, at about 1:45 P.M., a Palmach officer crawled into the headquarters house after a precarious climb up the hillside.

"We've only just arrived!" Nahum Arielly, commander of the force, gasped out to Gazit.

"How many are with you?" Gazit asked.

"Two others. The rest are down there. They couldn't make it. The firing's too heavy."

"Your men have got to push the enemy back!"

"We can't. We haven't enough men."

At that moment, one of Arielly's soldiers burst in. "The Arabs are here! They're taking the mukhtar's house!"

"What do you suggest now?" Arielly asked Gazit, still trying to catch his breath.

"I suggest we get the hell out of here! Let's make a run for it—down the hill to Arza!"

Braving a storm of lead, the Jews, carrying their wounded, dashed out the door toward Arza, a settlement at the northern foot of Kastel. They took cover in a house halfway down the hill, where some members of the Palmach company had been waiting. But when Arielly saw that a few were missing—he was unaware that they were fleeing to the southeast along a safer escape route—he ran out to find them, shouting that he would be right back.

Gazit and the others waited, while the firing grew louder. But Arielly did not return, and after several minutes, the Haganah commander said: "We can't wait any longer! Retreat to Arza!"

A Palmach corporal then aimed a pistol at Gazit's head, warning: "I'll shoot you if you don't wait!"

"Go to hell!" Gazit rasped, convinced that these reinforcements did not understand the gravity of the situation. And he ordered his own men to follow him.

As they ran out, the Palmach corporal lowered his pistol and cursed.

A few minutes later, after other Jewish defenders had fled past, the Palmach unit decided to retreat, too, though Arielly still hadn't returned. Shimon Alfasi, the platoon commander in charge, ordered: "All privates will retreat—all commanders will cover their withdrawal."

By the time the commanders started to leave themselves, the Arabs were practically on them. Only one squad leader made it to the safety of a thicket on the lower slope. The other 10 commanders were killed. They had waited too long for Nahum Arielly—who had himself been cut down shortly after he had gone in search of his missing men.

Bahjat Gharbieh was struggling up the northern slope of Kastel with his little band of men to join his comrades who had already captured the village proper when, to his flank, he saw the Jews dashing down the hill toward the woods. He ordered his men to fire, and smiled as he watched them drop like tenpins, particularly those in the last group to retreat. If they had reached the thicket they would certainly have escaped.

He and his fighters then climbed to the village and joined a mob of comrades who had streamed up the hill from all sides. Men were laughing and shouting, embracing each other, arguing excitedly over who killed how many Jews. Then someone yelled: "We found him! Abd el-Kader! . . . He's dead!"

The madness stopped abruptly. "Where is he? Where is he?" went the cry, and men surged toward the house that had been Haganah headquarters. In front lay a corpse in a leather jacket. A great silence descended over Kastel as fierce fightingmen sobbed gently.

Several men lifted the body and began to carry it down the hill toward the main road, and the crowd followed.

Bahjat Gharbieh was horrified. He and a few other commanders pleaded with the fighters to stay.

"After all the blood we've spilled, we can't leave now!" they argued.

But their pleas fell on deaf ears. The Arabs had fought an intensely personal battle—mainly to please and protect Abd el-Kader. Now their hero was dead. Some would go with him to Jerusalem to stay until he was buried. Others drifted off in all directions to their villages, having no more stomach for battle.

Bahjat gave up. He sat down on a rock exhausted and watched something die in hundreds of men—men who were brave and aggressive when fighting for a god but indifferent when fighting for a hill. He was as stunned as any man by Abd el-Kader's death, but wasn't this the hill for which the man had died?

Bahjat stayed to defend Kastel with only about 50 other fighters.[9]

"You must counterattack immediately and retake Kastel!" Yigal Yadin, the Haganah acting chief of staff, ordered brusquely over the radiophone in his Tel Aviv headquarters on learning that the height had fallen to the Arabs.*

Yosef Tabenkin, commander of the Palmach battalion assigned to Operation Nahshon, was silent as he watched the survivors of the Kastel rout limp, exhausted and bloody, into Harel Brigade headquarters at nearby Kiryat Anavim.

"But, Yigal," he argued, "I have only one platoon available. The rest are scattered. How can thirty men who haven't slept for forty-eight hours attack all those Arabs in daylight? We counted sixteen hundred and there may be more. We've got to wait!"

"This is an order!" Yadin retorted. "Recapture Kastel immediately!"

"I'm not going!" Tabenkin shouted.

Neither man spoke again for several seconds. Then a third voice broke in: "Yussefele, what do you plan to do?"

Tabenkin, a tempestuously aggressive man who didn't like to take orders from anyone, even from superiors, recognized the voice of Yadin's aide, Mundak Pasternak, a close friend. Now at least he was being "consulted," not ordered. Nevertheless, he began lecturing Pasternak on the

* Yigal Yadin had been the Haganah chief of operations but was appointed acting chief of staff when Yaacov Dori, the chief of staff, suffered a stroke. Normally Yitzhak Sadeh, founder of the Palmach, would have taken over, as he had done immediately after World War II when Dori went to the United States to work with the American "underground." But Ben-Gurion became furious with Sadeh when the latter publicly stated that an officer in some circumstances could ignore the commands of the political leadership. Also, Ben-Gurion preferred Yadin's more formalistic military thinking to Sadeh's concentration on guerrilla tactics. He was especially impressed by his vast knowledge of history and archaeology and his ability to use this knowledge to military advantage. The son of the country's leading archaeologist, Yadin was, in fact, to follow in his father's footsteps.

folly of past Haganah policies, which, he said, had permitted the Arabs to strike at the Jews with virtual impunity. Ben-Gurion and his crowd had only now awakened to the danger. It was rather ironic that the Palmach, which had always favored an aggressive attitude, should now be told how to attack.

"Please, Yussefele," Pasternak replied. "Leave politics to your father!" Yosef's father, Yitzhak Tabenkin, had broken with Ben-Gurion several years earlier after a bitter political dispute.

Then Pasternak reiterated: "Well, what is your plan?"

"I shall wait for our friend the night. *Then* I'll recapture Kastel."

That night, Tabenkin, undaunted by the possible consequences of insubordination, told a company of exhausted men he had managed to gather: "You aren't required to do more than you can."

The attack force marched toward Kastel and started to climb the hill, under cover of heavy mortar fire . . .

Bahjat Gharbieh knew that his 50 men, with no water or food and little ammunition, could not hold out long. True, Fawzi el-Kaoukji, when he thought he had crushed the Jews at Mishmar Ha'emek, had sent some 75mm. guns to the area under pressure from the Arab League—after rejecting a radio plea by Abd el-Kader, shortly before his death, for arms and men. These guns were now firing at Jewish concentrations, but it was too late. And a detachment of 75 men sent by Kaoukji "for show" was stalling in Ein Karem nearby, waiting until Kastel fell again to the Jews. Traitors!

On the morning of April 10, Bahjat and his men finally retreated from bloody Kastel, pondering the ways of God.

Other Arab forces were then pushed from a conquered corner of the Jewish colony of Motza and from the key Arab villages of Kolonyah, Bab el-Wad, Beit Mahsir, and Saris.

The day after Kastel fell, Sir Henry Gurney, the British High Commissioner's deputy, entered in his diary: "The Jews have now occupied [Kastel] and are supplying their Haganah there by air. So long as they are in it, there is little chance of getting any agreement with the Arabs regarding free passage on the road. It is a typical Jewish move. . . . They will now have to get out of Kastel before we can do anything more, and there will be the usual howls and screams about that."[10]

But the only howls and screams echoed from Jerusalem as the Jews of that city deliriously welcomed three supply-crammed convoys that had pushed through the remaining barriers to break the siege—temporarily.

5

The Fruit
of Deir Yassin

WHILE Bahjat Gharbieh retreated despondently with his men from Kastel in the early hours of April 10, Ahmad Radwan rolled restlessly in his bed unable to sleep. Ahmad, fourteen years old, listened with deep foreboding to the distant thunder of bombs and chatter of machine guns. The Jews, he guessed, were trying to recapture Kastel. Only a few hours before he had seen hundreds of Arab fighters streaming down the road to Jerusalem. They had come from Kastel, their heads bowed and their shoulders bent, even though they had won the battle. They were all on their way to attend the funeral of Abd el-Kader el-Husseini, which would take place later in the morning. And who was left to defend Kastel? To come, if necessary, to the aid of his own village—Deir Yassin?

A picturesque complex of flat-topped, sun-baked stone huts mounted in tiers to the crest of a hill, Deir Yassin was vulnerable indeed. Less than a mile eastward was Beth Hakerem, the fringe zone of Jewish Jerusalem; to the northeast was the kibbutz of Givat Shaul; and to the west Kastel. If that village fell to the Jews, Deir Yassin, with its terraced olive and apricot orchards and its vineyards, would be hemmed in even more menacingly, with Ein Karim, to the southwest, the only neighboring Arab village.

The elders of the four related family clans comprising Deir Yassin, Ahmad was convinced, had done their best to win the good will of the Jews. And wisely so since the surrounding Jewish districts purchased most of the village fruit produce; and some of the women worked as servants in nearby Jewish homes. But more important, why commit suicide? Recently, when four Arab strangers had fired at the Jews from the village, the mukhtar hastily conveyed his apologies. And only two weeks before, about 40 Arab fighters had asked for protection, and Ahmad's ninety-six-year-old grandfather, after politely inviting them to lunch, had refused their request. Moreover, had not the village leaders met with Jews from nearby settlements and agreed to maintain peace whatever fighting took place elsewhere? True, the thousand citizens of Deir Yassin had quietly armed themselves and stored away quantities of ammunition—just in case they were drawn into the war. But they wanted no part of this war.

At about 4:30 A.M., when the distant firing had died down, Ahmad heard shots that sounded much closer. He jumped out of bed and peered from the window. It was too dark to see anything. Then there were more shots—and screams. The Jews were attacking!

Two hours or so earlier, Mordechai Raanan, Irgun commander in Jerusalem, stood in the cellar of his headquarters pointing to a large map of Deir Yassin pinned on a board. With the final battle of Kastel still undecided, he emphasized to the two platoons of men seated on the cellar floor: "This will not be a hit-and-run operation. It will be the first time that a Jewish force will have captured an Arab village and held it."

Then (according to commander Raanan and other Irgun witnesses), he warned his men against looting and killing unarmed civilians. When one youth asked sarcastically what the Arabs would do if they captured a Jewish village, Raanan replied: "If a dog bites you, you as a man shouldn't act like a dog. I would not expect you to bite a dog."

About the same time, in Kibbutz Givat Shaul, Yehoshua Zetler, the Sternist chief in Jerusalem, was also briefing a platoon of his men who were to participate in the attack on Deir Yassin. He maintains that he, too, warned against killing unnecessarily; other Sternists add that he did so on the basis of an understanding with Raanan, though Raanan himself claims Zetler later commented that he did not consider it wise to "make such a speech" before a battle.

Actually, neither leader, it appears, conceived that his men would kill indiscriminately. The plan was to attack Deir Yassin from three sides—the Irgun from the east and south, and the Sternists from the north. A loudspeaker mounted on an armored car stolen from the British would give out a warning that all inhabitants should flee westward, and it seemed almost certain that the village would fall without a shot being fired.

Raanan had first seriously thought of attacking Deir Yassin when he had learned of Haganah's plan to take the offensive, though he had considered the idea earlier. David Shaltiel (Haganah commander in Jerusalem) had called him to his headquarters and informed him of Operation Nahshon.

"There is no room in a city under siege for three military organizations," Shaltiel had said. "Accept the Haganah's authority and help us attack Kastel."

Raanan's impetuous nature, gangling physique, and boyishly handsome face made him seem even younger than his twenty-five years. He loathed the balding, austere-mannered Haganah commander, who was some fifteen years older, disdainfully regarding him as prim, hypocritical and incompetent, a man he could not trust. Of course he would cooperate, he replied acidly—if he were assured that the Jews would fight to take all of Jerusalem. He strongly suspected, he said, that King Abdullah and Ben-Gurion had secretly decided to divide the city between them.

According to Raanan, Shaltiel then shouted: "I'm here to protect the life of the Jews in Jerusalem, not to initiate any attacks! If you're not going to cooperate, I'll deal with the Lehi and you'll be cut off from supplies."

Raanan went immediately to see Zetler, who told him that Shaltiel had threatened to deal only with the Irgunists when he had set forth *his* conditions for cooperation with the Haganah. Zetler then asked to join with the Irgun in an attack of their own, and Raanan agreed.

Deir Yassin seemed like a logical, and relatively easy, target. Strategically located on the outskirts of Jerusalem, it threatened to serve as an Arab base for an attack on the New City. They were convinced, moreover, that Arab fighters were even now using the village as a transit point from the Jerusalem area to Ein Karim and Kastel. Nor had they forgotten how in 1929 Arabs had emerged from that hamlet to massacre every Jew they could find. Even recently, their information was that the villagers had regularly sniped at Givat Shaul (Haganah could not confirm this).

Shaltiel, meanwhile, raged at the "arrogance" of the terrorist leaders, whom he despised as individuals, as well as for their extremist philosophies. As a former Haganah intelligence chief, he had done his utmost to clamp down on their activities. A veteran of the French Foreign Legion, he was himself sometimes ruthless. During World War II, he had helped to recruit Haganah fighters in Haifa by tarring and feathering a reluctant citizen and having him driven around the town in a jeep—an action he later deeply regretted. Nor had he been spared the role of victim in a world of brutality. When he tried to smuggle arms through Germany for the Haganah in prewar days, the Nazis captured and tortured him before the Jewish underground purchased his freedom. But though he was no stranger to violence and counterviolence, he viewed the Irgunists and the Sternists as straightforward thugs and murderers—who, furthermore, showed no respect for their elders.

Nevertheless, he reasoned after hearing of their attack plans, he *was* desperately short of fighters, partly because of what he regarded as the disastrous Haganah policy of tying up men in every outlying settlement.

So he would let the dissidents contribute their manpower to the cause. In any case, he felt, he didn't have the means to stop them if he wanted to.

Thus, on April 7, while the two groups prepared for the attack on Deir Yassin, Shaltiel sent identical letters to Raanan and to Zetler without—according to Ben-Gurion—consulting the Haganah High Command:

> I learn that you plan an attack on Deir Yassin. I wish to point out that the capture of Deir Yassin and its holding are one stage in our general plan. I have no objection to your carrying out the operation provided you are able to hold the village. If you are unable to do so I warn you against blowing up the village, which would lead to the flight of the inhabitants and the occupation of the destroyed and empty houses by foreign forces. This situation would increase our difficulties in the general struggle and a second conquest of the place would require heavy sacrifices.
>
> Furthermore, if foreign forces took over, this would upset our general plan for establishing an airfield. . . .

Neither Raanan nor Zetler responded. Nor did they request permission for the attack from their own superiors in Tel Aviv. It was difficult to communicate under siege conditions; and Zetler, in any case, had no intention of seeking approval from Friedman-Yellin.

So began the attack on Deir Yassin—which was to have a dramatic effect on the conduct and direction of the war—as the last bullets and shells pierced the dawn at Kastel.

The first shots that had shaken young Ahmad Radwan from bed had been fired at the eastern edge of the village. In a concrete pillbox there, his uncle, Mohammed Attieh, and two cousins were on guard when Attieh, noticing strange shadows in the first glimmer of day, cried "Who's there?" and received no response. All three opened fire, and the Jews answered with Sten fire and a shell that partially destroyed the pillbox. Attieh, wounded, ran to his house nearby for first aid, while advancing Irgunists, shouting *"Kadima! Kadima!"* ("Forward! Forward!"), shot his two sons who had remained behind.

Ahmad's ninety-six-year-old grandfather, Haj Ismail Attieh, who had just finished his morning prayer and was preparing tea for men in the guard post, rushed to bandage his son Mohammed, when two Irgunists burst in. The grandfather, shrieking defiance, leaped at one of them and grabbed him by the throat. It is not clear whether either Arab, or another of Haj Ismail's sons who was present, tried to shoot, but the surprised intruders fired, killing the three Arabs. Then they ran out of the house, leaving one of the old grandfather's wives cringing in a corner.

As the Irgunists poured in from the east and south, they were shocked and baffled by Arab resistance. Instead of empty houses, they found that each home was a bristling fort. The Jews were not used to capturing villages. Unless the residents fled or surrendered, how could a house be taken without killing the people inside? Hadn't the inhabitants been warned to run?

In fact, only a few had heard the warning. The armored car with the loudspeaker that was to accompany the Sternist platoon attacking from the north under the command of David Gottlieb arrived after the Irgunists had gone into action. It had been slated to smash into the center of the village for the announcement, but as it approached the first row of houses it skidded into a deep tank trap and could not be pulled out. There, while the village resounded with gunfire, it belatedly blared its message, heard by few other than the Sternists themselves:

"You are being attacked by superior forces . . . The west exit of Deir Yassin leading to Ein Karim is open for you! Run immediately! Don't hesitate! Our forces are advancing! Run toward Ein Karim!"

While these words resounded, Ezra Elnakam (the young Sternist who several months earlier had killed a British policeman for his gun) tried frantically with the help of his comrades to lift the armored car from the trap.

"They're shooting at us!" he gasped. "It's impossible!"

"Let's leave it where it is and attack without it," shouted Menashe Eichler. "We can't stay here all day."

The very thought aggravated him. It was Friday morning, and the Sabbath would start at sundown. Eichler was an ultra-Orthodox Jew, and wore the traditional full beard and long sideburn ringlets. And though God would excuse him for fighting an enemy that threatened his very survival, he wanted to get home and honor the Day of Rest if it was humanly possible.

The Sternists abandoned the armored car and began to return the Arab fire. They attacked the first row of houses (where most of the firing was coming from), throwing grenades into the windows and sweeping the interiors with gunfire as they crashed through the doors. As the smoke cleared in house after house, women and children lay dead and wounded with their fighting men. But still the Arabs kept firing, and as Jewish casualties steadily mounted, the attackers, angered and frustrated by a situation they had never contemplated or prepared for, started to kill with increasing ferocity.

He didn't want to kill women and children, Menashe Eichler thought as he lobbed grenades through windows and listened with sinking heart for the blast. But wasn't it better to kill than be killed? God would certainly approve. He understood the Sternists because they understood Him. Neither the Haganah nor the Irgun permitted true believers perfect freedom to observe His laws. But the Stern Group did. Orthodox fighters like himself could form their own units, go home for the Sabbath, eat their own ultra-kosher food. More important, the Sternists followed the instructions of the Bible more rigidly than the others. They honored the passage (Exodus 22:2): "If a thief be found breaking up, and be smitten that he die, there shall no blood be shed for him."

This meant, of course, that killing a thief was not really murder. And were not the enemies of Zionism thieves, who wanted to steal from the Jews what God had granted them? He didn't hate the Arabs as he did the British, who had no business at all in Palestine. But they were nevertheless "thieves."

Ahmad Radwan, who was alone in his house with five younger brothers and sisters when the fighting broke out (his father and elder brother were standing guard and his mother had gone to the bakery), did not need the advice of the loudspeaker close by. He immediately sent the young ones fleeing to Ein Karim, and they joined more than 200 other women and children who also took advantage of the unblocked route to that village. Through the window he saw his paternal grandfather shot dead as he ran out toward the stalled Jewish armored car to find other members of the family. The boy then dashed to the nearest pillbox and helped feed the men ammunition while women in nearby houses screamed encouragement. As the battle raged, Ahmad, on his way to an ammunition storage house, found the bodies of his father and an uncle. Tears rolling down his cheeks, he continued on—tormented now by the thought of his mother's possible fate.

At the village bakery, his mother Aziza was waiting in line with about 30 other women for the bakers, an elderly man and his son, to bake her dough in a large rusty oven when the fighting started. But the oven made such a noise that no one could hear the firing until someone came running up, crying: "The Jews are here! The Jews are here!"

The women panicked and began running toward their homes. But Aziza, who lived comparatively far away, crawled to the mukhtar's house at the top of a steep gradient nearby. The mukhtar's wife let her in—the mukhtar himself had fled for help—and she joined several other women under mattresses while a group of men manned the house, a highly strategic point which swiftly became the attackers' central objective.

*

Mohammed Kassim, the fifty-year-old village carpenter, lurched from
bed with the first shots and stumbled outside still half asleep. But the first
shell explosion shocked him fully awake. He started to dash through
the hills toward Ein Karim about five miles away as fast as his short, spindly
legs would carry him, having remembered his assignment—to run for help
the moment the Jews attacked. In little more than half an hour, he staggered into the Arab village, gasping: "Help! Help! The Jews are attacking
Deir Yassin!"

Several shabbily uniformed officers emerged from stone huts. They
were Syrian and Iraqi officers of the Arab Liberation Army contingent
that Fawzi el-Kaoukji had sent to Ein Karim in grudging response to Abd el-
Kader's desperate appeal for help at Kastel. But though within a few miles
of Kastel, they had not budged from Ein Karim to help in the battle for
that stronghold.

"Come with me!" Kassim cried.

"We have no orders!" one of the officers said despondently. "We can't
move without orders! All our top commanders have gone to Jerusalem for
Abd el-Kader's funeral."

"Well, then let's go to Jerusalem!" Kassim urged.

With two officers, he then set out for the Arab village of Maldha, about
two miles away, en route to Jerusalem, pleading all the time with his companions to hurry. In Maldha, the two officers took a taxi to Jerusalem and
Kassim stayed behind seeking help from the local populace. But his cries
met only silence. The villagers had either departed for the funeral or were
afraid to volunteer for battle.

In despair, Kassim started running toward Jerusalem to seek aid there
on his own. As he staggered into the Old City, he found himself amidst
wailing throngs of mourners surging toward the Mosque of Omar for the
funeral—heedless, dazed people who gazed silently at him with vacant
eyes as he plucked them by the sleeve and pleaded for assistance.

Finally, inside the teeming mosque, he found a well-known Arab
fighter—Sheikh Yassin el-Bakry—and, grabbing him by the arm, dragged
him outside. Bakry then ran with him to the nearest police station and
telephoned Allenby Barracks.

"It's your responsibility to stop the attack!" the sheikh yelled.

"I'm sorry," answered a British officer, "but I'll have to get orders. It
may take some time."

The Arab cursed, pulling at his small black beard for emphasis.

"Don't worry," Bakry assured Kassim. "I'll get you help somehow."

And he returned to the mosque to pray for the soul of Abd el-Kader el-Husseini.

As the battle in Deir Yassin continued, the attackers found themselves trapped in a murderous hornet's nest. Casualties were mounting steadily and even the operation commander, the Irgun's Ben-Zion Cohen, had been wounded. And for all the sacrifice, they had managed to capture less than 20 per cent of the village. They could only be thankful that they had found enough enemy ammunition to keep the battle going, since they had almost run out of their own.

"We've got to change our strategy," decided Yehuda Lapidot, who had taken over command from Cohen. "We'll fight them as we fought the British." And he sent a messenger to Raanan, who was watching the battle from a point near Givat Shaul. Within minutes, Raanan and several assistants were trudging to Deir Yassin with heavy bags of TNT tied to their backs.

After about an hour's respite, the attack started again, this time more systematically. Two men crawled toward a house covered by Bren fire, hurled a bag of explosives through a window or set it down by a door, and ran. No one inside could evade the dynamite, which virtually destroyed each house. Raanan personally directed the operation, ordering the destruction of each dwelling from which sniper fire was coming.

At last they were making headway, he thought, as blast after blast shook the village. His men might lack formal military training, but they certainly knew how to use dynamite. And if women and children happened to be inside after they had been warned to flee, was he responsible? Could a pilot who dropped a bomb on an enemy city be blamed for the death of innocent civilians? Raanan was responsible for the safety of his men—even if this meant they had to kill women and children, however unintentionally.

But not all the attackers were as careful to distinguish between intentional and unintentional killing of noncombatants. Increasingly enraged by the unexpected resistance that claimed so many comrades, some lost all restraint and cold-bloodedly shot every Arab they found—man, woman, or child. Raanan and Zetler disclaim any knowledge of such atrocities, but some of their men admit that they took place—confirming the charges of Arab survivors—though the Irgunists and Sternists tend to blame a "lunatic fringe" of each other's organization. At any rate, survivors say that Jewish fighters told them at the height of the battle that their leaders had ordered an end to the deliberate killing of women and children.

*

Although the dynamiting gradually eliminated the sniping, the mukhtar's house perched on a hill remained a center of fierce resistance, slowing down the whole operation. And the situation became desperate for the Jews as their casualties piled up, since the house overlooked, if from some distance, the evacuation route to Jerusalem.

What happened in the key battle that then took place is unclear. A Palmach unit, say the dissident leaders, volunteered its services, apparently without orders, and shelled the house with a mortar, departing immediately afterward. Then, according to Jewish participants, the Arabs in the house surrendered. However, as an Irgunist entered, the mukhtar's wife drew a pistol from her robes and killed him. Lapidot thereupon sent one man, Yossef Anvy, with a Bren to rush the house, and Anvy, though hit in the face by two bullets, continued to advance, entered the house, killed three men, and returned bloody-faced with the announcement that resistance had ended.

Ahmad's mother, Aziza, offers another version. As she lay under a mattress in the house, she heard a scream and several shots fired in the kitchen next door. After a silence of some minutes, she emerged from hiding and found the enemy gone and the mukhtar's wife and grandson dead. Several Jews then returned and one of them shouted from outside:

"Come out or we'll destroy the house over your heads!"

Aziza called out: "If we come out, will you spare us?"

"Yes!"

"Swear by your religion and the Ten Commandments!"

"We swear. We have received an order not to shoot women and children. How many men are in there?"

Without thinking, Aziza cried: "We have three men."

"Are they armed?"

"I—I don't know."

Aziza and all the other occupants then filed out with their hands raised.

As the women were led away to be locked in another house, they passed the bakery, where the father lay dead on the floor, and the son in the smoking oven.

When the fighting finally ended in mid-afternoon, the conquerors ordered all survivors to gather in the village square. Most of the men, including Ahmad, had fled to Ein Karim by this time, some dressed in women's robes; but about 10 still remained. Arab witnesses charge— and Irgunists and Sternists deny—that these men were herded into the square, separated from the women and children, and shot.

Then the women and children, including Aziza, were piled into trucks and driven through Jewish Jerusalem where the population watched the procession of crushed humanity in shocked silence. The prisoners climbed out at Mandelbaum Gate and dazedly shuffled into the Old City.

At about 5:30 that evening, Shaltiel drove to the edge of Deir Yassin to see Raanan.

"What have you done here?" he roared, gazing at a wilderness of smoking ruins.

"The place is completely under our control," Raanan replied, his wan face smudged with ash.

Then, after claiming to have found Iraqi uniforms and other evidence that the village had represented a grave danger to the Jews, Raanan demanded: "Now send some men to take over from us."

"We're not going to take responsibility for your murders!" was Shaltiel's reply. "You must bury the dead and hold the village yourself!"

He then left, and immediately sent some soldiers to cover the evacuation of the Jewish casualties. The next morning, he dispatched a platoon under an aide, Yeshurin Schiff. As Schiff inspected the scene he was horrified. Bodies were piled up in a quarry, some of them half-charred. When the corpses had begun to smell, the victors tried to burn them but found that the odor simply grew worse.

Schiff repeated Shaltiel's demands, but an Irgunist officer answered: "We're fighters, not pallbearers! We're leaving!"

Schiff said: "If you don't obey, my men will open fire!"

The two Jews breathed the putrid, sickening air as they stood facing each other under the hot sun. Schiff glanced at the hill of corpses. Then he withdrew his men.

Early the next morning, while the Irgun-Sternist detachment prepared to leave Deir Yassin, a jeep carrying Dr. Jacques de Reynier, the Red Cross representative, drew up to the village accompanied by an ambulance and a truck. The occupiers reluctantly allowed him to enter, escorting him as he tramped from house to house searching for dead and wounded. Amid the ruins, he found a number of corpses and three people—a ten-year-old girl and two women—who were still alive.

Later, he maintains, two Irgun commanders came to see him in Jerusalem and demanded that he sign a prepared document thanking the occupiers of Deir Yassin for receiving him courteously and offering him every cooperation. When he refused to sign, he says, they threatened his life, but finally left when he informed them that he had already sent a contrary report to his Geneva headquarters. After that, he adds, the Irgun cooperated wholeheartedly with him, turning over Arab hostages, for example, on request.[1]

As the Irgunists and Sternists, who had suffered 40 per cent casualties, withdrew from Deir Yassin, Schiff returned with a party of schoolboys. They dug graves and buried the Arab bodies, weeping and vomiting as they performed their macabre task. How many bodies did they bury? Paradoxically, the Jews say about 250 out of 400 village inhabitants, while Arab survivors say only 110 of 1,000 inhabitants.

The dissidents left, as it turned out, just in time. For High Commissioner Cunningham, on learning of the attack, had flown into a rage and, though reluctant to commit his few remaining troops to battle, urgently requested London to send Tempests based in Iraq (all had already been evacuated from Palestine) to bomb the occupied village. But by the time they arrived, Haganah forces had replaced the Irgun-Sternist units, and Cunningham saw no point in retaliating against the Haganah.

He was apparently influenced by a communiqué that Shaltiel, who had never expected the attack to turn out as it did, released on April 10:

> This morning, the last Lehi and Etzel soldiers ran from Deir Yassin, and our forces entered the village.
> We were forced to take command of the village after the splinter forces [Irgunists and Sternists] opened a new enemy front and then fled, leaving the western neighborhoods of the city open to enemy attack.
> The splinter groups did not launch a military operation. . . . They could have attacked enemy gangs in the Jerusalem area and lightened the burden which Jerusalem bears. But they chose one of the quiet villages in the area that has not been connected with any of the gang attacks since the start of the present campaign; one of the few villages that has not let foreign gangs in.
> For a full day, Etzel and Lehi soldiers stood and slaughtered men, women, and children, not in the course of the operation, but in a premeditated act which had as its intention slaughter and murder only. They also took spoils, and when they finished their work, they fled. . . .

The communiqué denied Irgun and Sternist claims that a Palmach force had participated in the attack.

Enraged by this declaration, Raanan and Zetler released the text of the letter Shaltiel had sent them guardedly approving the attack in advance. Israel Galili, the Haganah commander, then asked Shaltiel about this letter, which Tel Aviv had never sanctioned. Shaltiel cabled back on April 15:

I LEARNED THEY PREPARING ACTION AGAINST DEIR YASSIN STOP
AS I DIDN'T WANT TO MEET THEM I SENT LETTER STOP I WOULD
STOP TO THE EXTENT POSSIBLE FUTURE OPERATIONS OF DISSIDENTS

Ben-Gurion himself says he was filled with shock and disgust at this episode. Apparently he also feared that King Abdullah would now hesitate to reach an agreement with the Jews. He sent off a wire to Abdullah expressing his deep regrets and disclaiming responsibility for the bloody event. The King replied caustically that the Jewish Agency was indeed responsible for Jewish actions.

Odd as it may seem, Nathan Friedman-Yellin, the Stern Group chief and opponent of Zetler, was also embittered by news of the attack. Ill in Tel Aviv, he was visited in the hospital by David Gottlieb, who had led the Sternist contingent. Astonished, Friedman-Yellin asked him: "How could you have done it? It was inhuman and not consistent with the dignity of our freedom fighters. We're not a band of murderers!" He had wanted to disband the Stern Group as an activist organization as soon as the British agreed to leave Palestine, in any case, and would not listen now to arguments about unexpected Arab resistance.

The Arabs themselves shouted the loudest, exaggerating the atrocities to the point where even Glubb Pasha believed that virtually every one of the village's inhabitants had been slaughtered.[2] But if this propaganda, as intended, greatly intensified Arab hatred for the Jews, it also intensified Arab fears. Deir Yassin became not only a rallying cry for Arab vengeance, but a cry of panic that was to help propel the historic flight of hundreds of thousands of Arabs from Palestine, though many had started to leave before this incident. The effect, indeed, was immediate. After the fierce fighting at Kastel, which fell to the Jews just before the Deir Yassin attack, Haganah forces swooped into other villages along the Tel Aviv–Jerusalem road to meet little more than rearguard action covering the flight of the inhabitants.[3]

More spectacular was the exodus that began from large towns . . .

O PEOPLE OF TIBERIAS, we are in great trouble," cried Abu Abd el-Tabari, Mufti of that eastern Galilean town, as he stood amid his stunned people in the square. "We must decide whether to remain or to leave. The British say that they will provide transport if we leave."

The men remained silent, not wishing to admit that they would rather leave.

The Jews had always enjoyed a military advantage over them. Not only did they outnumber the Arab population, but most lived on the hill-side overlooking the Arab-dominated old city on the shores of Lake Tiberias. Even so, after the United Nations partition resolution, the Arabs had felt obliged to attack the Jews, with whom they had lived and worked for so long in amity. They had isolated the small Jewish population in the old city from the new city, and thereby, in effect, eastern Galilee from the rest of the country. The Jews in the old city had thus been forced to depend on supplies brought in by a few motorboats from the fishing kib-butz of Ein Gev on the eastern shore of the lake.

But then, on the night of April 18, as soon as British troops had with-drawn from the town, Haganah forces had attacked from the old city upward and from the new city downward to cut Arab Tiberias in two. Now the Arabs were the ones in trouble. King Abdullah had already dis-patched 30 trucks to Tiberias in cooperation with the British to evacuate the women and children. But should the men remain to be massacred as at Deir Yassin?

Early in the afternoon, the trucks arrived and were soon bulging with women and children. The men then climbed in of their own accord, encouraged by British officers who didn't want to have to intervene in the event of further fighting. The convoy pulled out of town, leaving behind a mountain of bundles the panicky passengers had had to relinquish for lack of room.

Three days later, it was Haifa's turn . . .

At 11:30 A.M., April 20, Major General Hugh Stockwell, commander of northern Palestine, handed a note to Captain Amin Izzedin, commander of the Arab forces in Haifa. As Izzedin sat reading it at Stockwell's desk, his hand began to tremble slightly. The note said that British troops had started to evacuate the positions they had occupied along a line roughly separating the Jewish and Arab zones, and that they would henceforth occupy only the port of Haifa and a few other points necessary to ensure a safe troop withdrawal from Palestine.

"In the last two weeks," the note read, "clashes between Arabs and Jews have increased to a great extent . . . I have no desire whatsoever to involve my troops or members of the police in these clashes."

When he had finished reading, Izzedin looked up at the General and said firmly: "We do not accept your decision. The British army must accept the responsibility for the well-being of the inhabitants . . . I don't see any chance of holding out against the Jewish forces. We protest this arbitrary division of the city, which amounts to turning over Arab Haifa to the Jews."

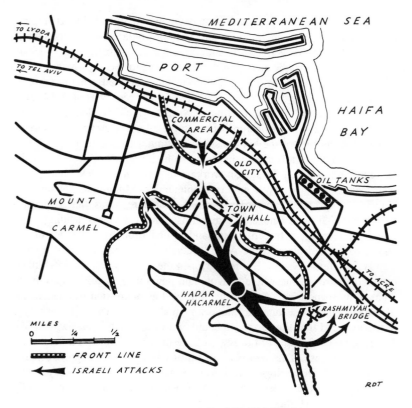

THE BATTLE OF HAIFA

Stockwell, a veteran of the Burma campaign in World War II, replied dryly: "These are my instructions and I'm not prepared to change them." Stockwell could well understand Izzedin's discomfort. The Haganah would certainly have the advantage in a free battle for Haifa, which, blessed with the greatest port in Palestine and an important oil refinery, was an invaluable prize. The Jews, who constituted 55 per cent of Haifa's 146,000 inhabitants, mainly occupied Mount Carmel, which overlooked the sea and dominated the strategic approaches to the city. The Arabs were largely bunched at the foot of the hill—a situation similar to that in Tiberias.

Furthermore, Arab morale in Haifa, so high after Arab workers at the oil refinery had killed 41 Jewish workers in December, 1947, had plummeted when the first Arab military commander, Mohammed Hamad al-Huneiti (a former Transjordan Arab Legionnaire) was killed in mid-March in a Jewish ambush of an arms convoy he was leading from Lebanon. Huneiti, a forceful commander, had brought order out of the quarrels that had plagued the Arab leadership and had organized a commendable defense system. But fear gripped the Arabs when the Jews killed him and destroyed the whole convoy, and new quarrels culminated in the flight of most moderate Arab leaders, as well as many rich businessmen.*

Stockwell, whose officers had dealt "realistically" with Tiberias, was now convinced that the Jews also could and would take Haifa, which, like Tiberias, was to be part of the Jewish State under the United Nations resolution in any case. This was perhaps unfortunate—he had opposed partition from the beginning—but nevertheless inevitable. The sooner the Jews took over, the easier it would be to evacuate British forces peacefully from the port of Haifa.

THIS CONVICTION HAD BEGUN TO CRYSTALLIZE AFTER TWO JEWISH officials, Abba Hushi and Harry Beilin, had come to see Stockwell in late February with a daring plan to end the street fighting that was going on. Hushi, who originated the idea, had said: "General, we wish to speak to you about an important matter, a matter that will perhaps seem to you madness . . . You must understand that the Jews will not give up Haifa, and a prolongation of the present situation may bring on a confrontation between the Haganah and the British army."

"Well, what do you suggest?"

"You should hand the city over to us."

"What?"

"After all, in the end the city will be part of the Jewish State."

"Well—. . . Give me time to think about it."

Finally, after four meetings, Stockwell had his answer ready—

---

* Information given the Haganah by a top official in the Arab League permitted the Jews to intercept 9 of 11 Arab convoys crammed with arms and reinforcements for Haifa. The Jews paid about £50 ($150) per convoy in bribes.

on April 18, in fact, two days before the meeting with Izzedin. "Gentlemen," he had said, "after consulting with General Mc-Millan I've thought a great deal about your offer . . . and I'm ready to accept . . . But my chief concern is about the lines of evacuation for the British army."

"We'll help you keep and secure those lines," replied Hushi.

"How much time will you need to complete the capture of the whole city?"

"Between twenty-four and forty-eight hours."

"You are pretentious and headstrong, Mr. Hushi," said Stockwell. "With the division and a half I have at my command, I wouldn't be able to do it in less than a week."

"Would you care to wager? Say, for a bottle of whisky?"

Hushi then wrote in a notebook: "Stockwell—one week; I—24 to 48 hours."

As Izzedin was now about to leave Stockwell's office, the General said that, of course, the Jews were only just being told the same news.

Deeply depressed, Izzedin, without informing Haifa's other Arab leaders, then took a boat for Beirut en route for Damascus where, he later said, he was convinced he had to argue personally for arms and reinforcements to bolster his 600 Arab fighters.

A few days earlier, Ramzi Hararah, an eighteen-year-old Arab operator in the Telephone Exchange at Haifa, had stood outside his house and watched glumly as several men carried furniture and other household goods from the house next door and piled them into a truck.

When the truck was loaded, a young man who had been helping strolled over to him and smiled sadly.

"Goodbye, Ramzi," he said, wiping the sweat from his brow. "Say goodbye to your mother and father. You have been dear neighbors."

Ramzi lowered his brown eyes. He would never find a friend like Josef again. No one could play soccer better than Josef. And his mother could cook such delicious food, especially on the Jewish holidays. After all, they were Oriental Jews. They appreciated the Arab tastes and understood the Arabs. Not like the Western Jews who lived apart and thought apart. Josef had had to go to a Jewish school and he to an Arab school. That was what the leaders of both people wanted. How foolish! If Josef had not lived next door in the Arab quarter, they never would have known each other or played soccer together. If all the Arab and Jewish kids went to the same school and played soccer together, maybe they wouldn't be fighting . . .

"I'm sorry we've got to move to the Jewish quarter," Josef added. "But there'll be fighting here . . . Look, you should move, too. You're too near the Jewish quarter."

"This is our house," Ramzi asserted firmly. "We shall never move."

Then the two youths embraced, and Josef jumped into the truck, which lurched away toward the Jewish quarter.

The battalion of Jewish fighters in Haifa did not wait for Captain Izzedin to reach Damascus with his demands for assistance. Spearheaded by students of the Technion Institute, they were preparing to take over all Haifa at the very moment when Izzedin learned of the British withdrawal. Indeed, the evacuation had begun the previous night, catching the Haganah, and even many British officials themselves, by surprise.

The Haganah plan, known as Operation Misparayim, or Scissors, was to cut Arab Haifa into three parts in a three-pronged attack, with forces from Mount Carmel to hook up with troops driving from the Jewish-held commercial center near the port. The main Jewish attack would start after dark. But at 1 P.M. on April 20, only about an hour after Izzedin learned the bad news, Mordechai Makleff, commander of the operation, sent a company of the Carmeli Brigade to occupy Nejidah House—a large concrete office building that controlled the strategic Rashmiyah Bridge, over which all eastward traffic from Haifa had to pass. By thus drawing Arab defenders to the eastern edge of town, the other Jewish forces, bolstered by a 3-inch mortar and several homemade Davidka artillery pieces, could more easily smash into the rest of the Arab section later.

After a vicious floor-to-floor fight, the Jews won control of the corpse-littered Nejidah House, only to find themselves open targets for Arabs in surrounding buildings who fired heavily through the shattered doors and windows of the crumbling fortress. While food, water, and bandages ran out, Jewish casualties mounted throughout the day and night as armored cars failed in desperate attempts to reach the building and reinforce the defenders.

"We've lost all our commanders," radioed a Haganah man from the building late in the day. "We have many wounded here. They are bleeding continuously . . . Please advance faster, advance as fast as you can!"

"We are coming nearer," came the reply. "Hold on. Don't lose hope. We are approaching you."

But even as the men in the building died, one by one—the survivors were finally rescued when armored cars reached the building the following night—they were winning Haifa. For shortly after midnight, while the Arabs were concentrating on the besieged house, Makleff struck with devastating force into the main Arab areas, taking house after house, partly with bullets and shells, partly with loudspeaker propaganda demanding surrender. By 7 A.M. on April 21, the Jews had made considerable progress, but the Arabs were still far from knocked out. The bitterly defended Huri Building had to be burned before the few Arab survivors retreated.

Thus, it was with a sense of joyous disbelief that Carmeli Brigade Commander Moshe Carmel and his deputy, Makleff, received a message from General Stockwell asking what Haganah's conditions were for peace. The Haganah leaders had been certain that the Arabs would fight until the situation was hopeless.

And this may have been the Arab intention, but Stockwell asked for Jewish terms apparently even before the Arabs requested them. For when he realized, to his amazement, that he would inevitably lose a bottle of whisky anyway, he saw no reason for letting the battle linger—especially since London might order him to intervene before the Jewish victory was decisive.

Actually, members of a hastily formed Arab Emergency Committee, most of whom were Christian and favored cooperation with the Jews (some were even ready to accept partition), had tried unsuccessfully to reach Stockwell after the fighting started. Finally, at about 9 P.M., after a committee member, Farid Saad, had made innumerable telephone calls, the British District Commissioner rang back and said that Stockwell would see him at 10:30 A.M. the following morning, April 21, more than three hours, as it turned out, after Stockwell had asked the Jews for their surrender terms.

At the meeting, Farid Saad and other members of the Arab Emergency Committee insisted with much agitation that it was the duty of the British as the mandate power to take over the city again and permit the 400 or so Arab reinforcements waiting at Haifa's barricaded borders to enter.

Stockwell stared at the visitors with cool blue eyes and refused the requests, exclaiming: "I am not prepared to sacrifice the lives of British soldiers in this situation. My only suggestion to you is to begin negotiations with the Jews for a truce."

When, in desperation, the Arabs asked what the truce conditions were, Stockwell hurried to another office where Mordechai Makleff was waiting for him.

"Here are our terms," Makleff said, handing him a sheet of paper.

Stockwell scanned it quickly and, returning to the Arabs, slowly read out 11 conditions to them. Principally, they were to agree to Haganah control over the whole city, the surrender of all weapons, and an immediate curfew in the Arab quarters. Jews and Arabs were to have equal rights and duties.

By this time, word had come that the Haganah forces had linked up in the center of the city, splitting the Arab areas in three. The Jews had lost only 18 men and the Arabs about 100 in the operation. Stockwell studied the Arabs hopefully. The conditions were fair, he felt, in view of the magnitude of the Haganah victory. But the committee members, though more moderate toward Zionism than most Arabs, were not yet prepared to risk the wrath of the less moderate. They agreed to meet at the Town Hall with a reply at 4 P.M. that afternoon.

Rushing to the home of Victor Khayat, a committee member, they called in Yunis Naff'a, the deputy military commander (who had taken charge of the Arab forces after the commander had gone off to Damascus) and asked him whether the Arabs could continue fighting. But he replied evasively: "I shall have to consult with my commander in Damascus."

Then, like his superior, he hired a boat to take him to Beirut en route for Damascus.

Nor was Naff'a the only Arab to flee. As the Jews tightened the vice round the Arab areas, the inhabitants, without commanders to guide them, panicked and ran toward the port, where they leaped into all available sailing craft.

With the situation disintegrating by the minute, committee member Elias Koussa went to the Syrian Consulate and via the Consul sent an urgent radio message to Syrian President Kuwatly, informing him of the Jewish demands and requesting instructions. But despite further reminders in the next three hours, no reply came. A terrible fear gripped Koussa. Either the Syrian government did not grasp the seriousness of the situation or it was incapable of deciding anything.

The committee, deeply split on whether to accept the truce terms, then agreed in despair to stall and force drastic amendments to the peace terms. When the members arrived at the town hall at 4 P.M., they saw for the first time in days Haifa's Jewish civilian leaders, with whom they had long been close friends. Jews and Arabs embraced one another and then sipped coffee together while waiting for the British to arrive.

Finally, the meeting opened and Shabetai Levy, the Jewish Mayor of Haifa, stated dramatically that the Jews did not want a single inhabitant of Haifa to leave. The Arabs and Jews, he said, could continue to live peacefully together as they had in the past. The Arabs would remain equal citizens in every way.

But the Arabs bickered over every point in the proposed truce agreement, until Stockwell snapped impatiently: "If you don't sign this truce I shall not be responsible if three or four hundred more [Arabs] are killed by tomorrow."

"What are you trying to do?" asked Victor Khayat. "We know Shabetai Levy, Jacob Solomon [a Jewish Agency lawyer], and all these people. We are old friends."

Stockwell replied stiffly: "If you are old friends, I understand that I can withdraw and that my services are no longer required."

The Arabs then asked for an adjournment of an hour and half to consider the revised terms, and appeal once more to Damascus for advice. They returned at 7:30 P.M., still without advice. Grimly fatalistic, they rejected the terms flatly as "degrading," having decided not to risk being branded as "traitors" for submitting to the Jews. Since the Arabs were panic-stricken and were running away, and since Stockwell was unwilling to intervene, they said, they could only ask the General to supply transport for these people and their household effects and let them go to the Arab countries. Actually, they knew the British could not supply adequate transportation, and hoped that their intransigence would force Stockwell to drive the Haganah from the Arab quarters so that the refugees would return.

The Jews later maintained that the Arabs of Haifa—and of other towns —had received orders from the Mufti's Arab Higher Committee and the Arab States to evacuate in order to clear the way for Arab invasion forces. When the Jews were pushed into the sea, according to this view, the Arab inhabitants would return to their homes and take over all Jewish property.

Makleff told the author that he recalled seeing an intercepted telegram sent by the Mufti to the Haifa Arab leaders issuing orders to this effect. Israeli leaders also cite a report that appeared in the *Economist* (London, October 2, 1948) in which its correspondent, explaining the reasons for the Haifa exodus, said: "There is but little doubt that by far the most potent [factor] was the announcement made over the air by the Arab Higher Committee Executive urging all Arabs in Haifa to quit . . ."

Whatever the intentions of the Arab leaders, the author was unable to find any evidence to back up these claims. Israeli military archives officials said they had no record of the telegram referred to by Makleff, or of any other messages of similar substance; and the British Broadcasting Corporation, which monitored all broadcasts from the area, had no record of the reported Arab radio appeal.

On the other hand, the Mufti-dominated Arab National Committee in Haifa had been issuing communiqués—the last appearing on March 20— ordering Arab citizens to stay and fight whatever the cost. Such evidence tends to support a claim made to the author by Emile al-Ghouri, one of the Mufti's chief lieutenants, that the Arab chiefs regarded the exodus from Haifa and elsewhere as disastrous to their cause—though it is possible, of course, that their views on this question shifted with the circumstances.

True, newspapers in some Arab countries have quoted Palestine Arabs as saying that they were ordered to leave so that the Arab armies could more easily come in. Perhaps the leaders in some individual villages did issue such orders, but no documentation pointing to any general policy of this nature appears to be available. Invariably, moreover, the quotations and commentaries have emanated from Arab sources wishing to discredit the Mufti's leadership during that period.

While the British chief of police did issue reports stressing that the local Arab leaders expressed determination to evacuate the Arab population, it is unclear whether these leaders *ordered* the evacuation or simply went along with the tide. And it is even less clear whether, if they did order the flight, they did so on instructions from above.

At the same time, no evidence could be found to support Arab charges that the Jews forced the Arabs to leave Haifa. On the contrary, Mayor Levy's appeal to the Arabs to stay seems to have reflected the general Jewish sentiment in that city. Thus, the British police chief, in a typical report, wrote on April 28: "The Jews are still making every effort to persuade the Arab population to remain and settle back into their normal lives in town." During the fighting, Jewish loudspeakers apparently advised the Arabs to evacuate only the women and children for their own safety.

No encouragement from either side was, in fact, needed to add fuel to the panic. The local Arab leaders—some of whom insist that they personally opposed the exodus—say that they could not have controlled this panic whatever their wishes.

When, during the evening meeting at the town hall, these leaders informed Stockwell that they rejected the Jewish surrender proposals, the General was furious. "You have made a foolish decision," he said. "Think it over, as you'll regret it afterwards. You must accept the conditions of the Jews. They are fair enough. Don't permit life to be destroyed senselessly. After all, it was you who began the fighting, and the Jews have won."

Stockwell then turned to Makleff, the Haganah representative: "What is your reply?"

"It is their own business," Makleff answered, "and they must decide on it alone. But I am determined to take over the city by force if necessary."

Shabetai Levy, tears in his eyes, then pleaded with his Arab friends to agree to the terms and urge their people to stay.

But the Arabs rose slowly, their faces gaunt and tormented, and walked out. Silently, they drove home through streets that seethed with half-crazed refugees clinging to meager belongings—running, jostling, stumbling toward the port. Forty thousand people, four-fifths of Haifa's Arab population, were thus to flee their homes.[4]

"We can't wait for Father!" cried Ramzi Hararah's mother. "He can meet us later!"

Ramzi listened to the din outside, the clatter of thousands of feet on the pavement, the screams and moans, the children's whimpers. Why hadn't his father come back from work? The refinery was certainly closed by now. His mother was right; every minute counted. A shell had landed next door; the next might kill them all. Jewish loudspeakers were demanding surrender, but he remembered Deir Yassin. And anyway, there was no one around to give orders. All their leaders had run. Military headquarters had been abandoned. Oh God, was this the end of the world?

Ramzi, his mother, sister, and three brothers darted out of the house, leaving their lunch untouched on the table. Swept into the frenzied stampede, Ramzi and another brother, each on one arm, virtually carried their mother through the narrow, debris-littered streets as people pushed and buffeted. They almost tripped over unfortunates who had already fallen under the surging, trampling mob.

At the port, they meekly submitted to a search for arms by British and Haganah soldiers working in complete harmony for the first time since the Palestine troubles started. Then . . . a boat! They had to find a boat! Ramzi spotted a small sailboat about to dock. He leaped into it and helped his family pile in before others could jump. The captain immediately pulled away from the dock with some 150 gasping, weeping passengers, while others dived into the water trying to climb in, some of them drowning in the effort. Once at sea, the Lebanese captain went round demanding £2 from each passenger.

"Where are we going?" Ramzi shouted into the shrieking wind.

"I wanted to go to Beirut," yelled the captain, "but the wind is taking us south."

The wind developed into a storm, and the captain ordered everyone to throw nonessentials overboard. A woman behind Ramzi threw something into the water, then screamed: "My son! My son!"

Ramzi looked back and saw the woman clasping a pillow under one arm. In her panic and confusion, she had hurled her infant son overboard instead of the pillow.

Day followed day, and many passengers died as the boat was carried out to sea, hopelessly lost: some of thirst, others from the effects of drinking sea water. All were slowly starving. Ramzi, in a near-coma, wondered what had happened to his friend Josef.

Finally, after 10 days of silent horror, an Egyptian vessel picked up the half-dead passengers and took them to Gaza.

On the evening of April 22, while the chaos in Haifa was at its height, Field Marshal Montgomery was about to leave his London flat to deliver a speech when the Prime Minister's secretary called and said that Attlee wanted to see him immediately. Montgomery, the army Chief of Staff, rushed to No. 10 Downing Street, where he found Bevin and Defense Minister Alexander also waiting for him.

The Prime Minister asked Montgomery if he had read the newspaper reports about the fighting in Haifa. The Field Marshal replied that he had, but that he did not believe everything he read in the press. He relied on reports from his generals, he said, and he had received none.

Bevin then stated angrily that 23,000 Arabs had been killed and that the situation was catastrophic. He demanded to know what Montgomery was going to do about it. The Field Marshal who, like Bevin, apparently knew nothing about Stockwell's "arrangement" with the Jews, expressed skepticism over the reports but said that he would try to get an accurate account. He then left to deliver his speech.

The next morning, Montgomery returned to No. 10, where he found Bevin more agitated than ever, arguing that the army should have stopped the chaos in Haifa and that the massacre of the Arabs had placed him in an impossible position with the Arab States. Montgomery replied that all reports he had received indicated that the press dispatches had been grossly exaggerated, and that the situation was not out of hand.

Bevin removed his cigar and said sourly: "I have been let down by the army."

Whereupon Montgomery stood up and demanded that Bevin retract the remark. When Bevin refused, the Field Marshal stamped out. He later went to see Defense Minister Alexander, complaining that Bevin had consistently refused to listen to the army's views—which usually were even tougher on the Jews than were the Foreign Minister's—and that he had been "led down the garden path" by the Colonial Secretary and the High Commissioner. Now, he charged, Bevin was trying to make the army the scapegoat for his own failures. Either the Foreign Secretary stood by his insult or he did not. And if he, Montgomery, were to be sacked, that would be all right with him since he would then have the opportunity to "say a jugfull" in the House of Lords about the handling of the Palestine crisis.

On May 7, Montgomery returned to 10 Downing Street for another meeting. By this time, High Commissioner Cunningham had wired that the Jewish attack at Haifa was a "direct consequence of continuous attacks by Arabs on Jews in Haifa over the previous four days." Attlee said diplomatically that he was sure Montgomery's anger over an "unfortunate remark" made in a moment of heat would be forgotten as soon as the remark itself.

Bevin smiled broadly and said: " 'Ear, 'ear!"[5]

And everybody laughed—including General Stockwell in Haifa, as he poured a bottle of his favorite whisky for the winners of one of history's most extraordinary wagers.*

---

* Following the fall of Haifa, the British apparently decided to help the Arab Legion reconquer that city after British troops had departed. A senior officer in Haifa explained the plan for such action to a group of his officers in early May.

WHILE the General would drink whisky to celebrate with the Jews of Haifa, he took tea with the Arabs of Safed in eastern Galilee, also under his command. The tea party took place on April 12 at the home of a Safed notable, Mohammed Yusef al-Khadra. It produced astonished Arab smiles not dissimilar from those on Jewish faces when Stockwell had announced that he would cooperate in the Haganah capture of Haifa. For Stockwell viewed an Arab military victory in Safed as even more certain than a Jewish one in Haifa—or in Tiberias, where his men also facilitated a Haganah takeover. And wasn't it in Britain's interest to end the fighting everywhere as soon as possible—no matter who won any particular battle —so that the withdrawal of British troops could continue unhindered?

He thus offered to turn over key strongholds to the Arabs when the British withdrew from Safed.

"You understand, of course," he emphasized, "you are not to attack the Jews until the British withdraw—on April 16."

"Of course," Syrian Colonel Adib Shishekli, commander of the small unit of Arab Liberation Army soldiers based in Safed, replied gravely.

Stockwell then posed other conditions for British cooperation. The Arabs would have to permit British intervention in the fighting if the Jews requested it, and they must treat the Jews humanely when they captured the town.

"Of course, of course," Shishekli promised.

Stockwell was satisfied as he left. True, Safed was supposed to go to the Jews under the United Nations partition plan; but they numbered only about 1,500 compared to 12,000 Arabs, and couldn't possibly win in battle. Ultimately, he felt sure, those stubborn Jews would ask the British to mediate a truce agreement—giving Safed to the Arabs.

Two days later, on April 14, the Colonel commanding the British force in the Safed region marched into the Central Hotel to see the Jewish leaders of the town, led by Meir Maivar, owner of the hotel, who had served in the British army in World War II.

"Really," said the Colonel, "the Haganah should leave the town and let the citizens here—Jews and Arabs—reach a peaceful agreement of their own."

When the Jewish leaders refused, the Colonel continued: "Well then, I suggest that you let us evacuate the women and children at least, because I predict a very unhappy fate for you."

THE CIVIL WAR
Maivar scowled. Things did indeed look bad. The British would certainly hand over the citadel to the Arabs—the remains of the great medieval fortress atop the steep hill on which Safed was built—when they left. From there, the Arabs could fire into the Jewish quarter on the slopes of the hill, while other Arabs attacked from the adjacent Arab quarter. Moreover, this hill was surrounded by other Arab-held heights, including one to the north, opposite Mount Canaan, crowned by a British "Teggart" fortress, a monstrous steel-and-concrete stronghold that the Arabs were also bound to inherit. Together with the Safed police station in town, these strategic places dominated and controlled every inch of Safed, including the road approaches. The town was, in fact, already under siege.

Furthermore, Jewish morale was low. Most of the inhabitants were ultra-religious shopkeepers, some of them descendants of Jewish mystics who had lived here 2,000 years earlier. They were people with almost no understanding of modern Zionism, like those in the Old City of Jerusalem. And this was one of the few towns in Palestine where the Jews were, in fact, less intellectually inclined—and motivated—than the local Arabs, who dominated the professions. They were not fighting material, Maivar realized. Indeed, many citizens were asking to reach an agreement with their Arab neighbors or else be evacuated. But evacuation—even of the women and children—meant the first step toward surrender.

Yet, despite the unpalatable facts, he and his few fighters would have to hold Safed. For it was not only a traditional Jewish spiritual center, but the key strategic town in northern Galilee. The town sprawled at the base of the upper, or eastern, Galilean "finger" that lay wedged between Syria to the east and Lebanon to the west. And since Jewish settlements within the "finger" were hopelessly trapped in a valley dominated by hilltop Arab villages, Safed might be all that stood in the way of an Arab sweep through the whole northern part of the country. Indeed, the Mufti was known to be planning to make Safed his headquarters for the conquest of Jewish Palestine.

From the hotel window, Maivar scanned the rugged, brown mountains that so majestically imprisoned Safed and then nodded to the Colonel.

"Everybody stays!"

The Colonel rose to go. "You do understand, don't you, that it will take only about two hours for the Arabs to clean you out."

On April 16, the Colonel put his prediction to the test, leading his British troops out of Safed to the shock and consternation of the Jews, who had expected them to stay at least two weeks longer. The Arabs, as planned, were already in the strongpoints. They promptly rained down mortar shells on the Jewish quarter, while others attacked on foot, blowing up houses which, ironically, some of the attackers had once frequented as welcome guests. Friendships died hard even at the peak of battle, as Jew and Arab took positions behind sandbags and wreckage within feet of each other.

"Fuad," yelled one middle-aged Jew wielding a rifle he had just learned to use, "why don't you go home? Your wife is worried about you. And anyway, the Palmach will be here soon, and then where will you be?"

"First," Fuad yelled back, "come out with your hands up!"

When another Jew cursed because his homemade Sten gun jammed, an Arab friend shouted advice: "You shouldn't fire so long with a cold gun!"

After 14 hours of shelling and cross-quarter battle and banter, peace settled over Safed. The Jews had held out despite the dire prophecy of the British commander. The next day, as the Jews had so casually forewarned their Arab comrades, a unit of Palmach soldiers infiltrated through the Arab blockade to be welcomed hysterically by the cellar-dwelling Jewish populace. Let Fuad and his comrades attack now. Was not the Palmach invincible?

The Palmach commander in chief, thirty-year-old Yigal Allon, was not so sure as he studied a wall map at his headquarters. Sandy-haired, blue-eyed, thin-lipped, Allon was a hard, earthy product of the kibbutz, brimming with self-confidence. But now he was alarmed. Only two weeks remained before the British mandate was to end and an invasion by foreign Arabs to begin. He must capture Safed before the invasion at any cost—but could he?

On April 28, his forces had moved into the police fortress of Rosh Pina literally on the heels of withdrawing British troops, who, in fact, fired on his men as they moved in. The fortress was now his headquarters. His plan, under Operation Yiftach, was to open a corridor between Rosh Pina eastward to Safed and thus break the Arab blockade and the Arab hold on the ancient town.

The attack by a battalion of the new Yiftach Brigade, which he personally commanded, was to start that night; but as luck would have it, the Arabs had just begun an offensive of their own, concentrating on the settlement of Ramot Naftali in the hills near the Lebanese border.

Allon left the map and walked back to his desk. He picked up a cable and read it for the third time; it was a desperate message from the Ramot Naftali commander, reporting that Lebanese armored cars had entered the courtyard and that the defenders would have to be evacuated if reinforcements didn't arrive immediately. If Ramot Naftali fell, the Arabs could sweep into the valley below, cut off his Palmach troops in Safed from their base in Rosh Pina, and perhaps even join with a force from the east to seal off all Galilee.

Yet the only men available were those in Safed or about to join them in the planned all-out attack. To dispatch these troops to the settlement would mean postponing Operation Yiftach and thereby letting the Arabs dictate his strategy. Would it not be better to redouble his efforts in Safed and force the Arabs to send troops from Ramot Naftali to that town? But was there time? He was appalled by the prospect that his decision could determine the fate of all northern Palestine . . .

. . . "THIS IS YOUR *bar mitzvah* PRESENT," HIS FATHER HAD SAID AS he pulled out the Turkish horse pistol from a desk drawer. "We'll see whether or not you're a man. Tomorrow night I'm sending you out on patrol—alone."

The blue-eyed youngster shivered slightly as he took the weapon, and he wondered whether he would have to die on the very day of his *bar mitzvah,* which was to symbolize his entry into manhood at thirteen. Arabs were continually harassing his settlement of Kfar Tabor. Could he, a boy who had just turned a man, chase them away all alone?

The next night, he waited silently in the fields behind an oak tree, jumping at every jackal howl or owl screech and suspiciously watching a camel caravan in the distance jingling along the road from Nazareth to Tzeniach in Transjordan. But as the hours passed, his fears diminished. Perhaps no Arab marauders would show up after all. Then he heard the dreaded sound—the pounding of hoofs. Within seconds, three Arabs dismounted and began cramming bushels of newly reaped grain into sacks.

Young Yigal tried to call out but no words came. Then, with a shaky hand, he cocked his pistol. The Arabs dropped their loot and started rushing toward him.

"Halt!" Yigal finally cried. "Halt or I'll shoot!"

The Arabs halted and saw themselves confronted by a trembling boy.

"*Andak!*" one of them yelled laughingly.

They had accepted the challenge and began moving toward the youth. Yigal closed his eyes and, with both hands clasping the pistol butt, began to press on the trigger. At that moment a shot rang out from behind him, accompanied by a husky voice shouting in Arabic: "You bloody thieves!"

His father! As the Arabs fled on their horses, the father laid his hand on the boy's shoulder.

"Were you frightened, son? . . . Never mind, I was there all the time."

"The whole time?"

"Yes, my dear. And you are a *bar mitzvah* boy now."[6]

Allon called in an aide and dictated a cable to the commander of Ramot Naftali: "At the bottom of the hill will be a Palmach machine-gun detachment. Anyone attempting to leave the settlement will be shot."

It was fortunate, thought Allon, that he had no machine gun to spare for such an assignment.

That night, the 3rd Battalion of the Yiftach Brigade attacked the Arab village of Ein Zeitun, which lay on the road to Safed about a mile to the rear of the besieged Jewish quarter. Moshe Kelman, the commander, watched with satisfaction as his men began firing the primitive Davidka "drainpipe" mortar, capable of killing few people but of frightening many with its deafening noise. He could think of no village he would rather attack than Ein Zeitun. For none had been more brutal to Jews over the years; the villagers, he had heard, had even burned some alive.

As the first shell exploded, the world suddenly lit up, and he heard a rumble that made him wonder if the mountain was about to collapse. Then, in the glare, he saw where the rumble was coming from. Every Jew in Safed, it seemed, was sitting on the slope facing Ein Zeitun and applauding lustily, as if at some surrealistic football game.

The applause encouraged his men, but deeply troubled him. The attack was supposed to be secret. How did everybody know about it? If all the Jews knew, the Arabs in Safed certainly knew as well and were prepared. For who kept his mouth shut in Safed? It was too bad the Arabs and Jews of Safed had to be so damned friendly with each other!

Ein Zeitun fell quite swiftly, in fact, and so did another nearby Arab village, Biria. The women and children of these villages were set free to spread exaggerated stories of the attack, and soon it was being said that the Jews had an atomic bomb! The fate of the hated men of Ein Zeitun who happened to fall into Jewish hands remains unclear.

With the siege of Safed broken, the Jews now prepared to attack the mighty citadel in Safed itself.

"Fuad, are you there?"

"What is it, Isaac?"

"Tonight's the night. Ha! We'll teach you a lesson!"

The night was May 6, and by the time the attack was to start, the Arabs in Safed were ready for it. But Netiva Ben-Yehuda, the Blond Devil who had killed 16 people singlehandedly in the ambush on an Arab bus several months before, wondered whether she and her fellow Palmach soldiers were ready to deliver another lesson. They were waiting in the darkness of the Central Hotel in Safed for the signal to dash up the hill toward the citadel, though they hadn't even had time to study the topography of the steep slope and must depend on a local inhabitant to guide them. If all went well, she was to follow with a mine detector.

The signal came. Netiva watched a platoon of her comrades start up the hill, slipping occasionally on damp pine leaves, and vanish into the moonless night. A few minutes later she heard heavy firing, and another platoon moved up swiftly to help. The firing grew even heavier. Moshe Kelman, after receiving desperate radio reports, then shouted an order for retreat.

As the attackers scrambled down the hill and piled into the Central Hotel, carrying their dead and wounded, Netiva asked what had happened.

"We learned too late that there was only room up there for one platoon," gasped a young soldier as he collapsed in exhaustion. "So in the dark the two platoons shot the hell out of each other!"

The next day, Yigal Allon arrived on foot to investigate, and was deeply chagrined. Not only had there been many casualties, but morale in the Jewish quarter had reached rock bottom. Their illusions about the invincibility of the Palmach shattered, citizens would no longer talk to the soldiers they had so gleefully welcomed, and some even took back clothes and other gifts they had lavished on them.

"You must evacuate the women and children, at least the children," the city elders demanded at a meeting with him.

"If I did," Allon replied, "we might lose Safed. One, I couldn't spare the men for the evacuation. Two, it would diminish the morale of the men —they will fight to the bitter end for their families. And three, the enemy would find out and be encouraged to fight harder."

Then, after working out a new attack plan with Kelman, he left on foot for Ein Zeitun. There he heard artillery shells bursting in Safed's Jewish quarter. From his information, the Arabs in Safed did not have such big guns; they must have come from Ramot Naftali. If so, his decision to dictate strategy had worked. He sat down on a large rock and, with mixed feelings, watched the black smoke rise in columns like the fingers of a pleading hand. Yes, the guns might well mean that he was right; but they might also mean the death of children he had refused to evacuate.

Apparently unknown to the Jews, Arab Liberation Army units had left Safed shortly after the British; only about 20 soldiers remained to support the local Arab fighters. After the abortive Palmach attack, a delegation from Safed rushed to Damascus to ask for help, but in vain. Two delegation members, Mayor Zaki Kaddoura and his local military chief, Amin Jamian, then hurried to Amman to ask King Abdullah for aid, but the King only said haughtily: "Why don't you ask [Syrian President] Kuwatly, who went into battle without being prepared for it?"

In any case, he added, the British had warned him not to intervene in Palestine until the mandate ended on May 15. If they were smart, they would withdraw their fighting forces to Transjordan and let them enlist in the Arab Legion.

The visitors were stunned. Abdullah, they concluded, was prepared to give Safed to the Jews without a fight. He apparently wanted the Jews to occupy it, in accordance with the United Nations partition plan—anything so that the Mufti would not take control.

They hastened back to see Kuwatly, who finally agreed to send 130 soldiers of the Arab Liberation Army to Safed. He omitted to say that they were untrained.

The recruits arrived in Safed on May 9 with Colonel Shishekli, the ALA commander of Arab Safed. On the same day, however, Shishekli returned to Damascus to obtain additional arms. And a few hours later, Sari Anfish, commander of the detachment, also left, taking with him all his baggage. Amin Jamian, the local military leader, was thus left in charge. And he was seriously thinking of pulling his men out as King Abdullah had advised.[7]

At 9 P.M. on May 10, Netiva Ben-Yehuda signalled an all-out Jewish attack on several key points in Safed by firing a bag of explosives from a Davidka. It blew to pieces a bunker protecting the citadel—pure luck, since there was no way to gauge the range accurately. (The next shell blew a hole in a hotel located only 15 feet away.) Infantry then charged up the hill, and were driven back three times by machine-gun fire. Finally, the wounded commander, Avinoam Hadash, called for a Piat to fire shells into the Arab emplacements. They were silenced and Hadash limped up the hill with his men to capture the citadel.

Meanwhile, the hardest fighting raged at the Arab-held police station at the base of the hill near the Jewish-held Central Hotel. Kelman sent several demolition men from the hotel to blow a hole in the thick wall so that others could pour through, but a sudden downpour of rain wet the explosives and they didn't go off. He then searched the city for TNT, which would not be affected by the rain and, having located some, sent Netiva with several men to the station. Under heavy fire, they set the explosives, which worked this time, blasting a large, jagged cavity in the wall. Netiva and her comrades rushed through it and took the first floor after vicious hand-to-hand fighting; in the confusion, the commander of the break-in unit was mistakenly shot dead by his own men.

Trapped in the building, the Arabs rushed upstairs, climbed through an iron door leading to the roof, and locked it shut behind them. Suspecting that Colonel Shishekli himself was one of the men on the roof after finding some of his personal documents (though in fact he was apparently not even in Safed), the Jews sought to break through the door. They even made a clumsy attempt to blow it open with a homemade flamethrower that almost set the whole building on fire and severely wounded several Jews.

Finally, after a siege of several hours, eight wounded Arabs came down sheepishly and surrendered. An embittered Haganah officer announced that he would find out if Shishekli was on the roof, even if he had to beat them mercilessly. As he grabbed one dusky Arab, the victim, a meek little man with rotting teeth, smiled and said with surprising calmness: "Six days ago, I was with my wife and children in Syria and knew nothing about Palestine. Then they came and asked me if I wanted thirty pounds and a white woman. I said 'Yes, of course,' and so I came here to Palestine."

Then, looking at Netiva, he added: "Now I see my first white woman— just before I die. The world is made of shit, I tell you."

Netiva's large blue eyes, magnified by thick lenses, stared fixedly at the meek Arab as the officer stood over him. She remembered killing sixteen people in a wet, rocky field; and then, shortly afterwards, while on another assignment, six cows. Why the cows? She couldn't find any Arab targets at the moment and her rifle was cocked, ready to fire. Killing had become so easy, almost like a game. And there stood the cows. . . .

Suddenly she rushed at the officer, yelling: "Don't touch this man, do you hear?"

And as she burst into tears, the officer, confounded, lowered his stick and walked away.

That night, the remaining Arabs on the roof managed to climb down and escape. Every other Arab in Safed had fled the town. Even the Arab defenders in the powerful Teggart fortress atop Mount Caanan had run—before they were attacked. Nor were the Arabs able to take Ramot Naftali.

As the refugees of Safed swarmed down the road, they came upon three large parked cars.

"What are you waiting for?" Mayor Kaddoura, who was leading, asked the men in the first vehicle.

"For Haj Amin [the Mufti]—to guide him into Safed."

The mayor could barely keep from laughing.[8]

THE ancient city of Jaffa, bordering on southern Tel Aviv, posed a delicate problem for the Jewish leaders. While Jaffa, the biggest Arab town in Palestine, was to be absorbed into the Arab State under the partition plan, the Jews had to capture it, they felt, to end the sniping into Tel Aviv, which had already taken many Jewish lives, and to prevent the harassment of Jewish traffic to the south and along the Tel Aviv–Jerusalem road. The question was how to deal with the city and its 70,000 people without provoking dangerous United Nations or British counteraction.

Yadin summoned Dan Even, commander of the new Alexandroni Brigade, to his underground headquarters and asked him outright: "Dan, if we decided to attack Jaffa, how would you suggest we go about it?"

"I would take the villages round Jaffa," he advised. "We would then be able to establish territorial continuity between the areas controlled by three brigades and perhaps open a road to Lydda Airport. Then, when the British leave, the city itself will fall into our hands."

"Like a ripe plum," Yadin commented. "Yes, that's exactly how I would do it. A frontal assault would be disastrous. Aside from the political questions involved, many men would be required to attack and police the city, and we need them elsewhere."

Even, who had served in the British army during World War II, smiled and asked quietly: "When will the operation start?"

"Maybe the first day of Passover. So let's call it Operation Chametz."

Even's smile turned to laughter. *Chametz*—leaven—according to Jewish tradition is not consumed during the Passover period.

It was largely because Jaffa, no less than Tel Aviv, was in danger of isolation that Arabs like mukhtar Abdel Bari were so trigger-happy. Abdel Bari, a tall, slender man with shrewd brown eyes and an imposing authoritarian air, was mukhtar and commander of southern Jaffa. He and his fellow Arabs well realized that, just as the Jews had to win control of the eastern part of the Tel Aviv–Jaffa–Jerusalem corridor in order to break the Arab siege of Jerusalem, so the Arabs must dominate the western part in order to extend the siege to Tel Aviv and prevent a Jewish siege of Jaffa.

At the time of the United Nations partition resolution, Abdel Bari and his fellows had been confident the Arabs could thus impose their domination. The Mufti had named one of his best fighters, Sheikh Hassan Salame, as commander of the Jaffa-Ramle-Lydda district. And Salame, who had divided Jaffa into three sectors, each commanded by a subcommander like Abdel Bari, had put considerable arms and ammunition at their disposal.

But subsequently, morale was seriously damaged by the economic effects of street clashes with the Jews. Factories closed down, fruit intended for export shriveled on the trees, public transport came to a standstill. As businessmen started moving elsewhere, the seeds of chaos and panic were planted, with civic leaders rushing to Damascus to seek aid from the Arab League's Military Committee.

As a result of this request, in early February Iraqi Major Abdul Wahab al-Shaykh Ali led a group of some 80 soldiers of the Arab Liberation Army into Jaffa, but the situation only grew worse. Hassan Salame, who had bitterly denounced Mayor Yusef Haikal for wanting to settle with the Jews, was soon at sword's point with Wahab as well, resenting the "intervention" of ALA troops in an area which the Arab League had earlier declared under the Mufti's military jurisdiction.

After weeks of wrangling, Wahab was replaced by Iraqi Captain Abdel Najim al-Din, who arrived in Jaffa on February 22 with another 150 men. But Najim proved even less capable of commanding the discipline of the various groups than his predecessor, and almost immediately he was exchanging charges of corruption and theft with Salame.

Abdel Bari's confidence was by now severely shaken.

JAFFA HAD BEEN A POWDER KEG THROUGHOUT THE THOUSANDS OF years of its history. It had been dominated in ancient times either by Sidon or Caesarea to the north, or by Ashkelon and Gaza to the south, with invaders storming in from the sea or marching down from the hills of Judaea. Its more recent agony had begun in 1921 when Arab mobs, enraged by international support of the Balfour Declaration, went on a rampage in the northern Jewish suburbs, including the infant district of Tel Aviv. The British administration then granted Tel Aviv a municipal autonomy that was eventually to produce the metropolis of today. In April, 1936, Arabs attacked Jews and British in Jaffa to set off the Arab revolt that lasted until 1939.

After that, relations between Arabs and Jews were surprisingly peaceful and—following World War II—even friendly to some degree as nationalists on both sides found common cause in trying to oust the British from Palestine.

Eli Sambo's relations with the Irgun, indeed, were not only friendly but almost brotherly. Most evenings Sambo, a virulently nationalistic Arab, would greet his Irgun friends at his little coffeehouse on Carmel Street, which borders on both Tel Aviv and Jaffa, with a flash of yellow teeth under his huge black mustache. His guests would slap him on the back and say: "*Salaam,* Eli, how many British did you poison today?" Then they would sit in a corner at a table with a dirty cloth and discuss plans for blowing up some British installation while Sambo loyally stood by the door to watch for the approach of Englishmen. Sometimes, when the heat was on, he would even hide his friends in his shabby apartment upstairs.

But then, in mid-1947, the Irgun boys stopped coming to Eli's coffeehouse. For Sambo and his fellow Arabs began to see that things were getting out of hand, that Jewish terrorist acts like those hatched in the corner of his café were, while forcing the British out, also paving the way for a Jewish State.

Only Arab fighters thenceforth frequented the coffeehouse, and Eli continued to watch at the door—but now on behalf of his Arab brothers. In fact, he became the leader of a group of Arab fighters and spent much of his time sniping at Jewish positions across the street, manned sometimes by his old Irgun friends.

With Arabs like Eli Sambo and Abdel Bari spraying the streets and even the marketplaces of southern Tel Aviv with rifle fire, and Jewish terrorists retaliating by bombing public places in Jaffa, the fuse had been lit by spring, 1948, for the biggest explosion in Jaffa's tempestuous history.

At about 8 o'clock on the morning of April 26, Abdel Bari, dressed in *khaffiya* and long robes, was sitting on a cushioned sofa in the home of his elder brother, Shaba'an Hissi, talking to a group of men in a calm voice that belied his excitement. His listeners, sprawled on chairs around the room, included a younger brother, Ibrahim, as well as friends such as Hamada Hassan Usrof. Only the sound of tinkling coffee cups interrupted the flow of Abdel Bari's imperiously delivered message.

"Early this morning," he said, "Haganah forces were seen moving into position along the edges of northern Jaffa, and a full-scale attack could come at any minute. You must go home, fetch your arms, and get to the northern sector to stop an enemy advance." He paused, then added, raising his voice slightly for emphasis: "The time for a showdown may have come."

"At last," said Ibrahim. "It had to come sooner or later."

"If I were not blind," Shaba'an interjected in a gruff, disappointed voice, "I should be leading you into battle." (Shaba'an, sixty-five years old, had lost his sight, as well as one hand and the fingers of the other, in 1925 in a premature explosion of a charge designed to kill fish.)

Suddenly, the men stiffened as a great blast shook the house, then another and another.

"It's started!" cried Abdel Bari. As the men rushed from the house, a youth came running toward them shouting almost unintelligibly: "Abdel Bari, Abdel Bari—your Uncle Mohammed—he's dead!"

"What happened?" Abdel Bari yelled, his fingers tightening around the rifle he had already grabbed.

"He was washing when the shell came through the roof of his house. He was hit in the chest. He's dead!"

Abdel Bari had been very fond of his uncle. Now he would kill some of those Haganah dogs.

Abdel Bari guessed correctly that a full-scale attack had started, but he misidentified the attackers, for it was not the Haganah but the Irgun that had launched the assault. Actually, Haganah leaders were just completing their plans for Operation Chametz, which would have avoided any direct attack on Jaffa. The Irgun command was less concerned about the diplomatic and military dangers of a direct attack; indeed, it thrived on direct action for its psychological effect both on the enemy and on the Jewish population.

Irgun leaders had been considering a major attack for some time, in fact. At first, they had planned to conquer the villages between Hadera and Haifa and thereby open the coastal road from Tel Aviv to Haifa. But at an informal talk with Haganah leader Israel Galili in his office, the Irgunists had been impressed with the stress Galili had placed on the need to protect the Tel Aviv–Jaffa–Jerusalem road. But Operation Chametz sounded to the Irgun leaders like a halfhearted way to meet what appeared to be potential disaster.

Among the least enthralled by the Haganah argument was Amihai Faglin, known in the Irgun as Gideon, or Giddy. Faglin, a tall, black-haired man with blazing brown eyes and a gaunt, brooding look, was the Irgun's chief of operations. A Sabra, born in 1922, he had joined Haganah when he was only fourteen, but switched to the Irgun four years later after he had been assigned by Haganah to post notices on walls discouraging Jews from using force to fight British White Paper policies. He swiftly emerged in the Irgun hierarchy as a genius in the application of measured ruthlessness, planning such masterful actions as the mass escape from Acre Fortress and the bombing of the King David Hotel in Jerusalem. The one act that still haunted Faglin was a particular reprisal . . .

THE BRITISH HAD CONDEMNED TO THE GALLOWS THREE IRGUN boys captured in the attack on Acre Fortress that set the prisoners free.

Near midnight of the day when the three victims were to be hanged, Faglin, afire with hatred and grief after hearing the grim news on the radio, drove to Menachem Beigin's secret hideout in Tel Aviv. (Beigin was commander of the Irgun Zvai Leumi.) He found Beigin discussing the situation with three other Irgun leaders who were trying to convince their chief not to carry out the organization's public threat of retaliation in kind if the Irgunists were hanged. At stake were the lives of two British sergeants, Martin and Plaice, who had been captured by the Irgun and held as hostages.

"We've got to go through with it," Faglin pleaded, when he had a moment alone with Beigin. "If we don't, there'll never be an end to the hangings and our future warnings will mean nothing." Beigin agreed.

Faglin then sped to Nathanya, where the two British sergeants were hidden. He rounded up several local Irgunists to help him in his task and drove his Morris 8 to within a few blocks of a sprawling diamond factory owned by an Irgun member. Two by two, he and his assistants entered and rushed upstairs into a huge warehouse-like room, where they were greeted by several other men.

"Okay, it's time," Faglin said in a quiet voice.

Two guards went to nearby windows, pistols in hand, to keep watch while others went into an adjoining room where one man bent down and lifted four large square tiles.

"Bring one of them up," Faglin ordered.

The man lowered himself through a hole 2-feet deep formed by a wooden frame. The hole led to a 12-foot-square underground room, a huge wooden box. Before the kidnapping of the two sergeants, this "room" had been fitted into place and covered with a layer of sand to insulate it. Here the sergeants had languished in the dark, equipped only with blankets, oxygen equipment, a week's supply of food, and a disinfected bucket that served as a toilet.

"Hurry up," Faglin called out impatiently.

His assistant climbed back through the opening with one of the sergeants sitting on his shoulders. Faglin helped to pull the soldier to floor level and studied him briefly. He was chilled at the sight of the white, stubbled face with its vacant, sunken eyes. He could gaze almost indifferently on torn flesh and decaying corpses, but somehow this confrontation with a broken human spirit horrified him. He swiftly placed a black hood over the blond head.

The Irgunists then led the British sergeant into the next room, where a rope with looped end hung by a hook from a rafter. The hooded sergeant was lifted onto a small chair under the rope. As his ankles and wrists were being bound, he asked in a tentative voice, like a child asking his mother whether she meant to spank him: "Are you going to hang me?"

When he received no immediate response, he asked with resignation: "Can I leave a message?"

Fagun steeled himself. He feared that the least display of human feeling might destroy his whole inhuman plan. "We won't be able to deliver any message," he said coldly. "You must prepare to die." Faglin gave a sign, and one of his men placed the rope around the sergeant's neck, and another kicked the chair from under him.

The youth swung gently, like some faceless phantom dancing on air, while the Irgun leader stood about six feet away, a pistol in each hand. If the British suddenly showed up, as they had done several times in the last week only to find a vacated diamond factory, the Irgun would not be cheated of its revenge. He would shoot the sergeant to make quite sure he was dead, and maybe kill another Englishman in the bargain. Faglin's damp shirt clung to his body as he watched in fascination. The silence was broken only by the distant hum of jeeps patrolling the area—and by the monotonous creak of the steel hook digging into the wood.

In a few minutes, Faglin noted, the sergeant's fingers grew limp and his khaki trousers grew sodden with urine released by non-functioning kidneys.

I am no longer a man; I am an animal, Faglin thought. Was not man created in the image of God, and am I not killing like a beast? He began to envisage the limp figure as his own. I am dead, he said to himself.

After about half an hour, his men brought the other sergeant, also hooded, into the room and hanged him side by side with his friend. And Faglin watched himself die again.

In another half hour, the bodies were taken down and wrapped in blankets. Faglin dispatched one of his men to fetch the jeep which other Irgunists nearby were to send when the area seemed clear of British patrols. The bodies were placed in the rear and the driver drove off, letting Faglin down at the outskirts of Nathanya. Then the jeep continued on to an orange grove where the two bodies, the ropes still round their necks, were hung from a tree. A mine was set underground a few feet in front of one of the corpses. Two dead British were not enough to compensate for the hanging of the three Irgunists captured in the prison break and another, Dov Gruner, who had also been hanged earlier. Perhaps the mine would even things up.

Faglin telephoned the British authorities (without identifying himself) and told them where the bodies could be found. He also spoke with Beigin, who informed him that the Haganah was helping the British in their search for the bodies. "We don't want any Jews to die," Beigin said. Faglin quickly warned the Haganah about the mine; when the bodies were eventually found, it was harmlessly exploded by the British, to whom the Haganah had passed on the warning.

The next day, Faglin read in the newspapers about the "great crime." He did not dispute the description, but felt that in the circumstances he would do the same thing again. What was the destruction of one man's soul if it helped revive the soul of a nation? . . .[9]

On the evening of April 21, 1948, Menachem Beigin and other Irgun leaders met at the home of Faglin's mother in Tel Aviv to draw up final plans for an attack on Jaffa.

"We shouldn't give the Haganah any advance notice about this," Beigin said, "or they might try to stop us."

"Who's going to lead the attack?" asked Faglin.

Beigin smiled.

"You are," he said.

Faglin immediately set to work planning the operation. Four days later, on the evening of April 25, about 600 men and 100 trucks—many stolen from British camps or off the streets—gathered at Camp Dov, named after the hanged Dov Gruner, in Ramat Gan, near Tel Aviv.

At about 2 A.M. on April 26, Beigin and the others emerged from the headquarters and faced the troops. This was the first time Beigin, who had kept his identity secret from all but his closest associates, had seen his men, and the first time they had seen him. He didn't say who he was, but they sensed that the bearded, slightly built man about to address them was their leader.

"Men of the Irgun," Beigin said dramatically, "we are going to conquer Jaffa. We are going into one of the decisive battles for the independence of Eretz Israel [Land of Israel]. Know who is before you, and remember whom you are leaving behind you. Before you is a cruel enemy who has risen to destroy us. Behind you are parents, brothers, children. Smite the enemy hard. Aim true, save your ammunition. In battle, show no more mercy to the enemy than he shows mercy to our people. But spare women and children. Whoever raises his hands in surrender has saved his life. You will not harm him. You will be led in the attack by Lieutenant Gideon [Faglin]. You have only one direction—forward."

Faglin then added his instructions, emphasizing the need to save precious ammunition. At about 3 A.M., the men filed out to the main road singing Irgun battle songs while Beigin watched, with apprehension and pride, from the window of the headquarters building. "May God protect them," he muttered.

Dawn broke at about 4:30 A.M., and Faglin, who had wanted to make a night attack, considered postponement until the following evening. But the Arabs, he knew, were now well aware of the pending attack. He couldn't wait. At 8 A.M. the first mortar shells, signaling the start of the assault, whistled over Jaffa, killing Abdel Bari's uncle and other waking Jaffa residents.

The Irgun plan was, first, to attack westward toward the sea with infantry and cut off the narrow panhandle of the Manshieh Quarter from the main part of Jaffa to the south. Then two motorized forces would attack from the northern end of the panhandle, race through it, and fan out into the heart of the town.

A continuing mortar barrage directed at the southern area began taking a steep toll in Arab lives and morale, but the machine-gun duel in the northern panhandle did not go well for Faglin and his men. Arabs such as Abdel Bari ferociously resisted the Irgun advance to the sea, and they enjoyed many advantages. Arab Spandaus were more than a match in firepower for the Irgun Brens, and the rows of ruined buildings in the area provided natural, concentrated defense positions which were well fortified. The Irgunists fought bravely and took over some of these positions but, in most cases, were forced to retreat under heavy Arab fire.

The Haganah did not seem unhappy about the Irgun setback, publishing a communiqué strongly critical of the Irgun action, while Tel Aviv newspapers, echoing this view, chided the Irgun for having launched a "barren" or "exhibitionist" attack. The Jewish Agency, feeling that Jaffa would fall anyway in Operation Chametz, quietly hoped that the Irgun's potential political power would evaporate in the disgrace of defeat.

But by the second day of fighting, Agency leaders, pressed by nonpolitical, militarily realistic Haganah officers, began to see the Irgun attack in a different light. With Operation Chametz about to be launched, the Irgun could perhaps be useful for the support of the Haganah operation. After all, it was more important for Haganah to win its battles than for the Irgun to be discredited.

Thus, during the second day, April 27, with the Irgun forces still tied down, Beigin and an assistant were invited to meet with Galili and Yadin.

"We will approve the continuation of the Irgun attack," Yadin said formally, "provided the Irgun fights under the Haganah's command and has a chance to succeed within twenty-four hours."

Beigin smiled, remembering the Haganah's previously contemptuous attitude.

Ironically, Beigin, while he agreed to these conditions, was himself highly skeptical at this point that success in Jaffa could be achieved within the prescribed time limit, if at all, and was seriously considering cancelling the whole Jaffa operation. On returning to Irgun headquarters, set up in an abandoned school in Jaffa, he found little reason to alter this attitude. His forces had captured several Arab positions, but the attack was still bogged down and seemed to promise little dramatic progress. He called a conference of his military chiefs in the map room and told them of the Haganah's conditional support.

"But," he said gravely, "I do not think we should go on battering our heads against fortified positions, which in any case are covered by British tanks. We have done our best for two days. In these circumstances it is no disgrace—not even for the Irgun—to suspend the direct assault. We shall defend the line we have taken with a strong holding unit. The rest of our troops, we shall withdraw."

There was an immediate stir. A few officers agreed with Beigin, but many did not. Faglin remained silent, exhaling the smoke from his cigarette in a deliberate fashion which Beigin knew signified displeasure. After considerable argument, Beigin stood by his decision. The Irgun would withdraw all but a few units from Jaffa. The assault would not be resumed.

Faglin left the room in silence to "tour the front lines." Shortly thereafter, groups of Irgun soldiers started coming to the map room. They had heard the news, they said (apparently from Faglin), and they could not accept the decision, being sure that they could push through to the sea if given another chance. Faglin then returned covered with dirt and breathing heavily.

"I have found some weak points in the enemy's positions," he said. "I am sure we can break through."

Beigin was visibly impressed with the ardor of his fighting men. He paused for a moment, smiling faintly.

Then he said: "All right, you win. I'll give you another twenty-four hours to reach the sea."

Immediately Faglin, endowed with new energy despite his extreme fatigue, began to work out plans with his officers for another attack. The Irgun, poorly trained in conventional warfare, was expert in the use of explosives and this skill, Faglin figured, could be applied to open fighting as well. It was useless trying to move over narrow roads that could easily be raked from entrenched positions. The answer was to advance through the houses to their front, utilizing the walls as natural cover. With picks and sledgehammers, they would break through, wall by wall, house by house, until they reached the Arab lines, and then they would place explosives near the Arab positions and blow them up.

"The operation will be backbreaking and slow, but it is the only alternative left," Faglin said, indicating each house on a detailed map.

At about 4 P.M. that day, April 28, the third day of fighting, the attack started. Hundreds of mortar shells were loosed upon Jaffa as Faglin's men began the task of carving two jagged parallel "tunnels" through blocks of houses, edging sandbags, ammunition, and other supplies forward yard by yard to consolidate their advances.

At 7 P.M., a runner dashed into headquarters: "We've reached a row of houses only 70 yards from the Arab forward positions, but we can't move any further. There's a road between us and the enemy and every inch is under fire!"

Faglin rose from the table he used as a desk, grabbed his Sten, and said: "We'll move further all right!"

He twisted his way through the "tunnel" to the most advanced position and surveyed the area. Then, conferring with his commanders, he pointed to three Arab strongpoints along the road.

"All we have to do," he said, "is knock them out."

When darkness fell, he sent a sapper to the left flank along the Irgun side of the road to blow up a three-story building just across the street from one of the Arab positions. When the building exploded, the debris fell onto the Arab position, as calculated, and knocked it out. At the same moment, two men dashed across the road to the other two Arab positions and placed explosives outside these houses. When they, too, blew up, groups of Irgunists dashed across the road. Faglin met the problem of flanking fire along the road by building two walls of sandbags, with soldiers throwing sacks into place as they inched their way across. Once across in force, the Irgunists continued to plow through the Arab defenses.

Finally, at dawn, April 29, Faglin heard one of his men yell ecstatically: "I can see it. The sea. Only two blocks away!"

Those near Faglin could see his eyes gleaming with excitement. A kind of mass hysteria rose as the Irgunists, almost to a man, rushed heedlessly into the open toward the sea, overwhelming the remaining Arab positions. The Arabs who could, fled in panic. Wild with joy, the men jumped into the sea, fired their weapons in the air, shouted and screamed like children.

Faglin looked at his watch. The whole maneuver had taken just over 24 hours.

Now, only one group of Arab fighters held out—in the Hassan Bek Mosque, the symbol for so long of Arab belligerence. While last-ditch fighting was raging there, an Irgun officer showed Faglin a photograph found among the piles of documents left behind by fleeing Arab leaders. Faglin looked at a picture of about 20 armed Arab fighters.

"What's so unusual about this?" he asked, looking up.

"Take a good look at the man in front, the leader. Do you recognize him?"

Faglin scrutinized the picture again. "Well, if it isn't our old friend!" he exclaimed.

"Yes, Eli Sambo. He's making his last stand at the mosque. The only one with guts."

Faglin remembered those evenings in the shabby little coffeeshop, Eli's broad, yellow-toothed smile as he welcomed them, his scrupulous loyalty.

"It's too bad he's on the wrong side," he said. "Can you get him to surrender?"

"He's fighting like a tiger. I don't think he'll ever give up."

"Yes, that's Eli, all right. I guess we'll just have to kill him."

A short time later, the Zionist flag fluttered triumphantly from the tower of the mosque. Outside, on the street, sprawled the bullet-riddled body of Eli Sambo.

With victory complete, the Irgun soldiers, never trained in conventional military discipline, sought loot. At first, they entered the gutted stores and selected specific items of jewelry or clothing for their wives and girlfriends, but soon they were rampaging through the desolate, abandoned shops and warehouses, carting off everything movable from furniture to refrigerators. Whatever was not movable—window panes, heavy machinery, chandeliers—they smashed in a frenzy of destruction.

Almost simultaneously with the Irgun victory, the Haganah launched Operation Chametz with a large-scale pincer movement from north and south. In the northern section, it captured several villages easily. But in the southern area, a battalion of the Givati Brigade, under the command of Yaacov Prulov, ran into disaster at Tel Arish, little more than a small hill crowned by a pillbox. It captured the hill at dawn, but Prulov learned the hard way the hazards of concentrating a large force in a small open area, for, with 180 men crowding the hill, the Arabs, counterattacking, had little trouble finding targets, and about 40 Jews fell.

Prulov radioed the Haganah command: "We're taking heavy casualties. We can't hold out. We're going to have to withdraw. Can you provide covering fire?"

A voice answered: "Yes, we'll put the Etzel [Irgun] mortars to work."

Faglin, whose men had just completed their spectacular march to the sea, replied to the request for mortar support: "We'll be glad to help the Haganah out of its difficulties."

*

The Irgun victory, which seemed to presage the fall of the whole city to the Jews, struck the British like a thunderbolt. When the attack had started, the British sat back and waited for what they anticipated would be an Irgun defeat. During the first day of fighting, a British officer had visited Jewish Agency officials and asked only that they use their influence to keep the Irgun from attacking British forces, promising to remain neutral if the Irgun agreed. And the Irgun did agree, having little desire to take on the British as well as the Arabs.

But now that the Irgunists were on the verge of total victory, the British had little stomach for neutrality. For one thing, General Mc-Millan's principal concern at this point was to make sure there would be no hitches in the scheduled British withdrawal from Palestine on May 15, and he was worried that if the Jews, particularly the Irgun, took over Jaffa, they might threaten the route of withdrawal from Ramallah, Lydda, and Latrun.

Even more concerned than McMillan was the British Foreign Office. Bevin at that very moment was being accused by the Arabs of having sold out Haifa to the Jews, and he was in no mood to see Jaffa—an all-Arab town that was to go to the Arab State under the partition resolution— also fall into Jewish hands.

He and his military colleagues agreed that the Jews had to be ousted from Jaffa at any cost.

At 11 A.M., on April 30, the fifth day of battle, British tanks counter-attacked along the three main roads leading from the main sector of Jaffa. When Faglin, viewing the scene from a rooftop, first saw the advance he didn't realize that the force was British. Though he believed that the British were actively supporting the Arabs, he had doubted that they would launch a direct attack that would involve them in a major battle so soon before their departure from Palestine.

But British or no, he immediately went into action. He sent a Piat team to a position along one of the roads, and it made a direct hit on the leading tank, knocking it out and stopping the whole line. When he saw another tank halt beside a tall building on a second road, he dispatched sappers to blow up the building, which collapsed over the tank. He sent an armored car to the third road, but a British tank shell hit it, killing four men inside. However, when the British tank crews on this road saw that the attack had failed on the other two roads, they turned around and retreated.

Faglin then went to the scene and embraced his sappers for their remarkable performance. "Now, to discourage them from coming back, let's dynamite some more houses along each of the roads and block them well," he said.

When evening came, all was quiet. The Irgun, incredibly enough, had stopped a determined tank attack by the British army.

Abdel Bari, his distinguished face grimy with dirt and dust collected in battle, sat amid the ruins of a front-line house with his rifle across his lap, staring into the wasteland of destruction that separated the Irgun troops from the Arab lines. His men had fought so hard, so courageously, yet somehow they could not withstand the onslaught of the Jews. Of course, it wasn't the Jews alone they were fighting. The British were naturally helping the Jews against the Arabs. Never could the Jews beat the Arabs without British support. As he desperately attempted to bolster his ego, Abdel Bari began to hate the British even more than the Jews.

Was Jaffa doomed, he wondered. Many of his friends and relatives apparently thought so. They were leaving by the hundreds because of the shelling. Soon there would be no Arabs left in Jaffa. Perhaps they were right. Why die for a lost cause? What was to be gained by fighting British tanks and Jewish artillery with rusty rifles like his own? Besides, eventually the Arab countries would invade Palestine and push the Jews out. But would they really? Had not these countries already betrayed the Palestine Arabs?

The Jaffa Arabs had requested help from King Abdullah of Transjordan, and from Egypt and Syria—but to no avail. Fawzi el-Kaoukji, who was supposed to be in command of the Arab Liberation Army troops, had never even bothered to leave his headquarters in northern Palestine to visit the city.

At the same time, Captain Abdel Najim al-Din (ALA commander in Jaffa), infuriated by the news that he was to be replaced, withdrew, taking with him his 300 men and all their arms.

As he was leaving, civilian leaders pleaded with him: "Jaffa depends on you. We need your men and your arms. You cannot leave us here to die."

But Abdel Najim was adamant. "I've tried to help you," he said as he got into a jeep loaded with equipment. "But what good are my efforts when they are constantly sabotaged by traitors?"

And he drove off.

Then, Abdel Najim's arch foe, Hassan Salame, abandoned his command, too, evacuating the city with many other Mufti supporters in his rage over increasing ALA domination.

"I cannot work with traitors," Salame charged.

Thus Jaffa was left virtually leaderless.

While chaos spread among the Arabs, General McMillan prepared to make a renewed attempt to push the Irgun forces out of Jaffa. The morning after the Irgun had repulsed the three-pronged British counterattack, British Spitfires dived on Irgun positions and a destroyer appeared offshore. At the same time, an infantry battalion, two Royal Marine Commando units, and a tank regiment all arrived from Egypt and Cyprus, though McMillan had not asked for these forces.

Before launching a second round, the British Commissioner of the Lydda-Jaffa District called the mayor of Tel Aviv to his headquarters and warned: "If the Irgun forces don't withdraw from Jaffa immediately, we will attack again and this time in greater strength."

The mayor, resentful of what he regarded as intimidation, replied: "All I can do is pass on the information."

But the Irgun leaders took this as an empty threat, Beigin even saying to Faglin: "You're exhausted. Why don't you go home for a rest until the situation clears?" Faglin went home and slept deeply for several hours.

He woke abruptly to the sound of his mother's excited voice: "Son, they're fighting. The British have attacked!"

As he dressed, Faglin heard explosions in the distance. Within moments he had dashed out of the house.

When he reached the front, one of his officers rushed to him and shouted almost hysterically: "They're hitting us with infantry and tanks . . . Killed some of our best commanders . . . Many of our positions are cut off and we can't get ammunition to them . . . How will we hold out?"

Without waiting to hear a full report, Faglin sprinted with several sapper teams toward an approaching tank force. Several men blew up a house that stood between the first two tanks, and when the structure exploded, the leading tank, fearing it was being cut off, hastily retreated. Other men, meanwhile, threw raw explosives at the stalled tanks, crippling several; but British firepower nevertheless tore isolated Irgun units to shreds. And though after two hours the Irgunists had slowed down the British attack, Faglin began to feel that all was lost. He returned to headquarters steeped in the agony of certain defeat.

But at about 6 P.M. that day, May 1, a runner burst in: "We've done it! The British tanks and infantry are retreating all along the road!"

Then two French reporters rushed in and asked to shake his hand. "The British have admitted their failure to crack your lines," one of them announced. "They say they won't try again."

Faglin smiled. He realized for the first time that the Irgun had broken the back of the British attackers—or at least that the British thought it had.

News of the latest British setback spread quickly among the Arabs who were now persuaded that this proved the British were conspiring with the Jews to crush the Arabs. The streams of refugees—including many fighters—pouring out of the city by land and sea converged into a flood. With the whole fabric of the Arab defense disintegrating, Michael al-Issa, the new local Arab Liberation Army commander, cabled Kaoukji several times for instructions. When he received none, Issa, feeling himself abandoned, joined the exodus with his men. They used transportation provided by the British, who had given up trying to control the chaos. Issa's flight broke remaining Arab resistance, and complete anarchy resulted.

Wild mobs of fighters and refugees, in their panicky flight through debris-strewn streets, broke into stores and looted every last article, much as the Irgun had done in the Manshieh Quarter. Some reports indicated that British soldiers permitted anyone to enter the customshouse during one short period and take whatever food, clothing, and other items he wanted—for a cash-and-carry payment of £80. And armed Arabs murdered other Arabs, settling old scores.

With Jaffa dying, mukhtar Abdel Bari called a meeting of about 50 local Arab leaders at the house of his elder brother, blind Shaba'an. His flowing robes still smudged from the trenches, Abdel Bari said with suppressed emotion:

"This is not a fight between Arabs and Jews but an organized imperialistic attack against unarmed Arabs, an attack planned by Britain and the United States. We must recognize this fact and flee, before our families are needlessly killed, taking with us only our souls."

One notable suggested the possibility of the young men staying to fight while the women, children, and old men fled; but the majority of those present vetoed this idea. The men were needed, it was argued, to protect their families in flight.

"I have a wife and eight children," said Hamada Hassan Usrof. "It isn't fair to gamble with their lives."

"If you run from the Devil, you'll meet him in flight," said another who was opposed to leaving.

But most argued that there was little use in continuing to fight when all was lost. Had not even the forces of the Arab Liberation Army deserted them? It was decided to leave by sea immediately after the last evening prayer.

General McMillan could not remember when he had been in a more difficult position. London continued to bombard him with demands that he retake Jaffa at any cost and reestablish Arab control there, yet circumstances were forcing him to help the Jews clear Jaffa of the Arabs he was supposed to reestablish in control. Unable to retake Jaffa by force without incurring losses utterly disproportionate, in his mind, to the limited and temporary gains to be achieved, he decided that the cost was too high, whatever the politicians at home might think. And this feeling was reinforced as the Haganah, with the Irgun's mortar support, helped to tighten the ring round Jaffa by capturing the villages of Salameh and Yazur east of the city, as well as bloodstained Tel Arish, which had been abandoned by the Arabs a few days after they had conquered it.

Finally, McMillan flew to the headquarters of British Middle East commander General Crocker in the Suez Canal Zone and told him bluntly that it was "quite impossible" to carry out the orders relayed from London.

"How can we give Jaffa back to the Arabs when there are hardly any Arabs left to give it back to?" he asked. "It seems to me we should concern ourselves only with keeping open the road from Jaffa to Egypt."

Crocker agreed and said he would explain the true situation to London and make suitable recommendations.

The Jaffa leaders made one final effort to save their city, renewing their plea for help to King Abdullah. They implored him by cable to send the Arab Legion units stationed in the Ramle-Lydda area immediately.

The Transjordanian government replied that fighters and civilians had to stay in Jaffa, and that the Arab Legion would come to their help as soon as the "Jerusalem operation" was completed. It was imperative, the reply said, that they hold out a few more days.

The Jaffa Arabs might have laughed if the situation had been less tragic. Hold out? With what and whom? Less than 5,000 of the city's 70,000 inhabitants were still in Jaffa.

McMillan now saw that there was nothing left for him but to negotiate directly with the Jews. At a hastily called conference, British officials informed the mayors of Tel Aviv and Jaffa that the British were ready to "stabilize the present situation"—on two conditions.

"You must give us control of Manshieh police station," one official said, looking at the Jewish mayor. "And we must be free to send armored patrols through the Manshieh Quarter."

The Jewish factions went away to discuss these proposals. Beigin later agreed to let the Haganah take over the occupied area, but demanded rejection of the British conditions on grounds of security and principle. When the Haganah insisted that the Irgun should give in, Beigin decided to render the question academic . . .

Faglin called an immediate press conference at the Irgun headquarters in Jaffa. One of the first questions asked was whether the Irgun would accept the British terms for peace. The Irgun commander looked at his watch. As he began talking, a tremendous explosion rocked the area.

"What's that?" someone shouted.

"That's our answer," Faglin said. The dynamite had exploded right on time (the press conference had been called for 10 A.M.). "There is no Manshieh police station."

After the last evening prayer, mukhtar Abdel Bari gathered together his family, his brothers and their families, his more distant relatives, and his friends; about 60 people in all. Burdened with cloth-covered bundles, they made their way to the port and climbed into five fishing boats, each only about 20 feet long, belonging to Abdel Bari and his four brothers. Their apprehension was fed by the scenes of panic and confusion along the shore as thousands of Arabs crowded the area, leaping into craft of all kinds, bargaining with hardheaded boat owners, shouting at wayward children, searching for mothers, fathers, husbands, wives.

Abdel Bari was in the first boat as the five overcrowded craft began to slice through turbulent, white-tipped waves that the brothers, as experienced fishermen, knew portended a storm. As the mukhtar struggled to stabilize his boat with a splintered oar, he began to wonder whether the dangers of staying in Jaffa would really have outweighed the threat now confronting them. But it was too late to think of that now. His only concern was to reach the shores of Gaza safely, out of range of Jewish and, he was certain, British, guns.

Suddenly the sea became the least of his worries. From a high building on shore, searchlight beams swung across the inky darkness, illuminating the restless, dancing waves. As there was constant sporadic shooting ashore, Abdel Bari could not tell whether any bullets were directed his way, but his heart froze when one relentless beam trapped his boat in its terrifying glare.

He and his fellow oarsmen rowed desperately and finally managed to

186 THE CIVIL WAR

break away into the open sea, past numerous bodies and overturned boats floating on the waves. Thank God, thought Abdel Bari, that he and his brothers were professional fishermen who knew how to deal with the sea. But as the waters grew wilder, he felt uncertain that even they could steer the boats to safety.

After about five hours at sea, there came a shrill scream from the second boat, about 20 yards behind. Then Abdel Bari heard the voice of his brother Ibrahim shouting: "My wife—she's having a baby! We must head for shore!"

Abdel Bari, his mind and body numb from fatigue, fear, and gnawing doubt, tried to believe he had misheard his brother and went on rowing relentlessly.

Meanwhile, on Ibrahim's boat, Sabra, the wife, began to give birth with the help of another woman aboard. The baby was finally delivered at dawn with the impact of a huge wave that sent torrents of water into the craft and nearly turned it around. A few minutes later, Abdel Bari thought he heard a strange sound over the roar of the waves. The first cries of his newborn niece, Aisheh—the name Ibrahim immediately selected for his daughter. It meant "life," and Aisheh became the symbol of hope for those who learned of her birth.

Abdel Bari, shaken at last from his stupor, was determined that the symbol should survive. This meant he had to take a chance and head for shore. He did not know whether he would land in Jewish-held territory, but he was sure the child would not live if the voyage continued. He raised his hand and pointed toward shore, hoping the oarsmen in the other boats would see him, and then, after eight hours at sea, headed in that direction with a prayer on his lips . . .

In one of the rear boats, Hamada Hassan Usrof sighed with relief as he observed the others turn toward the shore. He had been sure they could not survive another hour of the storm, and his heart ached at the sight of his seasick wife and eight children weeping in terror. In a few more minutes the nightmare would be over and his family safely on land. He caressed his two-year-old son, held tightly in his arms. As the pale, expressionless child —the only one of his children (four sons and four daughters) who was not crying—stared blankly into space, Hassan Usrof was certain his calm was a sign of courage. He would be a brave soldier when he grew up . . .

Abdel Bari's boat was about 20 yards from the beach when an enormous wave struck it. Amid a chorus of screams, the craft broke up and the passengers were tossed into the raging sea. But the water reached only to the waist, and Abdel Bari and the other able-bodied men were able to carry the women, children, and old men to shore. All collapsed on the sand, too exhausted and shocked to utter a word or even groan.

Refugees from the other boats soon arrived—most of them. Hassan

Usrof ran up, soaked and breathing heavily: "My children, my children!" he shouted despairingly. "Four of them are missing!"

His boat had overturned as it approached shore; gone were one daughter and three sons, including his two-year-old boy.

Etched against the orange sky, his wife Adila stood on the shore, her feet deep in the sand and her black-shawled figure a misty gray in the spray of the breaking waves. She gazed out to sea with strangely lifeless eyes.

"And my wife," moaned Hassan Usrof. "She won't move. She won't talk. She has gone mad!"

While the injured and the sick remained behind to receive treatment at a local Arab clinic (for they had landed in Arab-held territory), the remaining survivors, after resting and being fed by Arab families in the area, made their way overland toward Gaza. In the village of Joura, near Ashkelon, Hassan Usrof, his wife, and four surviving children stayed overnight at the home of friends.

Just as everybody was dipping their hands into a huge platter of chicken and rice, the guests' first real meal since leaving Jaffa, a shrill whistle rose to a screech that ended in an explosion right outside the house. The next thing Hassan Usrof knew, he was groping through the blackness trying to find the kerosene lamp. When he relit it, he saw that the house was a shambles, with pieces of furniture littering the floor and food splattered everywhere. In a moment his hosts, his wife, and two of his children gathered around him, in a state of shock but apparently unhurt.

"Where are the other two?" he asked.

He looked around feverishly in the lamplight and found, under a heap of debris, the bodies of a son, twelve, and daughter, ten.

"My God, two more are dead!"

As he suddenly lurched for the door, his host tried to stop him; but Adila grabbed the restraining arm. Despite her own unbalanced condition, she could not bear to see her husband suffer the disgrace of weeping in front of women.

And as Hussan Usrof plunged hysterically into the night, throwing himself to the ground, he remembered the friend who quoted the Arab proverb: "If you run from the Devil, you will meet him in flight."

In Jaffa, the last chapter in the fall of that city was being written. The British, faced with the *fait accompli* of the suddenly nonexistent Manshieh police station, settled for a cease-fire line at right angles to the sea approximating the Irgun's front line that separated the Manshieh Quarter from the main section of Jaffa. They were completely frozen out of the panhandle. Then, while kilted Scottish soldiers took positions behind sandbags on one side of Azen Street, the dividing line, a Haganah unit arrived to take over sandbagged Irgun positions on the other side.

"I've come to take command," the Haganah commander said stiffly to Irgun Commander Shraga Elis.

"Very well," said Elis. "But I'd like a receipt."

The Haganah officer ripped a piece of paper from a small notebook. On it he wrote carefully:

RECEIVED FROM IRGUN ZVAI LEUMI—ONE JAFFA.

A few days later, on May 11, with the British about to leave, Ahmed Abu-Laban, a wealthy Jaffa merchant and head of the new Emergency Committee, met with Commander Michael Ben-Gal on behalf of the 5,000 Arabs still in Jaffa and asked what Jewish conditions for peace would be. After Ben-Gal had stated his conditions, the meeting adjourned until the following day. The two sides then ironed out a surrender agreement.

At 3:30 P.M. on May 13, 1948, as the last British soldier departed, the agreement was signed. Haganah and Irgun units then marched jointly into Jaffa, which became a Jewish suburb of a city that had once been a suburb of Jaffa.

It is still debatable whether Operation Chametz, if it had proceeded according to plan, without an Irgun frontal assault, might have achieved the same objective at far less risk and cost.[10]

Wітн Deir Yassin burning in every Arab heart, and other strongholds falling fast, the Palestine Arab leaders decided that they must do something dramatic to lift plunging Arab morale; an act worthy of Abd el-Kader el-Husseini, whose memory was their most formidable weapon.

Mohammed Abdel Najar and Adil Abd Latif, two of Abd el-Kader's lieutenants, came up with what they thought would be an effective answer— an attack on a large Jewish supply convoy due to pass through the Arab-controlled Sheikh Jarrah Quarter to Hadassah Hospital on Mount Scopus. The convoy was supposed to carry only medical personnel and equipment, but they were convinced it would be used to smuggle soldiers and guns.

"Tomorrow," Najar assured Latif on the evening of April 13, "our people will find new spirit."

Dr. Chaim Yassky and his wife Fanny arose early on the morning of April 14 in their room in Jerusalem's Eden Hotel. Today they were to return to their home on Mount Scopus, in order to pack their things and leave again for an indefinite period. The High Commissioner and the British Colonial Secretary, Arthur Creech-Jones, had both personally offered assurances that convoys sending relief units to Hebrew University and Hadassah Hospital would be protected by British army and police forces. But, without undue interference, Arabs were shooting at every convoy and it was no longer possible to maintain these isolated institutions.

Dr. Yassky, director of the Hadassah organization in Palestine, had been searching for substitute hospital sites in new Jerusalem for four days and had finally found suitable buildings. They would now collect their belongings and move into one of them.

"Don't worry, dear," Yassky consoled his wife. "It'll be for just a short while. Then we'll be going home for good."

Mrs. Yassky did not have to see the despondent expression on her husband's face to know that he did not believe what he was saying. "Of course," she replied, as she set about packing a small bag.

For weeks, she knew, he had been tormented by the prospect of abandoning the hospital on Mount Scopus. To him, it was the symbol of the Jewish humanitarian endeavor in Palestine, the very meaning of the coming Jewish State. And he saw its abandonment now as possibly symbolic of a menacing future. He had worked to build up the hospital since 1921, only two years after they had arrived in Palestine from their native Odessa as a young married couple. Now Mrs. Yassky, who had worked alongside her husband all these years, was reluctant to look into his eyes, to see the fears of a man whose strength had always lain in an utter disdain of doubt.

After a brief pause, she said: "Well, we'll have at least one more night at home, anyway. I hope you'll be in voice tonight for our last party. It isn't often that we get to sing these days."

That same morning New York–born Esther Passman-Epstein was debating whether to leave on the convoy. In charge of the hospital's social welfare services, she had wanted to bring candy, cigarettes, magazines, and other items for the few remaining patients. She could, of course, send these things with someone else, but she felt it was her duty to deal personally with the patients' comforts. However, her teen-aged son, who was at home in new Jerusalem, had not recovered from burns resulting from premature explosion of a homemade bomb he had been experimenting with, and she hesitated to leave him alone.

"Don't worry about me, Ma," the boy told her. "Go on up if you think you should."

So she decided to go. Weighted down with cartons, she drove with a friend to the usual convoy takeoff point in front of Hadassah's out-patient clinic. As she reached the front of the queue, the man checking the names of passengers looked up from his list and said to her: "You're not supposed to be in this bus. You're to go in one of the ambulances."

This was a considerable blow. The two ambulances were leaving from the compound of the English Mission about four blocks away. Not only would she be late, but the packages she was carrying were getting heavier by the second.

"I'm late now," she begged. "I'll miss the ambulance. Please let me on."

"Sorry," the man said with finality. "There's no room on this bus for you."

She was starting off angrily for the English compound when Dr. L. Dojanski, a cancer research specialist and founder of the new faculty of medicine, called out to her: "Mrs. Passman-Epstein, please come and sit by me. You are my mascot."

But she shook her head and answered with a forced smile: "I wish I could."

Just as the buses were leaving, Dr. Moshe Ben-David, another founder of the faculty of medicine, and Dr. Alexander Geiger came running together to the takeoff point, a minute or so too late. Geiger said: "Well, that's that. We'll have to go tomorrow."

"Not me," said Ben-David. "If the others are going today, so am I." And he jumped into a passing taxi and ordered the driver to follow the buses.

Geiger reproached himself for giving up too easily.

Mrs. Passman-Epstein was breathing heavily as she rushed into the compound where the two armor-plated ambulances, painted white and bearing red shields of David, were just loading. She smiled as she saw her friend, Mrs. Yassky, who, with her husband, was about to enter the first ambulance.

"Don't forget to be at our house tonight," Mrs. Yassky cried out.

Then Mrs. Passman-Epstein stepped into the second ambulance in which a place was reserved for her. At about 8:30, three stretcher-borne patients were carried out of the mission, which had been converted into a casualty clearing station, and placed in the ambulances. The vehicles then set off.

At a point just outside Sheikh Jarrah, they joined with the two buses, as well as three trucks carrying equipment to the hospital, and the convoy remained there waiting for two armored escort cars, one to lead the way, the other to protect the rear.

After more than an hour's wait, the two cars were finally in place and a British police officer shouted: "All clear ahead." The passenger vehicles were checked to make sure all the steel shutters were closed, and the convoy, carrying 105 people, started to move off—the Yasskys' ambulance right behind the front escort car, followed by the second ambulance, the two buses, the three trucks, and the rear escort car.

The line advanced without incident for several minutes, and when the driver in the first ambulance announced that they were passing the large mosque in the center of Sheikh Jarrah, there was a feeling of relief among the passengers. Only a few minutes more and they would be past the danger zone. Dr. Yassky, who was sitting in the front seat next to the driver, smiled reassuringly at his wife, who was on a bench along the side of the ambulance. With the tension reduced, small talk began to break the silence.

Shortly after passing a British army post at a turning in the road, on the approach to Mount Scopus, the first ambulance was suddenly shaken by an explosion. An electrically detonated mine had gone off under the escort car about 20 yards in front, slewing it halfway round. The Yemenite ambulance driver, Zachariah, slammed on his brakes, then, fearing a trap, tried to move forward and pass the armored car. But in halting so abruptly the vehicle had skidded and the rear wheel was stuck in a deep side ditch.

"Forward! Forward!" Yassky cried.

"It's no use," the driver answered. "We can't move."

At that moment, bullets resounded against the steel sides of the ambulance.

"We've been ambushed!" someone yelled.

Yassky took his wife's trembling hand in his. *"Shalom,* my dear," he said softly so others couldn't hear. "This is the end."

As the second ambulance braked sharply, Mrs. Passman-Epstein, who had been kneeling by one of the wounded on the floor serving him tea, spilled it over a nurse next to her, and the nurse screamed: "Oh my God. I'm bleeding!" When the passengers realized what had happened, they burst into nervous laughter in the midst of the shooting.

The driver, Zvi Gershuni, tried to turn around on the narrow road, but as he peered through the slit in the windshield a bullet hit him in the face, and he screamed a Yiddish curse as he slid from his seat. While a doctor examined his wound, another driver, Joseph Cohen, took the wheel and managed to turn the vehicle. He headed off swiftly toward town through a hail of bullets, thus saving the ambulance and passengers.

As the second ambulance moved out of line, the two buses behind it, too large and awkward to turn around, tried to advance; but the driver of the first, unable to see much through the windshield slit, slid into the ditch like the first ambulance. When the driver of the second bus tried to pass, he skidded into the ditch on the other side of the road.

Benjamin Edelman, who was driving the second of the three trucks, struggled to turn around, managing to avoid the ditches by sighting one through a tiny hole in the steel plate on the side of his cabin where a screw had come out. His arms ached agonizingly as he turned the wheel one way and then the other, maneuvering on tires deflated by bullets. When at last he had got the truck around, he started down hill at great speed and almost went out of control, his brakes disabled and his numb arm muscles preventing a firm grip on the steering wheel, which trembled as steel frames ground over shredded rubber. Yet he was thankful for the truck's erratic movement, for only one bullet found the slit in the windshield and it missed him by a hair's breadth. Oddly enough, it appeared to have come from the direction of the British army post at the turning near the foot of the hill.

As Mohammed Abdel Najar watched all this from the window of a stone house just off the road, he was overjoyed by his success. He had expected to cause a number of casualties and to give the Jews a fright, but he had been far from sure that he and his 40 or so men, equipped only with small arms, grenades, and Molotov cocktails, could stop the convoy for long. After all, the Jews had guns too. And so did the British, who were stationed nearby and wouldn't be likely to let the situation get out of hand.

But now the first escort car was out of action, three vehicles were stuck in ditches, and most of the other vehicles were on particularly narrow stretches of road that didn't permit them to turn. The possibility that the steel-shuttered buses and ambulances contained armed Haganah men as he had suspected now seemed remote, since the only Jewish shooting was coming from the two armored cars at the front and rear of the convoy. The soldiers in the first car, apparently unhurt in the explosion that had stopped them, were causing some Arab casualties, but the situation looked ripe for exploitation—if only the British kept out of it. Behind almost every window, tree, and rock along the roadside there was an Arab, and each remembered Deir Yassin. Things were turning out very well indeed, he thought, as he aimed his Sten at a crack in the armor of one of the trapped vehicles.

*

Mohammed Gharbieh was in his house on the Mount of Olives enjoying a late breakfast and listening to the 10 o'clock news over the radio. As he glanced out of the window, he thought he saw columns of smoke spiraling into the clear blue sky, apparently from Sheikh Jarrah about two miles away.

"Look at that," he said to his German wife sitting across from him. "They must be fighting there." Then he remembered that a large convoy of Jews was scheduled to climb Mount Scopus that morning. "It must be an attack on the convoy!" he shouted. His excitement was mixed with resentment. He had himself been planning such an attack, and now someone had beaten him to it—without even being courteous enough to notify him in advance.

He set down his coffee and grabbed his gun from a closet. "I've got to get my men and join the fighting," he said to his wife, who was already standing by the door. He noted the familiar look on her face, the look that seemed to say: Why must you rush into every battle; why must you take such chances; why must you always be the hero?

"Why don't you at least stay and finish your coffee?" she asked quietly.

He smiled, his eyes shining with anticipation. "Don't worry, dear," he said as he stretched his short, stocky body to kiss her. And he added with half-serious bravado: "I am the equivalent of at least fifty Jews."

Then he dashed off in a jeep toward Jerusalem to gather his men for battle.

Jerusalem commander Brigadier Jones heard the first reports of the attack by radio while driving in a jeep in new Jerusalem. Yet another convoy attack! Maybe his men at the post near the foot of the hill and at Antonius House nearby could handle it, though there were less than a dozen at each post. Just to make sure, he decided to alert his battalion in the area. He could always send more forces if necessary. The Arabs, of course, couldn't be permitted to slaughter the Jews, but as usual the Jews were probably asking for trouble.

In the New City, Jewish leaders, listening helplessly to the gunfire in Sheikh Jarrah, were desperately trying to contact Jones and other British officials in the hope of obtaining swift aid for the convoy. Finally, Dr.

Reifenberg, the Jewish Agency liaison officer with the British army, begged a British officer to "give a Haganah unit permission to go up and rescue the passengers."

"I'm sorry," came the reply, "we're trying to arrange a cease-fire, and any interference could ruin everything."

Four Haganah armored cars, two from town and two from Mount Scopus, started toward the scene anyway, but were ambushed by Arabs and had to retreat.

The only early British intervention came at about 11:15 A.M., when a courageous British officer in a small, partially armored car drove up to one of the buses. Leaving his car, he braved Arab fire to reach the bus.

"I'll give you a fifty-fifty chance," he told the passengers. "If you'll risk the dash across the road, I'll try to get you back to the city in my car."

The passengers hesitated, then one of them said: "It would be suicide. I think we should wait for an organized rescue." The others agreed, and the officer went back to his car and drove away.

In the remaining ambulance, calm prevailed despite the feeling of almost all 13 passengers that they were doomed. Toward noon, Yassky peered out of a tiny hole in the side of the vehicle and said, "They're coming closer."

"We've got to get help," declared Dr. Yehuda Matot, who had been a British army officer during World War II. "Antonius House is less than two hundred yards away. If we make a run for it, maybe we can make it. It's better than being slaughtered here."

The driver disagreed. "We'd be killed as soon as we got to the door," he said. "We've no choice but to wait."

The others agreed with him.

"Very well, I'll go alone," Matot said. "If I make it, I'll send help."

Before anyone could reply, he had opened the door, jumped out, and slammed it shut behind him.

He crawled around the front of the vehicle on all fours and started up the small street leading to Antonius House, exposed to Arab fire from almost every direction. He had gone about halfway when a bullet hit him in the back. Falling flat on his stomach, he lay still for a moment, then started crawling ahead. Inch by inch he advanced, digging his fingers into the hard, crusty earth on the side of the road to pull his bleeding body forward.

He began to hear vague, pleading voices and thought he must be going mad. But as he focused weakly on Antonius House, he saw two British soldiers watching from the entrance. "Come on, chum," one of them was urging. "Keep coming. Just a little way now. Come on, come on. You can make it."

Matot, gradually losing strength, continued on, his face caked with dirt and dust, his shirt and trousers soaked in blood. "Come on chum, come on . . ." The words blended with the crack of bullets, a frog's croaking nearby, and the vengeful cries of men gone berserk. Mechanically he edged forward, hardly aware of his destination any more. The last thing he could remember was the flash of a smiling face looking over him, and the words: "Blimey, he's made it!"

Shortly after 1 P.M., Yassky, looking through the side peephole, saw in the distance a convoy of army vehicles approaching on the Nablus road, which crossed the Scopus road a few hundred yards ahead. "It looks as if help is coming," he said calmly, not wanting to raise anyone's hopes prematurely.

In one of the jeeps was General McMillan, who had received details of the ambush from Brigadier Jones. It looked to him as if the Jews were keeping the Arabs at bay with heavy fire, and it seemed pretty late in the game to risk British lives unnecessarily in their blasted scrap. Anyway, the Arabs were just trying to get even for Deir Yassin. And what, after all, was the Haganah doing to curb excesses by the Jewish terrorists? British intervention, it seemed to him, if needed at all, should take the form of mediation rather than fighting. The British convoy continued over the crossroads without halting.

A second British convoy a little later did the same.

Mohammed Gharbieh arrived with his men during a lull in the fighting as hundreds of other fighters who had just learned of the attack were streaming into the area to join in the kill. He conferred with Najar at his headquarters after ordering his men to spread out near the roadside. The fighting would probably be over soon, Najar told him, for a British officer was at that moment negotiating with Latif and two Haganah men from the first armored car. Najar pointed from his window to the negotiators standing beside a British armored car on the road. The Arab conditions were, Najar said, that all Jewish arms be surrendered and all Jewish men of fighting age be taken prisoner.

Suddenly new shooting broke out, and Latif fell to the ground.
"They've shot Adil," Najar cried. "Now we'll get them!"

Heavy firing ensued, and the two Haganah representatives fell dead.
Mohammed rushed outside and, taking up his position behind a rock, began
firing with the others. Too bad about Latif; but now at least he'd get a chance
to kill a few Jews.

At about 2 P.M., Esther Passman-Epstein stood on the roof of a casualty clearing station located just below Sheikh Jarrah and watched the
grim drama from which her ambulance had managed to escape. Suddenly,
flames erupted from one of the buses, and then from the other.

"My God," she cried, "they've set the buses on fire! They're burning
all the passengers alive!"

Then she recalled her anger that morning when the Hadassah official
had refused to let her onto one of the buses because she had been assigned
to the ambulance. She closed her eyes in horror and wondered why God
had singled her out to live.

At that point, the passengers in the trapped ambulance heard a frantic
knocking on the door. Yassky and the driver debated whether to open it;
perhaps it was an Arab. Then they heard a man scream: "Get out, get
out quick, or they'll burn you alive—like they burned the buses! Everybody's dead!"

The driver recognized the voice of one of the bus drivers. He was
about to open the door when a flurry of bullets bounced off it. Yassky
looked through the side peephole and saw the body of the bus driver
stretched in front of the door.

"They've set fire to the buses!" he gasped.

So insulated was the ambulance that its passengers hadn't previously
known what was happening, though they had heard two explosions. Arabs
had set the buses afire with Molotov cocktails, and all passengers had died
in the flames except a few who dashed out of the door only to be shot dead
like the driver lying outside the ambulance.

News of the tragedy greatly enhanced the terror in the ambulance.
Since no one knew of the "peace negotiations" that had failed, some passengers had thought that if worst came to worst they could surrender, and
saw some merit in the suggestion of the sick man on the floor, who had
said: "Why not put out a white handkerchief so they'll stop shooting?"

But now there could be no thought of surrender. Death would almost surely be their fate anyway, but somehow it was better to die even in fire than to surrender, which would probably mean humiliation, rape, and torture. What else could be expected of maniacs who burned helpless civilians alive?

While the shouting outside grew louder and closer, the passengers sat in silence waiting. But even when it seemed the end would surely come for all without distinction, Mrs. Yassky, feeling that her husband was too exposed to possible bullets or shell fragments through the windshield slit and the side peepholes, asked him to sit on the bench beside her. He refused, not wishing to make the driver, who was in an equally "exposed" position, feel any uneasier than necessary.

At about 2:30 P.M., Mrs. Yassky heard her husband groan suddenly and saw him stiffen, then slump in his seat.

"What happened?" she cried, grabbing him by the shoulders as he was about to fall. There was no reply. Sonya Astrakan, a nurse who had been sitting next to her, helped her to lay him on the floor, and the two women were horrified to see blood oozing from his side. Automatically, Mrs. Yassky removed her blouse and the nurse her white uniform for bandages. As the stricken wife held her husband's head in her lap, she murmured, "Darling, speak to me, please."

But she knew he was dead even before a doctor in the ambulance confirmed it. A bullet had apparently entered through the crack in the door, lodging in Yassky's liver and killing him instantly.

Mrs. Yassky sat silent, dry-eyed, on the floor, caressing her dead husband's forehead as if to assure him that everything would be all right. Only Sonya Astrakan wept, her sobs sounding to some of the passengers like a wordless prayer in the darkness. In fact, Sonya was praying that the end would come as quickly for her as it had for Dr. Yassky.

But not all the passengers were as resigned to death. The driver, who had previously opposed suggestions that the passengers run for it, now saw this as the only possibility of survival, and argued—as cries of "Deir Yassin! Deir Yassin!" grew ever louder—"What have we got to lose? It's our only chance!"

Mrs. Yassky looked up at him, her husband's head still resting on her lap. "I shall not leave my husband," she said in a quiet, determined voice.

Others who had been considering flight then decided they would not leave her alone, but the driver opened the door and jumped to the road. He was riddled with bullets before he could take a step.

Meanwhile, Brigadier Jones, some six hours after first receiving reports of the attack, had reached the British post near the foot of the hill behind

the line of vehicles, accompanied by three armored cars and troops armed
with mortars and machine guns. It had taken him all this time, he claims,
to round up the force. Within minutes, British guns swept the Arab positions, wounding Najar and causing many other Arab casualties.

Mohammed Gharbieh, who had advanced to within a few yards of
the ambulance, was out of the firing line because of his proximity to the
Jewish vehicles but, together with the other Arabs, he hastily retreated
under the withering barrage of British mortar fire. Well, he thought, it had
to come sooner or later. But he and his men hadn't done too badly. Most
of the Jews had been killed.

Inside the ambulance, no one knew what was happening. The door
was jerked open and the passengers, expecting the worst, were stunned to
hear an English voice saying: "I'm looking for Dr. Yassky and his wife.
Where are they?"

Mrs. Yassky stared at the British officer. "I'm Mrs. Yassky," she said
quietly. "And this is my husband. He's dead."

The Englishman, a major, looked at the corpse and said with genuine
sympathy: "I'm sorry. Is there anything we can do for you?"

There was no answer.

Within a few minutes—it was now about 4:30 P.M.—all the passen-
gers had been transferred to a British armored car and taken to Antonius
House, and later, to town. They were followed by truckloads of charred
Jewish corpses—76 in all, including those of Dr. Doljansky; Dr. Guenther
Wolfsohn, the physicist; Dr. Enzo Bonaventura, head of the university's
department of psychology; and nurses, students, and staff workers of
Hadassah Hospital and the university. A pharmacist in one of the buses
had disappeared, his body apparently carried off by the Arabs.

Also among the dead was Dr. Ben-David, who had managed to catch
up with his bus.

That evening Mrs. Yassky, one of only 28 survivors, went to the hospital building where she and her husband were to have lived for the duration of the crisis. As she entered their room for the first time, she switched
on the light and saw on the dresser a gay collection of almost unobtainable
items—a box of chocolates, a bottle of brandy, a carton of cigarettes, and

a vaseful of flowers. Her husband had left these things for her as "welcome back" mementos to be enjoyed when they returned from their home on Mount Scopus for the last time.

She bent over the flowers to breathe in their fragrance, then sat down on the bed.

Shalom, my dear . . .

6

Last Days of
the Mandate

THE tragedy of the Hadassah convoy was to drive home to the Jews of Jerusalem that Operation Nahshon had by no means ended their long, bitter night. The capture of Kastel and other strongpoints along the Tel Aviv–Jerusalem road had opened the way for convoys crammed with food, fuel, arms, and other supplies; but the Palestine Arabs, though severely shaken by Abd el-Kader el-Husseini's death, were still driven men. And their searing desire to avenge Deir Yassin and the killing of their godlike hero helped to compensate for their lack of central leadership.

On April 20, a week after the Mount Scopus ambush, Operation Nahshon was finally negated when thousands of Arabs swept down from the hills near Bab el-Wad to attack a bumper-to-bumper convoy—the largest the Jews had yet assembled—consisting of 350 vehicles. All but six vehicles did manage to break through to Jerusalem, including one carrying Ben-Gurion in secret. But as the hungry Jews sat down for the Passover Seder to enjoy chicken, eggs, matzoths, and other festival items brought in the convoy, and gave thanks in joyous song, they little realized how short-lived the miracle was to be. For the Arabs, in their attack, had retaken the heights above Bab el-Wad. Jerusalem was once more under siege.

Laughter and song again receded into the silence of fear and despair. Silent were the knots of Sten-bearing young men and girls in their khaki drill trousers and shirtsleeves as they waited for transport to their posts. Silent were the moonlit streets in the wake of heavy shelling, their dull glow accentuating weird shadows cast by roadblocks of square stone overlaid with sandbags. Silent were the mourners at the funerals of loved ones killed by a stray bullet or a jagged piece of shrapnel.

Once again the Eternal City, founded by King David almost 3,000 years before, was in grave peril. Twice it had been destroyed, once by Nebuchadnezzar II about 500 B.C., and again by the Roman general Titus in A.D. 70. For 2,000 years, the Jews had languished in exile, crying "Next year in Jerusalem!" Had the appointed year finally come—or would Jerusalem become a mass grave of Jews who had longed too deeply and too dangerously?

The Jewish leaders were not sure, but they decided that no Jew would go to the grave except in the fury of battle. The days of surrendering the ghetto were over. An Emergency Committee led by Canadian-born Dov Joseph was thus established with the central task of keeping the city alive. And this committee probably directed one of the most brilliant and imaginative programs in history for the conservation of life in a besieged area.

It took over a city whose administration had almost completely disintegrated as May 15 approached. It was a city without mail, buses, banks, courts, or railroads. Business had stopped, with many factories and office buildings isolated by Arab sniper fire. More important, it was a city with dwindling food, water, and fuel supplies—the essentials for a community's existence.

The committee immediately set to work on the food problem, and ran into equally swift resistance from people who wanted "business as usual." Requisitioning several firms that refused to cooperate, the committee consolidated the bakeries, which by the end of April were producing a daily ration of a third of a loaf per person. Without meat, fish, eggs, or milk (except for children), the people were encouraged to plant vegetables in their gardens with seeds from British stores.

Water was an even greater problem, since the pumping stations were all in Arab areas and could easily be sabotaged (they later were). With the help of Jewish officials in the British-administered Municipal Water Department, the Jews secretly pumped extra water into the main waterline and diverted water from pipes leading to British faucets. The water obtained was then quietly stored in hundreds of home cisterns, stone devices dating from ancient times when rainwater had been drained off from the roof.

Fuel was severely rationed, and housewives began cooking their meals over campfires in the garden.

At the same time, plans were laid for convoys to break through as soon as the road was cleared again, even temporarily. Arguments abounded over priorities.

"What about cigarettes, Dr. Joseph?" asked one committee member.

"Cigarettes? It's food we need. It would be criminal to waste three valuable tons of load on cigarettes."

"You say that because you are a nonsmoker, Dr. Joseph."

Joseph then called in five smokers and asked them their opinion. "Send cigarettes!" they shouted.

About the only people in Jewish Jerusalem who continued to eat and drink comparatively well were the news correspondents. They didn't mind the lack of water so much since the British supplied them with crates of surplus beer, which they used for shaving as well as drinking. And they had plenty of meat, since many cattle had been slaughtered in the fighting and the Jews were reluctant to eat nonkosher beef, despite the severe food shortage.[1]

The reporters needed all the energy they could muster to cover Operation Jebusi, which was designed to consolidate the Jewish areas of Jerusalem in preparation for the expected attack by the Arab States.* The operation had three major objectives: (1) to open a route to the enemy-surrounded kibbutz of Nevi Yaakov northwest of Jerusalem by capturing the Arab hilltop village of Nebi Samuel, which blocked the way; (2) to open a road to Hadassah Hospital and Hebrew University on Mount Scopus to the north by taking the Sheikh Jarrah area that isolated it; and (3) to connect the southern Jewish quarters of Mekor Hayim, Talpiot, and others to the rest of Jewish Jerusalem by seizing the missing link— Katamon.

The Jews ran into leadership troubles from the start. The overall commander of the operation, Yitzhak Sadeh—founder of the Palmach, and Orde Wingate's most illustrious pupil—had earlier had a bitter falling out with Shaltiel, the Jerusalem commander, whose Etzioni Brigade was to participate. Sadeh, like Mordechai Raanan of the Irgun, had wanted to continue through Sheikh Jarrah and force the Old City to its knees by surrounding it and attacking from the rear. But Shaltiel had refused to cooperate, insisting that he hadn't enough men for such an operation.

Then the assault on Nebi Samuel of April 26 ended in disaster when Palmach troops of Yitzhak Rabin's Harel Brigade neared the top of the hill at dawn only to find themselves caught in a murderous ambush. Many men were struck down as they retreated. The deputy company commander, Zehavi, though wounded himself, crawled down with his more seriously

* One reporter, Carter Davidson of the Associated Press, covered the war so energetically that he missed one of the biggest scoops in history. An assistant came running to him with the news that a Bedouin, while tending his goats on the western shore of the Dead Sea, had discovered some ancient manuscripts hidden in a cave. "Here we are in the middle of a war," shouted Davidson, "and you come to me with some fool story about antiquities!" The "antiquities" turned out to be the famous Dead Sea Scrolls, which offered evidence that a sect of Jews, the Essenes, originated Christianity 100 to 200 years before Jesus was born.

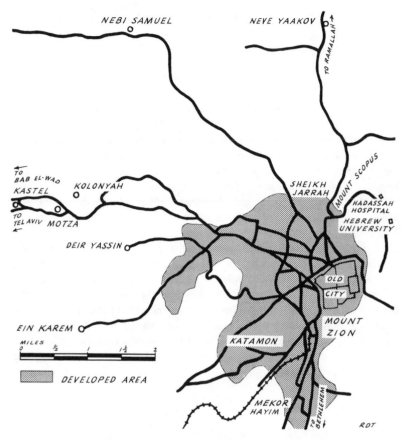

NEBI SAMUEL

NEVE YAAKOV

TO RAMALLAH

TO
BAB EL-WAD
KASTEL

KOLONYAH

SHEIKH
JARRAH

MOUNT SCOPUS

HADASSAH
HOSPITAL

TO
TEL AVIV   MOTZA

HEBREW
UNIVERSITY

DEIR YASSIN

OLD
CITY

MOUNT
ZION

EIN KAREM

MILES
0   ½   1   1½   2

KATAMON

DEVELOPED AREA

MEKOR
HAYIM

TO
BETHLEHEM

RDT

JERUSALEM AND ITS ENVIRONS

wounded commander, Poza, in his arms. Poza died on the way and Zehavi, after being hit again, was about to blow himself up with a grenade when a medical orderly rescued him.

The attack on the Sheikh Jarrah Quarter the same night fared better, as Jewish troops, in room-to-room fighting, dislodged Arab irregulars defending the area under Bahjat Gharbieh's command—that is, all but about five Arab snipers who, trapped on the roof of the Nashashibi house, kept lobbing grenades down the staircase. A British officer then intervened and negotiated with an attractive Jewish female squad commander for their evacuation. Intrigued by the girl, the officer kept negotiating for hours, and at one point, apparently to win her favor, even declared that of course he had nothing but contempt for the Arabs.

Meanwhile, higher British authorities had things other than romance on their minds. They ordered the Haganah, through the Jewish Agency, to evacuate Sheikh Jarrah completely since it was to be the British evacuation route, promising to maintain control of the quarter themselves and not to return it to the Arabs. When the Jews refused, British forces opened fire on the Nashashibi house. Haganah officers then agreed to retreat, having failed to call the British "bluff." As things turned out, the British kept their part of the bargain, and the Jews were able to reoccupy the quarter as soon as they departed.

While two Jewish columns were thus halted, if for different reasons, the third stabbed southward into Katamon, a quarter composed largely of luxurious Arab homes, and up a steep hill toward the massive Greek Orthodox monastery of Saint Simon, where an Iraqi unit of the Arab Liberation Army dominated southern Jerusalem.

Uri, the Jewish commander in charge of this operation, glanced at his radial watch dial as he lay behind a rock, then reached into his jacket pocket, pulled out his whistle, and blew it loudly. His men immediately began to clamber upward past wind-bent trees that bowed in eerie greeting until they reached the first of several stone fences. About 300 yards up, they could see the sign of the cross gleaming in the dark.

"Histaarut!" ("Charge!") Uri yelled.

Before the echo of his cry died, the hillside flashed to life with the rattle of gunfire while the Jews leaped fence after fence, guided by the shining cross.

"Draw knives!" Uri shouted as his men ran and crawled on up the hill, their knees bruised from the rocks, their hands bleeding from thorns.

Then, screaming once more "Charge!" he leaped over the last fence ahead of his men and sprinted forward like a man possessed. A machine gun spurted a deadly greeting, but still he ran. He caught someone by the neck, and drove his knife in deep, jerking it upward, then out. He slashed at another shadow, and fingers suddenly clawed at his face, ripping the skin from his cheek and thrusting into both eyes.

As Uri fell unconscious, his men piled through the iron gate and peppered the walls of the monastery and courtyard with bullets, toppling men off the roof and drowning out the cries of others already in flight. They smashed into the building, blindly spraying every room. In the commander's room, unlit, they heard a shrill scream and shortly after found the body of a young woman: secretary, girlfriend, prostitute?

The battle was over. Or so it appeared. But at dawn the Iraqis counterattacked, and seemed about to succeed when Palmach fighters climbed to the roof and dropped grenades on them.

In Amman, King Abdullah was deeply worried by the attack on Katamon but, despite the pleas of Palestinian leaders, refused to send in the Arab Legionnaires camped nearby and thus risk full-scale war with the Jews. But the King's commander in Jerusalem, Abdullah Tel, decided to help the Arabs, anyway. He supplied them with three armored cars and a number of soldiers dressed as civilians, and one of the cars spearheaded a new counterattack on the monastery.

By then, about half the Jewish force had been killed or wounded, but the rest managed to hold on encouraged by news that the Arabs were beginning to abandon the quarter. Jewish reinforcements finally arrived, and within hours all of Katamon had fallen. As the Jews tramped from house to abandoned house, they stared in amazement at the rich furnishings, the closets full of finery, the jewels, and the artwork. Amos Chorev, who had taken over command of the Jewish forces, saw the glitter in his men's eyes and ordered the homes to be blown up and burned. It was a pity to destroy such luxury, but it would be worse by far to see his disciplined soldiers break down and start looting.

KING ABDULLAH, alarmed by Katamon's fall, pleaded over the telephone with High Commissioner Cunningham for British intervention, but to no avail. Now he would have to take Glubb Pasha's advice. If he didn't make a final deal with the Jews immediately, they might take over the entire Old City and wreck his dream of ruling Jerusalem as the capital of a Greater Syria.

Unlike the Jewish leaders, who had come to regard an invasion by the Arab States as inevitable when the mandate ended, King Abdullah still thought that he could keep the other Arab countries from attacking while negotiating with the Jews for the peaceful division of Palestine. And an Arab League meeting held in Cairo on April 10 had confirmed his optimism.

In gloom and despair, the Arab leaders had listened to reports of Kaoukji's failures, the fall of Kastel, and Abd el-Kader el-Husseini's death. Finally, General Safwat had said: "In view of these latest developments, gentlemen, I believe we must now finally decide to dispatch our regular armies to Palestine."

Abdullah's delegate was ready to deal with this suggestion. He knew that Egypt, Saudi Arabia, and Lebanon wanted no part of an invasion by regular armies. And for all her outward belligerence, Iraq was still ruled by Hashemite kinsmen of King Abdullah who could be persuaded to support him. Even Syria, which so feared Transjordan, knew she wasn't ready for war. The Transjordanian representative thus announced that the Arab Legion would enter Palestine as soon as the mandate expired, and that it wasn't really necessary for the other Arab States to do so. As the King expected, the delegates reacted with mixed feelings of relief, concern, and confusion. Some seemed willing to let Abdullah bear the burden of a war they didn't want, but others, particularly the Egyptians, feared that Abdullah had made a deal with the Jews to grab for himself all the territory allotted to the Arabs under the partition plan.*

His main problem, now, Abdullah felt, was with the Jews, who had suddenly taken the offensive in April. He didn't mind them beating Kaoukji, who was far too ambitious. Nor did he grieve over the death of Abd el-Kader, the Mufti's only really able commander. And he had ignored Palestinian pleas for help in Tiberias and Safed, which, after all, were to be included in the Jewish State under the United Nations partition plan. But now the Jews were threatening to capture areas not included in their projected state. Even Jerusalem was in danger.

---

* It appears that Abdullah was well aware that Arab League secretary-general Azzam Pasha had secretly implored the British Ambassador to Cairo in late March to persuade his government not to withdraw British troops from Palestine as scheduled. And Azzam had been quietly encouraged to do this by both the Egyptian and Syrian Prime Ministers. Azzam told me that he had argued: "You've helped to build up Palestine for thirty years. You can't just pick up your things and leave the Arabs and Jews at each other's throats. If you agree to stay, the League will support your move. . . . We will even contribute to the cost of the administration. . . . And if you're leaving because of the Jewish terrorists, we will give you guerrilla support. . . ." But the British rejected the request.

Already they had taken Katamon. What would be next—the Old City? He must make a deal with the Jews before it was too late.

So he asked Glubb Pasha to send an officer through the lines immediately to conduct preliminary negotiations with the Jews.

On May 1, a few days after the fall of Katamon, Colonel Desmond Goldie, commander of the Arab Legion's 1st Brigade, stepped out of his car a short distance from Majami Bridge and returned the salute of Lieutenant Colonel Habis Majalis, who commanded one of his regiments (and who is today commander-in-chief of the Arab Legion).

"Habis," he said calmly, "would you please silence your guns for a while. I've got a mission over there and I don't want to get hit."

Majalis stared at him and exclaimed: "But it'll be dangerous, Colonel. You might get killed by either side!"

Goldie's driver immediately jumped from his car, saluted, and announced that he wasn't going.

Goldie shrugged, got in the driver's seat, and drove off, only to find himself in the middle of an angry Arab mob about a half-mile further on.

"Why are you going into Palestine?" one of the men demanded.

Before Goldie could answer, cries of "Kill the traitor!" went up, and the crowd surged toward the car. The Englishman thought the end had come when suddenly a voice cried out: "That's Goldie Bey!"

When the mob realized who he was, the leaders waved him past, and Goldie reached the relative safety of the Jewish zone. About an hour later, he was sitting with a group of Haganah officers in a house in the Jordan Valley village of Naharayim.

"I am authorized to speak in the name of Glubb Pasha," Goldie said as a Haganah girl set a cup of coffee before him. "We wish to prevent war and to maintain contact with you in the future. Is it your intention to conquer all of Palestine? The division of the country is a fact, you know."

He seemed to indicate that Transjordan still wanted to divide up Palestine peacefully on a permanent basis.

Shlomo Shamir, representing the Haganah, replied obliquely that borders were the work of politicians, but that in the event of an invasion the Haganah was capable of conquering the whole country. As for Jerusalem, it was Jewish, but if the Arab Legion did not attack the city there would be no armed confrontation there.

"We do not want to fight you," Goldie answered. But he added that care had to be taken that Transjordan was not made to appear as betraying the Arab cause. He conceded that in the first round the Jews had emerged victorious, and said that Arab morale had plummeted more quickly than had been anticipated.

"Insofar as the Legion will not fight and will act to prevent Arab aggression," the Jewish commander asserted, "there is no reason for us to fight you."

Goldie smiled and said that the Legion respected the Jewish fighters and was disgusted with most of the Arabs. Only the Bedouins (most Legionnaires were Bedouins) could be trusted.

When he rose to leave, the Haganah girl asked: "Weren't you afraid to cross the lines like this? How are you going to get back?"

"Oh, it's rather fun," Goldie said. "You know, a change in the routine . . ."[2]

When Goldie arrived back safely to say that the Jews seemed interested in a peaceful solution, King Abdullah was very hopeful. And he was delighted when Golda Meir and Ezra Danin, with whom he had dined in November, 1947, accepted an invitation to come to Amman on May 10.

But his hopes evaporated when he learned that the Arab League commanders had approved an Arab invasion plan at a meeting in Damascus. The League Political Committee was due to meet in Amman on May 11 to confirm this decision. How could he now make a deal with the Jews if other countries also entered Palestine?

There was only one possible solution. He would have to persuade the Jews to make major concessions. Perhaps they would agree if they thought they might be crushed in an all-out war. But it was unlikely.

Golda Meir and Ezra Danin felt they were speaking to a different man. The King, who had been cheerful and optimistic at their November meeting, was now sullenly fatalistic as he sat hunched in a chair. A close friend had secretly picked up the two Jewish representatives at Naharayim and driven them to his home in Amman through ten or more Arab Legion checkposts. The guards never suspected that the stout, black-veiled woman and the rotund man in a *khaffiya* were Jews, but it had been a risky ride, and now the visitors wondered whether the results would prove to have justified the risk.

Abdullah proposed that the Jews cancel plans for a Jewish State and retain autonomy for one year, after which all of Palestine would be absorbed by Transjordan. A joint parliament would be set up with 50 per cent Jewish membership, and the cabinet might also be 50 per cent Jewish. The only alternative, he said sadly, was war.

"But these proposals contradict the ones you made at our last meeting," Mrs. Meir pointed out.

Abdullah agreed, but explained that the situation had changed. The massacre at Deir Yassin had inflamed Arab feeling. And at that time he had been alone, while now he was only one of five. He regretted the inevitable ruin of great Jewish achievements in agriculture and industry if a war should occur, and could not understand why the Jews should be in such a hurry to declare a state.

"A people that has waited two thousand years can hardly be described as being in a hurry," Mrs. Meir replied.

She added that perhaps the Jews had been too patient, and then stressed that Jewish relations with King Abdullah had always been amiable and that they both had common enemies. The Jews had won important victories in the past weeks, and the Mufti's power had declined—to their mutual benefit.

"You must know," she said, "that the Jews are the only friends you have."

"I know that very well. I have no illusions. I know you and I believe in your good intentions. I believe with all my heart that divine providence has brought you back here, restoring you, a Semitic people who were exiled to Europe and shared in its progress, to the Semitic East which needs your knowledge and initiative. Only with your help and your guidance will the Semites be able to revive their ancient glory. We cannot expect genuine assistance from the Christian world, which looks down on Semitic peoples. We will progress only as the result of joint efforts. I know all this and I believe it sincerely, but conditions are difficult. One dare not take rash steps. Therefore, I beg you once more to be patient."

"We have no desire to mislead you," Mrs. Meir responded, "and we wish to make it perfectly clear that we cannot even consider your proposal. None of our responsible institutions, and not even ten Jews with any influence, would stand for such a plan. We can give you the answer here and now. If Your Majesty has turned his back on our original understanding and wants war instead, there will be war. Despite our handicaps we believe that we will win. Perhaps we shall meet again after the war when there will be a Jewish State."

As the King rose to leave after three-quarters of an hour of discussion, he hooked Danin's little finger in his own and walked with him to the door. Danin offered friendly advice that the King should more vigilantly guard himself against Arab assassins. Perhaps it was time, he suggested, to give up the old custom of permitting his subjects to kiss his hand or the hem of his robe when he visited the mosque.

"My son," Abdullah replied, "I will never depart from the custom of my fathers. I am a Bedouin . . . I will never prevent my subjects from expressing their affection for me."

As he stepped into his limousine, he said to Danin with a melancholy smile: "You didn't help me this time."[3]

When the King had left, the two Jews dined with his friend, but Golda Meir barely touched the food—to the chagrin of Danin, who was famished but would not be "impolite" by eating more than his fellow guest. The host then drove them toward Naharayim, and let them out about two miles away to avoid the checkposts.

"What will happen now?" Mrs. Meir wondered aloud as they trudged over the hills and crawled through barbed wire.

"If we win, we'll have ten thousand casualties."

"And if we lose?"

"We may have fifty thousand."

"You're a cruel man."

"No, I'm not cruel. It's the struggle that's cruel. The struggle to survive."

And Golda Meir was suddenly back in Kiev, watching her father and neighbors nailing boards across the doors and windows of their houses. Soon the peasants would be storming through the town shouting "Christ killer," beating and stabbing every Jew in sight.

PRESIDENT TRUMAN lived through some of his most painful days after the Austin speech proposing a trusteeship. He was filled with bitterness toward the State Department, and anxiety lest his friend, Chaim Weizmann, regard him as a dishonorable man. He did not blame Marshall personally for the policy reversal, feeling that he had been unwittingly led to believe that the trusteeship plan had official presidential approval.

But Truman regarded many of Marshall's subordinates less generously, persuaded that they were influenced by British traditional diplomacy in the Middle East or, in some cases, by anti-Semitic sentiments.

But what should he do now? Certainly he could not publicly repudiate the policy announced to the world at the United Nations, which would make the United States government look even more foolish. He would have to make the best of the new policy—and perhaps turn it to his ends.

The idea of a temporary trusteeship was not in itself so bad, he felt. It might be as good a method as any—and none were good—to postpone a dangerous international war in Palestine. The idea also had certain tactical advantages. Debate would be shifted from the Security Council, where Russia could always veto any American plan, to the Trusteeship Council, where decisions were reached by majority vote, and which, in any case, the Russians were boycotting.

Gradually, his approach began to take shape. First, he would personally reemphasize to the world that trusteeship was intended not as a substitute for partition but as a temporary means of filling a power vacuum. Then he would let the diplomats debate the problem—endlessly. It was not likely that they would agree on anything, and when the British left, an entirely new situation would arise; Harry Truman might just have a surprise or two of his own to spring on the State Department.*

Late one morning in mid-April, Joseph Linton was relaxing in bed when the telephone rang.

"Joe, come right over to my room, will you? I'd like you to meet an important visitor."

"All right. I'll get dressed," Linton answered Chaim Weizmann, who was staying just down the hall in the Waldorf-Astoria.

"No, never mind. Just put on a robe. It's urgent."

Linton went straight to Weizmann's room and found him sitting with a portly, gray-haired man.

"This is Judge Rosenman," Weizmann said, his face more lively than Linton had seen it for weeks; only the night before, he had been deeply depressed over the climate at the United Nations, where American representatives were pressing hard for trusteeship. The visitor, a White House adviser, had certainly brought good tidings.

Samuel Rosenman explained that the President had called him to the Oval Room and said: "I have Dr. Weizmann on my conscience." Truman had also said that he had not realized until the trusteeship proposal was actually announced that the State Department had gone so far in abandoning the partition plan, and that he wished to find his way back to the United Nations resolution. He would like advice, he added, but "the only man I'll listen to is my old friend the doctor."

"So if you would prepare some suggestions," Rosenman said, "I will submit them to the President."

Weizmann immediately volunteered that, first of all, the United States should recognize the Jewish State upon its birth.

A few days later, on April 23, Weizmann's spirits soared again when

* Truman's plan was reflected in a memorandum that William L. Batt, Jr., chairman of the Democratic National Committee, sent to Senator McGrath in reply to a query about what the trusteeship proposal meant. After checking with White House officials, Batt wrote:

The USSR will probably veto and the Security Council will not approve our trusteeship proposal. The next move is to call a special session of the General Assembly, for which we must obtain approval of 51 per cent of the membership. Whether or not we will obtain it is doubtful. . . . If we get the special session called, we will require a two-thirds majority to rescind the partition plan and another two-thirds majority to adopt trusteeship. It is extremely doubtful whether these will be forthcoming. . . . What happens if trusteeship does not pass? The United Nations will go ahead with partition.

Rosenman telephoned and asked him to come immediately to the Essex Hotel for a talk. He could tell from the tone of Rosenman's voice that it was good news.

"The President told me," Rosenman reported cheerfully (despite the fact that he was laid up in bed with a leg injury), "that he would recognize the Jewish State as soon as it is proclaimed. But he said that this must be kept absolutely secret."

Weizmann was speechless with joy. Now for the first time he was sure; there would be a Jewish State. As his visitor was about to leave, Rosenman grinned and said: "Have a nice Seder."

Weizmann and his wife were due at the home of their good friends, Siegfried and Lola Kramarsky, that night, Passover Eve, for the traditional Seder dinner. When they arrived Weizmann stopped at a bronze Epstein bust of himself in the hallway to place his hat on the head and a cigar between the lips. At the dinner table, he recited the first part of the Seder service and ate heartily. The others admired him for his uncanny ability to remain cheerful in the midst of distressing news from Lake Success.

As Truman had anticipated, the idea of trusteeship was meeting with severe resistance in the United Nations. Finally, when the proposal was hopelessly bogged down in partisan rhetoric, the State Department began to try for a simple truce under which the Jewish Agency and the Arab Higher Committee would supervise their own communities—without either declaring a state—after the British departed.

When the Jews showed reluctance, the Department, in desperation, started to threaten them. Lovett called Nahum Goldmann of the Jewish Agency to his office and said abruptly (according to Goldmann): "Dr. Goldmann, the United States is not going to risk getting involved in a war because of the obstinate attitude of the Jewish Agency. Will the Agency agree to our truce proposal?"*

"I can only say," Goldmann replied, "that I'll bring up the question again with the Jewish Agency Executive."

Lovett then lost his temper and pointed to a stack of files on his desk. "You see those files?" he asked. "That is all evidence of the violent, ruthless pressures exerted on the American government, mostly by American Jews. I wonder to whom they feel they owe their primary loyalty."

Goldmann, a Palestinian who had been born in Poland, was startled and incensed by this remark, but before he could reply, Lovett continued: "Unless you agree to our proposal we shall have to release this material

* The author tried but was unable to reach Lovett for comment on Goldmann's version of the meeting.

in a document that, I can assure you, will not be helpful to your cause."
Goldmann was not surprised by the warning. The Jewish Agency had
already received veiled threats that the United States might place an embargo against dollar remittances to Palestine as one form of sanction.
Ironically, he personally favored the truce plan, but he replied coldly that
the Agency would not be intimidated. He then took his leave and informed
Max Lowenthal, a presidential adviser, of the conversation. Lowenthal, in
turn, sent a memorandum to Clark Clifford dated May 11, 1948, reading:

> Suppose [the Jews] . . . base their action on their opinion, and con-
> trary to the advice we give them. Are we then going to engage in a policy
> of threat, of pressure, and of effectuation of threats? Such threats were
> already made by Lovett to Nahum Goldmann, though the threats were
> only of the issuance of a White Paper attacking Jewish leaders. [Under
> the note, Lowenthal had written: "Clark: Please do not let anyone else
> read this dynamite."][4]

At about this point, State Department officials began to mix their
threats with enticements. Egyptian diplomats, they told Sharett and Goldmann, had indicated in private talks that they would probably be able to
arrange for a meeting with Egyptian Prime Minister Nokrashy Pasha to discuss means of avoiding war—if the Jews would postpone proclaiming a
state. Department officials even arranged for Jewish and Arab representatives in New York to fly to Cairo on the President's private plane, the
Sacred Cow. But both sides rejected the proposal.

However, the better to gauge State Department intentions, Sharett flew
to Washington from New York on May 8 to see Secretary Marshall. Greeted
with smiles by Marshall—and Lovett, whose presence the Secretary had
requested—Sharett listened intently as the Secretary spoke of the danger
Palestine posed for world peace and of the urgent need for an immediate
truce and a postponement of Jewish national independence.*

As Marshall paused, Sharett opened a briefcase and removed a sheet
of paper, which he handed to the Secretary.

"I've just received this cable from Palestine," he said. "I think you'll
find it interesting."

Marshall read it, smiled briefly, and handed it to Lovett, who skimmed
over it expressionlessly. The cable reported that an Arab Legion colonel
representing King Abdullah had suggested an agreement between Abdullah and the future Jewish State whereby Transjordan would take over the
Arab portion of Palestine without Jewish interference, while leaving the
Jewish area to the Jews.

---

* Marshall told a Jewish Agency official at a cocktail party during the Arab
offensive that followed passage of the partition resolution: "I expected you Haganah
people to wipe out the Arabs as soon as they raised their heads, but you did not."

"There is nothing I would like more than such an agreement between Abdullah and the Jews," Marshall commented.

But Lovett said gravely as he turned to Sharett: "You seem to be assuming that the Arab Legion will not attack you and that you will reach an agreement with King Abdullah. But there will very likely be an invasion and you will be in trouble. In that event, you shouldn't come to us for help."

When Sharett replied that the United States had, in fact, forced the Jews to fight their own battle by refusing to come to their aid, Marshall (who basically sympathized with the Jews but doubted their ability to establish or maintain a state without the support of American troops), said gently: "It is not for me to advise you what to do. But I want to tell you as a military man: don't rely on your military advisers. They have just scored some successes. What will happen if there is a prolonged invasion? It will weaken you. I have had experience in China. At first there was an easy victory. Now they've been fighting two years and they've lost Manchuria. However, if it turns out that you're right, and you do establish the Jewish State, I'll be happy. But you are undertaking a very grave responsibility."[5]

After the meeting, Sharett hastened back to New York and told his Jewish Agency colleagues with deep conviction: "I am convinced of Marshall's good will. In my opinion, we should consider his plan for a truce and postponement of statehood. We can't afford to defy and antagonize the United States."

"I agree with Moshe," Nahum Goldmann said.

Other Jewish Agency officials, however, did not agree, but suggested that Sharett consult with Chaim Weizmann. Sharett then called on Weizmann, who was again ill in bed at his hotel, and repeated his view to him.

"Never!" Weizmann shouted in agitation. He wished he were free to tell Sharett of Truman's secret pledge. "I am an old man, and shall not live to see the state if we do not declare it now."

Weizmann then glanced at Joseph Linton, who was also present, and added: "He is a much younger man. And he will never live to see the state either."

The following day, as Sharett was about to board a plane at La Guardia Airport for Tel Aviv, he heard himself being paged over a loudspeaker and went to the telephone. It was Weizmann: "Tell B. G., tell everyone: it's now or never! Fear not, nor be dismayed."

But Sharett was still not convinced. On his arrival in Tel Aviv, he went immediately to see Ben-Gurion and tell him of the American proposal.

"What do you think of the idea?" Ben-Gurion asked casually.

"I think we should consider it."

Ben-Gurion's face hardened.

"Moshe," he said, "listen to me as a friend. If you don't want to ruin your life, don't say that in your report."[6]

*

When the Jews had rejected the truce plan, President Truman, at Clifford's suggestion, called a meeting in the White House for Tuesday, May 11, to discuss the question of recognizing the future Jewish State. The atmosphere was tense as Clifford, Niles, Marshall, Lovett, and McClintock gathered around the conference table.* After explaining that the issue of recognition had now become pertinent, Truman called on Marshall to give his views first.

Marshall said that he did not support immediate recognition of the Jewish State, if, indeed, it came into being. It must first prove its ability to stay alive in the face of what he considered the superior military force of the Arabs, and perform the functions of a state.

Lovett supported this view, maintaining that there was no point in deliberately alienating 40 million Arabs when they were so bitterly anti-American already as a result of United States support of the partition plan.

Truman then spoke to Clifford: "Clark, how about giving us your views now?"

Clifford, glancing at his notes only occasionally, asserted that recognition was consistent with traditional American policy, and that since the establishment of a Jewish State was inevitable anyway, the United States could better contain communism in that country by beating Russia to the punch.

"We must recognize the inevitable," he emphasized. "So why not now?"

Marshall exploded: "Mr. President, this is not a matter to be determined on the basis of politics. Unless politics were involved, Mr. Clifford would not even be at this conference. This is a serious matter of foreign policy determination, and the question of politics and political opinion does not enter into it."

Truman intervened calmly: "Mr. Clifford is here at my personal request since it seems sensible to air both sides of the question."

After further discussion, the President looked at Marshall and said: "Very well, General, I think we must follow the position you have advocated."

* McClintock represented Dean Rusk, his superior, who was unable to attend the meeting. It is interesting to note that Rusk and Clifford were completely at odds over Palestine, much as they were to be over Vietnam 20 years later, in 1968, when Rusk, as President Johnson's Secretary of State, maintained an uncompromisingly hawk position, while Clifford, as Secretary of Defense, helped to prevail upon the President to deescalate the war.

Israelis who dealt with Rusk regard him as having opposed the creation of a Jewish State with possibly more zeal than any other top State Department official, though later he did not appear to resist the generally pro-Israel policies of Presidents Kennedy and Johnson. An unsigned memorandum in Clifford's file detailing a conversation between Rusk and the memo writer (apparently Clifford) on May 8, 1948, one week before the end of the British mandate, reflects Rusk's bitter-end stance. Rusk, the writer states, insisted that a "simplified trusteeship" was still possible.

The conferees filed out of the room, silent and bitter. The President approached Clifford as he was gathering his notes and said: "I'm sorry, Clark. I hope you understand."

Clifford did. So strong was Marshall's opposition to recognition that to have overridden him on this issue would have been virtually tantamount to asking for his resignation. In the light of the dangerous world situation and Truman's deep, basic faith in the man, such action could not have been expected.

"That's all right, Mr. President," Clifford, a veteran attorney, replied. "This isn't the first time I've lost a case."[7]

Few men in the State Department were more coldly pragmatic than Robert Lovett, a Wall Street banker. He lacked both Marshall's underlying sympathy for the Zionists and the Lawrence-like attachment of many of his Middle East experts to the Arabs. He had been persuaded that support for 40 million Arabs better served American interests than backing for a few hundred thousand Jews, and he had opposed the establishment of the Jewish State on this practical basis. Since he did not have to overcome any emotional obstacles, it was possible for him to change his mind on this or any other question if the circumstances so demanded.

When he left the White House, therefore, he was in an unsettled state of mind. For the more he thought about Clifford's words, the more they seemed to make sense. Of course, he believed in the arguments he and Marshall had put forward, but he began to wonder if they necessarily applied to the rapidly changing situation. Forty million Arabs or no, the simple fact was that the establishment of the Jewish State now seemed, as Clifford had said, inevitable. Could one, from a practical point of view, ignore this?

Lovett mulled over these thoughts and spoke to some of his colleagues about his misgivings. A few of them, to his surprise, expressed similar doubts. Finally he made up his mind: he would call Clifford in the morning.

Clifford went to his office early on Wednesday morning, May 12, depressed by his rebuff of the day before. He was scanning the morning papers when the telephone rang. It was Lovett, asking to come over right away.

Less than an hour later Lovett was saying: "Clark, I've been thinking it over, and I'm a bit uneasy about the decision on Palestine. Maybe you were right about extending recognition."

Clifford's eyes brightened. "What do the others at the State Department think?" he asked.

"Well, I spoke with some of them yesterday, and they seemed worried, too. We're going to discuss it more today."

"I think you're headed in the right direction, Bob," Clifford said. "But what about Marshall? Do you think you can convince him? He's made a personal point of it. And the President will never act if Marshall doesn't give the word."

"Yes, I know. It won't be easy."[8]

ALTHOUGH an Arab invasion of Palestine now seemed inevitable, the big question mark was Egypt. She was still declaring to her fellow Arab States that she would not send her regular army, but only guerrilla volunteers, into Palestine. King Farouk, Prime Minister Nokrashy Pasha, and many senior generals feared that their regular army might well meet disaster if committed to battle, since it was essentially a parade-ground organization with virtually no training for combat. Nor was an army forged in combat necessarily the kind that Farouk could best depend upon to support his shaky regime.

Many ruling Egyptians conveniently blamed the British for the army's deplorable condition. It was the British who had trained and commanded the army for two generations, and until 1936, when an Anglo-Egyptian Treaty of Friendship and Alliance was signed, they had, it was charged, deliberately opposed every effort to develop it into an effective fighting force for fear that it might eventually be turned against them. Even since 1936, the British had done relatively little to build up such a force, these Egyptians complained.

A group of young officers, however, saw the situation in a different light. The British were indeed guilty—but of more than throttling Egyptian military development. They were guilty of maintaining in power a miserably corrupt class of pashas led by King Farouk himself. And these pashas —the big landowners, politicians, and military chiefs—were, in their view, no less evil than their British mentors. Heading this group of young officers was a hot-tempered captain named Gamal Abdel Nasser. . . .[9]

NASSER WAS BORN IN A DUSTY, MUD-HUT VILLAGE OF UPPER EGYPT. The son of a postal clerk, he had from an early age despised the King and the pashas who lived in gaudy palaces and played in Cairo's lavish gambling establishments with the profits squeezed from some of the world's most exploited peasants. But he detested them most of all for their role as "tools" of British imperialism. True, under the 1936 treaty, the British had evacuated all of Egypt except the Suez Canal Zone and given the nation at least nominal independence. But the British, in fact, still ran Egypt.

In his burning revolutionary fervor, Nasser joined as a youth the Young Egypt Party, an ultra-nationalist, green-shirted group with close links to Mussolini's fascism. And he regarded as a badge of honor the bandage he wore on his head after being clubbed by policemen in a student riot against the government and British imperialism.

Then, in February, 1942, his plans came to fruition. The Nazis had taken Benghazi, and King Farouk, pressed by demonstrating students and persuaded that the Germans would soon be in Cairo anyway, dismissed his pro-British government. But before he could install one that was anti-British, British tank-led units forced the gate of the palace, took Farouk prisoner, and released him only after he had signed a document appointing a pro-British premier.

The following day Nasser, overwhelmed with shame and rage, called together several other young officers and formed a Free Officers' secret society with the purpose of seizing power.

When the United Nations partition plan was approved in late 1947, Nasser—then a student at Cairo's Staff College—saw an opportunity to promote his objective: an invasion of Palestine. On the one hand, the Free Officers could help wipe out the stain of humiliation that had soiled Egypt's honor on that dark day in 1942; on the other, they would be able to take over positions of leadership in the army. For most top officers were upper-class "parasites" who had joined the army for the prestige and easy life, and would not dream of abandoning the officer club for the battlefield.

Nasser had no deep feelings about the crisis in Palestine, except for what he described as the "echoes of sentiment." But, he told a meeting of his colleagues, a cheap, spectacular victory in a war against the Jews who, after all, had never been reputed for their military aptitude, would serve the group's purpose. In his enthusiasm, he didn't share the misgivings of the more cautious and less ardently motivated senior officers.

Nasser decided to go straight to the Mufti, who was in Cairo hoping to organize volunteers for an invasion of Palestine. Without preamble, Nasser said: "You will need officers to lead the men in battle and train volunteers. There are a large number of Egyptian army officers ready to place themselves at your disposal any time you wish."

The Mufti smiled gratefully and replied that he appreciated Nasser's spirit, but that it would be necessary "to obtain permision from the government."

The government refused permission. Whereupon Nasser, bitterly disappointed, but by no means discouraged, decided simply to plunge Egypt into war on his own. He drew up a secret plan whereby certain Egyptian air force units would, without orders, take off and support Fawzi el-Kaoukji's operations against Jewish settlements. But the arranged signal from Damascus never came.

His hopes rose again, however, when the Cairo regime, under tremendous public pressure, agreed to permit some volunteers to attack in the Negev. This was only the beginning, Nasser was sure. When the British left Palestine, the government would have no choice but to send regular units to fight. And then, at last, the Free Officers would be on the path to power . . .

"Aziz, I've had my eye on you for a long time . . . I've decided to give you command of the volunteer guerrilla force . . . I want you to hit those settlements hard."

Lieutenant Colonel Ahmed Abd el-Aziz, a ruggedly built, tough-looking cavalry officer who lectured at Cairo's Staff College, felt that this was the happiest moment of his life.[10] Certainly it was a moment history would remember. The Minister of Defense, General Mohammed Haydar Pasha, was placing him at the head of a force that would attack the Jews in the Negev and, who could say, perhaps drive all the way to Jerusalem.

The government, until this moment, had opposed the dispatch of Egyptian volunteers to Palestine, and had made every effort to prevent them from going on their own. In particular, it had tried to control members of the Moslem Brotherhood, a fanatically religious pan-Islamic organization, whose principles were based on theocracy in private and public life, and which held foreign imperialism responsible not only for perpetuating Arab poverty, but for contaminating the Moslem spirit with heretical thoughts and customs. If the Brotherhood saw the Jews as lackeys of this imperialism, it little doubted that the Egyptian government was also such a tool.

Understandably, Farouk and Nokrashy, who worried enough about the loyalty of their own army, did not want openly anti-government groups forming their private armies. But they couldn't refuse a request by the Brotherhood to send a "scientific expedition" to the Sinai Peninsula, from where the "scientists" could easily infiltrate into Palestine. Nor could they ignore the public clamor, once the Brothers were in Palestine, for government support of their actions. So, belatedly, Nokrashy had agreed to organize a formal volunteer guerrilla force—with Ahmed Abd el-Aziz in command.

Finding little credible intelligence on Jewish armed strength, Aziz infiltrated personally into the Negev on April 7 to gather information. As he moved incognito through desert villages, dressed as a Bedouin, he was amazed to learn that the Jews were not nearly as weak as his superiors had thought. He wrote in his diary that the word "colony" in intelligence reports should actually read "fortification." Nor was his faith in the principle of hitting the enemy by surprise to remain unshaken when Arab notables in the villages he visited, having somehow learned of his identity, invited him to meetings to tell them how the Egyptians would crush the Jews.

Then, before he could prepare his men for battle, a group of Moslem Brothers that had already been in the Negev attacked on April 10—apparently on its own initiative—the religious kibbutz of Kfar Darom along the main Egyptian supply artery.

In an initial charge, the Egyptians reached a trench surrounding the settlement, but were chased back by heavy fire. A second attack with armored cars ended when an armor-piercing shell knocked the first one out, signaling a retreat during which many survivors were killed by their own artillery. The following day, an Arab tank broke through the front gate and smashed into the kibbutz, but a Molotov cocktail damaged it, frightening off the men in a second tank waiting outside the gate. Then, as the damaged tank gradually retreated, the Egyptian infantry charged, only to run into a minefield. The survivors, as they withdrew, were pursued by a barrage of ceremonial *tefillin* bags loaded with explosives.

When the battle was over, the Jews found a box of matches and a razor blade in the pocket of every dead Egyptian—the matches to burn down the settlement, the razor blade to castrate prisoners (according to Arab informants who lived nearby). Some wore, suspended around their necks by a string, a wrinkled parchment about 12 by 18 inches long, covered with Arabic script declaring the wearer "a true Moslem" fighting the *Jehad,* or Holy War, who was therefore immune "to all manner of lead and steel."

The Moslem Brothers, though possessed of a supreme courage born of religious and nationalist fanaticism, were convinced by their defeat that further frontal attacks would be suicide. And they expressed this view to Aziz, advising him that the volunteers should attack only Jewish communications and should sabotage the vital water pipeline to the Negev in order to force the Jews to fight on open ground outside their settlements. But Aziz would not listen. His orders had been to knock out the settlements, even though he led a supposedly guerrilla force.

It was all a question of surprise, he assured the Brotherhood leaders. And he would surprise the Jews when the time came.

Mohammed Abdel Aref, a scrawny Egyptian soldier, lay crumpled on the cement floor of his tiny isolated prison cell.

"Get up, Aref!" yelled the military warden, as he began to unlock the prisoner's ankle chains.

Another whipping, thought Mohammed. Oh God, not another! "What have I done now?" he whimpered.

"They're taking you away," the warden said. "They're giving you another chance."

Mohammed's sallow face, nearly hidden in a heavy growth of beard, lit up slightly. He had been in jail for almost a year. The fourth time in five years. And now that he was to be freed he was almost too tired to walk out. Salt and bread, salt and bread, sometimes lentils . . . it was hard to live on such a diet. Especially when he was sick with something called bilharzia, and had to carry sacks of rocks from one place to another day after day after day.

At last he would be going home again . . . Maybe this time they wouldn't find him so quickly . . . Why didn't they let him stay home at least for the planting and harvesting seasons so that he could help his sick mother and his blind father with the farm work? . . . How were they surviving? Begging again? . . .

He could still see his poor white-haired mother weeping and screaming as she followed while the policemen dragged him to the police station and locked him in a room with 70 other people whom they were also putting into the army. If only he were rich and had £20 to give the King, they would not have taken him. But his family hardly earned £20 in a year. How many *fellaheen* ever earned more that that from their landlords?

If he ran home again, of course, they would catch him sooner or later and whip him unconscious and throw him back into jail. Who cared about tomorrow? Today he would be back in his little village in the Nile valley. He would bury his feet in the green fields, and gaze upon the cotton, corn, beans, and clover, the tomatoes and vegetables. Then he would follow the narrow path leading to his little hut. And he would sit on a mat beside his mother and father and sip strong tea, surrounded by the animals that shared his dung-carpeted home—his chickens, geese, goat, and of course, his *gamoosa,* the beloved water buffalo who worked so hard and provided the family with milk, yogurt, and white cheese . . . Oh, if only Allah would lend him £20! . . .

"Don't think you're going to run away again," the warden said, when he had unlocked the chains. "It won't be so easy this time."

"What do you mean?"

"They're sending you to Palestine."

Mohammed, crestfallen, scratched his lice-ridden head.

"Palestine? Where is that?"

*

Mohammed Abdel Aref was one of thousands of Egyptian soldiers who learned a few days before the British mandate ended in Palestine that Egypt had decided to send its regular army into battle. When the Arab League Military Committee made the decision to launch a multiple invasion of Palestine—with or without Egypt and her ally, Saudi Arabia—Farouk had found himself in a serious dilemma. How could he explain to his restless people Egypt's aloofness from a war in which most of the other Arab States were participating? And without going all the way, how could he stop Abdullah from greatly expanding his kingdom and perhaps challenging Egypt for leadership of the Arab world? He reread the intelligence reports. Aziz almost alone seemed to think the Jews would be tough customers. True, the regular Egyptian army was in poor shape, but how good did it have to be to beat a few Zionist gangs?

Then Lebanese Prime Minister Riadh es-Solh and several other Arab dignitaries visited Cairo and urged Farouk not to let the Arab League down. Even Abdullah wanted him to join in the invasion, they said.

Farouk listened silently. He was a gambler, wasn't he—though never before with this much at stake. He decided to commit Egypt wholeheartedly to an invasion of Palestine . . .

Egyptian officers greeted the decision with sharply contrasting reactions. Young men like Gamal Abdel Nasser were overjoyed. But many of their seniors were shocked—none more so than Brigadier Mohammed Neguib, who was appointed second in command of the invading forces under Major General Ahmed Ali el-Mawawi. When he told Mawawi that only four of their battalions could be considered fit for battle, the General merely shrugged.

"We have our orders," he snapped. "Our duty is to carry them out, not to question them."

"On the contrary, sir," Neguib persisted, "our duty is to question every order that can't be carried out."

Mawawi then angrily reminded Neguib that he, not Neguib, was the commanding officer.

Neguib saluted and stalked out of the office. Moodily, he assessed his resources. Most of his soldiers were simple, sickly, illiterate peasants who should never have been conscripted. Many of his officers were heavily braided fops from "good families" whose relationship with their soldiers resembled that between man and buffalo. Well, at least he had the tall, powerful Sudanese. Though many were mercenaries, they fought like tigers. A company of them would lead each battalion.

He was also grateful that recently purchased arms were beginning to arrive—rifles, grenades, shells, planes, ships, from Belgium, Italy, Greece, and other countries. It did not occur to him that King Farouk was a man who did not gamble without making every effort to cut possible losses; that some of His Majesty's palace cronies, including Antoine Polly, his personal pimp, had bought millions of dollars worth of defective arms with government money—at a huge profit to the palace . . .

Perhaps even more astonished than Neguib about the Egyptian decision was Azzam Pasha. He learned of it, in fact, directly from King Abdullah at the very moment he was trying to persuade the monarch to follow Egypt's example and keep his regular army home.

"You can't be right!" Azzam exclaimed, ghostly pale.

The King merely smiled in bitter sympathy.

THE sudden prospect of invasion forced King Abdullah and Glubb Pasha to concentrate urgently on filling their arsenals while the British army, which had promised to equip a full division, still remained in Palestine. And the British, who depended mainly on Abdullah to safeguard their interests in the Middle East after their departure, were only too willing to cooperate in this crash program in the hope that he could force the Jews to accept peace on British terms.

British arms and other supplies were usually sent from the Suez Canal Zone through Beersheba and Hebron to Jerusalem and thence to Amman. But in the rolling gray hills overlooking the road north of Hebron sprawled the Etzion Bloc, which, though still isolated, had become a poisonous thorn in the Arab side. With the attack on Katamon about to start, the Haganah in April had ordered the Etzion settlers to stop all Arab reinforcements trying to enter Jerusalem from the south. After duly knocking out or damaging several Arab convoys in the next few days, the settlers were told to destroy all enemy communications with Jerusalem. They complied, blowing up a bridge and cutting telephone lines.

Glubb Pasha was infuriated, particularly since both he and the Jews hoped to avoid direct large-scale Legion-Haganah clashes even in the event of an Arab invasion of Palestine. The situation was further complicated by the public British commitment to clear Palestine of all Arab Legion soldiers by May 14, the last day of the mandate. Yet in military terms it was absolutely essential that British arms, and, especially artillery shells, should continue to flow from the Suez Canal Zone until the last minute. With the British gone, the road through Palestine would be closed. Glubb finally decided that he had to punish the settlers.

At dawn on May 4, Arab Legion tanks and armored cars—accompanied by infantry, mainly local Arab fighters—pounded Jewish outposts, particularly an old Russian monastery, in the most ferocious barrage of the war to date. The Arabs captured the monastery, but could not take the other outposts; the Jews, though greatly outnumbered, mowed down waves of attackers. By evening, the Arabs had withdrawn and the Jews reoccupied the monastery.

But the Jewish "victory" left the defenders with little to celebrate. They had suffered 42 casualties out of a total of about 400 men and women, and some of the fallen had been among the best Palmach fighters. At a meeting of the settlers and the small Palmach group of reinforcements, it was agreed that if it were not possible to strengthen the bloc very substantially within the next few days, its population—mothers and children had already been sent away—should be evacuated with British help. This view was transmitted to the Haganah High Command after much soul-searching and strong resistance by a minority who wanted to fight to the last.

But a few days later, on May 9, Moshe Silberschmidt, the bloc commander, addressed another meeting. His eyes calm and sad, he told his listeners that the High Command had decided the bloc must stand and fight whatever the consequences. There were too many weak and isolated settlements in the country and a voluntary evacuation of any one of them would sap morale and possibly affect fighting strength.

"But can we withstand an attack after last Tuesday's casualties?" someone asked.

"I'm not sure reinforcements can reach us before the decisive battle," the commander replied blandly. "So, let's face it. The next battle might be our last. But it must be a Masada."

The failure of the May 4 Arab attack burned away the last remnants of restraint in Glubb Pasha's pre-invasion strategy. By this time, it had become apparent that an invasion was inevitable and one of the biggest arms convoys yet—the last—was due to arrive in Amman on May 12. It had to get through at any cost. Glubb Pasha did not doubt that the cost would be extremely high (his intelligence reports indicated that the defending forces were many times more numerous and powerful than in fact they were). The Legion general staff therefore decided, apparently on

May 9, to destroy the Etzion Bloc once and for all before the convoy was trapped.

The role of the British army—if indeed it had any—in this decision is not clear. The British government was extremely anxious to arm the Arab Legion to the degree possible before it left Palestine. But an all-out attack by the British-commanded Legion on the Jewish colonies before the mandate ended would greatly embarrass London, which had, up to then, denied Legion involvement, at least of an offensive nature, in the Palestine war, and had categorically stated that Glubb's troops would not attack while mandate forces remained in Palestine. According to General McMillan, he and High Commissioner Cunningham had not been consulted about the pending attack and were "horrified" when they heard of what amounted to "mutiny" against the British army.

On May 10, Glubb drove to Hebron via a side road and was greeted by huge crowds clamoring to wipe out the Etzion Bloc. He met with Sheikh Mohammed Ali Jabary, mayor of the town, who had close links with the British, and Captain Hekmat Mehyar, commander of the Arab Legion troops based there. Together they formulated a plan for a coordinated attack by Legion forces and Palestinian irregulars on May 12—the day the final arms convoy was due. Glubb then returned to Amman and dispatched about 40 tanks and armored cars, as well as artillery, to Hebron, while Jabary sent out a call to villagers in the area to gather in the town. Four thousand men streamed in from all directions, bearing rusty rifles, Sten guns and, in many cases, large sacks—for loot.

"Tomorrow morning," shouted Sheikh Jabary through his bristly white beard when he came to greet them during the night of May 11, "we shall at last liquidate the Etzion Bloc."

Late that same night, Aliza Feuchtwanger was sitting on the floor of the recreation hall in Kfar Etzion, the largest of the four bloc settlements, listening to an accordion played by another kibbutz member. It was relaxing to hear music after concentrating on coded messages all day. Women weren't made to be soldiers—or radio operators. She wished she had back her old job of cooking for the soldiers based in Tel Aviv. Who wanted to be a heroine? The fighters had to eat, didn't they? And she was a pretty good cook. She had gotten away with it, too, until some hard-nosed officer found out she was a qualified radio operator and sent her to Kfar Etzion.

Aliza turned toward the stocky, rather homely young man sitting beside her and smiled. Actually, she had no regrets. Who could tell what manner of man she might have fallen in love with if she had remained a cook? Certainly she would never have found a man like Moshe Beginsky.

Such a funny name; yet it had been engraved on her mind before she even met the man.

"Beginsky, Beginsky, send Beginsky!" that was all she had heard over the radio. One would think he was more important than Ben-Gurion. He had arrived as a guard with the last convoy to reach the Etzion Bloc, and had started to return to Jerusalem when he was caught in the Nebi Daniel ambush. His truck had been one of the few able to turn around and smash its way back to the bloc, and he had been trapped here ever since.

Yet the Haganah command, apparently considering him its best platoon commander, demanded his return.

"Why doesn't he come? We're sending a plane for him. Send Beginsky! Send Beginsky!"

Who was this Beginsky without whom the war could not be fought? Finally, someone had pointed him out to her in the dining hall.

"Are you the important Mr. Beginsky?" she asked directly, having sat herself down next to him.

He stared at her merry eyes. "Yes, that's me."

And so they fell in love . . .

"Udrub! Wahad al wahad!" ("Strike! One after the other!")

This cry at dawn signalled a burst of bullets and shells and within seconds every outpost protecting Kfar Etzion was under heavy attack. The Jews had reached their positions and were cutting down wave after wave of attackers as they advanced from the hills and the valleys, but they could not hold out long and began to retreat either to Kfar Etzion itself or, if they were cut off, to the neighboring settlements not yet under direct attack. Among those who had to withdraw to one of these colonies was Moshe Beginsky, who commanded the mortar team atop Yellow Hill, the central stronghold of the bloc. He had run out of mortar shells.

By capturing the eastern outposts late that morning, the Arabs severed the bloc into three and dominated the airstrip; no more planes could land with reinforcements or supplies. They now directed the brunt of their attack against Kfar Etzion, assaulting all its defense posts—which were constructed in a wide circle around the crest of the hill—simultaneously. In desperation, the defenders pinned their hopes largely on an airdrop of arms and ammunition and on bombings of enemy positions.

Aliza kneeled at the top of the stairway leading to the cellar of the command post building and calmly sent messages to headquarters:

> 12:05 P.M.—We are heavily shelled. Our situation is very bad. Their armored cars are 300 yards from the fence. Every minute counts. Hurry the dispatch of planes.
> 12:53 P.M.—Hundreds of Arabs advance on Kfar Etzion . . . The

situation is desperate. We have many killed and wounded . . . Without immediate aerial support we will be lost.

1:45 P.M.—Heavy fire of artillery, mortars, and machine guns. The birds [aircraft] have not yet appeared. We have about 100 killed and many wounded. Establish contact with the Red Cross or help in any other way.

As Aliza tapped by the faint gleam of a kerosene lamp, she watched the wounded who lay on the damp cellar floor almost wall to wall, like rows of mummies in a dusty tomb. Many stared quietly back at her with anxious eyes, wondering what she was transmitting.

A young girl brought down some sardine sandwiches and water, but everybody stopped eating when a wounded man arrived with the news that Moshe Silberschmidt, their beloved commander, had been killed while leading a retreat from the Russian monastery.

The fighting finally slackened after dark. The kibbutz had managed to hold out despite severe casualties. At midnight, Haganah headquarters sent a query to the new commander, Yaacov A., asking whether he favored evacuation.

"Kfar Etzion," he replied, "prefers to remain where it is if it is possible to send reinforcements. If that is not possible, then we agree to evacuation."

Meanwhile, in the Jericho headquarters of Colonel Abdullah Tel, commander of the Arab Legion forces in the Jerusalem area, the telephone rang and Tel heard Glubb's excited voice.[11]

"Abdullah, Hekmat and his men have been fighting for sixteen hours now at Kfar Etzion and we don't know the result. I'm very worried. Hekmat, you know, is a police commander and he's had limited experience as an army officer. I suggest that you visit the battle area in the morning and see what's happening."

Tel was delighted. He had wanted to command the battle personally from the first, but Glubb had thought his presence unnecessary. Actually, he was convinced, Glubb hated him and simply wanted to keep him under his thumb.

Tel reached Kfar Etzion with some 50 men at about 4 A.M. on May 13, and surveyed the situation. He concluded that Hekmat Mehyar had made a mess of things. His forces were distributed all over the hills without plan, firing aimlessly. No one had eaten or drunk for more than 24 hours. Immediately, he shifted his troops around, assigned specific targets to the various units, and specified how many shells and bullets should be fired— though he ran into sharp resistance from Sheikh Jabary, who wanted to direct his own show.

Then the Arabs attacked again.

*

Lieutenant Nasri Effendi, commander of a Legion armored platoon, mopped the sweat from his face with a corner of his *khaffiya* as his armored vehicle plowed forward through a thick battle fog. He ordered the cars to halt at a point about 200 yards northwest of the settlement and start firing at the gate and the buildings commanding it. Then he ordered one vehicle to storm the gate and enter the farmyard. This would be his last attempt, he told himself. If his platoon didn't get through this time, it never would. He watched anxiously as the armored car sped ahead heedless of fire. It crashed through the gate and into the farmyard. Then several Molotov cocktails exploded and the vehicle jerkily withdrew. But the gate had been smashed! . . .[12]

"Okay, NOW!" shouted one of the defenders in a building close to the gate.

David D. pressed a button, but nothing happened. The electric anti-tank mine near the gate did not go off. As the armored car thrust at the gate, several Jews threw Molotov cocktails, most of which did not work, and forced it to withdraw, but immediately, under heavy covering fire, two other armored vehicles crashed through the breach, followed by hundreds of soldiers and irregulars.

As Aliza sat on the cellar stairs in the command post, she glimpsed through an open door some Arabs prowling around nearby buildings. Gasping, she contacted general staff headquarters in Tel Aviv without waiting to find the commander: "They've broken in! The Arabs are inside! What should we do?"

"Hold on!" came the reply. "Hold on!"

Aliza replied that this was impossible, that there weren't enough men and that ammunition was almost exhausted. Hundreds, thousands were pouring in. The hills were black with them, she reported.

But again the order was to hold on.

"Then send some birds [aircraft]!"

There were none to send, Tel Aviv answered.

The new commander, Yaacov A., came in, white-faced.

"Tell them we're surrendering," he groaned. "Then go up to the roof and hoist a white flag."

With tears in her eyes, Aliza sent her last message: "We are surrendering. I am destroying equipment and codes."

After smashing the radio set, Aliza grabbed a torn, bloody sheet from a cot, climbed to the roof, and fastened it to the antenna. Then, cupping her hands to her mouth, she yelled in all directions: "We're surrendering! Cease fire!" . . .

Yaacov Edelstein thought he was hearing things when a girl's voice shouted for a cease-fire. From his post, he wasn't able to see what was happening in the center of the kibbutz, but he was certain that his comrades were holding on just as the men at his post were. Every time the Arabs had attacked in his direction he and his comrades had halted them, even though the post commander had been seriously wounded.

He crawled to the command post to see what was going on, and Arab armor glinted all around.

"We've got to push them out!" he yelled to the bloc commander.

"The Arabs are in the settlement, and we haven't the force to get them out," the commander replied.

Edelstein looked around. Yes, it was too late. The shooting tapered off, and small groups of Jews emerged from the posts waving pieces of white cloth as they headed toward the command post. Everywhere Arabs were shrieking, shouting, laughing, some advancing slowly with guns cocked, others busy looting the charred buildings already in their hands.

When about 30 of the Jews, including Aliza and Edelstein, had gathered in a group near the command post, a number of Arab irregulars approached. Brandishing Sten guns, they ordered the prisoners to sit down, then to stand up and raise their hands. One Arab aimed his Sten at the group and another wanted to throw a grenade, but others cried out that the Jews should not be harmed. An Arab wearing a *khaffiya* then snapped a photograph of the group. An instant later another Arab opened up with a Sten gun, and others joined him in slaughter.

Most of the Jews died immediately, but a few scattered in all directions, miraculously still alive . . .

How could he be running, wondered Yaacov Edelstein as he groped through the fog of death. Was he really alive or was this the dream of a dead man? Minutes, perhaps hours, later, he found himself in a field near the Russian monastery, along with three other men who had escaped. So it was no dream. But why run? Reality bred a cruel logic. The Arabs were everywhere, and he was so tired. The four men dived behind some large rocks. After several moments, Edelstein rose to his knees to scan the countryside. The fog had lifted, and the world stretched before him with a strangely splendid indifference. The rocks all around shone in the sunshine—between them sprouted narcissi, cyclamen, anemones. The young forest seedlings were a vivid green, and the trees in the orchards were blossoming, their petals speckling the stony, black earth like snowflakes.

Then Edelstein heard a twig crack behind him and, startled, turned to look into the leathery, deeply seamed face of a frail, white-bearded old Arab wearing a dirty *khaffiya*. He held an ancient shotgun loosely under an arm.

"Don't be afraid," the Arab said with a toothless smile.

Edelstein and a comrade near him stood up and raised their hands.

"I won't hurt you," the Arab went on in a soft voice, his rifle still pointed to the ground. "All the people in Kfar Etzion are dead. They're all dead."

The two Jews were silent. Edelstein who, with the others, had left his rifle in the settlement, thought of grabbing the old man's gun. It would have been easy; the Arab was so old and weak. But what was the use?

At that moment, several other Arabs ran up and aimed their guns at the two prisoners.

The old man burst out: "You killed all the people in Kfar Etzion! What do you want from these two?"

"Shut up," said one of the group, "or we'll kill you too!"

"These men are under my protection," asserted the old man, invoking an Arab custom that forbids persons to harm anyone in the presence of a declared protector. "I won't permit you to kill them."

"We must kill them," one of the Arabs shouted.

"You've killed enough. Hundreds already. Why two more?"

During the heated discussion that followed two Arab Legion officers walked up, and one of them announced: "We're taking these two men as King Abdullah's prisoners."

The Legion officers then led the two Jews to their armored car. As they reached the car, Edelstein heard shots behind him. The irregulars had killed the other two men who had been hiding behind the rocks.

When the Arabs had started shooting at the Jews gathered near the command post, Aliza and several companions dashed blindly toward a nearby ditch and threw themselves down. The Arabs followed, firing into the ditch, and killing one after another. When one Arab aimed his rifle at Aliza, she screamed with such shattering force that firing in the area suddenly seemed to stop. The man standing over her pulled her out of the ditch, and in a moment other Arabs were crowding around her shouting at each other and trying to pluck her away from the original captor.

Finally, two Arabs, one on each arm, dragged her from the mob toward a forest bordering the farmyard, tripping over dozens of bodies as they advanced. The scene was chaotic. Looters were running in and out of buildings. Arabs shot at each other over a piece of furniture or a farm implement. No one noticed Aliza's hysterical screams any more.

As soon as they reached the woods, the two Arabs clawed at her, but fell out over who would rape her first. Each pulled an arm, like children fighting over a rag doll. Suddenly, the grotesque medley of screams, shouts, and curses ended with the abruptness of a Sten volley. In silent shock, Aliza saw both men drop dead at her side. Standing nearby with a smoking gun was an Arab Legion officer.

"Don't worry, you'll be safe with me," the officer said, leading her to his armored car close by.

He then practically shoved a piece of bread into her mouth. The bread was a symbolic form of hospitality guaranteeing her safety.

"Eat this," he ordered. "Now you're under my protection."

Then he covered her tangled black hair with his red and white checkered Arab Legion *khaffiya* to underscore the fact to the other Arabs.

"Who are you?" Aliza asked.

"I'm Captain Hekmat, the commander of the Arab Legion forces here."

As the girl stared, Hekmat demanded to know how many defenders there had been, where the arms caches were, and further items of military information.

"Everybody is dead," she answered vaguely. "Everybody is dead. I don't know anything."

Hekmat then led her to the command post and said: "You say everybody's dead?"

"Yes."

He removed a grenade from his belt, pulled out the pin, and handed it to her.

"All right, throw it into that building. If everybody's dead you have nothing to lose."

Aliza held the grenade in her hand. Thank God, she thought, that the wounded had been evacuated to the other settlements the night before. But she didn't know whether anyone was still in the post or not. Better to blow herself up . . .

Unnerved by her hesitation, the officer grabbed back the grenade and hurled it into the doorway himself. The explosion made the earth beneath them tremble.

"Yes, you're right," Hekmat said. "Everybody's dead."

The bodies of 20 or more girls were later found in the cellar, though it is not clear whether they were killed by Hekmat or earlier by other Arabs. Or had they killed themselves?

Hekmat then led the girl back to his armored car and, after they had got in, tried to put his hands on her.

Aliza pulled away crying: "You are an officer of the Arab Legion! And I thought officers of the Arab Legion were gentlemen! But I see you are no better than the men in that mob!"

Hekmat, clearly embarrassed, was silent for a moment. Then he stared at her and muttered with a smile: "All right, I'll take you home and make you my wife. You'll have a wonderful life with me."

Startled, Aliza replied: "You can't! I'm already married."

"Did your husband live here?"

"Yes."

"Well, everybody's dead. You're a widow now."

A shock went through Aliza as she thought for the first time of Moshe Beginsky. What had happened to him? She had not seen him since the battle began.

"Captain," she said finally. "I'm a soldier and I wish to be treated according to the Geneva Convention. I'm not interested in being your wife."

Hekmat ordered his driver to move on. Then he said: "How silly you are. I'll be forced to send you to prison. It's a shame. A nice girl like you. Do you know how dirty prisons are?"

Aliza could hear the Arabs lining the road shouting "Kill her! Kill her! Give her to us!" However, they continued safely to Hebron where another mob surrounded the car and demanded that the girl be lynched. A Legionnaire in an armored car to the rear fired into the crowd and Aliza and her escort finally arrived at the police station. Once more, Hekmat asked with a pleading look in his brown eyes: "Are you *sure* you want to go to prison?"

"Yes, I am!"

He guided her into the station and a sergeant at the desk asked her name. She glanced at Hekmat and replied: "Beginsky. Aliza Beginsky."

The sergeant then locked her into a cell.

"I'll come back tomorrow morning to see how you feel about it," Hekmat said.

In her exhaustion, Aliza collapsed on a cot and went straight to sleep.

The next morning, she was awakened by shooting, shouting, and other familiar noises outside the station. Prisoners from the other three settlements, whom the Haganah High Command had ordered to surrender after Kfar Etzion had fallen, had arrived. Within minutes, they were filing past her cell. One man halted and stared at her.

"Aliza!"

"Beginsky!"

A jailer led Moshe Beginsky to a cell down the corridor.

A short while later, Hekmat arrived.

"Well, have you changed your mind?" he asked with a grin. "Jail isn't so nice, is it?"

"But Captain Hekmat, my husband is here. He came in with the other prisoners."

Hekmat's jaw dropped.

"Oh, thank you so much for bringing him," Aliza said glowingly. "Would you do me a favor and put him in my cell?"

Gloomily, Hekmat replied: "No, it's against regulations."

When he left, Aliza and Moshe shouted to each other about their possible fate.

"Will they shoot us or hang us?" Beginsky pondered. "I'm an officer and I don't want to be hanged."

"Oh, don't worry, Moshe. I'm sure they'll shoot us."

A guard sitting in the corridor put his hands to his ears and yelled: "Shut up, you two, or I'll beat you both!"

"But he's my husband," Aliza cried. "Let him into my cell and I promise we won't make a sound!"

There was a further disturbance outside. Another batch of prisoners. As they crowded into the corridor, the guards, overwhelmed by the numbers, opened all the cells and jammed them with newcomers, not bothering to segregate the men from the women. In the confusion, Beginsky scrambled to Aliza's cell and crushed her in his powerful arms in the midst of other embracing couples. As they cuddled up in a vacant corner, Aliza said: "At last, Beginsky, you're around when someone wants you!"

At about 8 P.M. that night, May 14, a few hours after the State of Israel had been officially proclaimed, the Jews of Massuot Yitzhak, one of the four Etzion settlements, handed their arms to their Legion captors and climbed into trucks that would take them to Hebron—the last prisoners to leave the bloc. Ironically, one of the trucks struck a Jewish mine en route; among the several Jewish casualties was a pretty, blue-eyed girl.

Sheikh Jabary, who was accompanying the convoy, jumped out of his armored car, ran to the wounded girl, and carried her to his vehicle. The man who had whipped up so much fury against the Jews of Etzion then drove the girl to his home in Hebron at full speed, and attended carefully to her wounds. After making sure she was comfortable, he left to lead his people, as required by the political rules, in chanting before the Legion-protected police station: "Give us the Jews! Give us the Jews! Remember Deir Yassin!"

The prisoners were all sent to a camp in Transjordan, but after several months, toward the end of the war, they were released. As she was leaving, Aliza—one of only four Jews to have survived among those in Kfar Etzion at the moment of surrender—met Captain Hekmat again. He bid her goodbye and then, with a sheepish smile, said: "I've treated you like a gentleman, haven't I?"

"Yes, you have."

"Would you mind putting that in writing?"

Aliza was astonished, and somewhat moved. Yes, he—and the other Legionnaires—had treated the Jewish prisoners well, even kindly. They had permitted lovers—like Moshe Beginsky and herself—to have occasional rendezvous. And when the Jews, particularly the older ones, had quarreled among themselves, the guards had reacted like flustered parents. "Aren't you ashamed?" one Legion officer had lectured them. "You are insulting your country. Look at the other soldiers. Israel can be proud of *them!*"

"I'd be glad to put it in writing," Aliza replied.

Hekmat pulled a pen and sheet of paper from his pocket and handed them to her. Aliza scribbled: "Captain Hekmat has always behaved like a gentleman. [Signed] Aliza Beginsky."

"Thank you," Hekmat beamed. "Thank you and good luck."

Aliza then left for Jewish Jerusalem and married her fellow prisoner, Moshe Beginsky, thereby validating the signature on the character reference.

WITH the British about to depart, the time had come for Sergeant Major Desmond Rutledge, who had supplied the Haganah with considerable arms, to make his final move—and, incidentally, prove his love for his Yemenite sweetheart, Miriam. Indeed, he wondered if he hadn't waited too long. With the evacuation of British troops in progress, all leaves had been cancelled for his camp at Tel Hashomer near Tel Aviv. But he discovered to his relief that Tex, the sergeant who had helped him smuggle out arms, was free to come and go as commander of an armored unit escort.

"Then take me to see Miriam," Rutledge pleaded. "I've got to see her before we leave."

"Well, things are pretty tight now," Tex said. "But okay . . ."

And he suggested that Rutledge let him know via some Jewish civilian employees in the camp—Haganah contacts—when he wished to return so that he could be picked up.

"Good idea," Rutledge said with a smile—though he had no intention of returning this time.

A few days later, Rutledge jumped out of Tex's armored car to greet Miriam and other Haganah friends at the usual café near Tel Aviv. When the car had left, one of the Haganah men said thoughtfully that such a vehicle could be of considerable use to the Jews.

"I don't think Tex would give it to us," Rutledge responded. "They'd never let him out of jail if he did."

"Who says he has to *give* it to us?" asked the Haganah man.

The next day, Rutledge sent word for Tex to come for him. The sergeant came promptly—and found himself ambushed en route. Several Haganah men jumped into the armored car and ordered him to drive to the café, where he was heading anyway.

"I'm sorry, Tex," Rutledge apologized with a thin smile, as the two Englishmen and the abductors sat down for coffee. "But it's not your fault if the car has been forcibly taken from you. You'll be safely escorted to the police station in Nathanya. Then you can say what you like. Put the blame on me if you wish. I'm not going back."

After a silence, Rutledge resumed in a matter-of-fact voice: "But of course, you have another alternative. The Haganah is preparing for war. They need people with your experience. If you're interested, stay here. We'll fight the Arabs together."

To everyone's surprise, Tex didn't immediately reject the proposal. He reflected for several moments, then said: "I'll stay here tonight and think it over."

Whether from fear of returning without the car or from a spirit of adventure, Tex, no idealist, announced the next evening that he would stay.

Rutledge embraced Miriam joyfully. Then he walked her home—accompanied by a Haganah escort. The lovers no longer feared the British army but the Irgunists, who, unaware of Rutledge's role, had threatened to kill both of them if Miriam continued to "betray" the Jews by associating with a British soldier.

Meanwhile, Sergeants Michael Flanagan and Harry MacDonald were making *their* final move—the seizure of four Cromwell tanks. Having completed the two Haganah truck drivers' training by means of drawings and furniture props, they finally set off early one evening for Haifa Airport, which the tanks were guarding, and watched a small private plane land. The Jewish pilot and the owner of the plane stepped out, waving their passes to British officials—who did not bother to check whether anyone remained on board.

At midnight, when it was time for a change of guards, Flanagan and MacDonald, who were superior in rank to the guards, volunteered to take over the next shift.

"Everybody should do his share, even the sergeants," Flanagan explained with a grin.

At 12:30 A.M., three figures slipped out of the parked plane—the two

Haganah truck drivers and a man to cover them—and made their way
quietly to the tanks. There was not a word exchanged as Flanagan crawled
into the first tank, MacDonald into the second, and the two Haganah men
into the third and fourth.

Flanagan closed his eyes for a moment as if to shut out the thought of
what awaited him if the plot failed. The tank crews were asleep—he hoped
—in a hangar only about 20 yards away. He would have no time even to
make sure the rear tanks were following. Staring at the complex dashboard
with its switches and meter readings, he thought of the furniture arrangements that had served as the tank compartment and groaned quietly.

Then his tank, with a deafening roar, started up successfully, skidded
forward, and lurched toward a side gate in the fence leading to the Haifa
Bay area, which wasn't guarded. Within minutes, he had smashed through
the gate, which landed atop MacDonald's tank some 20 yards behind. Both
vehicles slithered down a side road to a rendezvous with three jeeps already
waiting. One jeep flashed a signal, and the tanks followed for about five
miles to a spot where two huge transporters were to take them on and
drive them to Tel Aviv.

"We've just had a radio signal," a Haganah man said as everybody
descended from their vehicles. "The transporters aren't coming. We'll have
to make our own way to Tel Aviv."

"The other two tanks—where are they?" another Haganah soldier
asked.

Flanagan looked back down the road, as if hoping for a miracle.

"I don't know," he said. "I thought they were following us."

The convoy then continued on to Tel Aviv where the plight of the
other two tanks was learned. The driver of the third tank had broken his
gear stick while trying to make a turn inside the camp, while the other
was unable to find the ignition switch and never got started. Both men,
however, had managed to reach safety.

And two Cromwells were better than none.

On the night of May 13, the British police in Jerusalem locked up their
stores and brought the keys to the United Nations representatives, who
had not been previously permitted to share in the administration of Palestine. A United Nations official indignantly refused to accept them, arguing
that the British were responsible for law and order until the mandate
ended at midnight on May 14.

"If you don't accept these keys," said a British officer, "we shall leave
them on your doorstep."

And he did.

The next morning an honor guard of Highlanders, dressed in shorts and khaki berets topped with red pompons, lined up outside Government House while tanks and armored cars fanned out around the palatial gardens. At exactly 8 A.M., 16 hours before the mandate was to end, Sir Alan Cunningham, the High Commissioner, stepped from the building, his eyes sad. He reviewed his guard of honor, made a short speech, shook hands with men in bowler hats and dark, doublebreasted suits, and climbed into a sleek Rolls-Royce. He had refused to leave in an armored car as advised by his assistants, being determined to depart "in style." As the Highlander bagpipers played a mournful Scottish funeral dirge, the car moved swiftly down British-guarded streets lined with sandbags—behind which Jew and Arab peered contemptuously from opposite sides at this final flutter of empire.

At Kalandia Airport, Sir Alan climbed into a Dakota bound for Haifa, from where he would sail home. As the plane flew high over swooping brown hills and green valleys, he pressed his face to the window. Thirty years before, General Allenby had entered Jerusalem on foot to be welcomed joyously as the liberator of both Arab and Jew from Turkish despotism. Could Allenby have envisioned the sullen, silent faces that would one day bid farewell to the British? Cunningham muttered in his agony: "How is it possible to divide this country . . . ?"*

I N THE Jewish Quarter of the Old City morale had plummeted. Abraham Halperin had achieved a miraculous psychological revolution among people sunk in despair, poverty, and hopelessness, but his sudden departure had a shattering effect. His successor, Moshe Rousnak, was unable to maintain the mood of determination Halperin had evoked.

Rousnak was a meek-looking man with a small, tightly knit face dominated by a large mustache and a prominent upturned nose. Born in Czechoslovakia in 1924, he had become an officer in the Haganah only in late 1947, after attending a noncommissioned officers' school for a short time. Now, a few months later, as the result of chance circumstances, he was top commander in this highly sensitive post.

He had chosen to turn over control of civilian affairs to a leading rabbi,

---

* Ben Oyserman, a British-Israeli film producer who was killed 20 years later while covering the Six Day War, was in the plane with Cunningham and heard him utter these words.

Actually, the last British troops, accompanied by General McMillan, left Haifa only on June 30, 1948. "I hereby hand over to you one port," McMillan said to an Israeli official as he was about to depart. "I hereby accept one harbor," the official replied.

though he retained ultimate authority, in order to concentrate on military activities. But he found time to relax with an attractive brunette nurse, Chava Kirschenbaum, whom he managed to see quite often since command headquarters was at that time located in the hospital building where she worked. Often she helped him with his paperwork. Leisure time, however, remained a luxury.

On March 28, Rousnak faced his first big test as a battle commander. He had received a message from Haganah headquarters in the New City the preceding day telling him to "be patient with the British," and not risk casualties by engaging in battle with them unless absolutely necessary in view of the quarter's critical shortage of fightingmen, every one of whom was essential for the confrontation with the Arabs when the British departed.

But the very next day he found himself openly challenging the British. What happened was that a detachment of British soldiers led by their local commander were searching a synagogue when they found a mortar hidden in a back room—the Haganah's only mortar. When Rousnak learned of this, he was aghast. It was essential to get the mortar back and prevent the British from confiscating the whole Jewish reserve of arms. He sent an officer to the British commander with a demand that he and his men give up the mortar and their own weapons and leave the synagogue area immediately—or prepare for battle.

The commander, a major, rejected the ultimatum and holed up inside the synagogue while the Jews opened fire.

"Send help urgently!" he shouted over his walkie-talkie from behind a window. "I've been hit in the shoulder."

But before British reinforcements could arrive the major, bleeding profusely, emerged into the street with hands raised.

"I wish to speak to your commander!" he yelled.

A messenger ran to Rousnak, who sent back word that his demands still stood. The major then agreed and a cease-fire followed after British troops had killed a number of civilians in a burst of rage. The British had been forced, in effect, to recognize the "Jewish army" for the first time.

Later that day, Rousnak was sitting in his office contemplating with satisfaction the magnitude of his victory when Rabbi Weingarten stormed in.

"What have you done?" he cried. "Are you mad, fighting the whole British army?"

"Calm down," Rousnak replied. "The British have agreed to let us carry our weapons openly and not to bother us any more."

"I don't care what they agreed to," Weingarten said heatedly. "It is utterly irresponsible for you boys to fight the British army. You'll end up getting us all killed and they'll stop the convoys coming through altogether."

Prime Minister David Ben-Gurion and his wife, Paula.

President Chaim Weizmann presents a torah to President Harry S Truman.

The Grand Mufti of Jerusalem, Haj Amin el-Husseini, greets a guest.

Palestine Arab officers; the top military leader, Abd el-Kader el-Husseini,
stands in the middle wearing crossed bandoliers.

Jerusalem's Ben-Yehuda Street after Arab bombing.

King Abdullah of Jordan.   *Zionist Archives and Library, New York*

Gen. Sir John Bagot Glubb (Pasha), left, commander of the Arab Legion,
meets with U.S. Col. William Riley, right, chief United Nations observer.

Arab Legionnaires at Mandelbaum Gate in Jerusalem.

United Nations

Fawzi el-Kaoukji, commander of the Arab Liberation Army,
accepts cheers of Palestine villagers.

Arab refugees flee Jaffa.

Arab refugees rest during flight.

Palestine Arabs charge up slopes of Kastel near Jerusalem.

Jewish forces occupy Kastel.

Prime Minister Ben-Gurion reads Israel's Declaration of Independence.

The Arab League holds a secret session in Cairo; Secretary-General Abdul Rahman Azzam Pasha is seated third from right.

The last British soldier to leave Palestine, Lt. Gen. Sir Gordon McMillan, commander of British forces in Palestine, sails from Haifa.

Count Folke Bernadotte, left, United Nations mediator for Palestine, confers with General Lundstrom, his assistant.

British United Nations Ambassador Sir Alexander Cadogan, British Foreign Secretary Ernest Bevin, American Secretary of State Gen. George Marshall, and Canadian Prime Minister McKenzie King attend the funeral of Count Folke Bernadotte.

Palmach Commander Yigal Allon.

Israeli Chief of Staff Yaacov Dori.

Israeli delegates sign Armistice Agreement between Egypt and Israel; left to right,
Eliahu Sasson, Acting Chief of Staff Yigal Yadin, Chief Delegate Walter Eytan,
and another Israeli.

Yitzhak Sadeh, founder of the Palmach and commander of the 8th Armored Brigade.

David Shaltiel, commander of New Jerusalem.

Israeli Commander Mordechai Makleff.

Givati Brigade officers confer; Commander Shimon Avidan is in center.

Israelis en route to El-Arish in the Sinai; Yeroham Cohen is at extreme left,
Yitzhak Rabin is second from right.

Rousnak looked at him coldly, then said: "Is there anything else, Rabbi Weingarten?"

"Yes. I suggest you turn over command of the Jewish Quarter to Yitzhak Dagani, who has had considerable military experience and who has the confidence of the people of this quarter."

Rousnak was startled. Dagani had married Weingarten's daughter, Rivca, only a week before. To put him in command would mean, in effect, putting Weingarten in command.

"I didn't buy my job on the market," Rousnak answered after a pause. "Do you think I can hand over my command to anyone who asks for it? *Shalom,* I'm quite busy."

If Weingarten was at odds with Rousnak, as he had been with Halperin, over policy and personnel, he did not hesitate to use his influence with the British on behalf of the quarter's defense effort, apparently feeling that if war with the Arabs had to come, however much at fault the wild-eyed Haganah men might be, it was best to be prepared for it.

His daring, high-spirited daughter Yehudit was a prime instrument in this effort, having been put in charge of her father's office in the New City, which had not been closed despite the transfer of his powers to the Haganah. Indeed, the Haganah did not want the office closed, for its existence gave Yehudit an excuse to travel between the Old and New cities as an agent.

Yehudit had often arranged for Haganah people to be smuggled into the Old City in food or Red Cross convoys, with certificates signed by her father saying they were civilian residents of the Jewish Quarter who simply wanted to be reunited with their families. Sometimes, she had also managed to smuggle in arms or other essential items hidden in crates of food. She was particularly effective at this because of her buoyant, impish nature, which lent credibility to calculated flirtations with key officers and drivers.

On April 28, Yehudit was faced with her biggest challenge to date. She was to smuggle in a vitally needed Lewis gun, the firepower of which could play a decisive role in the defense of the Jewish Quarter. Having been instructed by the Haganah to pick up a large suitcase containing the dismantled gun at the front gate of the Jewish Agency building, Yehudit walked over to the British officer in charge of a convoy bound for the Old City and said, smiling sweetly: "Lieutenant, my father asked me to bring him a suitcase with his personal possessions." She paused, then added: "Would you be kind enough to lend me two strong soldiers to help me carry it over here?"

"Why of course, Miss Weingarten," the officer said happily. "I'm always glad to be helpful."

A few minutes later, two burly British soldiers were taking turns carrying the suitcase from the Jewish Agency building about two blocks away to the compound where the convoy was preparing to leave. As one of them put it down for a moment, he wiped the sweat from his face and grinned: "I say, this is heavy, Miss. What have you got in it, a Bren gun or something?"

Yehudit smiled and said: "A fine sense of humor you boys have! Let's hurry or we'll miss the convoy."

With the suitcase safely in the rear of an armored scout car—Weingarten's "possessions" were never inspected—the convoy started toward Zion Gate. The scout car was moving fast when the car in front halted abruptly for some reason, causing it to brake suddenly. The suitcase skidded along the floor and struck the driver's seat hard.

The officer next to the driver looked around and said to Yehudit, who was in the back: "You must have a bomb in there! I don't want to get killed in a food convoy."

Yehudit's face whitened but she responded with a smile: "Sure I have. That's why I came along. There's nothing like being blown to bits to relieve one's boredom."

The officer laughed. "You Jews have all the answers, don't you? Incidentally, since you're so bored, perhaps I can see you tonight?"

Further back in the same convoy sat three girls, none of whom had met before, yet all experiencing at this moment equal excitement.

Judith Jaharan had finally been able to pester her Haganah superiors into getting her an accommodation, registered as a nurse, so that she could visit her sick mother. For months she had been unable to see her though living so close by. The Haganah expected her back after a few days; in fact, in the next convoy, but that was better than nothing. When she returned to the New City, she wouldn't mind so much having to stand guard on cold street corners at night.

Rika Menache sat with her arms hugged around her. At last she would be seeing Emmanuel again, after almost a year, ever since he had left for Cyprus and she for the Congo. So much had happened since then—the United Nations partition resolution, the fighting with the Arabs. She had still not completely recovered from her experience during the attack on the convoy at Nebi Daniel a few weeks before. As soon as she had got to the New City she had searched for Emmanuel and, having learned that he was in the Old City, tried to persuade the Haganah to send her there—in any capacity. She was going officially as a teacher; but she would be willing to be just a plain fighter if she could fight beside Emmanuel.

Beside her in the armored car was Esther Ceilingold, a slim, thin-faced girl with a haversack on her back who had just arrived from England eager to join in the struggle for a Jewish State. A grade school teacher just out of college, she had been determined to fight, not simply in Palestine, but in the Old City, the symbolic heart and soul of the struggle. There was something thrilling about risking death in Jerusalem as her forefathers had done thousands of years before.

"Don't be so ready to die," Rika said, amused by her ardor. "Jerusalem is important as a symbol, of course, but the most important thing is the practical business of setting up a state so that immigrants can come in. If you're going to be a fighter, always think in practical terms. Then you may live long enough to enjoy the symbol."

Esther contemplated this for a moment, then said: "Maybe so, but somehow you can identify yourself so much better with people in the Bible when you're fighting for a synagogue in Jerusalem than for a sand dune in the Negev."

As Independence Day approached, the Haganah guards watched from the roofs of houses and synagogues for the least sign of British withdrawal. The British had said they would leave Palestine by May 15, but it was considered likely they would march out of the Old City a bit earlier to join troops going from new Jerusalem. And the Jews of the quarter, with their small margin for survival, could not afford to let a minute pass between the time a post was evacuated and the time they occupied it.

Finally, on the morning of May 13, Rousnak received his first hint that the British were leaving that day when a short, blond British soldier approached him at one of the posts, saluted, and said nervously: "My name is Albert Melville. We're leaving now, but I'd like to stay here and fight with you."

Rousnak's first impulse was to regard the man as a spy.

"Why do you want to fight with us?" he asked suspiciously.

"I hate the Arabs. When I was in Algeria after the war they threw me out of a bar, right through a plate-glass window. Nearly killed me. Besides, I think you Jews have a pretty good case."

Rousnak examined the man's papers carefully. Then he relieved him of his rifle and 200 bullets, saying: "All right, if you want to stay you can. From now on, you're Private Albert Cohen."

About 15 minutes later, a Haganah liaison officer confirmed that the British were indeed leaving. "Major Allen just informed us," he said.

Rousnak urgently radioed the news to Shaltiel, and asked for an immediate response to a long-unanswered plea for more men and arms. He

then ordered his men to be ready to move on a moment's notice to implement Operation Horned Snake, the name given to a plan for seizing first
evacuated British positions, and then Arab posts separating the quarter
from the New City. Climbing onto the roof of a small stone house, he
watched scores of British soldiers march down the narrow, dark streets in
orderly files, looking straight ahead while two men from each squad walked
with their guns cocked observing every window and roof.

"They're really going," Rousnak muttered, with mixed feelings of joy
and apprehension. Now it was all up to him.

Major Allen, the British commander, halted his men in front of Weingarten's house and walked over to the old man, who was standing at the
front door. He saluted him and handed over the keys to Zion Gate, saying
in a voice faltering with emotion: "From the year A.D. 70 until today, the
keys of Jerusalem have never been in the hands of Jews. This is the first
time in more than eighteen centuries that you are so privileged."

Allen, who had been more friendly to the Jews than most British commanders, then gave Weingarten a Sten gun and a few magazines of ammunition and added: "Our relations have not always been too smooth
lately, but I personally did what I could for you. Your fighters are first-
class . . . Let us part as friends. I hope that you will have a complete victory. Good luck and *shalom.*"

Weingarten removed his glasses and wiped his eyes, and a Haganah
fighter standing nearby, moved by this farewell statement, cried out: "Good
luck!"

The British continued on their way, winding through the narrow
streets to Zion Gate and into the New City, leaving behind bitter memories
mingled with a strange affection for them as individuals. Within seconds,
six armed Haganah men in civilian clothes and steel helmets had occupied
the nearest British position, and within minutes, others had taken over
every British post overlooking the Jewish Quarter. By 6.30 P.M., stage 1
of Operation Horned Snake had been completed.

As the deadline for action approached, Jewish leaders on May
12 gathered in Tel Aviv to reach a decision that could mean life or death
for the whole Jewish community of Palestine. The question was: Should
the Jews proclaim a state immediately or wait until some future time as
the United States was demanding under her new truce plan?

The torment of that question was written on Ben-Gurion's haggard face as he entered the conference room for this historic meeting of the National Council of Thirteen, a body he had set up to replace the Jewish Agency Executive as the supreme ruling group and to assume the role of provisional government when the mandate ended. His own answer to the question was always: a state, of course. But then a hundred gnawing doubts overwhelmed him. The news from Kfar Etzion was terrifying; was this an omen of the future? He went over the situation again and again. On paper, the Jewish position did not look too bad. The Jews had, after all, won decisive victories over the Palestine Arab irregulars. They held the coastal strip of Palestine almost solidly from Tel Aviv north to Haifa; they occupied most of eastern and western Galilee, though the central belt extending south to Nazareth was still under Kaoukji's control; they had a firm grip on the Beisan Valley, and some control over a road network in the Negev which linked together 27 dispersed settlements; they were holding out in Jewish Jerusalem despite renewed Arab efforts to starve the city.

On paper, too, the Jewish forces seemed numerically a match for the combined Arab forces. Although drawn from a total population of about 40 million people, Arab troops likely to be committed to battle numbered only about 23,000 men, including 10,000 Egyptians, 4,500 Transjordanians, 3,000 Iraqis, 3,000 Syrians, 2,000 ALA volunteers, 1,000 Lebanese, and a few hundred Saudi Arabians—in addition to the many thousands of armed but largely untrained Palestinian irregulars already in the field. The Arab governments, it was evident, would keep most of their forces at home to protect themselves from domestic upheaval, and the armies they would send to fight were known to be deeply divided.

Against these armies, the Jews could hurl about 35,000 Haganah fighters, including 3,000 crack Palmach troops, assisted by some thousands of para-military civilian settlers and perhaps 3,000 poorly trained, undisciplined Irgunists and Sternists. The Haganah men and girls, who had fought only in small units before, had been organized into nine territorial brigades: Yiftach, Golani, and Carmeli in the north; Alexandroni and Kiryati in the center; Givati and Negev in the south; Etzioni in Jerusalem; and Harel in the Jerusalem corridor.* And these forces had the tactical advantage of operating in a tiny area near their depots and homes, while the Arabs would be converging from many different directions.

Yet an honest analysis of the situation, Ben-Gurion was persuaded, showed that this Jewish paper strength was as fragile as a desert flower. Despite the impressive military victories to date, the fact remained that the

* Each brigade was supposed to embrace 2,750 men, but some had barely 1,500 at this time. The non-Palmach Haganah infantry was called *Heyl Sadeh* (HISH), meaning Field Forces. Home guard troops, usually older and less qualified men and women, were organized into the *Heyl Matzav* (HIM).

Jews were dispersed everywhere. Even the coastal holdings had no depth; Arabs entrenched in the hills west of Tulkarm could, by cutting the Tel Aviv–Haifa road less than 10 miles away, snip Jewish-controlled Palestine in two. And the Arabs of Lydda and Ramle were a 20-minute car ride from Tel Aviv.

The enemy dominated the Judaean hill range from Jerusalem north of the Jenin-Nablus-Tulkarm Arab triangle and, with the Etzion Bloc making a last stand, would soon control fully the Hebron hill mass from Jerusalem to the vicinity of Beersheba. Most ominous of all, Jerusalem was still gravely endangered despite the fine spirit of the besieged people. And the latest news was that Jewish forces were failing in a desperate attempt to capture the Latrun salient along the Tel Aviv–Jerusalem road, which had replaced Kastel as the main barrier blocking the road to the Holy City.

Furthermore, until large shipments of heavy weapons arrived from abroad, the Arabs would enjoy a massive superiority in firepower. The Egyptians could blast through the Negev with a complete armored division —including tanks, armored cars, and heavy field guns—buttressed by two-engine bombers and a squadron of British Spitfires. The Arab Legion could attack with speedy armored cars and large mortars and cannons, including 25-pound guns. The Iraqis, Syrians, and Lebanese were also rich in tanks and field guns, and the Syrians had warplanes as well.

Against this enemy arsenal, the Jews had only a few hundred patchwork armored cars assembled in underground factories, about a dozen homemade Davidka mortars—though several other larger guns of ancient vintage were en route to Palestine—and a few unarmed Piper Cubs. The two Cromwells stolen from the British were the only heavy Jewish tanks. There were not even enough rifles or locally made Sten submachine guns to go around, with only one weapon available for every two or three fighters.

Nor did the plague of command disunity afflict the Arabs alone, Ben-Gurion was only too bitterly aware. He found himself commander-in-chief of a deeply riven army of his own, with some of his officers almost ready to mutiny against him. He had boldly tried to unify the various forces but this effort had served only to intensify the tensions.

The crux of the problem was the status of the Palmach. A proud, rigidly disciplined force—and until recently the only full-time fighting group— the Palmach had its own command network, which, though responsible to the general staff, sometimes neglected to take very seriously the plans and orders of non-Palmach officers. And the Palmach's warmest supporter within the High Command was Israel Galili, a stubby, vital man who had been Jewish Palestine's undisputed authority on defense matters since 1946.

In the Haganah's complex command structure, Galili bore the title of chief of national command, theoretically representing a token of the Jewish Agency Executive's authority in security matters. Actually, the Palmach regarded him as its own representative in the command, and his influence was vast. But when Ben-Gurion established the National Council of Thirteen to supersede the Jewish Agency Executive, Galili's official position grew increasingly ambiguous. Ben-Gurion planned to become Minister of Defense in the future government himself, and he wanted no other authority between himself and the general staff, particularly not Galili. For Galili championed the Palmach, and the Palmach, Ben-Gurion was convinced, wanted to be its own boss—though Galili insisted that it desired only a degree of "internal" autonomy, not the right to make its own military decisions.

In Ben-Gurion's view, the Palmach's tendency toward independence was not merely a matter of *esprit de corps*. The Palmach was rooted in the left-wing, though democratic, socialist ideology of the Mapam political party; the commander Yigal Allon and almost all of his subordinates and men sprang from the kibbutzim associated with this group. And they had little use for Ben-Gurion, from whose moderately socialist Mapai Party they had split in 1944, convinced that he was a power-hungry renegade from the egalitarian left. Ben-Gurion, for his part, suspected that the Mapam might try to use the Palmach after the war as an instrument for seizing power.

From a military viewpoint, too, he had his reservations about the Palmach—and about Galili himself. He did not doubt that the organization was made up of highly spirited, self-sacrificing fighters, but it was trained, he felt, for guerrilla struggle, not for conventional warfare against regular armies. The Palmach had to be molded into a larger unit framework, controlled by men with formal military training, particularly those who had served during World War II in the British army either individually or in the Jewish Brigade.

No, there was no room in the developing army for an "independent" Palmach, and he must start whittling down its power by abolishing Galili's job. On May 2, therefore, he delivered a letter by personal messenger to Galili curtly announcing this decision.

After angrily scanning the letter, Galili read it aloud to a group of staff officers.

"We'll never accept it!" one of them shouted.

"It's not for us to decide," Galili replied quietly, hoping to avoid a crisis in the army that could paralyze its fighting power. "We must accept."

Later, he telephoned leaders of the Mapam Party and asked them not to make an issue of it—but in vain. The Mapam Party's journal pronounced:

> . . . Any attempt to adapt the Haganah to the apparatus of an accepted regular army by disbanding the Palmach, eliminating the experienced and loyal commanders of the Haganah, would have one result: impairing the fighting capacity and pioneering strength of all Haganah brigades and paving the way for military careerism. . . . Disbanding the Palmach would mean breaking the backbone of the Haganah.

With the pressure rising, Ben-Gurion, five days after his decision, had to tell Galili that there had been a misunderstanding.

"Naturally I want you to resume your post," he insisted, but his eyes seemed to be saying: "The time will come." And Galili knew it.[13]

The time would come when all the Jewish defense problems would be solved—if the Jews could survive until then. But could they? The issue of the state, in Ben-Gurion's view, was really that of survival. The state was important to the extent that it would help the Jews to survive. And the truce proposed by Washington was less likely to postpone than to kill any future chance of proclaiming a state. The Arabs, Ben-Gurion was sure, would try to wipe out the Jews the minute the British left, whatever Abdullah or Marshall promised or intended. At least with a state it would be easier to buy arms, to bring in officers to train the army, to solicit international support.

As he sat at the head of the conference table that historic morning of May 12, Ben-Gurion posed the issue of statehood by asking whether the Jews should accept the American truce plan. If the majority answered No, a Jewish State would be born. He gazed at the faces around the table, faces even more anxious than his own. At least a third of the leaders of even his own Mapai Party had indicated that they shared Moshe Sharett's reservations about declaring a state immediately. He tried to relax; he must show absolute confidence. Otherwise the state was doomed—and also perhaps his people.

But as speaker after speaker rose, the mood became more desperate. Golda Meir told of her talk with Abdullah. Sharett discussed Marshall's views. Then, at the suggestion of some council members, Ben-Gurion called in Galili and Yigal Yadin. Certainly, Ben-Gurion felt, the military would support his view. Who could have more confidence in the outcome of a war than the commanders?

He put the question to the two men without embellishment: Would it be worthwhile to have a truce for three months? Galili answered in vague terms that a truce could bring great benefit militarily but, on the other hand, could not be divorced from political considerations. Yadin fingered his mustache and would not reply at first, explaining that any response would place an onerous responsibility on him. Then, his poetic countenance grim, he said that if a truce signified that the Jews could get the arms they expected and make other vital preparations for war, it was desirable. And hesitantly he added that even then he would give his forces only a 50–50 chance of victory.

There was a horrified gasp—only a 50–50 chance . . . of *survival!* One council member, Peretz Bernstein, suggested that a "government," as distinct from a state, should be declared as a compromise solution. Two others, Eliezer Kaplan and Joseph Shprinzak, made no secret of their desire to accept the truce plan.

Ben-Gurion felt that he must stem the tide and make them understand. Slowly, he summarized the picture as he saw it. There were three possible conditions under which an invasion might take place, he said.

"The first possibility: . . . No assistance will be permitted to reach either side, and the local balance of power will be left to settle the issue. . . . The Jews will win the whole country and its government, perhaps not soon but certainly not slowly. However, this is a remote possibility.

"A second possibility: The *Yishuv* will be left at its present strength, blockaded and prevented from receiving any new influx of manpower and arms. . . . The Arabs, on the other hand, will be able to obtain aid [from Britain]. The *Yishuv*'s position in such an eventuality will not be hopeless but it can only survive by a miracle.

"Actually there is a presumptive third possibility: the respective strengths of the Arabs and Jews will increase. We shall then have a none too easy struggle, not without losses . . ."

Ben-Gurion paused and the lines of his face tightened as if to accentuate his inner conviction.

"I return now," he continued, "to the main question: Do we envisage any realistic possibility of resisting invasion? My reply is: . . . given our moral values, and on condition that our manpower is wisely used and equipment is increased, then we have every prospect of success. . . . The Etzion disaster does not shake my resolution. I expected such reverses, and I fear we shall have even greater ordeals. The outcome depends on our wiping out most of the Arab Legion. Destruction of the enemy forces is always the determining factor in a war."

The audience was silent—aghast, yet enthralled. Wipe out the powerful Arab Legion? When they were all worrying about the prospect of mere survival?

"And now we will vote on whether to accept the armistice proposal," Ben-Gurion declared.

Had he made them understand? Could they hear the whispers of the fainthearted millions who had perished? Desperately, he tried to exclude from his own mind the stuttering, painfully revealing ambiguity of the testimony of his military experts.

When the vote was taken, Ben-Gurion announced the result with the same calm he might have shown in setting the date for the next meeting. Six of the ten council members present had voted to reject the truce plan. Ben-Gurion glanced with the faintest smile at Sharett, who had cast the deciding vote.

A state would be proclaimed.[14]

*

"You must have the auditorium ready within twenty-four hours. The state will be declared there. And remember, this is top secret!"

Otto Wallisch, a Czech-born artist, grumbled happily as Ze'ev Sharef, in charge of Independence Day arrangements, issued the order. For 2,000 years they had waited and now they wanted everything done in 24 hours! He had just finished designing the coming state's first postage stamp. He was sure it was the only national stamp in history without the name of the country on it. Who needed a name, he was told. They would think of one in good time. So he had marked the stamp simply *Doar Ivre,* "Hebrew Mail." He wondered if they had written the Declaration of Independence yet. Twenty-four hours! What a way to start off a country!

"And remember," Sharef admonished as Wallisch was starting to leave, "not more than a hundred and fifty pounds [$450] in expenses, eh?"

Actually, the Jewish leaders were still working on a draft of the Declaration, with almost every member of the Council of Thirteen fiercely trying to insert his or her view and personality into the historic document. One argument broke out over whether to define the state's frontiers as drawn by the United Nations. Ben-Gurion violently opposed this idea.

"Take the American Declaration of Independence, for instance," he argued. "It contains no mention of the territorial limits . . . The Arabs are making war on us. If we beat them, the western part of Galilee and the territory on both sides of the road to Jerusalem will become part of the state. If only we have the strength . . . Why tie ourselves down?"

His view finally prevailed.

Then there was the question of God's role in the affair. Some wanted to mention "the God of Israel," others "the Almighty and Redeemer of Israel." Some wanted no reference to God at all. For two hours, Ben-Gurion mediated a heated discussion on this question, finally suggesting the use of the phrase "Rock of Israel." He assured the anti-clerics that this expression did not refer to the deity—and the Orthodox that it did. Failing in this effort, Ben-Gurion demanded a compromise and eventually got it. "Almighty God" would be used, but "the Redeemer" would be omitted.

Tempers then grew short over what to name the infant state. "Judaea," demanded one member. But that was the Biblical name of only one region within the prospective state, others pointed out. "Zion," some insisted, arguing that the Jews would always have the last word at the United Nations and in other international forums since they would be voting at the end of the alphabetical list. But "Zion," came the rebuttal, was the name of a hill and might be confusing. Ben-Gurion suggested "Israel," and at the last moment this name was approved.

A committee under Moshe Sharett then drew up a draft of the Declaration, but Sharett's flowery, formal language did not please Ben-Gurion. On the night before the independence ceremony, he took it home with him and, over a supper of herring and cheese, rewrote it in strong, affirmative language, deleting the word "Whereas" from the start of each paragraph.

While the dreams of 2,000 years were being hastily compressed into an official proclamation by 13 quarreling council members, Otto Wallisch rushed to set the scene for the grand finale. The Tel Aviv Museum on Rothschild Boulevard had been selected as the site of the meeting because it could seat so few people—only about 200. The fewer the guests, it was felt, the fewer the possibilities of the secret leaking out. If the enemy knew the time and place of the Declaration of Independence, the site might well be bombed and the entire Jewish leadership wiped out at one blow.

Nor did the Jews want to risk a parting crackdown by the British. The ceremony was to take place at 4 P.M. on Friday, May 14, eight hours before the mandate would officially end. Since the Sabbath started on Friday night, no Jewish leader would sign the Declaration after sundown.

Wallisch hunted for a large portrait of Theodor Herzl, which was to hang on the wall behind the dais, and finally found one, coated with dust, in the cellar of a Jewish institute. He also discovered two huge Zionist flags that were to flank the portrait, but they were so dirty that he had to wash them in a launderette.

Then he went in search of a parchment scroll on which to inscribe the Declaration. After considerable difficulty he found one, but, deciding he must check its quality before it could be used for so noble a purpose, he rushed over to an engineering institute to demand a chemical analysis.

"It's late," snapped the only engineer around. "Why do you want it?"

"I can't tell you."

"Then I can't do it!"

So Wallisch stayed up all night testing the parchment himself at home.

The next morning, he discovered that the Council of Thirteen would approve the final draft only in the afternoon about two hours before the ceremony and that there would be no time to inscribe it on the scroll beforehand.

When Wallisch informed Dorit Rozenne, Sharef's secretary, of this highly irregular situation, she immediately ran to the nearest stationery store and bought a blue cardboard binding for the typed copy of the proclamation. Then she invited the director of a local bank to the ceremony so that he would keep his bank open until the ceremony was over to permit deposit of the signed Declaration in a vault. Bombs might destroy the signers, but never their signatures. After so many centuries, some people might not believe there was a Jewish State without written proof.

And thus the stage was set for one of history's most important, fateful—
and low-budgeted—Independence Day productions.

As his shiny new American automobile, rented for the occasion, drew up
to the white-painted museum, Ben-Gurion was startled to see a cheering, flag-waving crowd. The ceremony was supposed to be secret and
yet, it seemed, everyone in Tel Aviv knew where and when it was to take
place. (The Haganah radio had announced that it would broadcast the
ceremony, inadvertently revealing the time.) What would happen if the
bombs started to fall? But he managed to smile as he went into the building
and walked past an exhibition of paintings by Jewish artists.

The last official to arrive, he made his way through a mob of reporters
and photographers. He was wearing a dark blue suit and, as a concession to
history, a tie (he seldom wore ties—and indeed, three other members of
the council did not put one on even for this occasion). As he stepped onto
the dais to take his place behind a long table with the other council members, who were to make up the first Jewish cabinet, he glanced at the huge
profile of Herzl gazing down benignly on the packed gathering.

"Hey, B.G., please—a little smile," urged Robert Capa, the American
photographer, as Ben-Gurion took his seat.

The Prime Minister-to-be obliged . . . Yes, Herzl deserved the place
of honor at this impossible gathering. He almost seemed to be repeating the
memorable words:

"I created the Jewish State. Were I to say this aloud I would be greeted
by universal laughter. But perhaps five years hence, in any case, certainly
fifty years hence, everyone will perceive it. The state exists as essence in the
will-to-the-state of a people . . ."

After Capa had delayed the meeting for several moments taking pictures, he nodded to Ben-Gurion and the latter rose to rap a walnut gavel on
the table. His face a shiny pink, he soon began to read in a small, monotone
voice, trying to contain his inner excitement: "The Land of Israel was the
birthplace of the Jewish people . . ."

Throughout Palestine, enraged Arabs and enraptured Jews turned their
radio dials to the secret station broadcasting the proclamation—although in
Jerusalem they heard only the first part: The British-officered Arab Legion
had halted its bombardment of the Jewish sector for afternoon tea, and the
radio had come on. But when the officers finished tea, the shelling started
again, and no one in the city ever did hear the end.

". . . it is . . . the self-evident right of the Jewish people to be a nation,
as all other nations, in its own Sovereign State. Accordingly, we, the members of the National Council, representing the Jewish people in Palestine

and the Zionist movement of the world, meet together in solemn assembly today . . . by virtue of the natural and historic right of the Jewish people and of the Resolution of the General Assembly of the United Nations,

"Hereby proclaim the establishment of the Jewish state in Palestine, to be called the State of Israel . . ."

The audience rose and burst into prolonged applause.

Then, when the proclamation had been adopted by acclamation, Ben-Gurion put his signature to the blank scroll on which the Declaration would be inscribed later. Other council members followed, stepping to the front of the dais to sign while Sharett straightened out the slippery parchment for each of them.

Suddenly, the melancholy strains of *"Hatikvah,"* the Jewish national anthem, wafted over the audience (the Jewish Philharmonic Orchestra was hidden from view on an upper story). When the final notes died away, Ben-Gurion declared the meeting ended and Israel reborn.

Threading his way out through a surging, ecstatic mass of well-wishers, the first Israeli Prime Minister, his eyes reflecting both pride and anxiety, grinned at a British reporter: "You see, we did it!"[15]

EARLY that same day, May 14, the buzzer on Clark Clifford's desk in the White House summoned him and he made his way to the President's office. As he entered, Truman from behind his desk greeted him with a broad smile.

"Yes, Mr. President?"

"Just thought you'd like to know, Clark," he said jubilantly, "General Marshall called and he's agreed to *de facto* recognition."

He added that Marshall wanted to wait a few days so that he could consult with the British and the French.

Clifford's initial smile faded. "Mr. President, if we're going to recognize the country it's best to do it immediately."

Truman thought of the letter he had just received from Chaim Weizmann pleading for immediate recognition.

"All right, Clark," he said, "get a formal request for recognition immediately."

Clifford rushed back to his office, looking at his watch as he sat down at his desk. Almost 10 A.M. Only eight more hours until the Jewish State would be born, Palestine time being six hours ahead of Washington time.

He called up Eliahu Elath at the Jewish Agency headquarters and asked: "Are you people still determined to proclaim your independence today?"

"I haven't the slightest doubt," was Elath's reply.

"Then send me a letter immediately requesting United States recognition."

There was a pause. Elath was too stunned to speak. Finally, he replied: "I'll send it by messenger right away."

Elath promptly telephoned Benjamin Cohen, an adviser to the State Department: "Ben, can you come over here right away? The White House has asked for a request for diplomatic recognition and I need your help."

Cohen rushed over and began to write a draft immediately.

"Most unusual," he said with a dry smile. "Writing a request for recognition of a state that doesn't exist yet and hasn't even got a name."

"What'll we do about the name?" asked Elath in joyous confusion.

"Well, we'll have to use the designation referred to in the United Nations resolution—simply the 'Jewish State.' "

The request when completed read:

> My dear Mr. President:
>
> I have the honor to notify you that the Jewish State has been proclaimed as an independent republic within frontiers approved by the General Assembly of the United Nations in its Resolution of November 29, 1947, and that a provisional government has been charged to assume the rights and duties of government for preserving law and order within the boundaries of the Jewish State, for defending the state against external aggression, and for discharging the obligations of the Jewish State to the other nations of the world in accordance with international law. The Act of Independence will become effective at one minute after six o'clock on the evening of May 14, 1948, Washington time.
>
> With full knowledge of the deep bond of sympathy which has existed and has been strengthened over the past thirty years between the government of the United States and the Jewish people of Palestine, I have been authorized by the provisional government of the new state to tender this message and to express the hope that your government will recognize and will welcome the Jewish State into the community of nations.
>
> > Very respectfully yours,
> > Eliahu Epstein [Elath's original name]
> > Agent
> > Provisional Government of the
> > Jewish State

Elath read it over and guffawed. "Authorized by my government . . . that's a good one. As if there was time!"

A secretary typed up the draft. After signing it, Elath instructed Harry Zinder, the Jewish Agency press attaché: "Take your car and rush this to the White House! Deliver it personally to Clark Clifford!"

Zinder had been gone only a few minutes when Elath's secretary burst in shouting: "It just came over the radio. They've declared the state! They've named it the 'State of Israel.' "

"Quick," Elath exclaimed, "run after Harry and put it in the letter!"

The secretary ran out and sped in a cab to the White House. She caught up with Zinder at the White House entrance and told him the name. He removed the letter from the envelope and with a ballpoint pen crossed out references to "the Jewish State," substituting the words "State of Israel."

Shortly afterward, Clifford telephoned Elath and said casually: "Thanks for the letter. We'll recognize you, but keep it strictly confidential."

As Elath put down the phone, he ran one hand over his sweating forehead, and then realized that he wouldn't even be able to relay the good news to his "government" since it did not have a code system yet.

Clifford informed Marshall and Lovett of Truman's decision but told them that the President did not wish the news spread—even to lower State Department echelons or to the United Nations delegation in New York—until late in the afternoon. He did not explain why, but it was clear that Truman did not want any hitches to develop in his plan at this crucial time. Clifford and Lovett then met for lunch at the F Street Club and, over dessert, drew up a press release to be issued as soon as the state was proclaimed.

In mid-afternoon, Dean Rusk and other State Department officials, who had known earlier that the United States would recognize the Jewish State but were not certain when, learned of the White House plan for immediate action. They were infuriated. This would make fools of them all in the eyes of the world. And worst of all, the American delegation at Lake Success was just about to make a new appeal for a trusteeship, at least for Jerusalem.[16]

At 5 P.M., José Arce of Argentina, president of the second special session of the General Assembly, called the last meeting of the session to order.

"The General Assembly is . . . advised," he said, "that the work will be continued until it has been completed and each speaker will be allowed only five minutes . . . Mr. Sayre, representative of the United States of America, will address the General Assembly."

Frances B. Sayre walked briskly to the podium. "The time is very short," he said. "If a trusteeship agreement for the government of Jerusalem is to be got up, it is necessary that it be set up before the expiration of the present mandate." He looked at his watch and continued: "That will take place one hour hence . . ."

While Sayre was speaking, an usher moved down the aisle and stopped by the group of seats reserved for the American delegation.

"Ambassador Austin," the usher whispered. "Telephone."

Austin rose and walked quickly to a phone booth in the corridor. After listening quietly for several minutes, his face grew pale.

"But that's impossible!" he finally cried. "We're making a pitch for trusteeship at this very moment!"

A minute later, Austin put back the receiver and walked slowly to his seat in the General Assembly. He conferred briefly with members of his delegation who happened to be present. Then, wiping his face with a handkerchief, he strode out, got into his limousine, and ordered the chauffeur to take him to his hotel.

About half an hour later, after a long procedural wrangle in the General Assembly, Awni Khalidy of Iraq stood up and shouted: "There is a very important matter to consider before we proceed. The time is one minute past six o'clock. When he came to this rostrum, the representative of the United States declared that, if we had not arrived at a conclusion by six o'clock, the whole game was up. I present that to you, Mr. President, for your ruling. The time is past six o'clock."

Andrew Cordier, executive assistant to the Secretary-General, ignoring Khalidy's request, announced in a businesslike tone: "The amendment is to the Preamble which appears on page 4 of the document AC.1/298. It proposes that the fifth paragraph of the Preamble be replaced by the following text: 'Whereas the maintenance of order and security in Jerusalem is an urgent question which concerns the United Nations as a whole . . .' "

At that moment, an usher handed a note to Enrique Rodriquez Fabregat of Uruguay, a staunch pro-Zionist, who was seated with his delegation. Fabregat's face lit up. It was from an Israeli journalist friend, informing him that the United States was recognizing the Jewish State. The diplomat scribbled a note on the back of the message and passed it along to other Latin American diplomats nearby.

Raymond Hare, a member of the United States delegation, was on his way to his seat when Trygve Lie confronted him in the corridor with a flushed, excited look.

"What a surprise," Lie said.

"What do you mean?"

"You know, your country recognizing the Jewish State."

"But that's impossible."

"Well, go and look at the wires then."

Hare rushed to the ticker room and found it bustling with delegates as shocked as he. Glancing at the wires over someone else's shoulder, he read the news.

By now, pandemonium had broken out in the Assembly hall as word spread of the report from Washington. Delegates left their places and conferred with one another. Arguments broke out all over the hall. In the midst of the noise and commotion, the American delegates sat silently in their seats, doodling on pads or blowing smoke rings.

Above the confusion President Arce's voice droned on: "We shall now begin the discussion of the report of the First Committee to the General Assembly . . ."

Alberto Gonzalez Fernandez of Colombia then jumped to the rostrum and demanded bluntly: "I . . . wish to have information from the delegation of the United States concerning the truth of the information which has been distributed in the press room in regard to the recognition of the State of Israel by the United States government."

Sayre rose slowly. "I regret that we have no official information. Such a report has come over the ticker, but there is no official information that we have."

Finally, Philip Jessup, after telephoning Washington, went to the rostrum, cleared his throat, and said: "The delegation of the United States did not wish to comment on rumors before it was able to lay before the General Assembly the text of the statement issued by the President. I am now in a position to do so. It reads as follows:

" 'This Government has been informed that a Jewish State has been proclaimed in Palestine, and recognition has been requested by the Provisional Government thereof. The United States recognizes the Provisional Government as the *de facto* authority of the new State of Israel.' "

Mahmoud Bey Fawzi of Egypt rushed to the rostrum and shouted amid the general tumult: "The whole procedure through which we have been going for more than four weeks—the maze of proposals massed and heaped upon one another—was a mere fake."

The American delegates looked down, as if contemplating their outdated notes, some of them still doodling.[17]

In the Waldorf-Astoria Hotel, a few floors from the apartment where Ambassador Austin sat brooding, Chaim Weizmann lay in bed talking with friends who were congratulating him. In the next room, Joseph Linton was typing out letters, Weizmann's regular secretary having gone home early for the Sabbath. As people streamed in and out, interfering with his work, Linton, hoping to discourage them from standing around, turned the radio on loud. Suddenly, the blaring music stopped, and an announcer interrupted with a news report.

Linton burst into Weizmann's room.

"Chief," he said, then found himself unable to speak.

"The United States has recognized us," Weizmann volunteered with a calm smile.

"But how do you know?" Linton asked.

"Your face told me," Weizmann said. And he added: "Besides, didn't I tell you about President Truman?"

At the White House, the President telephoned David Niles: "Dave, I want you to know that I've just announced recognition. You're the first person I called, because I knew how much this would mean to you."[18]

Then he received Robert Lovett to discuss the new situation in Palestine. When Truman mentioned his difficulties with the State Department, the Undersecretary said quietly: "They almost put it over on you."

The President smiled and looked out at the rose garden, gray and serene in the cloak of dusk.

Y AACOV YANNAI, the Haganah signal corps commander, wondered whether the operator of his secret radio station had taken down the message from the United States accurately.

"Are you sure?" he cried into the telephone.

"Yes, that's what it says."

It seemed incredible. The time was just after midnight. The British mandate had hardly ended; and the United States had already recognized the State of Israel! Yannai slammed down the receiver and dashed from his house. He had called an aide of Ben-Gurion's earlier to pass on a request from some 60 American radio stations that the Prime Minister deliver a broadcast before dawn. But the aide had refused to disturb him. The news of American recognition, however, was too important to wait. He would awaken the Prime Minister himself, Yannai decided.

When he arrived breathless at Ben-Gurion's house, not far from his own, however, Yannai was barely able to get his foot in the door.

"Yes, what do you want?" demanded Paula Ben-Gurion, standing suspiciously in the doorway.

"I must see Ben-Gurion," Yannai replied, gently pushing his way in. "I have an important message for him."

"Ben-Gurion is exhausted. I will not let anybody wake him up!"

"But this is important."

"You will not go up this stairway!" Paula snapped, blocking the way with arms imperiously folded.

"Ben-Gurion would never forgive me if I did not wake him. I don't wish to use force, but I'm going up!"

And Yannai slid past and up the stairs to the Prime Minister's room. He jostled him awake and, feeling somewhat guilty, stared into the puffy, bloodshot eyes of a tired old man. Hardly had Ben-Gurion proclaimed Jewish independence the afternoon before than he had sped off to military headquarters at the dingy Red House and conferred for hours with the Haganah leaders. Alarming reports had come in of Arab armies concentrating on the borders. And then, to add to his troubles, the High Command had opposed his plan to make another strong thrust to seize the areas along the Tel Aviv–Jerusalem road. They had argued that they did not have enough troops and did not know the enemy's plans. Not enough troops to save Jerusalem? Bad news. Nothing but bad news. Now he heard himself crying: "I don't believe it!"

"But the operator took down every word."

"Take me to the station. I want to check it myself."

He jumped out of bed, slipped into a robe, and ran down the stairs, with Paula at his heels crying, "Come back! Come back!" Yannai then drove them both to the Haganah radio station, located in a small wooden hut along the beach on Hayarkon Street. Within minutes, Yannai had contacted New York and confirmed the message.

"It's definite," he told Ben-Gurion. "Truman has recognized us."

The Prime Minister embraced him.

"They want me to speak to America? Tell them it's okay. I'll do it."

So Yannai drove them home and picked them up again some two hours later for the broadcast. While contact was being made with New York, the three waited outside the hut. Suddenly they heard an ominous hum, and within moments, Egyptian bombs were screeching down on a nearby power station. The invasion had begun!

After the explosions, there was another screech—from Paula. "You are killing Ben-Gurion!" she yelled, rushing to her husband's side. "Let's get out of here before he's killed!"

At that moment, the radio operator called out that New York was ready. Yannai was trapped. Should he whisk Ben-Gurion to safety as his wife demanded or encourage him to make the broadcast despite the risk? Certainly Israel needed the world, and especially America, behind her at this critical moment. He watched the planes as they circled for another go.

"Ben-Gurion," he said, "let's go inside."

And as he guided the Prime Minister into the station, Paula followed, still crying: "You are killing him! You are killing him!"

Yannai slammed the door shut to keep Paula out, and Ben-Gurion sat down by the microphone. At 5:20 A.M. (10:20 P.M. the night before in New York), the Prime Minister began his talk from hastily scribbled notes while his wife pounded on the door, shouting and wailing. The planes swooped down again to drop more deadly loads nearby. The walls of the hut shuddered, the microphone shook, and lights winked on the control panel. Ben-Gurion paused for a moment, then interpolated in a low, rather monotonous voice, as if nothing unusual was happening: "The explosions you can hear are Arab planes bombing Tel Aviv."

Then he went on with what he had been saying. And the walls continued to tremble—from the desperate exhortations of Paula Ben-Gurion, noisily pleading with her husband to come home and get some sleep before he was killed.

Eventually he did go home, but not before he had slipped away to the airport with some soldiers to see what damage the planes had done there. On his return, he sat down at his desk and drowsily wrote in his diary: "Outside stood people in pajamas. I looked at them and saw that there was no fear in their eyes. I knew then we would win."

PART **II**

THE INVASION

7

The Roadblocks

As the dining hall at Kibbutz Nirim echoed to the voices of the folk singers, Shulamith Ram wanted to join them in song, to dance and laugh and cry with happiness at this long-coveted moment in Jewish history. Yet a deep foreboding filled the girl's heart as she listened to the trio who had come from Tel Aviv to help her isolated kibbutz celebrate the founding of the State of Israel that day, May 14.

Nirim was situated in the western Negev only about four miles southeast of Rafa on the Sinai border, closer to Egypt than any other Jewish colony. Egyptian troops would therefore almost certainly attempt to storm it while racing northward from El Arish through Rafa along the coastal road, a likelihood already confirmed by local Bedouins who were paid well by the kibbutz for useful information.

But despite the risk, Shulamith, a sturdily built girl with a mop of black hair, was glad that she had volunteered to help found this paramilitary settlement three years earlier. She only regretted having fallen into a trench about a week before and broken her arm, which was now in a sling; she would still command the four men in her pillbox, but she herself would not be able to fire.

As the entertainers finished their last song to prolonged applause, the kibbutz commander shouted: "All right, everybody to bed, except those on guard. Our Bedouin friends have just told us that the Egyptians are planning to attack at about three in the morning. So get some sleep while you can."

"What about us?" asked the visiting guitar player, a boy called Grisha. "It looks like we won't be able to get to our own units."

"We've got one telescopic sight," said the commander. "You can be our sniper. I hope you can shoot a gun as well as you play the guitar!"

While the inhabitants of Nirim slept fitfully in their clothes, a gun beside each bed, about 10,000 Egyptian soldiers equipped with tanks and artillery were gathering in the Sinai at El Arish, a short distance beyond the Egyptian frontier. To capture the Negev, they would have to win control of the four main roads running through it: a north-south highway extending along the Sinai-Palestine coast; an inland artery roughly parallel to it running from the Sinai through Beersheba; a road branching off from Beersheba to Hebron and Jerusalem in the northeast; and an east-west highway reaching from Majdal on the coast to Hebron.

The Egyptian attack force was divided into two brigade groups, one led by Brigadier Mohammed Neguib and the other, largely made up of Moslem Brother volunteers, by Colonel Ahmed Abd el-Aziz. Neguib's much larger force was to move swiftly up the coastal road through Gaza all the way to Tel Aviv. Aziz's troops were to disengage from fighting along the coast and advance to Beersheba, Hebron, and Bethlehem, just south of Jerusalem, to link up with the Arab Legion, a maneuver largely intended to deprive Transjordan, no less than Israel, of territory in the Negev.

Under pressure from the other Arab States, which wanted the Arab Legion's help in the invasion, Egypt had agreed to accept King Abdullah as the commander-in-chief of a United Arab command. But she had little intention of submitting to his authority, and, indeed, was determined to limit both his power and his booty.

The attack, after considerable delay, finally got under way. A Bedouin guide led the 6th Battalion of Neguib's force toward Nirim and stopped as they drew near.

"There it is, over there," he said, indicating a small settlement in the distance. "That's the colony."

The battalion commander peered through his binoculars at Kibbutz Nirim, known to the Egyptians as "Dangour." It was too bad that he had no time for reconnaissance first. Indeed, he might not even have found the colony without the local guide.

"Do you know anything about their defenses?" he asked.

"No sir, but I've seen them digging a lot."

The officer shrugged and ordered his artillery unit to zero in on the colony.

*

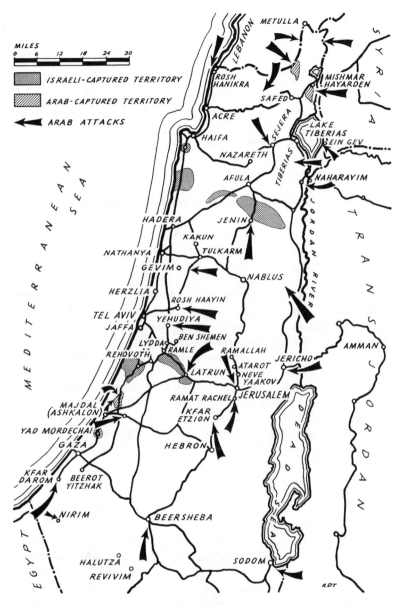

MILES
0   6   12   18   24   30

ISRAELI-CAPTURED TERRITORY

ARAB-CAPTURED TERRITORY

ARAB ATTACKS

LEBANON

METULLA

SYRIA

ROSH HANIKRA

MISHMAR HAYARDEN

SAFED

ACRE

SEJERA

LAKE TIBERIAS

HAIFA

EIN GEV

NAZARETH

TIBERIAS

AFULA

NAHARAYIM

JORDAN RIVER

HADERA

JENIN

KAKUN

NATHANYA

TULKARM

GEVIM

NABLUS

HERZLIA

ROSH HAAYIN

TEL AVIV
JAFFA

YEHUDIYA

AMMAN

BEN SHEMEN

LYDDA

RAMLE

RAMALLAH

JERICHO

REHOVOTH

LATRUN

ATAROT
NEVE YAAKOV

MAJDAL
(ASHKALON)

RAMAT RACHEL

JERUSALEM

YAD MORDECHAI

KFAR
ETZION

DEAD SEA

GAZA

HEBRON

JORDAN

KFAR
DAROM

BEEROT
YITZHAK

NIRIM

BEERSHEBA

EGYPT

HALUTZA
REVIVIM

SODOM

RDT

MEDITERRANEAN SEA

TRANS

OPERATIONS FROM INVASION TO FIRST TRUCE

Shulamith Ram was thankful that the attack had not started at 3 A.M. as expected and that the guards had therefore let the settlers sleep until about 7:30. As soon as she was awakened, she went to her dugout position at the northern corner of the kibbutz and, within half an hour, heard the long-awaited scream of shells. After a furious bombardment, she peeked from her dugout and saw an Egyptian column consisting of four tanks, several armored cars, 27 Bren carriers, and a number of trucks laden with infantry advancing under intensifying cover fire to within 400 yards of the settlement.

She froze. All the kibbutz had to stop this formidable force were four Stens, one light machine gun, one Bren, seven Italian World War II rifles, and about ten British rifles—leaving most of the defenders without any weapons at all. With ammunition equally scarce, the only person permitted to shoot consistently was Grisha, the guitarist, with his telescopic rifle. As the Egyptians began to advance in small groups, he aimed carefully at one soldier in each and fired, and the units immediately retreated in disorder.

But when the attacks continued and other defenders fired, the situation grew more precarious. "Fire! Fire!" cried Shulamith to her men. But their rifles wouldn't work. Then the machine gunner was hit. All seemed lost as a column of Bren carriers advanced to within 30 yards of the surrounding barbed wire. But then one Israeli dashed toward the fence firing a desperate burst with his Sten, and the attackers retreated. And with the armor apparently intimidated by signs reading "Caution! Mines!" no further frontal assaults were launched.

The Egyptians decided to bypass Nirim, leaving artillery units behind to shell the settlement. The resistance of Shulamith and her comrades had set the pattern for the fighting that was to follow.

While the 6th Battalion of Neguib's brigade had been diverted from the main drive in order to eliminate Kibbutz Nirim on the brigade's eastern flank, the 1st Battalion pushed northward on the morning of May 15 toward Kfar Darom, the religious kibbutz which volunteer Moslem Brotherhood forces had failed to take some days before. The 1st Battalion was to assault the settlement anew, permitting Aziz's volunteers, who were besieging it, to start on the drive toward Beersheba, Hebron, and Bethlehem.

Anticipating an attack by the regular Egyptian army, the Israelis planned a desperate thrust, on the night of May 13, to break through Aziz's siege with reinforcements and supplies. A convoy was sent off at top speed toward Kfar Darom, exposed to enemy eyes—and guns—but it bogged down in the deep sand of a wadi bed about two miles from the kibbutz.*

Aziz, watching the scene through his binoculars, smiled with satisfaction. He had already ranged his guns and deployed ambushes along the supply route. Now he gave the order to his artillery officer, Hasan Fahmi Abd al-Majid, standing near him: "All right, open fire. They're sitting ducks!" . . .

"Artillery!" exclaimed Aharon Davidi, as the shells started to scream overhead. This was the first time the 60 men with him had ever encountered big guns. Davidi, a communications officer in Negev Brigade headquarters, had come along to repair the kibbutz's communications system, which had broken down, isolating the settlers. He wished now that he had had more infantry field training.

As shell after shell slammed into the convoy, all but two vehicles were hit. Then, miraculously, a Piper Cub appeared to bomb the Egyptians and, in the confusion, the Israelis set fire to the vehicles and dashed through the fields carrying the wounded and all the arms and ammunition they could hold. Remarkably, only one man was killed during the run, though about half were wounded.

"We're glad you got here," one settler grumbled to Davidi as they sipped the few drops of water now available for each individual in the intense heat. "But did you really have to come?"

Early the next morning, May 15, Neguib's troops arrived. From his viewpoint in a trench, Davidi could see seven tanks moving through a wheatfield from the west like ships in a yellow sea, with about 70 dark-skinned Sudanese soldiers following close behind. Simultaneously, five armored cars closed in from the north. Davidi and his comrades fired rapidly, but the Egyptians kept advancing.

Annihilation seemed certain until an officer, Yitzhak Ahituv, though wounded in one leg, crawled through a hole in the barbed wire and limped toward the first tank with the settlement's only Piat. Some yards from the target, he kneeled down, took aim, and fired. The tank, though apparently not hit, began to retreat, and the others followed suit. The Sudanese infantrymen continued to advance without support but were finally driven back by murderous fire. The attack was over.

Davidi went to survey the damage and found everything in ashes except the Holy Cabinet containing the Torah scriptures. He kissed the velvet

* *Wadi* is Arabic for the bed or valley of a stream in the desert region of the Middle East and North Africa. It is usually dry except during the rainy season, when it often forms an oasis.

covering, then went to work to repair the communications system so that he could tell the world Kfar Darom was still alive.

On May 16, Captain Gamal Abdel Nasser rose early and breakfasted with his wife Tahia. He scanned the bold newspaper headlines announcing that the war had officially begun, and looked across at Tahia, who was trying to suppress tears. He wished she would let herself cry as a woman should. He rose and went into the children's room, where he hugged his two small daughters, Huda and Mona. Then he grabbed his khaki bag, kissed his wife swiftly, and ran downstairs while he was still able to keep from weeping himself.

A taxi took him to the home of Major Abdel Hakim Amer, a fellow Free Officer. From there the two men, joined by Captain Zakaraya Muhieddin, a third conspirator from the Staff College, went to the station, all of them depressed by family farewells. But as they boarded the train heading for El Arish in the Sinai, the world narrowed down to the concerns of war. They turned their compartment into a miniature operations room, spreading a large map across their knees and talking excitedly of strategic plans. And the laughter and zeal of the other soldiers on the train nourished their own sudden euphoria.

Gradually, however, they felt nagging doubts. Why had the government not mobilized a larger number of battalions by calling up the reserve for immediate active service? Why had an official communiqué described the first operations as merely a punitive expedition against "Zionist bands"?

The three men separated at El Arish and Nasser reached Rafa by jeep. There he finally found his 6th Battalion, which had just returned from its ill-fated adventure in Nirim. When he heard what had happened from a fellow officer, he was almost speechless. Was it possible—his battalion turned back by the "Zionist bands"?

"How did it happen?" he asked.

"Well," explained the officer, "towers worked by electricity rose out of the ground, fired in all directions, and then disappeared again into the ground."

"But how do you know the towers were powered by electricity since you never got inside the settlement?"

The officer drew on his cigarette and ignored the question. Nasser was silent, too. If the Egyptian forces couldn't capture a relatively small settlement like Nirim, or for that matter Kfar Darom, what would happen at Yad Mordechai, the next Jewish colony en route to Tel Aviv? It was defended by some 1,000 trained soldiers, according to the rumors he had heard, and since it actually straddled the main road, must be taken in order to keep communications open in the thrust northward.

May 18 dawned hot and dry in the Negev. A car, followed by a Red Cross ambulance, sped down the road and stopped abruptly at the entrance to Kibbutz Yad Mordechai. Two men, a Swedish doctor and Arie Harel of the Haganah, stepped out, to be greeted by Grisha Mirhov (not the same Grisha who fought at Nirim), the commander. Grisha's perpetual frown, caused by a deep crease between his dark eyes, gave way to a welcoming smile.

"This Red Cross team," Harel explained, "is bound for Kfar Darom to evacuate the wounded in exchange for release of three Arab commanders we captured recently. I'm going along as a Haganah observer, but we need someone who can guide us."

Grisha agreed to go with them, and climbed into the car. When the group arrived in Gaza, the Swedish doctor and Harel went to Egyptian headquarters to request passes while Grisha, disguised in a white Red Cross smock, strolled around this enemy stronghold. Everywhere he saw troops, artillery, armored cars, Bren carriers. Officers were shouting orders, soldiers grumbling, motorcyclists storming up with messages. This army, he concluded, was ready to move.

He approached an Egyptian major who was watching his men load a truck with ammunition and asked casually in English: "Where will you be going next, Major?"

The Egyptian replied, smiling: "One column is on its way to Beersheba and Jerusalem, and my brigade will go to Tel Aviv. Tomorrow we shall surround Deir Seneid."

Grisha knew the Egyptians referred to Yad Mordechai as "Deir Seneid," and they had, of course, no intention of surrounding the nearby Arab village of that name. He waited impatiently for his two companions, who finally returned with glum faces.

"We spoke with Colonel Taha, the commander, and he refused to give us passes," Harel reported. "He said the Egyptians had conquered Kfar Darom and would treat it in accordance with the Geneva Convention."*

At this point the three men were arrested, but managed to elude their guard and leave hastily in their car. On arrival in Yad Mordechai at about 6 P.M., Grisha shouted to the sentry: "Find Munio [Brandwein—the field commander] immediately and tell him to put our defense plan into action!"

* Taha, like most Egyptians, believed reports from Cairo that Kfar Darom had fallen, though it was only besieged.

He then ran to his command post to help prepare the kibbutz, with its limited force, to face the Egyptian army in a struggle that could determine the fate of Tel Aviv.

Shortly after the Red Cross car had pulled out of Gaza, a train from Cairo arrived at Gaza Station with more Egyptian troops to reinforce the 1st Battalion that was to march on Tel Aviv. Among the officers aboard was Captain Zakaraya Muhieddin, Nasser's close friend, who had come to join Colonel Sayed Taha's staff.

"How ready are we for this attack on Deir Seneid?" he asked Taha on entering the Colonel's headquarters, set up in a railroad car.

"Cairo is pushing us too hard, but I think we can do it."

"What do we know about the settlement's strength, sir?"

"Not very much, I'm afraid," was the reply. "There hasn't been time for reconnaissance."

"But, sir, how can we attack if we're not even sure where their strongpoints are?" Muhieddin said. "Perhaps I could take a reconnaissance patrol out in the morning."

"Very well, but you only have until noon. If we don't attack by afternoon, Cairo will have my head."

The Egyptian leaders were anxious indeed for a quick victory at Yad Mordechai; while they calculated that they could simply bypass Nirim and Kfar Darom, they were persuaded that they had to take "Deir Seneid" if they were going to capture Tel Aviv. The first two colonies were quite far from the coastal highway and, in their view, could not obstruct traffic appreciably if placed under siege. But Yad Mordechai, lying three-fourths of a mile north of the Gaza Strip, sprawled directly across the route.

While officers in the field were agreed on the need to capture this colony, many felt that the settlements left behind posed a serious danger to their flanks and should be eliminated first, and could be, if the government and the "Cairo generals" were not basing strategy more on political than on military considerations.

Nasser, for one, became convinced that the war was a "political affair" when he read a Cairo communiqué announcing that his battalion had "successfully carried out a mopping-up operation" at Nirim. And his agitation grew when he received orders to send his battalion from Rafa to a new camp about two miles away, apparently without reason, and then again, to move his soldiers to Gaza. He watched a sergeant ordering one soldier to pull down the tent he had spent hours putting up. The man looked up in bewilderment and remarked: "How frustrated we are!"

To Nasser, these words were like a sword to the heart. The Egyptian soldier, in his own cynical way, was expressing his lack of faith in his leaders and his disgust with the whole war.

Nasser felt deeply depressed on the train to Gaza as he watched the dunes roll past in barren splendor. But his mood changed slightly on arrival when he found his good friend, Abdel Hakim Amer, waiting for him on the platform. Amer, now adjutant of the 9th Battalion, was preparing to leave Gaza with a support group for the battle of "Deir Seneid." Nasser was his counterpart in the 6th Battalion.

The two men embraced, but their smiles soon dissolved as they discussed their mutual disappointment over the progress of the war.

"I understand how you feel," Amer said finally, "but you'd better leave high strategy to the High Command. You'll have enough worry just trying to feed your troops."

"What do you mean?"

Amer opened a briefcase and handed Nasser a stack of pound notes. "The command sent a thousand pounds for cheese and olives. Here, buy what you can with it. Nobody took the trouble to supply us with emergency rations for the men in the field!"

"You mean our men will have to sit like rats in a hole eating only a bit of cheese?"

Amer shrugged in disgust.

As Shoshana Klarman was about to close the small grip into which she had hurriedly piled a few items, her husband Moshe handed her some photo albums.

"Here, take these for the children," he said.

His wife glanced at them briefly. "Why? There's no need. The bag is full as it is."

"Please take them," he repeated.

But Shoshana was adamant. It was difficult enough to leave her husband at this moment when Yad Mordechai was about to be attacked. Most of the other women, including mothers, were remaining, a few to fight alongside the men, most to provide meals and other services during the fighting. But as a children's nurse, she had to accompany the kibbutz children, among them her own two, in the evacuation that was to take place that evening of May 18. Somehow, she felt, to take the albums would be tacit recognition of the possibility that her husband might die, a thought that she would simply not tolerate.

"No," Shoshana said, as she snapped the suitcase shut. "There's no room for the albums. Don't worry, they'll still be here when the war is over . . ."

Throughout that hot, muggy night, the people of Yad Mordechai—which was named after a resistance fighter of the Warsaw Ghetto from where most of the settlers had come—worked ceaselessly. Dawn came upon them with stifling swiftness as a *khamsin* swept in from the desert borne by a shifting wind. Bathed in sweat, the men and women took their first break at about 6:30 A.M., when they trickled into the dining hall for breakfast.

At 7:45, before they had all finished their coffee, the air raid alarm sounded. Within seconds, three Spitfires had released incendiary bombs and mortars were pounding the kibbutz. Wooden buildings went up in flames against a murky sky that was curiously speckled with white chicken feathers.

To the occupants of the pillbox at the southeast corner of Yad Morde-chai, several hundred yards from the center of the settlement, it seemed that the whole area had suddenly disappeared in the billowing storm, leaving them in terrible sunlit isolation. The commander, Yitzhak Waldman, tried to contact headquarters, but the line was dead. Perhaps all the people were dead too, he thought.

"How could they live through that?" Mendel Zeidman asked, watching the massive destruction through a slit in the wall.

Then the men in the pillbox heard a whimpering sound just outside.

"What the hell is that?" asked Yitzhak.

Mendel strained to see through the slit.

"It's one of the Doberman pinschers," he said (referring to the dogs that were being trained to guard the fields). "He's scared. He wants company I'll let him in."

"No, you won't," Yitzhak said hastily. "What if he goes mad with fright and starts to bite?"

"But it's inhuman just to let him stay out there."

"We'll have to shoot him," Yitzhak said.

The men were silent for a moment, while the roar of the bombs and the dog's whimpering both seemed to grow maddeningly loud.

"Mendel," Yitzak said in a hard voice, "you shoot him."

"But, Yitzhak . . . "

"You heard me. Shoot him!"

Zeidman put his rifle to his shoulder and aimed at the animal, which stood trembling, staring at him. But each time he tried to pull the trigger, the stock somehow slipped from his shoulder.

Finally, Yitzhak, pushing Mendel away, aimed and fired.

Lowering his rifle, he watched horrified as the dog, mortally wounded, crawled up to the window, poked his nose through the slit, and resumed his whimpering. Yitzhak pushed him from the window with his rifle barrel. As he fell to the ground, the dog was silent at last.

One of the men, Joseph Steinberg, began to sob. Yitzhak Waldman dug the rusty sight of his rifle into the palm of his hand until it bled. All were roused from their horror only when someone shouted: "Look, two armored cars!"

They leaped to the windows and watched the two cars crawl up the sandy road that ran from the Arab village of Deir Seneid toward the sea. The vehicles stopped in a row of carob trees about 700 yards away on the other side of a flat field, and Yitzhak through his binoculars could see the small cannons mounted on the back wheeling round toward the pillbox.

"It's our turn now," he cried excitedly. "Every man to his place!" . . .

Moshe Baron, the kibbutz electrician, sat in one of the trenches lamenting that all his work had gone for nought. He had spent hours the day before setting up an electric light system around the kibbutz and now they had to shell the place.

"Everyone of those two hundred bulbs must be smashed by now," he said gloomily to his companions, one of whom, Aaron Korn, commented: "My wife is sure to say you're a lousy electrician. Now she won't be able to knit in the shelter between bombardments!"

Aaron always looked lightly on misfortune. He had to in order to survive. During World War II, he had escaped from Nazi-invaded Poland to the Soviet Zone, where he was arrested for illegal entry. After a short period in jail, he had been put to work in a Soviet factory welding cannons for the struggle against Hitler—a "forced" labor that he was only too glad to perform. He was finally released and came to Palestine with General Anders' Polish army in exile, from which he had deserted to join the kibbutz he had preferred since before the war.

Baron took out a bottle of wine from the niche in the trench where he kept supplies, and pulled the cork with his teeth.

"For every lamp one Egyptian," he said. *"L'chaim*—to life!"

As he took the first swallow, a shell landed in the trench, killing him and Aaron Korn, and wounding five others.

Late in the morning, after about three hours of bombardment during which an estimated 2,500–4,000 shells were lobbed into the settlement,

there was a sudden startling silence, broken only by the whine of an airplane releasing, not bombs, but leaflets. As they came fluttering down, the
men in the trenches grabbed them and read the message (written in faulty
Hebrew):

> In the name of Moses and in the name of Allah, the prophets of the
> true God who has mercy on us; God has said that if your enemy wants
> peace, be at peace with him. God listens and God knows the truth.
>
> With these holy words from the Koran we approach you, the inhabit-
> ants of this settlement. Our aim is to bring peace among you on condition
> that you act peacefully toward us. Thus you will be able to save your
> lives, your property, and your children.
>
> It was not our intention to start a war. It is your resistance which has
> caused us to attack you, but your resistance will be of short duration and
> in vain.
>
> Therefore we ask all inhabitants to lay down your weapons peace-
> fully, to give up your weapons, your mines, and all your battle equip-
> ment, to raise a white flag, to destroy no property, and to gather into one
> place to await us. You are commanded to put these orders into effect
> within one hour after this proclamation has reached you. After this time,
> if you do not obey our orders, you will be considered an aggressor and
> will have proven to us that you wish to fight.
>
> God said, "If you are attacked, answer with attack, and know well
> that God is on the side of the righteous."
>
> The Almighty God always speaks the truth.

The settlers laughed as they read this, particularly at the references to
the desirability of saving property, since virtually all Yad Mordechai's
property had already been blown to bits in the bombardment. The leaflet
had obviously been designed to influence settlements before they had been
heavily shelled.

But the defenders were grateful for the hour in which to redig trenches,
tighten defenses, clean weapons, and care for the wounded. The kibbutz
doctor, a man named Keller, spoke with Grisha and Munio Brandwein,
the field commander, after they had visited the underground shelter where
the wounded were taken. "We must summon the Red Cross to come
in and evacuate these men. I cannot treat them properly under these conditions. There's not even enough room to lay them down."

"We are surrounded," was Grisha's answer. "The bombardment will
begin again any minute now and we have to expect infantry attacks. Maybe
it will be possible tonight, although I doubt it."

"But in every war they evacuate the wounded!" cried Keller, who had
served in a German hospital during World War I. "Mundek must be
operated on at once—it's his only chance. If you don't get him to a hospital,
I won't be responsible for his life!"

The two commanders looked at Mundek Halperin, who lay on a bunk with tourniquets on both legs. They understood the special affection Keller felt for him, for they shared the same feeling. Mundek had been born with a deformed foot and until he was thirteen had not even been able to walk without help. But after he joined Yad Mordechai he forced himself to do hard work and had earned an appointment as a post commander. Now the legs he had trained himself to use with such tremendous effort were nothing but bloody stumps from which his life was ebbing.

"Do what you can, doctor," Grisha said. "We'll try, God knows we will. But we're cut off."

Mundek died later that day.

Captain Muhieddin, back from his reconnaissance mission, was making feverish last-minute preparations in Deir Seneid for an infantry attack on Yad Mordechai. One company of his 1st Battalion was already encamped in the banana plantation from where the attack was to be launched, and a second was about to leave for the plantation.

Soldiers sat around under the trees waiting for the order to advance. Muhieddin, standing with one of the officers, glanced at his watch. "Zero hour is only half an hour away. Everything all set?"

"Yes, sir," the officer replied.

"How many wirecutters has your company got?"

"Wirecutters? Nobody gave us any."

Muhieddin paled. "You mean you have no wirecutters, and we're supposed to attack in half an hour?"

"That's right, sir. There hasn't been time to arrange everything."

"Just how do you expect your men to get through those barbed wire fences without cutters?"

The officer was silent for a moment. "I don't know, sir. I guess we'll have to use our bayonets."

Muhieddin looked around at the soldiers relaxing in the sun. They were being led to slaughter!

Artillery began to pound the Israeli positions again as soon as the hour's grace was over, and shells came in with even greater intensity than before, particularly in the pillbox area. The pillbox squad, now lined up in the trench behind the half-destroyed fortification, had felt the earth tremble around them for perhaps half an hour when one of the lookout men yelled: "They're coming!"

Joshua Katzir, a member of the squad, stuck his head above the trench. "Look at them! You'd think they were on parade!"

As the Egyptians, mostly tall Sudanese, emerged from the cover of the banana plantation, they advanced at a leisurely pace fully erect, as British colonial troops might have done in past wars with Pathon tribesmen.

Pinhas Marmor, who had now replaced Yitzhak Waldman (who had been wounded) as commander of the pillbox position, watched in amazement through his binoculars as the great human tide edged forward in magnificent textbook formation, followed by smartly dressed officers waving their revolvers, presumably to prevent a retreat, and shouting: *"Aleihum!* Onto them!"

The Egyptians advanced to within 300 yards—200 yards—100 yards. The covering artillery barrage then ceased abruptly in order to avoid hitting the attackers.

As Pinhas ordered his men to fire, cries of agony echoed across the field, and the attackers stopped and began running back to cover behind a small hill.

The Israelis also halted a second assault; but they could not stop a third along a broader front.

"Run!" Pinhas yelled. "Take all the ammo . . . Scatter out!"

The men dashed through burning wheatfields toward the center of the kibbutz about 50 yards away. Simultaneously, the Egyptians, seeing them run, turned around and retreated in the opposite direction, apparently calculating that the flight of the Jews indicated their position was about to be blown up. Later, however, they returned to occupy the post.

All other posts managed to hold out until night enveloped the settlement in a new savagery, the savagery of sudden peace that permitted members to reflect on what had happened that day.

Throughout the fighting, Haya, Aaron Korn's wife, had worked with frenzied efficiency keeping order and helping the lightly wounded in the underground shelter where she was in charge. As these wounded took turns lying down on the only two bunks in the shelter, she saw to it that the women cared for them as best as they could—giving them something to drink or eat, wetting their lips with gauze, or simply stroking their foreheads.

As darkness fell, men from the trenches started trickling in to see their wives and friends, but as the hours passed and her husband did not come, Haya began to worry. No one, it seemed, had seen him. Fearing that he was lying wounded somewhere, she went out alone into the trenches, flattening herself against the dirt walls each time a stray shell whistled nearby.

Finally, exhausted, she returned to the shelter and lay down on the cold dirt floor.

"You know that guy who sang so nicely and was always laughing?" she heard a Palmach reinforcement near her say. "He was killed this morning and the shell buried him in the sand . . . "

Haya lay in shock, listening to the terrible cries of wounded animals.

In another shelter, Munio Brandwein was discussing tactics with his fighters when a woman pointed to a young man lying under a bunk and asked: "What shall we do with him? He won't fight."

Munio pulled the man roughly from under the bunk. But breaking into hysterical sobs, he grabbed Munio's knees and began to kiss his shoes.

"Please sir," he pleaded, "don't send me to the trenches. I was in a concentration camp. I only got to Palestine three weeks ago. I want to live a little. I want to see my sister."

Munio pushed him away and lifted him to his feet. The man, ashen-faced and weeping, towered over Munio's muscular but smaller frame.

"I can't! I can't!" he sobbed.

Munio, as he held him by the shirt collar, wanted to drag him outside and shoot him. A tough, Palmach-trained fighter, Munio—who had migrated to Palestine in 1938 after serving for more than a year in the Polish army—believed in the simple battlefield credo: "Win or die." And those who were not willing to die were "traitors."

But as he stared into the frenzied eyes of this man, he felt he was looking at a ghost. The man was already dead. He had died in Hitler's camps, just as surely as the others had been asphyxiated in the gas chamber. Who knew what courage had died with him?

Munio released his hold on the man, who scurried like a frightened animal under the bunk again.

"All right," Munio said. "Go and dig trenches."

Early the next morning, in one of the shelters, the women were taking turns standing in the corridors that connected trenches at either side of the stifling underground room. There, at least, they could breathe fresh air and see the sky. But then shelling was resumed and Mira Givoni, who commanded the shelter, ordered all the women into the safer central section where they stood in the aisle, leaning against one another, or lay crushed together on narrow shelves. The shelter, almost airless and mercilessly hot, smelled of the 30 people bathed in sweat, some of them lying in excrement loosed by fright as the interior trembled with each nearby shellblast.

One fifteen-year-old girl refused to move from the corridor despite the danger. "Please, Mira, don't make me go inside. I can't bear it any more."

"But it's dangerous out there," Mira said firmly. "Now come inside immediately."

"I don't care. I'd rather die here."

Mira dragged the girl to her feet and pushed her inside. "Now you get in there and don't make any trouble!" she said.

But a few minutes later, the girl was outside again. Abruptly brought back, she went out once more and sat with her head buried in her hands. No, she would not return to the days of Bergen-Belsen. She would not lie all day next to another stinking body. She looked up and saw the sky, a mass of brown clouds. Even the heavens were filthy.

As she sat weeping, Mira did not disturb her again.

In the midst of the resumed shelling, the Egyptians fired smoke bombs for the first time as their 2nd Battalion prepared to attack along the whole southwestern front.

"We should have used smoke yesterday," Captain Mohammed el-Mogy, commander of the attacking company, said to Lieutenant Saad el-Gammal, whose platoon was to remain in reserve in the banana plantation. "Now that we have proper wirecutters, we'll be able to get through before they realize what has happened."

"Good luck," Gammal said. "We'll give you plenty of covering fire."

And the Egyptian troops started to advance toward the screen of smoke, as yet undetected by the defenders . . .

"Where the hell are they? Can anybody see them?"

"Never mind, keep shooting!"

The men in the trenches at Post 1 and what was left of Post 2 fired blindly into the smoke, hoping at best to frighten away the unseen enemy. Then, abruptly, the wind began to shift from east to west, as often happened at Yad Mordechai at about 11 A.M. during a *khamsin*. The attack had been timed to start at 11 A.M. precisely.

Within seconds, the smoke thinned out and finally disappeared altogether, and, like actors in the midst of action when the curtain goes up, dozens of Egyptian soldiers were suddenly exposed at the barbed wire busy with their wirecutters. Shaken, the defenders lobbed hand grenades and raked the Egyptians with gunfire. A mortar then pumped shells into the area along the fence.

When the battle was over, lying dead at the fence, together with about 40 per cent of his men, was Captain Mohammed el-Mogy.

At Palmach headquarters in nearby Nir 'Am, Gershon Dubinbaum (or Debambam, as he was nicknamed) was called to a staff meeting and—while the windows rattled from the shelling at Yad Mordechai—asked by his superiors for his estimate of the situation. He had been listening to the battle and reading reports from the commanders with some anxiety. From a distance, it looked as if the kibbutz had been turned into a furnace of death that no living being could survive. But whenever a bombardment slackened and an infantry attack presumably began, there was always heavy answering fire.

"I know their defenses well," he told the officers, "and I know the people of Yad Mordechai. We can count on them for a fight to the end. They are better prepared to hold off the Egyptians than any other settlement on the main road. Let's give them everything we have."

Nahum Sarig, commander of the Negev Brigade, said: "I agree as to the strategic importance of Yad Mordechai. It's holding up the main Egyptian column in its march on Tel Aviv. But the sad fact is that we are short of both men and guns. We have only two platoons—sixty men—available for reinforcements."

At that moment, the wireless operator entered the room with a message from Yad Mordechai. Sarig read it aloud:

> 18:30. The fifth attack, covered by machine guns, mortars, and heavy artillery, beaten off. We have 16 dead and 20 wounded. There is no place to lay them. The doctor is at the end of his strength. We must have help. S.O.S.

After a brief pause, Sarig said: "We'll do this. We'll send in one platoon. We can't do more; it would be wrong to send in every man to a surrounded point."

"What about the wounded?" Debambam asked.

"You know as well as I do that every truck is tied up evacuating the children," Sarig responded.

The seriously wounded would just have to die.

*

"We've got to surrender," one Yad Mordechai defender said in a high voice at a kibbutz meeting held around 10 o'clock that night in the headquarters shelter. "How can we few men hold up the whole Egyptian army? We haven't got a chance. Why should we die here? I say surrender!"

Grisha dissented, reminding those present of the massacre at Kfar Etzion only a week before. Could Yad Mordechai expect any better treatment, he asked.

The question of the women then came up for the first time, reflecting the dropping morale. Previously, the men had not wanted to frighten the women by voicing their secret fears and the women had not wanted to frighten the men. But late that afternoon, a hysterical young runner had reported that several posts had fallen and that the Egyptians had driven to the center of the kibbutz. Panic had swept the shelters as the hidden fear of rape and other atrocities against the women, who were now demanding hand grenades with which to blow themselves up if necessary, suddenly emerged as uppermost in everyone's mind. At that moment, the Haganah's theory that keeping nonfightingwomen in besieged fortresses would strengthen morale proved directly contrary to the reality.

As the men began demanding that the women should somehow be evacuated that night, Zvi Mayer burst into the shelter waving his rifle wildly.

"I've shot all the cows!" he sobbed. "All the animals. I've shot them! I couldn't bear to see them suffer. We're all going to die here anyway. Why should the animals suffer?"

There were gasps throughout the shelter, but Munio, pragmatic as usual, shouted: "What right did you have to use up bullets without an order?"

"I shot them all," Zvi said again hysterically. "I found Atziel—he was still alive by the swimming pool. I shot Atziel and one of the mules. I shot the cows . . ."

"Go and lie down," said Grisha gently. Someone led Zvi out.

A heavy silence ensued. Atziel, the beautiful white horse that had been the pride of the kibbutz . . . and all the other animals that had signified growing prosperity and diversified farming . . . Each animal, it seemed at that moment, was as important as any human member of the settlement.

Suddenly, Shabtai Weiner appeared from his wireless set to interrupt the meeting. "Egyptian headquarters is reporting to Cairo," he announced. "They say they have two hundred casualties. They say that they are unable to capture the place. They are asking for reinforcements."

"Reinforcements!" someone shouted. "They need reinforcements?"

And at 2 A.M., the new lift given the defenders by the knowledge that

the Egyptians considered themselves practically beaten was buttressed by
the arrival of the Palmach platoon. Oddly, Munio was among the most
depressed that morning. While inspecting the posts, he felt something tick-
ling his hand from behind. He looked around and saw a calf, the only
animal still alive, licking him. He wept.

Lieutenant Saad el-Gammal, whose platoon was in reserve in the village
of Deir Seneid, awakened at dawn on the fifth day of fighting and walked
over to 2nd Battalion headquarters to find out if a new attack against that
stubborn Jewish settlement had been scheduled yet.

"Good morning, Gammal," said Colonel Abdel Raouf, the battalion
commander, with a tired smile. "I'm going to give you the most important
assignment of your life."

"What is it, sir?"

Raouf got up from his chair, walked over to the Lieutenant, and, putting
one hand on his shoulder, said: "Gammal, I want you to take the colony
today. Your platoon will lead the attack."

Gammal was silent for a moment. This assignment was not altogether
unexpected, since he was one of the few officers in the battalion left alive;
but he was nevertheless stunned by the responsibility, and horrified by the
thought that he would almost certainly be dead before that pleasant spring
day was over. For days he had watched his closest friends being mechanically mowed down. Now it was his turn. It would have been better earlier
in the battle, he reflected, before he had seen those scores of bodies hanging
on the barbed wire.

Nevertheless, he replied: "All right, sir. But I'd like to do this my own
way."

"What do you mean?" the Colonel asked.

"I want to attack with only fourteen of the best men. And since the Jews
always concentrate their fire on men with automatic weapons, I don't want
anybody to carry a Bren gun, and I will be the only man with a Sten. I'd
like two tanks, five Bren gun carriers, and three armored cars. When we're
inside the colony, I'll signal for the rest of the company to reinforce us."

"Very well," said Raouf, "your request is granted."

Gammal then assembled his platoon and spoke to the men.

"We're going to attack again today, and this time we're going to take the
settlement. We'll succeed even if some brothers are killed, won't we?"

The troops, affected by his enthusiasm, shouted in a single voice: "Yes!"

"All right," said Gammal, somewhat encouraged. "This time only
fifteen men will assault in the first wave. Which of you want to join me?"

Most of the soldiers raised their hands, and Gammal selected 14 whom he knew well as brave, seasoned fighters. He then tore the officer's insignia off his shoulders, saying: "You know who your leader is, but I don't want the enemy to know."

And he smiled, his face flushed with the hope that perhaps he could pull off a miracle after all.

That morning, the Yad Mordechai defense committee agreed, over the objections of Munio, to send a delegation of three men through the Egyptian lines after dark to plead with higher authorities to evacuate the women and wounded and send reinforcements. Munio had argued that such a mission would not only be futile, but would deprive the kibbutz of three fighters when every person was vitally needed. But the others, in their desperation, wishfully assumed that the dispatch of reinforcements and evacuation trucks would now be almost automatic.

The meeting started to break up at about 2 P.M., when the air was suddenly split by the fury of massive shelling, the worst yet. After about an hour of unceasing bombardment, two runners burst into the shelter, almost simultaneously, one from Post 2 on the south and the other from Post 10 on the southeast. Both carried the same message: "Tanks are advancing from the pillbox!" . . .

Lieutenant Saad el-Gammal and his platoon moved slowly from the pillbox area across the charred wheatfields toward the southern defense perimeter of the kibbutz, two or three men behind each Bren carrier, with two tanks leading the way. Gammal felt somewhat numb as he walked along behind one of the vehicles toward what other commanders had found to be certain death. Other forces attacking the western defenses, he hoped, would draw Israeli attention from his own unit.

He began to pray, and then suddenly remembered that a few days before, his good friend Captain Mohammed el-Mogy, who had died in the attack on the second day of the battle, had asked him on the train bringing their battalion to Gaza whether he had brought a Koran with him.

"I forgot to bring it," Gammal had replied.

"Well, I have one here," Mogy had said, removing a small Koran from his inner jacket pocket. "There's a paragraph in it which is supposed to make you immune from death on the day that it is read."

"Do you believe that?"

"I don't know, but that's what it's supposed to do."

Though highly skeptical, Gammal had copied the passage on a slip of paper. Now he wondered whether Mogy had remembered to read it before going into battle. Where was the paper? He groped in his shirt pocket, pulled it out with a feeling of satisfaction, and read it. Whatever the powers of the Koran, he felt less fearful and more confident now.*

"Listen," he said suddenly to the two men beside him. "It is said that he who reads this paragraph from the Koran won't die on the same day. I'll read it aloud, and you repeat it."

Then he dashed forward from Bren carrier to Bren carrier, reading the prayer while the men repeated it.

He looked up to find in horror that he had advanced almost to the outer barbed wire fence without realizing it, though he was supposed to have stopped about 50 yards away, signalled the artillery to change its range, and laid a smoke screen. Now his platoon was virtually within the target area of his own guns, with no smoke cover. He and his men were dead already, he thought, as an Egyptian shell exploded nearby. If his own artillerymen did not get them, the Jews would. And he waited for the Jews to open fire at any second.

But, oddly, they did not. And there were his men right at the fence. The prayer had saved them! By continuing to advance under heavy bombardment and without a smoke screen, they had thrown the enemy off guard. The Jews were almost certainly hiding in the trenches under the tremendous shelling and could not believe the infantry would attack until the firing had slackened.

"Okay, blow the wire," Gammal ordered, and a man went forward with a Bangalore torpedo (an explosive device for cutting wire). Then he ordered two other men with torpedos to get ready to cut the two inner wires once the outer one was broken. Within a couple of minutes, all three fences had given way without a single Israeli bullet fired.

Gammal sent up a red flare to let his command know that the wires were cut and that the other platoons should follow. Then he signalled "forward," and the first tank plunged through the gap toward the heart of Yad Mordechai . . .

When the kibbutz commanders learned of the Egyptian advance from the pillbox, they were almost sure that the attack would be directed against

---

* The passage from the Koran that Gammal read was Sura IX: 128, 129: "Now hath come unto you An Apostle from amongst Yourselves; it grieves him That ye should perish; Ardently anxious is he Over you; to the Believers Is he most kind and merciful. But if he turn away, Say: 'God sufficeth me; There is no God but He; On Him is my trust, He is the Lord of the Throne [Of Glory] Supreme!' "

Post 10, on the eastern side of the defense perimeter along the main road. The Egyptians had not yet attacked this area, apparently believing signs that indicated it was mined (though in fact it was not).

"Everybody to Post 10!" Munio yelled, as the post commanders dashed from the headquarters shelter into the smoking wasteland. Only Munio and three Palmach men ran to Post 2 to check on the defenses there.

At Post 2 (next to Post 1 at the westernmost point of the defense perimeter), Joshua Katzir and his men crouched in the trenches behind the dugout as shells exploded all around them. He didn't think it likely that the infantry would attack during the barrage, but decided to make sure. So he ordered a Palmach man, a new immigrant, to go to the dugout and see what was going on.

Although the dugout was only about five yards away, there was no connecting trench, and to reach it the man would have to crawl under heavy fire. He stared at Katzir and shook his head.

"That's an order!" Katzir shouted.

"You go first," the man replied.

Katzir considered shooting him, then felt he could not force his men to do anything he would not do himself. He crawled out of the trench, scraped along the ground, and threw himself into the dugout. As he peered down the steep incline that led to the barbed wire at the bottom, he froze. Hardly 30 yards away, between Posts 1 and 2, tanks and armored cars, shielding squads of infantrymen, were advancing slowly in a jagged line, firing heavily. Just behind, more troops were disembarking from a large green bus.

Katzir hastily crawled back to the trench, yelling: "Tanks are almost on the position!"

Just then, Munio arrived with the Palmach men, who fired their only three Piat shells and missed. The post's lone Bren gun then stopped working, and a heavy machine gun was knocked out.

Ordering the post to hold on as best it could, Munio started toward Post 10 near the main road. Suddenly, he halted in shock. In the center of the kibbutz stood an Egyptian tank, spitting fire at the wooden huts and houses all around . . .

Lieutenant Gammal and his platoon had followed the spearhead tank into the kibbutz and edged their way toward the zigzag trench that led to Post 1 on the west. Gammal's plan was to race through this trench, surprise the post's defenders from the rear, and link up with Egyptian forces advancing westward. He left the second tank, together with the Bren carriers, outside the fence to await the expected reinforcements.

As the attack unit advanced, several men ran toward the trench, but only a few, including Gammal, survived Israeli fire. One of them then threw a grenade toward Post 1 . . .

Holding the post at the time were Moshe Klarman and three other defenders, who did not suspect that their rear had been breached. Klarman was cool as he watched the enemy advance from the front. His men regarded him as resigned to death, fatalistic, as he had been when he had insisted that his wife take the family albums while she was being evacuated.

As he fired steadily from the dugout window, a bullet hit him; he died instantly.

A moment later a grenade, hurled from the rear, exploded nearby and a second man was killed. The two survivors then ran to Post 2, abandoning their station . . .

In the trench behind Post 1, Gammal and his men, not realizing that the position was now unoccupied, paused in their advance to fire to their rear at Jews shooting at the tank from various directions. But they soon ran short of ammunition. Gammal was furious. Where were the reinforcements that were supposed to follow his detachment into the kibbutz as soon as he had fired a flare? He now hesitated to storm Post 1.

Finally, he decided to return to the vehicles waiting outside the fence, in order to obtain more ammuniton and send new signals. He ordered his men to hold fast until he came back, and set off toward the fence . . .

Shmulik Koiler, a defender who, the night before, had wanted to evacuate the kibbutz, now changed his mind as he watched the tank moving steadily toward him.

"We've got to stop it!" he yelled to his companions. And with grenades in both hands, he dashed directly at the tank.

The tank machine gunner immediately swung his gun and fired just as Shmulik hurled his grenades, which exploded in front of the machine-gun slit. As Shmulik fell screaming, almost cut in half by bullets, the tank stopped. Three Egyptians climbed out of the turret and ran for the fence.

But the enemy was forgotten in that moment as Shmulik lay writhing in agony, yelling: "Kill me! Kill me!"

"We can't let him suffer like that," said Zvi Kestenbaum. "He's a dead man already—maybe I should give him a round and help him to go."

At that moment, someone shouted: "They're coming in!"

Zvi swung around and fired his Spandau in the direction of the fence just as several Egyptians ran through, firing as they came. Two fell and the rest retreated. As he turned back to Shmulik, a bullet hit him in the forehead, killing him.

Someone else then put an end to Shmulik's agony.

Lieutenant Gammal, after again failing to attack successfully with the handful of men still in condition to fight, was almost weeping with rage and frustration. Though he had managed to penetrate the settlement, head-quarters had apparently abandoned him. He had fired dozens of red flares into the sky, but to no avail. And when he radioed for help, he received only promises—and congratulations on his "victory." News of the feat, he was told, had been sent to King Farouk as soon as the first flare burst. Were they mad? Did they expect him to take this fortress all alone?

Only he and two of his men were still alive and unwounded—those in the trench had been killed—and ammunition was virtually exhausted. He radioed Major Salah Salem in brigade headquarters and explained the position.

"All right. It's almost dark, anyway," Salem said. "You might as well come back."

That evening, Grisha dictated a message, transmitted to Palmach head-quarters by toy flashlight.

"We are at the end of our strength. We have no more ammunition. Give us permission to release our surviving members."

Shortly afterward, at about 10 P.M., blinker signals from Nir 'Am re-plied. Reinforcements and armored trucks to take out the wounded would arrive within the hour.

But Debambam arrived alone, with the news that three armored trucks were waiting in a wadi on the other side of the railroad tracks some 400 yards from the fence, but that five additional trucks loaded with reinforce-ments and arms had not been able to get through.

"How long could you hold out in case of another infantry attack?" Debambam asked members of the defense committee.

"Not more than two hours," Grisha replied. "I think we should retreat while there's time."

"We will be false to the fighters of the Warsaw Ghetto," Munio pro-tested bitterly, "unless we do everything possible to stay and hold this place."

Then Joshua Katzir summed up the majority view: "I do not be-lieve that in the few hours that remain, help can be brought in to us. We must do a Dunkirk. We must leave here, so that we can fight again some-where else."

Debambam thought this over. "I cannot give you permission to leave," he said finally. "The orders are that you are to keep standing. I will take out as many of the women as I can. I will report what I have seen here. We will let you know by flashlight signals or by runner what help can be sent."

"We will prepare to stay," Grisha replied. "But we must also prepare to go. If we don't get an answer by three o'clock we'll start retreating."

When Lieutenant Gammal arrived back at headquarters shortly after dark, Colonel Abdel Raouf, the battalion commander, greeted him brusquely.

"What happened? I thought you had taken the colony."

"I fought for four hours," Gammal said, his face drawn with fatigue and restrained fury. "But the rest of the company did not come to help me as planned. If they had come, we could have taken it."

The company commander who had replaced the dead Captain Mogy was then called in. Pale-faced and shaky, he explained that he had not led the rest of the company into battle because he had been wounded in the right hip.

"That's a reason to halt operations?" Raouf demanded. Then he looked at Gammal and said: "Get some rest. In the morning, you're going to Gaza. General Mawawi wants to see you."

A few minutes before 3 A.M., just after the trucks had left Yad Mor-dechai with the wounded, Munio came to headquarters with the news that a runner had just arrived from the Palmach.

"No help can be sent," he said.

Even Munio realized that this message was an invitation for the sur-vivors to leave.

Nevertheless, some members were reluctant to accept the order that they prepare for evacuation. Israel Weiss, a one-legged veteran of World War II, who was busy repairing trenches, threw his shovel into the dirt and cried when Haja told him the news: "Leave? Leave here? Leave when we're beating them? I won't go. I can't go. How am I going to march all that way?"

"You can't stay here," Haja Rotstein said sympathetically. "Come along with me—I'll help you."

Shortly after 3 A.M., 110 people began the trek to safety, including 25

walking wounded, 17 women, a dozen young boys, and two stretcher cases
who had been left behind by the trucks. Abraham Mordish, who was helping to carry one of the stretcher cases, tripped over a rock and fell at one
point and the wounded Palmach man almost slipped off the stretcher; but
Libka Shaeffer, the kibbutz treasurer, quickly took over as bearer, though
she soon found her knees buckling under the heavy burden.

"Don't leave me! Please don't leave me!" the wounded man, Asher
Landau, cried, thinking for a moment that he might be left behind.

"We'll soon be safe, Asher," Libka said as she struggled along. "We all
thought we would die there, but now, you see, we are saved."

About a third of the way to Gvar' Am, the nearest Israeli-occupied
village, with the column stretched for a distance of about 500 yards, mortar
shells suddenly screamed over them and burst nearby, and a machine gun
rattled in the night. The Jews panicked, some dashing for cover behind piles
of rubble in a dismantled British army camp, others flinging themselves
into orange groves or into any indentation in the ground they could find.

One-legged Israel Weiss hopped along the road, then fell and tried to
crawl, pulling his artificial leg behind him as he slowly advanced with groans
and grimaces.

"Better leave me," he said to Haja and Rachael Winman, the chief cook
of the kibbutz. "I'll never make it."

Ignoring his protestations, the two women, though both were short,
lifted the 6-foot Israel and dragged him along, his arms draped around
their shoulders.

Finally, they were out of range of the Egyptian guns and began to make
their way, exhausted and breathless, toward a checkpoint behind the hills to
the east where armored cars were waiting for them. Munio and Shalom
Wachtel waited at the approach for them, and as they trickled past, Munio
asked where the stretcher cases were, but no one knew. At last, as a sliver
of orange creased the horizon, a group came into view carrying a stretcher,
each bearer panting and about to collapse.

As Munio and another man grabbed the stretcher, Munio asked:
"Where is the other stretcher?"

"It must be with Grisha and the rearguard," someone said.

"God, I hope so," said Munio, as he went with the stretcher to the
armored cars waiting behind the hills.

Shalom Wachtel, waiting alone at the approach, suddenly saw shadows
materialize into the three missing people—Libka Shaeffer and Yitzhak
Rubenstein barely stumbling along with the wounded Asher Landau.
Shalom was running back to get help when he heard voices shout in English
and Arabic: "Who's there? Hands up!" Then shots pierced the morning air.

In desperation, Shalom ran on to the armored cars, and brought back
some Palmach soldiers to help the three, if they were still alive. But when

they reached the area where Shalom had heard the voices, no one was in sight.

A little later, on a distant ridge Shalom saw the silhouettes of the bearers still carrying the stretcher, surrounded by Egyptians—the last that was ever seen of the three missing Israelis.

General Mawawi looked gravely at Lieutenant Gammal after returning his salute.

"Lieutenant," he said, "you know where you were yesterday?"

"Yes, sir."

"Well, I want you to radio me at twenty-three hundred hours [11 P.M.] tonight from the same position."

"You want me to attack at night, sir?"

"Yes. They won't be expecting a night attack, and you know the layout of the colony pretty well by now. They've tied up about half the force we have on the coastal road for five days. You *must* take the colony tonight."

"Yes, sir," said Gammal, trying to force the memory of the previous afternoon from his mind.

"Good. I want May 24, 1948, to go down as a proud day in Egyptian history."

May 24. Gammal's birthday. What a day to die!

That night, after heavy shelling, Gammal led a company of more than 80 men along the path he had followed earlier—and read the Koranic passage to himself once more. After all, it had worked the first time for him even if it had failed for some of his men.

On reaching the fence, the column poured through the still unmended gap and sped to the area where so many had fallen the day before. Gammal was amazed to find no resistance. Then he realized what had happened.

"They've gone!"

As his soldiers started to shout and shoot off their rifles in glee, Gammal walked back to an armored car at the fence and radioed headquarters:

"This is Lieutenant Gammal. Please inform General Mawawi that I am speaking from the Jewish colony of 'Deir Seneid.' I have captured it."

Then he took from the armored car a guitar he had brought along just in case of victory, and returned to his men to celebrate his birthday.

8

Tombstones in the Dust

WHILE the fall of Yad Mordechai cleared the way for a renewed Egyptian thrust to Tel Aviv along the coastal road, the volunteer battalion under Colonel Ahmed Abd el-Aziz pushed from Rafa to El Auja and thence to Beersheba—all Arab towns—without meeting any opposition.

Aziz, who had begun the trek shortly after leaving Kfar Darom in the hands of regular Egyptian troops, was greeted in Beersheba by cheering crowds waving Egyptian and Palestinian flags and firing wildly into the air.

Among the happy inhabitants lining the dusty main street as the convoy rolled in was Hamdi Hirzallah, the young, good-looking assistant postmaster of the town, who was convinced that Aziz's arrival guaranteed that Beersheba would never fall to the Jews. Hamdi pushed to the front of the throng surrounding the Colonel as he stepped out of his jeep.

"Save your bullets," Aziz ordered good-naturedly, "you'll need them to defend yourselves."

"You must stay here to help us," a city elder cried.

"I shall leave a small detachment and some arms," Aziz replied, "but the rest of us must push on immediately."

A sigh of disappointment hung in the desert air.

Hamdi pleaded: "But you must at least help us occupy Beit Eshel. It is heavily fortified and a constant threat to us."

Aziz had seen the Jewish colony of Beit Eshel in the distance as he had approached Beersheba. Indeed, he had ordered his artillery to fire at it, provoking a reply that had killed an officer. Local Arab forces, and some of

288

his volunteers, had attacked the colony many times before but had always been hurled back, although the settlement was defended by little more than a dozen men armed with rifles and two machine guns and supplied by a daring airlift.

"I have no orders to attack Beit Eshel," Aziz said now. "Anyway, I have more important things to do. I must be in Jerusalem tonight."

Mawawi had apparently authorized him to advance only to Bethlehem, but why stop there when he could go down in history as the conqueror of Jewish Jerusalem?

Aziz deployed a small part of his forces for defense of the area. Then, as Hamdi and his companions watched silently, the main convoy rolled out of the town into the scorched reaches of the desert.

Aziz's next stop was Hebron, where local Arabs greeted him with joy almost matching that of the Beersheba populace, though, oddly enough, less because they feared an Israeli attack than because they preferred Egyptian over Transjordanian rule. Loyal followers of the Mufti, the Hebronites violently opposed King Abdullah's plan to absorb them, regarding him as a British agent.

The Hebron notables took Aziz and his men on a tour of the tombs of Abraham, Sarah, Isaac, Rebecca, and Jacob. As the visitors entered the small chamber containing Abraham's huge tomb, Aziz was enthralled by the thought of his soldiers being blessed by Abraham before setting out to kill the Jewish enemy; a blessing, he was sure, that would lend a special holiness to the war.*

The Egyptians then hurried on to Bethlehem, where they encountered hostility from Transjordanian officials, who refused to permit the Egyptian flag to fly beside the Transjordanian banner atop the police fortress of the town.

But Aziz found that the official line of the Transjordanian government, firmly supported by Glubb Pasha, did not correspond with the feelings of some of the top Arab commanders in the Arab Legion, who hated Glubb and thought that he was influencing King Abdullah against the other Arabs. Major Abdullah Tel, Legion commander in Jerusalem, sent Aziz a message welcoming him to the area and saying that he was placing his men at Aziz's disposal for use in operations in south Jerusalem.

Then Aziz received further good news. About 300 Arab Palestinian irregulars under Ibrahim Abu Daya (who had led the assault on the 35 kibbutz soldiers near the Etzion Bloc and later on Kastel) would attack Ramat Rachel on the road leading north to Jerusalem, and thereby clear the way for a march on the Holy City.

*

* Moslems as well as Jews claim descent from Abraham.

Abraham Halperin had never felt more depressed than on the morning of May 22, as he sat in Haganah headquarters in the New City reading desperate messages from the beleaguered Jewish Quarter in the Old City on the one hand, and from Ramat Rachel on the other. He rued his luck in having been expelled by the British from the Jewish Quarter some weeks before. Maybe if he were still in command there, he could have rallied the handful of defenders to continue resisting until reinforcements came.

Ramat Rachel was another story. There he *could* do something and, in fact, had been ordered by Shaltiel to defend the kibbutz at any cost. So he called in an aide and ordered: "Dig into our last reserves. Send a platoon to Ramat Rachel immediately. It may fall any moment now."

Ibrahim Abu Daya looked grim but confident as he waved his men forward from the main Bethlehem-Jerusalem road toward Ramat Rachel. He would now score his biggest victory since the fighting started. He had about 350 determined fighters, three artillery pieces, and six armored cars—more than enough men and equipment to take the colony.

They approached the grade leading toward the kibbutz.

"Forward! Forward!" yelled Abu Daya, and hundreds of Arabs raced up the slope.

But as they reached the barbed wire that surrounded the settlement, a blast of fire issued from within. Among those who crumpled to earth was Ibrahim Abu Daya himself, fated to remain a cripple until he died some years later in the hospital.

Abraham Halperin put down the phone in disgust. All seemed lost. The bus carrying his reserve platoon had been ambushed en route to Ramat Rachel and over 10 men (about a third of the force), including the commander, killed. Now came the news that the settlement had fallen completely except for the concrete dining hall, where survivors were still holding out. He would have to counterattack with the last two reserve platoons in Jerusalem.

Late that afternoon (May 22), he accompanied the two platoons on foot through the Talpiot and Arnona quarters to the vicinity of Ramat Rachel, arriving early in the evening.

Fires were still blazing when they reached the kibbutz, a mass of charred ruins. Except for occasional shots, the only sounds that echoed in the warm evening air were the raucous voices of Arab fighters shouting and laughing as they scrambled to the road carrying furniture and other household goods and pushing reluctant cows. Some were fighting over their loot; others were chasing fat, frightened chickens around the rubble-strewn grounds; while still others, having caught their prey, sat by the burning buildings happily roasting their dinner . . . Within minutes, the Arabs had scattered in panic as the Israelis interrupted the fun without sustaining one casualty.

During the night, the reserve force—being the only one available in Jerusalem—left the kibbutz in the hands of some older home guardsmen. The next day, May 23, about 60 villagers from the neighboring hamlet of Sur Baher led a new attack on the settlement. After an intensive artillery barrage laid down by Aziz's Egyptian battalion, the Arabs captured Ramat Rachel again—excepting, once more, the dining hall. Aziz's Moslem Brothers and some Legionnaires then arrived, sent the villagers home and, like their colleagues the previous night, were also caught weighed down with furniture and munching chickens as the same Israeli reserve unit stormed into the kibbutz again to recapture it.

Colonel Aziz was distressed as he leaned on the railing of the veranda of his headquarters at the Hotel Windsor and saw silhouetted against the dawn sky the Israeli flag, still fluttering from a burned-out chimney in Ramat Rachel. His own brave, dedicated soldiers had cheapened their cause by looting instead of fighting.

He decided that he would now direct the attack personally. The Legion had promised to support him, with 50 Legionnaires, 3 officers, and 2 armored cars; the Palestinians with over 100 fighters. Abdullah Tel, moreover, had promised to shell the Jewish Quarter of the Old City relentlessly to keep the Jewish forces occupied.

Yes, the settlement would fall for good that day, May 24, and the next morning he would attack Jerusalem and win immortality as its conqueror.

The morning before, shortly after the reserve Haganah unit had taken Ramat Rachel the first time, Shaltiel, despite misgivings, called Mordechai Raanan, the Irgun commander in Jerusalem, to his office. As Halperin had pointed out to him, he had no choice. The reserve unit could not be tied down in any single battle. It had to evacuate the kibbutz, and the only adequate fighting force available to replace it was the Irgun. Using the Irgun was, after all, preferable to losing the kibbutz.

"We've got to send some men quickly to Ramat Rachel," Shaltiel told the Irgun commander brusquely. "I'd like you to contribute two platoons. You will, of course, have to accept Halperin's command. Can you send your men immediately?"

Raanan readily agreed, feeling a certain satisfaction that Shaltiel had felt it necessary to call upon his forces.

"I'll get the two platoons together as quickly as possible," he said.

By that evening, before the Irgunists, under the command of Yehuda Lapidot, could arrive, the kibbutz had fallen in the attack launched by the Sur Baher villagers, and the reserve Haganah unit had gone back and recaptured it a second time. When Lapidot arrived late that night, the victorious Haganah unit again departed, leaving a squad of 10 Haganah men to support the 65 Irgunists.

A stubby Irgun fighter from New York, Moshe Brodetsky, set up a machine gun on the roof of the dining hall, aimed toward the road, and waited for daylight, which came together with a great flurry of enemy shells. Then, at about 10 A.M., Brodetsky witnessed a bizarre scene. While hundreds of armed Arabs dotted the brown landscape in the distance preparing to charge, a group of well-dressed civilian dignitaries and officers stood beside jeeps on the main road casually chatting, smoking, and watching the show as if at a drive-in movie . . .

"Once we've softened them up with the artillery, our infantry will overwhelm them," Colonel Aziz predicted as he gazed through field glasses at the smoking remains of Ramat Rachel. "Before the day is out, you'll see the Egyptian flag flying from that building."

Mohammed Hassenin Heikal, a young Egyptian journalist, conscientiously took down every word in a small notebook. "This will be a great victory for you, Colonel," he said reverently.

Lowering his binoculars, Aziz—a winner of many sharpshooting contests—responded reflectively: "You know, I have three dreams in life. One, to be the world's best sharpshooter. Two, to win glory in war. Three, to write a book on military strategy—one that will be thought as great and authoritative as that of von Clausewitz. I've even selected a title."

Pausing to watch a wall at Ramat Rachel crumble in a haze of smoke, he said: "I'm calling it *Surprise*."

The two men then climbed into a jeep and roared back down the road.

At the Hotel Windsor, they went upstairs to headquarters and Aziz introduced Heikal to his staff officers, who were standing on the veranda watching the performance.

"Egypt has a right to be proud of her soldiers," Aziz said to Heikal. "If they enter a village or a town, no power on earth can prevent them from keeping it. And they are disciplined, too. We have issued orders that no soldier can take even a straw from any place we conquer, because we are Arabs, and our principles do not permit plundering or looting. When our soldiers find such things as food or clothing, we send them to the nearest Arab village and tell the mukhtar to distribute them to the poor as a present from the Egyptian army."

Then all eyes turned to the fields below as troops began to march forward and armored cars bristling with guns started up their motors . . .[1]

From his position on the dining hall roof, Brodetsky watched the long line of more than 100 enemy soldiers advancing, most of them dressed in British khaki rather than in the mixed garb of irregulars. They marched swiftly, jumping from terrace to terrace into the shallow valley below, led by several armored cars and half-tracks. Brodetsky, a decorated veteran of World War II in Europe, held his fire, as did the Israelis in the trenches to the east and west, even when the enemy infantry reached the road to Jerusalem, cutting off the route over which reinforcements were expected. But he could barely control his trigger finger. For his mind throbbed with the words: "Six million, six million . . ." Now he would avenge his ravaged people. Now he would kill those who wanted to finish the job.

Troops attacking from the east began overrunning the trench in that area, forcing the defenders to take refuge in the dining hall. By noon, the Arabs occupied the whole eastern part of the settlement. However, Brodetsky—by firing in spurts—managed to keep them away from the dining hall, though shell after shell sought him out. Finally wounded in one eye, he stumbled downstairs and fell on a cot, joining a whole roomful of wounded men—about half the defense force.

When a comrade had bandaged his face, Brodetsky sprang to his feet, crying: "Get up! Get out out there and fight! To the last bullet! All of you who are wounded and can still fight! Come on, let's go!"

At that moment Lapidot came in and ordered Brodetsky to sit down and be quiet. The American sat down but wouldn't remain quiet, leading his comrades in a medley of battle songs. Lapidot then called all his men into the dining hall, saying: "No more shooting. Don't make a sound. Let them think we've evacuated the place. But stand by the windows and door and be ready to give it to them if they try to enter. Our radio contact is out. We can only try to hold on until dark. Reinforcements will be sure to come then."

So the Israelis waited in silence for the sun to go down, each gripping

a grenade or gun, while Arab fire also tapered off and jubilant voices nearby
replaced the boom of artillery . . .

Colonel Aziz stood near the entrance of Ramat Rachel in the late
afternoon and rejoiced with his aides as an Egyptian soldier climbed to
the top of a half-shattered building and attached an Egyptian flag to a
pole. But, within minutes, scores of civilians from nearby villages started
converging on the kibbutz and Aziz's joy turned to horror as he saw a
repetition of the nightmare he had witnessed on the two previous nights.
Like vultures, the civilians dragged off all objects and animals that still
remained, and his own men, as well as the Legionnaires, were joining in
the wild orgy of plunder.

"Stop them! Stop them!" he shouted to his commanders.

But it was too late. His men would not listen to their officers as they
fought with each other for everything from old shoes to broken-down chairs.

Aziz got into his jeep and drove back to headquarters. He went out
on his veranda and quietly watched the Egyptian flag fluttering in the
distance against the gray dusk sky. A great victory! A great victory! Wait
until Cairo learned of the glory he had won for Egypt.

When Brigadier Norman Lash, Glubb Pasha's deputy, heard at his
headquarters in Ramallah of the Legion's involvement at Ramat Rachel
and of the looting that followed, he telephoned orders to chief of staff
Colonel Ahmed Sedky el-Gendy to withdraw Transjordanian troops from
Ramat Rachel immediately. Gendy then called Captain Hekmat Mehyar,
the Arab Legion commander in the Bethlehem area, relaying the order:
"Get your men out of Ramat Rachel without delay!"

But when Hekmat drove to the settlement to organize the withdrawal,
some of his soldiers, preoccupied with the spoils, ignored him as the
Egyptians had ignored Aziz. They did finally leave, however, and Aziz
withdrew his forces, too, apparently on orders from Amman. Though shattered, he continued to work on his book, *Surprise.*

"We're Jews! We're Jews!"

An officer leading about 50 members of a Harel Brigade unit that had
been sent from the Jerusalem corridor to Ramat Rachel crawled in the
moonlight toward the voice coming from behind the barbed wire fence.

"You're still alive!" the officer said incredulously. "We thought you were all dead or taken prisoner. It was announced on the radio that an Arab flag was flying."

The two men embraced.

"The Arabs thought we were dead, too."

And so the Jews once more were in command of the southern route to Jerusalem.

S̶HIMON AVIDAN, commander of Israel's Givati Brigade, was shaken as he read in his Negev village headquarters the latest report from an observation post near the coastal road north of Yad Mordechai. A long column of about 500 vehicles, including artillery and tanks, had been seen rolling northward that morning of May 29, heading toward Ashdod, only about 25 miles from Tel Aviv.

Avidan urgently requested the High Command to send him reinforcements and to order the southern settlements to lend him every possible man and gun. He asked also for support by Israel's first Messerschmitts, which had just been assembled, though they had been scheduled for duty elsewhere. As word spread among his units of the advancing enemy column, near panic broke out among the new recruits, some of whom promptly deserted. Even the veterans were alarmed; never before had they come face to face with a force of such power and magnitude. Moreover, only one company was sufficiently rested to engage in the immediate task of confronting the Egyptians in Ashdod. Despite the fact that many members of this company were suffering at the time from food poisoning, the unit was rushed into battle in a frantic effort to stop the relentless enemy drive toward the heart of Israel.

Mohammed Neguib was worried as he jumped out of his jeep and, with other Egyptian officers, examined the damage done to the bridge just north of Ashdod.

"Have it repaired immediately!" he said to an aide.

Then he surveyed the bare countryside, and his uneasiness increased. One of the most elementary rules of warfare was to protect one's flanks and supply lines. But here he was, moving into the interior recesses of Israel in a single column that the enemy at any moment might isolate and cut to pieces. Cairo was not prepared to wait. The politicians wanted Tel

Aviv, no matter what the cost. But didn't they realize what a terrible price in blood had already been paid to subdue a few isolated colonies? What would the price be when the column met the great concentration of "4,000 Zionists" that local Arabs reported was waiting a little farther north? He had only 2,300 men. Even with 10 tanks, 6 field guns, and some 2-pounders, how could a single column, unprotected on the flanks, crush so large an enemy force entrenched in its own territory?

As work on the bridge proceeded, Neguib thought he heard a familiar drone . . . but he had not asked for air support. He looked up into the clear sky and saw four dots rapidly approaching his column.

"Messerschmitts!" an officer near him yelled. "Enemy planes!"

Anti-aircraft gunners immediately adjusted their sights and everyone dived into ditches along the side of the road. The planes swooped over the vehicles, which were standing bumper to bumper, and dropped bombs while the anti-aircraft gunners fired frantically. Although some vehicles were hit, the sight of one plane falling in flames drew a cheer from the Egyptians.

"Thank God they didn't do more damage," was Neguib's reaction after the planes had turned away.

But the assault damaged morale severely. No one had dreamed that Israel had Messerschmitts. Neguib was now more reluctant than ever to surge ahead, and Israeli harassment that night seemed to confirm his instincts. Local Arabs reported that an enemy artillery observation officer dressed like an Arab was directing fire from the tower of the village mosque. They also claimed that the Israelis had poisoned the wells. And the howling in the desert? Not wolves . . . the Jews were sending signals.

"Have the men dig in along the road," Neguib ordered his officers. "We've got to consolidate our position before we move on."

"They're digging in, but we don't know how long they'll stay in Ashdod," Avidan informed Yadin at GHQ that night. "We should try to wipe them out before they start moving again."

"Very well," Yadin agreed. "It should take about two days to plan the operation and get the force together. We'll attack on the night of June 1. The U.N.'s arguing about a cease-fire. If we're not ordered to stop fighting before we're ready, we'll attack."

In the feverish effort to organize the operation, three battalions were ordered to participate, including one Irgun battalion that had joined the Israeli defense forces, and a company of armed jeeps from the Negev Brigade, a special mobile force organized by Colonel Marcus.

Close to midnight on June 1, the units were at their jumping-off stations when Avidan received a message from Yadin. He then had to inform his officers at the pre-attack briefing in his headquarters: "We're too late. The Security Council has called for a truce, effective at midnight. Withdraw your units to their bases."

But the Israelis had erroneously thought that the Arabs had agreed to the terms of the proposed cease-fire. In fact they had not, and were, indeed, busy planning to attack Kibbutz Negba, the settlement closest to the point where the east-west road crossed the interior north-south highway. Negba represented a permanent threat to Egyptian traffic going both north and east.

"Come down! Come down!" the commander of Negba yelled over the radio to Zeev Wirovnik, who stood at the top of the settlement's water tower at dawn observing enemy movements while bullets and shells sang by.

"Just one more minute!" Zeev shouted above the explosions. But the next moment the men in the trenches below saw Zeev Wirovnik's dead body dangling by one foot from the ladder. It was quickly removed and another man, Menachem Kenigsberg, took his place against orders.

"The enemy is advancing from the south and west," he cried over the radio at about 7 A.M. "And I can see seven tanks and about a dozen armored cars!" . . .

Aron Schneider, a mild little man in charge of Post 6, a dugout at the southwest corner of Negba, strained his eyes to see through the enemy smoke screen, but in vain. As he and his four fellow defenders kneeled ready to fire, they suddenly found themselves facing a khaki wall gradually revealed through the wispy screen. Not two yards in front of them athwart a narrow trench squatted an enemy tank. As an Egyptian started to crawl from the tank into the trench, Schneider fired at him and heard a scream. At that moment a bullet struck the girl beside him (one of the defenders) and Schneider ordered a man to take her to the rear. Then he looked around and found that the remaining two defenders had disappeared.

He shivered. If only he were Samson and could take the tank in his hands and twist it into a heap of metal! But he was a peaceful man, a forty-year-old farmer (a founder of Negba in 1939), who had never been close to a tank before.

He began to fire at the small window, but with little effect. He then hurled his only Molotov cocktail but it failed to explode. In desperation, he ran to Post 5, about 50 yards to the west, and returned with two men and some more Molotov cocktails.

"It's gone!" exclaimed Schneider as they neared his post.

"Are you sure you weren't seeing things?" one of the reinforcements asked.

The two men then raced back to hold off tanks approaching their own post while Schneider, dazed by the experience and wondering if he wasn't going mad, sat down in a trench. . . .

The Piat team, Yoel Gises and Arie Back, were creeping to Post 5 when they saw six tanks groping their way forward, guns blazing, hardly 100 yards away. Gises, who had had only abbreviated crash training in the use of the Piat, fired and the first tank exploded.

Then they both wheeled around to face a tank already inside the kibbutz. Gises fired again hurriedly and the vehicle, though not exploding, slithered at full speed out of the settlement. The two men then turned around once more and with six further shells hit four more tanks . . .

A short time later, the defenders of Negba braced themselves for a new attack as another cloud of smoke puffed up in the west. But when it cleared, they saw armored cars dragging the disabled tanks away and the casualty-ridden infantry running in the distance.

Aron Schneider, still dazed, hobbled toward the command post. When two of his fellows saw him, they went pale.

"You!" one cried.

"Somebody must have screwed his head back on!" exclaimed the other.

The two men then dashed off and returned in a few moments, one explaining: "There's a headless body in the trench near your post, and it's wearing a khaki uniform just like yours. But we've looked at his papers and he's an Arab. Everybody thought the tank sliced *your* head off!"

"Give me a cognac, will you?" Schneider murmured.

Shimon Avidan was jubilant on hearing that Negba had withstood the Egyptian attack. He immediately prepared to carry out the attack on the enemy column at Ashdod that had been cancelled the previous evening. With the morale of his men soaring in the wake of the Negba stand, he was now more confident that the attack, the largest yet to be launched against the Egyptians, would succeed.

Shortly after dark, the units that had dispersed the night before set out again. The main task force raced over the sand dunes north of the enemy column in a westward line of advance, with the aim of attacking the enemy from the rear. The second task force, Israel Carmi's company of armed jeeps, half-tracks, and armored cars, advanced from the south to attack the village of Ashdod. A third force was to attack from the east in a diversionary move.

The Egyptians were ready for the attack, having learned of it in advance. As the main task force assaulted from the rear, it was met with withering fire and forced to retreat shortly before dawn. But before the retreat could be completed, day broke and the Egyptians mowed down the troops as they ran. By the time the Israelis were out of enemy range, about 30 men, a third of the force's strength, lay dead.

The second task force, under Carmi, also ran into trouble. Slogging through heavy sand dunes, it assaulted an enemy unit just before daybreak. But once again while bloody fighting was in progress the darkness lifted, revealing the paltry Israeli force in Egyptian gunsights.

The Israelis then began a desperate retreat, but their vehicles would barely move in the deep sand. As Carmi's men feverishly pushed and hauled their jeeps and half-tracks, which were loaded with wounded, one of them shouted: "Look, enemy armored cars!"

"We're trapped!" Carmi exclaimed.

But after a few tense moments of further effort to advance the caravan, the Israelis realized they were saved by the very curse that was threatening them. The Egyptian vehicles, too, were deeply bogged down in the sand. Finally freeing their own cars, the Israelis escaped encirclement, but only after having suffered (like the main task force) more wounded in retreat than in attack.

When news of the disaster reached Ben-Gurion, he immediately called a meeting of the High Command. A sense of desperation pervaded the conference room. With the Israeli attack force broken and the Egyptians little more than 20 miles from Tel Aviv, could that city now be saved? Some commanders thought that only a quick truce would stop the Egyptians. But how could the Egyptians be expected to accept a truce when the heartland of Israel lay practically open to them?

At an Egyptian staff meeting in Cairo, Lieutenant General Mohammed Haydar, chief of the armed forces, read out several cables from General Mawawi, then commented:

"Our forces, as you can see, have repulsed the enemy attack at Ashdod. But there are likely to be more attacks. Although about a tenth of the four thousand Zionists gathered to strike at us south of Tel Aviv were killed in the battle, according to these reports the rest pose a grave threat to us. It might be wise now to change our tactics and consolidate our gains. After all, we have all but cut off the Negev from the enemy. With a truce in the offing, why take a chance on a disaster south of Tel Aviv? We can always take Tel Aviv later. Let us concentrate on completely isolating the Negev from the Jews."

The staff agreed, and so did King Farouk.

S HORTLY after the battle at Ashdod, Gamal Abdel Nasser joy-fully received orders for his 6th Battalion to move from Gaza to Ashdod to replace the 9th Battalion there and dig in. At last Egypt would consolidate her gains, mopping up centers of resistance in the rear and on the flanks of her lines of communications.

The next day, June 6, he arrived with his troops at Ashdod and immediately embraced his friend Amer, who was waiting for him. That night the two men lay on blankets in a trench by the trunk of an orange tree. They were too exhilarated to sleep. When they weren't excitedly discussing the war, Egyptian artillery was shelling the settlement of Nitzanim nearby and Amer's radio set was communicating the minute-by-minute progress of the devastation.

"Tomorrow my battalion is to attack Nitzanim," Amer told Nasser. "It's the main threat to our flank at Ashdod."

"I hope this won't be another Deir Seneid or Negba," Nasser said cynically.

"Don't worry, we learned valuable lessons at Deir Seneid. Our young officers are tremendously enthusiastic. When I suggested drawing lots to determine which company would lead the attack, Mahmoud Kheleif [a Free Officer] immediately volunteered to have his company lead the assault."

But Nasser remained skeptical.

At about 1 o'clock on the morning of June 7, Akiba Peled stumbled through the narrow trench leading to command headquarters in the center of Kibbutz Nitzanim, crouching as he ran to avoid flying shrapnel. The Egyptians had been pounding the settlement with a continuous rain of shells since midnight, and Akiba wondered if he were wise to have left his dugout post. But with radio communication broken, he had to find out what was happening and what his distant post should expect.

Suddenly, he saw a figure running toward him along the trench.

"Shula!" he cried. Both fell flat as a shell screeched to earth nearby. Then the girl, Shula Dorchin, got up again. "Get into a shelter!" said Akiba.

"There's some wounded . . . ," the girl said breathlessly. Then she removed a gold watch from her wrist.

"Please keep this for me, will you?" she said, handing it to Akiba.

"Sure, but why?"

Shula's soft, dark eyes smiled, though her mud-streaked oval face was immobile. She dashed on as another shell scattered shrapnel nearby.

Akiba glanced at the watch and then turned to see the girl disappear in the shadows cast by the flaring sky. He wondered how long her luck could hold. Just the other night she had run to headquarters in the middle of a bombardment and, without catching her breath, had grabbed the radio microphone and sung "Believe, the Day Will Come!" into it. Cowering in a trench with his head down, he had nearly wept at the sound of her soft, passionate voice. He and others had scolded her for taking such chances, even though she had made them stronger. But it was useless.

Akiba put the watch carefully in his pocket and hurried on to headquarters . . .

"Do you think they'll attack with infantry?" Dvora Epstein asked, as she sat on the floor of a dugout facing east next to Arie Barelko.

"Probably," Arie replied. "They've never hit us so hard before. You should have evacuated with the other women."

"But I'm single," Dvora said, her large eyes glinting gaily. "And I'm not even a mother. You know as well as I do that every person is needed."

"But you've only been here six months. You haven't lived the kind of life to prepare you for something like this."

Yes, she had lived a good, secure life in Uruguay. She had had wealth, servants, doting parents . . . everything.

"I'm quite prepared for something like this," she asserted. "It was the kind of life I lived that made me realize I had to fight for something . . ."

"We're not receiving a thing," Issahar Hirschler muttered resignedly, "and there's no way of knowing if they're receiving us."

"Well, keep sending," Mira Ben-Ari, his assistant, advised. "For all we know they may be hearing us very clearly."

Mira smoothed back her short black hair and Issahar knew that she was trying to ease the throbbing in her head as she sat on a cot against the wall in the communications shelter, her face oddly placid. Of the 10 women not evacuated, she was the only mother. This was unfair, Issahar thought, but who else could help him operate the radio? She was the only other trained operator in the kibbutz.

As shells continued to shake the cavelike shelter, Mira seemed almost unaware of the storm. It was nearly a week now since she had sent a letter to her husband (by one of the mothers who were evacuated) . . .

My love:

I shall write only a few words. I'm sure you will understand that it is difficult to write. . . . I have never felt [so depressed] before, but I shall overcome this feeling. In these times, we have to overcome everything! Perhaps because of the ability of our people to suffer and not to lose hope; perhaps because of our stubborn refusal to give up even though we are very few—in any event, we shall gain what we have longed for for 2,000 years.

There is no separation more difficult than that of mother and child, but I have separated from my child so that he will be able to grow up in a safe place, so that he will be a free man in his country. Visit him often and when you do tell him how much I love him. . . .

"They'll certainly send reinforcements," Issahar said, adding skeptically: "If they hear us . . ."

Abraham Schwartzstein, the Palmach commander at Nitzanim, sat at a wobbly table in the headquarters shelter talking to Akiba Peled and other post commanders. His sensitive countenance was gaunt and pale, and his disheveled hair curled down to his heavy brows.

"We're almost surrounded," he said calmly. "They'll probably attack after sunrise. But we can hold them until reinforcements arrive."

He did not feel as confident as he sounded, for the kibbutz occupied low ground and had a defending force of only 130 settlers and Givati Brigade soldiers armed with light arms, one 2-inch mortar, and one Piat.

"Better get back to your posts," he told his officers with a smile of encouragement. "It's almost dawn . . ."

Less than half a mile away, Brigadier Mohammed Neguib and officers of the 9th Battalion, including Abdel Hakim Amer, sat behind a half-shattered house in a former British camp discussing the final details of their attack plan. Spreading a map on the radiator of a jeep, Neguib pointed to the main features of the settlement. The battalion, supported by a platoon of tanks, a company of armored cars, a regiment of 25-pounders, a battery of anti-aircraft guns, two batteries of anti-tank guns, and a squadron of fighter planes, would carry out the assault in three phases.

First, the force would capture a small hill in the northeast dominated by the water tower. Then it would take the higher ground centrally, where the dining hall and living quarters were situated. And finally it would seize the Palace, an abandoned Arab house to the south also higher than its surroundings.

"The colony is heavily fortified," Neguib emphasized grimly, "but we have the courage to capture it. And I'm going along to help you do it."

At about 9 A.M. an Egyptian infantry unit began to advance toward the settlement from the northwest, but it ran into heavy fire about 40 yards from the outer barbed wire surrounding the kibbutz. After Captain Kheleif, the young Free Officer leading the charge, had been killed, the attackers retreated behind a line of tanks a few hundred yards away. A second wave attacked shortly thereafter and was again thrown back. Then two planes suddenly materialized and swooped down to strafe and bomb the Israeli positions, while several tanks began advancing from the east and northeast, their guns firing point-blank at the three gun positions facing them.

In a trench inside the settlement, an Israeli armed with the defenders' only Piat kneeled and aimed carefully. He hit one tank and a second. Then he screamed out as a jagged sliver of shrapnel entered his body.

"Quick," he yelled, "somebody fire this thing! I'm wounded!"

But no one else in the kibbutz knew how to use the Piat, and within minutes the guns of the advancing tanks had knocked out all three Israeli strongpoints, killing most of the occupants . . .

Issahar Hirschler had just sent the last of scores of desperate S.O.S. messages to Givati Brigade headquarters, praying that at least one had gotten through, when a soldier rushed into his dugout crying: "Leave the radio! The infantry is breaking in! Go to the top of the hill and help us hold them off!"

Issahar and Mira Ben-Ari grabbed their rifles and dashed to the crest of the hill in the center of the kibbutz where they joined several other defenders, including commander Schwartzstein. They lay in the dirt firing away at Egyptians who had broken into the kibbutz from the north and northeast. After about 15 minutes, Schwartzstein yelled: "We can't stop them! Our only chance is to retreat to the Arab house! Hold them off while I pass the order around for everyone to gather there!" . . .

Dvora Epstein, her fair, patrician face a white mask, watched impassively as scores of defenders rushed past her.

"Come on, Dvora, they're breaking in!" a comrade shouted to her as he ran by. "Everybody to the Arab house!"

But she shook her head as she sat in the trench gently stroking the forehead of Arie Barelko, who lay with his head in her lap moaning from severe wounds in his arm and leg.

"No," she said calmly. "Arie can't be moved, and I won't leave him here alone."

"But they're coming!" the man insisted. "They'll kill you both!"

Silently she went on stroking Arie's forehead . . .

Shula Dorchin burst into the first aid bunker and shouted to Dr. Perlmutter, the settlement doctor: "Come quickly! Two of our boys are seriously wounded in the bunker near the Arab house. They may be dying!"

"But Shula," Perlmutter reasoned, "the Egyptians are breaking in, shooting everywhere, and it's a long run from here. We'll have to wait. It's too dangerous."

"If you won't come with me," said Shula, "then I'll go alone. Maybe I can at least ease their pain."

"But Shula . . . "

"Please give me some first aid equipment."

The doctor knew she wouldn't give in—any more than she had given in to the Russian occupiers during World War II when she had been a student in Poland. They had closed her Jewish school and had tried to burn all Zionist books, but she had hidden the books in her home despite the risk—and even smuggled some into Russia when she, together with other Poles, was sent to a Siberian labor camp. . . .

Perlmutter shrugged. He gave her some bandages and first aid materials, which she put into the knapsack on her back. Then she ran out.

Brigadier Neguib was exuberant as he marched alongside his men through the ruins of the old British army camp toward the enemy settlement. The fences and gate had been breached and his troops had already captured the northern area, taking trench after trench, just as he had planned. It wouldn't take long now to sweep through the colony and kill or capture the Jews gathered in the south.

Suddenly, the world seemed to explode in his face . . . a tank just two paces in front of him had hit a mine. Several of his men rushed up to him and one officer asked: "Are you all right, sir?"

Neguib, ashen with shock as he lay on the ground, could feel multiple pains in his chest and right loin. Little throbbing pains. He was certain that his wounds were superficial. Yet if General Mawawi, who was cool toward him anyway, learned of his injuries he might have an excuse to transfer him back to Cairo. Neguib decided he would undergo secret treatment in Gaza after the battle.

"I'm all right," he said as two men helped him up. "Just a little shaken up, that's all."

At about 3 P.M., almost 100 people crowded into the Arab stone house —all but a few wounded and their volunteer attendants, and some men in distant posts to whom the order had not been communicated. (A handful of these, among them Akiba Peled, later escaped.) The mood was one of desperation, as the fighters sniped sporadically through the small windows at the broken lines of Egyptian infantrymen gradually making their way south and west through the kibbutz ruins, all concentrating their fire on the house.

"The kibbutz is lost," commander Schwartzstein told his officers. "We have two choices. Either to try to escape or to surrender. Those who want to risk a withdrawal should be given a chance."

But an escape attempt failed when Egyptians pinned down the fleeing Israelis and drove them back to the Arab house with heavy casualties.

"What do we do now?" asked Moshe Peleg, one of the surviving Givati men.

"We have no choice," Schwartzstein—who had led the group—replied, breathing hard. "We must surrender."

"We need a white flag," one officer said.

"Everyone take off their undershirts and we'll use them," the commander ordered.

He then told his fighters to cease fire, and several men crawled out behind an embankment nearby waving rifles with the undershirts attached. When the Egyptians continued to fire, Schwartzstein said: "I'll go to them waving one of those things myself. Then maybe they'll believe we're serious."

Mira, the radio operator, said: "Abraham, let me go with you."

"No, it's too dangerous."

"It will be safer. They would be less likely to fire at a woman."

The commander reflected for a moment.

"All right, come on. But your husband will never forgive me for this."

When the shooting finally slackened, Schwartzstein, waving his undershirt in one hand, walked side by side with the plump radio operator through the southern gate and then eastward toward the Egyptians in the old British army camp. They crossed a narrow wadi a short distance from the camp and, as they emerged, found themselves staring into the startled faces of a group of Egyptians not 10 yards away. Shots rang out and the Israeli commander fell to the ground. Mira whipped out a pistol from her belt and fired at the Egyptians, killing three of them. The other Egyptians then shot her dead . . .

About 10 minutes after Schwartzstein and Mira had left on their mission, Moshe Peleg crawled outside and saw several Egyptians lurking behind the fence.

"Come out with your hands up!" an enemy officer yelled in English.

Peleg went back and relayed the order to his colleagues, who were busy dismantling their guns and burying the parts in the earth. Then, their hands raised, they marched to the fence where the Egyptians were waiting for them with guns pointed . . .

In a bunker just behind the Arab house, Shula Dorchin was kneeling beside two seriously wounded youths, Meir Entin and Moshe Rowed, who were on the ground moaning in severe pain, when Issahar Hirschler rushed in, crying: "Shula, it's all over! We're surrendering! Come with us!"

The girl glanced compassionately at the wounded. "We'll have to take them, too," she replied.

But when she started to lift one of them, the youth whispered: "It's no use. Leave us and go."

Shula held his trembling hand and smiled at him.

"But Shula," Hirschler persisted, "the Egyptians have ordered us . . . "

"No, I'm staying with these boys. I'll come later, when the Egyptians bring an ambulance for them . . . "

"Sit down and put your hands over your heads!" an Egyptian officer ordered, as the prisoners filed through the southern gate.

The Israelis obeyed, and then some, their throats parched from the intense heat, asked for water. An Egyptian officer told one of his men to fetch a canteen of water, and within minutes the prisoners were taking turns pressing it to their lips.

When an officer asked for someone to accompany him on a search of the kibbutz for Israeli stragglers, Moshe Peleg volunteered to go. As the two men walked toward the kibbutz gate, the Egyptian, a lieutenant, scrutinized the Israeli and asked: "Are you afraid?"

"Yes."

"I give you my word as an Egyptian officer that you will return in good health to your group."

Peleg stopped abruptly as he saw two figures sprawled nearby. He ran over to them and kneeled by the first, crying: "Abraham! Abraham!"

There was no response from commander Schwartzstein. Then he turned to the second figure and saw immediately that Mira, too, was dead. As he closed his eyes in anguish, his Egyptian companion said in an awkward effort to comfort him: "Well, it's war, you know."

They continued on toward the kibbutz gate, from which dozens of local Arab looters were streaming, burdened under the weight of sewing machines, crates of food, drums of oil, furniture, and other items. The looters virtually stepped on someone lying on the ground, face down, just outside the gate.

"Shula!" Peleg screamed, as he ran to the girl.

As she started to turn slowly on her side, Peleg put his hand to his mouth in horror. Her abdomen had been ripped open, apparently with a bayonet, and her entrails were dragging in the sand. She looked up at Peleg with glazed eyes trying to recognize him, her face waxen. Then she whispered faintly: "Please shoot me."

Peleg stared at her, then said prosaically: "I have no gun. Anyway, I'll bring a doctor and he'll get you well."

He touched her arm gently, and got up.

"Get one of your doctors, will you?" he urged the Egyptian officer.

"I'm sorry," the Egyptian replied uncomfortably, "but our doctors are all busy with our own wounded. Where is your own doctor?"

"I didn't see him in our group. Maybe he's still in the first aid station. Can we go and look for him?"

"Very well."

But then Peleg looked around again and he began to crack as he saw Shula's intestines protruding from the lacerated body. He knew it was too late. She was dying.

"You Egyptians are responsible for this," he shouted, crazed with grief. "Now at least finish the job. Kill her!"

The officer swallowed, and his tan face reflected confusion.

"If you want to shoot her," he said, "I'll give you my pistol and you can do it yourself."

But Peleg knew he could not.

"I didn't start it, you people did," he cried, almost in tears. "Now finish what you started!"

"Come on," the officer replied. "We'll look for your doctor."

The two men then went in search of the doctor, but could not find him.

Dazed and heavy-hearted, Peleg could hardly bear to watch when he passed some Egyptian soldiers trying to help a wounded Israeli to his feet. The youth was resisting their efforts as he lay sobbing, clinging to the body of a beautiful girl. Dvora Epstein had been lying dead in Arie Barelko's arms since the last stage of battle.

"No, I won't leave her!" Arie cried out.

"We've got to get back to your group now," the Egyptian officer told Peleg.

"But the wounded girl . . . "

"I promise to find a doctor."

A little later, trucks carried 90 men and 7 women to Majdal, en route to a detention camp in Cairo. Arie Barelko and most of the other wounded were among them and were to receive good hospital treatment. But Shula was missing, and so were the two youths she had refused to leave in the bunker. They had also been stabbed to death. Missing, too, were more than 30 other Israelis killed in the battle.*

At Givati Brigade headquarters a few miles away, Akiba Peled, who had

---

* Nitzanim members say Arab informants told them (after the war) that on the day following the kibbutz's fall, local Arabs marched triumphantly through a nearby village parading the heads of two women on sticks.

escaped, sat holding a cup of coffee with shaky hands and pondering the lot of his comrades. Radio reports of the battle had come in clearly until the Egyptians began to overrun the kibbutz, but there had been no units available to reinforce the defenders. Could everyone be dead?

Suddenly, he remembered the gold watch Shula had given him in the midst of the final battle. He took it from his pocket and examined it. She had had no money . . . It must have been a gift from someone. Her mother? A boyfriend? Why had she given it to him for safekeeping? Perhaps she had sensed that something would happen to her . . . and wanted to make sure that she would not be forgotten.

THE fall of Nitzanim lent urgency to an earlier Israeli decision to capture Hill 69, a former British army camp about a mile west of the kibbutz. For occupation of this height, which overlooked the coastal road, would not only cut off the Egyptian force in Ashdod from its base in Majdal, but would provide a takeoff point for a counterattack on the enemy units occupying Nitzanim. Actually, control of Hill 69 would reduce the strategic importance of Nitzanim, but the Israeli command was determined to recapture that settlement in order to keep up the morale of others holding out against great odds.

Neither Israeli nor Egyptian troops had tried to capture Hill 69 previously, since neither command had felt it could spare the men. But now, a few hours after the attack on Nitzanim, Givati forces marched on the unoccupied hill post.

At about 3 A.M., Aharon, a captain who commanded B Company of the Givati Brigade's 51st Battalion, arrived with about 75 men after trudging 1,200 yards from the village of Beit Daras to the north. He had orders to harass Egyptian traffic on the coastal road about half a mile to the west and to hold the hill at all cost, but as he quietly toured the area he wondered: how high would the cost be?

He did not even know the exact location of all the Israeli mines that had been laid earlier. And while he himself had served six years in the British army, he had only two adequately trained subordinates—his second in command, Dani Delogi, and a platoon commander, Issar Berski. The unit as a whole had experience only in minor skirmishes and mopping-up operations in coastal villages.

Moreover, though his company had more and better weapons than most units, they could not compare with those of the enemy, while its defense area had a radius of only about 60 yards, far too small to accommodate all his men; a concentrated barrage could be disastrous. And the earth was so soft and sandy that trenches were difficult to dig and would be even more difficult to keep intact under fire. To add to his distress, three enormous mushroom-shaped water towers were perched atop the hill like tombstones in the desert. Shining in the moonlight, they constituted perfect markers for enemy gunners.

As Aharon gazed at all this, he could see the silhouettes of orange trees outlined dimly against the sky. The grove outside Beit Daras—somehow, it seemed like the other end of the earth. An open field separated the hill from the orchard, and only a narrow path threading across it was free of the Israeli mines.

When the first shell burst at about 5 A.M., Milek Slonsky poked his head out of a foxhole dug into the northern side of the hill and saw a line of half-tracks and Bren carriers moving along the road from Nitzanim to the northeast.

"Tanks!" he yelled (misidentifying the armored vehicles).

He began to fire with his rifle at the first half-track as a machine gun nearby also opened fire on the approaching convoy. Within minutes, Milek was shouting joyfully as two half-tracks drove wildly into a ditch and turned over.

Dani Delogi, the company's second in command, came by at that point.

"How are you doing? We're holding 'em, aren't we?"

"We sure are."

"Okay, keep firing. Remember how they stopped the tanks at Negba."

As Dani moved away to lend his strength to other fighters, Milek felt invincible. Let them come with their tanks! Had not Negba proved that a single Israeli with a bottle of gasoline could stop one?

But as the line of armor kept edging forward, breathing fire, Milek's morale began to sink again. Why wasn't the Piat team firing? How close would the tanks be allowed to come? . . .

In a nearby trench, a member of the Piat team asked Dudu (David) H., a reconnaissance squad leader, if he should start firing.

"No," replied Dudu firmly. "Under no circumstances are you to open fire before being ordered to do so. We've got to tempt them into range and then knock them out."

But a few minutes later, an impatient Canadian volunteer, unable to hold back as the deadly armor advanced, fired a Piat shell, which fell far short of his target. As the Egyptian column stopped and began edging back, new shouts of glee from Milek and other defenders echoed through the area.

"We've won! We've won!"

But the Egyptians responded thunderously when the column had re-treated to a safer position, peppering the hill with missiles at point-blank range. Dani Delogi, so revered by his men for his courage and ability, looked out from his foxhole to see what was happening and a bullet struck him between the eyes. Issar Berski, the platoon leader, was sitting in another foxhole with his knees drawn up to his chin when shrapnel from a shell bursting overhead nearly sliced his leg off. The casualties mounted as the Israeli positions—dug into the soft earth—began to cave in under the pounding.

At about noon, the barrage let up and two tanks and several half-tracks, followed by a battalion of infantry, began to close in on the hill from three sides . . .

Aharon, the company commander, was shocked when messengers reported that Delogi and Berski were casualties. That left him as the only officer in the company, and no one else had more than a smattering of com-bat experience. He had already pleaded with battalion headquarters in Beit Daras to send reinforcements, though he realized afterward that any rein-forcements would have been cut down running through the open field. For some time, he hadn't even been in radio contact with headquarters or with his own platoons, since the explosions had disrupted communications. And now his only commanders had been hit!

How could his company keep fighting? Whenever a runner arrived with news of more casualties, more weapons knocked out, his despair mounted. As the shelling gradually diminished, he looked over the edge of his trench and saw the Egyptians trying to encircle the hill. But they still had not blocked the mine-free path leading eastward to Beit Daras.

There was nothing else to do. He must order a retreat, even though the men would have to run in the open in broad daylight. Normally, only higher headquarters could decide on a retreat, but since the radio was out he would take full responsibility. Actually, an artillery observer at another position on the hill was in radio contact with his gunners, but in the con-fusion, Aharon maintains, he did not think of that means of communi-cation.

Some armor was almost at the fence. There was no time to lose. He would go with the platoon facing Beit Daras, near his command dugout. With platoon leader Issar Berski wounded, the unit needed someone to show the way through the minefield. The other two platoons deployed in more distant sectors of the hill could follow. This seemed to be a logical plan; at least it was less suicidal than waiting to be killed on the hill.

At about 1:15 P.M. he called for a runner and, his eyes blazing, ordered: "You are to go to the first and second platoons and tell them that I am issuing an order for a retreat to Beit Daras. The third platoon will leave first with me and the first and second are to follow, removing the wounded with them. Do you understand?"

The messenger had already started to run toward the positions occupied by the two more distant platoons, but before he could deliver his message, a shell exploded in his path and a piece of shrapnel decapitated him . . .

Shraga Gafni, an engineer and machine gunner on the northern side of the hill whose gun had just been destroyed by a shell, watched dubiously as he saw an Israeli running past his position toward the fence ringing the base of the hill.

"Stop, you fool!" he shouted. "You're running toward a minefield!"

The man halted and yelled back to Gafni: "Are you the demolitions man? Where is the break in the fence? Quick!"

"What happened?"

"They're surrounding us! Retreat!"

Gafni was astounded. Who had ordered a retreat? No one had informed him of such an order. And besides, from what he could see, most of the enemy armor and infantry were keeping their distance, apparently afraid of mines, and had come near the fence only in the west. Even without his machine gun he could still kill a lot of Egyptians. Why retreat now, especially across an open field? It was safer to stay where they were. But then he saw dozens of other men dashing down the hill. Order or no order, the retreat was on and he certainly couldn't let them cross the minefield.

He jumped out of his hole to lead them toward the break in the fence that opened on the mine-free path to Beit Daras. But when he reached it, he groaned in consternation as he saw enemy armor slithering across the field toward the narrow lifeline . . .

Milek Slonsky raised his eyes to ground level and peered over the edge of his foxhole. Tanks, armored cars, troops—they were tightening a noose around B Company. There was nowhere to go, and almost no shelter. His foxhole had diminished into little more than a slit trench; moreover, his rifle had become jammed with dirt and wouldn't fire. It was hopeless. He would die. Many would die . . .

AS THEY HAD THAT STEAMY SUNDAY IN JULY, 1946 WHEN HE HAD visited a friend in Kielce, Poland. About 120 Jews had lived there—all who had survived the Nazi slaughter of the 20,000 prewar residents. He had watched from a window while citizens of the town, frenziedly engaged in a pogrom, trapped his friend as he was trying to escape. While church bells tolled, they had kicked and stamped on him until he was dead, then drawn away and silently contemplated their deed—before finally going off to celebrate mass . . .

"Retreat!"

Milek watched, stunned, as his comrades scurried down the slope, dropping their weapons as they ran.

"Retreat!"

The rumble of panic began to sound like an avalanche. Everywhere Milek looked people were running, jumping, stumbling, gasping, moaning, crying. He sat back in his foxhole and observed the scene for a few more moments with the detachment of a psychiatrist analyzing a nightmare. Then he knew it was time to run again, and found himself swept up in the avalanche—managing somehow to ride it to safety.

A supporting company rushed to the area near the orange grove to cover the retreat, but Egyptian armor, spotting the unit, crawled to within 50 yards of it and fired point-blank.

"Mortar fire! Mortar fire!" the company commander shouted into his walkie-talkie.

Almost immediately, Israeli mortar shells sang overhead exploding by mistake amid the supporting company. By the time further shouts over the radio had been heeded by the mortarmen, about 20 shells had hit the unit, eliminating it as a fighting group . . .

"Come on, keep running!" Dudu, the reconnaissance squad leader, panted as he and three other Israelis reeled across the plowed cornfield toward Beit Daras bearing Issar Berski on a stretcher.

They were following in the path of the company commander, who was far ahead, but were desperately afraid they would step off the track (it was scarcely visible) and blow themselves up. Then they forgot the mines as mortar shells exploded all around them and tanks standing in the field swept the area with bursts of machine-gun fire.

"Faster!" urged Dudu at the front end of the stretcher.

Then he was pitched forward by a tremendous explosion. As he lay on the ground, he felt something wet on the nape of his neck and cautiously reached for the spot, expecting to find his fingers dripping with blood. Instead, he found himself staring aghast at a human eye. The two men who had been carrying the rear end of the stretcher had been blown to bits, though he and the other man in front, as well as Issar, had been untouched by the exploding shell.

The two surviving bearers decided that nobody would get through alive if Issar were carried any farther. Dudu crawled over to the platoon leader, whose leg was hanging by a strip of flesh, and stammered: "Issar, we'll hide you and come back for you a little later. It's the only way any of us can survive. Okay?"

Issar, drugged with morphine, nodded his approval. The two men left him under a bush with a rifle and a grenade and dashed off crouching low to evade tanks that were seeking out the Israelis . . .

Meanwhile, Shraga Gafni stood by the fence showing other soldiers the way to Beit Daras until finally the stream diminished to a trickle of stragglers. Then, armed with a Molotov cocktail to use against a tank if one got too close, he ran across the field as fast as he could, ignoring the bullets mowing down men in front of him. The single file had now fanned out in all directions like rabbits fleeing the hunter. Some were blown up by mines. One soldier, chased by a tank, finally turned and raised one hand in surrender, only to be riddled with machine-gun bullets. Another approached a half-track in which an Egyptian sat smiling, beckoning him to advance. The Egyptian then took the Israeli's weapon and beat him with it . . .

Abba Kovner, educational officer of the Givati Brigade, narrowed his large, melancholy eyes as he stood beside two other brigade officers at the edge of the orange grove watching the disaster. Gripping a pistol in a slim hand, he muttered: "We've got to stop them before they cross the grove. If our reserves in the rear see them, they might panic, too. And then we would have no defense at all!"

He raised his pistol a few inches as the heavy-set figure of the company commander materialized in the distance, straining, puffing ahead. Kovner would have liked to shoot him. What greater crime was there than for an officer to retreat without orders, and to leave his men behind? . . .

He would almost certainly have shot such a man in the Nekomah (the United Partisans organization), which he had led in the guerrilla fighting in the woods near Vilna during World War II. He recalled the subzero nights in the forest when he had slept in wet caves with a grenade in his hand—the same hand that had once wielded the sculptor's knife. What fire had fused an artist's soul with a soldier's heart? The instinct for survival? The desire for vengeance? Both. But more powerful than either had been the passion for a Jewish resurgence within a just society, for an ideology that would renew the spirit of his tortured, depleted race . . .

Now, as he surveyed the chaos on Hill 69, he saw the whole fabric of his dream undermined. He wondered whether the Egyptians knew how clear was the way to Tel Aviv, and whether the company commander, the first Israeli officer to retreat without an order, deserved to live. He had learned in the ghetto of Vilna the wages of docility. And it didn't much matter in the end whether retreat resulted from tactical miscalculation or from fear. Retreat to where? To the gas chamber? To oblivion?

"Stop! Stop! Why are you retreating without orders?" Kovner shouted as Aharon approached the three brigade officers. (Kovner maintains that he pointed his gun at Aharon as he spoke, although Aharon denies that he was greeted by this or any other sign of belligerence. The company commander, says Kovner, stumbled to a halt, his eyes staring blankly as if he were in shock.)

"I was surrounded by tanks . . . what else could I do? I gave orders to retreat . . . ," Aharon gasped. "And there was no way I could contact headquarters."

"I am arresting you," Kovner claims he replied, his pistol still aimed at the commander.

But the steadily mounting chaos rendered the moral issue, at least temporarily, academic, and the brigade officers ordered Aharon to help them stop his fleeing men in the orchard before their panic spread to other units, and to reorganize them for immediate defense of the area. Even so, it seemed clear that if Egyptian tanks attacked the grove, there would be little to stop them from plunging northward toward Tel Aviv.

Shraga Gafni finally reached the orchard to find clusters of nearly hysterical survivors looking for the path through it leading to Beit Daras. He called to several of them to follow him, but a few did not trust him and began dashing in other directions. Inside the orchard, his group met the company commander, who was attempting to bring order among the survivors seeking their way through the grove.

"What do you need that for?" Aharon asked, pointing at Gafni's Molotov cocktail.

"To honor a tank with."

"There's no longer any need for that," snapped Aharon. "Throw it away. There are still wounded in the orchard. Go and find them."

Something at that moment died in Shraga Gafni. He had been fully aware of the extent of the fiasco, but he had not permitted himself to admit defeat. He had still been hoping for some miraculous counterblow, for some undefined event that would turn the tables. But Aharon had extinguished his last spark of hope. With some other Israelis, he found and evacuated Issar Berski, who died of his wounds two weeks later . . .

Unknown to Shraga Gafni, or to most of the Israelis, one man still remained on Hill 69—a young artillery observer, Zvi, who continued to spot targets for Israeli guns even after the retreating survivors had all reached

Beit Daras. When Egyptian tanks began to ascend the hill, he yelled into his walkie-talkie: "The Egyptians are on the hill! Fire on me!"

When this call came through, the commander of the artillery mortar team radioed battalion headquarters and asked what he should do.

"He's asking to die!" Abba Kovner told Meir Davidson, the battalion's second in command.

The battalion leaders were caught in a dilemma. They might still be able to keep the enemy from occupying the hill if they could knock out some of the armor. But could they order the death of one of their own men—a soldier who had refused to retreat even after everyone else had done so? Kovner remembered the Vilna ghetto—how the young and able-bodied had refused to leave the old and sick to fight in the forests, and so had died in the same gas chambers with them. The Jews could not afford sentimentality.

Davidson made the difficult decision. "We're going to fire on your position!" he radioed. "Save yourself! Run!"

Then he ordered the artillery team to fire.

A few moments later, Hill 69 exploded with shells, which knocked out about two tanks and forced the others to flee. And when the smoke cleared, Zvi's body lay amid the guns, helmets, and ammunition left behind by the other men.

Two days after the retreat, Abba Kovner stood before a group of men sprawled on the grass at the battalion base.

"I wish to address myself to B Company," he said deliberately. "You have lost one battle, but the war is still before us. This was our first encounter with tanks and artillery. You have learned much . . . "

He paused for a moment, then continued: "We're going to give you a chance to decide for yourselves whether the company should be broken up and all of you dispersed to other units, or whether it should stay together and try to prove itself in the future. Let's have a show of hands. How many want to break up the company?"

Not an arm rose among the handful of company survivors.

"How many want to stay together?"

Kovner smiled as he saw the unanimous response, not revealing that the brigade command had already decided to keep the company intact.

Then he read out an order issued by Givati Brigade commander Avidan: "From this day onward, any man who runs in the face of an enemy attack will be considered a traitor to the homeland, and all soldiers are granted permission to shoot him on the spot."

The men were silent, and Kovner knew that the order was not really necessary. Nor was the problem so simple. The battalion leaders wanted to court-martial Aharon, but the trouble was finding qualified judges. For what man could judge another's action on the field of battle without himself having undergone a similar test?

And so, though the case was investigated, Aharon was never tried, and eventually retired from the army with full honors as a colonel.

After Hill 69 had fallen, a jerry-built Israeli defense line held against halfhearted efforts by the Egyptians to exploit their victory and advance northward. A truce was slated at last to go into effect the following day, June 11, and despite the possibility for a major breakthrough to the heart of Israel, the Egyptians were in no mood to risk disaster at this point. Indeed, they were more convinced than ever that they should concentrate on consolidating their gains and completely sealing off the Negev from the Israelis, though the Jews, in their highly vulnerable condition, feared an attack on Tel Aviv until the last moment.

As the fighting came to an end, Gamal Abdel Nasser drove his jeep to Hill 69, climbed to the top, and surveyed the results of the grim weeks of battle. Enemy dead lay all around him. In the distance he could see the sea rimming the horizon like a delicate blue brush stroke, and beyond, the red and gold streaks of sunset. It was a miracle, he thought, that he should be standing there, hardly 25 miles from Tel Aviv, overlooking part of a vast sweep of territory—from the sea almost to Jerusalem—under the control of a scattered, untrained, politically manipulated Egyptian army. A miracle!

9

The Guns of Galilee

COLONEL Abdel Wahab Bey al-Hakim, commander of a Syrian force, stood on a grassy slope overlooking the Israeli-held Arab village of Samakh on the southern shore of Lake Tiberias, listening to the disconcerting sound of tanks and trucks moving into the Jordan Valley to reinforce the enemy. He could even see their headlights from his position east of Samakh. The Jews, it appeared, were stronger than he had expected.

Why hadn't he been given adequate information about enemy strength? Nothing seemed to be going well. As commander of the Damascus garrison, he had been ordered to prepare his men for an attack only three weeks before, though they needed at least three months more training. First, he was told to attack Safed. Then, on May 13, his government had acceded to demands from Amman that he attack Samakh and the rich Jewish settlements in the Jordan Valley instead. So now, only 48 hours later, he was poised for an attack on Samakh, about which Syrian intelligence knew almost nothing.

True, he had a strong force—on paper: an infantry brigade consisting of two battalions, an armored car battalion, and an artillery regiment, in addition to the company of tanks. But the Jews, who knew every square foot of the area, were apparently even better armed, unless his eyes and ears were deceiving him. And they had built powerful fortifications. They had even won control of the police fortress of Samakh from local Arabs who had occupied it as soon as the British had withdrawn from the town some days before.

Wahab returned to his headquarters (in a small village house) and gloomily ordered a staff officer: "Let's start the bombardment and probing attack. We've got to test the enemy's strength before we risk an all-out assault."

In Samakh, Shalom Hochbaum, a member of Kibbutz Degania A, which, with neighboring Degania B, stretched just to the west of Samakh, paused in his trench-digging to watch the line of trucks approaching from the hills. How wonderful they looked—truckloads of "supplies and reinforcements." He wondered if the Syrians further up in the hills were falling for the trick. Every truck in every nearby settlement had been rounded up and sent into the mountains to the west with their lights dimmed so that they could return, lights ablaze, to deceive the enemy into thinking reinforcements were pouring into the area. He had lost count of the number of trips the trucks had already made. And the rumble of the "tanks"—could the Syrians tell that this was just the sound of tractor engines kept running?

Maybe the deception would win the Israelis enough time to organize the settlements for defense. Foolishly the settlers, misled by intelligence reports, had not expected an attack in this area and were unprepared. In fact, the evacuation of children and old and sick people had only just started. If the Syrians attacked that night, Shalom thought, how could Samakh and the settlements hold out? Only three platoons of the Golani Brigade plus some reinforcements like himself from nearby settlements were available to defend Samakh. And a few hundred yards beyond was Degania A, which had started to build fortifications just two days before.

At about 7 A.M. on May 15, after several hours of constant artillery and aircraft bombardment in the area, Shalom cautiously lifted his head from the trench he had helped to dig and saw a long column of infantrymen approaching from the foothills. They were already about 150 yards away. With his comrades, he opened fire and hit four men in a row. Within a short time the attackers were driven back with considerable casualties.

Meanwhile, another Syrian company, supported by artillery fire and armored cars, advanced toward the two settlements of Masada and Shaar Hagolan south of Samakh. It was halted only near the perimeter fences of the two colonies, which remained critically threatened.

The bitter Jewish resistance to these initial probing attacks convinced commander Wahab that his troops, even with tanks, could not successfully attack Samakh and the settlements without reinforcements.

"I need another battalion of infantry," he radioed GHQ in Damascus.

"All right," came the reply. "Harass them until the reinforcements arrive."

Wahab felt somewhat relieved, though he would have to delay the attack for two or three days.

"Keep shelling at intervals," he ordered his artillery commander. "Don't forget we've only got about a hundred shells per gun and two thousand bullets for every machine gun."

At dawn on May 18, a few hours after a third battalion arrived, Wahab watched from a hill as his big attack ground into gear. His swarthy face was tense, though he was now more confident of the ability of his force to roll over the Jewish strongpoints and all the way south to Haifa. He would not submit the infantry to the withering Israeli fire this time. It would move only when his armor had overrun Samakh.

The armor advanced toward the town in a wide arc, directing well-aimed shots into enemy positions while artillery blasted away. To Wahab's surprise, many of these positions were poorly constructed mud houses that collapsed easily. In a flanking movement to the south, the tanks then threatened the town's communications from the rear. They were running! The Jews were running! And so precipitously that they were unable even to evacuate their wounded. Only the police fortress was still holding out, but as the tanks closed in, firing point-blank, it, too, finally fell, with all the defenders dead. As he drank in the full glory of his victory, Wahab looked at his watch: 8 A.M. The battle had lasted only about three hours. He wondered how many hours it would take to link up with invading Arab forces in central Galilee en route for Haifa.

"You must take back the police fortress," Chanan Belkind, commander of Degania A, exhorted the group of 20 settlers at about 9 A.M. that same morning. "Otherwise our kibbutz will be the front line. We've got to gain time, at least until the children and old people are evacuated."

As Belkind spoke, survivors from Samakh limped and stumbled into the settlement one by one, bleary-eyed and shocked.

"Give the wounded first aid and send the rest to the trenches," Belkind ordered a subordinate. "Unless we can stop them at Samakh, every man who can hold a gun will be needed to save the kibbutz."

The group of 20 counterattackers, led by Shalom Hochbaum, then started running across the corpse-strewn fields that separated the settlement from the town, hoping to knock out the tanks with Molotov cocktails. But as they dashed through a spray of dust and shrapnel, flying pieces of metal lodged in Shalom's leg and shoulder.

"Go on without me," he cried to the others, and he limped back to the kibbutz.

Shortly afterward, the survivors of his platoon dejectedly returned. Their counterattack on the police station had failed, and five men had been killed. No one realized at the time that the assault had nevertheless delayed a Syrian attack on the kibbutz, giving it more time to prepare its defense.

"Netter, will you go to Haifa to look after the children?" Joseph Baratz, one of the founders of the kibbutz, said to the settlement doctor as he was dressing a wounded man in the first aid shelter shortly after the retreat from Samakh. "The lorries with the mothers and children are leaving now."

Netter looked up at Baratz, his eyes pained. "But don't you need me here?"

"Yes," said Baratz, "we need you, but you'll be more useful there."

As they were talking, two men brought in a body on a stretcher, the face covered with a blanket, and placed it almost at their feet.

Baratz then took his friend by the arm and shouted: "You must go! You must get into the lorry at once!"

Netter stared at him. He remembered how, early in World War II, he had had a chance to escape from Germany, where he had been born. But his people had needed his help, and so he had stayed with them and gone to a concentration camp and tried to heal the sick, the few who had escaped the gas chambers. When he had come to Degania after the war with his Irish Catholic wife, he finally laid down his instruments, which his withered hands could no longer manipulate with dexterity, and had gone to work in the poultry yard. But now he felt he was needed with the same urgency that had kept him in Germany during World War II. Yet, ironically, he was also a creature of his early German training.

"Is that an order?" he asked.

"Yes," replied Baratz, "it is an order."

Netter glared at him for a moment, then turned and went out to the lorry. As it drove off, he called out to Baratz from the rear: "This is against my conscience, Joseph."

Baratz went back to the shelter. He raised the blanket covering the face of the body that had been brought in. Such a young, handsome boy, he thought, recalling how as a member of the Jewish Brigade in Europe after the war the youth had found his parents in a concentration camp and brought them to Degania. Thank God Netter—his father—had left without seeing him.[1]

*

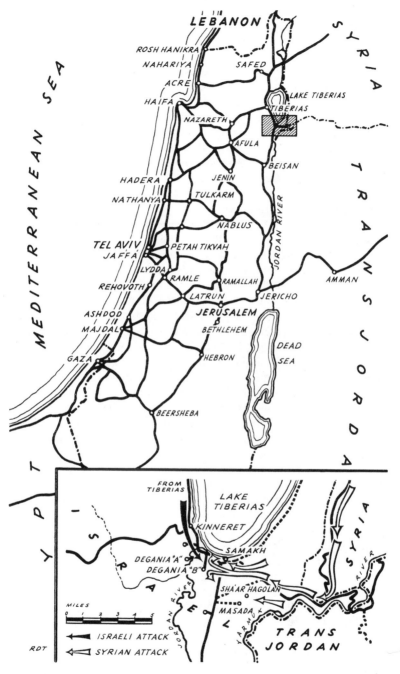

THE BATTLE OF SAMAKH AND DEGANIA

While Wahab redeployed most of his forces for an attack on the two Deganias, the Syrian troops who were dug in near Shaar Hagolan and Masada to the south prepared to assault those settlements. On receiving information that the defenders were planning to evacuate, the Golani Brigade command, which was responsible for the defense of this area, sent orders that they should hold their positions. But the message arrived too late. The settlers abandoned the two colonies on the night of May 18, and the Syrians walked in the next morning.

Coming in the wake of the defeat in Samakh, this new setback further sapped Israeli morale. However, new hope arrived with a special commander named Moshe Dayan, a son of Degania famed for his raiding exploits against the Arabs in the 1930's as Orde Wingate's *aide-de-camp,* and against the Vichy French in the Levant during World War II. His orders now were to hold the Jordan Valley settlements at all costs.

Standing outside his headquarters in the hills, Dayan, lean and wiry, a black patch over one eye, scanned the valley stretched stunningly before him as if for the first time; the green fields and gardens, the olive groves, the fishponds, the scarlet acacias and wild cyclamen, poppies and cornflowers. Yes, it was a good name, Degania—"cornflower." Along the northern fence, the Jordan flowed lazily between banks lush with willows and eucalyptus trees that formed a canopy of leaves. Beyond, as a natural setting for the jewel, soared the jagged mountains of Syria and Transjordan, with the snowcap of Mount Hermon poking into the distant sky . . .

Was this really his birthplace? He remembered playing here on the brown, burnt grass and romping in the scrubby swampland that had sucked the boots off his feet. The steamy air (below sea level) had buzzed with malaria-carrying mosquitos that had covered his feeble body with red welts. Here, too, he had often gone hungry, making do with only milk, eggs, and vegetables bought from Arab villages until the kibbutz could produce enough food of its own. Here, Bedouin bandits had found the Jews, whom they called "children of death," easy victims of robbery and murder. Over there in the olive grove was buried brave young Moshe Barsky, the first member of the settlement to die fighting thieves; he had refused to give them his mule. It was indeed an honor to be named after him . . .

It had been difficult—being only the second child born on the very first kibbutz to have been established in the Holy Land. His Russian-born parents, among the founders of this communal settlement in 1910, had had to fit a child into an untested egalitarian society, in which a woman worked as hard as a man and no member owned even a shirt or a pair of socks. His mother never had time for him. If she wasn't working, she was ill from overwork. And then his father Shmuel would have to act as mother, too.

"Why should I try to hide the fact," Shmuel had once written Devora (Dayan's mother), who was in a Jerusalem hospital at the time:

> . . . that, however much effort I make, I cannot look after Moshe the
> way you do? He misses you a lot. Rainy days are the worst of all. . . .
> Do not cry, darling. What if we do miss you? It is good to miss some-
> one. I can supply the boy's needs, entertain him, and hold his hand.
> Sometimes I scold him. In the evenings I wash him and slip into bed
> beside him. He snuggles up to me and embraces me, putting his little
> arms around my neck. My heart melts, and tears roll onto our dear little
> child's face and eyes. I kiss him and fall asleep . . .[2]

Dayan remembered his father's tears, and his own, too, the tears of a child born into an experimental world cruelly exacting of body and soul. Yet now, as he surveyed the fruit of the experiment, how exquisite was the agony of memory. And the cornflowers, barely stirring in the dry, breezeless heat, were just as gloriously golden as the ones he used to pick.

But there they were . . . enemy tanks poised like giant beetles ready to devour the harvest . . .

"Congratulations on your victory," said Syrian President Shukri al-Kuwatly, when Colonel Wahab had helped him to ease his great bulk out of the jeep.

"Thank you, Mr. President," Wahab said proudly. "Our men fought bravely and well . . . We shall take next the two Deganias," he predicted confidently to his distinguished visitors who included, in addition to the President, the Defense Minister and the army chief of staff.

"Very good," said Kuwatly, as he strolled with the group past abandoned Israeli positions. "But, Colonel, you reported that your men fired about four hundred and fifty shells in the period before the attack by tanks and infantry. You seem to forget that we have a limited supply of ammunition. The war may be long and we must make the supply last for at least six months. Do not fire on them so lavishly in the future."

"Very well, Mr. President," Wahab replied, looking dejected. Here he had won a glorious victory, and the President was reprimanding him. Why, if he hadn't saturated the Jews with bombs he might never have broken their morale, and it wouldn't be so easy to overrun the Deganias.

"We've got to get some artillery to stop those tanks," Moshe Dayan said, swiftly analyzing the situation with Chanan Belkind in Degania A about the time that Kuwatly was touring Samakh. "I think we should send a delegation to see B.G. personally. The command has got to understand that if Degania falls, the whole of Galilee may be finished."

Almost immediately, Joseph Baratz and two other elderly kibbutz members drove to command headquarters in Tel Aviv, where they found Ben-Gurion talking with Yadin.

The Prime Minister looked tired and worn, but he listened sympathetically to their request. Then he replied sadly: "We have nothing. We have a front in Jerusalem, a front in Galilee, a front in the Negev. There are not enough arms anywhere."

There was a pause, and suddenly one of the delegates broke into tears.

"What can I do?" Ben-Gurion repeated. "We have nothing. I will gladly come with you if you wish, and stay with you in Degania. But we have no arms."

After another pause, he added: "We'll see what we can possibly do."

The three men then drove home, arriving at about 4:30 A.M., May 20, during a bombardment as 8 Renault tanks supported by some 10 armored cars advanced toward Degania A and halted about 150 yards away . . .

At about 7:30 A.M., Shalom Hochbaum burst into the kibbutz headquarters shelter crying: "We're running out of ammo, and the tanks have started to move! They're coming in! What'll we do?"

Chanan Belkind looked distraught, but said calmly: "I've got three Molotov cocktails, that's all. You can have one. The other two are for me."

Shalom ran back to his machine-gun position at the northern end of the trench that zigzagged just inside the barbed wire fence facing the Syrians, who were attacking with tanks, followed by infantry, along the whole eastern perimeter of the kibbutz. As he jumped into his position, which was camouflaged with leaves and secured with bags of cement, Shalom saw a tank break through the fence about 50 yards to the south and take up a position squarely on the trench, its gun raking the southern defense area. His sudden fear was tempered by the fatalism of the concentration camp survivor whose whole family had perished.

Gripping the neck of his Molotov cocktail, Shalom crept along the trench toward the tank, hoping it wouldn't swing its gun northward. When he was about five yards away, he stood up and threw the bottle, which had once contained beer. Simultaneously another defender, Yehuda Sprung, hurled one of the few remaining cocktails from another point. To their mutual delight, flames engulfed the vehicle, as well as several trees in the area.

At that moment, Shalom saw enemy infantrymen about to break through the fence further to the north. He ran back to his machine gun and sprayed them. Meanwhile a Syrian in the flaming tank, lifting himself out of the turret, fired with a revolver at Israelis in the trench but was cut down as he jumped to the ground. The other man had died in the operator's seat.

The defenders then knocked out two more tanks and an armored car, and the rest of the armored force hurried away, with the infantry, seriously depleted in number by Shalom's raking machine-gun fire, following in panic.

The Syrians, in their frustration, now attacked Degania B, which was separated from Degania A to the north by a large garden. But this attack also failed.

Much of the Syrian force then regrouped in the fields between Samakh and the Deganias, reorganizing for another attack.

Shortly after noon, while the fighters of the Deganias kept their eyes riveted on the tanks, Moshe Dayan saw a truck approaching his mountain headquarters. When it halted and he looked into the rear, he thought he was seeing things. He was—two ancient 65mm. field artillery pieces. After hours of argument, Yadin had persuaded Ben-Gurion to send these two Napoleonic relics to Degania. The Prime Minister had wanted to dispatch them, as well as two others that had just arrived from abroad, to the Jerusalem area.[3] Dayan immediately ordered them brought into position on the Yavniel range, overlooking the Jordan River and Lake Tiberias. The inexperienced crew, finding no sighting equipment, began to zero in by firing practice shots into the lake. When they had achieved some accuracy, they redirected their fire on the Syrian armor concentrations between Samakh and the two Deganias.

Colonel Wahab observed the fighting from atop the police station in Samakh in some bewilderment. His forces had been stopped before the gates of both Deganias and had retreated. Many of his men were being killed with their own artillery. The Jews had managed to cut into his radio system and issue false orders to his artillerymen to fire at their own troops, against all rules of civilized warfare . . .

At this point, an officer rushed up to him. "Sir, those are Jewish shells! They've got artillery!"

Wahab was silent for a moment. Jewish artillery? Why hadn't his intelligence warned him? How could his paltry force hold out against artillery when there were hardly any fortifications in Samakh? His enemies would, of course, blame him for not having fortified the town after its occupation. They would ignore his explanation that he hadn't had enough time.

"Head the troops into the hills!" Wahab brusquely ordered the officer.

Early the next morning, May 21, Israeli fighters reentered Samakh without opposition. The Syrians had fled the whole area, including the settlements of Masada and Shaar Hagolan, which they had completely gutted, leaving behind scores of their own dead sprawled amid the poppies and cornflowers that were to sway over their graves.

RECHAVAM ZE'EVY—whose lean body and drawn face had earned him the nickname of "Gandhi"—sang loudly with the rest of his men as they pulled out of their base heading north toward Malkieh near the Lebanese border. When he heard Micky Marcus remark, while watching them leave, that "any unit that sings like that" could not lose a battle, Gandhi wished he could sing even louder.

It was May 13, Independence Eve, and he was participating in the first Jewish offensive mission against a regular army. Yigal Allon, commanding the Yiftach Brigade, had received information that the Lebanese army, supported by the Arab Liberation Army, was planning to invade through Malkieh southward along the Rosh Pina–Metulla highway and so cut off the Jewish-held "Finger" of eastern Galilee. He had therefore ordered his brigade's 1st Palmach Battalion under Dan Laner, one of his best officers, to advance cross-country and make a surprise attack on Malkieh and the hills surrounding it.

Such action, in addition to shutting the "Malkieh Gate," would isolate the powerful police fortress of Nebi Yusha that dominated the highway at a point some miles to the south and permit an assault on it from the rear. Even if the Lebanese counterattacked and recaptured Malkieh, they would be thrown off schedule and the Jews would have more time to prepare their defenses. But the prospect of facing an estimated 3,000 Arab soldiers poised for invasion with a single battalion made Gandhi's voice tremble slightly—especially since about 100 of the men didn't even carry arms, but would have to scavenge those of dead and wounded comrades.

After several hours of marching, the battalion temporarily lost its way in the mountains of eastern Galilee, but finally arrived at its destination shortly before daybreak. One company began to occupy the hill village of Kadesh, another the former British military camp outside Malkieh, and a third Malkieh itself. A reinforced platoon under Gandhi, attached to the company occupying the camp, positioned itself along the valley highway just south of Malkieh to prevent Arab reinforcements from arriving via an intersecting road from Sasa.

Gandhi immediately deployed his men and ordered them to dig in, patting Dov Reines, his number two Bren gunner, on the shoulder as he inspected the positions. What the hell was a sixteen-year-old kid doing behind a Bren gun? he wondered vaguely. Then a flash of artillery fire lit up the horizon like a premature dawn as the Lebanese launched a fierce counterattack on the occupied villages and camp.

While shells exploded nearby, Gandhi lay in a slit trench muttering curses. His unit would certainly be wiped out if it remained so vulnerably exposed in the valley. Surveying the landscape despairingly, he focused on a hill south of the military camp. He quickly examined a map but could find no trace of the height. Well, what the hell, it was there, wasn't it? He radioed Dan Laner at battalion headquarters in nearby Ramot Naftali and received permission to move his men to the uncharted hill.

While the other Israeli units began to retreat, Gandhi marched his men to the new objective, where they dug in once again.

When the Lebanese offensive accelerated and several commanders were killed or wounded, Laner ordered a general retreat. But Gandhi still demurred.

"My unit can stay here on the hill and cover the retreat," he shouted over the radio.

Hardly had the military camp fallen when the Lebanese began attacking the hill with concentrated artillery and mortar fire, followed by wave upon wave of armored cars and infantry.

Then the number one Bren gunner, Arie Pauker, was hit in the head and died instantly. His youthful assistant, Dov Reines, pushed the body out of the way and began firing furiously without anyone to supply magazines. All through the unbearably hot day he fired from a shallow trench, though it seemed that the whole Lebanese army was determined to knock out his deadly gun.

When darkness finally descended, Gandhi sent his runner, a one-armed boy who had pleaded his way into the army, with a message for Reines.

"Gandhi says get ready to withdraw."

Reines looked at him strangely. "Give me a few drops of water, will you?"

The runner, who had been crawling from position to position with a helmetful of dirty water dredged from a small pool, handed him the helmet and the Bren gunner took a sip, then started firing again.

"I can't go," the gunner said suddenly, as he again loosened his grip on the gun.

"Why not?"

"I've been hit in both legs. I can't move."

"We'll carry you."

"You'll be lucky to get out with the wounded you have. Leave me here and I'll cover you."

"But we can't leave you . . . "

"Never mind! Take off! I'll be all right."

As Gandhi and his men struggled southward carrying their wounded, the echo of Bren gun fire from the crest of the hill rattled in their ears like the voice of an angry god—until the voice was abruptly silenced.

Gandhi's stand had permitted a classic, orderly retreat by the survivors of the battalion, who carried with them, mostly on their backs, about 120 casualties. One of the company commanders, who had been wounded when he had kicked a grenade away from his men, refused to be carried on stretcher or back, hopping on one foot or crawling on his knees. Finally, when he could hardly move further, he sat on a rifle carried by two men.

When Allon learned the details of the retreat, he was convinced he had scored a "victory." The Lebanese, he calculated, would certainly have to delay their advance southward a few days after such bitter fighting—perhaps long enough for his forces to nip the invasion in the bud.

The next night, May 16, his optimism grew when an Israeli force, supported by Piper Cubs (whose pilots hand-dropped bombs to greater psychological than military effect), overran the Nebi Yusha police fortress south of Malkieh, where 28 Jews had died some days before in an abortive attack. The Israelis could now block the invasion road south of Malkieh.

But Allon was not satisfied. He wanted to recapture Malkieh itself.

"Now that we have Nebi Yusha, they probably expect us to attack from the south," he told his staff in Safed. "Let's help them to expect it— and then attack from the north." It was thus decided to feign an attack from the south, and to launch the actual assault from the rear within Lebanon.

Under a moonless sky, an armored column with dimmed lights rumbled through open fields from Manara into Lebanon, thence to a point on the road leading southward to Malkieh just inside Palestine.

Meanwhile, in Malkieh, the Lebanese commander radioed his headquarters: "We can hear the Jews approaching from the south, from Nebi Yusha. Send reinforcements as swiftly as possible!"

Shortly thereafter the commander received word from headquarters that reinforcements were on the way.

Lebanese villagers near the border shouted greetings as an armored column sped southward on its way to drive back the enemy, and some of the soldiers in the convoy returned the waves and smiles appreciatively.

After a short battle, this convoy of Israelis, still glowing from the warm reception accorded them by the villagers of Lebanon, took over Malkieh from the startled Lebanese occupiers who, like the villagers, had taken them for the expected reinforcements.

*

While Israeli forces thus thwarted invasion attempts in the Jordan Valley and in eastern Galilee, other Jewish units stormed up the coast in western Galilee toward Lebanon to repel a possible invasion from the border village of Rosh Hanikra. They were led personally by Moshe Carmel, the northern front commander.

When Carmel and Mordechai Makleff, his successor as commander of the Carmeli Brigade, arrived in Nahariya near the frontier, they were met by the Jewish mayor, who reminded them that the United Nations had allotted his town to the Arabs. Handing Carmel a bouquet of flowers, he addressed him expansively:

"I welcome you to Nahariya and request that you annex this town to the Jewish State."

Carmel and Makleff glanced at each other and smiled.

"Very well," said Makleff, "we hereby annex Nahariya."

By May 15, only one coastal town remained in Arab hands—Acre. Carmel, who had been imprisoned by the British in Acre Fortress from 1939 to 1941 for "illegal" Haganah activities, decided to attack that besieged town, though reports indicated that it was well defended despite the flight of many of its leaders. Ben-Gurion didn't object, but questioned the need for such action at this time in the light of Israel's scarcity of troops. He also remembered that Napoleon had been defeated at Acre in 1799 and had started his long trek back to France afterward, relinquishing his territorial gains in Egypt on the way.

The Israelis struck on the night of May 19.

Attacking from the north, they captured the Acre police station after hours of bitter street fighting, cracking Arab morale. Thus, 22 hours after the battle started, a priest carrying a white flag walked from the old to the new city and asked to see the Haganah commander to whom he sulkily surrendered the town.

Carmel glowed as he led a detachment the next morning into Acre Fortress. He remembered all too well the ancient walls that had sealed him and 42 other Israelis from the world for two years, ironically enough, for carrying arms . . .

CARMEL HAD BEEN CONDUCTING A COURSE FOR HAGANAH OFFICERS under the camouflage of a sports camp in 1939, when, one day about two months after World War II had broken out, two British police officers visited the camp and found some rifles. The Haganah men immediately sent most of their arms and equipment on three trucks, under the supervision of Yigal Allon, to a new underground camp.

But the trainees, including a young officer named Moshe Dayan, were arrested with 20 rifles, 6 grenades, and some ammunition in their possession. Carmel could still hear the judge pronouncing sentence: 10 to 15 years' imprisonment. Who could have guessed then that two years later most of these men, including himself, would be liberated to undertake dangerous war missions for their British wardens—and to receive military training that would later permit operations against both the British and the Arabs? . . .

Now, the prison guards were waiting for Carmel at the entrance to hand over their pistols.

"The war is over for us," one of them mused in resignation. "At last there is peace."

Carmel smiled at him.

"Do you remember me?" he asked.

The guard studied the heavy-set figure with the unruly hair and, the lines around his mouth crinkling slightly, replied: "Yes, you were among the forty-three."

Carmel shook the guard's hand, recalling his kindness; he had brought the prisoners cigarettes and letters from their families, though these privileges had been forbidden.

HAVING failed on all fronts, the Arabs in the north paused to reorganize and rethink their military aims. Many no longer viewed the elimination of the State of Israel as a realistic ultimate objective. A new Syrian command under General Husseini Zaim, taking over after the rout in the Degania sector, now thought mainly of local victories. It hungered after the eastern shore of Lake Tiberias and the Finger of Galilee, which would give Syria control of the Jordan headwaters.

Lebanese leaders were divided over military policy. All had been opposed to formal war from the start, though never saying so openly for political reasons. But with the Arab League decision to go to war, Prime Minister Riadh es-Solh felt that it was politically essential to Lebanon to implement League plans calling for her to thrust southward to Haifa. And he had the support of Fawzi el-Kaoukji, who was determined to regain lost glory. Kaoukji planned to send his newly reorganized Arab Liberation Army all the way to Nazareth in central Galilee, from where he hoped to fan out throughout Galilee in cooperation with the regular Arab armies.

However, General Fuad Shehab, the Lebanese military commander, opposed as possibly disastrous any deep military penetration into Israel, at least until it was clear that the Arabs were winning the war. Nor, since he was a Christian, did sentiment dominate military considerations in a war fought principally on behalf of Moslems.* He had thus halted in his advance after taking Malkieh in the first battle for the village, offering the excuse that he must reorganize his forces. The success of the Israeli counterattack during which the Jews invaded Lebanese territory confirmed him in his caution. He agreed that his forces should attack Malkieh again for security and facesaving purposes, but he opposed any further advance southward.

"I am responsible for the army, and I don't believe our forces are large or strong enough to fight the well-armed Jews," Shehab snapped at one meeting in Beirut. "If we must fight, we should do so on a defensive basis."

"In a war, one must attack," Solh retorted.

Finally, they consulted with President Bishara al-Khouri in an effort to reach a compromise, and Khouri, a Christian, sided with Shehab. The Lebanese army, in conjunction with Syrian and ALA forces, would attack Malkieh again, but advance no further. However, Kaoukji's troops, who could suffer a defeat without disgracing any regular army, would continue to drive southward into central Galilee.

On the Israeli side, the High Command decided to move the Yiftach Brigade to the Latrun area, where the Jews were making a supreme effort to capture the strongholds blocking the road from Tel Aviv to Jerusalem; and most of the Carmeli Brigade to the central front for a confrontation with an Iraqi invasion force.

As a result, the Finger of eastern Galilee, which the High Command regarded as relatively secure after the initial Israeli victories, was largely left in the hands of the new Oded Brigade, a ragtag organization composed mainly of home guardsmen and other marginal defense groups. It was not difficult for the Arabs to observe the pullout of the troops they had learned to respect, and to calculate that they were being sent to more active fronts.

It was with renewed confidence, therefore, that, on the morning of June 6 three Arab battalions—Lebanese, Syrian, and ALA—launched a new concerted assault on Malkieh. Though the Israelis had for some days received reports and rumors of military activity on both sides of the Finger, the inexperienced Oded defenders were caught completely by surprise. At first, they managed to stop the advance of Kaoukji's battalion, while

* With Lebanon about equally divided between the two faiths, the Premier is always a Moslem and the President always a Christian.

the Syrians suffered heavy casualties when they walked into a minefield.
But the Lebanese force succeeded in driving the Israelis from Malkieh.

The next day, Kaoukji's troops flowed into the interior of Galilee to
the cheers and applause of Arab villagers who had had little to cheer about
since the Jewish victories of April and early May.

Kaoukji, zooming by jeep from one advancing column to the other,
waved to the welcoming crowds whose adoration he had finally rewon.
Fanning to the west and east, his troops, as he had pledged, finally smashed
into Nazareth on June 11, just before the United Nations—imposed cease-
fire.

Kaoukji was ecstatic, though he was a bit ruffled that the Jews were
too busy fighting elsewhere to put up more than a token defense.

While Malkieh, on the western edge of the Finger, was falling on June
6, the Syrians simultaneously assaulted the colony of Mishmar Hayarden,
just across the Jordan from Syria on the eastern edge of the Finger. This
old village, established in 1884, was ill-prepared for an attack. The inhabitants had known it was coming for some time from the movement of
men and vehicles on the Syrian side of the river, but they could not impress
the need for military help upon the authorities.

"All you have to do," one Israeli officer advised the colony's defense
committee, "is to dig trenches along a line parallel with the river, and you
will be able to hold out against an attack long enough for reinforcements
to arrive."

But the settlers could obtain no weapons to supplement the few rifles
and other light arms they already possessed. Finally, in their desperation
they propped up irrigation pipes against a fence, hoping to convince the
Syrians that the settlement was bristling with artillery.

One reason for the official neglect appeared to be that an important
segment of the community was Irgunist, and the government was not anxious to distribute arms to people whom it suspected might try to use them
one day against the authorities. Moreover, Mishmar Hayarden, being a
conventional village, lacked the close ties with the military that the kibbutzim had developed over the years. For under the British mandate,
Haganah units had found the collective settlements excellent hiding places
—the Palmach, indeed, was rooted in the kibbutz system—while it was
far more difficult to lose oneself in a village, where cooperation among the
inhabitants could not be achieved to the same degree.

Yet, strategically, few points in the north were more important than
Mishmar Hayarden, which controlled the Daughters of Jacob Bridge across
the Jordan where in ancient times the Via Maris, from Egypt to Syria,

traversed the river. By capturing the settlement, the Syrians would be in a position to thrust to Tiberias and cut off the Finger.

Most of the mothers, children, and old people were evacuated when an attack became imminent, though some families refused to leave regardless of the danger. Sixty-year-old Abraham Baleshnikov who, with his wife, was among this group, continued to hobble into the fields each morning before dawn to tend his herd of cattle, armed with a Mauser, wearing a *khaffiya* on his head to look like an Arab, and carrying a flute in his hand and a knapsack containing a prayer shawl and *tefillin* on his bent back.

But on the morning of June 6, Abraham had to neglect his cows when a furious artillery barrage sent the inhabitants running to the shelters. The Syrians then forded the river. But to the surprise of the settlers themselves, they managed that day, with the help of Oded troops belatedly rushed to the rescue, to prevent the Syrians from transferring their armor to the west bank of the Jordan, forcing them to withdraw across the river.

The Syrians, however, with a cease-fire imminent, swiftly assembled a larger force of two brigades for a renewed attack, which they launched on the morning of June 10. By about noon, they had stormed into the colony despite desperate resistance by scattered individuals that continued into the afternoon. The other settlers, including Abraham Baleshnikov and his wife, were taken prisoner. No one knew what happened to Abraham's cows.

Finally having driven a small wedge into eastern Galilee, the Syrians joyously proclaimed the fall of Mishmar Hayarden as the *Fatih-Allah*— the Capture of God.

While Syrians and Lebanese tried to cut into the northern tip of the Finger, Iraqi troops preoccupied themselves at the base of the Finger on the central front. On the eve of the invasion, Iraq, having no common border with Israel, sent a brigade of about 3,000 men and an armored car regiment through Transjordan to the east bank of the Jordan River opposite the Israeli settlement of Gesher. The Iraqi plan was to ford the river, overrun Gesher, and drive southwestward toward the sea, cutting Israel in two at her narrow waist. The Iraqis apparently had in mind less the destruction of Israel than control of the pipeline from the Mosul oilfields in Iraq to the Haifa refineries.

Over hastily laid pontoon bridges replacing spans blown up by the Jews, Iraqi forces, on May 16, struck across the Jordan and, after intense fighting, managed to seal off Gesher. Iraqi soldiers in armored cars then assaulted the front gate of the neighboring police fortress, blew it up, and were about to enter the building itself when a defender hurled a Molotov cocktail at the leading armored car, which had penetrated the courtyard.

The vehicle burst into flames and the attackers fled. Discouraged by their failure, the Iraqis satisfied themselves thereafter with keeping Gesher under tight siege.

But Transjordan, which was fighting crucial battles in the Jerusalem area further south, was far from satisfied. Glubb Pasha had hoped that an Iraqi drive across the waist of Israel from Gesher would divert large Israeli forces from the Jerusalem fighting, but with the Iraqis pinned down in a siege this strategy wasn't working. The next best thing, he calculated, was to strengthen the Jerusalem front—at Latrun—with an Arab Legion battalion that had been occupying the vital Triangle that linked the three Arab villages of Jenin in the north, Tulkarm in the west, and Nablus in the south (the Triangle was the central front).

The Iraqis, he figured, could replace the Legion battalion in the Triangle—which controlled virtually the whole northern and central road network—and at the same time launch a diversionary attack from Tulkarm toward the coast. The Iraqi leaders agreed to the idea, and on May 24 Iraqi units entered the Triangle to relieve the Arab Legion battalion, leaving only a token force to continue the siege of Gesher. Some of the Iraqis then prepared to drive westward from Tulkarm toward Nathanya on the coast.

The Israeli High Command, oddly enough, believed that the Arab Legion had attacked Gesher and that the Iraqis had been occupying the Triangle since the invasion started. Thus, unaware that the Iraqis had, in fact, replaced the Arab Legion battalion to free it for duty in Latrun, the Israelis began planning an attack on the Triangle under the illusion that such action might keep the Iraqis from going to Latrun. If they had known that the Iraqis had not been slated for transfer there, they would hardly have contemplated such an attack at that time.

The Triangle, with a completely Arab population, was to have composed the heart of the new Arab State under the United Nations partition plan, and the Israelis had no wish to antagonize world opinion at so critical a moment, particularly over territory which, except for western fringe areas, was not essential to Israeli security or development. Even more important, with such vital regions as Jerusalem, the Negev, and eastern Galilee in desperate danger, it would have made little sense to squander urgently needed men and arms on a secondary objective. But owing to faulty Israeli intelligence, the Triangle became a primary objective.

"Jerusalem is in a critical situation," Israel Baer, a general staff officer, told Moshe Carmel—whose command was stretched to include the central front—at Carmeli Brigade headquarters. "We must make an attack at Jenin to keep Iraqi forces away from the Jerusalem corridor."*

---

* After the war, Baer was convicted of spying for the Soviet Union and sentenced to prison.

Glancing at Carmeli commander Mordechai Makleff, Carmel asked with concern: "Are we to attack only one point in the Triangle?"

"No," said Baer. "The Carmeli and Golani Brigades will attack Jenin while the Alexandroni Brigade attacks Tulkarm."

Under this coordinated plan the enemy would have to divide its forces between Jenin and Tulkarm.

Israeli troops started moving south toward Jenin on May 28—by coincidence, the same day that Iraqi forces began striking westward from Tulkarm, forcing the Alexandroni Brigade, which protected the coastal area from Haifa to Tel Aviv, to concentrate on preventing a breakthrough to the sea. By dawn on June 3, three Carmeli battalions had taken the high ground surrounding Jenin, including two dominating hills, one on either side of the main road south of the town. Makleff, leading his troops, sent scouts into the village, which was nestled picturesquely in a deep brown valley, and they returned shortly, sweating in the morning heat.

"From what we could see," one reported, "it's like a ghost town. No troops and no civilians."

Makleff's blue eyes shone with satisfaction. But gradually he grew doubtful as he examined the eerily silent scene from afar. The situation somehow didn't seem right. There must be some troops in the town. He could not take a chance, he decided, on occupying it in daylight, but would wait until night.

"The Jews are all around!" a soldier of an Iraqi detachment that had fled from positions south of Jenin informed Major Nuh, the commander of Iraqi forces that were taking refuge in the town's police fortress. "They're ready to attack Jenin!"

Just as his intelligence had expected, thought Nuh. The Jews had pulled out most of their forces *from the Jerusalem area* in an effort to take the Triangle and prevent an Iraqi drive to the sea. The diversion had worked —but what would happen to his small surrounded force? Most of his men had gathered in the police fortress with him—about 200 paratroopers, some soldiers who had retreated from nearby hills, 40 Palestinian fighters, and a group of civilian refugees.

Nuh urgently radioed Iraqi GHQ for help:

"We're surrounded. Send reinforcements immediately or we won't be able to hold out. Meanwhile, though we're low on ammunition, we'll start firing with everything we have."

"What did they say?" asked an aide after the radio conversation.

"They're sending us planes and the infantry detachment that was heading for Nathanya," Nuh said with relief.

Then he ordered artillery units in the fortress area and in the hills to start firing . . .

"Shells and bullets are hitting all around us . . . yes, yes . . . "

As the commander of the Carmeli 21st Battalion on a hill west of Jenin shouted into the radio microphone, battalion headquarters, behind a large rock, was suddenly transformed into a swirling whirlpool of dust and flying stones. A shell had exploded only a few feet away. When the air began to clear, David A., a company commander who was present, saw the battalion commander moaning on the smoking earth, and his second in command lying silent, his face a bloody mass.

As a medic ran up, the battalion commander said feebly: "Go back to the men and see what's happening . . . Remember, it's too dangerous to retreat in daylight . . . "

David ran to his company and found the living cowering behind rocks and in shallow depressions in the hard, stony earth. The dead lay sprawled everywhere. Hardly had he arrived when a messenger came up.

"Retreat!" he yelled. "You're supposed to retreat!"

David grimaced in astonishment.

"Who gave that order?" he demanded.

"The battalion commander."

"You're crazy! I just saw him and he said no one could retreat in daylight . . . "

But the messenger had already dashed off, apparently to deliver his message to other units, and David was unable to clarify the matter—then or afterward, since the runner was killed about half an hour later.

He glanced at his men. Looking into their eyes, he knew that they had heard; animals' eyes, fearful, bereft of reason. As some of them started to retreat, David cried out: "Come back, you fools, or you'll all be killed!"

But the trickle of men broadened into a flood and he realized that he had no choice but to try to lead them to safety. He raced to the front of the mob and desperately attempted to achieve a semblance of order. When he saw some men discard their guns, he shouted disgustedly: "I know the way, but I won't take anyone without a weapon!"

The men without arms immediately scrambled to nearby corpses and grabbed guns and ammunition.

This was insane, David raged to himself. The only possible route of

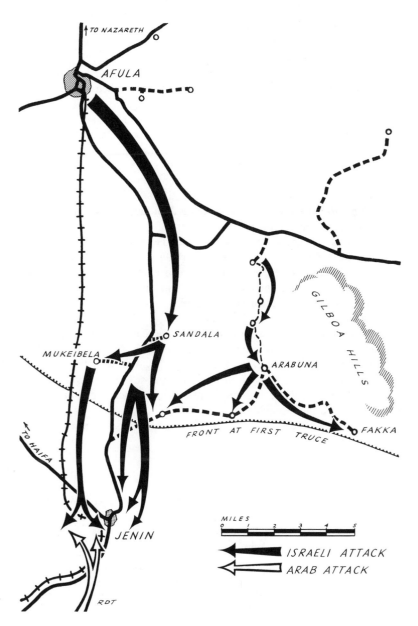

TO NAZARETH

AFULA

GILBOA HILLS

SANDALA

MUKEIBELA

ARABUNA

TO HAIFA

FRONT AT FIRST TRUCE

FAKKA

JENIN

RDT

MILES
0 1 2 3 4 5

ISRAELI ATTACK
ARAB ATTACK

THE BATTLE OF JENIN

retreat was through the town into the northern hills. God knew what they would find in town, where people in every house might fire on them.

The men did succeed in reaching the town, however, and David shuddered as they sauntered past deserted houses as if on a casual stroll in the park, their eyes blank, their expressions indifferent. Then he spotted a group of armed Arabs on the street about 20 yards ahead. They were waving and smiling, mistaking the retreating Israelis for fellow Arabs.

"Start shooting," David muttered to his men, "before they start shooting us!"

But the men just jogged along, numb with shock. David alone began firing, pouring Sten bullets into the startled group of Arabs, killing some and frightening the others off. His men were still walking at the same casual pace, taking no more notice of the shooting than they might of a sidewalk brawl that didn't concern them.

David was sure their luck couldn't last; they must move faster; certainly no one would get through alive carrying the wounded. He led the men into a deserted house, where they spread blankets on the floor. The wounded were set down, and David left them the group's only canteen, promising: "We'll be back for you. *Shalom!*"

They simply stared at him in silence.

Eventually, David led most of his men to the relative safety of a northern post and sent a unit to bring back the wounded. Then he reported to Carmel's outdoor headquarters in the nearby village of Sandala.

Carmel was horrified as the visitor, in sweat-soaked, bloody clothes, grabbed up a pail of water and gulped it frenziedly, then wiped his mouth and sat down on the ground.

"It's bad, very bad over there," he muttered to himself, his eyes blank and bewildered.

When the Iraqi counterattack was in its first stages that morning, the Israeli commanders were still cautiously optimistic that they would be able to capture Jenin—if the full coordinated attack plan was carried out. Carmel radioed the High Command at about 8 A.M.:

> The attack on Jenin develops according to plan. Already we occupy the strongholds on either side of the road dominating the city. Enemy resists severely with all arms, including guns. The battle continues. It is imperative that a diversionary attack be undertaken by Alexandroni to prevent reinforcements from being sent to this sector.

Carmel did not know that Israel Baer had inexplicably neglected to inform Alexandroni commander Dan Even that he was to attack Tulkarm.

Nor that Even had his hands full, in any event, stemming the Iraqi drive to Nathanya by the sea. The Iraqis had captured a village only about five miles from there and were shelling the Tel Aviv–Haifa road.

On receiving Carmel's plea, Yadin radioed Even and asked him if he had the strength to launch a counterattack against the Iraqis—who had all but cut Israel in two—and to drive on to Tulkarm. Even was taken aback. The area between Tulkarm and Kakun, several miles to the west, was exposed flatland and only a pincer movement from two directions could succeed, he felt. An assault by his forces alone would be suicide, especially against the strong Iraqi forces moving on Nathanya, and when one of his best battalions had been wrenched away from him to fight at Latrun.

"I haven't the forces to attack Tulkarm," Even told Yadin, "but we'll stage a holding attack in the general direction of the town if that'll relieve the pressure on Jenin. I'll round up men for an attack on Kakun, but we couldn't be ready before tomorrow night. Anyway, Kakun is as far as we can go."

Compounding the comedy of miscalculations, Even was unaware that the greater part of the Iraqi force pushing toward the sea had been ordered that very morning to backtrack to Jenin to reinforce Major Nuh's beleaguered defenders, and that he could actually have attacked Tulkarm with little risk of strong Iraqi resistance.

At 10:50 A.M., after the Iraqis, running out of ammunition, had reduced the ferocity of their artillery and machine-gun attack, Carmel and Makleff received a radio message from a southern post: "A convoy of about 40 vehicles seen moving in the south toward Jenin. Are they our vehicles or the enemy's?"

The Israeli commanders, expecting no reinforcements of their own from the south, immediately calculated that an Iraqi force was coming from Nablus, probably troops who would have been sent to the Jerusalem front if they hadn't been diverted northward to Jenin. At least the main objective of the Israeli attack on Jenin had been achieved, they thought, however the battle itself turned out. The pressure on the Israeli forces in the Jerusalem area would certainly be lessened. But would their own troops in Jenin, already badly battered, be able to deal with the strengthened Iraqi force—especially if the Alexandroni continued to delay an attack on Tulkarm?

A message immediately went back to the southern posts: "They are enemy vehicles. Start firing!"

*

Major Omar Ali, commander of the Iraqi reinforcements, was stunned by the fury of the reception he was accorded as his detachment approached Jenin. He wondered if his force would be enough to overcome the Jews solidly dug into the hills around Jenin. If only he hadn't been diverted from his original task, he might have been in Nathanya already and the Jewish State would be split in two. Instead, his men were supposed to commit suicide in Jenin . . .

From a ditch on the side of the road where he was taking refuge from Israeli fire, he radioed Major Nuh in the police fortress.

"The Jews control the hills," he said. "It would be very difficult to dislodge them. I suggest that you retreat with your forces from the fortress."

"No, that's impossible," came Nuh's reply. "For one thing, we're under siege and could never withdraw alive. But I wouldn't retreat if I could. We have women, old men, and children with us and we couldn't leave them. There's no choice. We must fight."

Within minutes, the Iraqis unleashed a savage storm of artillery, mortar, and machine-gun fire. Soon, Iraqi planes joined the battle, strafing the Israeli strongholds. The Israelis fired back, but could not match the Iraqi firepower. The two 65mm. cannons that had played an important role at Degania and were brought to Jenin now contributed little to the Israeli cause, being too far out of range to inflict meaningful damage. In addition, Israeli Messerschmitts promised to Carmel did not arrive, having been sent instead to the Negev to head off the Egyptian drive toward Tel Aviv.

Omar Ali's reinforcements, at the same time, left the road and, supported by Palestinian Arab fighters, began attacking through the mountains where they made less conspicuous targets. These troops, badly trained, attempted to capture Israeli positions by running upright directly toward them, even in the face of point-blank fire, and Jewish guns mowed them down by the dozens. But they kept coming and the Israeli units, particularly in the south, dwindled steadily, further sapping morale that had already been ravaged by the elimination of a battalion command and the wild retreat of David's group.

Finally, another commander in the south radioed headquarters for permission to lead a retreat before all his men were exterminated, but was angrily told: "Your request to retreat is refused. You must stand fast regardless of cost."

Carmel and Makleff were persuaded that any further local withdrawals would completely demolish the morale at other posts and end in a disastrous general retreat. If there was to be a retreat, it should take place at night under orderly conditions.

Makleff, that afternoon, decided to storm Jenin itself with his reserve, an "armored column" consisting of several armored cars and four civilian buses, each carrying an infantry platoon. But to the column's surprise, it found the town unoccupied. The fierce if threadbare Israeli resistance in the hills had prevented the Arab reinforcements from entering the city, though a new Iraqi detachment had arrived in the afternoon and coordinated its fire with Omar Ali's force. The only Arab troops in the town were holed up in the police fortress, and they were in a precarious condition. The Israelis intercepted a message from Nuh to the Arab reinforcements: "The Jews are in the town! The police fortress is in danger! Save us!"

In the evening, a picked group of men from the Golani Brigade, which had helped in the capture of the approaches to Jenin, advanced to the fortress and took shelter nearby while sappers crawled to the concrete wall around the building to set explosives. There was a tremendous flash and roar, and the Israelis rushed through the choking smoke and dust to the hole that had been blown in the wall.

"It's too small!" one shouted.

"Never mind, we can squeeze through," said another.

But when he tried to work his slim body through the gap, he got caught and could only be extracted with difficulty. The men looked at each other in anguish; they had used up all their explosives. They retreated under heavy fire, their mission a failure.

"Mordechai," said Moshe Carmel, as he and Makleff sat that evening under an olive tree in a trench at Carmeli Brigade headquarters, "after the casualties we've taken, I think it would be foolish to carry on the fight unless Alexandroni attacks Tulkarm and takes the pressure off us."

Makleff, who had barely escaped death shortly before when shrapnel had ripped a map out of his hand, agreed; the two men drove in a jeep northward to Afulla from where Carmel telephoned Yadin at about 11 P.M.

"Yigal," Carmel reported, "the battle for Jenin has not yet been decided. Bitter battles are being fought at the strongholds and in the city. The enemy is throwing in additional reinforcements. It's impossible to hold Jenin as a lone wedge in the Triangle. All enemy forces there will be hurled against it. If you plan to attack Tulkarm and to capture it soon, it seems to me that we ought to hold Jenin at any price. However, if there is no intention of attacking the Triangle at any other point, it may be preferable to abandon Jenin before we suffer additional casualties. Can you give me an immediate reply?"

"Let me have half an hour," Yadin said.

Exactly half an hour later, Yadin called back with instructions: "If Jenin cannot be held, an orderly withdrawal should be ordered."

The Alexandroni Brigade, he explained to Carmel (who had known nothing of Dan Even's situation or intentions up to then), was unable to attack Tulkarm. "Deliberate and make a decision immediately," Yadin ordered.

Carmel and Makleff discussed the alternatives for about 15 minutes, cursing Even in the process, and decided that their troops should withdraw. In any case, they agreed, Carmeli troops were more urgently needed in the Galilee Finger. Mishmar Hayarden was about to fall, and if the Carmeli troops arrived in time perhaps they could save it—a hope that was to prove in vain.

At midnight, Carmel called Yadin again and reported: "I've decided to withdraw from the town and its strongholds before dawn."

When the conversation with Yadin had ended, Carmel turned to Makleff with a sad smile. "Actually, the battle hasn't been a failure," he said. "Our objective, after all, was to divert the Iraqis from the Jerusalem front, and we did it."

In Amman, Glubb Pasha was delighted when an aide rushed into his office to inform him that the Jews were retreating and the Iraqis were reoccupying Jenin. But his joy was tempered by concern. To achieve the victory, the Iraqi force pressing toward Nathanya had had to be diverted to Jenin, where it had suffered grave, perhaps crippling, casualties. Thus, with the pressure on Israel's coastal area relaxed, the Jews were free to divert some of their own forces from that sector to the Jerusalem front. The Iraqis, he felt, had failed to accomplish their main objective—to keep Jewish troops away from the Jerusalem-Latrun front.

On June 4, the night after the Israeli retreat from Jenin, Alexandroni forces captured Kakun, and held it the following day against several counterattacks. Even's move came too late to affect the situation in Jenin, but it ended the immediate menace to Nathanya, since Kakun lay between Iraqi-held Tulkarm and that coastal town. Nor did the Iraqis undertake another diversionary drive westward, to Glubb's chagrin, since they placed little faith in the plans of a British commander—or in their own ability to drive the 10 long miles to the sea.

10

The Siege of Jerusalem

BLAST it, I can't hear a thing!" Jean Nieuwenhuys, the Belgian Consul in Jerusalem and chairman of the three-man Consular Truce Commission, shouted over the telephone. "Can't they stop firing for one minute?"

In the French Consulate the new United Nations–sponsored commission, composed of the French, Belgian, and American Consuls, was desperately trying to bring peace to a Jerusalem that had disintegrated into a bloody battleground within minutes after the British withdrawal from the city at noon on May 14.

"It's no use," Nieuwenhuys fumed, slamming down the receiver. "Now I've been cut off."

Never mind," Dr. Pablo de Azcarate, a United Nations representative, remarked wryly. "You'll save Jerusalem with your telephone calls."

In a few minutes, the phone rang again. Then again and again. The room was muggy and tense. Mosquitos buzzed through the shattered windows. The occupants sat round a long table sweating and sipping *arak,* which an aged servant kept pouring into their shakily held glasses.

An Israeli military official, Colonel Chaim Herzog, had braved his way to the Consulate (with a driver who had been wounded en route) to negotiate an extension of a truce that had brought uneasy peace to Jerusalem in the last days of the mandate. But local Arab leaders had not come, claiming in response to the Belgian Consul's frantic phone calls that the Jews were sweeping with fire the area they would have to cross. Finally, the telephone stopped working and the *arak* ran out. It seemed pointless to stay any longer in so dangerous a position.

343

The people in the Consulate slipped out silently one by one and squeezed into Herzog's large sedan in the garden. The vehicle, without lights, sped around the corner to the abandoned King David Hotel, former British headquarters, where some of them had been living. The peace-makers dashed through the shabby grandeur of the dark lobby and up to their rooms, gathered their belongings quickly, then continued on to the Salvia Hotel in a relatively safe Jewish sector.[1]

Whatever the Arab intentions, the truce officials, as they trudged into the building, had little doubt that the Jews had done their best, with well-placed bursts of fire, to discourage the Arabs from coming to the meeting, while making sure that Israel could not be blamed for refusing to discuss a truce.

Whether this suspicion was justified or not, the Israelis, already threat-ened by the Arab stranglehold on the Tel Aviv–Jerusalem road, had, in fact, no intention of ceasing fire until Operation Pitchfork had culminated in success. Carefully detailed plans for this operation, completed by Shaltiel and his lieutenants the previous afternoon, May 13, called for a three-pronged advance through Arab or mixed zones to the south, north, and center to create a solid Jewish area embracing all of western Jerusalem up to the Old City wall. The plans called also for the capture of the Arab-inhabited Sheikh Jarrah Quarter sprawled at the base of Mount Scopus and separating the mountain with its Jewish hospital and university from the New City.

To the Israelis, an immediate cease-fire smacked of suicide.

Within 10 minutes after the last British soldier had drawn out of sight, the Jews captured the British security zone they contemptuously called "Bevingrad," which, surrounded by barbed wire, concrete emplacements, and dragons' teeth, symbolized to them the foreign character and "tyranny" of British emergency rule. Strategically located just west of the Old City, this zone embraced the Criminal Investigation Department, the General Post Office, the Generali Building, and Barclays Bank among many other important buildings. Ironically, the British had permitted Haganah patrols to occupy the area the night before—vastly simplifying the seizure—in the hope of deterring a possible last-minute Sternist or Irgun raid.

Certainly the dissidents were impatient. Under the command of Yehoshua Zetler and his deputy, David Gottlieb, the Sternists sat in trucks parked just behind the barbed wire barrier and smashed into Bevingrad even as the British rearguard pulled out. The attackers, among them Orthodox Menashe Eichler, jumped from building to building, room to room, guns blazing and grenades exploding. Those Arabs who had not already fled were soon either taken prisoner or killed. Eichler and several other Sternists and Haganah men then ran to the central prison in the Russian Compound nearby, freeing the Jewish prisoners and capturing the Arab inmates. Then they stormed into Barclays Bank, which faced the Old City wall, on the heels of retreating Arabs who had occupied it before them. Eichler immediately kneeled at a window on the second floor and began firing at Arabs on the wall.

After shooting for some hours, he glanced at his watch and saw that it was after 5 P.M. He rose and made his way down the bullet-swept street to Sternist headquarters in the post office building. Finding Zetler there, bent over a map, he said: "The sun is going down and we have everything under control. May I go home for the Sabbath?"

"Sure. But be back at sundown tomorrow. And don't be late. We'll need every man."

Operation Pitchfork had originally called for the encirclement and capture of the Old City, but this part of the plan, strongly supported by Ben-Gurion, was cancelled when Shaltiel insisted (during the Jewish leader's secret visit to Jerusalem in the Passover convoy) that insufficient troops were available.[2]

However, Shaltiel was faced with an old problem—the dissident groups. Menachem Beigin, though claiming that the Irgun force in Jerusalem was free to act on its own until the Israeli government proclaimed the city a part of Israel, had agreed that he would at least consult with the government before taking independent action. But the Stern Group in Jerusalem had no such agreement with the government and was determined to initiate actions it considered appropriate with or without the Haganah's support. And it wanted most of all to capture the Old City.

Though exhausted after the first day's fighting, David Gottlieb was unable to sleep that night as he lay on the floor of the post office, several hundred yards from the Old City wall. His soldiers, sprawled around him, had helped to take the post office and then been told by Haganah officers to remain where they were. But sleeping made no sense at a time like this. Why did the Haganah refuse to move further than Barclays Bank down the street? The bank stood just across from the wall. Gottlieb decided to take a few men with him to the area of the wall and study the possibilities of breaking through the New and Jaffa gates. As he started to get up, a girl's voice whispered: "Where are you going?"

Gottlieb looked down at the shadowy figure lying next to him and said: "Go back to sleep, Rachel. I'm just going to look around. I'll be back soon."

"Let me go with you," Rachel Seltzer, one of eight girls in the Sternist detachment, pleaded.

"No, go back to sleep," Gottlieb said. "I'll be back soon." He had already made a mistake, Gottlieb decided, in giving in to her pleas to take her this far. Yet what else could he have done without giving the impression to the others that she was enjoying special protection because she was engaged to him? But he would take her no farther—at least until he had some idea of the dangers that lay ahead.

With several men he made his way down the street to Barclays Bank, and shortly afterward was back to awaken the rest of his fighters.

"The firing isn't too heavy now," he told them "Let's see if we can break through the gates and relieve the Jewish Quarter."

"This time I'm going," Rachel insisted.

"No, you stay here!"

"I won't! I'm going!"

Gottlieb turned his flashlight on her and was struck as always by her beauty—the long, black hair curling over her narrow shoulders, the dark eyes and tight, determined lips. In a way, he was responsible for her passion for action. As Hebrew University students, they had argued endlessly about the teachings of Lenin, Sartre, and other political philosophers, and finally, under his influence, she had forsaken communism for the cause of Zionist nationalism. Now she was not satisfied unless she was taking the most daring risks. What could he do? Everyone was looking at him, waiting.

"All right, come on," he muttered.

He led his fighters, about 150 in all, down the street to the rear of Barclays Bank, and split them into two columns. One would march west to Notre Dame Hospice, directly across from New Gate, the other south to the Fast Hotel near Jaffa Gate to establish bases for a breakthrough.

"You go with the group to the hotel," he told Rachel. "I'm going to Notre Dame first and then I'll join you. Take care of yourself."

He grasped her hand in his for a moment and a smile lit his thin face. He hoped he was sending her to the right place. The road leading to Jaffa Gate seemed clear, but he was sure there would be hard fighting at Notre Dame.

In the gray dawn light, Gottlieb then led his column eastward through the ruins to Notre Dame while machine guns crackled on the wall. As they entered the fortress-like monastery, built by the French in the days of Turkish rule to shelter their pilgrims, they were greeted by a group of frightened priests and nuns. Gottlieb asked a priest in hesitant French: "Are there any armed Arabs here?"

"There were, but they've all withdrawn."

"Give me your word that there are no armed Arabs still here and I promise that we will respect this place."

"There are none."

Part of the group then ran up to the roof and immediately found themselves under heavy fire from Arabs on the wall just across the narrow street. Others ran to the French convent nearby to fire from what was to be called "death's roof" because of the large number of casualties inflicted by the Arabs.

On receiving an urgent call for reinforcements from Gottlieb, Zetler rushed to Shaltiel's office in the Jewish Agency building. He found himself repelled by the Haganah commander's neat, polished appearance, which somehow seemed to mock the men writhing in blood and smoke by the Old City wall.

"Shaltiel," Zetler says he begged, "the Arabs are in disarray. They're running. We've cleared the whole area south of Barclays Bank. There is no one there and the Legion is nowhere to be seen. We can advance and take it. It depends only on you now. Come on, let's do this together, you, me, and the Etzel."

Shaltiel, disdainful of Zetler as a ruthless terrorist with no understanding of military tactics, retorted: "Taking the wall would be a heroic act, but it would have no real value since we haven't got the force to capture the Old City."

"Well, at least we can capture a strip leading to the Jewish Quarter."

"The Jewish Quarter has enough food and weapons for a while. I'm ordering you to pull your men back to Barclays Bank. You can do nothing alone and we won't help you. Neither will Etzel, as we have an agreement."

Zetler then went immediately to the Irgun headquarters of Mordechai Raanan.

"I'd like to cooperate with you," sympathized Mordechai Raanan, "but my hands are tied . . ."

David Gottlieb, waiting for word from Zetler on his appeal for assistance, crawled through intense fire from Notre Dame to the Fast Hotel to see how his troops there were holding out. He reproached himself bitterly for having let Rachel talk him into sending her to the front line. When he finally stumbled into the hotel, he noted a soldier staring at him oddly.

"What's the matter?" Gottlieb asked.

When there was no answer, he pressed: "Well?"

The man then mumbled: "Rachel . . ."

Gottlieb felt a sudden chill. "Where is she?"

The soldier nodded toward a door, and Gottlieb rushed in. Rachel lay on a cot, a large bloodstain in the center of her khaki shirt.

Kneeling down beside her, Gottlieb felt for her pulse, then slowly drew his hand away.

"When did it happen?" he asked.

"A few minutes ago," replied the soldier, who had followed him into the room. "A bullet came right through the building."

Gottlieb gazed at the girl for several silent moments, then lifted her body in his arms, the long black hair rippling loosely, and carried her through the ruins to the post office, almost unaware of the storm engulfing those who lived.

After a day of rest and prayer, Menashe Eichler returned to the Barclays Bank area in the evening just as Haganah troops were replacing the battered Sternists, who had been forced to retreat from Notre Dame and the Fast Hotel. Having missed the fierce fighting that day, he was determined to stay—especially after Shaltiel decided to launch an attack on New Gate in the hope of reaching the Jewish Quarter in the Old City, which had been completely isolated by Arab attackers. He thus joined the Haganah force in a futile attempt to retake Notre Dame.

Israeli loudspeakers then blared into the Old City: "Take pity on your wives and children and get out of this bloodbath! Surrender to us with your arms! No harm will come to you."

But while the Arab fighters behind the wall had no intention of giving up and, in fact, continued their attacks on the beleaguered Jewish Quarter within, the Israelis, in little more than 24 hours, had captured almost all of their objectives under Operation Pitchfork.

Ｎｅｗｓ of the Jewish offensive in the New City had not yet reached Amman on the sultry morning of May 14 when four Arab Legion regiments (or battalions) departed from their camp in the desert and headed for the Transjordanian capital on the way to Allenby Bridge. There they would cross to the west bank of the Jordan River to occupy the Triangle.

Glubb Pasha, waiting to join the troops in Amman for the trip to the Jordan River, was exuberant as he watched the long convoy rumble into a bedlam of greeting. Boisterously shouting men stood in packed columns along the streets, while women and children crowded the flat roofs and small windows waving and giggling. The jubilant troops themselves clapped and cheered and waved back, their vehicles decorated with green branches or bunches of pink oleander flowers picked beside the road.

Was this an army going to war or a carnival? Never were soldiers more eager for battle. This was the army he had developed into a splendid fighting force, an army adored by the people and utterly loyal to the King—and to Glubb Pasha himself. He got into his car as the convoy moved slowly through the town. When he passed the various units many soldiers saluted with broad grins, and some called out: "Long live the father of Faris!" referring to Glubb's young son Godfrey, whom the King had "rechristened" Faris, an Arab name. Very proud of parenthood, Arabs often identify themselves as the fathers of their children.

Toward evening, the convoy, after twisting through the mountains into the Jordan Valley, swung off the road into bivouac areas, and soon thin columns of smoke were spiraling into the sky from clusters of campfires throughout the sprawling gray plain. As Glubb gazed around, he drank in the primitive beauty of the peaceful scene at dusk. Ever the romantic, he "almost felt as if the Angel Host might, at any moment, come pouring down from Heaven, in a tumble of white wings, from out of those scarlet clouds." He could "almost catch the first distant strains of their music . . ."

Glubb drove back to Amman in an exalted mood.

"The Jews are advancing everywhere. The city is in confusion! The noise of shooting is deafening! All Arabs will be massacred! For God's sake, come and save us! Come! Come quickly!"

Glubb found his mood abruptly shattered the minute he arrived at the royal palace in Amman, where the King and the Prime Minister were on the telephone constantly, in response to desperate appeals from Arab Jerusalem.

"What are we going to do?" asked Abdullah, his face tense with alarm.

Glubb advised urging the Consular Truce Commission to arrange an immediate cease-fire. If the Legion moved into Jerusalem, he said, not enough men would be available to hold the rest of the country. And if the

Jews occupied the rest of the country, Jerusalem itself would be outflanked and fall.

"Perhaps you're right," the King murmured, and immediately telephoned Nieuwenhuys in Jerusalem.

"The Truce Commission is in touch with both sides," the Belgian Consul told him. "Fighting is still going on, but we hope to make progress tomorrow. I suggest, Your Majesty, that Transjordan refrain from taking any immediate action."

The King agreed, and Glubb then left the palace and drove home, deliberating in his mind the relative strength of the opposing forces. Of his two brigades, one, composed of the 1st and 3rd Regiments, would occupy the Nablus area to protect the Triangle, while the other, consisting of the 2nd and 4th Regiments, would concentrate at Ramallah. The 6th Regiment would stay in the Jerusalem region with headquarters in Jericho. In addition to these forces, which were bolstered by eight 25-pounders, a company that had been cut off in Hebron and unable to return to Transjordan before the British evacuation was protecting the area between Hebron and Bethlehem. The Legion had considerable artillery, ranging from 6-pound anti-tank guns to the 25-pounders, though only a limited amount of ammunition.

But what was this strength compared to that of the enemy? His intelligence indicated the Jews had powerful, well-trained forces in the New City backed by almost unlimited reserves from the para-military population of 100,000 people.

As things stood, his forces would not initiate attacks on areas allocated to Israel by the United Nations; but they could stave off any Israeli attacks on areas earmarked for the Arabs. That is, if he did not have to divert any of these forces to Jerusalem. Yet, in the last analysis, the Old City must be kept out of Israeli hands at any cost. Not only was its retention absolutely vital to Arab morale, but the area was of overriding strategic importance. The Arab Legion had to defend the three districts of Samaria (the Triangle), Judaea, and Hebron, which extended the length of the Palestine mountains from north to south. The Jews occupied the flat coastal plain between the mountains and the sea, and might normally, as had other armies in history, fail in any attempt to fight their way up the hills.

But as Jerusalem was perched on the very crest of the mountain range, capture of the whole city would permit the Jews to drive down the main road to Jericho and turn the whole Legion position in Palestine. At the same time, the seizure of Allenby Bridge would cut off the Legion forces in Palestine from Transjordan.

On his arrival home, Glubb hurried to his study and went down on his knees.

"Oh God," he prayed, "I am not equal to these events. I entreat Thee to grant me Thy help. I beg Thee to direct everything to a good ending—if it be Thy will."³

"Some more have just arrived. Go on out and help bring them in, will you, Tanya?"

The doctor moved on to treat the wounded who had been brought earlier to the makeshift Hadassah Hospital in the middle of town. And Tanya Liebkovich, looking older than her twenty-six years, rushed to the entrance to help carry the stretchers bearing the latest civilian victims of the relentless artillery shelling attack on the New City from Arab emplacements in the Old City and nearby areas.

Tanya had treated many wounded since the artillery assault on the besieged city had begun on April 10. But from the moment the British had marched out of Jerusalem, her patients multiplied rapidly as the indiscriminate shelling tore houses apart, killed people in the street, and shattered the city's nerve—if not its heart as intended. Sometimes planes flew over dropping incendiary bombs which started many fires. And the Jews had no deterrent except for a few homemade mortars, which were constantly moved from place to place to offer the impression of a mighty arsenal. But life in the New City somehow ground on.

Whenever Tanya went with an ambulance to pick up wounded, the scenes of siege she witnessed gave her the feeling that she was playing a role in some absurdly unreal melodrama. With shells singing overhead and sniper bullets whizzing nearby, a man determinedly walked his dog before breakfast, which would probably consist of a slice of bread; a mother brought out her baby in its playpen from a cramped, crumbling, depressingly airless home and placed it in the garden during an occasional lull; a boy ran from house to house hurling into doorways abbreviated newspapers mimeographed by candlelight in hidden cellars; women bent over small wood fires in the street boiling coffee, while others darted to corner queues with pots to obtain their miniscule water rations from carriers making the rounds with horse-driven carts; a pair of sweepers with wheelbarrows and brooms cleared and cleaned a rubble-strewn, shell-pocked street as if for some holiday parade; a pigtailed little girl rushed curiously to the window to see the results of some great "boom," then returned to her piano to practice Beethoven, undeterred by the competitive thunder of war . . .

But there was nothing unreal about the ripped bodies left in the wake of that thunder. Tanya worked with cool control, but she could never accept the open, bloody wounds or—even worse— the dazed, somehow accusing eyes, eyes she had seen over and over again, a brutal reminder that she had survived Auschwitz.

Now she grabbed one end of a stretcher and helped to pull it from the ambulance and carry a wounded woman into the hospital. The victim this time was elderly, her face seamed and sallow. She kept murmuring someone's name. Perhaps her husband, her son, her daughter? In a stuffy, crowded ward, Tanya and her fellow porter transferred the woman to a bed and a doctor immediately came over and examined the shattered leg. The woman, semi-conscious, did not moan or cry; but she continued to mumble, almost inaudibly, the same name, over and over again. Tanya stood by her side, hypnotized by the shriveled, pained countenance, the low, monotonous voice.

"Let's get her out of these clothes," the doctor said . . .

"REMEMBER, THREE PILES . . . CLOTHES IN GOOD CONDITION, clothes no longer usable, and clothes usable but requiring repair work. Then you make a package of the clothes in good condition so they can be shipped to Germany. Take the repairable stuff to the repair shop. Do you understand?"

"Yes," Tanya said quietly to the *kapo*—a tall, blond Jewish woman whom the Nazis had recruited to police the other Jews.

"And don't get too fat in your new job," the *kapo* smirked. "Anyway, it's only temporary. All the jobs around here are temporary."

Tanya could hardly believe her good fortune. This was the job every female prisoner in Auschwitz prayed for. As she joined the other inmates rummaging through the pyramids of clothing, she could almost taste the food she would find. And if she discovered valuables like jewelry or money, she could bribe guards to give her an extra ladleful of the watery soup they poured into cupped hands, or an extra slice of the wormy black bread.

She found herself throwing most of the clothes into the "unusable" pile—ripped, frayed dresses, dirty, patched children's garments. Not much luck this time. But the other girls were finding food. One was gnawing on a slightly rotting apple, another was devouring a stale sandwich. So greedy. Why didn't they share what they found with the others?

Then, as she went through the pockets of a torn blouse, she felt something hard and flat and pulled it out eagerly, hoping to find a candy bar. It was a comb in a leather case. How long had it been since she had seen a comb? She ran it through her short-cropped hair. What a wonderful feeling!

"I found a mirror," said a fellow worker. "Why don't you look at yourself?"

But another grabbed the mirror out of Tanya's hand, stared at her, and threw it into a trash can. Tanya was startled and angry, but before she could protest she glanced around and understood. The women here were healthier than any in the camp, yet they looked like decaying cadavers, without flesh on their protruding bones or life in their hollow eyes. Such a condition had come to seem so normal that she hadn't realized they barely resembled living beings. She felt her own face with bony fingers and quickly drew them away. Maybe she could swap the comb for a few crumbs of bread.

At last! She scooped a piece of cheese out of some grimy pocket and flung it into her mouth, consuming it in a single gulp.

"Do you think another group will be coming soon?" she asked.

Another came the next day. Through the electrified fence, Tanya watched truckloads of prisoners pull into the compound where the gas chamber and crematorium were located. They would enter a barracks in the compound and disrobe, then their clothes would be brought to Tanya's barracks on her side of the fence. Tanya felt quite detached as she watched the prisoners climb out of the trucks—old women clinging to frightened children, elderly men, the lame, the sick, the crippled, the feeble. The new prisoners were silent, and looked more confused than worried. None of them had guessed, apparently. She watched a little boy nibbling on some bread and found herself almost wishing he wasn't wasting it like that.

Then she noticed a figure shuffling hesitantly toward the fence from the truck nearest her.

"Mother!"

As the two women rushed toward the fence separating them, a German guard who had been supervising the unloading ran up and grabbed Tanya's mother, a thin, middle-aged woman, by the hair.

"Where are you going?" he yelled. "That fence is electrified! Do you want to get killed? Get back with the others!"

"She's my mother," Tanya cried. "Let me talk to my mother!"

"This is no social gathering," the German replied brusquely.

"Have you a mother, a wife, daughter?" Tanya blurted.

The guard was silent for a moment, then released his hold on the prisoner.

"All right, you may look," he said. "But you are forbidden to talk."

Mother and daughter silently gazed at each other. Only the elder woman sobbed; Tanya was too weak. After a few moments, the guard grabbed the mother by the shoulders and led her away while Tanya watched numbly. Then there was nothing but the rusty barbed wire fence.

"Come on, Tanya, back to work," said a companion, taking her by the arm. "We eat again today." . . .

In Hadassah Hospital the doctor pulled a blanket over the old woman who had been wounded, saying: "It's too late. Maybe we can save some of the others."

AT DAWN, May 18, Secretary-General Azzam Pasha of the Arab
League, Iraqi Regent Prince Abdul el-Ah, and the Prime Ministers of Iraq,
Syria, and Lebanon drove to the palace in Amman to see King Abdullah.
The Regent, a Hashemite like his uncle (the King), spoke with amusement:
"Your Majesty, Azzam Pasha says that he will denounce the Hashe-
mites as 'traitors' if you don't dispatch a force to Jerusalem."

With some embarrassment, Azzam burst in: "Your Majesty, you are a
descendant of the Prophet. You must know how deeply I respect you. But
if you don't agree to act at this urgent moment, I shall have to inform the
world."

Abdullah stared at Azzam. He knew that the secretary-general had
opposed a formal war in the first place, and that made his appeal all the
more impressive. Abdullah now reached a decision that had been shaping in
his mind for some time.

"Don't worry, Jerusalem won't fall," he said. "I'll send the necessary
troops. My ultimate objective is the head of the snake—Tel Aviv. That
should make you happy."

"If you take Tel Aviv," said Azzam joyfully, "I shall place the crown
of Palestine on your head myself whether others like it or not!"

And the two men rose and clasped each other in a fond embrace.[4]

Only when the distinguished delegation left the palace did Abdullah
realize the full import of his promise. He would now be risking all in a
military confrontation with the Israelis—just what he had been trying to
avoid. But there was no other way. Glubb Pasha seemed more concerned
about defending other parts of Palestine than Jerusalem, but he would just
have to give in.

Later that morning, a soldier rushed into the headquarters of Legion
troops based in Palestine and handed Glubb (who was visiting the force)
an urgent message from Amman. It read:

> His Majesty the King orders an advance toward Jerusalem from the
> direction of Ramallah. He intends by this action to threaten the Jews, in
> order that they may accept a truce in Jerusalem.

Glubb was puzzled and alarmed. What if the Jews would not accept a
truce immediately? Did the King want the advancing force to attack in that

case? He found out about a half an hour later when a messenger arrived with a second message:

> From the Minister of Defense to Glubb Pasha. His Majesty the King is extremely anxious and indeed insists that a force from Ramallah with artillery be sent to attack the Jewish quarters of Jerusalem. The Jews are attacking the gates of the Old City in order to break into it. An attack on the Jews would ease the pressure on the Arabs and would incline the Jews to accept the truce for Jerusalem. The Belgian Consul has been here and His Majesty has gathered from him that such action on our part might frighten the Jews and make them less obstinate. His Majesty is awaiting swift action. Report quickly that the operation has commenced.

"Sir, they've broken in!" an officer reported, as Glubb finished reading the message. "The Jews have broken through Zion Gate and made contact with the Jewish Quarter!"

Glubb knew he could stall no longer. He summoned an aide: "Send an order to the 1st Infantry Company on the Mount of Olives. 'Advance at once into the Old City and man the wall.' "

A few hours later that same morning (May 18), he received the first report from the company. On entering the Old City, the troops, according to the report, had "driven out" the invading Jews. But Glubb was still apprehensive. How could 100 Legionnaires, thinly scattered in the 35 towers of the wall, with rifles thrust through medieval holes shaped to accommodate crossbows, face 100,000 soldiers? Jewish forces already occupied Sheikh Jarrah, and soon they would attack the Mount of Olives and surround the Old City completely. Was there any alternative to an Arab Legion attack in force? He then thought of Fawzi el-Kaoukji and his Arab Liberation Army. Kaoukji had abandoned his positions in the Latrun area without even informing Glubb of this, but perhaps he would return if he were persuaded that Jerusalem was about to fall . . .

That day, May 18, Kaoukji was camped with a detachment of his men near Jericho, on his way back to the Jerusalem area from battle in central Galilee, where he had gone in hasty response to an Iraqi appeal for assistance.

"A very urgent message, sir," said the messenger as he entered Kaoukji's headquarters tent. Kaoukji looked pleased as he reached for it and read:

> 3:15 P.M.—Situation Jerusalem very critical. City about to fall. We are asking you fervently to extend help soon as possible using shortest route. Commander of Arab Legion.

Just as he had thought; they needed him! First they criticized him, then they asked for his help. Hardly had he ordered his men to get ready to move when another message arrived from a commander in Jerusalem:

> Very urgent—3:55 P.M.—Situation is dangerous. Enemy is launching general attack in all sectors of city. Artillery is shelling heavily from every direction. We must have reinforcements or else obliteration will be our fate. And I repeat . . . obliteration and the fall of the city . . .

At 5:20 P.M. still another message from the same commander reported:

> Situation is deteriorating. Alas for the Holy City. Advance to save the situation. The people are waiting for your immediate help.

Yes, the people were waiting for him, Kaoukji agreed. At 5:35 P.M., he radioed back: "Maintain your stand. I am on my way to you. Fawzi."

Kaoukji then led a battalion of men to a village near Jerusalem and began pounding the New City with cannon shells, though contributing no infantry to the defense of the Old City. He later claimed: "I saved Jerusalem!"[5]

In the evening, Glubb ordered headquarters in Palestine to attack Sheikh Jarrah at dawn on May 19 and commanded the 8th Infantry Company on the Mount of Olives to join the 1st in defending the Old City.

Then he went to the palace to see the King, whose leathery cheeks, he noted, were sunken and pale.

"I conjure you by God to tell me the truth," Abdullah urged. "Can we hold Jerusalem, or will the Jews take it?"

"If God wills, they will never take it, sir!"

"I want you to promise me that if you ever think the Jews will take Jerusalem, you will tell me. I will not live to see them in the Holy Places. I will go there myself and die on the walls of the city."

"If God wills, that will not happen."[6]

"The Legion is coming! Armored cars! Dozens of them!"

In the Police Training School at the northern edge of Sheikh Jarrah, Yehuda Lapidot looked grim but unsurprised by this news brought to him by a runner. As commander of an Irgun unit that had taken over Sheikh Jarrah from the Haganah, he felt abandoned. The Haganah had not supplied him with a single anti-tank weapon, not even machine guns. How was he supposed to stop tanks—with his bare hands?

Military critics were later to blame Lapidot for not pressing his men to dig in sufficiently—a defense measure which had never preoccupied the Irgunists, traditionally geared to hit-and-run tactics.

Major Slade's armored Legion unit poured shells into the school and other buildings as it advanced, forcing the Israelis to retreat to the cemetery south of Sheikh Jarrah. Finally, it came to a halt in front of a massive concrete barrier on the road leading out of Sheikh Jarrah into the Old and New Cities. Slade jumped out of his car under heavy mortar fire to assess the situation, and was wounded. But a 6-pounder quickly demolished the roadblock.

Whether the Arab armor then advanced further is disputed. Glubb Pasha says that by 2 P.M. the armored car squadron had reached Damascus Gate, but withdrew at dusk because of its uselessness in narrow streets at night. Lapidot maintains that the cars never moved beyond the southern edge of Sheikh Jarrah.

Glubb was delighted to learn that Sheikh Jarrah, at least, had been captured. And now that the Legion had committed itself in Jerusalem, he decided to bolster his forces there with the 3rd Regiment, which was based in the Nablus area. This meant leaving the defense of the Triangle—an area of more than 1,000 square miles—to the 1st Regiment alone (and later to the Iraqis), but no other unit was available.

At 4:30 P.M. on May 21, Major William Newman, the Australian commander of the 3rd Regiment, assembled his soldiers in the olive grove where they had been camping.

"Men, we're going to Jerusalem!" he announced.

Legionnaires who had been sprawling listlessly under the olive trees suddenly jumped to their feet, overwhelmed with the honor of being selected to "save" the Holy Places from the Jews.

"What? Jerusalem? *Al hamdu l'Allah!* Praise be to God! What did you say? O Hamed! O Qasim! O Abdullah! Jerusalem! We are going to Jerusalem! We are going to Jerusalem!"

"Yes," said the commander, "and we're leaving immediately."

When the men had gathered their equipment, they moved southward on trucks from Nablus along the road for Jerusalem. As they passed through Ramallah, wounded soldiers rose en masse from hospital beds to join their comrades in battle.

"Take us with you, brothers," they cried as they scrambled aboard, many of them still wrapped in bloodstained bandages.

Proceeding on foot from the village of Shafat, the infantry plodded into Sheikh Jarrah at dawn, May 22. Tired from the five-mile march—some Arab officers were furious at Newman for not permitting their men to ride farther—the regiment moved rapidly ahead through blistering fire that greeted them when they emerged into the open area separating Sheikh Jarrah from Jerusalem proper.

*

In his Amman headquarters, Glubb Pasha sat nervously playing with a string of amber beads. The attacking regiment was to speed southward to Damascus Gate, its western flank exposed to enemy fire from the New City along most of the way, then regroup for an attack on its final objectives: Notre Dame and Barclays Bank at the edge of the New City.* He shuddered at the thought of his desert fighters making their way through unfamiliar alleys under enemy fire.

Yet he could barely suppress a smile as he reflected on the delight of his soldiers at the prospect of fighting in Jerusalem. They were like children going to the movies. He stared at a teacup on his desk . . . If he broke it, of course, he would have to buy four more as a penalty. That had been the rule of his desert force. Sometimes the troops, as they squatted in the desert under the stars, even held mock trials to determine which culprit had broken a cup—like the trials of men accused of stealing camels. A whole body of law had risen from the disputes. Should a man who volunteered to make tea for his comrades be fined if he broke a cup? Should a guest be fined? . . .

The telephone rang.

"They're *lost?* What do you mean? How can three whole companies simply vanish?"

After a pause, Glubb smashed his fist down on the desk. "Oh, my God! Well, *find them!*" . . .

Major Bill Newman crouched in the corner of a house in Sheikh Jarrah amid the deafening roar of mortar shells vainly demanding over a walkietalkie that someone out there in the smoke and dust answer him.

"God damn it, where are they?" he grunted to an aide nearby.

It was not until noon, May 22, that a message finally came through reporting that one company had reached the Old City walls at Damascus Gate. But the other two companies were still missing.

"We've got to find the rest of our regiment," Newman said then. "We're moving up!"

Accompanied by a troop of armored cars, Newman and his whole regimental command raced forward into the twisting streets of the city toward Damascus Gate, running the murderous gauntlet of the Israeli-controlled flank . . .

* The Israelis firmly believed that the Legion attacks represented an all-out assault on the New City, but the Legion leaders deny this, and I was unable to find evidence to support the theory. The details presented here come from Legion officers and from Aref's book.[7]

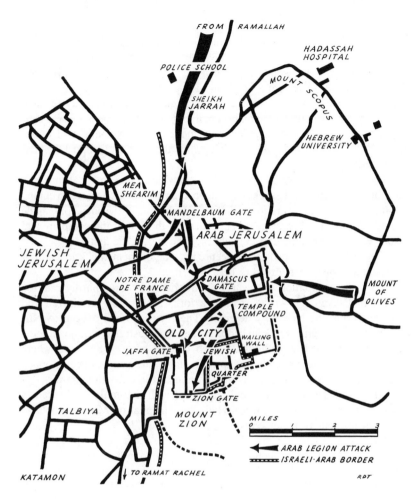

FROM RAMALLAH

HADASSAH
HOSPITAL

POLICE SCHOOL

MOUNT SCOPUS

SHEIKH
JARRAH

HEBREW
UNIVERSITY

MEA
SHEARIM

MANDELBAUM GATE

ARAB JERUSALEM

JEWISH
JERUSALEM

NOTRE DAME
DE FRANCE

DAMASCUS
GATE

MOUNT
OF
OLIVES

TEMPLE
COMPOUND

OLD CITY

WAILING
WALL

JAFFA GATE

JEWISH

QUARTER

ZION GATE

TALBIYA

MOUNT
ZION

MILES
0   1   2   3

ARAB LEGION ATTACK
ISRAELI-ARAB BORDER

KATAMON

TO RAMAT RACHEL

RDT

THE ARAB LEGION ADVANCE INTO THE OLD CITY

Ghazi el-Harbi was a tough Saudi Arabian veteran with a wrinkled, weatherbeaten face. He had been given little orientation on the route he was to take, and he wondered now if his armored car would ever find Damascus Gate. Give him a target in the desert and he'd find it even if it were only a stick in the sand. But how was he to thread his way through this crazy maze of city streets? The small map he held in his hand was simply a jumble of crisscrossing lines that made no sense at all. And to aggravate things, Newman wasn't giving him the artillery support he had promised.

Suddenly, an explosion rocked the car, which came to an abrupt halt in a burst of flame and smoke. The men crawled out and started running to the rear, but many were mowed down. Harbi, one of the survivors, made his way toward the two armored cars carrying the rest of the company and shouted to the commanders: "Quick, save the men in the first car!"

The two vehicles sped to the scene, but one of them was knocked out en route and the other forced to flee.

In its preoccupation with survival, the depleted force hardly realized that it had taken the wrong road at a fork south of Sheikh Jarrah and blundered into the New City defenses. The Jews who had bagged two armored cars were elated, convinced that they had frustrated a major Legion attempt to attack the Orthodox Jewish quarter of Mea Shearim, where some inhabitants had already put up white flags. The cars had been stopped near the Mandelbaum houses as they were about to enter the quarter.

Meanwhile, a second lost unit equipped with anti-tank guns raced in another wrong direction—toward Hadassah Hospital on Mount Scopus— and was also halted by fierce resistance . . .

Newman and his regimental command careened into the square outside Damascus Gate, and broke into some abandoned houses to prepare frontline defensive positions while troops who had already arrived poured shells into the Israeli-held Notre Dame Hospice overlooking the area. The agitated commander later located the missing companies, and sent armored cars to guide them to Damascus Gate, where they arrived exhausted and casualty-ridden late in the day.

"Let's hope the Jews are as tired as we are," Newman said to his officers in the headquarters hotel that night. "I'm not sure it'll be possible to wake up the men if the Jews attack before morning."

After a quiet night, the battle for Notre Dame, the doorway to the New City, began at dawn, May 23 . . .

While two 6-pounder anti-tank guns and four 3-inch mortars pounded the nearly invulnerable walls of Notre Dame, a Legion armored column flanked by infantry wormed its way from Damascus Gate through narrow debris-cluttered streets toward its majestic objective. House by house, men and machines advanced in a storm of fire until the spearhead of the armor reached the street outside the monastery.

When the first armored car passed in front, an Israeli (a sixteen-year-old veteran of the French maquis) hurled a Molotov cocktail from inside the monastery which set the car on fire, providing an effective anti-tank obstacle. The other vehicles turned and retreated, except for a second one which was also hit and damaged, reinforcing the barrier. At the same time, Arab irregulars in the area poured fire into Legion troops who had entered the garden of the monastery, mistaking them for Israelis.

Ghazi el-Harbi, the Saudi Arabian leading this forward group, was undiscouraged despite the fire from two sides; and after a bloody battle he managed, at about 9 A.M., to break through into the basement of Notre Dame with some 10 men. But they soon discovered that they were cut off and surrounded, with few infantrymen left to attempt a linkup. Nearly half of the 200-odd infantrymen who had set out to attack Notre Dame had been either killed or seriously wounded, and one company had lost all but one of its commissioned and noncommissioned officers.

Late in the afternoon, Harbi was sitting at a window firing at Israelis in nearby buildings when a regimental officer radioed him: "We have orders that you must evacuate Notre Dame immediately."

"Evacuate? After all the trouble we had getting in?"

"Never mind. We have too many casualties. We can't send you any help."

"I won't leave!"

When Glubb Pasha heard of Harbi's defiance, he was furious.

"Tell him," he radioed Newman, "that we won't send him any food or ammunition. He must leave immediately!"

Harbi still refused to leave. Finally, when his superiors said that the Legion had laid TNT charges and intended to blow up the building, he reluctantly agreed, withdrawing with his men at about 5 P.M. The Israeli commander on an upper floor was incalculably grateful. His men had begun to run out of ammunition and some, poorly trained, had become jittery. The Legion force, he had feared, would take over the building completely if it continued to press its assault.

Harbi went with some of his men to the Jericho headquarters of Abdullah Tel, now a colonel, and found a sympathetic ear as he bitterly complained that the British officers had "betrayed" him, first by sending his company from Sheikh Jarrah to the New City without adequate information or artillery support, and then by forcing him to evacuate Notre Dame.

"This fits in with Glubb's refusal to help the Egyptians at Ramat

Rachel," Tel said to his visitors. "He doesn't want to fight the Jews, but only to implement the partition plan. And he has hoodwinked the King into supporting him."

Tel then telephoned the King in Harbi's presence, hoping to influence him against the British officers.

"The 3rd Regiment attacked Notre Dame and failed," Tel reported.

After a pause, King Abdullah fumed: "How did it happen?"

"Newman is responsible, Your Majesty. His handling of the attack resulted in many deaths."

"That's enough," interrupted the King. "In the name of God, let's hear no more such talk!"

"As you wish, Your Majesty."

Tel hung up and turned to Harbi. "It's no use. The King will not listen to a word against the British."

Ousted by Glubb from the Legion, Harbi became a sort of martyr to Tel and other Arab Legion officers. He represented to them the fighting spirit that British commanders were trying to suppress, on orders from London. Tel was determined to reduce this British control of the Legion and, incidentally, to play a heroic role himself—fighting the Jews, in co-operation with the Palestinian irregulars, independently of Glubb's authority.

First, he decided, he would score a devastating victory over the stubborn defenders of the Jewish Quarter in the Old City.[8]

HARDLY had Moshe Rousnak (the quarter commander) received the news that stage 1 of Operation Horned Snake had succeeded when an aide handed him a radio message from David Shaltiel:

> Take over British positions but . . . don't be the first to open fire. British positions in Jewish areas are of course coming to us. Observe cease-fire rules as the continuation of food convoys under Red Cross supervision depends on this. You cannot have reinforcements of men and weapons at this time. Take into consideration your forces in all your actions.

Rousnak crumpled the message in his hand. He was not to pursue the next stage of Operation Horned Snake, not to attack Arab positions, and this at the very last moment, when the fate of the Jewish Quarter—and the entire Old City—hung in the balance.

"What they're asking is suicide," he told Chava Kirschenbaum. "They're handing us over to the Arabs on a silver platter."

Even before Shaltiel's shattering message arrived, Haganah soldiers were automatically following up the first stage of Operation Horned Snake on May 13 by moving into the vacuum left by the British in the Armenian Quarter, which lay athwart the path to Zion Gate and the New City. They were amazed by the ease with which they could advance, and Rousnak decided not to stop them unless he received a direct order to do so. The Arabs, incredibly, seemed to have been unaware of the sudden British departure and were making no effort to take over the vacated posts.

As the Jews quietly occupied the Greek monastery of St. Georges, which bordered on the Jewish and Armenian quarters, a black-robed priest in the Armenian monastery, or *Vank,* entered the study of Armenian patriarch Guregh II Israelian and said excitedly: "Your Beatitude, the Jews are taking over the British positions in our quarter. They are already in the Greek church."

The patriarch, his head framed by a pointed black hood, stared at the priest with shocked eyes. "The Arabs will think we permitted them to enter," he said, nervously caressing his long, furry beard. "Evacuate all Armenian families to the monastery immediately. The Arabs may come any minute."

But by midnight, the Haganah had occupied more than half the deserted Armenian Quarter and no Arabs had showed up, being apparently still unaware of what was happening.

The patriarch, who had long since discovered that the better part of valor was to remain neutral in the Arab-Jewish struggle, called two priests to him and spoke to them in some despair: "Go to the Jews and tell them that they must leave at once. Try to make them understand that if they do not want to be attacked, they must withdraw immediately from our quarter."

The two priests quietly crossed the barricade into the Jewish area and asked Haganah guards to take them to Rabbi Weingarten, an old acquaintance of the patriarch.

Awakened from a troubled sleep, Weingarten greeted the priests warmly. "What brings you here at this time of night?" he asked. "It's dangerous. Shooting could start any time."

"That's the point," said one of the priests, as the rabbi served them some wine. "His Beatitude fears that the occupation of the British posts in the Armenian Quarter by Jewish forces will result in widespread bloodshed among the Armenians. He asks you to use your influence to have them withdrawn immediately."

Weingarten drew his robe tighter around him and slowly sipped his wine. It seemed ironic that everybody still respected him as the leader of the Jewish community—everybody but the Jews in control.

"I can do nothing," he admitted. "It is a military matter and the area is apparently considered essential for Jewish security."

When the priests found they were making no progress, they returned to the patriarch, who sent them back again with the injunction: "Tell him that I will order an attack immediately if he does not come at once!"

While the priests were on their errand, the patriarch, who had at his disposal only a few small arms and light machine guns, ordered an assistant to gather at least 100 tough-looking men and post them along the street and in front of the monastery armed with every weapon in the arsenal to give the impression that he possessed a mighty army.

About an hour later, Weingarten and the two priests emerged from a dark cobblestone alley and were shocked to find themselves threading their way through lines of scowling Armenians armed to the teeth. The rabbi was shown into a huge, luxurious reception room and he and the patriarch discussed the crisis until about 4 A.M. (May 14). He would do his best to influence the Haganah leaders, Weingarten promised, on condition that the Arabs would not be permitted to take over the posts in the quarter either.

Weingarten then rushed back to the Jewish Quarter and arranged a meeting with Rousnak and other Haganah chiefs, as well as civilian notables, at Haganah headquarters.

"I have seen with my own eyes," the rabbi said when all had arrived, "that the Armenians are well armed and they will fight us unless we vacate their quarter. The patriarch promises that he will not permit the Arabs to take the positions."

After considerable argument between the civilian leaders, who supported Weingarten's plea, and the Haganah people, who did not, Rousnak said firmly: "The answer is No, and that's final!"

Weingarten returned to the patriarch and told him of the Haganah's decision. The Armenian leader then called Shaltiel's headquarters in the New City and protested to him directly, pointing out that occupation of Armenian holy places was contrary to an agreement he had reached with the Consular Truce Commission.

Shortly thereafter, Rousnak received a radio message ordering him to leave the Armenian Quarter. Though enraged, he had no choice but to obey, and his men vacated their posts at about 2 P.M. on the afternoon of May 14. At about 3 P.M., the Arabs walked in from the east and north and told the patriarch they were there to stay, truce violation or no. Within another couple of hours, the Arabs attacked the Jews who had taken over British positions at Zion Gate. The defenders, cut off from the Jewish Quarter by the Arab occupation of the Armenian Quarter, were forced to flee in the evening—only minutes after Ben-Gurion had proclaimed the birth of the State of Israel.

The Jewish Quarter was now completely isolated from the outside world.

*

Mohammed Gharbieh first learned of the Jewish advance into the Armenian Quarter from a friend who knocked ferociously on his door shortly after dawn on May 14. Mohammed shook himself out of bed, trying not to waken his German wife, and on opening the door was greeted with the words: "The Jews have taken over the Armenian Quarter! Let's go!"

Within minutes, Gharbieh was dressed and running out of the door with his Sten, glad that his wife was still asleep. He hated to see the look of anguish on her face whenever he left for battle.

By the time he had gathered his men and reached the edge of the Armenian Quarter, Armenian officials had passed the word that the Jews had agreed to leave the quarter peacefully.

Mohammed, as he stood on a street corner with his men, smiled and said: "We should be able to take the Jewish Quarter in a couple of hours —once we have the Armenian Quarter."

His group was only one of many that gathered that day to defend the Old City against Jewish attack and to prepare for an attack of their own on the Jewish Quarter, and, if possible, the New City. Since the death of Abd el-Kader el-Husseini, no one man seemed to be capable of exerting effective authority over all the guerrilla forces, though Munir Abu-Fadil, a Lebanese in his mid-twenties, seemed to wield the greatest influence. Fadil's principal handicap was that, as a closer associate of the Mufti than many of the Palestine fighters, he had incurred the wrath of King Abdullah, who was reluctant to give him either moral or material support, particularly for the struggle in Jerusalem. Indeed, Abdullah Tel had once called him on the telephone and warned: "Munir, His Majesty has ordered me to arrest you—so I suggest you do your best to avoid me!"

At the same time, Tel, who favored an immediate advance by Arab Legion troops into Jerusalem though knowing that the King and Glubb opposed such a move, quietly helped to organize more acceptable groups of Palestinian fighters for the battle of Jerusalem.

Various groups of fighters thus prepared to conquer the Jewish Quarter and move into the New City—which was fine with Mohammed Gharbieh, who was the general of his own small army in the great Arab crusade.

Late in the morning of May 14, Emmanuel Meidav, the popular and much respected Haganah officer, stood before his troops in the Jewish Quarter and addressed them in a low but forceful voice:

"We have gathered in our first military formation as legal soldiers . . . Forget that you have families here . . . This is simply a battleground . . . Every bullet must count . . . We won't be able to get reinforcements of men and ammunition easily, and perhaps we won't get them at all. Every one of you, every pair of hands is dear to us. Take care of yourselves . . . You are not to leave your positions until the last bullet and the last man . . . "

Then he added: "We may be at war, but I want to see you all clean and polished every morning."

The soldiers, men and women, laughed. Living in dirty cellars, sleeping at posts in the street, short of clothes and soap, they took Emmanuel's order as a joke. Most of the men wore dirty khaki trousers and sweaters and torn shirts. And Judith Jaharan, who had joined the forces in the Jewish Quarter after having entered the Old City, found herself without any khaki at all and had to wear the old Kelly-green skirt she had arrived in. She had not realized that the convoy which brought her to the Old City would be the last, going either way, and that she would not be able to return to the New City.

When Emmanuel had finished his talk, the troops returned to their posts—all except Rika Menache who, since her arrival in the quarter, had been serving as a secretary to Rousnak.

"Emmanuel," she said now, "I'm fed up with deskwork. You just said yourself that every person is needed to fight. Let me fight in your unit. Then I'll be doing something more useful and at the same time we'll be together . . . "

She took his hand and looked at him, her dark eyes pleading. "Please, Emmanuel."

He tried to avoid her look. "Someone has got to write the reports, and you're an expert at it," he muttered. "You're as important here as anyone with a Sten gun. There's no use your getting killed doing something you're not really trained to do."

"But I can shoot a gun as well as the next man."

He was silent, and as she searched his sensitive face for a reaction she knew she had conquered him.

"Well, all right," he said. "But no heroics, and if you disobey orders I'll court-martial you and send you back to the Congo!"

Since the Arabs were not yet organized they agreed, as did the Jewish Quarter, to an extension of the cease-fire that had been in force before the British departure. Fighting therefore was only sporadic on May 14 and during daylight on May 15, with Israeli fighters engaged mainly in dodging grenades and digging last-minute entrenchments.

The Israeli commanders were thankful for the relative quiet, since troop morale had plummeted as the result of the pullout from the Armenian Quarter and Zion Gate and the knowledge that the Jewish Quarter was now completely isolated. Many civilians were already prepared to surrender and, on May 14, used the fact that it was the Sabbath as an excuse not to engage in defense work, though the rabbinate had authorized such labor.

Emmanuel, enraged by this attitude, went to one of the troop billets. "Take your weapons and bring people, if necessary by force, to help on the entrenchments," he said firmly.

As soldiers went from door to door, some civilians refused to answer, or else shouted *"Shabbos!"* ("Sabbath!"). A few even poured down water on the callers from windows. Finally, the soldiers fired into the air, and people reluctantly started coming out. Others, after their doors had been broken in, were carried out bodily. Bitter shouts of "Desecraters of the Sabbath!" echoed through the area, as did the clatter of boots on cobblestone as some civilians fled to take refuge with friends or in synagogues.

At about 7:30 P.M. on May 15 the cease-fire, to the extent that it had existed, came to an abrupt end with a heavy Arab mortar bombardment.

"Move all civilians into Bate Mahseh," Rousnak ordered, though he wondered, in his frustration, whether some of them were really worth saving.

During pauses in the bombardment, Israeli soldiers swiftly herded terrified, weeping civilians out of their homes into the subterranean synagogues and basements of the Bate Mahseh, a forest of stone tenements near the city wall normally inhabited by poor people and *Yeshiva* students.

In one of the buildings, when the bombardment had subsided that night, Emmanuel and Rika lay side by side on dirty blankets in a large room occupied by about 20 soldiers trying to grab a little sleep. Rika watched Emmanuel in the dim light as he tossed restlessly in a vain effort to sleep. His normally full cheeks were hollow, his wavy blond hair covered his ears, and there were deep, dark circles under his eyes. How different he had looked before the trouble started, when they had been students together at Hebrew University. He was so tired now, so crushed by the accumulated tension of the last six months.

As Rika watched him, he opened his eyes, smiled weakly at her, and, gripping her hand in his, clung desperately to the night.

Early the next morning, May 16, the Arabs launched an attack from all sides, and the Israelis defended themselves fiercely. Mohammed Gharbieh was in the forefront of the assault as he and his dozen or so men crawled down a narrow street leading into the Jewish Quarter, keeping as close to the wall as possible. They fought their way through one house, killing two Israeli defenders. Then Mohammed climbed through a window and was trying to reach the window of an adjoining house, when a bullet hit him in the buttocks. He managed to get to the next window anyway, and dived inside, riddling the room with bullets as he hit the floor just in case there were Jews present.

He pressed a handkerchief to his wound and cursed his luck. Couldn't he have received a more dignified wound? To be shot in the ass! . . .

Esther Ceilingold's wish was being fulfilled; she was in the very thick of battle. Her job was to run from one position to another, supplying food, ammunition, and other needs, and to join in the actual fighting if necessary. But her principal contribution, as far as the soldiers were concerned, was the constant encouragement she gave them.

Leaping from roof to roof with a haversackful of supplies, she would clap them on the back and say: "Come on chaps, let's get cracking. We can hold them, we can." Then she would plump down a bag of sandwiches or bullets and head for the next position, apparently oblivious of the danger.

Nor did the gore and filth of war affect her concern for high standards. Once, she entered a house under fire and gasped when she saw the sandwiches she had brought earlier now blackened with soot and dust. "I was in England during the bombing," she said tartly, "and sanitary conditions remained good throughout."

She left, returning in about 15 minutes with a new batch of carefully wrapped sandwiches.

"Now I don't want you to kill anybody else until you've eaten them," she admonished.

On May 16, as the Arabs began their big attack, Esther was hit in the hip by a stray bullet as she ran from one post to another. She started to hobble down the Street of the Jews toward the hospital, grimacing with pain, and met a number of fighters rushing to stem the Arab attack. They offered to help her, but she pointed to the battle area and said: "Go and help over there."

And she hobbled on alone . . .

As the Arabs stepped up their attack that morning and casualties began to mount, Rousnak and the other Israeli commanders, feeling utterly abandoned by Shaltiel, radioed urgently: "The situation is desperate. They are breaking into the quarter from all sides!"

In his New City headquarters, Shaltiel conferred immediately with his aides.

"What forces are available to send them?" Shaltiel asked an officer.

"We'll have to scrounge from here and there."

"Well, do what you can," Shaltiel said crisply.

A few minutes later, Rousnak received a message saying that help would be on the way within an hour and a half.

"At last!" he cried, as he read the message at the height of a deafening bombardment.

But as the day wore on and no reinforcements arrived, the depression among the commanders grew worse than before. After a savage battle had taken place that afternoon in the *Yeshiva* of Porat Joseph, a vital position, the Jewish Quarter appealed once more:

"Help us immediately. Otherwise we will not be able to hold out."

To which the New City replied laconically: "You are to hold out at all cost."

Shaltiel was shocked when he received the immediate response—that the Jewish Quarter would not be able to hold out for more than 15 minutes . . .

While Shaltiel absorbed this message with rising fury and frustration, Rousnak was also reading it in his headquarters and reacting similarly.

"What in hell have you done?" he shouted at Mordechai Wager, his second in command, who had sent the message without consulting him. "Couldn't you have said that we may not be able to hold out for longer than, say, a few hours? Who will believe us now? You know very well we can hold out longer than fifteen minutes!"

"I thought we had to frighten them enough to send reinforcements immediately," Wager replied. "What's the difference—fifteen minutes or a few hours? We're being overrun, aren't we?"

Rabbis Weingarten, Mintzberg, and Hazan then arrived and, after more commanders had been called in for a conference, stressed that the quarter was indeed being overrun.

"It is stupid to hold out any longer," Weingarten said. "They're coming right into the center of the quarter. We'll all be slaughtered."

Rousnak leaned heavily on his desk and said nothing while the rabbis went on describing the situation in desperate terms. Maybe they were right. What was the use of sacrificing the whole population for a lost cause?

"Very well," he said finally in a husky voice, "we'll surrender."

But although some of Rousnak's commanders agreed, others did not; some had not even been asked to participate in the conference. Among these was the Irgun's Isser Nathanson; he only heard about the meeting by accident from Emmanuel Meidav, who had just come from headquarters.

Nathanson, whose 40 Irgun fighters were defending the northeast part of the Jewish Quarter, dashed through the narrow alleys to headquarters where he saw a Haganah leader, Shaar Ishuv Cohen, just emerging.

"What's happening?" the Irgunist cried.

Cohen repeated what Emmanuel had said.

Nathanson burst into the headquarters office and interrupted the informal meeting in progress. He looked at Rousnak icily and said: "You've decided to surrender, but don't you know that the irregulars will have no mercy on us? They'll kill us all. We must fight to the last round!"

He then left the room, and encountered a group of soldiers outside.

"We want to continue to fight," one of them said.

"Who says no?" Nathanson asked calmly.

"We know they're making a deal in there to surrender," another man said.

"Never!" Nathanson replied. "Get back to your posts and fight!"⁹

At this point, Emmanuel Meidav crept along a twisting street and entered the evacuated Tiano Building. He put his Sten gun on the floor, kneeled down, and began fiddling with a wired contraption he had brought with him. He did not know much about setting up booby traps, but then neither did his men, and it would have been unfair to ask any of them to do the job. As he worked, the shooting outside grew louder. He had told his men that with luck this mine could hold up the Arab advance long enough for them to counterattack and possibly end the talk of surrender at headquarters.

Suddenly, the house resounded with an explosion. As Emmanuel's men, who had been guarding nearby, came running, they saw smoke pouring out of the window. They climbed through the wreckage in the doorway and found Emmanuel lying amid the debris . . .

Rika Menache lay propped up behind the window of a small house, resting her elbows on a pile of sandbags and firing occasionally in the direction of fleeting targets that flung themselves intermittently across shadowy alleys or showed in relief against other small, square windows. Somehow, it all seemed unreal. She tried to imagine herself on some kind of maneuver, with the targets merely stuffed dummies, controlled by strings, that could not possibly shoot back . . .

RIKA MENACHE HAD SPENT MOST OF HER 22 YEARS FAR FROM THE harsher realities of life—in Elizabethville, the Belgian Congo, where her father had owned a shoe factory—living a sheltered life surrounded by servants and a small, tight community of white Gentiles.

She had gone to a Catholic mission school and all her friends were Christians. She had hardly even heard of Zionism or Palestine—until, to her shock, she had been banned from the local Girl Scout organization because of her religion.

At fifteen, she had gone to South Africa to learn how to organize a Jewish Scout movement among the 2,000 Jews in the eastern Congo, and there she had been introduced to Zionism. She had returned to Elizabethville with a suitcaseful of books about Palestine and had translated them from English to French so that other Jews in the Congo could read them. Then, with the help of her brother, she organized a Zionist movement in the Congo and was eventually offered a year of free study in Palestine, where she decided to stay . . .

For all her military training, she did not feel herself psychologically prepared for this kind of experience. It was only Emmanuel who gave her the strength to fight, as he gave strength to everyone who came into contact with him.

Rika fired again, automatically, at something she thought she saw moving.

She began to wonder when Emmanuel would return. He had been gone for about an hour. She hoped he would be in a better mood than when he had left . . . Poor Emmanuel, he was so intense, so nervous, so exhausted . . . Just before leaving, he had shouted at his men, the men who loved him so dearly, because they were too slow piling up sandbags on the street. "What's the matter with you lazy bastards," he had yelled. "Don't you know that unless we fight they'll slaughter us all?"

And then he had gone off somewhere and the last she had seen of him was when he looked up at her briefly and waved, his haggard face smeared with dirt, his hair tumbling over his forehead. For him, the war was so real. For her, only Emmanuel was real . . .

About an hour later, when the fighting appeared to have stabilized, Rika started back toward Bate Mahseh. On the way she met someone who yelled to her: "Did you hear? Emmanuel has been wounded."

Rika paused, shocked, then ran all the way to the hospital, a large building located in Bate Mahseh. She burst in and made her way through a milling throng—doctors, nurses, ambulatory patients, civilians who had taken refuge there—until finally she found Dr. Abraham Laufer, the hospital director.

"Doctor," she cried. "Emmanuel—is he all right?"

Laufer silently took her arm and led her to a room. Inside, a mummy-like figure, the whole face bandaged, lay on a stretcher placed on a table.

"Will he live?" she asked.

"I believe so."

Rika sighed with relief. Thank God. At least he would no longer have to fight and risk his life recklessly. Perhaps he had had to be wounded in order to be saved. In any case, she would take care of him until he recovered. She wouldn't leave him for a minute.

Then Laufer continued, placing his arm around her shoulder: "But my dear, you may as well know . . . He has lost his eyes and his hands."

On the morning of May 17, the Jewish Quarter was still holding out, Rousnak having changed his mind about surrender. An observer dashed into Rousnak's office.

"They're coming. They're moving down the Street of the Jews—right toward the center of the quarter!"

Rousnak, his eyes bloodshot from lack of sleep, said in a hard, calm voice: "Go back and tell them to hold. They've got to hold until reinforcements arrive."

That afternoon, Jean Nieuwenhuys, the Belgian Consul, and Dr. Pablo de Azcarate, the United Nations representative, were returning to Jerusalem from Amman where, as members of the Truce Commission, they had spoken with King Abdullah, when they decided to stop at Arab Legion headquarters in Jericho. Abdullah Tel received them cordially and over coffee told them he had heard reports that the Jewish Quarter was almost ready to surrender, but only to regular Arab troops. He expressed the hope that his own forces would soon be sent to the scene.

The two diplomats then continued on into the Old City of Jerusalem and made their way to the headquarters of Munir Abu-Fadil, who summoned other Arab commanders to the meeting.

The Belgian Consul related what Abdullah Tel had said and added that he himself would be glad to offer his good offices if they could contribute to a just peace.

Fadil and the other Arabs did not hide their irritation. This was a Palestinian affair and they didn't want the Legion taking the glory, and possibly the territory, when it was the irregulars who were bringing the Jews to their knees. With their approval, at about 7:00 P.M. Nieuwenhuys telephoned Dr. Leo Kohn of the Jewish Agency and communicated the Arab terms of surrender. The gathering tensely awaited the reply amid sparse conversation and the nervous tinkle of coffee cups.

At 8:30 P.M., Kohn called and spoke to the Consul, who then informed the Arabs: "Gentlemen, Dr. Kohn says that he has communicated with the Haganah commander in the Jewish Quarter by radio and the commander has indicated the situation is not nearly serious enough to justify surrender on your terms."

Fadil, his round face gray, slowly put down his coffee in the deadly silence.[10]

When Leo Kohn received the call from Nieuwenhuys about Arab surrender terms, he was not in fact at all sure he could afford to turn them down. Only about an hour before, at 5:55 P.M., the Jewish Quarter had radioed a frantic message to Shaltiel's headquarters pleading for help: There will be no use soon. The need is now. The hour and a half has already continued 36 hours. By what watch are you going?

Nor were the messages any less desperate when Kohn checked on the situation after the Consul's call. At 7:30 P.M., a message read: "They are bombing the Jewish Quarter." At 7:50, another: "Our situation is lost. Our last request. Send help." At 8:01: "We urge you please bomb the quarter heavily so we can hold on. It is matter of minutes for us." And at 8:05: "It's a matter of minutes. Send help immediately, immediately, immediately."

These messages shook Shaltiel into making two swift decisions. He would order troops to break in that night at any cost, and he would send in another officer with these troops to take over the Jewish Quarter command from Rousnak, who, judging by the messages, had gone to pieces—though it appears that other officers rather than Rousnak personally had in fact framed most of them. When Shaltiel told Kohn of this decision, the Jewish Agency official telephoned Nieuwenhuys and rejected the surrender proposal.

Though Rousnak and his colleagues were not fully aware of it, their forces had actually managed to blunt the Arab attack. The attackers, largely untrained and undisciplined, had failed to push their advantage and, indeed, placed obstacles in their own path by looting and then burning each building they captured. But possibly the decisive factor was the heroic defensive action of fighters like Judith Jaharan and the use they made of homemade hand grenades manufactured by local residents in large quantity with tin cans, nails, bits of metal, and any other small, sharp objects.

Despite this fierce resistance, many Jewish homes had fallen to the Arabs, including that of Rabbi Weingarten. The rabbi had held out to the last moment in the face of the gravest danger. Even after the Arabs, the day before, had rolled a barrel of TNT down the narrow hill to his house—it missed—he refused to budge from this last tangible reminder of his dignity and prestige.

But when the Arabs, the following day, shelled his house and the Haganah position on the roof, the end had come. The Weingarten family dashed to refuge in the hospital, carrying only two suitcases of mementos and valuables that Yehudit had packed in advance.

"Don't worry, Papa," she said, as she helped her father through smoldering black alleys. "I didn't forget your silver collection."

After this misfortune, Weingarten and other rabbis had come to Rousnak that same day (May 17) and demanded that he reach a peace agreement through the Red Cross, which made the commander wonder whether they had negotiated with the Arabs themselves in a plot to surrender without authorization. His own desperate pleas for help to the New City were one thing, he felt, but to let civilians make military decisions was another.

"Get out of my office," he said violently to Weingarten. (He even thought of killing him, but then, on reflection, concluded that he could not kill a Jew, even for what he considered near-treason.)

That evening, Rousnak received a message from New City headquarters informing him that reinforcements would arrive before dawn, May 18, and that a new commander, Mordechai Gazit (who had commanded the Haganah defenders at Kastel), was being sent with the detachment to relieve him of duty.

Rousnak absorbed the news with mixed feelings. His pride was hurt by the abrupt decision, but he was glad to be turning over the responsibility to someone else. He was exhausted to the point of collapse, and he had never really wanted so enormous a burden anyway.

"Well, if I'm lucky," he said to Chava that evening as they chatted over coffee at headquarters, "I'll be just another officer tomorrow."

Shaltiel's plan to relieve the Jewish Quarter called for the Etzioni Brigade to break through Jaffa Gate in the main attack. Irgun forces were to penetrate Nablus Gate, and units of the Palmach Harel Brigade to capture Mount Zion and threaten Zion Gate at its base in a diversionary move to draw Arab forces away from Jaffa Gate.

Yitzhak Rabin, the commander of the Harel Brigade, agreed to this plan only with reluctance. For one thing, to attack through Jaffa Gate rather than Zion Gate, which was located closer to the Jewish Quarter, seemed questionable tactics. Nor did he like the diversionary role reserved for his crack troops while less seasoned forces were assigned the main task.

But Shaltiel insisted on the plan. He then called in Raanan of the Irgun and asked him to cooperate.

"You'll need a reinforced platoon of forty-five men," Shaltiel said. "When they reach the Jewish Quarter they're to stay there to reinforce its defenses."

Raanan was skeptical. "Are you making this offer," he asked, "in order to tie up our forces in the Jewish Quarter so that we won't be able to operate here?"

"I'm asking you to cooperate," Shaltiel replied, "because we need fighters in the Jewish Quarter to save it from annihilation."

Despite his suspicions Raanan then agreed, and immediately appointed Ben-Zion Cohen, who had led the attack on Deir Yassin, to command the Irgun detachment.

The coordinated effort was to start shortly after midnight on May 18. But it never got off the ground because of a breakdown in Etzioni administrative arrangements. As for the Irgun force, instead of being sent to its scheduled takeoff point for the attack, it was driven in armored buses to the Tanus Building some distance away and simply told to remain in the buses until further orders.

Ironically, only the "diversionary" Palmach attack on Mount Zion succeeded. The force ascended the steepest slope and surprised the irregular Arab forces.

Uzi Narkis, deputy commander of the successful battalion, radioed Shaltiel before dawn of May 18 and asked (referring to a pledge Shaltiel had made before the attack): "Where are the replacements you promised?"

"Don't worry," Shaltiel replied, "they'll come."

A little later, Shaltiel called and asked Narkis to attack Zion Gate that night and make contact with the Jewish Quarter, simultaneously with the delayed attack by the Etzioni force on Jaffa Gate.

"I'll try," Narkis replied, smiling at having forced Shaltiel to ask him to play a major role in the operation after all. "But again, only on condition that we are replaced as soon as we take over the area between Zion Gate and the Jewish Quarter. We are not garrison troops, and we're certainly not going to hold both Mount Zion and the Jewish Quarter when we're needed desperately elsewhere."

Shaltiel apparently agreed to this demand.

At 1 A.M. on May 19, Mussa, commander of the Etzioni force that was to attack Jaffa Gate, led his men from the ruins of the new commercial center toward the Old City wall. Daniel Spicehandler, an American volunteer, dashed forward with his machine-gun crew to a wrecked sandbag position abandoned by the Arabs. They mounted their gun, waiting, as ordered, for two minutes before opening up to give cover to other men who were charging past them toward Jaffa Gate.

Then the storm broke as Arabs on the wall and by the gate fired frantically into the attacking force. Spicehandler and his men fired, too, but it was hopeless. Within moments, they heard Mussa, fatally wounded, screaming: "Every man for himself!"

Into view sprang a mob of retreating soldiers, running, stumbling, moaning, their faces contorted in the eerie glow of a phosphorus bomb. All the sappers who had breached the wall near the gate lay dead or wounded, and an armored car whose driver had taken the wrong road of retreat burned brightly against the wall, its damaged horn screeching in the night like some horribly injured beast.[11]

Ben-Zion Cohen and his Irgun detachment lay sprawled on the street in front of the Tanus Building near Jaffa Gate watching the night explode. While his men fired at Arab targets near the gate as directed by the Haganah command, Cohen cursed violently, beating his fist on the pavement. He considered ordering his men to charge the gate in direct support of the Etzioni troops, but decided against such action. He did not, after all, know what the Haganah had in mind. He could not disobey orders at this point.

Yet he was sure that Shaltiel had tricked the Irgun, promising it a major role in the attack, but in fact simply tying it up in a diversionary action so that it would not enter the Jewish Quarter on its own and possibly push on to take the rest of the Old City.

Shaltiel would do anything, he thought, to prevent the Irgun from sharing the glory.

"Raise the Red Cross flags!" shouted Dr. Egon Reis above the din of panic and pain in the Jewish Quarter hospital.

Within a few minutes, patients had fashioned several flags from red and white cloth with sticks and safety pins, and the doctor climbed personally to the roof of the hospital to install them. But the shelling grew louder and more devastating than before.

"They're zeroing in on the flags!" someone yelled.

The hospital was the core of what remained of the Jewish Quarter. During the terror of May 17, the wounded had all been brought down from the second to the first floor, where they were a few degrees safer, and the floors of the wards were blanketed with mattresses, bloody and filthy, on which lay scores of men, women, and children, many in the blood-soaked clothes in which they had arrived.

Moishele, a sixteen-year-old boy, had refused to be divested of his undershirt.

"Don't take it off!" he cried, trying to inject a lighthearted note into the panic-stricken ward. "I'll never see it again and the quartermaster won't issue me a new one."

"Don't be so clever!" snapped Masha Weingarten, the head nurse, her usually soft blue eyes giving him a sharp glance as she ripped his clothes off and bandaged his shrapnel-pocked leg.

"All right, get the next batch ready for the operating room," Dr. Reis's voice ordered, reminding the patients that night was approaching at last. Only then did the bombardments let up sufficiently for operations to be performed, in the dull glare of flashlights and sometimes under a rain of falling plaster.

Masha Weingarten and the other nurses immediately hurried to obey. Masha had not slept for two nights, and the agony of her exhaustion was compounded by the sight of her father, who had fled to the hospital the day before, strolling around in a daze, unable to accept the collapse of his world. Yet she worked on, the only one with the energy and will to wash the patients, and one of the few (including her sister Yehudit) to brave the horror of identifying the dead in the small, stinking room into which they were piled, body upon body. Wearing a theater mask, she examined each grotesquely staring face by flashlight, matching severed limbs to torn trunks and placing them together as specified by Jewish law (which requires that anyone who dies unnaturally be buried in the clothes he expires in, however dirty and bloody, with all his limbs).

Haganah officers, meanwhile, went from room to room ordering all unwounded civilian refugees to go to nearby Rothschild House. With the hospital finally cleared of aimless wanderers, it was easier to locate the wounded. Some were not to be found. Esther Ceilingold, for one, had limped out during the day with her Sten gun.

Emmanuel Meidav lay silent and unmoving in a small, smelly room. Seated by his bed was Rika, her face sunken and deathly white, her eyes inflamed and heavy-lidded, her black uncombed hair streaking her high forehead. She had sat there for two days and two nights, watching over him, helping him to sip tea with a spoon through the bandages, listening to him breathe, now in gasps, then almost imperceptibly. Every few hours she would lay her head next to him and doze off; but as soon as he stirred, she would wake and run for the doctor.

As she stared at the form before her, she could hardly imagine that this was only part of a man—a man without eyes, without one arm, and with only two fingers on the other hand. He had been so brilliant as a student. Now he would never read again, never be able to embrace her again with his large gentle hands, or smile at her with his eyes. She kept pushing these thoughts from her mind, thinking only of Emmanuel as he had once been—buoyant, vital, energetic—an image so real that the reality itself seemed only a nightmare from which she would eventually awaken.

Nurse Adina Shirion, a close friend of theirs, entered the room that morning (May 19) and implored Rika to go into the next room and get some sleep.

"You can't go on like this," she said. "This isn't doing you or him any good. We still need healthy people here."

Finally, Rika agreed to sleep, but on the floor at the foot of Emmanuel's bed, while Adina took up the vigil beside him. Soon, he started to move and seemed to be trying to say something. Frightened, Adina was about to wake Rika, then decided to look for another nurse instead. She ran into the corridor. The shooting had stopped and the hospital staff seemed to have disappeared. Adina began to panic. Had the Arabs come and taken them off, neglecting to look into her small room? She sobbed as she ran from room to room calling for help. Finally, she returned to Emmanuel's room shouting: "Rika, Rika, wake up!"

Just as the girl woke, footsteps sounded in the corridor, and Adina dashed out again. She saw another nurse, Ora, approaching with a bearded soldier.

"Adina," Ora exclaimed, "I want you to meet a friend of mine. He has just come in with the Palmach. They've come!"

Gasping, Adina paused to absorb the news, then ran back to Emmanuel's room.

"Emmanuel! Emmanuel!" she cried. "They've come! They've come! We're saved!"

As her flashlight settled on Rika's face, Adina saw the wide, dilated eyes of a madwoman.

"Rika, what's wrong?"

Rika was immobile for a moment, then laid her head on the lifeless form on the bed and sobbed: "No, no, no . . . !"

At about midnight that same night, the sky over Mount Zion had shone with the glow of embers and hot bricks as Arabs in the Old City fired a steady, rhythmic barrage into the area occupied by Palmach troops, hoping to stave off an attack through Zion Gate.

But Uzi Narkis' men were not discouraged as they lay in the shadows of trees on the hallowed slopes of the hill, where Christ had held his Last

Supper and appeared to his disciples and his mother after the Crucifixion. They were about 30 yards from the Dometian Church, waiting for the signal to attack, and could hear the radio operator announcing: "Zero hour is beginning!"

At 2 A.M. (May 19), light machine guns opened fire on Arabs on the wall, covering a heavy machine-gun team that scrambled down the hill and set up the gun near Zion Gate. Then two men fired a Davidka.

At 3:15 A.M., two young sappers with dynamite on their backs crawled to Zion Gate and, while enemy fire poured down from the wall above, placed the explosives against the sandbags and concrete blocking the gate. They retreated quickly. At 3:25 A.M. precisely, a shattering explosion blasted a hole in the great wooden gate.

At that moment, Mordechai Pincus, a Jewish Quarter commander who had been watching from the roof of the Sephardic Talmud Torah, ran down to the street, accompanied by an aide, and dived into the smoke and dust billowing around the wall. The Arabs in the area, shocked by the force of the explosion, held their fire just long enough for the assaulting platoon to scramble through the breach.

"Who's there?" Pincus called out through the choking brown cloud.

"*Aportzim!*" ("Those who break in!"), came back the password.

Pincus and his aide embraced each other and shouted for joy, then ran to greet the reinforcements like children running to their mother.

The commander of the attackers immediately reported back to Uzi Narkis, who was waiting nervously in his headquarters at the church: "We have carried out the great task and have reached the Jews of the Old City . . . 1,700 souls have been saved."

Thus, contrary to the original plan, the Palmach, which was to play only a diversionary role in the attack, managed to break into the Old City at least in part because the Arabs had been diverted by the abortive assault on Jaffa Gate by the Etzioni Brigade—the brigade earlier earmarked for the main breakthrough . . .

As Palmach men streamed down the road leading from Mount Zion through the Armenian Quarter to the Jewish Quarter, bearing crates of ammunition, sacks of explosives, guns and medical supplies to the beleaguered Jews, scores of shouting, ecstatic people poured into the road to greet their saviors with kisses and embraces. When the first reinforcements entered the Rabbi Yochanan Ben Zakkai Synagogue, where hundreds of civilians (including Judith Jaharan's parents) had been wasting away, they were welcomed, after the initial moment of shock, with the cry: "The Messiah! The Messiah!"

There were more kisses, embraces, and tears, and suddenly men and women, though old, sick, and underfed, burst into spontaneous dance and song.

Meanwhile, Uzi Narkis, for all his immediate pleasure, was concerned as to what would happen next. He was determined to remove his men from the area as soon as they had finished unloading the supplies. It was all up to Shaltiel now. If he wanted to keep Zion Gate open and maintain the connection with the Jewish Quarter, he would have to send new soldiers to replace the Palmach unit—or use Mordechai Gazit's men, mostly untrained, overage home guardsmen who had come with the Palmach. Narkis felt that he had already made a large enough sacrifice. About one-third of his men had fallen at the gate.

Narkis' deputy, Raanana, found Gazit at Zion Gate as the last crates were being carried in. Raanana remarked casually: "We're leaving as soon as we've delivered all the supplies. You've got to hold the area from Zion Gate to the Jewish Quarter."

"My dear fellow," Gazit replied tartly, "I haven't got enough men to do that. And the men I have hardly know each other and have no training."

"But Shaltiel promised us we would be replaced."

"I'm sorry, but that has nothing to do with me. I can't hold the area alone."

"Well, we're leaving!"

Moshe Rousnak headed for Zion Gate to greet the relief troops, after having gone from post to post warning his fighters not to fire on the newcomers as they moved through the Jewish Quarter into Arab areas in an attempt to capture the entire Old City. (A Palmach radio message just before the breakthrough had stated: "We'll be with you in half an hour, and in another hour we'll have the whole Old City.")

On the way to the gate, he was intercepted by Beni Marshak, a Palmach officer, who had been looking for him.

"We've finished what we came to do and we're leaving now," Marshak said. "Keep pressing Shaltiel to send you adequate reinforcements."

Rousnak could hardly believe his ears.

"Leaving!" he exclaimed. "You've just come! You can't abandon us like that! I thought you were going to take the whole Old City."

"We'd like to," Marshak replied, "but we haven't got enough men left."

"But the Arabs are in disarray. The Old City is largely undefended."

Marshak made a gesture with his hands, palms up, indicating that he could do nothing.

Utterly dejected, Rousnak then returned to his headquarters, where he found Mordechai Pincus with a soldier he did not recognize.

This is Mordechai Weinstein [Gazit's original name]," said Pincus.

Rousnak's morose expression dissolved. "It's so good you've come. Now I can get some sleep," he said happily.

"You can't sleep now," was Gazit's brusque reply.

"I've got to."

"You can't. I don't know anything about the military situation here."

"I haven't slept for five nights."

"Who has?"

"I'm totally exhausted and I'm going to bed. You're the commander now."

And Rousnak left abruptly for his dingy living quarters.

Pincus, for his part, collapsed on a cot in the office and immediately fell asleep. Gazit tried to shake him awake, but in vain. He was aghast as he stood by the snoring officer. The whole command had suddenly been dropped into his lap. And no superior had even told him that he was to take over from Rousnak.*

When Shaltiel received a message that the Palmach, after breaking into the Old City, was about to leave, he, too, was incredulous.

"This is impossible," he said to the officer who handed him the message. "I don't believe it. They couldn't do that!"

"But there it is, in black and white."

"Quick," Shaltiel cried, "collect people from all our positions and send them in as replacements."

As the officer rushed out, Shaltiel yelled: "For God's sake, hurry!" And he sat down at his desk, his face buried in his hands.

The officer returned swiftly, saying: "The Palmach has left and the Legion has entered the city and shut Zion Gate. It looks like we'll have to fight our way in again!"

Later in the morning (May 19), Narkis stormed into Shaltiel's office.

"How in God's name could you leave the Old City once you got in?" Shaltiel roared, his face reddening. "How could you even think of such a thing after all the sacrifice?"

"I didn't come here to argue," Narkis snarled. "I came to get reinforcements for my troops on Mount Zion, or we'll leave there, too. Don't forget that you promised to send them."

"I never promised you any more than you got!" Shaltiel shot back.

* Though Rousnak says he received an order to turn over his command to Gazit, Gazit claims he had been ordered into the Jewish Quarter as Shaltiel's "personal representative," but that he was not to replace Rousnak. It appears that the officer giving Gazit his orders did not know that Shaltiel wanted him to take over the command, for Shaltiel told me that this had been his intention.

After a further bitter exchange, Shaltiel finally ordered: "Leave my office at once!"

Narkis turned, marched out, and slammed the door behind him.[12]

Yosef Tabenkin, Narkis's superior, later negotiated with Shaltiel to replace the Palmach force on Mount Zion.

In the Old City, while Shaltiel was confronting Narkis, Chava Kirschenbaum rushed into headquarters and found Rousnak, who had just returned from a fitful sleep, cleaning out his desk. He expected to turn it over to Gazit.

"Moshe," she cried, "Weinstein [Gazit] has been wounded in the chest."

Rousnak, as he looked up, dropped some papers he had just removed from a drawer. He stared at her open-mouthed.

Before going off for his sleep, he had asked her to show Gazit the positions, but instead the new commander, imbued with a sense of mission, had personally led a counterattack against a Legion armored car advancing along the Street of the Jews. After Israeli grenades and Bren fire had chased the vehicle off, he had climbed to the top of the Talmud Torah building to inspect the area, followed by Chava, who had seen him enter.

"I was with him on the roof looking at the Arab positions," Chava explained to Rousnak, almost in tears. "I told him to keep down, but he wanted to see everything. He said 'Don't worry.' And at that moment they shot him."

Rousnak remained silent, still staring at her.

Chava grew frightened. "Don't worry, Moshe," she said, "you'll do a good job."

Then she left for the hospital to see how seriously Gazit had been wounded, wondering if Rousnak really would be able to make the people fight, especially after the shattering letdown by the Palmach, when they had thought the Messiah had come.

Somehow the fighting went on. That night Palmach troops tried to break through Zion Gate once more, possibly moved by conscience, but were thrown back with heavy casualties. The Legionnaires, who had now taken over from the irregulars, let the Israelis go through the gate into the casemates, then opened concentrated fire, converting the gateway into a death trap.

Unknown to the Legionnaires, as the days wore on there was almost no organized defense. Little groups of defenders simply fought their own independent wars as circumstances dictated, with most of the field commanders killed or wounded and no post strong enough to permit reinforcement of another.

Among the bravest fighters was Albert "Cohen," the British deserter who had joined the Jews just before the British withdrawal. Rousnak, at first distrustful, had him carefully watched and would not let him near the front-line posts. Some of the Jewish fighters were so sure he was a spy that they wanted to shoot him. When several Irgunists suggested this to their commander, Isser Nathanson, he had to threaten them with court-martial to prevent such action. But after some days the command agreed to let Albert fight, and he did—even after being wounded in the hand.

No less aggressive, despite their youth and sex, were Judith Jaharan and Esther Ceilingold, who ran from place to place firing and throwing grenades to offer the impression of strong resistance. Perhaps their greatest value lay in the example they set for some of the men who were reluctant to fight.

Once, when Judith, who served as both medic and infantryman, discovered that one of the men assigned to assist her in an attack had disappeared, she searched until she finally found him hiding in a synagogue with civilians. She walked over to him, Sten gun cocked, and ordered: "Back to your position!"

The youth, who was about two years older, looked up at her from the floor where he had been squatting and, as he stared into her piercing brown eyes, knew she meant business. He rose and silently plodded back to the trench he was convinced would be his grave.

The Jews and Arabs fought a seesaw battle for Nissan Beck Synagogue, which was situated virtually on the doorstep of the hospital and headquarters. Two days after the Palmach left, the Legionnaires managed to capture it, lending a new meaning to the engraving on its wall showing a lion of Judah mourning the downfall of ancient Israel. But Rousnak ordered a counterattack and it was retaken after bitter fighting.

Rousnak then went to look for the Bren gunner to congratulate him on his key role in the victory, and ran across an eleven-year-old boy carrying the gun.

"What are you doing here?" he shouted angrily. "Go back to your mother."

The boy looked at him with hurt blue eyes and, rubbing his dust-coated face, said: "But Moshe, I'm number two man on the Bren gun. There's no one else."

Rousnak smiled bitterly.

"Congratulations," he said.

Soon, on May 22, the Arabs were attacking again, They dashed from one house to the next, ever closer, meeting little resistance from exhausted, retreating defenders who found themselves outmanned and outgunned. Judith Jaharan lay with an Irgun companion on the roof of a house next to the synagogue, expecting to die that day. What was the difference, she thought. Surrender would almost certainly mean death anyway, and perhaps in a far more horrible form. She rubbed her knees, which hurt from contact with the stone roof. If only she had a pair of trousers. This ridiculous green skirt . . . whoever heard of fighting a war in a skirt?

She thought of her mother . . . her poor mother who was crowded into another synagogue with hundreds of people. She would certainly get sick again, without the right food, without the pills she needed.

Suddenly the Arabs down the street started running toward Judith's post, shouting slogans to each other. Judith aimed her rifle, bracketing one of the Arabs in her sight. Mechanically, she pulled the trigger and watched the attacker drop in his tracks like a suddenly emptied sack of potatoes.

The surviving Arabs took cover in doorways or behind obstacles. Judith put down her rifle and reached for her Sten. She regretted having fired the first shot, because now she knew definitely, for the first time, that she had taken a human life. She would use her Sten after this if possible. It was better to spray death aimlessly and not be sure which, if any, bullets hit the target. As the Arabs began advancing again, she fired, but some managed to reach the synagogue.

Soon, these men were shooting at Judith and her companion, Zahavi, from the synagogue roof. At the same time, Arab bullets poured in from their rear. Through the crackle of fire, Judith heard someone's voice calling in the distance. "Come down, come down . . . "

Judith then realized that she and her companion were trapped. The other Jews had retreated without their knowledge. She glanced over the edge of the roof and saw several Arabs on the street below preparing to scale the wall. She took a grenade, pulled out the pin, and dropped it. There was an explosion, followed by cries of pain. Then she noticed incredulously that she had been shot in the leg without even knowing it. She bound the wound with a bandage from her first aid kit and continued to fire. Finally, she and Zahavi managed to climb down and flee to safety— after forcing the Arabs to retreat.

"You killed so many they thought they were confronting a whole army," a comrade said in greeting.

Judith, as if in a trance, kept limping along.

"Come on Judith, let's go to the hospital," the man said.

"No, I'm going to see my mother . . . "

"But your leg. You can't just stroll around like that." He took her by the arm and led her to the hospital.

As Judith Jaharan later that day approached the Yochanan Ben Zakkai Synagogue in which her mother and father were penned up with more than 800 other people, she forgot the pain in her leg. She had been so frantically busy the past few days that she had not had the opportunity to visit them and it seemed as if weeks had gone by. She longed to embrace her mother and cry on her shoulder.

As she entered the synagogue, she found herself in a cage of terror in which women, children, and old men, all white-faced and trembling, clung to each other on dirt-encrusted blankets and mattresses spread over the floor, weeping, praying, shouting hysterically, or—most horrifying of all— just gazing vacantly into a world far distant from the insane reality of explosions and machine-gun fire that shook the building like an earthquake.

Judith discovered her mother and father in a corner of the stinking, rubbish-littered room, sitting on a torn mattress. They were among the silent ones. Her father smiled, his dark eyes, set deeply in a brown, wrinkled face, seeming to look straight through her. Her mother also stared. Neither moved. Judith silently sat down beside them. Her mother glanced at the Sten and her bandaged leg, and for the first time Judith noted a stir of emotion in her eyes. Then tears gradually came, and finally bitter sobs.

As explosions continued to rock the building, her father reached for some food on the floor beside the mattress. Judith took it and began to nibble, and her father, smiling again, sat back against the wall with an air of resignation. Not a word passed between parents and daughter.

Judith began to feel that she could not bear to sit another minute. Yet she could not afford to display any sign of weakness, either to herself or to those around her. She could not indulge in the luxury of being sixteen, or even human.

She got up to go, and her mother reached for her, but then withdrew her hand and placed it over her eyes. As the young girl left, she looked back and saw her father still smiling meaninglessly.

While the Jewish Quarter hovered on the edge of extermination, Yaacov Tangy, hospital orderly, emerged from the morgue where he had been attaching identification tags to the most recent batch of bodies, and put on a clean white shirt he had been saving for this day. It was *Lag b'Omer*, the one day during an extended period after Passover on which, under

Jewish law, marriage could be performed.* At last he could be united with
Zvia Carmon, the gray-eyed beauty with whom he had been in love since
she had come to the Old City as a teacher shortly before the British left.
He desperately wanted her to have his child in case he did not survive the
siege; and—like most of the other defenders—he harbored little hope of survival for himself.

Early in the afternoon, Zvia arrived at the hospital from her front-line
post, changed her dirty khaki for a blue and white dress, and then, with
Yaacov, went into the street just as shells began exploding nearby. Among
the people they met running for cover was the sole baker in the quarter.

"My oven is destroyed," he shouted, grabbing hold of Tangy. "Now
we will all starve!"

"Let's starve later," Tangy replied. "First, I'm going to get married!"

And the couple dashed along the smoky street to the Gates of Heaven
Yeshiva, where Rabbi Meir Hamo and a few guests, including Yaacov's
mother, awaited them. The rabbi, dressed in a long, black robe and a black,
wide-brimmed hat, took Tangy's hand and hurriedly led him to the front
of the candlelit cellar, while the youth's mother embraced Zvia and placed
on her wrist an old gold bracelet, a family heirloom. In a mortuary-like
atmosphere, with bursting shells making it almost impossible for anyone
to hear the rabbi's words, the couple took their vows.

"Stay for a glass of wine," the rabbi said after the ceremony, as the
couple embraced.

"Sorry," said Tangy, "save it for the *briss* [the Jewish circumcision
ceremony for the male child]. We must get back to our posts—if they're
still there!"

Many posts were no longer "there" that deadly afternoon. While the
Legion plastered the quarter with shells, Arab irregulars, in an all-out
attack, captured a third of the remaining Jewish territory, including the
area adjacent to the Yochanan Ben Zakkai Synagogue. All they had to
do now was to cross an alley 2 yards wide in order to wipe out its 800
helpless occupants.

In desperation, Rousnak sent Chava to find Yitzhak Mizrachi, one of
the few first-rate fighters still alive.

"Yitzhak, we've got to capture the Magen Club," Chava urged the
youth.

---

* *Lag b'Omer* is the thirty-third day of the *omer,* or harvest season, which, in
ancient times, extended for a period of about two months from Passover. During this
period, which recalls the suffering the Jews endured under Roman persecution, no
Jew, according to Orthodox tradition, may marry or cut his hair—except on *Lag
b'Omer,* a day of celebration. On that day, in the early second century, the Jewish
General, Bar Kochba, won a great victory over the Romans; simultaneously, a plague
that had been raging among student recruits is supposed to have suddenly ended.

As he lay on a mattress in the *Yeshiva* where the wedding had just taken place, Yitzhak stared at Chava with blurred eyes. He knew the importance of the Magen Club; it was a key building near the threatened synagogue. But he replied: "I can't. It's hopeless trying."

"But, Yitzhak," Chava insisted in a slow, soft voice, "try to understand. We need just the club, that's all. Take six men with you and capture it."

"But I can't," he pleaded, turning his head away. "I haven't slept for two weeks. I run every day from one end of the quarter to the other. I'm in every battle. In every hole. I'm tired. I can't."

"But Yitzhak," Chava persisted, "we must. The Arabs are only a few yards away. If we don't, they'll sweep us out of here within an hour. There are women and children, Yitzhak. Go with six men. Don't let the Arabs break into the street!"

"Leave me alone," Yitzhak begged. "I can't. I'm too tired. There's no use anyway. In the end we'll surrender."

Chava then looked at him and began to smile as he started to get up.

"All right," he said, "I'll go. But I have a feeling this will be the last time."

From nearby posts, Yitzhak gathered the six men, saying in a voice full of confidence: "Men, we're going to take the Magen Club. Don't be afraid. Follow me."

As they neared their objective, an Arab threw a grenade from a roof, and when it exploded, blood from all of them stained the street. Yitzhak, holding his head, got to his feet and ran crazily toward the hospital, yelling: "My eye! My eye!" He died on arrival.

With him died the last glimmer of hope, in the minds of the quarter's civilian leaders, that the people in the synagogue, in the whole area, could survive another day without surrender.

In the basement of the Armenian School of the Holy Translators adjoining the Jewish Quarter, Captain Mahmoud Bey Mousa, the quiet-spoken Arab Legionnaire in command of the Legion attack, rose from his classroom chair behind a desk and walked to a shattered window to watch the show he was directing.

From windows upstairs, that night of May 27, machine guns relentlessly showered bullets into the Jewish Quarter, while below, on the street, big guns pumped shell after shell into the area at point-blank range. When the firing stopped occasionally, the air, putrid from the stench of dead bodies, reverberated with the sound of buildings crashing to earth, among them the two hundred-year-old Horva Synagogue. It had collapsed upon its fighting occupants, who had not budged even in the face of an ultimatum from Abdullah Tel. Flames licked the whole zone and the sky had turned an eerie pink.

The devastation finally stopped at midnight, and Abdullah Tel sent word that the Legion would cease fire until 1:30 P.M. the next day, May 28, to give the Jews one last chance to surrender before he destroyed the quarter completely.

"I think negotiations will begin in the morning," Mahmoud Bey Mousa told an aide, as Legionnaires began to pry open new barrels of ammunition lining the basement from wall to wall.

The Haganah command now found itself in an impossible position. Shaltiel had promised to attempt a new break-in on the night of May 28, several hours after the Arab deadline for surrender. But even if the Jews could hold out one more day, the hundreds of trapped civilians would probably be dead by the time a rescue unit arrived, if indeed it did. The quandary sharpened the already bitter conflict between military and civilian leaders.

At about 7 A.M. on May 28, the day of decision, Shaul Tawil, commander of the Gadna Youth Brigade (which embraced runners and fighters from eleven to seventeen years of age), received a telephone call from Rousnak.

"A couple of rabbis are preparing to cross the lines to surrender," Rousnak said. "Stop them as they go past."

Tawil, whose headquarters bordered on the alley leading to the Arab sector, immediately issued orders to his men, and Rabbis Mintzberg and Hazan, carrying a white flag, were turned back a few minutes later at a sandbag barricade.

At 9 A.M., with the sun still blotted out by a huge dark cloud that had settled over the quarter, the two lonely figures again approached the Haganah men.

"Who are they?" one of the guards asked.

"Looks like the same rabbis again."

"Still trying. Well, they won't get far."

"Those damn civilians are just trying to cause trouble."

"Okay, go back. You're not going through."

The two rabbis halted. Hazan, a tall, white-bearded man in black garments, stood proudly erect despite his seventy-two years, though he leaned on a cane with one hand while carrying the flag in the other. Mintzberg, wearing a shiny black ankle-length cape, stared in fright with small, shrunken eyes.

"You can't stop us," Hazan said. "We have permission from head-quarters."

"You're not going through until we get specific orders. Now turn around and go back."

"But we have permission . . . "

The officer in charge ordered a soldier to find out who had sent them and the soldier ran to headquarters to see Rousnak.

"What?" exclaimed Rousnak. "I'll take care of this myself."

He removed the pistol in his belt and ran out, reaching the rabbis just as they were starting back. He pointed the pistol at them, shouting: "What do you mean trying to surrender without any permission? We're continuing to fight whether you like it or not!"

"It's not important who kills us—you or the Arabs," Hazan replied, trembling with emotion. "We are lost. Even if you shoot us, we will go."

"We'll give you half an hour to give us formal permission," Mintzberg added. "Then we'll go even if you shoot us."

Rousnak took the two rabbis to his headquarters and ordered them to wait there. Then he visited the various posts and took a quick inventory of the ammunition remaining. He concluded that his forces, controlling an area no larger than 200 by 100 yards, might be able to hold out for one or two hours, no more. And during that time, the civilians in the synagogue would be undefended. He saw only one chance for holding out until dark: if he could stall the Arabs with talk about a truce to permit the removal of dead on both sides. The possibility of the Arabs accepting such a proposal was slim; they had refused similar proposals in the past. But nothing could be lost by trying.

Rousnak returned to his headquarters after two hours and called all his officers together to ask them what they thought of his idea. All supported it.

Then he turned to the two rabbis and said: "Very well, you can go. But you are not to discuss surrender, only a truce to permit the evacuation of the wounded. Keep them talking as long as you can. Do you understand?"

The rabbis agreed, and, though forced back by gunfire once, set out again, accompanied by a few companions. The grim parade advanced through the wilderness, past the Israeli posts and along the street bordered by the great wall, as a thousand pairs of eyes gazed on them. Beyond the wall, startled Palmach troops preparing for an attack that night silently watched from the Dometian Church on Mount Zion while their commander, on the roof with his binoculars, kept murmuring to himself: "Only a few more hours, a few more hours . . . "

Onward the delegation walked, with only the steady tap of Hazan's cane on the cobblestones breaking the tense silence. A Legionnaire emerged from the entrance of a tower along the wall to guide the party, and gradually others appeared, keeping excited local Arabs at a distance while the group threaded its way along the narrow path leading to Legion headquarters in the Armenian School of the Holy Translators. Finally, they reached an arched doorway at the rear of the school and were led to the basement, where they sat down on a bench to await Captain Mousa. The rabbis could hear the protests of the armed irregulars besieging the entrance that the Jews were being treated too well and deserved to die.

Mousa arrived and said stiffly but politely: "I cannot order a ceasefire until a representative of the Haganah and your mukhtar, Rabbi Weingarten, come and agree to our terms."

Holding Mintzberg hostage, he then sent Hazan back to deliver his demand. Rousnak agreed to it, but took his time in the hope of stretching out the talks as long as possible, designating Shaul Tawil, who spoke Arabic, to represent the Haganah. Weingarten, when asked to go, was delighted. This was the first recognition he had received since the fighting started—though it was the Arabs who had asked that he go, knowing nothing about his present status. He put on his only suit and a borrowed white shirt, shaved, and brushed back his hair, determined to look his best for what he regarded as the diplomatic assignment of his life. If the Jews were to surrender, he would see to it that they surrendered with dignity.

As he prepared to set out from headquarters for the Armenian Quarter with Yehudit, who insisted on accompanying him, he shouted with a smile to grim-faced Israeli troops: "Don't worry, boys, I'll do what I can for you . . ."

The party left as the Legion resumed shelling to remind the Jews of its impatience . . .

As the new delegation walked down the Street of the Jews, shots suddenly rang out from the quarter's police station, which had been captured by the Arabs. Haganah soldiers returned the fire while members of the group rushed for cover in ruins nearby, Tawil and Yehudit yelling: "Stop firing, stop firing!"

The shooting stopped after several moments, and Yehudit, dressed in a white, bloodstained nurse's smock, ran to the middle of the street and waved both arms in a frantic plea to the two adversaries not to resume fire. An Arab machine gunner in a nearby building put down his Bren, folded his arms, and leaned on the windowsill. Zion Mizrachi, a machine gunner at one of the Israeli window positions, also laid his weapon down and exposed the upper part of his body, the two men gazing at each other across a stretch of smoking desolation occasionally making obscene signs with their hands.

When the delegates reached the wall at the end of the Street of the Jews near Zion Gate, Abdullah Tel, surrounded by his aides, was there to greet them. After a polite exchange of "Good morning," Tawil explained: "I have come as a representative of the Haganah to discuss a cease-fire."

Tel replied without expression: "It's very simple. You must surrender."

"Let's go somewhere and discuss the matter," Tawil suggested.

"Very well, we'll go to my headquarters," Tel replied. "But there isn't much time . . . "

Meanwhile, at about 1 P.M., Rousnak received a radio message from the New City: "What is the meaning of the delegation with a white flag . . . ?"

At 1:20 P.M., Rousnak radioed back "We've begun negotiations to remove dead in order to permit rest. First result was that Arabs ordered a cease-fire. Details are not yet known."

At 1:30 P.M., Shaltiel sent a reply: "Agree to cease-fire to remove dead. No negotiation on an armistice may be made without my permission."

In the Yochanan Ben Zakkai Synagogue, where more than 800 people had expected to be slaughtered that morning, pandemonium broke out as reports of the cease-fire reached them. Amid shouts of joy and thanksgiving, the few men with any remaining strength got up and tried to break down the locked door in an uncontrollable lunge for freedom and salvation.

"Let us out! Let us out!" hundreds of voices chanted. One yelled, "Mama, we're saved," and another, "Thank God, our problems are over!"

Despite the efforts of Haganah soldiers to keep the door shut, it opened sufficiently for some people to squeeze through and join other Jews who were streaming out of almost every house and cellar in a great human flood that surged toward the border area of the quarter, there to be swallowed up in a sea of merrymakers. Haganah youths tried to use poles to block the advancing mob, but were swept up in the tide.

Arabs and Jews who had been killing each other a short time before mingled and embraced; old friends shook hands, discussed old times. Opposite the threatened synagogue, a Legion officer and a Jewish fighter talked and laughed together. One elderly Jew opened the shutters of his coffeeshop and yelled: "Mohammed, Ahmed, let me treat you to a cup of coffee. I'm sorry there's no cake."

At the synagogue, Haganah soldiers finally managed to slam the door on most of the occupants, and held it shut while Moishele, the sixteen-year-old

youth (now recovered from his wounds), ran to headquarters to request
orders, as did runners from every Israeli position.

Rousnak met them at the door, his hands clenched into white-knuckled
fists.

"What shall we do, Moshe?" Moishele asked on behalf of all present.
"They're running wild in the streets."

"Get back to your posts!" Rousnak ordered, infuriated. "The war isn't
over yet. And by God, keep the people in the synagogues. Tell them they'll
get killed in the streets. Now take off!"

Rousnak then went out into the streets and found himself swept up in
the maelstrom, the Arabs drunk with victory, the Jews with gratitude for
their miraculous survival. He slowly made his way back out of the crowd
and returned to headquarters, where he sat at his desk for a while, crushed
and defeated, watching the shifting shadows on the wall cast by a flickering
candle. Then, taking the candle in hand, he removed his last cigarette from a
drawer and lit it . . .

"Ejou! Ejou!" ("Here they come!")

The Arabs shouted with glee as the "peacemakers" entered a low stone
structure surrounded by a thick, high stone wall opposite the School of
the Holy Translators. As the heavy iron doors slammed behind them, they
proceeded through a dark passageway into a courtyard bordered by stone
buildings. The party crossed in front of the Armenian Church of the Holy
Archangel, with its slightly bent belltower, and into a building on the site
of the House of Annas, where Christ, after his betrayal at Gethsemane, was
dragged for a preliminary examination by Annas the Priest before being
tried and condemned on Mount Zion.

When the delegates had entered a large room and seated themselves,
Tawil suggested that a cease-fire be called to permit removal of the dead
and wounded from the Jewish Quarter.

"I must reject your proposal," Tel said gently but firmly. "This is war.
We have dead and you have dead. We don't remove ours, and you don't
remove yours. The only answer for you is surrender. We will offer reasonable conditions."

"I am not authorized to discuss surrender," Tawil responded, "But if
you tell me your conditions, I'll submit them to my superiors."

Tel glanced at a sheet of paper on his desk and recited the conditions:
(1) The surrender of all arms and their seizure by the Arab Legion; (2)
all able-bodied men to be taken as prisoners of war; (3) old men, women,
children and all seriously wounded to be allowed to choose between staying
in the Old City under Arab control or entering the New City through

arrangements with the Red Cross; (4) the Arab Legion to guarantee the welfare of all Jews who surrendered; and (5) the Arab Legion to occupy the Jewish Quarter.

"Bring your commander to us," Tel said, glancing at his wristwatch. "I'll give you half an hour to get back."

"But my commander will have to discuss the situation with his officers," Tawil argued, "and it will take longer than that to get them together."

"All right, I'll give you two hours, until three o'clock . . ."

Tel extended the deadline to 4 P.M. when Tawil's party was delayed in its return by Legionnaires who arrested members by mistake.

When the delegates finally arrived at headquarters after Legionnaires had cleared a path through a bristling multitude of armed Arabs, they found Rousnak raging that the Arabs were taking advantage of the cease-fire to advance into Israeli-held territory.

"The Legionnaires have even entered the synagogue to talk with the inhabitants, and our men let them. If fighting breaks out again, our people will all be killed."

Yehudit then ran to seek the help of Legion officers. When she found several, she led them to the synagogue, and they ordered their men, who had been talking with the excited civilians, to leave immediately. When some civilians, seeing that the door was open, attempted to leave, Yehudit stood in the way and, shaking with anger, shouted: "None of you can leave! Don't you realize that you're endangering your own lives?"

A man tried to push past her, but she slapped him in the face, and then did the same to a woman who protested.

"No one leaves here!" she said again.

Then she saw Moishele standing by the door, one of the two soldiers guarding the synagogue.

"And you, Moishele," she ordered, "go inside and hide among the inhabitants because they'll be going to the New City. God knows what they'll do to the prisoners!" . . .

At headquarters, Tawil and Weingarten briefed Rousnak and the other Haganah officers on the meeting with Tel.

"He won't give in on the cease-fire proposal, I'm sure," Tawil said.

"The surrender terms are reasonable," Weingarten chimed in. "Who can fight now with everybody out on the street?"

Rousnak had seldom agreed with Weingarten, but he had to admit that what he said now made sense. How, indeed, would it be possible to get the inhabitants back into the synagogues and cellars to wait for massacre— or to get the Arabs out of Jewish territory? The Arabs, by mixing with the Jews, had in fact infiltrated the Jewish Quarter. Some had already started

to loot Jewish homes and stores, though Legionnaires, he knew, were doing
their best to prevent this. For all practical purposes, the quarter was already
occupied.

He pointed out the ugly truth to his subordinates and said that, under the
circumstances, he saw no alternative to accepting Tel's terms.

"Couldn't we stall a few more hours?" one officer suggested. "Just long
enough for the Palmach to come?"

"Tel made it clear," Tawil said, "that he'll start firing at four o'clock
sharp. They'll slaughter all the Jews on the street."

In the end, Rousnak would not make the decision himself. "This is too
important a question for any one man to decide," he said. "We'll put it
to a vote. Should we or should we not accept the Legion's surrender terms?"

He asked each officer in turn his opinion. All voted for acceptance except
the Irgun's Isser Nathanson, who abstained . . .

As Rousnak, Tawil, and Weingarten entered an inner courtyard of the
Vank, Tel saluted and shook hands, greeting them warmly in English. At
last the man had come who had the authority to surrender. Rousnak, dressed
in shabby khaki with a beret on his head, started to remove the pistol from
his belt to give it to Tel in the traditional symbol of surrender, but the
Legion commander raised his hand, saying: "Never mind, you may keep it."

As the Israelis seated themselves around his desk, he suggested with a
smile: "How about tea, gentlemen?"

In their nervous exhaustion they all gladly accepted.

"What are your conditions?" Rousnak asked.

Tel reread the paper he had earlier read to Tawil.

They agreed to slight modifications, then to send an officer from each
side to Mount Zion to inform Israeli forces of plans to evacuate the civilians.

While the peacemakers awaited the return of the two emissaries, a
strange silence settled over the scene as each man quietly sipped tea, puffed
on a cigarette, or doodled on scratch paper. Running through everyone's
mind was the thought that perhaps the two men would not return, that the
Palmach forces might not be able to resist the opportunity to "liberate" the
Jew and take the Legion officer prisoner.

Abdullah Tel looked at his watch. Only a few more hours until dark,
when, if everything were not settled, the Israelis might attack the gate after
all. He exchanged glances with some of his subordinates who were standing
around him. Perhaps he had made a mistake. Perhaps he should not have
offered the Israelis such a temptation at so fateful a moment in history, a
moment for which the world would long remember him.

Moshe Rousnak savored his tea with the appreciation a condemned man might feel for the smallest remaining comfort. How would history judge him, he wondered. Would his people understand that he had stayed in the field against impossible odds, in the face of almost total destruction of his forces, until the last conceivable moment, when further resistance would mean wholesale slaughter of the entire population?

He realized that he was not a born leader, and he was pained by the fact that some of the fighters did not treat him with the respect that a Halperin would have commanded. But he had done his best under the circumstances. He had held out despite his moments of weakness; despite what he regarded as the cruel indifference of New City headquarters, which answered his pleas for help with laconic, cynical responses or outrageous lies; despite the psychological sabotage of the greater part of the community. He had held out with a few squads of wounded boys and girls, mere children, armed with guns but virtually no bullets. Had he any choice now but to surrender? Was it undignified to reject total, unnecessary martyrdom?

He was sure the two officers would come back—but what if they did not? He, too, glanced at his watch. So close to dark . . . But what of the hundreds of Jews running loose in the streets and crowded into synagogues; how long would they survive another attack? And he himself was already a prisoner.

He studied the men standing around Tel, some of them fair-skinned. The *khaffiyas* wrapped around their blond heads did not fool him. They were British deserters, he was certain, and they stared at him with hatred in their blue eyes. But Abdullah Tel, it seemed to him, had a pleasant face, and, though an Arab, acted like a real English gentleman, the sort he had liked and respected even during the mandate. Civilized and reasonable . . . perhaps the kind of person he would choose for a friend if it were not for this damned war. And yet this man, with a flick of his finger, could (and he knew he was quite capable of doing it) order the complete devastation of what remained of the Jewish Quarter . . .

At one end of the courtyard, a group of Legion soldiers started beating up a helpless man they had dragged in.

Dr. Pablo de Azcarate, representing the United Nations at the meeting, asked Tel with some alarm: "What are they doing? Attacking a Jew?"

He wondered if this was a sample of the fate awaiting the Jewish population about to be delivered to the Arabs. Tel ordered the soldiers to bring the victim to him, and he turned out to be an Arab irregular.

"We caught him looting," one of the soldiers said.

"I admire the discipline of your men," the U.N. representative said, "but let him go free this time."

Tel agreed, and silence again reigned.

Rousnak was impressed. At least it looked as if the population would be protected from the local Arabs.

At last, the two officers who had gone to Mount Zion reappeared. "It's okay," said the Jewish officer. "They'll be waiting for the inhabitants."

Abdullah Tel smiled broadly.

"Very well, gentlemen," he said, "now we can sign the papers."

After Rousnak had signed the surrender agreement—one copy in Arabic and another in Hebrew—Weingarten volunteered: "Now I'll sign."

Abdullah Tel casually responded: "Oh, that won't be necessary. As long as we have the signature of the Haganah commander."

"But I'm the mukhtar," Weingarten said, a child's hurt look on his face. "Why can't I sign, too?"

"It's only necessary for the military commander to sign," Tel explained.

"But I am the leader of the community," Weingarten insisted, almost in desperation.

Tel raised his eyebrows and muttered: "Very well, if you wish. Sign."[13]

While the surrender party headed back for the Jewish Quarter surrounded by hundreds of shouting, restive Arabs, word was swiftly passed around that all inhabitants of the quarter were to gather in the square near the hospital to be processed for evacuation to the New City.

Mordechai Pincus, meanwhile, sent runners to the various positions, ordering all fighters to deposit their weapons in the square and mingle with the inhabitants in the hope that some might be able to avoid identification as combatants and be sent to freedom. One runner arrived at a post just in time to prevent a fistfight between two men who were arguing over whose turn it was to clean the guns. A few men fired bullets in the air or at convenient targets in the area, just to enjoy the freedom of shooting without having to worry about saving ammunition—a sport that almost created panic among the inhabitants and other soldiers who thought the war had resumed.

Many of the fighters dashed into the hospital—which had been moved, together with military headquarters, to another building a few days before for security reasons—to ask the commanders and doctors what they should do. Some quickly changed into civilian clothes in an attempt to pass as noncombatants. When Judith Jaharan ran in, Dr. Laufer stopped her.

"Judith, a Legion officer just told me that some of the local Arabs are looking for a girl with a green skirt who killed a lot of their men. He said they call her the Black Devil. They mean you, of course."

Judith now understood why Arabs she had passed on the way to the hospital had pointed at her and whispered to each other. She had always told herself that she would never surrender, never submit to the tortures and humiliation that she was sure to suffer if she were captured. And now the nightmare was materializing. The Arabs might do anything to wipe out the disgrace of suffering at the hands of a woman.

"What should I do?" she asked fearfully.

"Change your clothes and cut your hair," Laufer said. "You can pass as a nurse."

She ran into one of the wards, found scissors and, in front of a broken mirror, cut her long, black hair almost as short as that of a boy. So they called her the Black Devil, did they? She stared at the scarcely recognizable figure in the mirror. It was not so much the short hair as the eyes, eyes set in deep black caverns, beast's eyes. Then she removed her green skirt and khaki shirt and put on a soiled nurse's smock that Masha supplied . . .

The hospital grew silent as the first Legion officer entered, accompanied by two sergeants. Twirling his large brown mustache, he smiled as he brushed past the Jews gathered near the entrance, and sauntered to a table in the hall. A nurse who had been serving coffee to the patients poured some for the Arab visitors, and the officer, lifting his cup as for a toast, said to the apprehensive, incredulous spectators: "Cheer up. That's the luck of war, you know!"

As Albert Cohen left the hospital and walked toward the square, he met several fellow British officers.

"You're British, aren't you?" one of them asked as he passed, noting his uniform.

"Yes," Albert said.

"Well, what the hell are you doing here?"

"I've deserted, that's what, just like you."

"You mean you're fighting with these Jew bastards?"

"I'm fighting with the Jews, yes."

"Well, they've lost now. Come with us and we'll see that you're treated well. You've been fighting on the wrong side."

"I've been fighting on the right side, and I expect to be treated just like them."

"But the Jews are going to prison."

"If they're going, so am I."

"Don't be a fool. You're an Englishman."

Albert paused, and then said forcefully: "I insist on being taken prisoner."

And he joined the Jews who were lining up in the square.

Heavy bluish smoke hung over the square, enveloping aged, black-robed men mumbling prayers, sickly-looking women in soiled print dresses with bundles under their arms, dirty-faced children, silent and bewildered, people in filthy hospital smocks or ripped khaki.

Abdullah Tel scanned the motley remnants of the ghetto population, whose initial joy was now dissipated in a growing realization of the horrors of refugee and possibly prisoner status. He shouted in English: "All soldiers are to identify themselves."

When there was no response, he spoke to Moshe Rousnak standing beside him, and Rousnak said in Hebrew: "All soldiers step forward."

Still there was no response, until seventy-eight-year-old Rabbi Moshe Isaac, bent and unsteady on a cane, advanced a step, clearing his throat as he tried to stand at attention. Immediately, men who had hoped to bluff their way into the New City followed suit. At Rousnak's order, Pincus gathered them into a separate unit in parade formation. Abdullah Tel surveyed the group with a disturbed expression.

"Are they all the soldiers?" he asked Rousnak in amazement. "Thirty-five men killed more than two hundred of ours?"

"That's all we have," Rousnak replied. "I can't give you more than we have."

"Had I known this before," Tel said glumly, "I would have sent people armed with sticks to fight you."

He then walked over to the melancholy group of civilians huddling amid cloth-wrapped bundles and broken suitcases, glancing at people as he slowly threaded his way among them.

He spoke to Rousnak, indicating various individuals: "I'll take this one, that one, that one over there . . . "

Among the people he chose were old men up to eighty years old and boys of only twelve. Rousnak protested: "But some of these people are too old to walk even"; and he said of one boy: "Why, he's just a child!"

"Don't worry," Tel said, "I'll separate them later."

But Rousnak knew he would not. He was simply trying to pad out the prisoner list so as not to look foolish with a bag of only 35 men. In the end, the Legion commander took about 340 people, most of whom had never fired a gun.

Among the group were Rabbi A. Mordechai Weingarten and his ailing wife, who asked to be taken prisoner.

*

"All right, get up, we're moving," Yehudit Weingarten, who was in charge of the civilian evacuation, called out, and the refugees, most of them sitting on the ground or on their baggage, rose laboriously and lifted their bundles to their backs for the 500-yard trek to Zion Gate. Slowly they hobbled through odorous alleys strewn with blocks of masonry from fallen buildings, pieces of furniture, decaying garbage, and other charred debris, dragging their bundles behind them. Children whimpered as they clung precariously to their exhausted mothers, and old men in greasy skullcaps and bristly fur hats wept unashamedly as they left behind the ancestral homes and synagogues, mostly in ruins now, that had constituted their whole life. Occasionally, if one was lucky enough to pass his own beloved house, he would stop to kiss the *mazuza* in the doorway.

As the refugees reached the esplanade along the wall, a building collapsed in flame and rubble across their path. They surged back in panic and snaked down another street over other piles of wreckage, helped by Legionnaires who carried baggage and took the aged by the arm.

As Zion Gate loomed up ahead at last, several shots rang out, and people fell to the pavement or lunged into doorways, wailing and crying anew. Judith Jaharan was in the middle of the street, firing a pistol into the air. Finally, a youth grabbed her and took the pistol from her hand.

"Why are you shooting?" he asked, looking around fearfully to see if any Legionnaires had witnessed the incident.

She stared at him with glazed eyes, vaguely remembering him from some forgotten battle, then burst into tears and screamed hysterically: "Mother! Mother!"

"Cry, Judith, cry," the youth said gently as he put his arm around her shoulder and guided her toward Zion Gate. "It doesn't matter now who knows you're only sixteen."

As dusk blended into darkness, a nurse who had been outside dashed into the hospital, where the wounded were being prepared for evacuation to the New City the following day, shouting: "A mob of Arabs . . . They're coming this way . . . setting fire to everything . . . "

Dr. Laufer ran out to see flames leaping into the black sky only a few hundred yards away. He returned hastily and went over to several Legionnaires who were sitting in the hallway.

"They'll burn us all," he said. "You must stop them, or the world will say you are not soldiers."

One officer went out to examine the scene, returning with a dejected look. "It's probably too late to stop them," he said. "But maybe we can move you to the Armenian convent where we have our headquarters. You'd be safe there."

When Laufer agreed, the officer hurried out to get authority for the action.

Masha and a handful of other remaining nurses began preparing for the ordeal of removal, dressing wounds, packing instruments, collecting stretchers. Then Masha went from ward to ward, announcing: "Every patient who can stand on his feet, even if his legs are wounded, must walk. Form lines in the hallway and help each other."

The nurses went from mattress to mattress, helping the patients to put on their shoes and encouraging the reluctant ones to try to walk since there was a shortage of stretchers and people to carry them.

"I'd walk if I could."

Masha looked around to see Esther Ceilingold's delicate, pale face peering out from under a blanket. She had been wounded a second time when the Arabs had blown up a house she had entered with 10 other fighters. She was paralyzed from the waist down and was able to consume only liquids; but although she was in constant pain, it was manifested only by her heavy breathing and an occasional moan.

"Don't worry, darling," Masha said with a smile, "you'll be walking soon. Is there anything I can do for you?"

"Yes, would you get me a Bible, please? And maybe later you can read me the Psalms . . . "

The flames crackling toward the hospital lit up the heavens, providing the caravan of wounded with a ghastly light to guide them along the winding path leading to the Armenian convent. Men and women limped ahead carrying stretchers on which lay their more seriously wounded comrades. Arab Legionnaires, feeling a certain communion with these people whom they had maimed in meeting the terrible demands of war, helped to carry them to safety, even offering words of consolation.

"Just a few more minutes and you'll be safe," a young Bedouin, who held one end of Esther's stretcher, said almost cheerfully. "We'll protect you, don't worry."

Esther clung silently to a Bible.

In the frantic race against time, the hospital personnel left most of their equipment behind. When, after many trips by the stretcher bearers, all 119 wounded had been carried up to the third floor of the convent, Masha, out of breath from her part in the ordeal, asked the other nurses if the Jewish Quarter was now clear of all Jews.

"I don't think anyone is left," one answered.

Then Masha, with a sense of shock, remembered the 10 women, each about ninety years old, who had been moved during the fighting from a home for the aged to a synagogue. Every day, before and after their removal, she had taken them food from the hospital, given them medicine, made them comfortable. Now she realized that she had not seen them among the civilians who had left for the New City.

She ran downstairs and into the street, dashing into the Jewish Quarter toward the synagogue, heedless of the mobs now running wild everywhere, looting buildings, setting them afire with flaming torches, all the while howling like wolves in the night.

As Masha rushed on, someone grabbed her wrist, and when she looked around she was staring into the smiling, unshaven face of an Arab with a white *khaffiya* on his head and a curved knife at his belt. He roughly tried to tear off her wristwatch. With other Arabs closing in, she screamed, and at that moment a Legion officer pushed his way through the crowd and broke the Arab's grip on Masha's arm. He fired several shots into the air with his pistol, and the mob dispersed.

"If you value your life," he warned her, "run to the convent as fast as you can."

She did, weeping all the way for the fate of the 10 old ladies.

Chaos reigned on the third floor of the convent that Saturday, May 20, because of the shortage of equipment needed to operate a hospital. A severely wounded girl cried for a bedpan, but all that could be found was a dirty dustpan. Patients vomited, but there was no paper or cloth with which to clean up the mess. Flies swarmed everywhere, worms crawled in open wounds, the few sheets of toilet paper that remained were used to plug bullet holes. Pervading the whole room was a sickening stench which diminished even the small pleasure of drinking lemonade contributed by sympathetic Legionnaires.

After examination by Israeli doctors and a Red Cross representative, the list of wounded considered well enough to be taken prisoner was finally announced at about 5 P.M. Fifty-four persons would be taken to Amman, including three whom the Israelis had placed on the critically wounded list; the remainder would go to the New City. Masha and Yehudit Weingarten asked to go with the wounded so they could be with their parents, who had volunteered as prisoners.

As the nurses began to prepare the severely wounded for evacuation, Ora walked over to Esther, who seemed to be asleep, and said with a wan smile, gently trying to wake her up: "We're leaving, Esti, isn't it wonderful?"

But Esther did not wake.

"Esti!" Ora called as she shook her.

Then, trying to suppress her tears, Ora pulled a blanket over the girl's face and picked up a Bible that had fallen to the floor.

As the sun went down, everyone who could, including the Legionnaires present, helped to carry the wounded evacuees to Zion Gate, shuffling to the melancholy rhythm of a Jewish partisan song emanating from the third floor window, where the Jordan-bound prisoners remained.*

---

* Chava Kirschenbaum went with the prisoners to Jordan "by mistake." She left for the New City with the civilians, but returned the next morning to help old people and children who had still not made the crossing. Legion officers then decided to send her with the prisoners. In the prison camp near Amman, she was permitted to see Rousnak occasionally. The Weingarten family was released and sent back to the New City shortly after arriving in Jordan. Chava blames Rabbi Weingarten, who has since died, for not exerting his influence sufficiently to get her and one other nurse —the only two women prisoners—released promptly, though it is not clear that the rabbi was in a position to do very much.

Abdullah Tel permitted another Israeli, Nisan Zeldes, to enter the New City to attend the funeral of his father, who had been killed by a shell that day—on condition that he would rejoin the prisoners. After the funeral, Zeldes returned to the Old City as he had promised.

II

Latrun

WHILE Israeli fighters desperately defended every square foot of Jewish-held territory in the New and Old Cities, their leaders grew alarmed at the prospect of losing all Jerusalem to the Arabs. Prime Minister Ben-Gurion, in particular, felt that Israel could somehow survive even a temporary enemy occupation of Tel Aviv, but not a knifewound in its Biblical heart.

At a High Command meeting, he stressed this to his companions.

"The three places we must defend with the greatest vigor," he asserted in a cool voice, "are Tel Aviv, Haifa, and Jerusalem. If we lose Tel Aviv, we can establish a bridgehead in Haifa. If we lose Haifa, the major part of our national strength will still be intact in Tel Aviv. But if we lose Jerusalem, the blow to our morale will be so great that I cannot visualize how we could keep Tel Aviv and Haifa."

Yadin and most of the other commanders were less inclined to view the position of Jerusalem through an emotional prism. They had to do what was possible to save Jerusalem, they felt, but within the context of the total military situation. And some still calculated that Jerusalem could most easily be saved by continuing to concentrate mainly on the defense of the rest of the country. Nevertheless, no one doubted that even from a strictly military viewpoint the salvation of Jerusalem was vitally important; for if large Arab Legion and Egyptian forces linked up there, they would be able to launch a concerted attack on Tel Aviv. And feeding the High Command's apprehension were frantic pleas for help from the New City, which sounded much like those sent earlier to Amman by Arab irregulars in the Old City.

403

Thus, paradoxically, while Amman's fear of a Jewish attack on the Old City had sparked the Arab Legion intrusion into Jerusalem, Tel Aviv's resultant fear of a Legion attack on the New City provoked the Israelis into planning the very action Amman had hoped to prevent.

Indeed, the High Command meeting had been called after the Legion entry into Jerusalem to determine strategy for dealing with this threat. Members who had previously given low priority to an assault on the Old City now agreed that they should launch such an attack in order to ward off a Legion occupation of the New City. But first, they decided, they had to open the Tel Aviv–Jerusalem road so that military personnel and supplies, as well as food for the hungry population, could flow into the New City. The immediate Israeli target, therefore, would be the hills surrounding the Arab village of Latrun, the ancient home of the "good thief" crucified at Jesus' side.

A Givati Brigade force had occupied these hills after Kaoukji had withdrawn his troops without bothering to consult Glubb. But Yadin, in his frantic effort to halt the Egyptian drive on Tel Aviv, had hastily transferred this unit to the Negev front after persuading a reluctant Ben-Gurion that the Egyptian threat was more immediate. Thus, for almost 48 hours, the Latrun hills had been largely unmanned by either side. The Israelis now thought that Kaoukji was still responsible for Arab defense of the area, and were unaware that Glubb had since dispatched the 4th Arab Legion Regiment to occupy it (and the Iraqis to replace this unit in the Triangle).

Latrun overlooks the Tel Aviv–Jerusalem highway at a point where a branch road leads north to Ramallah, which straddles the north-south road connecting Transjordan with the Old City. Once Latrun fell and the road to the New City was open, the Israelis would attack Ramallah via the branch road and strike from the rear at the Old City, isolating the occupying Legion forces within its walls.

However, the question of a drive on Latrun precipitated a controversy within the High Command similar to that which had strained relations between King Abdullah and Glubb Pasha.[1] Ben-Gurion, fearing that the New City might fall any day or that the United Nations might impose a truce before the blockade could be lifted, wanted to make a head-on attack instantly and at any cost. Yadin favored a delay until Israeli forces were better prepared and a more sophisticated flanking strategy could be worked out. With all experienced brigades embattled in other areas, an embryonic 7th Brigade consisting of scattered units from various fronts and virtually untrained new immigrants would have to carry most of the load. In addition, Yadin was reluctant to see the other fronts, already short of defenders, weakened even further by the transfer of troops to Latrun.

History, too, played a role in his thinking. Many bloody battles had been fought through the ages in the region of Latrun, a series of high rolling ridges that dominated the Valley of Ayalon, where Joshua bade the sun stand still. These foothills of the Judaean mountain range had seen David hurl back the Philistines to the coastal plan, and the Saracens weather the fanatical charges of Richard the Lion-Hearted, whose ferocity still lived in the ruins of a castle etched against the sky.

And such frustrated invaders had not had to contend with the massive, thick-walled police fortress built by the British atop the westernmost ridge; nor with a stone artillery post on a 1,300-foot crest, called Gun Hill, east of the fortress; nor with the system of trenches and strongpoints established near an old Trappist monastery and in neighboring Arab villages.

At the High Command meeting, Yadin therefore insisted: "Jerusalem can still hold out for a while. We must have time to prepare the attack. We haven't even made detailed plans yet."

"Plans!" shouted Ben-Gurion. "There is no time for that. We'll have to improvise. And I'm not interested in the obstacles. It's your job to overcome them."

"A direct attack will be sheer suicide," Yadin warned.

"Our intelligence reports," the Prime Minister stressed, dismissing the protest with a curt wave of his arm, "indicate that Latrun is being defended by Kaoukji's irregulars and perhaps a small unit of Legionnaires. It shouldn't be so difficult to take."

"But the defensive positions are formidable," Yadin argued. "I implore you again to postpone the attack for just one week."

"Not for one day," Ben-Gurion asserted.

This decision crystallized on May 22. The Israelis were to trigger Operation Ben-Nun—the "Son of Nun," referring to Joshua—the following night.

Yadin was crestfallen. Though he respected Ben-Gurion, a civilian politician, for having grasped so well the essentials of military science, he considered the Prime Minister's dictation of battle strategy irresponsible. And he was equally disturbed by his strong preference for officers trained in the British army over the locally developed officers, particularly of the Palmach, who had little or no training overseas, but who understood battle tactics suited to local conditions. Yadin, who was himself trained locally, tried to strike a balance between the two groups, but he nevertheless favored the more imaginative and independent-minded domestically developed soldier.

He was particularly cool toward Ben-Gurion's choice of Shlomo Shamir, who had been an officer in the Jewish Brigade during World War II, to command the new 7th Brigade. But precisely because he considered Shamir "Ben-Gurion's man," Yadin, after his own futile confrontation with the

Prime Minister, asked the British-trained officer to exert his influence on him.

"A tremendous responsibility has been placed on your shoulders," Yadin told Shamir, as the two men were about to enter Ben-Gurion's office to discuss final details of the operation. "Personally, I feel that a direct attack may be catastrophic. Try to impress on B.G. the need to postpone the operation."

Actually, Shamir did stress at the meeting the obstacles he faced, apparently hoping for at least a short postponement. But when Ben-Gurion asked flatly, "Can you do it?" he said he could.

"Well then, go ahead."

"Your decision is, of course, an order."

But Shamir clearly harbored misgivings, and not without reason. It was only on May 14, a few hours before the proclamation of the State of Israel, that the Prime Minister had asked him to organize a new brigade. Thus, he had had only a week in which to obey this order, a week in which to create a fighting organization that would normally take months to mold. He still wasn't sure how he had managed to scrape together four battalions.

He had "borrowed" a battalion, commanded by Zvi German, from the Alexandroni Brigade that was protecting the narrow, 10-mile-wide Israeli waist in the Nathanya area—one reason why that brigade had been unable to attack Tulkarm in support of Moshe Carmel's force in the Triangle. He had formed personnel of the Armored School, together with their few steel-plated cars and jeeps, into an armored battalion under the schoolmaster, Chaim Laskov, a Jewish Brigade veteran. And he had persuaded each front to contribute a company to a third battalion.

Finally, he had funneled an undisciplined group of Eastern European immigrants fresh off the boat from former British detention camps in Cyprus into a fourth battalion, though they had learned to pull a rifle trigger only just before embarkation and could not even speak Hebrew. Moreover, the battalion commander, Zvi Gilat, had only junior officers who had not yet completed an infantry officers' course to lead these newcomers into battle.

Nor did the prejudice and narrow-mindedness of officers who had scorned foreign training raise the morale of his troops, Shamir felt. The Palmach had strongly opposed creation of the brigade, the first mobile one that it was not to organize, for its leaders saw this new unit as a threat to their own semi-independent power. Shamir himself was hurt by the knowledge that Yadin had little trust in him, though he personally had promoted Yadin to prominent rank before World War II.

Shortly after Shamir was ordered to prepare for the attack on Latrun, he met at GHQ with Colonel Chaim Herzog, the Haganah intelligence chief, who had just flown in to Tel Aviv from Jerusalem to become the operations officer of the 7th Brigade.

"When do we attack?" Herzog asked.

"Tomorrow night."

"But how can we?" Herzog exclaimed. "We barely have time to get the troops together and orient them."

"We won't even have time to see them," was Shamir's reply.

Shamir and Herzog then backed Yadin fully in a new effort to persuade Ben-Gurion to postpone the attack for at least 24 hours.

"Ben-Gurion," urged Yadin, "you cannot ignore the appeal of the brigade commander, the man who is going to carry out the operation."

Ben-Gurion reflected for a moment. Then he replied hesitantly: "Very well, twenty-four hours. But no more!"

Relieved, Yadin flew to Kibbutz Hulda, west of Latrun, where most of the brigade was to gather for the attack. He strolled under the pine trees watching No. 5 civilian buses pull into the settlement from Tel Aviv and discharge the men who were to storm the strongholds of Latrun within hours. Still largely unequipped, most of them wore civilian shoes or sandals and bright-colored, short-sleeved shirts and shorts. Only a few carried arms or any other military equipment. They might have come for a picnic under the pines. No one seemed to know what to do or to show much interest in finding out. And there would not even be enough time to scatter these recruits among the more experienced companies; they would have to remain a single unit.

Yadin felt ill.

When most of the troops had arrived, Shamir, late on May 23, briefed unit commanders on their mission as they sat crammed into children's chairs in the kindergarten bungalow used as a staff room. Only two of his four battalions would attack the Latrun area, he said, mapping the operation on a blackboard. Three companies of the 32nd Battalion, borrowed from the Alexandroni Brigade, would play the main role, attacking the Latrun police fortress west of the Ramallah-Latrun road and the village itself.

"Our intelligence," he announced, "indicates that most of the enemy force is situated in the police station and in the woods west and south of the village."

Simultaneously, two companies of the 72nd Battalion, mainly the new immigrants, would bypass Latrun to the south and attack the Arab village

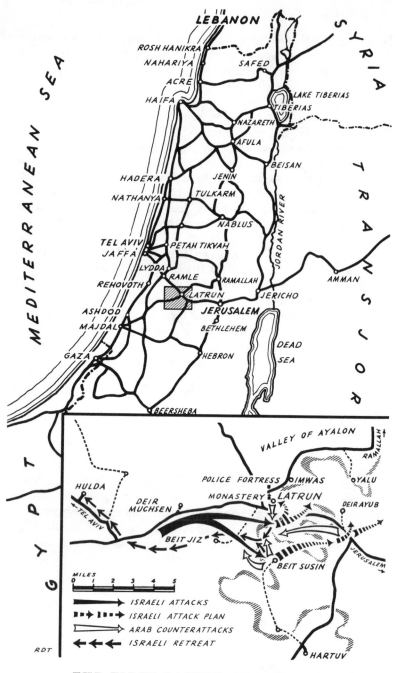

THE FIRST BATTLE OF LATRUN

of Deir Ayub about three miles east of Latrun in a diversionary flanking movement. Shamir assured his listeners that the Arab villages of Beit Jiz and Beit Susin that lay along the path this battalion would follow, as well as the mountainous area east of Beit Susin, were unoccupied.

"Resistance probably won't be very heavy anywhere," he concluded. "The Legion appears to be concentrating for an attack on Jerusalem and therefore is not strongly defending Latrun."

As soon as Latrun fell, he added—as if to dismiss any other possibility—the two attacking battalions would join the two in reserve in guiding to Jerusalem a long convoy of food and arms already waiting on the road nearby. Meanwhile, the Harel Brigade would start the next phase of Operation Ben-Nun—a thrust toward Ramallah.

Squeezed into one of the miniature chairs listening to Shamir was stocky Colonel Mickey Marcus, whom Ben-Gurion had sent to "observe" the attack. Marcus volunteered several suggestions diplomatically; at intervals, to emphasize his passive role, he tipped his chair against the wall and thumbed through a paperback volume of poetry by Longfellow. But when the room had cleared, he slipped the book into his hip pocket, and with a broad smile walked over to Shamir, the man who had recruited him.

"Very good briefing, Shlomo," he commented. Then, his smile dissolving, he expressed doubt about the accuracy of intelligence information indicating that Latrun was not strongly defended. "The information I've seen just doesn't ring true," he said uneasily.

Marcus then went back to his quarters, removed his rumpled khaki, and, wrapped only in a bath towel, went out to sunbathe on the grass. He spoke cheerfully to the nervous soldiers. "Come on, what are you guys waiting for? It's a beautiful day. Enjoy the sun. Relax!"

And they did. After all, if an American colonel with full knowledge of the situation could be so at ease, perhaps things weren't as wrong as they thought.

At about 7:30 P.M. the next evening, May 24, an aide rushed into the headquarters hut with an urgent radio message: "120 enemy vehicles, among them a large number of armored cars and artillery carriers, left Ramallah in the direction of Latrun."

Shamir looked up from his desk but remained silent. One hundred and twenty vehicles! That was a large force. Perhaps a company or two. Well, after all, he would attack with two battalions. Two others were in reserve. A major battle was still unlikely.

By 8 P.M., the troops had assembled in lorries and Tel Aviv buses which were to take them to the Latrun area and were sweating in the heat of a blistering *khamsin*. Yet, no one knew when they would leave.

"What's holding us up?" a soldier in one of the buses demanded after several hours.

"Take it easy," replied Sergeant Yussef S. "You've got to expect these things."

But Yussef, platoon sergeant in B Company of the Alexandroni's 32nd Battalion, moved restlessly in his seat. When they had first boarded the bus, they had laughed and joked, confident that before the night was over they would be celebrating their victory in Jerusalem, where they were to head after Latrun had fallen. But now they were sweaty and itchy in the stifling heat, and increasingly suspicious that something had gone awry.

Yussef looked at his watch. After midnight. If they didn't get started soon, dawn would break before his unit achieved its objective, and then casualties would mount. The three companies of his battalion did, after all, have the toughest targets: the police fortress of Latrun and the village itself. And even if sparsely manned, these positions, perched on high ground, could spell trouble—though, of course, no real resistance.

He detached the beer bottle hanging by a cord to his belt and took a sip of water. Warm as hell! To think that on a hot night like this there were enough canteens for only half the men!

"Well, is it true or isn't it? We can't move until we find out."

Shlomo Shamir, beads of sweat trickling down his face, glared at the leader of the patrol he had sent out to determine the validity of a mysterious report that the road to Latrun was still blocked by iron stakes driven by Israeli troops some days previously.

"We went as far as we could without encountering the enemy," the soldier said breathlessly, "and we couldn't find anything."

This was the second patrol Shamir had sent out to check, so he concluded the report must have been baseless. On top of the fruitless delay, the support weapons—half-tracks, machine guns, and mortars, which had arrived at the port of Tel Aviv that very night—had still not reached Hulda. It was 2 A.M. already. This meant that fighting might rage into daylight. Indeed, the 72nd Battalion of new immigrants could hardly avoid such battle since it had to bypass Latrun and attack Deir Ayub several miles east of it after a long, time-consuming march. Well, it was too late to repair matters now. He would order the vehicles to carry the men as far as possible to save a little time.

He strode out of the headquarters hut and shouted last-minute orders to his commanders by the road. As he and Mickey Marcus watched the vehicles rumble down the road toward Latrun and beyond, motors groaning and headlights piercing the black wall of night with dimmed but visible beams, they were filled with mingled relief and foreboding.

First Lieutenant Mahmoud al-Rousan, adjutant of the Arab Legion's 4th Regiment, tingled with anticipation as he inspected the posts in the Latrun police fortress. Arab Legion patrols had indicated that an Israeli attack was imminent and he was more than ready. The 4th Regiment had dug in deeply since its arrival about a week earlier to fill the gap precipitously left by Kaoukji. It now occupied the fortress, Latrun Castle, and Gun Hill overlooking Deir Ayub. And the arrival that night of the 2nd Regiment from Ramallah injected new vigor into the Legion defense system. All 120 vehicles of the unit, which entrenched itself in the eastern hills, had already been unloaded and the equipment set up.

Suddenly, two red rockets streaked through the black sky. The signal— the Jews were advancing! Rousan's tan, handsome face broadened into a smile. He marched briskly to the west tower where he had installed a mortar team.

"Keep your eyes open! The enemy is advancing from the west. Lob a few shells to draw fire so that we can locate them."

Then he hastened to inspect the gun positions in the northern tower and at other strategic points.

He would wait until they came within close range to hit them hard. With every hill and wadi already pinpointed, he could then let go with his 2-inch and 3-inch mortars and his 6-pounders. The 25-pounders set up in Beit Nuba, about three miles to the northeast, would also start hitting them. And the defenders in the eastern hills—the newly arrived 2nd Regiment plus local Arab fighters—would take care of any enemy forces trying to outflank Latrun.

Standing behind a stack of sandbags on the roof, he gazed at the foothills stretching away like an ebony sea and happily contemplated the next few hours.

At about 3:30 A.M. (May 25), 10 buses drew to a halt in the tiny deserted village of Deir Muchsen, three miles west of Latrun, and the three Alexandroni companies piled out with their equipment. Hardly had the troops gathered to march toward their target when a shell whistled overhead and exploded some distance away.

As Yussef S., who had dropped rapidly to earth along with the others, scrambled to his feet he commented wryly: "Must be a stray shell. They're not supposed to know we're coming."

"Maybe we're not supposed to know they're there," joked one of his men.

They all laughed. No one took the "stray shell" seriously . . .

At about this time, in a nearby village, the second in command of the Alexandroni Battalion decided that he would further strengthen the morale of his troops by giving them immediate artillery cover with two Napoleonic 65 mm. cannons, twins of the two that had been sent to Degania and later to Jenin.

"That would be a mistake," argued Chaim Laskov, commanding the reserve armored battalion. "It'll only alert the enemy and permit them to pinpoint our positions."

"The most important thing is to keep up the spirit of our men," the second in command retorted. "They should know we're supporting them."

And he ordered a barrage from the two ancient guns, which were located nearby. Shortly afterward, Legion shells responded, saturating the area and knocking out both cannons.

Yussef's platoon, one of the three composing Alexandroni's Company B, trudged warily through the Valley of Ayalon just south of the Tel Aviv–Jerusalem road toward Latrun. Simultaneously, Company A headed for Hill 314, which dominated a series of heights sloping into the sky south of the valley. From there it was to provide cover for Company B in the valley as this unit advanced across the road toward the police fortress and Latrun village. Company G remained behind to guard the area between Deir Muchsen and Latrun.

As the new day dawned in deadly splendor, the sporadic enemy mortar fire escalated suddenly into a full-scale barrage accompanied by machine-gun fire.

"Get down!" Yussef shouted, as his men leaped into a wadi and lay flat.

The platoon commander David G., crawled over to him. "We've lost radio contact with the other two platoons!"

"We'll have to catch up."

"How can we? The fire is too heavy. We're stuck here!"

Twenty-five pounders exploded into huge fiery clouds nearby and irregular Arab troops could be seen darting down the hills toward the road. As the platoon started firing at them, Yussef grunted ironically to David:

"What the hell are you worrying about? Our intelligence experts said resistance would be light . . . "

While Yussef's Alexandroni Company B, split in two, found itself pinned down by murderous fire, the battalion of new immigrants, moving southeastward in a semicircle around Latrun in an effort to outflank it, suddenly became the target of the same guns. However, this force pushed ahead until it neared Beit Susin, where an Arab Legion patrol greeted it with a concentrated volley of fire—despite Shamir's information that the village was deserted. Soon, hordes of irregulars were assaulting from the east.

Zvi Gilat, at battalion headquarters to the rear, radioed his commanders: "Dig into the hills around Beit Susin until we find out what's going on. And keep firing at the irregulars trying to cross the road from the north. They've got the 32nd Battalion tied down with heavy fire."

But his orders were only partially obeyed. In the confusion of the unexpected resistance, some of the troops in one company, hearing the cry "Follow me," mistakenly followed the leader of another. And the third company scattered in panic after the initial firing, some joining different units, others getting lost, still others retreating wildly to the west, while Arab sharpshooters picked away at the disintegrating ranks.

The officers tried to bring order out of the chaos, but were severely handicapped by the lack of a common language with many of the immigrants. Some communication was possible in Yiddish, but mostly the officers gestured, pulled, pushed, swore, and finally surged recklessly into battle hoping to lead through example. But for the most part it was a lost cause.

As one youth fell mortally wounded, the safety catch of his rifle still closed and his blue sport shirt splattered with blood, he moaned in Yiddish to an officer bending over him: "I didn't have a chance to see my mother after getting off the boat. Tell her, will you, that I died for Israel?" . . .

Yussef, crawling through the wadi in which his platoon was trapped, grabbed a canteen from a man about to take a sip and snapped: "There's only enough water for the seriously wounded. No one else drinks!"

But even worse than the lack of water were the flies, swarms of vicious *barhash* flies, which buzzed round open wounds, attacked the eyes, clustered in the sweat, devoured the will and even the wish to survive.

"Yussef," said David, the platoon commander, "we've got to get out of here! Do you think you can make it to Hill 314? Find out if A Company got there. Maybe if they give us cover, we can retreat there. It's our only chance."

Ignoring the storm of lead, Yussef crept out of the wadi, dashed southward from rock to rock, then crawled up the slope of the hill, pulling himself by aching fingers scrabbling in the hard earth. Ahead he saw a mirage. Only a little further to the cool stream. He rubbed his crusted lips. Then, dazed and exhausted, he rose and walked the last few yards to the crest of the hill as if on a stroll in the sunshine.

He was met by Captain Ram Ron, commander of A Company, whose troops had occupied Hill 314 as planned without undue trouble. Yussef told him of his platoon's desperate plight.

"Go back and lead your men up here. Your platoon can help us cover the retreat," said Ron . . .

"We must retreat. We have no choice," Chaim Laskov shouted at Shamir in 7th Brigade headquarters. "It's clear we won't be able to attack the enemy or even hold the territory we have taken in daylight. And casualties have made our forces ineffective. I'll cover the retreat as best I can."

"All right," Shamir agreed, shattered by the disaster. "I'll order a retreat."

Then his face brightened slightly. Apparently the Legion was defending Latrun with two full battalions. That meant he might have saved Jerusalem after all. Glubb Pasha would be storming the New City right now if he hadn't had to divert such large forces to Latrun.

Laskov, justifying the abortive attack with similar rationale, then ordered the stranded units to withdraw to Hill 314, where a general retreat would be organized. The men would dash down the western slope to the road leading to Beit Jiz. At about noon, he radioed the commander of the company on the hill (there had been an interruption in communications):

"Hello Jonah 2 [codeword for the unit]. You are severing communications. The fault is with you. Don't move before all the other forces are out. Waiting for you at Beit Jiz."

Strategically located between the Alexandroni Battalion's B Company isolated to the north and the new immigrant battalion under attack to the south, Hill 314 thus became the primary center of refuge for both—and the primary target for the Arabs.

Only the two casualty-ridden platoons of B Company that had been separated from Yussef's platoon retreated via another route—directly to Deir Muchsen, the way they had come.

Laskov had hoped to cover the retreat with his armored cars but because enemy fire was so heavy the vehicles could not get near enough. He then led a machine-gun unit to a point where it could pepper the Latrun hills, but one gun was knocked out by artillery and the other soon ran out of ammunition, leaving the withdrawing forces with little more than machine-gun fire from atop Hill 314 itself to provide cover.

With Yussef leading the way, his platoon, carrying its wounded, threaded its way through burning fields and scrambled up the rocky slope to the crest. From the south, meanwhile, surviving new immigrants straggled in panic up the hill.

As the remnants of shattered humanity made their way painfully to the top, the Arabs began to surround the hill. Only an immediate withdrawal could prevent entrapment.

"Every able man must carry a wounded man," an officer shouted. "We'll have to leave the dead behind."

"But some of the wounded are too badly hurt to be carried," a soldier cried.

"Then we'll have to leave them, too. A rearguard will stay behind holding back the enemy until the rest of you reach safety."

While the officer was still drumming out orders, some of the immigrants, glassy-eyed and white-faced, unable to understand the language anyway, were already racing in disorder down the dusty road to Beit Jiz, frantically fleeing their Tower of Babel.* Many were killed or wounded by shells as they stumbled along in the stifling heat. Some owed their lives to Yussef, who forced them to continue on after they had collapsed from wounds, exhaustion, or thirst, threatening to shoot them if they did not move.

When he finally reached Beit Jiz, supporting a wounded man, Yussef fell to his knees before a barrel of filthy water and greedily drank his fill, leeches and all. Then he sat back and admired the changing hues of Latrun at sundown, as men throughout the ages had done in the midst of carnage.

DAVID BEN-GURION refused to accept Yadin's view that the attack had been a failure, despite the disorderly retreat and heavy casualties, including about 140 dead.

"You must look at the general picture," he insisted at a meeting of the High Command, which had already decided to attack again. "By hitting Latrun when we did, we saved Jerusalem. We forced the enemy to divert forces to Latrun that would certainly have attacked the New City."

Yadin did not dispute the danger of an Arab Legion attack on the New City, or even the success of the Latrun operation in pulling Legion

* "Then they said, Go to, let us build us . . . a tower, whose top may reach unto Heaven, and let us make a name for ourselves, lest we be scattered abroad upon the face of the whole earth. . . ." And the Lord, angered by this effort to penetrate his heavenly realm, "came down to see the tower, which the children of men builded. And the Lord said, Behold, the people is one and they have all one language. . . . Go to, let us go down, and there confound their language, that they may not understand one another's speech." (Genesis 11:4-7).

units out of Jerusalem. But he argued forcefully that a diversion of Legion troops from Jerusalem had not been the objective of the Latrun attack.

"If a diversion had been our aim," he contended, "it would have been much easier and cheaper to attack elsewhere, perhaps in the Jordan Valley. The immediate objectives of the attack were to open the roads to Jerusalem and Ramallah, and we failed miserably."

Both men agreed that the attacks might have gone better with a strong overall command authority, and that a supreme commander should be selected for the second attack. But while Ben-Gurion wanted to choose a British-trained officer, Yadin preferred a Palmach officer.

The Prime Minister then proposed a "compromise"—actually the more he thought about it, the more he felt it was the best solution. He suggested that Mickey Marcus should be appointed to the post. (The Israelis called Marcus "Stone" in order to avoid embarrassing the American government.)

Yadin readily agreed to this proposal, seeing in Marcus a valuable blend of military experience and flexibility of mind. The Palmach commanders, however, were not overjoyed by the prospect of taking orders from a foreign professional soldier, particularly one so close to Ben-Gurion. Yet, they apparently looked far more favorably on Marcus's selection than on that of any British-trained countryman.

Thus, on May 28, the provisional government issued an order signed by Ben-Gurion:

> Brigadier General Stone is hereby appointed Commander of the Jerusalem front, with command over the Etzioni, Harel, and the 7th Brigades. General Stone is authorized to select officers and noncommissioned officers from the aforementioned three brigades to form his staff.

As head of the largest body of Israeli troops yet put under a single field command, Marcus became the first Aluf, or General, since Judah Maccabaeus held the rank 2,000 years earlier.

Marcus, as the Palmach had feared, immediately tipped the scales in favor of a second head-on attack.

"We haven't got the time or the men to outflank Latrun," he advised his colleagues. "We have the capability to capture it. It's a matter of proper preparation and execution. I think we can do it."

Ben-Gurion was delighted. "When will you be ready to attack?" he asked.

"In two days." Marcus grinned, adding as he characteristically pounded a huge fist into his hand: "And this time we'll take the place!"

His confidence convinced even Yadin that the Israelis could, after all, seize Latrun by a direct attack if it were well prepared. But most of the home-trained commanders were still dubious.

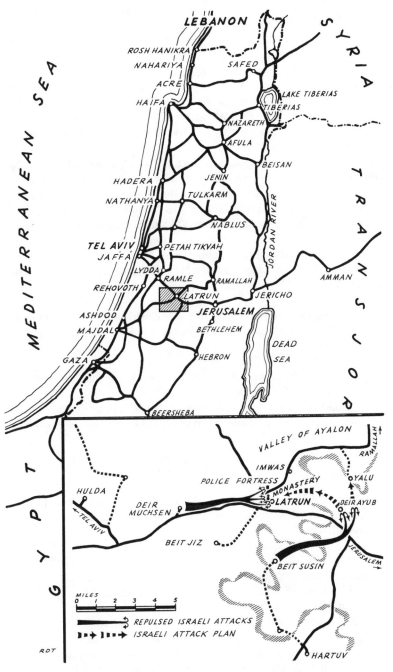

THE SECOND BATTLE OF LATRUN

Marcus immediately sat down with Shamir, Laskov, and other staff officers to plan the new assault, which was again to be a 7th Brigade operation. This time, they decided, Laskov's armored battalion which had remained in reserve in the initial battle, would lead the main striking force, smashing into the police fortress, taking Latrun village, and demolishing the artillery on the hill near the Trappist monastery. A company of infantry would then thrust into the fortress to relieve the armored force and consolidate Israeli control.

At the same time, an experienced infantry battalion borrowed from the Givati Brigade to replace the badly mauled Alexandroni force would make a diversionary attack northeastward from Beit Susin, which the Israelis had occupied after the first Latrun attack. This battalion would capture Deir Ayub and Gun Hill overlooking it, then Yalu further north in a diversionary strike on the eastern flank of the Latrun strongholds.

"Everything will depend on coordination," Marcus stressed as he traced the attack plan on a wall map. "Tomorrow we'll go through the whole thing at Hulda. Yaacov will be there, won't he?"

Yaacov Prulov, commander of the Givati Brigade's 52nd Battalion, listened with a skeptical expression as Shamir and Herzog outlined his part of the operation to him.

"How do you like it?" Marcus asked.

"That's quite an order," Prulov said. "You know that my battalion was badly cut up in the Negev."

His confidence was not increased on being told that a company of Zvi Gilat's immigrant recruits would be attached to two companies of his own battalion.

"I hate to think about the casualties," he remarked sourly.

"We'd better think about making this operation succeed," Marcus replied.

When Prulov had gone, Marcus sat silently for a moment, then turned to Gilat. "Zvi, I'm a bit worried about Yaacov. Just in case, be ready to take over his battalion."

After this meeting (according to Shimon Avidan, the Givati Brigade commander), Prulov radioed Avidan the projected plan and asked whether he thought it feasible. Avidan contemplated it carefully in his Negev headquarters and decided to visit Prulov personally.

When he arrived at Prulov's headquarters, the two men discussed the attack plan with contempt. They condemned the basic strategy of a frontal assault, as well as the decision to assign their battalion, so experienced and battle-tested, to a diversionary role in an operation undertaken largely, in their view, by officers and troops of lesser ability and stature.

They expressed particular concern about casualties. Many of the men had been recruited from the Tel Aviv region where Prulov had been raised, and he had known them since childhood. Moreover, Avidan had taught him and other loyal disciples the principle of "no advance without security," the need to avoid, if possible, any engagement with the enemy that would eat too deeply into the ranks.

Prulov, therefore, was not surprised when Avidan, as he was about to leave, advised him not to push a direct attack and risk having his men ripped to pieces by artillery.

"How many times do I have to say 'no'?" exclaimed Chaim Laskov on the morning of May 30, as he watched his armored force conduct a final skeleton exercise in preparation for Operation Ben-Nun No. 2 that night.

Hadassah Lempel, a plump brunette, stared at the commander and persisted: "But Chaim, *why* can't I go? I'm a good radio operator. Why should you discriminate against women?"

Laskov, his slightly Oriental eyes expressionless, walked away. Yes, a good radio operator. But how could he let an eighteen-year-old girl join the attack on the police fortress? If anything happened to her, what would he tell her mother? Though he admired her courage, he had to refuse.

But she was the least of his worries at the moment. The operation had already been postponed for 24 hours because Prulov had started out too late toward his objectives and had to stay overnight in Beit Susin.

After giving orders to his men maneuvering in the field, Laskov eased his great hulk against a tree and sat brooding. The Palmach commanders resented him for his British training in modern military strategy. Yet they knew nothing about fighting with large units against regular armies, while he understood guerrilla strategy as well as any of them.

Laskov had joined Haganah when he was only ten, shortly after his father had been murdered by an Arab outside his home in Haifa.* During the 1936–39 Arab revolt, he had fought with Orde Wingate, whom he could still remember holding a Bible, moving his finger across a thumbworn page as he read a favorite passage relating to the prowess of Gideon's soldiers. Yes, Chaim Laskov's roots were in Haganah, even if he was "British-trained." . . .

"Let's get ready to move, Chaim."

Laskov looked up into the calm, smiling face of Mickey Marcus. Mickey understood how to fight this war. How to fight regular armies. How

* At a meeting of his top military commanders shortly before the Arab invasion, Prime Minister Ben-Gurion ordered all who had not already done so to adopt Hebrew names on the spot so that history would remember them by such names. Only one commander was permitted to keep his original name—Chaim Laskov—in honor of his father's memory.

to smash the enemy head-on if necessary, to throw him off balance and keep hitting at any cost. As Laskov rose, he could hardly wait for the scorching dusk to dissolve into night, when the flash of artillery in a moonless sky would signal the start of his greatest battle.

It was about midnight when Laskov and Marcus climbed into their command car and, flanked by two jeeps, pulled out of Hulda along the pocked asphalt road leading toward Latrun. Behind them moved a long convoy of three attacking columns. About 20 armored cars, 5 machine-gun-equipped half-tracks, flamethrowers, infantry, and a support company including light mortars made up the column that would assault the police fortress. Three armored cars and a platoon of infantry made up each of the other two columns, which would advance to the village and the monastery.

Reaching the takeoff point for the multiple attack at about 2 A.M., the three columns split up. Some units stayed put, others advanced toward their respective objectives. The command car and two jeeps moved along a side road to a grassy embankment about 300 yards from the police fortress, where the two commanders set up battalion headquarters.

"Well, let's make ourselves at home," said Marcus, settling languidly under an acacia tree. "There's nothing more we can do but hope for the best."

As Laskov sat down beside him, he glanced at his watch.

"Prulov should be on his way to Yalu by now," he murmured.

"Don't worry," Marcus said, putting on his steel helmet. "Everything is going to go all right."

Laskov looked northward toward Imwas—the modern name for Biblical Emmaus, which Judah Maccabaeus, in his campaign against the Syrians, destroyed in 165 B.C.

Then the thud of a mortar shell being released shattered the dense silence and his thoughts. Within seconds, the projectile burst in a corner of the police fortress silhouetted to the west, and a clump of trees vanished in an orange and yellow inferno.

"That's where they've got an anti-tank gun," Laskov exulted, pointing toward the raging flames. "We must have knocked it out!" . . .

"They've destroyed an anti-tank gun," Lieutenant Abdel Majid Maitah, commander of the police fortress, shouted over the radio. "And we can hear their armored cars and trucks mobilizing nearby. Send some armored cars immediately or we may not be able to hold! We only have thirty-seven men!"

"I'll relay your request to brigade headquarters," Lieutenant Mahmoud al-Rousan shouted back in 4th Regimental headquarters at Imwas. "Meanwhile, we'll hit the Jews with our artillery."

Maitah paced the roof of the fortress, then paused to watch the embers of the trees that had caught fire. What deplorable luck! With the anti-tank gun knocked out, how could he stop a determined enemy attack? The brigade command should have given him the armored cars much earlier.

Suddenly, he heard a distant rumbling. An aide ran up to him. "Do you hear, Lieutenant?" he shouted. "They're here! Our armored cars! We're saved!"

Maitah strained his eyes to see into the black distance. "Thank God!" he mumbled.

"It sounds as if they've reached the grove of the monastery," the aide added.

After a short pause, Maitah remarked: "It's strange that the commander of the reinforcements hasn't informed us he's on the way."

Maitah watched with mixed puzzlement and relief as a column of eight shadowy vehicles wound around a bend and approached the fortress. Then a burst of machine-gun fire crackled out, followed by a shrill scream.

"They're firing at our guards!" Maitah shouted. "Quick, order everybody on the roof!" . . .

As the column of Israeli armored cars and half-tracks fired furiously, a bullet entered the barrel of a Piat held by a Legionnaire guarding the front fortress gate and exploded the detonator. The guard (a cousin of Lieutenant Mahmoud al-Rousan) and a comrade standing nearby were killed instantly.

A crew of Israeli sappers then ran forward and blew the gate open. Four of the vehicles smashed into the courtyard spurting bullets and flames, while the other four stayed outside the gate.

In the midst of the storm, a girl's voice exclaimed into a radiophone in the rear of an advancing half-track: "We're inside the courtyard!" . . .

Laskov was both exhilarated and enraged to hear Hadassah Lempel's voice.

"Wait till I see that girl!" he fumed.

Then he rejoiced at the good news coming in from almost every commander.

"It seems we're advancing everywhere as planned," Marcus said.

"What about Prulov?"

"Haven't been able to get him yet."

As flames burst from the roof of the fortress, lighting up the sky, Laskov radioed orders to two infantry companies nearby to advance, one of them to Latrun village, the other to the fortress to take over from the armored spearhead.

A few minutes after 4 A.M., Laskov and Marcus heard the whir of motors approaching.

"That must be our buses with the men," Laskov ventured.

An explosion ripped the area, followed by several more.

"Land mines!" exclaimed Marcus . . .

"That's it, Mama! You hit one of the tanks! You hit it! Listen to them scream!"

The thirteen-year-old Arab boy slapped his brother, a year older, on the back, then hurled another grenade from the trench the family had dug outside their little stone house near the road leading to the police fortress.

After the first grenade exploded, some of the men in the buses got out, thinking one of the vehicles had hit a land mine. They were soon ducking a barrage of grenades, drawn from a neat pile in the trench.

"Look, Mama! They're getting back in the tanks and turning around! We've scared them! Papa would be proud of us!"

And the woman and two children threw several more grenades toward the attackers, who were convinced that they had run into a full-fledged ambush . . .[2]

In the fortress courtyard, the Israeli half-tracks careened crazily round the building spraying bullets and fireballs into every window and setting aflame part of the roof. The sappers, meanwhile, ran to the iron door of the fortress to set explosives. Everything appeared to be going well—until the flames shooting from the building spread to two adjacent wooden barracks, lighting up the entire scene as brilliantly as day.

From the roof, shouts of "God is great and Mohammed is his Prophet!" echoed in the air as the defenders lobbed grenades and fired directly into the open half-tracks and at the team of sappers, targets illuminated as if by spotlight . . .

Three hundred yards away at battalion headquarters, Laskov and Marcus listened to Hadassah Lempel's calm voice: "Enemy has brought up twenty-five-pounders . . . Direct your shells to right . . ." Then after a pause: "Our car has been set afire!"*

"Hadassah! Hadassah!" Laskov shouted into the night. But there was only silence.

---

* According to Arabs who were present, a young girl cried out in Arabic as one of the Israeli half-tracks sped around: "God and Mohammed are not here! Only the Jews are!" Shortly afterwards, these Arabs say, she was wounded and, as she lay on the floor of the half-track dying, she yelled: "Mohammed has won!" Laskov describes this story as "ridiculous."

"It looks like we're finished," Laskov groaned. "The infantry has turned back, and the armor is trapped in that hell over there."

"We're not finished yet," Marcus assured him. "We haven't heard from Prulov. He should be hitting them from the rear at any moment. Then, when they turn their guns on him, we can regroup and attack again."

A thunderous roar punctuated his words. Seeing a flash just beyond the monastery, Laskov exclaimed: "That's an enemy eighteen-pounder! And it's being fired from Imwas!"

The two men were silent for a moment as they stood under the trembling leaves of the acacia tree. Their concern over Prulov's tardiness now mounted to alarm.

"Where the hell is he?" shouted Marcus, who expected Prulov to strike at Imwas. (Laskov later insisted that Prulov was supposed to capture or neutralize Imwas after taking Yalu—though Prulov has denied that he received such an order. Prulov's official battle orders, in any case, did not mention Imwas.)

Their alarm was compounded when enemy artillery, in an accelerated barrage, turned the Valley of Ayalon into a seething cauldron of fury.

"I'm going to find him!" Marcus said, starting down the bullet-peppered slope.

Laskov had the presence of mind to send a jeep after him, and Marcus ordered the driver, Gaby Anakov, to circle through the rear area of the firing line close to the route he thought Prulov would follow. But no one could provide a clue as to the whereabouts of the missing battalion. After distributing water to the troops and taking two wounded men aboard, Marcus said: "All right, let's get back to Laskov."

But hardly had the jeep wheeled around when a bullet hit the rear bumper.

"They've spotted us! Let's go!" the American shouted.

Gaby zigzagged precariously up the bumpy slope through a hail of machine-gun fire and finally escaped into the shadow of Laskov's headquarters.

"Boy, that was close!" Marcus exclaimed as he jumped out of the jeep, adding: "We didn't learn anything. Prulov seems to have disappeared."

"No, he hasn't," Laskov retorted, his voice broken. "Brigade headquarters finally heard from him. He got as far as Deir Ayub and reported that he could not advance. He was granted permission to withdraw."

"You're kidding!" Marcus cried. "That means he hardly got started!"

"There's no chance of holding out now," Laskov said. "Dawn will be breaking soon and then they might encircle us. I'm going to radio Shlomo and ask him to order a general retreat."

"Okay. Let's get back to Hulda."

"You go. I'll follow in a little while," said Laskov.

After requesting Shamir to order the withdrawal, Laskov, alone now, sat down on a large rock facing the blazing police fortress. He picked up a pebble, and rolled it vehemently between thumb and forefinger, muttering: "God damn!" He repeated the curse more loudly.

Then he stared into the fiery sky and shouted: *"God damn!"*

After about two hours (at 8:30 A.M.), a voice disturbed his bitter reverie: "So there you are!"

Laskov looked around and saw the American photographer, Robert Capa.

"Mickey sent me with this canteen," Capa said. "He says you're probably thirsty."

Laskov took the canteen and, putting it to his mouth, swilled down about half the *arak*.

"He says you should come back, and that you shouldn't worry. We'll have another go at it."

At 7th Brigade headquarters in Hulda, Marcus and Shamir sat by the radio waiting for reports that would throw some light on the Givati failure. How could Prulov have suffered so disastrous a defeat so soon in an area known to be defended only by small and scattered enemy units? Finally, a code message from the battalion came in:

"Hello, Korah One, Korah One . . ."

"A casualty report," said the radio operator.

"Yes, what is it?" Marcus pressed.

"Givati lost two dead, sir."

"That can't be right," the American exclaimed. "Ask for a repeat."

A few minutes later the operator showed the new message he had scribbled on a sheet of paper, saying: "They said it twice, sir. There's no question about the number."

Gradually, some of the details followed. After his battalion had captured Deir Ayub without opposition, Prulov sent the immigrant recruit company attached to Givati to take Gun Hill overlooking the village. But as soon as two men were killed on the way up, it retreated. Prulov then sent his two other companies to outflank the hill and attack it from the north, but by the time they were in position day had dawned. Prulov apparently remembered Avidan's advice not to push a direct attack if severe casualties seemed likely. In any event, he asked Shamir at that point to authorize a general withdrawal—rendering academic the question whether he was to drive on to Imwas.

In his official report to Yadin, Marcus wrote: "I was there, saw battle . . . Plan good. Artillery good. Armor excellent. Infantry disgraceful."

Yadin then sent a note to Marcus: "Ben-Gurion has issued an order to remove Prulov from command. Maybe he's right and maybe he's wrong. In any case, we must have an investigation."

"Yigal," Marcus wrote back, "I'm going to see Prulov, and then I'm either going to hang him or exonerate him."

Shortly after dawn on May 31, Lieutenant Mahmoud al-Rousan and other officers from higher headquarters arrived at the police fortress to congratulate Lieutenant Maitah on holding out even though the armored cars he had requested arrived after the Israelis were in full retreat.

"You were brave, but lucky, too," said Rousan. "After an enemy force occupied Deir Ayub, our troops in the east pulled back toward Ramallah and left a big gap between the 2nd and 4th regiments. Do you realize what would have happened if the Jews had continued on and attacked us from the rear?"

"Do you realize," Maitah countered, his face black with soot, "what would have happened if the force attacking the fortress had walked in the front door while we were all up on the roof?"

"What do you mean?"

"The Jews lost time trying to blow the door open, and we killed most of them," explained Maitah. "Thank God they didn't know that we had neglected to lock the door!" (Maitah died later that day in an artillery bombardment.)

WITH the Israeli command more desperate than ever after its second defeat at Latrun to crack the blockade of Jerusalem, a soldier's homesickness was destined to play a key role in the new strategy.

Amos Chorev, the Harel Brigade officer who had helped to lead the Jewish offensive in the Jerusalem corridor before the mandate ended, had been yearning to visit his wife and baby in Tel Aviv for weeks. Just after the Arab armies invaded, therefore, he asked Harel commander Yitzhak Rabin for a few days' leave, pointing out that the Jerusalem–Tel Aviv road at that particular time was open.

"Kaoukji seems to have withdrawn from the corridor," he said, "and convoys are getting through. I've almost forgotten what my wife and child look like and this may be my only chance to see them for a long while."

"Okay," Rabin replied, "but you'll have to go and return at your own risk."

Chorev thus left for Tel Aviv from the Harel camp near Jerusalem on May 17, rejoiced with his family, and was about to return to his post when the Arab Legion entrenched itself at Latrun, cutting off the road again. Chorev decided to infiltrate back to Jerusalem regardless, but when he reached a kibbutz just west of the Latrun barrier, an Israeli officer advised him: "Wait a couple of days and you'll be able to use the highway straight through to Jerusalem."

"But the Arab Legion controls the road," Chorev pointed out.

"It won't for long. We're planning to attack Latrun."

Chorev waited. When the wounded and dead started arriving, he knew the assault—the first one—had failed. Mickey Marcus then came through and, grasping Chorev around the shoulders, grinned wanly.

"Amos, don't worry. We'll attack again. We've got to get you to Jerusalem," he quipped.

"Well, if you don't," Chorev replied, "I think I know of a way of getting myself there, and maybe everyone else, too."

"What do you mean?"

"After all the time I spent in the Jerusalem area I'm familiar with almost every stone. We control Beit Jiz and Beit Susin now, don't we?"

"Yes."

Chorev drew a map on a sheet of paper then and there, showing how the Israelis already possessed part of an alternative route to Jerusalem, a dirt path that wound southward from the main road near Deir Muchsen and then ran parallel with the road eastward to Beit Susin. He penciled in an extension of this path to a point three miles to the east, on the north-south road leading to Hartuv. The point was just south of Bab el-Wad and the Tel Aviv–Jerusalem highway.

"Our Harel troops are positioned on the Hartuv road," said Chorev. "That means if we can connect Beit Susin with that road—a distance of only three miles—we'll be able to use the sector of the Jerusalem road starting at Bab el-Wad."

Marcus studied the crude map for a moment, then said carefully: "It's worth looking into."

Leaving the project in suspension, he departed to prepare for the second attack on Latrun.

On May 31 (the day after this attack had failed), Chorev, accompanied by Marcus, Shamir, and Herzog, drove to Beit Susin to investigate the feasibility of building a new road that would bypass Latrun to the south.

They climbed out of their jeep at the eastern edge of the village, and Chorev ordered some guards to provide machine-gun cover while he led the group down a precarious slope to a creek flanked by several date palms. A barely discernible footpath from the opposite bank of the stream threaded upward between uneven columns of gnarled fig trees to vanish into the rocky brown hills.

"You wait here and I'll take a look and see where it leads," Chorev said. "The machine guns will cover me."

He clambered up a stony incline and disappeared over the other side while his three companions waited expectantly. A few minutes later, he reappeared somewhat breathless and reported: "The terrain is pretty rough for about a mile, I'd say. But then it dips into a wadi below Latrun. The going would be fairly easy from there to the Hartuv road."

"But can we forge a path for vehicles through these hills?" Marcus asked.

"I think we can."

As the group sauntered back to Beit Susin discussing the situation, Marcus slapped Chorev on the back and said: "Okay, Amos, get yourself a couple of boys and try to make it across those hills in a jeep. If you get through in one piece, maybe we all can."

A few hours later, at dusk, Chorev and two other Palmach soldiers started on the test trek, bulldozing through bushes, skidding across slabs of rock, lurching upward in a desperate zigzag on wheels that spun hot with friction and often slipped to within inches of oblivion. Finally, the battered, steaming vehicle came to a halt at the crest of the last height, and Chorev, leaning against a fender, removed his helmet, mopped his perspiring brow with his sleeve, and gazed at the starlit wadi that stretched out from the base of the 400-foot eastern slope.

"The jeep will never make it down this hill," one of his men commented as he collapsed exhausted on the hard earth.

"Yes it will," Chorev rejoined. "It's carried us most of the way. Now it's our turn to carry it."

And the three men, groaning and cursing, their fingers bleeding and numb, edged down the precipitous slope inch by inch with the jeep in tow until they reached the bottom. Then they climbed in and bumped through the wadi to an Israeli post near the Hartuv road, arriving some three hours after they had started up the first hill.

"My God," exclaimed a delighted company commander in greeting. "This is a miracle!"

Chorev immediately radioed Marcus the good news.

"Great! We'll give it top priority," the American said jubilantly.

After a short rest, Chorev hurried back on foot to Beit Susin and then to Hulda where Marcus was waiting for him. They charted his course on a large topographical map.

"You'd better get some sleep," Marcus suggested after studying the map. "Tomorrow night you're going to lead a convoy of jeeps loaded with supplies over those hills."

He then radioed GHQ: "Give Amos a few guns and mortars for Jerusalem."

The next night, ten jeeps piled high with military supplies left Hulda, with Chorev in the first vehicle. All but one succeeded in reaching Jerusalem.

In the morning, Marcus met with Shamir, Laskov, Chorev, and other commanders at Hulda and proposed that a road be built immediately through the hills.

"Until it is completed," he said, "we can send a small but continuous stream of supplies to Jerusalem, using jeeps and human porters to carry the stuff as far as the wadi, where trucks can meet them. But only a real road will break the blockade of Jerusalem completely and persuade the United Nations that the city cannot remain isolated if a truce is ordered on the basis of the territorial status quo."

"But is it possible to build a road through such rough terrain in so short a time?" one officer asked.

"We made it across the Red Sea, didn't we?" Marcus retorted.

"It still sounds fantastic, building a road right under the barrels of enemy guns."

"We'll just have to keep them from finding out what's going on."

That night, an endless procession of mules, jeeps, and oxcarts began hauling tons of food and equipment from Beit Susin to the crest of the hill overlooking the wadi. There, convoy after convoy was met by some 200 members of the Jerusalem Home Guard (men in their forties and fifties), who took over from the animals and machines, each carrying a 45-pound burden on his back while clinging to the shirttails of the man in front of him as he moved precariously down the hazardous slope. Hardly had the porters staggered into the wadi, where trucks were waiting to carry the material to the New City, when they returned for a second load.

Spurring the bearers on as they fought their way up and down the hill was the scratch of chisels, the crack of wooden mallets on rock, and the scrape of shovels scooping up the limestone gravel. Histadrut—the Israeli Labor Federation—had appealed for an army of laborers to help in the massive construction job, and within hours hundreds of middle-aged men and women with reddish dust clinging to their sweaty, often wrinkled faces, were groaning and puffing as they clumsily wielded their tools.

After five nights of punishing work, tractors ground wire netting into

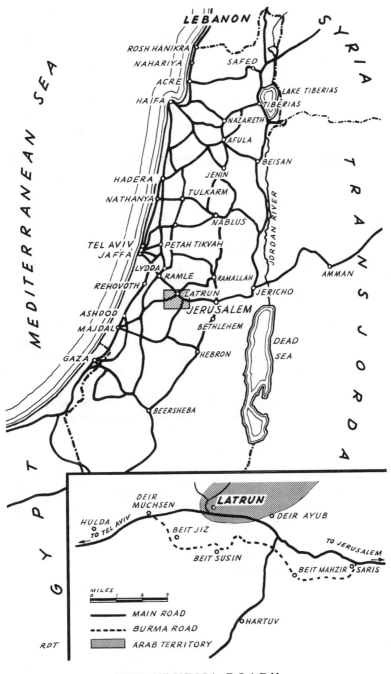

MEDITERRANEAN SEA

LEBANON

SYRIA

TRANSJORDA

ROSH HANIKRA
NAHARIYA
SAFED
ACRE
HAIFA
LAKE TIBERIAS
TIBERIAS
NAZARETH
AFULA
BEISAN
HADERA
JENIN
NATHANYA
TULKARM
NABLUS
TEL AVIV
JAFFA
PETAH TIKVAH
LYDDA
RAMLE
RAMALLAH
AMMAN
REHOVOTH
LATRUN
JERICHO
JERUSALEM
ASHDOD
MAJDAL
BETHLEHEM
DEAD SEA
GAZA
HEBRON
JORDAN RIVER
BEERSHEBA

EGYPT

DEIR MUCHSEN
LATRUN
HULDA
TO TEL AVIV
DEIR AYUB
BEIT JIZ
BEIT SUSIN
TO JERUSALEM
BEIT MAHZIR SARIS

MILES
0 1 2 3

——— MAIN ROAD
- - - BURMA ROAD
░░░ ARAB TERRITORY

HARTUV

RDT

THE "BURMA ROAD"

the section of the new roadbed, which wound unevenly round the perilous height leading to the wadi; the time had come to test the feasibility of the road. A volunteer jeep driver waited expectantly at the precipice, staring nervously into the yawning valley 400 feet below. Behind him, in a taxi, sat a second driver.

The jeep driver, holding a handkerchief to his face, inched down the narrow, serpentine road, slipping, skidding, pitching. Every few moments he stopped to let the smothering dust settle so that he could see ahead. With a final bounce, the jeep ground into the soft earth of the wadi. The man in the taxi had a more difficult time and nearly plunged over the cliff, but after a wild descent, he, too, bumped to safety.

The link to Jerusalem—the Burma Road, as it was called—had been forged.

The danger, however, that the Arabs might discover the project and destroy it, or at least hold up work with artillery and possibly infantry attacks, persisted, particularly during the third night of work when Arab Legion guns started a concentrated barrage in the area.

"They probably don't know exactly what we're doing," Marcus speculated to some officers as he searched for damage in the construction zone during a pause in the shelling. "But they know we're up to something."

The Israelis did their best to conceal what. Prowling mobile units and entrenched ambush patrols covered every approach point, preventing curious enemy scouts from penetrating the intricate screen. But not even the most tightly meshed screen could keep the Arabs completely in the dark.

Lieutenant Mahmoud al-Rousan paused on a hillside as he conducted Glubb Pasha on a tour of the area where the second battle of Latrun had been fought. Pointing southward to some naked, scrub-patched hills, he said: "They're building a road behind those hills over there. And our scouts say it's almost completed."

"It's hard to believe," said Glubb, peering into the distance. "But if it's true, what do you think we should do?"

"We need a third infantry regiment to take over those hills overlooking the road. The two regiments now based in the Latrun area are too thinly spread out to do it."

Fully recognizing the importance of keeping the New City besieged, Glubb wished he could agree to Rousan's suggestion. But where was he to get the troops? While suffering 20 per cent casualties, the Legion was spread over a 70-mile front. And it had already been demoralized by an order from the British government received on May 30, a few hours before the second Israeli attack on Latrun, that all British army seconded officers were to leave their commands immediately. (Under pressure from the United Nations and his own Parliament, Bevin had agreed to this.)

Glubb had shuddered upon hearing the news. The Legion had been expanded from a *gendarmerie* into a military force only in 1940, and the most senior Jordanian officer had, therefore, only eight years of genuine military service. Without British officers, the army might well collapse. To add to his worry, even his own position was in question. The British Legation had informed him that while he was not a regular army officer himself, under the Foreign Enlistments Act he might be subject to a charge of having taken service, "without His Majesty's cognizance," with a foreign power engaged in war. Glubb's furious reply had been that if His Majesty had no cognizance of his presence in Jordan, His Majesty must be suffering from loss of memory.

Actually, he had managed so far to evade the expulsion order for his officers—with the connivance of some Foreign Office supporters.

On the day that Bevin was to tell Parliament that not a single regular British soldier was still in Palestine, Glubb had sent all of his officers across Allenby Bridge into Transjordan. On receiving word that Bevin had completed his speech, he ordered the men back to their posts.[3] Thus, no one could say that the Foreign Secretary had lied if what happened to the officers was investigated. But Glubb knew he was treading on uncertain ground and if renewed pressure were exerted on Bevin, the officers might have to be expelled again—without notice. He certainly couldn't take the chance at this point of spreading his lines thinner than they already were, and he told Rousan so.

"But, sir," Rousan argued, "if the Jews complete the road, they'll break the siege. Then our control of Latrun will be almost meaningless."

"I can't believe they'll succeed."

Shortly afterward, Mickey Marcus bounced down the final slope of the Burma Road in the second of three jeeps, each of which carried the parts of a 4-inch mortar, bound for Jerusalem. Finally, after many requests, Yadin had come through with the weapons, and Marcus, eager to see the faces of the besieged Jerusalemites when they saw the powerful guns, insisted on accompanying the convoy despite the admonitions of his driver, Gaby Anakov, who told him bluntly: "The road isn't safe enough yet for commanders."

Marcus shrugged and joked each time Gaby negotiated a precarious turn or screeched uncertainly along the edge of a precipice. Within an hour, the three vehicles halted outside Etzioni Brigade headquarters in the center of Jerusalem, to be surrounded by hysterical crowds materializing from every nearby street. Marcus leaped out of his jeep just in time to avoid the smothering embrace of hundreds of grateful people, people who had no idea that an American colonel was helping them to hold fast against the invader. Marcus stood musing in the midst of the joyous tumult . . .

"You see, colonel," the young lieutenant from texas had said on the guided tour of Dachau after World War II, "here's where they piled up the bodies."

Marcus gazed into the pit of skeletons.

"And here is where they gassed them."

Chaim — Rachel — Miriam — Joseph — Abraham — names scratched on the concrete wall . . .

"And this is the oven."

"What does that sign over it say?"

"Please wash your hands after your work; cleanliness is next to godliness!" . . .

In Etzioni headquarters, Marcus met with David Shaltiel, who greeted him resplendent in an immaculate, brass-buttoned uniform.

"This is Mordechai Kaufmann," Shaltiel said rather sourly, introducing him to a young man also immaculately dressed.

Marcus was surprised to be welcomed so regally, particularly since "Kaufmann" (the original name of Mordechai Raanan) was the Irgun commander in Jerusalem, basically trained as a "terrorist" rather than as a military man. Other than Shaltiel himself, Marcus had, in fact, never seen a spit-and-polish Israeli soldier.

Raanan looked self-conscious as he shook hands with "Stone." Two days before, Shaltiel had called him into his office and told him that Marcus would soon be coming and that he wanted to meet all the commanders in Jerusalem.

"Haven't you got a neat uniform?" Shaltiel had asked, contemptuously surveying the dirty, torn khaki Raanan was wearing.

"What for?"

"Stone is an American colonel. He will expect to see an army. You must look like a military commander."

"But I have no other uniform."

"Don't worry, you will have."

Shaltiel called in an aide and barked: "You know that tailor on Ben Yehuda Street? Find him and tell him to go to Kaufmann's headquarters immediately!"

"His shop is closed," Raanan exclaimed.

"He'll open it!"

"But his sewing machines are electrically operated and there is no electricity in the city."

"I'll supply him with a special generator."

A few hours later, the tailor arrived at Irgun headquarters in the midst of an artillery barrage, and took the commander's measurements. The next morning he returned with a perfectly fitting uniform.

"Sorry about the leather buttons," the tailor had apologized. "I couldn't get hold of any brass ones."

At the meeting, Marcus discussed possible action in Jerusalem with Shaltiel and Raanan and found himself caught up in a violent argument. Indicating Mount Scopus on a huge wall map, Raanan advocated its immediate capture.

"Once we capture it, we'll have cut off the Arab Legion's supply line across Allenby Bridge and it will have to withdraw from the Tel Aviv–Jerusalem road."

"Nonsense," shouted Shaltiel. "Our job is to reopen the road to Tel Aviv directly. That's what we must concentrate on."

Finally, Marcus thanked the two men for their views and departed. Then Raanan, as he followed, ripped off his new, elegantly cut jacket so that he could be as comfortable as Marcus—who was wearing rolled-up shorts and socks, an open shirt, and sandals.[4]

Despite the crack in the siege of Jerusalem, Marcus continued to fear that the Arab Legion would attack the still uncompleted road in an effort to repair the breach. And his fear was reinforced by the belief that a full Transjordanian brigade (three regiments) was operating in the area; in fact, only two regiments were based there. He was further concerned that the Legion might strike at Kibbutz Maale Hahamisha east of the junction of the main highway and the Burma Road, and thereby nullify the value of the new artery.

As he sunbathed on the grass in Hulda, he decided that the Israelis would have to attack the Latrun area again. The primary objective would still be to open the Tel Aviv–Jerusalem road, but this time the success of the attack would not be measured solely by this criterion. Even if the Israelis failed to clear the main road, the attack would serve to keep the Legionnaires too busy and off balance—at least until a truce, now imminent, took effect—to launch an assault of their own on the new road or on Maale Hahamisha.

With the 7th Brigade still suffering from the heavy blows it had sustained in the first two attacks, Marcus now planned to use two Palmach brigades—Yiftach and Harel—for the main thrusts. He had reservations about this plan, for he knew the commanders of these Palmach units were totally opposed to direct attacks on such strongholds as Latrun. And his experience with Givati's Prulov in the second attack demonstrated what could happen when independent-minded commanders were ordered into battles they regarded as ill advised. However, no other adequate forces were available; in any case, the Palmach leaders would have to learn to take orders whether they liked it or not.

At a meeting of the High Command, Marcus won support of a plan for his main forces to strike in the east this time and envelop Latrun from the rear. After a series of diversionary attacks from both west and east, a battalion each from the Harel and Yiftach Brigades, based near Bab el-Wad, would storm Gun Hill overlooking Deir Ayub, which Prulov had only halfheartedly assaulted in the second battle of Latrun. The 7th Brigade would provide artillery support and protect the Burma Road. Simultaneously, a Yiftach unit would encircle an Arab Legion garrison that had captured Radar Hill, which dominated Maale Hahamisha.

Thus, even if the police fortress could not be taken in this attack, the forces on Gun Hill—the Latrun stronghold nearest the Burma Road and the most likely jump-off point for an infantry drive on it—would be neutralized. And so would the forces on Radar Hill east of the new route.

But Marcus's reservations about the Palmach attitude were again to prove well founded as obstacle after obstacle delayed the start of the assault, named Operation Yoram after one of King David's army commanders. Marcus knew that more than logistics were responsible for the slow pace. Four precious days went by after the attack plan had been drawn up. In three more days, Marcus now learned, a cease-fire would take place.

In the fading glow of dusk on June 8, Marcus headed in a jeep over the Burma Road toward central front headquarters near Abu Ghosh, a tiny stone village inhabited by friendly Arabs. He would brook no further postponement, and he would make this clear to Yigal Allon, the Palmach commander-in-chief who personally led the Yiftach Brigade.

As Marcus hoisted a canteenful of *arak* to his lips, he thought how great a commander Allon would be if only he could learn not to question orders. He was aggressive, imaginative, utterly devoted to his men, like the other Palmach leaders. Few armies, in fact, would match the Palmach man for man if only it would learn greater discipline and combine its native knowledge with formal training. In any event, he had already decided to recommend to Ben-Gurion and Yadin that Allon be appointed the commander in Jerusalem in place of Shaltiel, who would become military governor of the city, a civilian position.

*

"I know your men are tired, Yigal, but so are the enemy. You have one mission, only one: Latrun. And don't forget it!" Marcus pounded his fist into his palm for emphasis as he and Allon sat on a stone fence marking the edge of the camp outside Abu Ghosh.

"Mickey, it's unnecessary to hit Latrun," Allon persisted. "Look what happened in the last two attacks. Let's bypass Latrun and take Ramallah, and from there we can surround the Old City. Once isolated from its supply lines, Latrun will fall automatically."

Marcus looked at Allon with fiery brown eyes devoid of their usual good humor.

"The decision has been made, Yigal," he said. "You are a soldier. Your job is to fight. You will attack in four hours!"

THIS ORDER WAS REMINISCENT OF ANOTHER ISSUED TO ALLON IN 1941 when he was about to lead a Palmach spearhead into Axis-controlled Syria to clear the way for an Australian invasion. The Australian commander had demanded that he make a head-on attack on an enemy pillbox just over the frontier despite Allon's objections. Allon reluctantly obeyed—and his troops were forced to retreat after a disastrous battle.[5]

"All right," he now answered Marcus, "you're the boss."

"There it is! The lone cypress! Just as the scouts said!"

As he whispered eagerly to a fellow officer, Isachar Shadmi, commander of the Harel 5th Battalion, noted that he had reached this landmark right on time, shortly before 3 A.M. At 2 A.M., three companies of his battalion had jumped off from a point just south of the Tel Aviv–Jerusalem road and were now moving northwest toward Yalu Ridge, which was believed to be only lightly defended. After capturing this height, the Yiftach 3rd Battalion under Moshe Kelman would march through and attack the main objective about a mile further to the northwest—powerfully fortified Gun Hill.

The tree marked the place where the force was to turn due north along a shallow wadi leading to Yalu Ridge. In the inky darkness, the battalion officers surveyed the ground nearby.

"Here's the wadi," one whispered.

The troops then resumed their advance, and within an hour were fighting their way up a steep hill, advancing foot by foot against bitter resistance.

Finally, the Israelis captured part of the hill, overrunning several enemy positions. They occupied an artillery observation post and then made use of a trick (according to Arab Legion officers) that had often proved profitable in the past. An Israeli intelligence officer, knowing the names of the various Legion commanders, radioed Lieutenant Mustafa Khasawneh, who commanded the artillery battery.

"Mustafa," the Israeli said in Arabic, "this is Mahmoud al-Rousan. The enemy has captured the police fortress. Fire on it!"

Lieutenant Rousan, at regimental headquarters in Imwas, happened to tune in to the same radio frequency at that moment to give genuine orders to the artillery commander and overheard the false ones being issued in his name.

"Mustafa, don't believe him!" he cried. "It's the Jews trying to trick you. *I* am Mahmoud al-Rousan. And the police fortress is still in our hands."

After a pause, the artillery commander asked: "But how do I know who is lying? Both of you sound like Mahmoud al-Rousan!"

Rousan then shouted: "I am Abu Ziad Rousan."

Khasawneh then knew that the second speaker was indeed Rousan, for he had said: "I am the father of Ziad." The Jews were not likely to have known the name of Rousan's son.

So Khasawneh concentrated his fire on Israeli positions while Rousan desperately formed a makeshift company to launch a counterattack on the Israelis. At about 4 A.M., while a Moslem priest called out his dawn greeting from the tower of the village mosque: "God is great! God is great!" the troops, repeating the words in unison, drove off spiritedly in armored cars toward Gun Hill to repel the enemy attack there.

Shadmi's men had followed the wrong wadi at the cypress tree, bypassed their objective, Yalu Ridge, and unwittingly assaulted Gun Hill beyond it instead—still thinking they were on Yalu Ridge.

At about the time the Legion armored column started eastward toward Gun Hill, Moshe Kelman, whose 3rd Yiftach Battalion was gathered south of the Tel Aviv–Jerusalem road, finally received the signal for which he had been waiting impatiently. Shadmi radioed that his troops had conquered about two-thirds of "Yalu Ridge," though Legion defenders were still holding out in the western trenches. Kelman's force could now advance over the height and smash toward Gun Hill.

Kelman led three companies northward to a point east of Yalu Ridge and then turned west to face it. As he halted his men, he was puzzled. The hill was quiet, though Shadmi had reported that fighting was still in progress on one side. At the same time, tracers looped through the sky in the direction of Gun Hill and explosions seemed to echo from there although he had not begun his assault on it yet. He would try to figure it out later; his job now was to get to the top of Yalu Ridge and then turn north for the assault on Gun Hill.

Leading a support company loaded down with heavy equipment to the top of the ridge, he concluded that Shadmi must have subdued the whole hill. That would certainly make it easier for him. He could now set up his mortars and machine guns at the top—pointed toward Gun Hill—without grave danger of harassment. He looked back. His men, groaning under their loads, were walking in rather too close a formation to suit him. Well, with the hill in friendly hands, the danger wasn't too great. About 20 yards from the peak, he stopped, cupped his hands, and called out the password: *"Aportzim kadima!"* ("Those who break in, forward!").

A grenade sailed through the air and landed near him.

"Down!" he yelled to his men, and the grenade exploded harmlessly.

Then he shouted out: "What the hell's going on up there? You'll kill us if you don't watch out!"

Several more grenades exploded nearby, wounding some of his men. Then shells began to whistle over their heads, hitting too far in the rear, however, to cause much damage.

Kelman was stunned. Who the hell was up there in the shadows trying to wipe him out? He called Yiftach Brigade headquarters on his walkie-talkie and bellowed to Mulah Cohen, Allon's deputy: "What's going on? We're under fire from the top of the ridge."

"I haven't the foggiest idea," Cohen replied.

Kelman then turned to the 5th Battalion's wavelength and heard the commander of the lost force report to his headquarters that he had taken heavy casualties and that he wasn't sure where he was.

"Now we're being attacked by armor," he was shouting. "We must retreat!"

Kelman switched back to Cohen, who had also heard the report. "Go with your men and help them," Cohen ordered. "They must have attacked Gun Hill by mistake."

"How can I?" Kelman retorted, while grenades continued to explode all around him. "They're a mile away and it's almost daylight. We'd be slaughtered. In fact, we're being slaughtered right now . . . I can't conquer my hill!"

By dawn, the survivors of the two battalions—about half of the Harel force had been killed—straggled southward across the main road. At least, this time, no dead or wounded were left behind. All soldiers were connected to each other by rope so that casualties could be pulled to the rear. (In the first two attacks, Palestinian irregulars had shot all the abandoned wounded, stripped the dead of equipment and clothes, and left the bodies to be devoured by jackals and vultures.)

HAVE all guard units been put on special alert?" asked Mickey Marcus, just returned from Jerusalem headquarters to central front headquarters near Abu Ghosh.

Yigal Allon, his face gray with fatigue, said: "Yes, there's nothing to worry about."

Marcus glanced at his watch. It was about 1 A.M., June 11.

"Well, I'm going to bed," Marcus said. "I'm beat."

The American had had an active day, and now he could rest. The long-negotiated truce was fixed for 10 A.M., just a few hours away, and it appeared that fighting would be over for its duration. Since the Arabs might make a last-minute effort to improve their positions before the deadline, he had ordered a special alert in the command area, but he guessed they had already exhausted themselves—just as his own men had.

Little more than 12 hours before, an Arab Legion unit, following up its third victory at Latrun, had attacked the settlement of Gezer near the main Israeli regional base of Hulda. After a fierce battle, it succeeded in breaking in and capturing the surviving defenders. Marcus immediately dispatched a Yiftach unit to counterattack and toward evening it recaptured the settlement, now reduced to cinders.

Despite this ultimate hard-won victory, Marcus felt that his exhausted troops had reached the limits of endurance and he stalled off GHQ pleas for a new Israeli attack on Latrun. Upon learning that Gezer had been recaptured, Marcus and his commanders, in a surge of relief and good cheer, had gathered late in the afternoon of June 10 round a campfire to consume their first real meal in weeks. Ingenious aides had managed to forage from the countryside a lamb, a variety of fruit, *arak,* and even black caviar—found in the kitchen of Jerusalem's King David Hotel. As the impromptu banquet was ending, Alex Broida (Marcus's aide) approached, his slender, distinguished face reflecting his pique at not having been invited, and reminded Marcus, happily groggy with *arak,* that he was expected in Jerusalem shortly.

Now, several hours later, on their return to central front headquarters, they could enjoy the luxury of a good sleep for the first time in days. It seemed a fitting way to usher in the truce. And what more fitting place was there than atop the hill where the Holy Ark of the Covenant, containing the tablets dictated to Moses on Mount Sinai, was brought in 1100 B.C. after being recovered from the Philistines?

Marcus and his commanders were billeted in the monks' quarters of the abandoned Monastère Notre Dame de la Nouvelle Alliance, built on the spot where more than 2,000 years ago an ancient synagogue marked the holy place. Broida, still disturbed by his omission from the list for the feast, was further agitated when he learned he was not to share a room with the commander he revered, but had been assigned to the room next door. Marcus was to stay with Mulah Cohen, Allon's deputy.

As they entered their respective quarters, Marcus grinned at Broida. "See you in the morning," he said cheerfully . . .

Eighteen-year-old Eliezer Linski, a one-year veteran of the Palmach, glanced at his watch; only 20 more minutes to go.

It was 3:40 A.M. At 4 A.M., his hour on guard would be up. Another man would replace him and he could go back to sleep. He wouldn't get much more sleep, for he would be awakened early to take part in the squad leaders' course that was being conducted in the monastery area. But every minute he could squeeze in somehow seemed important. Besides, guard duty that night was more harrowing than usual, and his post, facing west, was one of the most dangerous since it crowned a gentle terraced slope on which local Arabs cultivated wheat. It would be far easier for Arabs to attack there than to climb the steep grades isolating the camp on the other three sides.

As Linsky stood with his Czech rifle slung over his shoulder in the humid, moonless night, he wondered whether the cease-fire due to start in a few hours would permit him to take some leave with his family in the village of Rishpon near Tel Aviv.

He looked at his watch again. Only 15 minutes to go. Perhaps it would be quiet that night after all.

Suddenly (according to Linski's later testimony) he heard the sound of stones rolling about 30 yards away. Nervously, he removed his rifle from his shoulder, advanced about five yards, and cried:

"Mi sham?" "Who is there?"

He waited hopefully for the password, *"Haderech shelanu"* ("The road is ours"), but no reply came. He recalled the verbal orders that had been given all Palmach guards. If someone did not answer the first challenge, the guard was to fire a shot in the air. If the person continued to advance, the guard was to act according to circumstances. In peacetime, he would try to avoid shooting at the trespasser regardless. At a time of alert, he was normally to fire.

As Linski waited anxiously for an answer, he saw a figure in a white garment standing on the low, broken wall that surrounded the monastery area.

Once more, the guard shouted: "Who is there?"

When again he received no reply, he fired a shot into the air, and the figure jumped from the wall and ran toward the monastery, mumbling incoherently in what sounded to Linski like English; the guard had learned some English in elementary school, but his knowledge of the language was very poor. What Israeli in the camp would be speaking English, he wondered in alarm. He did not know of any American or Englishman there, but his battalion had often fought Arab Legion forces led by British officers and had even captured some. The intruder might be an Arab masquerading as a Briton. Perhaps a saboteur!

Linski, sweating profusely, yelled: "Halt or I'll shoot!"

But when the figure went on running, the young guard maintained in his testimony, "I fired a nondirect shot from the hip, an instinctive shot, a shot that was not aimed by sight with the intention of hitting, but only of stopping."

At the same moment, Linski testified, "they fired from the other position also. The figure ran a few meters and fell. I shouted to the other position to stop firing and they stopped."

Linski ran to the figure sprawled on the ground and found a man clad only in shorts and undershirt, wrapped in a white blanket. He turned his pocket flashlight onto the face. The man looked dead. Linski then felt his pulse and was sure that he was. Another guard from a position about 20 yards to the north of Linski's post, the position from where Linski testified he had heard firing, then joined him.

"Go get Menachem!" Linski exclaimed (referring to Menachem Kupinski, who was in charge of the guards).

Kupinski, who had been sleeping in his clothes and boots with a weapon at his side, was awakened by the shout: "There's an Arab in the camp and he's probably dead!"

Dashing to the scene, he sent his men away and examined the body with his flashlight. From the clothes and blanket he doubted that the victim was an Arab. Soon the camp commanders were surrounding the body.

Colonel Michael David Marcus lay with a bullet hole in his chest, one of the last fighters for Israel to die before the truce . . .

Alex Broida had been turning restlessly in bed unable to sleep when, about the time of the killing, he heard several shots nearby—he did not remember afterwards how many—with a pause of a few seconds between them. Some minutes later, he heard Mulah Cohen's voice in the garden and then someone replying: ". . . He answered in English."

Broida, feeling instinctively that something had happened to Marcus, went down to the garden and asked a soldier if anything was wrong.

"Nothing as far as I know," the soldier replied.

Broida, though still uneasy, went back upstairs and finally fell into a fitful sleep. At 5 A.M., he was awakened by Yosef Tabenkin, the commander of the Harel Brigade's 4th battalion.

"Alex, get up! Yigal wants to speak to you."

Broida jumped out of bed and into the corridor, where he met Yigal Allon. He could tell what had happened from Allon's eyes before the Palmach commander spoke.

Broida was silent. They hadn't even bothered to tell him until more than an hour after it happened . . .

Later that morning, Dr. Issachar of the Palmach wrote in a deposition:

At 0400 on June 11, I was called to the wounded man Stone [Marcus] who was brought to Abu Ghosh. I examined his wounds and declared that the wounds he suffered caused his immediate death. As far as could be seen, he was wounded by a *Sten* bullet . . . [The bullet was apparently never found.]

Eliezer Linski testified that he had fired a Czech rifle.

Awakened at his home when a radio message from Allon arrived, Ben-Gurion, in his pajamas, stood rigid with shock as he read the news of Marcus's death. Of all the men to die! A man of such heart . . . and the one real military expert in Israel. As he sat on his bed, his despair turned swiftly to bitterness and suspicion. The message said Marcus had been killed accidently by a guard. That certainly seemed odd—and just when he had been appointed commander of the Jerusalem front. He began to wonder just how far some Palmach men would go to make sure the Palmach would determine strategy.

Later that day, he summoned Yaacov S. Shapiro—an old lawyer friend whom he intended to appoint Attorney General in the Israeli Ministry of Justice—to his office.

"Yaacov," he said, "I want all the facts in the Marcus case. I want you to make a thorough investigation and then report to me."

Shapiro agreed and immediately set out to work. However, he later wrote in his report:

I didn't find it necessary to visit the Abu Ghosh monastery since I am well acquainted with the monastery and the surrounding area from past visits. . . . The sketch prepared for me . . . gave me a good idea of the area and the surroundings.

Shapiro also considered it unnecessary to question personally most of the witnesses, requesting only signed statements. He did not attempt to square Dr. Issachar's declaration that "as far as can be seen" Marcus was killed by a Sten bullet with Linski's testimony that he fired a Czech rifle; nor did he even refer in his summary to this discrepancy. The exit hole left by a 9-caliber Sten bullet is usually considerably larger than that left by a 7.92-caliber Czech rifle bullet, though the size of the aperture may be influenced by the proximity of the gun (Linski was about 10 yards from Marcus when he fired), or by obstacles the projectile strikes. Ignored also was a statement by the doctor that there were "two surface wounds" on Marcus's right arm. What might have caused these wounds?

These unanswered questions are related to still another omission in Shapiro's report: reference to Linski's testimony that he had heard other shots fired almost simultaneously with his own, and to Broida's statement that he, too, heard a series of shots.

Significantly, Linski stated: "I think that the man fell from my shot, but I heard that others think that he might have fallen from shots from the other post."

Moreover, the guard at the other post, who carried a Sten gun, was never questioned, at least for the record, or even identified in the report—possibly because the fatal bullet appeared to have entered Marcus's body from the side nearest Linski.

But perhaps the chief mystery was what Marcus was doing at all outside the perimeter of the camp, particularly in the most dangerous zone. Having had a good deal of liquor before going to bed, he might have gotten lost trying to find the latrine, which was located to the west but within the camp itself. And "the general assumption," Shapiro wrote in his report,

> . . . is that he went . . . to attend to his needs. But if this assumption is correct, a few problems arise: The deceased was well acquainted with the camp. He was there two days a week, and for two days before the incident. He walked around there quite often (he even took sun baths). It is difficult to believe that he lost his way. . . . The deceased knew that the camp was on the alert and the guards had been told to keep especially on their toes. As an experienced soldier, he certainly knew of the danger entailed by leaving the camp at such an hour, beyond the border of the camp and a guard post. He was acquainted with the Palmach soldier and he undoubtedly knew that it is difficult to identify oneself in English to a Palmach guard.

At any rate, Shapiro concluded flatly that "Commander Marcus was killed by a shot fired upon him by Private Eliezer Linski" in the line of duty.

No evidence came to light that anyone might have deliberately tried to kill Marcus, who was well liked even by those who disagreed with his tactics and might have resented the appointment of an "outsider" to the highest field command. Eliezer Linski, as he himself conceded, may well have fired the fatal bullet. But though the investigation report, kept secret for 20 years, expressed this conclusion unreservedly, no real attempt was ever made to prove it.[6]

12

Lull in the Storm

$\mathbf{A}$ TRUCE came into effect on June 11, crowning the sluggish United Nations peacemaking effort that had begun almost immediately after the Arabs invaded Palestine. On May 15, the day of the invasion, Arab delegates argued that their countries had entered Palestine because the Palestine Arabs had invited them to restore order in the wake of the British withdrawal. But the White House and the State Department both pressed for an immediate cease-fire since continued fighting might force the United States to land marines—if the Jews were about to be massacred, as Marshall had long feared, or if the Russians unilaterally sent troops into the area.

Ironically, American diplomats who had opposed the creation of Israel for fear of a Middle East explosion now supported, at least temporarily, policies favorable to the new-born state because of this same fear.

Thus, on May 17, American Ambassador Austin demanded that the Security Council order a prompt truce and apply sanctions against belligerents who failed to comply. But British Ambassador Sir Alexander Cadogan, after learning that the Arabs were advancing on all fronts, stalled off such moves, expressing doubt, in line with Bevin's aims, that the Arabs had broken the peace or committed an act of aggression as the Americans charged. What he failed to say was that it was not yet time to rescue the Jews; the Jews would first have to realize that only Britain could save them from catastrophe, and that she would be glad to do so in return for agreement on a new partition plan under which the Negev, or at least part of it, would go to the Arabs.

Finally, Cadogan, though privately revealing to trusted friends his misgivings about this effort to "blackmail" Israel, skillfully maneuvered a defeat of the American proposal.

With Washington's fear that American troops would have to intervene rising rapidly, Lewis Douglas, Ambassador to Britain, met with Bevin in London on May 22 and urged him to support a cease-fire order. The Foreign Secretary was noncommittal, demanding that Israel accept conditions he knew she would not or could not fulfill.

The State Department then recommended in a top secret memorandum to President Truman that "if the Security Council is unable to take effective action to bring about a cease-fire or to impose a general arms embargo, the United States will inform the Security Council that we shall resume our freedom of action with respect to the licensing of arms shipments."[1]

Truman readily agreed to this suggestion, which represented a thinly veiled warning to Britain that unless she supported a truce and stopped sending arms to the Arab States, the United States would dispatch arms to Israel. British diplomatic blood pressure soared. The large-scale arming of Israel could sink the Bevin plan for forcing the Jews to accept a territorial compromise.

At any rate, Cadogan the same day (May 29) proposed a modified resolution that referred only indirectly to the possible imposition of sanctions, and simply called for a cease-fire to remain effective for a month. Israel immediately accepted this appeal which, however, was apparently intended only to take the heat off Britain, since Cadogan, supported by Arab diplomats, stalled his own suggestion to death.

The British Ambassador coupled his delaying tactics with a proposal that a United Nations mediator for Palestine be appointed to negotiate peace on the spot. He supported for the job Count Folke Bernadotte, a member of the Swedish royal family and president of the Swedish Red Cross. Bernadotte had gained fame during World War II by saving thousands of Jewish and other prisoners from extermination in negotiations with Nazi SS chief Heinrich Himmler, though it is not clear whether he or Felix Kirsten, Himmler's personal physician and intimate adviser, deserved most of the credit.[2] In any event, Bernadotte's reputation for humanitarianism and his neutral nationality made him acceptable to all members of the Security Council, including the United States, which had suggested the appointment of a mediator even before the Arab invasion.

The British backed a man they felt they could trust—not necessarily because Bernadotte would make any "deal" with them, but because his personal convictions were consistent with theirs. Like the British, the Count, apparently unknown to most United Nations representatives at the time, had personally opposed the 1947 partition plan and supported the establishment of a unitary Arab State in which the Jews would have special rights. Thus, it would probably not be too difficult to persuade Bernadotte that pursuing British aims was the only realistic way of succeeding in his mission—especially since the British-supported Arabs were winning the war.

En route to the Middle East, Bernadotte met with British officials and learned what Britain wanted: a revised partition plan, with Transjordan getting the southern Negev, and possibly Haifa, and the Jews western Galilee as compensation. His amenability even led these officials to suggest that Transjordan should be given all of Jerusalem—though Bevin had previously been satisfied with the internationalization of that city.

Bernadotte, who had left Lake Success with a United Nations mandate simply to mediate a truce, began to see the possibility of broader service. He had, after all, always considered the 1947 partition plan a mistake. The artificial frontiers granted to Israel, and the solid Arab resistance to the creation of a Jewish State, had inevitably produced war, in his view. But if it was to late to establish a unitary Arab State, it was not too late to change the boundaries. And the British suggestions did seem reasonable. To test international reaction, he asked French Foreign Minister Georges Bidault whether France would be "willing to agree to Jerusalem being made an Arab center?"

Bidault replied in no uncertain terms: "The whole Christian world would join a new Crusade!"

But Bernadotte was not discouraged. If the United Nations partition plan had been a mistake, his duty, he felt, was not to compound the error by implementing the plan, but to correct the error by formulating a new plan. This was the only way to produce a permanent peace. He would make enemies on both sides, of course. The Jews would say he had no right to scuttle a United Nations–sponsored partition plan, and the Arabs would excoriate him for permitting the existence even of a smaller, less dangerous Israel. But this would only prove that he was, in fact, neutral, as indeed he was convinced he was.

When he landed in Transjordan, Brigadier Norman Lash of the Arab Legion met him at the airport and, noting his blue and white United Nations armband, remarked with a smile: "I am sorry to see, sir, that you are wearing an armband in the Israeli colors."

"Ah," Bernadotte replied, his long, aristocratic face alight with amusement, "but I do not wear my heart on my sleeve. My heart is of a strictly neutral tint."

*

In the last days of May, the British began to wonder if the time was not drawing near for the cease-fire they had been warding off. The Egyptians had won control of most of the Negev, so there was no need now to pressure Israel into giving up what she had already lost—though the presence of some troublesome settlements behind the Egyptian lines was still a problem. And since Abdullah controlled most of Arab Palestine and the Old City, including the Jewish Quarter, there was little reason for him to continue to fight much longer—especially with Britain, under international pressure, about to cut off ammunition supplies to the Arabs. The main problem now was not to fight Israel, which was resisting more fiercely and causing more casualties each day, but to ensure, with the help of Bernadotte if possible, that the Legion somehow entrenched itself in the Negev.

On May 29, therefore, Cadogan introduced another resolution in the Security Council, appealing to all parties for a four-week cease-fire. As a concession to the United States—and to public opinion at home—he also agreed that if the order were rejected or later repudiated, sanctions would be "considered." But few United Nations diplomats doubted that Britain would veto, if necessary, any effort to clamp sanctions on the Arabs.

Count Bernadotte began selling the cease-fire to the belligerents almost as soon as he arrived in the Middle East. He found the Israelis, who were about to launch offensives in the Triangle and at Latrun and were doing well in the north, less eager to buy an immediate truce than they had been earlier, and the Arabs, who were lagging behind, more eager.

The Israeli leaders rejected Bernadotte's demand that they restrict the immigration of men of military age during the truce so that Israel would not gain a military advantage. Foreign Minister Sharett argued angrily that "the cease-fire resolution forbids only their mobilization or training."

Also controversial was the mediator's plan to limit food and other relief supplies going to besieged "urban areas," meaning the New City, so that they would not be "substantially greater or less at the end of the truce than they were at the beginning."

"Your control measures," Sharett insisted, "cannot affect the supplies brought into Jerusalem via our new Burma Road, since it is being used before the truce."

The Arabs took another view. At his palace in Amman, King Abdullah addressed Bernadotte in the majestic, lavish manner that the mediator was to find refreshing compared to what he regarded as the cool and abrupt Israeli attitude:

"I should like to say first," the King emphasized, "that I, in common

with the governments of the other Arab States, am fully convinced of your
sincerity as mediator and your desire to reach a just settlement. Like myself,
you are of royal blood, and you must know what it means to govern a kingdom. I am always at your disposal as your counsellor, if you wish to talk
things over with me, but I would not force my help upon you. I will call you
brother, and I hope that you will place the same confidence in me as in your
brother. I regard your views as just and correct. But as to Jerusalem, I
cannot allow that a single drop of water or a single pound of provisions
should be taken into the city during the truce."

Bernadotte replied: "I humbly thank Your Majesty for the kind words
Your Majesty has addressed to me personally. Your Majesty must understand, however, that as head of a humanitarian organization like the Red
Cross, I cannot share Your Majesty's view that the starving Arabs and Jews
in Jerusalem should not receive any humanitarian aid. I cannot accept a
view that goes against my conscience, and I am convinced that Your
Majesty, being a great king, would not give me advice, the execution of
which would mean that I was acting against my conscience."

Abdullah was impressed. It would make little sense to argue over
details with a man who could be of help to him; in any case, he had
achieved his basic aims in the war and might lose more than he would
gain if the fighting continued. So he agreed to the feeding of Jerusalem and
then, just as the mediator was about to leave, said with a dry smile: "Transjordan, for its part, is prepared to accept the cease-fire."

Arab politicians and military commanders met in Amman to consider
the cease-fire order, and most of the politicians expressed reservations for
the record. For it was not easy to accept a truce when Arab radio commen-
tators and domestic newspaper headlines had proclaimed that the invaders
had all but wiped Israel off the map. Lebanese Prime Minister Riadh
es-Solh, one of the most peace-minded of the participants, urged: "We
must continue to fight, regardless of the consequences."

King Abdullah, however, showed no reluctance to express his true
opinion: "Why my good friend, es-Solh, you're a bright man. This is June
and the fruit season has passed and we won't be able to find even one
orange on the trees to throw at the Jews!"

The military commanders agreed that the ammunition shortage was
critical and that other military considerations as well dictated the need for
a cease-fire. The "United Arab Command" had disintegrated. The Egyptians, bogged down near Ashdod, badly needed reorganization and supplies. The Iraqis, influenced by Transjordan's pro-partition policy,
complained bitterly that they were operating along a "vast front in

different directions" and hesitated to venture beyond Jenin. Only the Syrians insisted on postponing a truce, hoping to continue their advance in the north. The Arabs voted for the cease-fire.

As for the Israelis, whose late offensives had not gone so well, Moshe Carmel expressed the prevailing view when he said of the truce: "It came to us as dew from Heaven."

TANYA LIEBKOVICH awakened on June 11 to the loudest storm of shells over the New City she had heard since the war began. As she got out of bed she glanced at the clock on her night table. Only four more hours to go. At 10 A.M. the cease-fire was to go into effect. But the incessant din, apparently issuing from all over the city, at once made her doubt that a truce was really imminent. Having worked late the previous night, she was not supposed to report to the hospital until noon. She had gone home instead of staying there, expecting to return to work through a safe and quiet city.

Tanya dressed and listened to the radio. There was talk only of peace, peace, peace—while the shells still whistled through the air. Finally—10 o'clock. Still the din of death. Then, at 10:04, sudden silence. She waited for the next inevitable explosion. But this time it did not come.

She ran out into the street and scanned the stone houses of Rehaviah, with their neat little flower gardens shaded by blossoming carob trees. All was calm and bright in the sunlight as she walked tentatively to the bus stop and caught a bus into town. She looked through the open window at a strangely numb world. People emerging into the streets, many of them from shelters, were all as dazed as she, their eyes darting everywhere, watching perhaps for the flash of a gun on some distant hillside that would return them to reality.

Tanya got off the bus in town and watched shopkeepers roll up steel shutters for the first time in a month. The people on the streets, their shabby clothes rumpled and dirty from sleeping in the shelters, walked silently, doubtfully, looking back over their shoulders every few steps. There was no conversation, no jubilation. Only the crunch of boots trampling on uncollected garbage, broken glass, fragments of tile and furniture, branches from uprooted trees, twisted, rusting shutters. A man leaned a ladder against his house to replace his shattered staircase. The Jerusalem buildings, being mainly of stone, had stood up well to the shelling; even so, many had gaping holes in them, and others that had received direct hits by incendiary bombs were simply burnt-out shells.

Children began to join in the silent processions, their faces pale and scrawny. If the truce really had come, perhaps they would soon be eating normally again. Almost everyone had exhausted their stocks of food. There were no more cans of sardines or packets of macaroni, no coffee, sugar, rice, or fat. The daily bread ration had been cut to about five ounces —four thin slices of soggy, crumbling pulse. Apart from that, the food ration consisted only of seven to eight ounces of dried beans, peas, or groats —to last for a week. Few people were consuming more than 800 calories a day. And there was hardly any fuel available, even wood, to cook these paltry rations. Tanya watched a man in a long queue forming outside a grocery store; at least he could wait for his rations now without risking his life.

She stopped to join a little group gathered around a loudspeaker announcing the cease-fire. Then she walked on past the Orion Cinema, glancing idly at a poster in English and Hebrew advertising the last film, *Something to Sing About,* with James Cagney.

But no one was singing, and she understood why. Like all the other citizens, Tanya was drained emotionally and physically. She felt no joy, nor even relief yet. Her mind could only cling to the routine of going back to work . . .

"I FEEL FINE, DOCTOR. I WOULD LIKE TO GO BACK TO WORK."
"Open your mouth!"

Tanya, sitting up on her cot, obeyed, and the doctor probed her throat with a short, flat wooden stick. As he did so, she looked over his shoulder at the nurse behind him, holding a pencil in one hand, a notebook in the other. A flick of the pencil and that was the end. It meant one was too ill to work, therefore no longer eligible to live. It meant "selection."

Perhaps it was inevitable. It was a miracle that she had escaped the gas chamber this long. Eating barely enough to stay alive; sleeping amid sweating, stinking inmates on the hard, cold floor in a bug-infested barracks; how long could one avoid illness? And the doctor came almost every day with orders not to take chances. Epidemics were to be prevented at all costs. Tanya and many of her Auschwitz comrades, desperately struggling to remain well, washed their bodies and their clothes at least twice a day in the cold-water trough that ran along one wall. They spent nights picking lice out of their ragged garments. But still they wallowed in the filth of human decay. Still they woke in terror with skin rashes, sore throats, and other infections.

"Hospital!" the doctor would murmur to the nurse.

And if the patient did not recover almost immediately, the nurse would enter the fateful mark in her ledger of death.

Only the day before, Tanya had felt a soreness in her throat. As she stood lined up in the barracks with the other women, her skeletal body shaking uncontrollably, the doctor had examined her and muttered the dreaded word.

Now she was in the hospital, and the doctor was judging her condition one final time. She watched the nurse open the notebook and thumb through it, and suddenly remembered being thirteen and playing the violin at her birthday party in the great white house in Yugoslavia, where her family had been accepted as good converted Christians.

The doctor removed the wooden stick from Tanya's mouth and whispered something to the nurse.

"Yes, doctor," the nurse said, seeming to tighten her grip on the pencil.

Then she shut the notebook and followed the doctor to the next cot, and Tanya listlessly, almost apathetically, returned to work . . .

She walked on in a daze through the rubbish-littered streets of the New City toward Hadassah Hospital, wondering how many patients would die that day.

In Amman, Glubb Pasha, too, was counting casualties. As soon as the truce took effect, he went to see Prime Minister Tawfiq Pasha to explain that the Arab Legion, with many men killed and wounded and no reserves to replace them, could not resume the war unless the government recruited new soldiers. Actually, Glubb dreaded the idea of renewed war in any event. Transjordan would have little to gain, he felt, since she already controlled almost all the land she had set out to control and what Britain intended her to keep. But she would have much to lose, perhaps everything, if the war started again.

While Israel would undoubtedly stockpile a mountain of arms during the truce, Transjordan would probably remain critically short of ammunition, mainly because of the Egyptian "pirates." In May, two British ships loaded with ammunition had sailed from Suez to Aqaba, but only one of them arrived. As the other had steamed out of Suez Harbor, an Egyptian launch gave chase and ordered it to return to port, whereupon Egyptian soldiers unloaded the vital crates, piled them on trucks, and drove off. While Cairo closed its ears to Transjordanian protests, Britain, under increasing United Nations pressure, was hesitant to resupply Amman.

But Glubb's greatest worry was the situation in Lydda and Ramle. These two towns, stretching along the flat coastal plain only 15 miles from Tel Aviv and almost surrounded by Jewish colonies, had been awarded to the Arabs under the United Nations partition plan. But even before the war started, Glubb had warned the King and the Prime Minister that they could not be defended. Both the King and Tawfiq had agreed and, when the war broke out, did not send Transjordan military governors to the two towns as they did to Hebron, Jerusalem, Ramallah, and Nablus.

"We have decided," Tawfiq explained to a grateful Glubb, "that we cannot hold Lydda and Ramle. If we appoint a military governor, and then the Jews take them, it will look worse."

Twenty-four hours before the truce began, however, Glubb, with the government's approval, sent a token force to Ramle so that Transjordan could claim the twin cities in any eventual peace settlement in line with Abdullah's plan to absorb Arab Palestine. If new fighting broke out, Glubb was sure, Israel would pounce on the two cities and find them largely undefended. Such a disaster would not only deprive Transjordan of a valuable strategic wedge in a Jewish-held area, but would produce devastating political repercussions throughout the Arab world.

Even so, the Arab Legion would have to be prepared to fight elsewhere. But when he now asked Tawfiq Pasha for new recruits, the Prime Minister replied forcefully: "There won't be any more fighting. No more fighting! I and Nokrashy Pasha are agreed on that, and if we two are agreed, we can sway the rest. No! No more fighting!"

Glubb, while delighted by this decision, nevertheless insisted that the Legion must be ready in case the Jews attacked.

"No more fighting," Tawfiq reiterated impatiently. "And no more money for soldiers!"[3]

In Tel Aviv, the attitude was just the reverse. Israel, the leaders universally felt, would sooner or later have to fight until she recovered the Negev and cleared the main road to Jerusalem once and for all. Nor could Israel permit Syrian troops to keep their foothold in Mishmar Hayarden, since from there they could cut eastern Galilee in two. And then there were other strategic objectives to be captured: the dangerous wedge formed by Lydda and Ramle, more breathing space along Israel's 10-mile waist, the whole of Galilee. Since the Jews had accepted the original partition plan and the Arabs had tried to scuttle it by force, Israel was perfectly justified, the Israelis felt, in seeking to improve the original borders.

In the first round, Israeli defenders had miraculously held out against the regular armies of the Arab world at almost every settlement within the territory earmarked for Israel, losing, in addition to Mishmar Hayarden, only Yad Mordechai, Nitzanim, the Jewish Quarter in the Old City, and some outposts around Jerusalem. But the Israelis had fought virtually to the breaking point, as their inability to launch a new attack on Latrun demonstrated.

With new arms and fresh troops, however, the Israelis would be ready to take the offensive again. At least this was the idea. But, too close to the situation to recognize the magnitude of their defensive achievement, the Israeli commanders were anything but optimistic when they met, haggard and perspiring, at GHQ in Tel Aviv when the cease-fire had taken effect on June 11. Moshe Carmel opened the meeting with a gloomy report on the northern front.

"The fighting units are worn out," he declared. "There are at least a hundred dead in every battalion, each of which has shrunk to miniature proportions . . . On the Jenin front, we are under continuous artillery fire and attacks from the air. If the enemy is to use this firepower as cover for an infantry attack, we will not be able to withstand them."

Dan Even of the Alexandroni Brigade offered an equally dismal picture:

"The units have reached a stage of crisis. The main reason is fatigue, and a perennial shortage of everything. There were cases of men going to battle in pajamas. There were those who returned from battle in their underwear and who received clothes only three weeks later . . . "

And Nahum Sarig of the Negev Brigade warned that the southern settlements were near collapse.

"They are subjected to artillery barrages by night and artillery plus air attacks by day . . . And there are units which have had no leave for seven months."

David Shaltiel stated that his troops were hungry and weak because of the shortage of food. More than 50 artillery pieces had been firing on the New City, including 100-pounders, he said, in an attempt to force the Jews to surrender.

Then the Palmach Harel and Yiftach Brigades reported massive casualties. Some commanders complained bitterly that the neglect of soldiers' families had seriously affected troop morale.

"When a man is pinned down in his foxhole," grumbled one officer, "he should not have to worry about his family."

And a colleague added: "There were cases where my men refused to eat their meals because they knew that their families were hungry . . . "

Prime Minister Ben-Gurion sat at one end of the conference table listening intently to the flow of long-festering battlefield grievances. Finally, he summed up his own relatively cheerful view that, despite certain failures, the past four weeks had yielded a major accomplishment.

"If the battle is renewed," he said, "and it must be assumed that it will, we shall be entering the decisive phase."

Then the characteristic lines on his face deepening, he touched upon a problem that in the following days was to plague the infant State of Israel and even threaten civil war:

"Because of lack of discipline we have lost positions; because of lack of discipline we have not fully exploited possibilities and have not gained achievements that were in our reach. If we had one army rather than a number of armies, and if we had operated according to one strategic plan, we should have more to show for our efforts."

W HILE the Israeli commanders were meeting in Tel Aviv, Mordechai Raanan, the Irgun commander in Jerusalem, was on a mission that he believed would determine the fate of Jerusalem. He had hitched a ride in a convoy of over 100 empty trucks that had been trapped in Jerusalem since the British left, but was now permitted to return to Tel Aviv over the main road under United Nations supervision. Every driver had taken a "relief man," actually a Jerusalem fighter going home on leave or elsewhere on army business.

Raanan planned to return to Jerusalem again soon—but not in an empty truck. He would come back over the Burma Road with truckloads of arms for the conquest of the Old City when war broke out again. He was fed up with what he regarded as Shaltiel's pussyfooting, defensive attitude. He had been pleading with his Haganah counterpart since mandate days for a cooperative drive on the Old City, but the answer was always the same: "We haven't got enough men or arms." And the Irgun force in Jerusalem—only about 150 able men, armed with too few weapons to go around—had been unable to launch such an attack alone. Ironically enough, the Irgun had a bulging arsenal of weapons stored in Tel Aviv (weapons stolen from British camps before independence), but had been unable to transfer these arms to Jerusalem during the siege.

As the convoy leaving Jerusalem stopped at a checkpoint near Bab el-Wad, United Nations officers inspected the trucks and noted that each had two drivers.

"I'm sorry," ruled one officer to a gathering of the Israelis, "but we can permit only one driver for each truck."

Raanan asked his driver friend: "How about letting me go on?"

"Have you ever driven a five-ton truck before?"

"No, but don't worry. I'll make it."

On arriving in Tel Aviv with virtually stripped gears, Raanan rushed to Irgun headquarters, where Beigin greeted him enthusiastically.

"I'd like to take back with me all the men and equipment you can mobilize," Raanan said without preamble.

Beigin smiled. The Irgun detachment in Jerusalem was the only one that still had not been integrated into the newly formed Army of Israel, an exception made possible by the government's hesitance to absorb the New City officially into Israel in defiance of the United Nations. This one force could operate independently; and Beigin was determined to make the most of it.

"Of course," he replied. "We'll give you everything we can make available to you at the moment. And we'll try to talk the government into letting you pass over the Burma Road."

Three days later, four trucks were loaded up with 100 or so men and innumerable crates of arms. The arms—gathered from the Irgun's Jaffa headquarters—included 10 Brens, 2 3-inch mortars with some 300 shells, 3 Browning machine guns, 200 homemade Sten guns, a Piat, more than 100 rifles, and 10,000 rounds of ammunition.

A messenger, Raanan maintains, then arrived with the good news that Yaacov Meridor, Beigin's deputy, had extracted permission from Israel Galili for the Irgun convoy to use the Burma Road—though Galili denies he ever granted such permission.

Raanan jumped into the leading truck beside the driver and ordered him to head for Jerusalem. Near Hulda, Haganah guards halted the convoy in front of an armored car blocking the road.

"Where's your pass?"

"This is an Etzel convoy going to Jerusalem," Raanan replied. "Israel Galili approved the trip."

"I'm sorry," said the guard, "I have clear instructions not to let anyone through without a pass."

"Listen, young man," Raanan retorted contemptuously, "I suggest you remove the car blocking the road or we'll do it ourselves."

The guard glanced up to see a machine gun pointing down from the roof of Raanan's truck.

"I'll call up my commander," he said nervously.

"You won't call up anybody! Now get that car out of the way!"

The guard hesitated, then ordered the driver of the armored car to let the convoy pass.

The trucks turned off the main highway and were soon lurching up the Burma Road to a point where army tractors had to help vehicles over a precariously steep grade. Raanan jumped out of his vehicle and strode to a Palmach headquarters tent nearby, where he found the commander sitting behind a desk.

"My name is Raanan," he announced. "I'm commander of the Etzel in Jerusalem. We'd like the tractors to help us up the hill."

The Haganah officer—whom Raanan has identified as Moshe Kelman, though Kelman denies it was he—rose slowly and replied: "Do you really think you're going to do here what you did at Hulda?"

"That's exactly what we intend to do. You can be sure that we'll get through to Jerusalem with or without your consent. Anyway, Galili gave us permission to pass."

"I have orders not to let you through. Galili gave no such permission."

"We're going through. I have my own tractor drivers. Now I don't suggest that we have a battle here. You'd better call up your superiors and ask for instructions."

Raanan left the tent while the officer radioed his headquarters. He returned half an hour later, after ordering his trucks to block the route to all other vehicles.

"My headquarters is checking now," the officer said.

"We can't wait any longer."

"Take it easy. I should have an answer in about five minutes."

"Well, no longer."

As Raanan emerged from the tent again, he was startled to see a familiar figure approaching.

"Menachem, what are you doing here?"

Menachem Beigin was grim-faced. "About an hour after you left Tel Aviv," he explained, "Haganah called us and said they withdrew their consent to the trip. They said they wanted us to wait."

Ben-Gurion, he indicated, had apparently vetoed Galili's decision.

"I drove out here as fast as I could to let you know. I don't want any bloodshed."

Beigin then spoke calmly with the Palmach commander, who claimed he still had not received instructions. Finally, when the commander realized that the Irgun outnumbered and outgunned his Palmach force, he agreed to furnish the tractors.

The convoy arrived in Jerusalem at about 11 P.M. that night.[4]

Shortly after dawn, Raanan strode into Haganah headquarters and said to the Jerusalem commander: "Shaltiel, I've come from Tel Aviv with a convoy of arms and men. As soon as the truce ends, we're going to attack the Old City. I suggest we carry out the operation together. If you don't agree, we'll do it ourselves. And we're strong enough to do it now even against your opposition."

Shaltiel reacted mildly, and there was even a glint in his blue eyes.

"Well, if we have enough arms," he said, "of course we'll attack the Old City when the fighting starts again—your forces, mine, and Lehi."

Representatives of the three groups then met to discuss plans. All agreed that not enough men were available to take the Old City by surrounding it and cutting it off from Transjordan. They would have to launch a direct attack. And Shaltiel had a suggestion for storming the ancient wall. A scientist at the Weizmann Institute, Aharon Kachalsky (father of the Palmach officer, Amos Chorev, who conceived the Burma Road), was developing a huge, 350-pound V-shaped bomb, called the Conus, with enough explosive power to blast a hole in the formidably thick barrier. It would probably be ready for use by the time the truce ended.

The Irgunists and the Sternists were skeptical. Was this a typical Shaltiel trick, they wondered. But they agreed to the plan. There was still a better chance of taking the Old City with the Haganah than without it.

Shaltiel was driven by mixed motives. Since the Irgun had the means of acting on its own, it was better that it act under Haganah leadership. Arms were arms, after all, and if the Irgun had enough for an effective attack on the Old City, why not take advantage of the opportunity? Considering that the United Nations had failed to intervene in the Jerusalem fighting so far, it seemed unlikely that it would or could act at this stage. And he would go down in history as the man who returned Jerusalem to Israel, the Jerusalem that his ultra-Orthodox parents had taught him to revere as the repository of the Jewish spirit and soul.

So obsessed did he become with this idea that he had two sheep placed in his donkey stable. As soon as the Old City was liberated, he would perform the ancient rite of sacrificing the sheep in thanksgiving at the site of the fallen Temple.

DESPITE the ample swelling of the Irgun arsenal in Jerusalem, Menachem Beigin looked forward to bolstering his independently operated force there even more dramatically. He planned also to fit out the Irgun battalions that were to be integrated into the regular army with the latest modern arms. His aim was to make the Irgun the best-equipped military force in Israel, and he thought he had the means to achieve this.

Beigin's hopes centered on a ship called the *Altalena,* a World War II LST which an Irgun official, Abraham Stavsky (known by his underground name, Palest), had purchased in the United States before the partition resolution in order to transport refugees from Europe to Palestine. When the resolution had passed, the ship was earmarked to carry arms instead—if some could be found. Finally, the Irgun's representative in Paris, Samuel Ariel, persuaded the French government to come to the Irgun's aid.

Foreign Minister Georges Bidault—like other French leaders bitter toward Britain for forcing the French out of Syria and Lebanon—was only too anxious to support a cause that would reduce British power in the

Middle East. Moreover, Ariel convinced them that the Irgunists, many of whom had fought in the French maquis, would come to power after the new state was born and would support France in her disputes with her North African territories.

The French government therefore agreed to supply the weapons without cost, and to permit the Irgun to set up a military base for the training and collection of Irgunist refugees from throughout Europe until they could be sent to Palestine. The quantity of arms offered was so great that the *Altalena* would have to make about five trips to carry it all. As he pondered the fruit of his efforts, Ariel was persuaded that the Irgun would soon be far more powerful militarily than the Haganah, and therefore in a position to control the Jewish government—though Beigin denies that the Irgun ever intended to use force to achieve political power.

Eliahu Lankin, another Irgun official, was the military commander aboard, and Monroe Fein, an American from Chicago, was the ship's captain. Fein had offered his services after seeing Ben Hecht's pro-Irgun play, *A Flag Is Born,* and had been appointed an officer because of his experience on an LST during World War II.

In his crew was Richard Fallon, a chunky, blond American of Irish extraction, who sympathized with the Zionist cause. Fallon had been recruited under strange circumstances. He had tried to sign up for work on a Haganah refugee ship but had been told that, as a Gentile, he would be more valuable in the propaganda section. Altogether he was thoroughly fed up with the "Yiddishe mamas" running Haganah.

Then one night he had just fallen asleep, around two o'clock, when he was awakened by loud knocking on the door. He opened it and a dark-skinned little man asked in a strange accent: "Are you Fallon?"

"Yes."

The visitor entered without invitation and waved a manuscript in Fallon's startled face.

"You wrote this?"

Fallon took the clipped pages and thumbed through the script for *The Cross and the Star,* a skit about Christian-Jewish good fellowship. (He had written it for New York's Station WNEW, but the Jewish producer had rejected it, saying that he was too "socially conscious," and eventually fired him. Fallon felt that the producer was too "self-conscious.")

"Yes, it's mine," Fallon said. "But how . . . ?"

"Do you believe what you wrote?"

"Of course."

"Then get dressed and come with us."

At that moment, another man entered. He was tall and powerfully built, with a jutting jaw, smoldering black eyes, and a broken nose.

"Sure!"

While Fallon dressed, he tried to find out who these men were and where they were taking him, but they were silent. What the hell was all this about? A practical joke or something?

He was taken downstairs, put in a car, and blindfolded. About 20 minutes later, he could smell the waterfront. Then the car stopped, and his blindfold was removed. He got out and found himself standing on a dock overlooking what he recognized in the flat dawn light as an old LST.

When he had gone aboard, a huge man greeted him with a smile.

"Welcome aboard!"

"Who are you and why am I here?"

"They call me Palest," the man said. "Have you ever heard of the Irgun Zvai Leumi?" . . .

Still another American aboard was Harold Kraushar of Brooklyn, who had joined the New York branch of Batar, the Irgun youth group, when he was fourteen and, with the encouragement of his militant girlfriend, became intrigued with the writings of Vladimir Jabotinsky. But the more he read about the Irgun's activities, the more he favored the still bolder Sternist philosophy. He became completely disillusioned after the bombing of the King David Hotel, feeling that the Irgun had revealed its "softness" by warning the occupants in advance that the attack would take place. In war, you could not give any quarter.

And so Kraushar, a tall, gangling youth, joined the small Sternist organization in New York—until Batar offered to send him to Israel to fight the Arabs. Stopping over in Paris, he had learned that the *Altalena* was about to leave and immediately flew to Marseilles to join the 900 Irgunists preparing to head for Israel. The Irgunists were too soft for him, but at least he was getting a free ride to the battlefront.

While Irgunist forces were being rounded up and the French army was shipping the promised arms to a central warehouse in Miramar, near Marseilles, Beigin met in Tel Aviv with Yadin, Galili, and other Israeli military leaders to sign an agreement dissolving the Irgun and incorporating it in the new Army of Israel. After many long talks a compromise had finally been reached whereby the Irgun would be integrated into the army in complete battalions with their own officers. Beigin also agreed to turn over to the army all the arms and ammunition the Irgun possessed.

As he was preparing to sign the agreement on the morning of June 1, he thought of the men and arms being loaded aboard the *Altalena*. Would his Irgun boys, after all their efforts, reap no special advantage from this miraculous windfall, an advantage which would have been theirs automatically if the ship had arrived a few weeks earlier before the establishment of the state? Was it not reasonable that the Irgun battalions should be strengthened by arms the Irgun itself had obtained?

He looked up and, seeing that everybody was impatiently waiting for him to sign the document, scrawled his signature and smiled. As he walked out, army officials had no inkling that a mountain of arms was jamming a warehouse in southern France.

Near midnight on June 9, Ariel, Lankin, Fein, Stavsky, and a French official stood on the dock in Port du Bouc beside the *Altalena,* anxiously peering down the road into the blackness of a starless night. Suddenly Fein exclaimed: "Look, lights! They're coming!"

A string of lights wound slowly toward the dock like fireflies in formation. Ariel and the French official (the chief of security services in southern France) got into a car to meet the ghostly caravan, which halted as they drove up beside the first jeep.

"Where are you going?" the security chief asked.

"We're looking for Monsieur Ariel," a French officer replied.

The men then got out of their vehicles, and when Ariel presented his identification documents, the French officer glanced at them and saluted. "I am Major Sasso, in command of the convoy," he said formally. "Where do you want us to unload the material?"

Ariel and the security chief led the caravan to the dock where the *Altalena*'s hull shone brilliantly silver in the carlight. One by one the trucks drove up, while French soldiers jumped out of the rear to start unloading heavy wooden crates.

Finally, after more than two hours, the job was completed and the officer asked Ariel to sign a receipt for 5,000 rifles, 300 Bren guns, 150 Spandaus, 5 caterpillar-track armored cars, 4 million rounds of ammunition, several thousand air-combat bombs, and other equipment. He then saluted, and the convoy headed back into the night, leaving the Irgun officials surrounded by crates containing enough explosive power to change the geography of a nation, or, in the view of some, a government, if necessary.

Shortly after dawn that day (June 10), French stevedores started loading the crates aboard the *Altalena*. Lankin was watching when Ariel came running toward him, a look of panic on his face.

"What's the matter?" Lankin asked.

"Have you seen the newspapers?" Ariel asked excitedly, waving one in his hand.

Lankin took it and read a short article on the front page about an Israeli ship that was loading arms in a French port.

"It's out," he muttered. Now the pressures on the French government to stop the whole operation would be enormous. As an afterthought, it struck him that the Israeli government would also learn what the Irgun was doing.

Hardly had he considered the possible ramifications when he noticed a commotion on the loading dock. A crate, while being lifted aboard, had fallen to the dock and burst open. Lankin and Ariel rushed to the scene and saw precious rifles scattered all over the dock. This was part of their game, Lankin thought. Israel's enemies had gotten to the right people.

The stevedores stopped loading, and urgent pleas by Ariel to the union leaders proved futile. They wouldn't load war materials, the unionists said; they were not prepared to encourage a continuation of the war in the Middle East. Ariel knew it was hopeless. Many of the stevedores were North African Arabs, who had no intention of helping Israel in her struggle against their fellow Arabs. Irgun recruits, as they arrived from Marseilles, were thus put to work loading the heavy equipment without even the help of cranes, which the stevedores refused to let them use.

"Faster, faster!" the Irgun officials urged. At any moment the French government could break under the pressure and cut short their dream.

The recruits, about 120 of them, worked without pause throughout the day and night, finally completing the task at noon the next day, June 11. By that time, the bulk of recruits had arrived by truck from Marseilles, and they were immediately herded aboard the ship. But before they had all arrived, impatient French port authorities came aboard, inspected the vessel according to regulations (though not too carefully, since officially they knew nothing about the arms), and gave Fein clearance to depart.

Fein stalled them to give the remaining recruits time to arrive. Also, though an Irgun representative had arrived the day before from Tel Aviv confirming orders that Fein was to land in that city, he was not sure that Tel Aviv was, under the conditions of the truce that was about to take effect, the logical place to disembark.

That evening, French authorities boarded the vessel once more and, more abruptly than before, ordered Fein to leave immediately.

The last recruits arrived just then, and late on June 11, the *Altalena* headed out to sea into an unknown adventure. Anxieties were not put to rest by a BBC broadcast that evening announcing the departure of the highly vulnerable ship, as well as the details of the truce agreement, including a pledge by both Jews and Arabs not to bring in arms while the accord was in effect.

In Tel Aviv, Beigin was also shaken by this broadcast. If the *Altalena* came in at this point, all could be lost, for the Ben-Gurion government, which now probably also knew of the sailing, might feel it necessary, in view of the cease-fire agreement, to prevent the ship from landing. Moreover, though he condemned the truce as a "submission to shame," he was reluctant to bear the responsibility for the possible consequences of a breach, with the very survival of the infant nation at stake. The crew should never have left without consulting him, he complained loudly to his aides.

Then it struck him that perhaps the BBC broadcast was inaccurate, that the British simply wanted to alert the United Nations to the *Altalena*'s plans. He immediately cabled Samuel Katz, an Irgun official, in Paris:

DON'T SEND THE BOAT   STOP   AWAIT INSTRUCTIONS

Katz, who, like his colleagues in Paris, had assumed that the Israeli government would give its blessing to an accomplished fact, replied, after a two-day communications delay, that the cable had reached him the day after the ship's departure and that he was unable to contact her. He advised Begin to communicate directly with the vessel. Begin then radioed the *Altalena* on her third day at sea:

KEEP AWAY. AWAIT INSTRUCTIONS!

Then he telephoned the Israel Ministry of Security and asked for an urgent meeting with top government officials.

"But it's almost midnight!" a voice said crossly.

"I don't care," Begin replied. "It's extremely urgent and I must see them tonight."

On the *Altalena,* deep depression gripped the crew. The communications system had broken down and the ship was completely isolated from the world.

The tension was broken only on the second day at sea when a young Frenchman came to Fein and said he wanted to marry a girl recruit on board, "just in case something should happen to one of us." Fein found an American rabbi among the recruits, but he refused to perform the marriage, saying: "They've no proof that they're single and, frankly, I doubt the girl's Jewish origin."

When Fein saw their disappointment, he agreed to perform the ceremony himself. He gathered witnesses and, in a ceremony following Jewish tradition, married the couple on a cargo hatch surrounded by crates of explosives. That evening, crew and passengers danced and sang at a wedding party before the couple finally retired to a storage locker that had been converted into a bridal suite and decorated with paper flowers cut out by the brawny boatswain.

When the party was over, Fein, Lankin, and Stavsky went to the radio room and tried once again to contact Israel. Suddenly, they heard the ship's whistle blowing frantically and were convinced the vessel was under attack—until they learned that the bridegroom's foot had got entangled in a halyard, setting off the whistle mechanism.

Hours later, as they continued to call on the radio, a woman's voice came through with the barely audible message: "Keep away! Keep away!" Contact died after the words "Await instructions" had come over garbled almost into gibberish.

"I recognized the voice," Lankin said eagerly. "It's our secretary in the Tel Aviv office."

Fein immediately tried to acknowledge the message and ask for a re-transmission, but he could not establish contact.

At about 1 A.M., shortly after Beigin's secretary had made contact with the *Altalena,* the Irgun chief and his aides met at his headquarters with Israel Galili, security chief Levi Eshkol (later Prime Minister), security official Pinhas Vaze, and David Cohen, the liaison officer between the Irgun and the government. Despite the BBC broadcast announcing the departure from France of the *Altalena,* they apparently did not know about the cargo it carried.

Now Beigin announced dramatically: "The *Altalena* is carrying men and iron to Israel that can win the war for us. She's carrying enough arms to equip ten battalions. She will arrive in five days."

In view of the cease-fire, he asked, what did the government want to do about the *Altalena?* If she landed, he added, it seemed only fair that the Irgun, which had gone to such trouble getting the arms, should receive 20 per cent for its fighters in Jerusalem.

The government representatives appeared shocked, particularly in light of the agreement calling for the absorption of the Irgun into the Israeli army. But they felt that this was no time for accusations and recriminations. They were faced with an extraordinary development that could, depending on the way it was handled, tip the scales of war one way or the other. On the one hand, the Irgun now posed a threat to the state, and so might the United Nations if Israel were caught violating the cease-fire. But on the other, Israel vitally needed the arms.

"Get in touch with the ship and tell the captain to slow down," said Galili. "We'll consider the situation and give you further instructions later."

After the meeting, Galili immediately telephoned Ben-Gurion and informed him of the substance of the conversation. The Prime Minister raged at what he regarded as the Irgun's deception.

"Well, it's a *fait accompli*," Ben-Gurion finally said, "and we need the arms, cease-fire or no cease-fire. Let the ship come, but the arms will go to the army whatever happens."

Later in the morning, Galili and his staff worked out the details. Galili then telephoned Beigin and informed him that the government wanted the *Altalena* to land and that his representatives would coordinate plans with him.

"What about the arms for Jerusalem?" Beigin asked.

"We'll work that out," Galili replied. "I think twenty per cent can go to Jerusalem."

Beigin was delighted. He would also insist that the Irgun forces elsewhere received a priority share of the remainder; but the important thing was that his men in Jerusalem would get 20 per cent of the total.

He hadn't listened very carefully, as Galili appears to have calculated; Galili had said nothing about the *Irgun* forces in Jerusalem getting 20 per cent.

Galili then told Pinhas Vaze to find a suitable place for the unloading and to arrange for the transport of the arms from the shore to army warehouses. Vaze met with Beigin and his assistants, including Amihai Faglin, at Irgun headquarters, and insisted that the arms be unloaded at Kfar Vitkin —a strongly pro-Ben-Gurion settlement—and stored in government warehouses. The Irgunists reluctantly agreed to Kfar Vitkin, but Faglin retorted: "I say that the arms should be stored in our warehouses and that the guards should be our men. And if the government doesn't agree, then I think we should unload the ship ourselves."

The meeting ended with Beigin stating simply (Vaze maintains) that he would "have to consult with my friends."

Vaze telephoned Galili and asked him to come urgently to army headquarters in Ramat Gan (near Tel Aviv, from where it had been moved). There he informed him of the stiffening Irgun attitude.

"Do they think they can get away with this?" Galili asked, stunned by the news.

He arranged a meeting with the Irgun leaders immediately at their headquarters and found Beigin adamant on the question of storage. Other army units could help Irgun troops to guard the arms, but the arms must be stored in Irgun warehouses, Beigin maintained (according to Galili's account). Moreover, Beigin insisted, aside from his demand that the Irgun units in Jerusalem receive 20 per cent of the arms, Irgun battalions newly integrated into the army should have priority in receiving the weapons. And (again according to Galili, though Beigin denies this) Beigin further suggested that the weapons should be distributed to these battalions at a special ceremony.

The two men looked at each other across the table with growing rage— as they had done two years before in another agonizing dispute. . . .

IN JULY, 1946, GALILI HAD APPEALED TO BEIGIN TO CALL OFF A
planned bombing of Jerusalem's King David Hotel, British headquarters, after the Haganah had withdrawn from the plot. But when
Beigin angrily responded that the Irgun would go ahead with the
bombing alone if necessary, Galili, without consulting Ben-Gurion or
other political authorities, decided to cooperate with Beigin so that
the Haganah could retain at least some control over him. In the
ensuing bombing almost 100 people, including many Jews, were
killed because the British refused to heed a warning to evacuate the
building. A bitter quarrel consequently broke out between Galili and
Beigin over who was responsible, with the Irgun leader charging that
his Haganah counterpart was a hypocrite for refusing to admit
publicly the role of Haganah in the plot . . .

Now the two men confronted each other again with charges and threats.
Stonily, Galili passed on Ben-Gurion's warning about the arms on the
Altalena:

"You will have to accept our demands or you will bear full responsibility
for the consequences, and the responsibility will be very heavy indeed.
Unless you change your mind, we wash our hands of the unloading of the
arms."

"Very well," replied Beigin, "then we'll unload the arms ourselves."

He spoke almost with a sense of relief. Galili had not forbidden the
Irgun to land the ship or even to unload her alone, orders which the Irgun
would have had to obey. He had simply indicated that the army would not
help unload. Apparently, Beigin thought, Galili was just trying to save
face. In fact, once the ship arrived, the army, in its enthusiasm to get the
arms, might even agree to help after all.

It did not occur to Beigin that Galili might not have wanted to say anything sufficiently strong to divert the shipload of arms from Kfar Vitkin. Nor
did Beigin interpret Galili's warning of "consequences" as more than an
empty threat.

The next morning, June 19, the *Altalena* was within 220 miles of Israel
but still had received no word from Irgun headquarters in Tel Aviv.

"Well," Lankin said to Fein, "it looks like we'll have to make a run for
Tel Aviv, land, and hope for the best. We can't go drifting forever without
instructions."

But before Fein could order preparations for a landing, cable communications were suddenly established with the Irgun office. Fein eagerly gave
their location and asked for landing instructions.

The laconic reply read:

ADVANCE TO KFAR VITKIN.

Lankin slapped Fein on the back and said gleefully: "Head for Kfar Vitkin, Captain. We're going home!"

Fein asked Irgun headquarters to designate the landing point with two vertical red lights as the ship approached, estimating she would land at about 9 P.M. that night.

At about nine, the *Altalena* steamed in and Fein managed to sight the two red lights flashing from a fishing pier. He maneuvered to within about 40 yards of the end of the small pier (which extended 100 yards from the shore of Kfar Vitkin) and could go no further in the shallow water.

Under Richard Fallon's supervision, the Irgun recruits started disembarking into a motor launch, which tried to reach shore but was forced to return because of rough seas. Two rowboats obtained from shore were also used in the attempted disembarkation, one of them, Fein noted, a fishing boat rowed by a fisherman whom he assumed was an Irgunist.

Finally, Lankin, aboard the ship, heard someone calling his name from shore. Begin was yelling: "It's almost daylight. Sail back to sea until darkness."

Thus the *Altalena* pulled out to sea again at about 5 A.M. on June 20, and remained some 50 miles offshore waiting for darkness in order to reduce the chances of observation by United Nations officials. At least, thought Fein, nothing but the weather had interfered with the landing so far . . .

But unknown to the Irgunists, the government was at that very moment planning drastic action to end the "revolt." The "fisherman" who had tried to help disembark the passengers was in fact a government agent seeking necessary information. On the basis of his and other reports, Galili sent an urgent memorandum to Ben-Gurion on the morning of June 20 maintaining that the Irgun was challenging the authority of the state and recommending "swift and clear action" to counter what he regarded as an internal threat to Israel.

In this memorandum, he laid the groundwork for a charge that was intended to reap the fullest possible international advantage for Israel from any action the government might take. He criticized the Irgun for trying to bring in soldiers and arms in violation of the cease-fire, though the government had been perfectly willing to commit such a violation itself provided that its conditions for the landing were accepted.

That afternoon, at a secret meeting of the Israeli cabinet, Moshe Sharett, while stressing the danger to the state's authority, also deplored the fact that "it is possible we are about to break the cease-fire in a most embarrassing way. It will be broken by Jews, but we personally will not be responsible for it. It will be done by the Irgun . . ."

Sharett then suggested that the army should concentrate 500 men on the shore to scatter Irgunists who had deserted the army to help in the unloading, and to disarm and arrest persons disembarking from the ship with weapons.

Yigal Yadin reported that he had already sent 600 soldiers to the landing point and that he could send two battalions if necessary. But he added: "Before such a force is concentrated, it should have clear orders under what circumstances it should go into action."

Ben-Gurion supported Yadin, saying: "The army can only threaten if it is ready to carry out the threat."

Finally, the cabinet decided unanimously to give the High Command the authority to use whatever means were necessary to take the arms if it could gather a sufficient force in time.

The meeting ended at 9 P.M., just about the time the *Altalena* started back toward shore . . .

Fein maneuvered the *Altalena* to the same position where she had anchored the night before, and the passengers began to go ashore, though about 50 of them were kept on board to man Bren guns and an anti-aircraft gun, all mounted on steel pipes around the ship.

The first passengers to go ashore were women and the sick, who were greeted by an attractive Yemenite girl, Malka Jaffet—or Topsy, as her fellow Irgunists called her. She helped to gather them together, led them to a waiting truck, and drove them to a reception base near Nathanya. On her return more than an hour later, she ran to a group of Irgun officials and reported: "The Haganah is barricading the road. I was barely able to bluff my way through."

"It probably doesn't mean anything," an officer said. "Better load up again. We've got a lot to do."

Among the hard-working volunteers was Harold Kraushar, who stayed to help in the unloading of the arms, lowering the crates on ropes into the small boats and removing them on reaching shore. Topsy was usually on shore to greet him and the other workers, and she helped to open the crates and remove the thickly greased arms, which could be more easily handled unpacked. To the disappointment of Fallon, Kraushar, and their fellow "stevedores," it became evident that only the small arms could be unloaded after a boom broke during an attempt to lower an armored car, resulting in several injuries.

As dawn once more approached, Beigin decided that the unloading must continue through the day. But this decision was opposed by Faglin, who was in charge of the work on the shore side. He had been frustrated and annoyed from the beginning by the holiday atmosphere on the beach, where Irgun sympathizers from all over the country had gathered, as if at a picnic, to watch this glorious episode in Irgun history. At one point, he had ordered everyone who was not working off the beach, explaining to Beigin, when he protested, that the crowds were interfering with the work.

"Never mind," said Beigin, "let them celebrate this great day."

But now Faglin saw a more serious hindrance to the operation. Topsy's concern about the Haganah barricade had not been misplaced. A patrol confirmed that Haganah soldiers were closing in, and inevitably they would take over the whole area, arms, men, and all. Therefore, he decided on his own that the ship would have to go out to sea again—with all the men and arms. When the next boatload of weapons reached shore, he ordered the coxswain to reload the arms on the vessel.

Beigin, who was then visiting the *Altalena* amid tumultuous cheers from those on board, was incredulous when the boatload of weapons returned. He immediately radioed Faglin.

"Who gave you instructions to reload the ship?" he demanded.

"I'm doing it on my own responsibility," Faglin replied.

"Why?"

"Because the Haganah is preparing to attack us."

"Are you out of your mind?" Beigin said, infuriated.

"I can't discuss this on the radio. You had better come ashore."

When Beigin arrived, Faglin said: "My assignment is to unload these arms safely. Now we're surrounded by the Haganah. The only way I can carry out my mission is for the ship to go back to sea with all the people and arms, and then we can organize ourselves and disembark when and where we choose—perhaps after the truce when it will be easier."

"And where do you propose to unload?" Beigin asked.

"Maybe in Gaza or El Arish. We've got enough men and arms to take over an Arab area."

"You must be dreaming," Beigin shouted. "Our worry is Bernadotte and the United Nations, not the Haganah."

"If any U.N. people come," Faglin replied, "someone can keep them waiting a few days in an orange grove while we reload and leave. It's not an important factor. The only sensible alternative to leaving is to surrender to the Haganah. The government, after all, has a right to do as it wishes with these arms. If we don't want to let them exercise their right, that's another thing. But we'll lose everything if we stay here and fight. If you disagree, maybe you should give my command to someone else."

"I will," Beigin responded sharply. "I'm giving it to [Yaacov] Meridor."

Faglin then made his way along the seashore to Nathanya, where he went to a friend's house and promptly went to sleep . . .

A Haganah officer drove to the beach early that morning and delivered an ultimatum to Beigin. Signed by Dan Even, the commander of the Alexandroni Brigade based in the area, the document warned him that unless he agreed to turn over all arms to the army, military units would confiscate them, by force if necessary.

"You have ten minutes in which to give your answer," the message concluded.

As Beigin looked up, he said wryly: "This isn't a matter that can be decided in ten minutes. I'll be glad to discuss the situation with the brigade commander if he comes here carrying a white flag."

But Beigin was now almost alone among the Irgun leaders in his determination to defy the government at any cost. To him, the situation had become a question of personal honor. Justifiably or not, he felt betrayed by the government. To give in now would mean a deep humiliation that would forever besmirch his record of defiance of any "unjust" authority.

Meridor argued that the Irgun was literally under siege at Kfar Vitkin but might be able to extricate itself if the vessel proceeded to Tel Aviv, where there would be more Irgunists to help in the unloading with, no doubt, the support of the people of the city.

Beigin was skeptical, but Meridor insisted: "Here you won't be able to do a thing for us. I want you to go so that you can straighten out this muddle."

Beigin finally agreed that perhaps he was right . . .

Toward 5 P.M., Beigin ordered a break for his exhausted men, and sent Topsy to the ship to obtain 400 sandwiches from the vessel's kitchen. As she climbed aboard, she asked for the captain and, since she could speak little English, made her request in Hebrew through an interpreter, then departed.

"Say, that was something, wasn't it?" Fallon, who had been standing nearby, said to Fein. "Those shiny white teeth and that body!"

Fein, who had barely noticed the girl, replied firmly with a smile: "There's no time for that now, Fallon. Get back to work."

Then, from the railing, he looked toward the receding boat carrying the girl to shore. She smiled as she glanced back and Fein suddenly wished there were time for that now.

During the break, Fein went ashore with Stavsky on the boat carrying the food, and the two men joined Beigin and a small group of Irgunists who were sitting on the pier. Beigin, unshaven and dressed in a short-sleeved sports shirt and dirty khaki trousers, looked tired and worried as he ate his sandwiches.

"Anything could happen now," he said morosely. "Maybe Meridor is right. Maybe I should go to Tel Aviv with the boat."

Fein returned to the ship after a short while and had hardly stepped aboard when he heard machine-gun fire ashore and saw the people on the beach diving behind an embankment (built in a semi-circle around the loading area as protection against attack). Fein's first thought was that the Arabs had broken through. He immediately tried to make contact with the beach and heard Stavsky's husky voice shouting: "We've got some trouble on the beach. We're coming back to the ship."

Fein replied: "I'm moving out to sea for protection. You follow us out."

The firing had started, according to government officials, when Irgun trucks loaded with men and arms tried to break through the army barricades that had been set up on the road leading from the beach. As Irgun men fell in their tracks under the heavy fire, they were carried, bleeding and moaning, under the pier, where Topsy, crying as she worked, bandaged them with ripped shirts and rags.

Begin lay flat on the sand behind the embankment watching Irgun soldiers rake the surrounding area with Brens and rifles. Then he heard Stavsky, who was lying nearby, shout: "Let's get back to the ship, or they'll kill us all!"

"No," Begin yelled hysterically, "we're going to stay and fight! We're going to break through their barricades! I won't leave!"

At a sign from Stavsky, Fallon and other crewmen grabbed Begin and dragged him to the motor launch. When about 30 other Irgunists had climbed aboard, the boat took off, with Begin cursing incoherently in Yiddish over the sound of machine-gun bullets whizzing in all directions.

As the motor launch started toward the *Altalena,* Fein was swinging the bow around in order to head out to sea. At this point, two corvettes which had been lying offshore began to fire at both craft. Fein, while returning the fire, skillfully maneuvered his ship between the corvettes and the small boat and spun around again, thereby shielding the latter from fire. The launch finally reached the *Altalena* and was hauled aboard, Begin still cursing.

When he had recovered his breath, he ordered Fein to steam southward to Tel Aviv, where he believed (as Meridor had said) that he could arouse the people in support of the Irgun's operation. Almost simultaneously, Fein received a signal from one of the corvettes that the ship should follow the government craft southward. With everybody in agreement, he therefore started toward Tel Aviv, keeping as close to the coast as possible so that the corvettes, further out to sea, would be unable to fire again without risking casualties ashore.

One corvette turned back, and after about half an hour, Paul Shulman, American commander of the embryonic Israeli navy, who was in the second corvette (the *Wedgewood*), approached to within 150 yards of the *Altalena* and made radio contact with Fein.

"You are in the territorial waters of Israel," Shulman said, "and must adhere to orders of the government. You are ordered to move west, out to sea." (He wanted to be in a position to fire at the ship in the direction of the sea if it didn't surrender when they reached Tel Aviv.)

Fein quickly thought of an excuse to stall his fellow American navy veteran. "I haven't enough fuel to head out to sea," he said.

"I order you again to move west," Shulman repeated.

Fein had his radio operator reply with nonsensical messages, including matchcover advertisements, in the hope of stalling a little longer. About 15 minutes out of Tel Aviv, Shulman fired a cannon, hitting the ship's bow and wounding several people. At that moment, Fein saw several American merchant ships lying off between Nathanya and Tel Aviv waiting for clearance to head for Haifa and unload their cargoes. He wove a zigzag path through the line of ships, thus preventing heavy fire from the corvette.

With Tel Aviv in sight, Shulman received urgent orders to stop the ship at any cost before she reached the city, since Fein clearly had no intention of surrendering. He fired again as the *Altalena* emerged into the clear, but the ship was now off the shore of Tel Aviv and heading into the deeper water of the harbor. In a last desperate effort, Shulman finally swung his corvette round between the LST and the shore and fired, but he missed. Then it was too late.

Fein decided to run the ship right up on the beach, where Irgun men would presumably be waiting to help the crewmen establish a beachhead and unload. But less than 100 yards from shore, the vessel caught on the remains of an old refugee ship that had been sunk by the British before World War II.

When Stavsky noted the location, he cried: "We're stuck on top of my ship!" He had himself bought and sent the ill-fated refugee ship, loaded with Jews, to Palestine.

The location also brought back other memories for Stavsky. It was on shore just opposite the ship that Chaim Arlosoroff had been murdered one hot June evening in 1933 while strolling along the beach with his wife . . .

ARLOSOROFF, WHO WAS DIRECTOR OF THE JEWISH AGENCY'S POLITical Department, had just returned from a grim trip to Germany where he had conducted preliminary discussions with the Nazis for the transfer of the nation's persecuted Jews to Palestine despite British reluctance to let them in. As he walked along in the moonlight, a man approached him and asked for a light. Arlosoroff was about to strike a match when the stranger, without warning, removed a pistol from his inside coat pocket and shot him dead.

Who was the murderer? The Jewish Agency and the British were convinced, or wanted to be, that it was a young Revisionist extremist—Abraham Stavsky. The Revisionist movement, which later produced the Irgun, had intended the murder, they claimed, as a violent protest against the Agency's moderate approach to the refugee problem, and particularly its unwillingness to employ force if necessary to get the British to open Palestine's gates. Stavsky, they charged, had been the instrument of this protest. He was convicted by a court but was later released on grounds of insufficient evidence, with some indications pointing to an Arab as the killer.

His case had created the fiercest controversy in Zionist history. Now here he was involved in what could turn out to be an even fiercer controversy . . .

Beigin contacted Chaim Landau, the Irgun representative in Tel Aviv, and asked him to negotiate some arrangement with the government that would permit the Irgun to unload the *Altalena* without regard to the details of arms distribution.

Then Fein said: "Well, it's after midnight. Everything's quiet now, and there's nothing more we can do tonight. Let's go to bed. We may need the sleep."

While the *Altalena* was threading its way southward to Tel Aviv, Bezalel Stolnitzky, an Irgun official, had called on Faglin in Nathanya and told him what had happened.

"What can we do?" Stolnitzky asked. "Maybe we should go to Tel Aviv to help them land."

"It'll be a waste of time," Faglin responded, dressing hastily. "We'll go to Tel Aviv, all right, but only to get some men."

"And then what?"

"Then we'll head for Ramat Gan [a suburb of Tel Aviv and the government seat] and take over the government!"

There was silence for a moment as Faglin contemplated this pronouncement. It was the only way left to prevent the government from exercising its undeniable right to end the glorious history of the Irgun in defeat and humiliation. After all, Ben-Gurion had not come to power as the result of a popular election but only because he had had the backing of military force. What he could do, the Irgun could do—provided, of course, that it was able to demonstrate superior force.

If government leaders resisted, the Irgun would simply "wipe them out."[5]

*

The next morning, June 22, several hours after the *Altalena* had come
to rest in Tel Aviv Harbor, Ben-Gurion called an emergency cabinet meeting. His eyes inflamed from sleeplessness and his white hair more unruly
than ever, the Prime Minister spoke solemnly:

"The situation is very serious. What is happening endangers our war
effort and even more important, it endangers the very existence of the state,
because the state cannot exist until we have one army and control of that
army. This is an attempt to kill the state. If we have to fight, we have to
fight, for on these two points we cannot compromise . . . I am no less a
compromiser than you, but there are things that are not open to compromise because they are the soul of the state . . . "

Ben-Gurion then asked the cabinet to approve an order that the ship
be turned over to the government and that all measures necessary to assure
compliance be taken. A resolution calling for such an order was passed
by a vote of 7 to 2.

Shortly after the cabinet meeting, Ben-Gurion, in his capacity as Defense Minister, telephoned Yigal Allon at Palmach headquarters (which
was located by the beach within sight of the *Altalena*) and said: "Yigal, we
are being faced with open revolt. Not only is Tel Aviv in danger of falling to
the rebel forces, but the very future of the state is at stake. You are to take
command of the Tel Aviv area. Your new assignment may be the toughest
one you've had so far. This time you may have to kill Jews. But I'm depending on you to do what is necessary for the sake of Israel."

"I'll do my best," Allon responded.

"What's our strength in Tel Aviv at the moment?" Ben-Gurion asked.

"There are very few troops in the city, and a large percentage of them
are women or wounded men not fit for battle."

"How are they armed?"

"Just with pistols and rifles and a few submachine guns."

"The Irgun has caught us at the right time," said Ben-Gurion grimly,
"when most of our forces are defending the border settlements or on leave.
Can you gather enough men to do the job quickly enough?"

"I'll call immediately for a company each from the Yiftach and Carmeli Brigades. And I can use a company from the Negev Brigade which
infiltrated through the Egyptian lines last night."

"Okay," Ben-Gurion answered, "but don't start firing unless they fire
first—or unless they start unloading despite our warnings."

Ben-Gurion then ordered the evacuation of all civilians from the beach
area and, realizing his own home was within firing range, telephoned his
wife, Paula.

"Tell the neighbors to leave their houses until the trouble is over," he said, "and be sure that you go, too."

Paula warned her neighbors but remained at home herself to finish the housework, though she did not dare to answer the telephone that afternoon for fear that her husband would discover her presence and worry about her.

With Tel Aviv poised on the brink of civil war, government troops cracked down hard on the besieged beachhead at Kfar Vitkin. As firing there continued, casualties grew, and the encirclement tightened, Meridor decided in the early morning of June 22—a few hours after the *Altalena* had arrived in Tel Aviv—to surrender. He met with army officials in the town hall and agreed to give up all the unloaded arms, about one-fifth of the total.

When Israeli troops took over the beachhead at dawn, Topsy was still bandaging the wounded under the pier—18 Irgunists had been wounded and 6 killed, as compared to 2 dead and 6 wounded for the government forces.

"Give us your name and then you can go," an army officer told the girl.

She finished bandaging one of the victims without looking up, then rose and said icily: "My name is Malka Jaffet—you murderer!"

In the crisp bright morning, the crewmen of the *Altalena* routinely cleaned up the mess left by 900 passengers—and less routinely rigged a loudspeaker on the bow so that it faced shore. While Ben-Gurion was addressing the cabinet, Beigin addressed the local population: "People of Tel Aviv, we of the Irgun have brought you arms to fight the enemy, but the government is denying them to you . . . "

Then, directing his appeal to the army, he shouted: "Use your heads. Help us unload these arms, which are for the common defense. If there are differences among us, let us reason later . . . "

On the veranda of the Kaete Dan Hotel, due west of the ship, a group of United Nations observers, who had their headquarters there, listened in astonishment over a breakfast of herring and eggs. In a nearby building at the government press office, foreign correspondents, many of them dazed from having filed stories all night, took down notes with the help of interpreters as Beigin spoke. At Palmach headquarters in the Ritz Hotel, slightly to the north, Yitzhak Rabin, who had become deputy Palmach commander, began distributing hand grenades to his small staff.

As Beigin spoke, troops under the command of Tel Aviv commander

Michael Ben-Gal cleared the beach front of civilians. But people watching from the numerous hotels and houses along the waterfront, many of them from balconies equipped with machine guns, could see a small motor launch lowered from the ship and putting in to shore. On arrival, about half a dozen men jumped out and established a beachhead hardly 20 yards from a group of army men, while about a dozen others unloaded several large crates.

Beigin, Fein, and the others aboard the *Altalena* greeted the returning crew joyfully. They had made a test run and it had succeeded, with the army simply standing by while the arms were unloaded. Beigin's appeal had apparently worked. Jews would not kill Jews.

"Load up the boat again," Fein ordered, his concern about the three corvettes that had been encircling the ship since early morning now much diminished.

But just as the reloading was completed, Fein, through his binoculars, saw dozens of army trucks pull up to shore and hundreds of soldiers disembark and spread out along the beach front, many of them taking up positions behind a concrete wall enclosing a large restaurant.

Whatever might happen, Fein and Beigin decided, the second boat had to test the government's intentions.

At about 1 P.M., the launch started for shore again. With each chug of the motor, the hundreds of spectators—soldiers, sailors, diplomats, United Nations observers, politicians, and others who just happened to be in the area—felt that they were about to witness a spectacular moment in history. And some were reminded of the fate of the Second Temple almost 2,000 years before . . .

THE ROMANS, ENTRENCHED IN JUDAEA, HAD BEEN RULING OVER A deeply divided Jewish society. The aristocrats, who controlled all the cultural, religious, and economic institutions, hoped to conserve their power by collaborating with the Roman regime; members of the moderate mass social and cultural movement, the Pharisees, were willing to fight only if victory were virtually certain; and a relatively small group of zealots wanted to fight regardless of the cost.

Finally, Jewish forces, sparked by the zealots, drove the Romans from Judaea. The aristocrats and Pharisees then formed an independent Jewish "coalition" government—without the zealots. As Roman legions counterattacked in the year A.D. 67, the zealots simultaneously struck for power. Within the sacred walls of Jerusalem, Jew slew Jew, and in the next three years tens of thousands lay dead or dying in the narrow, twisting streets, their bodies pierced by arrows or split by the sword, their souls too numerous for the rabbis in the great Temple to bless properly. Nor did a zealot victory end the fighting; the greatest savagery occurred in endless bloody struggles among power-hungry zealot factions.

Only in the year A.D. 70 did the civil strife end—in the face of the final Roman assault. Piercing the wall with machine-driven drills, the Romans entered and destroyed the Temple, scattering the Jews throughout the earth.

Was history about to repeat itself? . . .

Beigin, as he stood on the bridge of the *Altalena* gripping the railing, his jaw set, his eyes squinting in the sun, mentally measured the white trail of foam as it gradually lengthened in the boat's wake. No matter what a few narrow-minded, hypocritical men like Ben-Gurion ordered, he thought, their soldiers would not shoot former schoolmates, fellow Jews with whom they had shared a dream. Yes, it had happened at Kfar Vitkin, but on a small scale, far from the centers of popular influence. But what Jew could kill another within view of people haunted by six million ghosts . . .

Fein stood next to him, his long face rigid, his thick brows knitted anxiously. He became aware suddenly of the screech of sea gulls in the clear blue sky. And he wondered how he had ever gotten entangled in this absurd situation. Everything had been so clear when he was fighting the Japanese in the Pacific. There the enemy had been a stranger, the universal object of hatred and vengeance. Now, within moments, he might have to order the killing of his own people, of people he had come to help . . .

To Yigal Allon, as he watched the boat approach from the roof of the Ritz Hotel, which was already surrounded by Irgun forces, the situation was clear enough. The enemy was anyone who threatened the Jewish State, and the motorboat was an enemy craft. It was not the individual Jew, but the collective race that was important. And he knew his men. They would shoot if given the order. They would kill fellow Jews in the service of Judaism . . .

The motorboat was about 20 yards from shore when, as Tel Aviv stood still, a machine gun on the beach sputtered a murderous welcome. As bullets sprayed the water, the boat zigzagged crazily through the waves, finally making it to shore. But on the bridge of the *Altalena,* Fein heard over his walkie-talkie the gasp of the boat's pilot: "I'm hit in the chest!"

While Beigin stood apparently mesmerized, Fein shouted orders for the four Bren guns set up on the bow to give the boat and the Irgun men on shore covering fire. Then, when the full force of what was happening at last struck home, Beigin ran to the radio room, contacted Chaim Landau ashore, and hysterically ordered him to persuade army leaders to cease firing. Then he roared into the loudspeaker: "Stop shooting! Do not kill your own brothers!"

Seconds later the loudspeaker on the bow was blown off its mounting. Engineers tried to remount it, but were shot as bullets tore into the ship from buildings all along the shore.

Stavsky, Fallon, and a Cuban volunteer, David Mitrani, who had all been below when the firing started, raced toward the bridge to coordinate plans with Fein. But while climbing the ladder to the bridge, they were exposed to fire. Suddenly, Stavsky fell heavily to the deck while Mitrani crumpled nearby. Fallon was looking toward shore at the time and was convinced the bullets that hit them came from a machine gun operated from the balcony of a beach house by a girl in a yellow dress.

"The dirty bitch!" he yelled, as he ran to the two men to give them first aid.

He found that the Cuban's jaw had been torn away and his chest perforated, and that Stavsky had been hit in the leg and was bleeding profusely. While other crew members carried Stavsky downstairs to the messhall where most of the wounded were being taken, Fallon dragged the Cuban into the wheelhouse and gave him morphine shots.

The Cuban died in Fallon's arms after about 20 minutes of agony, and Fallon wept over his bleeding body. Then he picked up a rifle and, looking through a porthole in the wheelhouse, saw the girl in the yellow dress still behind the machine gun firing. He framed the girl in his sight, then hesitated for a moment as he squinted at the target. I'm going to kill her, he told himself. But somehow his finger lingered on the trigger. The long flowing black hair . . . the big breasts under the tight yellow dress . . . Who could tell, perhaps he would be taking her out that very night if it were not for this stupid killing, even going to bed with her and feeling those lovely breasts and screwing her . . . Or maybe they would just talk, and she would tell him what it was like in a concentration camp and how her parents were burned in an oven and their fat turned to soap . . .

Fallon glanced at the grotesque form of his Cuban friend sprawled a few feet away, and such thoughts vanished abruptly. He was about to press the trigger when a voice cried: "For God's sake, don't shoot! Do you want to draw more fire?"

Fallon looked around to see a crewman who had crawled into the room.

"Maybe you're right," he said, taking a deep breath . . .

The firing on the motorboat was the signal not only for a barrage of government fire toward the LST, but also on the group of Irgunists who had already been taken ashore by the launch to establish a beachhead. But no sooner were most of them killed than other Irgun men, mainly deserters from the army, began storming toward the beach from the city. All along the waterfront and on the adjacent streets, Jews shot at Jews in scenes of chaotic mass hysteria. To add to the confusion, friend and foe were dressed in the same khaki uniform, making them indistinguishable to the outsider.

As bullets flew, United Nations observers on the Kaete Dan veranda dived under tables and waiters dropped their trays and joined them, all watching the show, horrified, from ringside seats. Only Dov Joseph, the civilian leader of Jerusalem, and his guest, a British member of the United Nations team, sat at their table quietly eating lunch, each preferring to risk death rather than show himself less collected, dignified, or courageous than the other.

Initially, the Irgunists appeared to have the edge, for they outnumbered the Haganah troops immediately available in Tel Aviv. They had deserted the newly integrated Israeli army en masse the night before or early that morning to participate in the conflict. One Irgun battalion left the front line in the vicinity of Lydda Airport without any warning, permitting Iraqi troops to fill the vacuum. Another battalion abandoned its positions between Arab-held Ramle and Sarafand Camp and arrived in Tel Aviv after being slowed down by a fierce fire fight with Haganah troops in Beit Dejen on the way. (A third battalion was later prevented from heading for Tel Aviv by Haganah forces who halted it near Sarafand Camp.)

Soon after the shooting started, these troops took over Ben-Gal's seashore Haganah headquarters and threatened to take over Palmach and naval headquarters. Yitzhak Rabin and other Palmach soldiers stood by the windows in the Ritz Hotel and shot or threw hand grenades at Irgunists, but as bullets penetrated the building from all sides, the Palmach position grew increasingly precarious.

To all intents and purposes, the Irgun forces—though few people in Tel Aviv realized it—had won control of Tel Aviv.

Moshe Kelman, commander of the 3rd Battalion of the Yiftach Brigade, was awakened early that morning in his room in Sarafand Camp by a messenger who handed him a note from Palmach headquarters. It read: "Be on alert. Gather all soldiers you can and await further orders."

At about 10 A.M. Kelman, who was thoroughly confused, knowing nothing about what was going on in Tel Aviv, received another message, informing him this time of the struggle with the Irgun. The headquarters was surrounded, he learned.

"Come immediately with any force at your disposal," the message ordered.

Kelman gathered his men together within minutes and addressed them:

"Men, we have orders to perform an action that is a bit unusual. However, this country has one government and only one government, and we, as soldiers, take orders only from that government."

He paused for a moment, then continued: "We may have to shoot Jewish people. And I expect everyone to carry out all orders. If any order is not obeyed, I will have to deal with the situation as I would on the battlefield. I don't want any misunderstandings. There is a little trouble with the Etzel. I don't know exactly what it's all about, but they've surrounded Palmach headquarters. So we're going to Tel Aviv. You'll get further orders on the spot. Now get on the buses."*

As his men filed into the nearby buses, Kelman studied the faces of the soldiers in Squad 8. It was made up of Irgun men who had been integrated into the company—Irgun militants whom the Haganah had hidden from the British before independence, after they had committed terrorist acts.

He would have to treat them like the other soldiers; otherwise, this was no army. But as he vainly sought some clue to their feelings in their expressionless faces, he chilled at the thought of what he would have to do for the sake of company morale if they refused to act against their fellow Irgunists . . .

KELMAN HAD ONCE BEFORE HAD TO KILL A FELLOW JEW, ABOUT A year earlier. But that had been a formal—though secret—execution. The man was a traitor and there was no question of his guilt. He had been observed behaving suspiciously at Kibbutz Ayelet Hasachar (Palmach headquarters for eastern Galilee) and was arrested and persuaded to confess that he was a British agent. His story was that the British police had charged him with some petty crime, and a "Sergeant Keeley" had then offered him a deal. If he would go to Ayelet Hasachar, his old settlement, and arrange for the Jews to buy arms, he would receive a ticket to Australia and £100. The British, the man asserted, wanted to capture the Jews in the act of buying arms—a crime punishable by death—and use this "crime" as an excuse to raid the settlement and search for weapons they believed were already hidden there.

"How were you to maintain contact with the British?"

"Well, there's a certain coffeehouse in Tiberias . . . "

Haganah agents checked and confirmed the information.

The full Haganah High Command then deliberated the case and finally ordered the captive executed. The method was left to Kelman, Palmach commander in the area, to decide.

___

* The commander of another Israeli unit gathered in Tel Aviv to help Allon's beleaguered troops asked those of his men who had compunctions about killing other Jews to step forward. Shocked when about two-thirds of his 60-man force stepped forward, the commander announced in anger and frustration that these men would all be court-martialed.

Kelman decided that the "operation" would take place at Kibbutz Dafna in the north, for the earth was soft there, unlike many parts of rocky Galilee, and an unmarked grave would be difficult to detect. But he told the Dafna commander, since he knew he would object to submitting the settlement to possible involvement in a "murder" charge, that some arms being smuggled from Lebanon would be buried on the grounds. Several handpicked gravediggers then dug a grave, carefully placing samples of dirt from each level on a piece of canvas to make sure that the same shades would be returned to the proper strata when the grave was filled in. Nothing could be left to chance.

When the prisoner arrived, he was fitted out with brand-new khaki shorts—the clothes he had worn were burned—and guarded by the gravediggers under a plum tree in the kibbutz orchard. Having no idea what was in store for him, he waited patiently. Toward midnight, Kelman guided the prisoner to a spot near the gaping hole. While his platoon commander stood beside the man, Sten in hand, Kelman, facing them, started reading by moonlight from a statement sent to him by the High Command. He read slowly, in jerky phrases, as he strained to see:

"The High Command has considered the case of the accused . . . and has found him to be a traitor to the Zionist cause . . . "

Kelman paused and looked at the man, who stood listening indifferently. He breathed in the fragrance of freshly turned earth, choked slightly and continued in a shaky voice:

"It is our decision that the accused be executed immediately."

"No! No! . . . "

The platoon commander lifted his Sten, and a single bullet fired directly at the head cut off the piercing scream.

The gravediggers then buried the body, making sure that the earth was meticulously replaced almost grain for grain as before. A tractor evened out the ground, and a missing Jew had disappeared without trace . . .[6]

Now, more than a year later, Kelman wondered if his second Jew would be any easier . . .

Kelman's bus convoy smashed through an Irgun roadblock on the street leading into Tel Aviv and raced to within a few blocks of Palmach headquarters. Then, approaching on foot along two parallel streets leading to the sea, his men sealed off the area and disarmed motley groups of Irgun soldiers as they advanced. By the time they reached Palmach headquarters, the Irgunists who had been besieging it, realizing they were surrounded, had scattered.

Kelman's company then began to round up Irgun forces throughout the city with the help of half-tracks brought from Tel Letvinsky Camp on the outskirts of Tel Aviv. In one chase, he led 13 half-tracks at breakneck speed in a race to catch an Irgun armored car, their sirens screaming and their wheels screeching as they careened wildly round corners. Finally, the car halted and four Irgunists jumped out and held up their hands as the whole convoy came to a halt.

Kelman got out of his jeep and looked at the men in the first half-track.

"All right, Squad 8, get down and disarm them," he ordered, unable to resist this opportunity to test its loyalty.

The men obeyed and surrounded the fleeing Irgunists.

"Gentlemen," said the squad leader, a huge, powerful man, "please surrender your arms."

His soldiers took the rifles from three of the captives, but the fourth struggled fiercely, shouting: "You're soldiers just like I am! Would you give up your weapons to anyone?"

The men seemed to relax their hold on him, and Kelman trembled slightly. Then the squad leader said: "Give it to me or I'll take it!" And he grabbed the man, shook him, and seized his Sten gun.

"Okay," said Kelman casually. "Now let's find a few more."

While sporadic fighting continued in the city, Allon, about 45 minutes after the exchange of fire with the ship had started, agreed to a request from the vessel that the firing stop while the wounded were evacuated, provided there was no more unloading.

But during the lull, he was sure he saw Irgun men setting up a heavy machine gun on the deck and aiming it at Palmach headquarters (though these men were apparently doing so without the authority of their leaders). He immediately telephoned Ben-Gurion's office and received permission from the Prime Minister to fire cannon and mortar shells, first as a warning to surrender and then, if necessary, to sink the ship.

Meanwhile, Mayor Israel Rokakh of Tel Aviv, heading a four-man delegation of local dignitaries, appealed to Ben-Gurion in the Prime Minister's office to enforce a government cease-fire in order to permit Rokakh to board the ship and negotiate a surrender.

"After all, they are our children," Rokakh pleaded passionately. "They bled yesterday at Jaffa and Jerusalem, and they will bleed tomorrow again that we may live."

Ben-Gurion listened attentively. Then he looked the mayor directly in the eye and said, with what the delegation regarded as something less than sincerity: "I understand your feelings, but I have no power to interrupt military operations without a cabinet decision."

The telephone rang and Ben-Gurion picked up the receiver. After listening silently for several moments, he said: "I see. When did it happen?" Then after a pause: "Keep me informed as things develop. Thank you." And he replaced the receiver.

He looked at his curious visitors.

"Gentlemen," he said quietly, "I think the situation is reaching a climax. I've just been notified that the ship has been hit by an artillery shell and is burning . . . "

At about 4 P.M., shortly after the cease-fire was to have gone into effect, Fein and the others aboard, while anxiously waiting for the army evacuation boats, heard the boom of a cannon and saw water gush nearby as a shell landed in the sea. A second and third shell also fell short. Fein immediately signalled for the firing to stop and received assurance that it would. But a few minutes later a shell hit the middle of the deck, pierced the soft steel, and exploded in the cargo hold below. Smoke poured out and ammunition went off like firecrackers.

With the fire starting to rage, Fein and Fallon ran along the deck, literally dodging bullets, and hooked up three sprinkler systems, flooding the hold and managing to keep the flames under control.

Fein then ran to the bridge, where he found Begin enraged. "I've called the Palmach commander, but he won't answer. It looks like we'll all die here . . . Monroe, you and the other Americans aboard are free to get off. You came as navigators, not soldiers."

"I'm staying," Fein answered. "But we've got to hoist the white flag. Otherwise the ship is sure to blow up with all that explosive stuff down there."

"We'll never put up that flag!" Begin shouted. "I'm the commander here and you'll obey orders!"

"We're putting it up!" Fein bellowed, and he ordered his radio man, who was standing nearby, to make sure Begin did not interfere.

A few minutes later, Fallon came rushing up to the bridge.

"Captain, we've got to surrender," he said breathlessly. "The wounded are bleeding to death!"

Fein pointed to the mast; a white sheet was flapping in the afternoon breeze. On the floor, stomach down, was Begin, with the radio man on top of him, a knee in his back.

"Take it down, take it down!" the Irgun leader shouted. "It's better to die here. Then at least people will see how evil the government is."

And he continued to rant hysterically . . .

As shells splashed relentlessly into the water around the ship, Fein finally got through to Palmach headquarters: "You promised to stop firing if we surrendered, but we've raised the white flag and you're still firing. Why are you shelling us?"

The answer came back: "There is a general cease-fire but the order has not yet reached all units of the army."

By now, in any event, flames had started to engulf the main deck. Fein issued orders to abandon ship. As he stood on the bridge waving a white flag and shouting for a cease-fire, the evacuation proceeded with remarkable calm. The wounded, including Stavsky, who died later in the hospital, were lowered on life rafts, and the healthy men, equipped with life preservers, jumped into the water and swam while bullets "pinged" around them. Some men were picked up by Irgun boys, mostly in their teens, who had paddled out from shore on rafts and surfboards.

With only seven men left on board, Fein and Lankin insisted that Beigin jump next. But he grabbed hold of the railing and refused.

"I shall be the last one off!" he yelled.

Fein ordered two seamen to throw him overboard, and the Irgun chief was heard cursing until he struck the water, to be picked up by a raft.

Finally only Fein, Lankin, Fallon, and another seaman remained. Fein looked at Fallon and said: "Haul ass!"

The last two aboard—Fein and Lankin—glanced at the spreading fire, then at each other. Fein smiled briefly, remembering that moment when, in the crushing boredom of civilized Chicago, he had decided to "do something worthwhile."

"I guess we'd better jump," he said. And the two men, dressed only in shorts, dived through the smoke into the debris-strewn sea.

Early that morning, Faglin and Stolnitzky had found a cab at a taxi station in Nathanya and started off on their extraordinary mission—to seize the government. But hardly had the taxi left Nathanya when it was flanked by Haganah armored cars and halted—the result of a tip by another taxi driver who recognized Faglin at the taxi stand.

The two men were arrested, but Faglin was determined to escape. While in one of the armored cars, he made a break for the door, shouting to the guards: "Give my best to Ben-Gurion!" but the latch caught before he could jump out. Placed in the guard room of an army camp in Nathanya, he had removed all but two bolts from a barred window. Then he was dragged off to an underground bunker in a kibbutz near Tulkarm and guarded by many soldiers. But with a jagged piece of knife, he opened the lock of the iron door and, dressed only in shorts, dashed right past the guards, climbed a high barbed wire fence, and ran through a minefield to freedom!

Arriving in Nathanya ready to go through with his plan, he collapsed exhausted in his friend's house after learning that the *Altalena* had been sunk and that the Irgun was on the run.

The survivors of the *Altalena* reached shore just as the ship started

to explode and found that, because of the danger, the government troops
had been withdrawn from the beach. Most were met by jeeps which took
them, naked and drenched, to Irgun headquarters. Felled in the battle
on shore and at sea were 83 casualties, including 14 dead.

That evening, Beigin went on the Irgun's secret radio and delivered a
highly emotional speech, stating that "Irgun soldiers will not be a party
to fratricidal warfare, but neither will they accept the discipline of Ben-
Gurion's army any longer. Within the state area we shall continue our
political activities. Our fighting strength we shall conserve for the enemy
outside . . . "

Ben-Gurion, whose forces had suffered only two dead and six wounded,
replied before the National Council: "Blessed be the gun which set the ship
on fire—that gun will have its place in Israel's War Museum."

And he continued to round up and arrest all the Irgunists who could be
found, despite the token resignation of two cabinet ministers who opposed
this dedicated, and successful, effort to destroy the Irgun in one lightning
thrust.

While the army thus vigorously hunted down Irgun fighters, Beigin,
brooding in a Jaffa hideout, was visited by Israel Sheib, the Sternist leader.

"I haven't come to scold or to console," the fiery little professor said
as he sat down on the edge of a chair, tense and impatient. "I've just come
to ask—What next?"

"Who can say?"

"Well, I, for one," Sheib replied. "Look, Menachem, we are not obliged
to subject ourselves to a government such as this. We can exploit the incident, gather all our men, and break through to Jerusalem. Jerusalem is in
danger and there is still foreign rule there. We are strangers, useless
strangers, here. Our place is in Jerusalem."

Beigin stared at Sheib, silently contemplating his words.

"Maybe it's worth a try," he allowed. "Maybe we can unite our forces,
take over Jerusalem, and declare it 'Free Judaea.' "

"I suggest that our forces attack the Old City immediately as well as the
Arab strongholds all the way from Jerusalem to Ramallah," proposed
Sheib, outlining a plan that Zetler had long advocated. "By doing this, we
will increase the area and prestige of our 'Free Judaea.' And it would give
us more mobility in case Ben-Gurion lays siege to the area."

But as the conversation progressed, Sheib began to feel that Beigin,
emotionally confused by the *Altalena* disaster, was not really serious about
setting up a Free Judaea.

At this point an Irgun soldier burst into the room crying: "Military
police are approaching!"

"What are you going to do?" Sheib asked.

"We'll defend ourselves."

"Then they'll finish the job they started yesterday. They'll kill you!"

"Maybe, but I'm going to stay to the end with my men."

Sheib couldn't help smiling. The same old Menachem; the same old romanticist! He recalled how Beigin had come to him in Tel Aviv during World War II dressed in a Polish officer's uniform . . .

AFTER THE RUSSIANS HAD DRAGGED BEIGIN FROM VILNA, LITHU-ania, to a Siberian prison camp during the Moscow-Berlin detente, he was finally liberated, as were most Poles, to join the Free Polish Army. Units of that army went to Transjordan, and Beigin thus had the chance to enter Palestine, which he had intended to do anyway. Moreover, he helped to persuade the Poles—who were violently anti-Soviet despite their common battle with the Germans—to arm and train his Irgunist friends in return for a campaign by the Revisionists to disseminate anti-Russian and anti-Communist propaganda in the United States and Britain.

Sheib, who had earlier smuggled himself into the country, had met Beigin and inquired caustically: "Menachem, when are you going to take off that Polish army uniform?"

"I've asked to be released from the Polish army," was the reply.

"And if they don't agree? Why don't you do what hundreds of other boys are doing and just leave?"

"You mean that I should desert?" Beigin was incredulous.

"Of course. Why not?"

"Don't you think I have a sense of honor?" . . .

A sense or honor! Menachem still failed to see that the only true honor lay in the redemption of God's promise—the creation, for the first time, of an Israel stretching from the Euphrates to the Nile, to revolve around a reconstructed Temple in Jerusalem.*

"Menachem," he asked now, "what kind of heroism is this? Lenin would not have done it this way. Lenin hid in the forest, managed the campaign from there, and won."

"Perhaps so," mumbled Beigin, "but I've decided. I won't leave my men."

The matter was resolved when the military police marched past the house without searching it. Sheib left gloomily, his dream of a "Free Judaea" shattered.[7]

Fein and Fallon were among those arrested and questioned by the

---

* Although Israeli extremists maintain that the "river of Egypt" mentioned in the Bible is the Nile, Israeli moderates say that the Bible refers to the El Arish River, a muddy stream that flows a few miles inside the Sinai. The Arabs have long charged that Israel wants to conquer all the territory between the Euphrates and the Nile.

army before being freed several days later. Fein, who fell ill while under detention, was blindfolded, taken to a Tel Aviv hotel, given a £5 note, and left on his own. Irgun friends came and sent a doctor to treat him. The doctor provided him with a nurse, an attractive Yemenite girl with a rounded figure and shining white teeth.

"Haven't I seen you somewhere before?" he asked, as she popped a thermometer in his mouth.

"Yes," she replied in uncertain English. "I am the sandwich girl, remember? They call me Topsy."

Fein smiled, nearly cracking the thermometer. Well, at least now he had time for this.

And a few months later they were married.[8]

IF Ben-Gurion was willing to sacrifice a shipload of Irgun arms for the sake of military unity, he combined his unification efforts with feverish acceleration of his own arms-gathering program in quiet defiance of truce regulations. Czechoslovakia, with Russia's blessing, remained his chief source, even after the British had left Palestine. Having helped to achieve the principal Communist objective, Moscow wanted to make sure that Bevin would not return through the back door in the wake of an Arab victory.

The Israelis looked for planes and arms elsewhere, too, even from such an unlikely donor as Britain herself, which had stopped sending arms to her Arab allies. But the British were eventually alerted to Israeli activities and began to crack down. Even so, Emmanuel Zur, an Israeli agent in London, managed to obtain several Beaufighter bombers and was determined somehow to get them out of Britain. As he pondered the problem, a pilot he had hired came to his hotel one day and introduced him to a beautiful young woman.

"The finest actress in New Zealand," the pilot said. "She may do a film here based on New Zealand's role in World War II."

"Really?" asked Zur, his eyes brightening.

Within days, Zur himself had provided the funds for a film about the courage of New Zealand pilots in the war. With the help of contacts in the British movie industry, a production company was formed and actors, all of whom had to be real pilots, were hired. One scene in the script called for a mass take-off of Beaufighters. The cameras rolled away as the actors played impeccably. The film might have been a good one—had the Beaufighters returned . . .

*

Agents in the United States were also busy buying bombers. Nahum Bernstein, the New York lawyer in charge of acquisitions there, and his air force expert, Al Schwimmer, purchased four B-17 Flying Fortresses and four A-20 medium bombers. The B-17's were to fly from Miami Airport to Puerto Rico on June 12, the second day of the truce, and then on to the Azores and finally to Ajaccio, Corsica, their last stop. That was the announced flight schedule. Actually the planes would fly directly from the Azores to Czechoslovakia to get arms, and thence to Israel. Friends at Ajaccio were to "confirm" to the Azores that the planes had "landed" there.

Two of the planes took off from Miami on schedule without incident; the third took off the next morning (June 13) after a tire burst on the runway. The fourth was not ready to leave. Everything went smoothly, except that in one of the planes the navigator stepped on a pane of glass set into the floor to facilitate aerial photography and fell through. Spreading his arms as he dropped, he miraculously managed to hold on for half an hour until other crew members finally discovered him, numb with cold and fear.

Bernstein and Schwimmer waited anxiously in New York for word of the bombers' fate, and were frantic when they heard nothing for 24 hours. Then, on the morning of June 14, Bernstein glanced at the *New York Times* over breakfast and turned ashen. Three Flying Fortresses, frontpage headlines blared, had disappeared off the Azores en route to Europe. Rescue ships had found wreckage on the ocean.

"Don't worry," Schwimmer calmed him on the phone. "I've seen reports like this before. Just hold tight."

Later that day, Schwimmer received a call from Paris. The three planes had arrived safely in Czechoslovakia.

"What about those reports that they cracked up?"

"Well, you see, the Azores gave the alarm when they didn't receive 'confirmation' that the planes had landed in Ajaccio. Our friends in Ajaccio forgot to tell them!"

The funny thing was, Schwimmer learned, that the planes actually *did* land in Ajaccio en route for Israel.

The newspapers soon forgot about the "lost" aircraft, but the FBI and the State Department, irked by Israel's graceless refusal to accept the arms embargo, were more vigilant. American Embassies throughout Europe enjoined host governments to seize all planes of American origin that appeared to be heading for Israel, and to confiscate the passports of American crews suspected of participating in the arms traffic.

It did not take the FBI long to learn that the Israelis had acquired a fourth Flying Fortress and four A-20 bombers that had still not left American soil. And their interest in Israeli international operations was not quelled by the storm of intrigue centering around the hairbreadth exploits of amateur secret agent Hank Greenspun . . .

"I'm on my way, baby doll," Greenspun had assured his lonely wife, Barbara, in a telephone call to Las Vegas.

Dazed and exhausted after the nightmarish voyage of the *Idalia* from Los Angeles to Acapulco, Greenspun was in Mexico City awaiting the arrival of some C-46's and Constellations Schwimmer was smuggling out of the United States. The arms unloaded from the *Idalia* were to go to Israel on those planes, due to arrive at any moment.

"I'll believe it when I see you," said Barbara, who still thought he was in Mexico on "business." "Sometimes I've had the most terrible feeling I'll never see you again. I've been so lonely and so worried, Hank."

"Just a few more days. Nothing on earth can stop me from coming home."

But something on earth did: a phone call from Haganah headquarters in New York. He was to come to New York immediately. Greenspun protested bitterly. Poor Barbara; another broken promise; and he couldn't even confide in her.

"Well, what is it now?" he asked resignedly on arrival at New York headquarters.

Yehuda Arazi, Israel's top arms procurement chief, came right to the point. He informed Greenspun that the arms from the *Idalia* would be shipped to Israel not in the smuggled planes, but in the freighter *Kefalos,* which was on her way to Tampico Bay. Since the vessel could carry 6,000 tons of goods, Greenspun was to acquire additional arms to fill her up.

"You will be responsible for the success of Israel's whole arms procurement program in the West," Arazi told him. "The fate of the new state could hinge on the results."

"It's too much for me to handle," Greenspun responded, awed by the task. He was just a newspaper editor and a guy who dabbled in the nightclub business. And anyway, he wanted to get home to "baby doll."

"You may be right," Arazi replied, "but we have no one else."

Setting up an office in a suite in Mexico City's Hotel Reforma, Greenspun and several aides made the rounds of Mexican government arsenals, prying up tarpaulins, inspecting and testing firing mechanisms, and finally signing a check made out to the government for over $1.2 million that covered thousands of rifles and machine guns, as well as aerial bombs, howitzers, and cannons.

One night, Greenspun's hotel doorbell rang and went on buzzing insistently, but there was no one there. A pin had been jammed in. Greenspun found a copy of the newspaper *Excelsior* on the floor. Picking it up, he saw a red circle round an article about the *Kefalos* being loaded with weapons for Israel. Across the story was scrawled in the same red crayon: *"Itbach el Yahud!"* ("Kill the Jews!")

The next day, an Arab banker, Miguel Abed, and his followers demonstrated against the sailing of the *Kefalos,* and the Mexican government couldn't ignore the pressure. It indicated it might indeed have to crack down.

Greenspun invited a government contact for a drink at the Reforma bar and asked for advice.

"A neutral country could buy and ship arms without any trouble," the Mexican said. "Can you think of any possibilities?"

Greenspun chewed on a long black cigar, then, eyes flashing, asked: "Your government hasn't had any trouble with Chiang Kai-shek lately, has it?" . . .

Generalissimo Chiang Kai-shek, the great leader of Nationalist China, needed arms urgently and was confident Mexico would cooperate.

In stuttering Spanish, Greenspun explained this the following day to General Cuenca, deputy chief of staff of the Mexican army, at the presidential palace. The General listened politely, though apparently understanding little of what his guest was saying, and then replied: "For the time being, the Mexican government will accept your statement that you represent an official Chinese Purchasing Commission."

Smiling and shaking hands, he added: *"Buena suerte, Coronel* Greenspun."

While Greenspun waited for delivery of the equipment he had purchased and for sailing clearance from the Mexican government, he decided to fly home for two days to avoid a possible rupture of his marriage. But hardly had he been tearfully welcomed home than Teddy Kollek, who had replaced Arazi, telephoned him from New York.

"Get back to Mexico City at once!" Kollek ordered. "The Mexican Foreign Minister and delegate to the U.N. has stood up in open session demanding that they take official action . . . Now the U.N. has sent a message to President Aleman [of Mexico]. They want him to slap an immediate embargo on the *Kefalos.* Do you know what that means?"

"You don't have to draw me a picture," Greenspun said bitterly.

"The Mexican government can't use the Chinese story much longer— it's a myth and everyone knows it . . . ," Kollek stormed on.

"All right, I'll go back on the next plane. Tell the boys to keep their pants on."

As he hung up, he avoided Barbara's eye.

"You're leaving *again?*" she exclaimed incredulously. "But you've only been here for a couple of hours!"

"Be patient for a little while longer, baby. A few days, maybe a week. It will be all over by then. I promise you."

"You're quite right, Hank. If you leave again, it *will* be all over between us. That's *my* promise . . . "

The next day, Greenspun arrived back in Mexico City—with his wife and little daughter, Susi, plus two family friends in tow.

At the hotel, a colleague shook his head.

"Hank, when I told Teddy Kollek you were bringing Barbara and the kid, *and* a couple of friends, I thought he'd swallow the phone!"

Greenspun, while agreeing that he had hardly acted in the orthodox tradition of the secret agent, replied: "There was no way to avoid it . . . Okay, what's up?"

It soon became evident that only a meeting with President Aleman himself could free the *Kefalos.* After a somewhat surrealistic night on the town with his still unsuspecting wife and friends, Greenspun was shocked awake at about 9 A.M. by the phone. The President would see him—in 30 minutes.

Bleary-eyed and half-shaven, he stumbled into the presidential palace to be met by General Cuenca, who presented him to President Aleman. As they sat in the President's austere office, Aleman expressed his profound sympathy for Greenspun's undertaking and for "the terrible problems confronting the Jewish people of the Holy Land." But matters of state, he said somberly, had to take precedence over his personal feelings. And grave, seemingly insuperable difficulties had arisen. As he nodded to Cuenca and took his leave, the General reemphasized: "It is quite impossible for the Mexican government to defy the United Nations."

"Can't they insist the shipment is going to China?"

Cuenca looked at Greenspun sternly. "There is only one condition that would permit the government to let the *Kefalos* sail. You would have to produce supporting documents to prove that the ship is loaded with arms for Nationalist China . . ."

"I'm interested in making heavy capital investments in Formosa," Greenspun announced imperiously to the bespectacled young Chinese sitting in the reception room of the Nationalist Chinese Embassy. "Can you supply me with detailed information about the possibilities?"

The man took out some glossy folders from his desk and discoursed on the great "economic opportunities" in Formosa. After Greenspun had listened with apparent interest, the man said eagerly that he would get more detailed commercial literature from an adjoining room. Greenspun then whispered in Yiddish to a colleague who had accompanied him: "Go with him and keep him busy as long as you can."

As it was Sunday and the Embassy was officially closed, Greenspun was uninterrupted as he prowled through the hall trying doorknobs. When one of them turned, he slipped into an office, opened a desk drawer, and grabbed bundles of stationery, envelopes, two large metal seals, and stamp pads inked in red and purple. Stuffing everything into the pockets of his trenchcoat, he bounded out and got back to the foyer just as the Chinese returned.

"Thank you for your gracious assistance," Greenspun beamed, as he hurried out with his confederate, their arms piled high with commercial literature . . .

As the last trainloads of arms arrived at Tampico, Greenspun delivered "official" Chinese documents to the Mexican government "proving" that the arms were intended for Nationalist China. Then he sent his protesting wife home, together with his daughter and friends, and waited impatiently for the precious clearance papers. Finally, on a Saturday, a Mexican contact tipped him off that an order would be issued at 8 A.M. Monday to the officer in charge of the army detachment stationed on board the *Kefalos*.

"What kind of order?" Greenspun asked, holding his breath.

"To unload the ship and confiscate her cargo."

Within minutes, Greenspun, with a set of the false Chinese papers in one pocket of his trenchcoat and his Mauser in the other, dashed out and chartered a small plane to Tampico. Arriving early Sunday morning, he banged on the door of the customhouse, and a petty official on duty finally opened it. The startled official gaped as he found himself confronting a man waving a sheaf of papers and demanding to see the chief inspector. Greenspun then cooled down and, shortly after slipping the man *mordida* (a tip), was introduced to the chief inspector. Clasping a 1,000-peso note in one hand, the inspector perused the documents and, picking up the telephone, summoned the immigration officials to the pier to clear the *Kefalos'* crew.

Greenspun boarded the *Kefalos* drenched in sweat and already nauseous from the stink of bunker oil. A stout Major in charge of the troops on guard, whom he had met before, approached him with an impressively official air. Praying that the order to confiscate the cargo had not been delivered yet, Greenspun blustered in broken but authoritative Spanish: "I am acting on orders from the deputy chief of staff, General Cuenca! The *Kefalos* has been given sailing clearance!" He waved the documents in emphasis.

"And you may remove your detachment of troops from the ship," he continued. "You, Major, will be the last man to leave. *Para seguridad!*"

"*Si, mi Coronel!*"

Greenspun then strode to the bridge, where he found Captain Adolph Sigmund Oko, a journalist and public relations man like himself who had volunteered to smuggle refugees to Israel through the British blockade. Oko, having heard of Greenspun's "high living" in Mexico City while he moldered in the filth and heat of Tampico, felt little but resentment for the man on the other end of the operation.

"A visitor on Sunday?" Oko sneered. "I'm deeply flattered, Colonel Greenspun . . ."

"Drop it, Oko. We don't have time to argue. Customs and immigration are coming aboard at any moment to clear you. The *Kefalos* has to get out of Tampico Bay no later than six tomorrow morning."

"That's a laugh. Don't you realize that some of my crewmen are still ashore in the hospital being treated for their crummy diseases? Under Mexican law, I can't leave port until the entire crew is aboard."

"We've already arranged to post bond for those who can't make it. They'll be shipped out later. Look, Oko, this is serious . . ."

Greenspun moved closer and lowering his voice told Oko of the confiscation order.

But the captain jerked his arm viciously toward shore, his thumb extended, and shouted: "Off! Before I have you thrown off!"

Greenspun hesitated for a moment; not the *Idalia* all over again! He drew his Mauser from his pocket, holding it pointed toward the deck, and said softly: "Get ready to leave Tampico. If you don't, I'll take over this stinking tub and sail her all the way to Haifa without you!"

As he heard men climbing the ladder to the bridge, Greenspun pocketed the Mauser again.

The Major appeared at the top of the ladder, followed by the immigration officials. Oko looked at him, then at Greenspun.

"Okay," he growled. "Let's get this lousy business over with."

"Hank, I hear you need Chinese documents before the *Kefalos* can sail," Teddy Kollek said anxiously over the telephone. "We're friendly with the Chinese Ambassador in Washington. Maybe we can explore the possibilities . . ."

"The ship left at six o'clock this morning. Everything is okay."

"This is no time for jokes," Eliahu Sacharov, an Israeli aide, chimed in. "Your humor can destroy us! The *Kefalos* must sail—everything depends on it."

"She *has* sailed."

"Look, Hank," Kollek pleaded. "The situation is desperate. B.G. himself has been sending us urgent messages."

"The ship sailed this morning!"

"You know what, Eliahu?" Kollek said suddenly. "I think Hank is sincere. Maybe the ship really *has* sailed."

"She's gone, Ted," Greenspun insisted, "she's on her way."

Then, hearing the quiet sobs on the phone, he, too, found himself sniffling.[9]

WHILE Israel prepared for new victories on the battlefront, the Arab States prepared for new victories on the domestic propaganda front. Even Arab leaders who had been wary about plunging into a new round began yielding to public demand that they themselves had whipped up with tales of great Arab conquests.

Only the Transjordanian leaders continued to insist that a resumption of battle would be disastrous for the Arabs. Glubb Pasha, in line with British policy, pressed this view on King Abdullah incessantly to make sure he would not bow to other Arab States. The Jews were smuggling in arms, he pointed out, while Britain had cut off arms shipments to the Arabs. Instead of making war, he insisted, the Arabs should fight in the United Nations for a substantial modification of the original partition plan—with the Negev going to Transjordan.

But Abdullah needed little persuading. And he agreed with Glubb that Transjordan nevertheless had to replenish her arms in case events pushed her into war again. If possible, they decided further, Transjordan should insist once more on a unified command headed by Abdullah—who could then better control events. In the first round of fighting, they were convinced, the Arab States had failed to achieve their ends largely because they had rejected such unity. Egypt had not even permitted Abdullah to review Egyptian troops, though she had accepted him as commander-in-chief.

Abdullah decided now to press his views personally in Cairo and other Arab capitals, though an Iraqi government delegation had already failed in a similar effort to promote Arab unity, even agreeing to support an Egyptian as commander-in-chief.

King Farouk, his bitter competitor for dominance in the Arab world, greeted Abdullah coldly on his arrival at his palace on June 22. Abdullah had hardly sat down on a richly embroidered sofa when he was served coffee in a cup smaller and of inferior quality to that placed before

Farouk—a pointed insult. It was his own fault, thought Abdullah, for assuming that the descendant of a Balkan farmer (Farouk came from an
Albanian commoner's family) could be transformed into a gentleman
merely by becoming King. The Transjordanian leader nevertheless pressed
hard to achieve his aims; but in vain.

On June 27 he flew off to Riad, Saudi Arabia, to patch up affairs with
King Ibn-Saud, whom he had not met personally for 25 years—since
Saud had expelled Hussein, Abdullah's father, from the Sherif's throne in
Medina. But while their talks were friendly, they were no more productive
than the meeting with Farouk. Abdullah then left for Baghdad, where he
received word that the Arab League Political Committee, meeting in Cairo,
had voted unanimously to resume the war . . .

In Amman, Tawfiq Pasha nervously explained to Glubb and the King,
who had returned urgently from Baghdad: "I was in a minority of one. All
the others wanted to renew the fighting. If I had voted alone against it, we
should only have been denounced as traitors, and the truce would still not
have been renewed. Transjordan cannot refuse to fight if the other Arabs
insist on fighting. Our own people here would not stand for that."

"But how can we fight without ammunition?" asked Glubb despairingly.

"Don't shoot unless the Jews shoot first."

This had, in fact, been the strategy agreed upon at the Cairo conference,
according to Glubb. All the Arab chiefs of staff wanted to prolong the truce,
pleading that their armies were not strong enough to beat the enemy, especially with their depleted arsenals. However, the politicians, led by Egypt's
Nokrashy Pasha, who had earlier pressed for peace but gave in under irresistible pressure at home, demanded renewed hostilities. As a compromise, says Glubb, the meeting decided that the Arab armies would assume
only a "passive defensive." The Arabs, of course, could not gain anything
by such tactics but with luck they would not lose anything, either.

However seriously the Arabs contemplated such a war—subsequently
they did shoot first and try to gain ground, though possibly intending only
limited offensives—Iraq alone substantially improved her military position
during the truce. She doubled her army in Palestine (raising it to about
10,000 men) and smuggled into Transjordan and Palestine, past United
Nations observers, 11 large convoys of arms and ammunitions hidden in
crates of food and clothes. Some of the ammunition was later to be fired
from long-starved Arab Legion guns.

But if the commanders were wary of facing the far more strengthened
Israeli forces, the politicians felt they had no choice.

U.S. Col. David (Mickey) Marcus and his aide, Alexander Broida.

United Nation

Moshe Dayan (with patch) and
other Israelis meet with Arabs for
peace talks.

Miriam and Desmond Rutledge
atop a Cromwell tank in the Negev
after a battle with the Arabs.

Miriam Rutledge

Orthodox Jewish fighters.

Israeli female soldier in front-line position.

Israelis capture Arab village near Ramle.

United Press International

Israelis hoist flag at Elath.

Emmanuel Meidav, Israeli officer who died in the Old City Jewish Quarter.

Rika Menache, fighter in the Old City Jewish Quarter and fiancée of Emmanuel Meidav.

Moshe Rousnak, commander of the Old City
　　Jewish Quarter.

Daughters of Rabbi A. Mordechai Weingarten,
　　mukhtar of the Old City Jewish Quarter;
　　left to right, rear: Masha, Rivca, Yehudit;
　　front: Rachel, Ceremia.

Rabbi Weingarten, his daughter Yehudit, and a wounded Israeli discuss the surrender of the Old City Jewish Quarter with Arab Legion officers.

Two old rabbis meet with Arab Legionnaires to discuss surrender of the Old City Jewish Quarter.

Arabs fire at Israelis from the ruins of a synagogue in the Old City Jewish Quarter.

Col. Ahmed Abd el-Aziz, commander of Egyptian irregular forces.

Maj. Gamal Abdel Nasser, left, and his battalion commander, in Faluja.

Col. Sayed Taha (looking up at camera), commander of the Faluja forces, and other Egyptian officers meet with Israelis in peacemaking effort.

Ralph Bunche, Acting United Nations mediator for Palestine, signs the
Egyptian-Israeli Armistice Agreement.

above: Mordechai Raanan, left,
commander of Irgun Zvai Leumi forces
in Jerusalem, and Menachem Beigin,
the Irgun commander-in-chief, visit
Washington, D.C.

left: Amihai Faglin, Irgun chief
of operations.

opposite page, top: Irgun soldiers defen
position in the Sheikh Jarrah area of
Jerusalem.

opposite page, bottom: Spectators watc
the *Altalena* burning in Tel Aviv Harbo

Crew members of the *Altalena;* Captain Monroe Fein is in the bottom row, center.

Nathan Friedman-Yellin,
commander of the Stern Group.

Israel Sheib,
Stern Group ideological leader.

British prison photo of Yehoshua Zetler, Stern Group commander in Jerusalem.

A̶s ARABS and Israelis braced themselves for another round at the end of the truce period, Count Bernadotte and his staff worked desperately to draw up a new partition plan that they hoped might lead to a permanent, negotiated peace. [10]

Day and night, Bernadotte and his aides, including his American Negro deputy, Dr. Ralph Bunche, met at United Nations headquarters on the island of Rhodes to thrash out ideas. Bernadotte, who had done little homework on past solutions considered by various international commissions over the years, felt that with his fresh eye he might perceive what had eluded dozens of experts—an answer acceptable to both Arab and Jew.

Finally, he and his staff came up with a fresh and original creation, incorporating these main features:

(1) Palestine, as defined in the original British mandate of 1922, that is, including Transjordan, would form a union of two members, one Arab and the other Jewish.

(2) Each member would exercise full control over its own immigration policy, but at the end of two years either member would have the right to demand a review of the other's policy by the governing Council of the Union. If the Council could not reach a decision, the matter would be submitted to the United Nations Economic and Social Council.

(3) Territorially, the two states would be homogeneous geographical entities. All or part of the Negev would go to the Arabs, all or part of Western Galilee to the Jews. All of Jerusalem would become Arab, with municipal autonomy for the Jewish community. Haifa would be a free port and Lydda a free airport.

"I was perfectly well aware," Bernadotte later wrote in his diary, "that my proposal would be exposed to severe criticism. . . . If the United Nations General Assembly had not adopted its, in my view, unfortunate decision of 29th November 1947 and if the State of Israel had not been recognized by so many nations, I should not have chosen this solution."

But he was saddled with a Jewish State, and the best he could hope for was that the two sides, despite the expected criticism, would agree broadly to his plan. After all, if they did not, "the war would flare up afresh. And the fortunes of war must in the end turn against one side or the other. It was hardly likely that the losing party would get better terms than the ones I proposed."

The Arabs were the first to impress Bernadotte with their view of his logic.

"The Arab world would rather go under than give up the fight," Azzam
Pasha, secretary-general of the Arab League, proclaimed imperiously when
the mediator confronted Arab representatives on July 3 in the Prime
Minister's office in Cairo.

But Bernadotte remained strangely confident. He was, in any event, delighted with Transjordan's reaction; at least, her unofficial one. Abdullah
could hardly believe his eyes when he read the plan. Even the British could
not have proposed a better one. Not only would he be getting almost the
whole of Arab Palestine as defined by the original partition plan, but the
Negev and all of Jerusalem as well. For that, he would be more than willing
to agree to a loose confederal union with an emasculated Jewish State. But
conversely, the other Arab States, though they did not make this delicate
point to Bernadotte, were frightened as much by the prospect of a vastly
more powerful Transjordan as by the likely domestic reaction to the creation of a Jewish State in whatever form. And Abdullah, ironically, had to
reject the plan officially or stand accused of "treason" to the Arab cause.

Perhaps the Jews would prove more "logical" than the Arabs. Bernadotte clung to this hope—until he saw Sharett's tense, somber expression
when they met in the Foreign Minister's Tel Aviv office on July 6.

"Here is our reply," Sharett said, handing the mediator several typed
pages.

The plan, commented the Jewish document, represented an unauthorized
repeal of the original partition project approved by the General Assembly,
and completely ignored territorial changes achieved by Israeli defenders
repulsing Arab aggression. Israel would never agree to restricted sovereignty or immigration policies; and the idea of giving Jerusalem to the
Arabs was "disastrous."

Bernadotte's gloom was only slightly dispelled when Sharett said that
Israel would agree to an extension of the truce.

Israel needed it. Only a few days remained before the truce was to
end, and the government was in turmoil. Technically, at least, Israel did not
even have a Prime Minister or a High Command . . .

"Who is behind this—Galili?" Ben-Gurion had fumed on the morning
of June 29, when he had glanced over the High Command's recommendations for new front commanders.

"Several of us consulted on it," replied Moshe Tsadok, the adjutant-
general. "Galili, Yadin, [Yossef] Avidar [director of arms and materials],
[Zvi] Ayalon [deputy chief of staff], and myself."

"Well, some changes will have to be made."

The Prime Minister was furious.

The Palmach, that is, Galili and the Mapam Party, were not satisfied with monopolizing 8 of the 13 brigade commands. Now they wanted to make the Palmach chief, Yigal Allon, central front commander, the job Mickey Marcus had held briefly before he was so "mysteriously" eliminated. Well, he had taken care of the Irgun, if with the Palmach's help, and now it was the Palmach's turn, thought Ben-Gurion sourly. The High Command and the cabinet would not dare stir up a major crisis when the war was about to be resumed.

The Prime Minister met in his office with several members of the High Command and announced that Shlomo Shamir would take over the central front.

"We believe that Yigal Allon is the best man for the job," Yadin interrupted sharply.

Allon was better fitted to command the Negev front, Ben-Gurion replied firmly, knowing that in the renewed fighting the Negev would be secondary in importance to the central front, which extended from Tel Aviv to Jerusalem, The central front, he argued, had to be commanded by a man with formal military training who knew how to handle large units. On the other hand, Allon would be suitable for the Negev operation since it would be of a "guerrilla" nature.

"Nonsense," Yadin retorted.

"You must accept my decisions," said Ben-Gurion.

But since he knew of Yadin's special hostility toward Shamir, he agreed to appoint another British-trained officer instead—Mordechai Makleff, the Carmeli Brigade commander.

"If you do not name Allon as central front commander," Yadin persisted, "I shall be forced to resign."

"If you do," the Prime Minister raged, "I'll court-martial you."

Yadin and his colleagues then stood up, announced their resignations, and marched out of the office.

But this setback, which promised to be far more serious than the earlier rift over Galili's position, only fed the Prime Minister's determination to reshape the army. Upon receiving formal letters of resignation from members of the High Command, Ben-Gurion called in Yadin and pleaded with him to change his mind.

"Only if you change yours," replied Yadin.

Ben-Gurion then met with members of his cabinet and immediately went on to the attack.

"The letters I've received," he asserted bitterly, "are the result of our not having accepted the proposals of three people—Galili, Yadin, and Ayalon—for the reorganization of the High Command. I did not approve their plan as it appeared to me to be yet another attempt to transform the whole army into the army of a certain party . . . What this business really amounts to is an attempt at revolt by the army. A war is being waged on me . . . I demand that a committee of three ministers be appointed to examine the matter and draw conclusions . . . "

Ben-Gurion had decided to stake his whole political career, and possibly the security of Israel, on the outcome of this secret investigation . . .

"Mr. Ben-Gurion has consistently intervened in military operations on the tactical level. I pleaded with him to delay the first attack on Latrun. But he would not listen."

Staring coldly at the Prime Minister, who sat with a look of calculated indifference several seats away at the long conference table, Yigal Yadin added: "Ben-Gurion, I told you it would be suicide, and it was."

Ben-Gurion dryly repeated his argument that the attack, even though it failed, had saved Jerusalem by drawing Arab Legion troops away from the city.

From the moment a five-man cabinet committee had begun its hearings, on July 3, only five days before the truce was to end, the Prime Minister found himself on the defensive. The issues involving the Palmach's "independence" and the relative merits of home- and foreign-trained commanders had stretched to encompass the entire question of Ben-Gurion's military authority and competence. The Prime Minister himself was clearly on trial.

Witness after witness attacked him. They called him a "dictator." They complained that not a company of troops, or even a mortar, could be transferred without his approval. They criticized him for creating conditions that made possible the Tubianski Affair. Meir Tubianski, a Haganah officer in charge of the Schneller army camp in Jerusalem, had been sentenced to death for allegedly passing military information to the enemy (though after the war he was cleared posthumously of the crime, an exoneration that the Palmach commanders, who executed him, even today regard, possibly for political reasons of their own, as a political whitewash).

Quietly counterattacking, Ben-Gurion accused the Palmach of gross insubordination, claiming the Yitzhak Rabin had issued an order, approved by Galili, to obey only those commands emanating from Palmach headquarters. Galili conceded that such an order had been issued, but only by a junior Palmach commander with no authority in such matters. The Palmach leaders also admitted that a Harel unit under Uzi Narkis had "confiscated" arms destined for Shaltiel, saying that this action was a "mistake," but that Shaltiel had promised to send arms to Harel anyway.

Despite Ben-Gurion's efforts, however, he was overwhelmed. It was only at the concluding session on July 6, about 48 hours before the war was to start again, that the Prime Minister's cultivated expression of bored indifference dissolved as committee chairman Yitzhak Gruenbaum, Minister of the Interior, read off the list of recommendations.

The committee called on the government to appoint a War Cabinet to decide on war strategy, and two directors-general to assist Ben-Gurion. One of them, presumably Galili, would serve as liaison officer with the High Command; Galili, in other words, would again function, if under a different title, as chief of national command, the position Ben-Gurion had abolished in his earlier encounter with him.

When Gruenbaum had finished reading the report signalling Ben-Gurion's defeat, the Prime Minister rose in silence and walked out of the meeting.

In his office, he picked up a pen and wrote in heavy Hebrew script:

> I offer my resignation as Prime Minister and Minister of Defense . . . I am ready to place myself at your disposition as adviser on matters of security, without the right to vote. . . . In order that the government's time not be wasted, I ask you to put aside your proposals for reorganizing the Defense Ministry, if the intention is to have me continue at its head . . .

After completing the letter, Ben-Gurion read it over carefully. He could almost see the shock and shame on the faces of the committee when they read it. The truce was about to end, and they were to find themselves without a Prime Minister or Defense Minister—unless they suddenly saw reason.

Meanwhile, he decided to get sick . . .

A few hours later, Foreign Minister Sharett, one of the dissenting minority on the investigating committee who had defended Ben-Gurion, slid past Paula at the front door of the Prime Minister's house and ran up to his bedroom.

"B. G." Sharett exclaimed. "What in heaven does your letter mean?"

A doctor by Ben-Gurion's bed put his finger to his lips and whispered: "Please, Mr. Ben-Gurion is ill."

"No, I'm all right," the Prime Minister groaned, opening his eyes slightly and breathing sluggishly. "But no business, Moshe. I just want to rest."

Sharett stared at his old friend with restrained sympathy, not sure whether he was quite as ill as he seemed.

"I understand, B. G., but the letter . . . "

"Moshe, it's necessary to meet immediately with the High Command to complete the planning . . . "

"Who will meet them?" Sharett replied. "Are you Prime Minister or not?"

"No," Ben-Gurion moaned, grimacing suddenly.

The doctor whisked Sharett from the room . . .

The committee was stunned when Sharett reported back.

"Maybe the committee should withdraw completely, as if it had not begun its hearings," chairman Gruenbaum, one of Ben-Gurion's bitterest foes, suggested.

"I doubt that Ben-Gurion will accept even that," replied Moshe Shapiro.

"The advice you give, Gruenbaum, would mean the destruction of the army . . . ," said Aharon Zisling, another antagonist of Ben-Gurion's.

But Gruenbaum, despite his personal feelings toward the Prime Minister, regarded the matter pragmatically: " . . . Who would be the fool to accept responsibility while being advised by Ben-Gurion? Would you do that? If Shertok [Sharett] were to say to me: I am willing to sacrifice myself and will take on the job . . . with Ben-Gurion as adviser, I would agree immediately. But Shertok is not prepared to say such a thing."

Sharett quietly confirmed that indeed he was not.

Pinhas Rosenbluet then concluded: "I suggest we tell him that we accept all his proposals except his resignation, and at the same time tell him that if he resigns the whole government will resign. He must be made to understand the gravity of the situation . . . "

Gruenbaum then spoke in another room with Galili, Yadin, and Yohanan Rattner, a staff planning adviser.

"Well, *chaverim* (comrades)," he said, "we are facing the first big crisis of our new state, and it could have severe repercussions. We must pay the price to solve it."

"I am the price and you may pay it," replied Galili, who, with the other commanders, continued to work, resignation or no resignation. "I'm ready to resign my post permanently and to do everything necessary to influence the other commanders to act in a responsible way."

Gruenbaum returned to the committee room and reported happily that Galili was willing to sacrifice himself if necessary. A messenger then entered with a note for Gruenbaum. It was from Ben-Gurion. He was prepared to withdraw his resignation and work together with a two-man "committee," but the proposals of the Gruenbaum group would have to be shelved.

When Gruenbaum had read the message aloud, there was a moment's silence. Then everybody smiled with relief.

At the same time, Mordechai Makleff, after being told by Yadin that the general staff did not want him to command the central front, voluntarily sent a message to Ben-Gurion gratefully declining the job. He explained that he was needed to command the Carmeli Brigade's projected offensive in the north. This note permitted Ben-Gurion to reach a face-saving compromise with Yadin on the dispute that had sparked off the crisis in the first place. There would be no central front commander, but

Yigal Allon would lead the offensive in that area—which amounted to the same thing.

Ben-Gurion had not yet achieved his goal of placing the Palmach under the control of "nonpolitical," British-trained officers (though he compelled officers of that egalitarian force to wear distinguishing insignia for the first time and tried, if not very successfully, to make them eat in officers' messes).

Still, the Prime Minister, in showing that he was virtually indispensable, at least while the war was in progress, could all but call the tune in the future.

A few hours after Ben-Gurion returned to his post healthier than ever, the Egyptians attacked in the Negev. The war had resumed. Even as the first shots rang out, Count Bernadotte's plane was on its way from Rhodes to Amman in response to an urgent call from King Abdullah. As he rushed up the steps of the royal palace, the monarch greeted him with a worried expression.

"Perhaps there is still time to avoid a renewal of war. You must do what you can to stop it," he said.

Bernadotte agreed to leave for Lake Success immediately to urge the Security Council to take emergency action. But both men knew in their hearts that it was too late.

PART III

THE COUNTEROFFENSIVE

13

The Ten-Day Whirlwind

MORDECHAI MAKLEFF knelt on the muddy, moonlit west bank of the Jordan River, just south of Lake Huleh, and anxiously watched his men pulling boats and rafts across the river toward the eastern bank in Syria while bullets and shrapnel peppered the water. Their objective was to encircle the Syrian force occupying the Israeli colony of Mishmar Hayarden on the western bank, but progress was slow and difficult. All four Israeli columns taking part in Operation Berosh (Cypress) were in trouble that early morning, July 10.

The one Makleff was watching, made up largely of undertrained, inexperienced soldiers, had reached the river bank after a swift march southward from Hulata along the shore of Lake Huleh. Engineers were to build a pontoon bridge over which the infantry would enter Syria in a surprise attack; but the Syrians had been waiting with guns at the ready, and they forced the Israelis to attempt a precarious crossing by boat.

Makleff, commanding the Carmeli Brigade under Moshe Carmel (who was now the northern front commander), had hoped to start this new phase of the war with an impressive victory at Mishmar Hayarden, one of the few Israeli settlements in Arab hands. Success would not only enhance Israeli prestige, but would block a Syrian drive to cut off the only road connecting upper—or eastern—Galilee with the rest of Israel. He had been confident of success, even though intelligence reports had estimated that Syria had two infantry brigades, powerful artillery units, and a battalion of 25 tanks committed to the area, as opposed to an Israeli force of only two battalions of 1,200 men, unsupported by tanks or anti-tank guns.

While he watched some of his men struggle across the river on foot, groaning as they dragged along boatloads of other soldiers as well as equipment under fire, he wished he could stretch the night to give his force a chance to cross and consolidate its position on the opposite bank. At dawn, the Arabs would certainly counterattack, and possibly trap his men. And Makleff was very sensitive to casualties—perhaps in part because he was haunted by the memory of his family being massacred during the anti-Jewish rampage of 1929; only he and his sister had managed to escape a knife-wielding mob.

Finally at 4 A.M., he gave up hope.

"Bring the men back," he ordered an officer. "It's almost daylight. They'll get slaughtered over there."

On receiving the order, most members of his unit already on the opposite bank swam back across the river without waiting for boats to fetch them. The other three columns either retreated as well, or dug in near the river.

The Syrians, as predicted, counterattacked at dawn with tanks and infantry on both sides of the river, and the Israelis retreated north in disorder toward Hulata, from where they had started their attack, and took up positions in trenches just south of the town. But as Syrian tanks appeared in the distance, the panicky recruits started to resume their flight—when Makleff blocked their path with a Sten gun.

"Are you mad?" he yelled. "Get back into the trenches before those tanks machine-gun you in the back! If you don't, I'm going to give it to you in the front!"

As some of the men, dazed with terror, kept running, Makleff fired over their heads and they lurched to a halt, staring at him as if abruptly awakened from a deep sleep. They returned to the trenches and fought off the enemy attack.

A nine-day stalemate resulted, and Makleff had to depend as much on psychological as on military tactics to prevent a Syrian breakthrough. At night, he sent convoys in varying directions with the lights of every vehicle blazing. Each time, the Syrians, in confusion, rushed forces to meet an expected attack that never materialized. The Israelis also used high-screaming wooden-nosed shells, which frightened many Syrians into thinking that the enemy had a secret weapon and even influenced some to give themselves up.

The attacks and counterattacks became simply killing matches, in which some 800 Syrians and 150 Israelis died, and more than half of the 1,200-man Israeli force was knocked out.

At Lake Success, news of the ill-conceived Israeli venture reinforced Arab-British determination to prevent another truce. Thus the Israeli failure, by producing a United Nations impasse, actually furthered Israel's

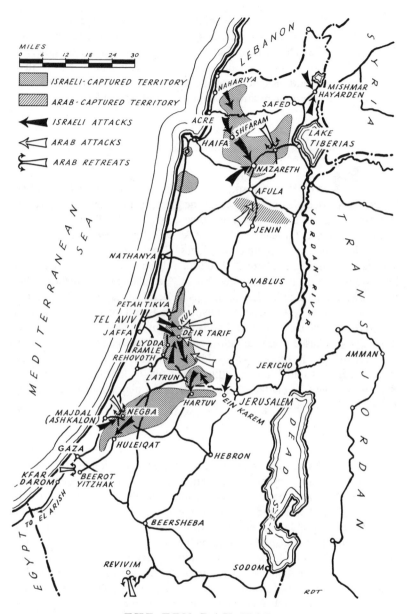

MILES
0   6   12   18   24   30

ISRAELI-CAPTURED TERRITORY

ARAB-CAPTURED TERRITORY

ISRAELI ATTACKS

ARAB ATTACKS

ARAB RETREATS

LEBANON

SYRIA

MEDITERRANEAN SEA

NAHARIYA

ACRE

HAIFA

SHFARAM

NAZARETH

SAFED

MISHMAR HAYARDEN

LAKE TIBERIAS

AFULA

JENIN

NATHANYA

NABLUS

JORDAN RIVER

TRANS

PETAH TIKVA

TEL AVIV

JAFFA

KULA

DEIR TARIF

LYDDA
RAMLE
REHOVOTH

LATRUN

HARTUV

JERICHO

AMMAN

JORDAN

NEGBA

MAJDAL
(ASHKALON)

HULEIQAT

EIN KAREM

JERUSALEM

DEAD SEA

GAZA

KFAR DAROM

BEEROT YITZHAK

HEBRON

EGYPT

TO EL ARISH

BEERSHEBA

REVIVIM

SODOM

RDT

THE TEN DAY WAR

cause, for Yigal Allon, the central front commander, had more time to prepare for the most ambitious Israeli campaign of the war to date: Operation Dani, named after Dani Mass, leader of the 35 students killed earlier in the year near Kfar Etzion. The aim of this central front campaign was first to eliminate the Lydda-Ramle wedge pointed toward Tel Aviv, and then to open the route to Jerusalem through capture of Latrun and Ramallah.

HAFEZ ABU KUWAIK, the mukhtar of northern Lydda, knitted his brows worriedly as he squinted in the glare of the noon sun. Scores of men were running down the street, ancient World War II rifles in hand, threading their way through hundreds of fleeing refugees who were crowding into Lydda from nearby conquered villages. Now Lydda itself was menaced, and the town had only about 300 full-time defenders, most of whom had been trained to do little more than shoot. Yet, though Glubb Pasha had withdrawn the bulk of his Legion troops to Beit Nabala, about three miles northeast of the city, they would surely halt the Israeli forces marching from Tel Aviv before they reached Lydda, thought Kuwaik. Nor would the Legion troops based at Latrun allow an attack from the south.

Nonetheless, the fifty-one-year-old mukhtar grabbed the rifle that stood in a corner and told his wife: "I'm going out to look at the positions. Stay in the house no matter what happens. They may bombard us heavily before the Legion attacks. . . "

Glubb Pasha always wore the cool, melancholy look of the British military aristocracy, despite his exuberant nature. But his melancholy was now painfully real as he sat at his desk thumbing through appeals for help from people in Lydda and Ramle. These two Arab towns in the coastal plain filled a 15-mile gap between Majdal Yaba, at the tip of the Iraqi army's southern flank, and Latrun, which was occupied by his Arab Legion. If they fell, the flanks of both armies would be exposed. But if he sent one of his two Latrun battalions forward to protect these towns, which together projected like an arrow toward Tel Aviv, it would be cut off and surrounded.

The Israelis could then contain Lydda and Ramle and concentrate their assault against the one battalion left in Latrun, which, he calculated, was the main Jewish objective. And if Latrun fell, the Israelis would not only have opened up the road to Jerusalem, but also the road to Ramallah from where they could turn southward to outflank Jerusalem or northward to Nablus behind the Iraqi army. He was grateful that King Abdullah had agreed with him, however reluctantly, that Lydda and Ramle must be sacrificed in order to save Latrun.

Yet he knew what the fall of those towns would mean politically. Many Arabs would call the King a "traitor" and Glubb a nefarious "British agent." They would conveniently forget that he had been serving Arab interests since 1920, when he had arrived in Iraq with British forces . . .

GLUBB STILL HAD FOND MEMORIES OF HIS MEETING IN 1939 WITH King Abdullah, who was then an Emir, or Prince. Glubb was to replace Colonel Peake Pasha, founder of the Arab Legion, who had resigned as Legion commander after 17 years of service. From the wary look in Abdullah's eyes, Glubb knew that the Emir was wondering if he would measure up to the man in whom he had placed such trust.

"You are English," Abdullah had said, "and this is an Arab country, and an Arab army. Before you take over command, I want you to pledge me your word that, as long as you remain in this appointment, you will act always as if you had been born a Transjordanian . . . I know you would not wish to fight your own countrymen. If it should ever come to fighting between us and the English, I will hold you excused. You may leave us then and stand aside. But if, by God's will, this does not happen, I want you to be one of the people of Transjordan."

"Sir," Glubb had replied, "I give you my word of honor. From now onwards I am a Transjordanian, except under the conditions you mentioned, and which I pray God may never come . . ."

Nine years had gone by and he still felt that he was a Transjordanian. Yet, as a military man, he must close his heart to the Arabs of Lydda and Ramle.

Late on the morning of July 10, Moshe Kelman, commanding the Yiftach Brigade's 3rd Battalion, stood in the hillside village of Daniyal, about a mile east of Lydda, and scanned the outskirts of the city. To his surprise, he could see no trace of Legion forces. So far, he thought, lowering his binoculars, everything had gone well. Since starting toward Lydda the night before, the two Yiftach battalions attacking from the south had captured several Arab villages, including Daniyal, and had "liberated" the Arab-surrounded Jewish village of Ben Shemen.

Meanwhile, Yitzhak Sadeh's 8th Armored Brigade, advancing southwest from near Tel Aviv, had taken a number of other Arab villages and

Lydda Airport, north of the city, though it was now bogged down in a struggle near Beit Nabala with Glubb's armored cars. In this north-south pincer operation, Lydda and Ramle were practically surrounded.

It was only noon. That meant Kelman would have to waste several hours awaiting night. Allon, he felt, was overcautious about casualties. The time to strike was now, when surprise would be greatest. He could feel Lydda out, anyway. Test its defenses. He decided to order a company to penetrate as far as it could into the city.

The commander of the company sent out reported back quite swiftly that his unit controlled the eastern outskirts of the city. Kelman's face lit up. It seemed to be easier than anyone had suspected. He then sent two other companies into Lydda.

Hardly had these units left when a jeep ground into Daniyal. Yigal Allon, Yitzhak Rabin, and Mulah Cohen, who had replaced Allon as the Yiftach Brigade commander, entered the small stone house where Kelman had established battalion headquarters.

"There's a hell of a lot of shooting in Lydda," Allon said brusquely. "What's going on?"

"Three of my companies are in there taking over the place," Kelman replied casually.

Allon looked aghast.

"Who told you to do that?" he shouted. "It's suicide attacking a city like that in broad daylight. You'll pay for this with your head!"

"Look, gentlemen," Kelman then said coldly to his three superiors. "Would it be wise to change horses in mid-stream? I'm busy fighting now. Let's discuss the matter tonight—when the battle's over."

Mukhtar Kuwaik and his fellow citizens poured into the streets cheering wildly when the rumor spread that Arab Legionnaires were approaching.

"We're saved!" they cried. "Long live the Arab Legion!"

They raced to the edge of town, where they saw marching toward them a long column of men, some wearing *khaffiyas*. But as they ran to meet the "Legionnaires," waving their rifles in greeting, a hundred firecrackers seemed to go off at once and dozens of Arabs fell in their tracks. Amidst screams of shock and confusion, the rest of the "welcoming" party scurried back into town shouting: "They're Jews! The Jews are coming!"

Then mortar shells rained down, and men and women, dragging children after them, dived into doorways or any shelter they could find. After each explosion they bolted out again, leaping over the dead and wounded, until they had made their way home.

The Israelis edged along the streets, meeting little opposition from the panicked citizenry until they reached the police station, where about 150 Legionnaires halted the assault after a third of the town had been captured.

Toward dusk, after the police station had been holding out for more than two hours, Kelman received a message from his commander in the city asking for help. He relayed the appeal to Mulah Cohen, who contacted a unit of the 8th Armored Brigade which, in its southward drive, should have reached the "liberated" Jewish village of Ben Shemen by then.

"I want to speak to your commanding officer," Cohen said.

"Yes, sir, I'll get him," a voice replied.

After a few minutes, another man identified himself as the commanding officer.

"One of my units is in Lydda," Cohen explained, "but it has encountered heavy fire in the southeast part of the city. Can you give us help?"

"Yes, we can. We've got to finish things here, but it won't take long."

Cohen was very relieved. A tank battalion would soon take care of the police station. What he did not realize was that he had been talking to the commander of the 89th Commando Battalion, which consisted mainly of jeeps and half-tracks—a force excellent at shooting up villages with small-arms fire, but not at destroying fortresses. Nor did the commando leader, Moshe Dayan, know that Cohen had mistaken his unit for the tank battalion, which was still busy fighting Legion forces at Beit Nabala.

Dayan and his men were enthralled at the prospect of attacking Lydda, despite their exhaustion after a successful but bitterly fought battle for the village of Deir Tarif, north of Beit Nabala. Their advance southward to Ben Shemen, where they were to link up with the forces that had attacked northward, was behind schedule. Now they would race through Ben Shemen and on into Lydda.

His battalion had suffered heavy casualties in the last 24 hours, but it was now, Dayan felt, more coordinated, more confident, and more daring than ever. It included a platoon of Sternists and a jailful of prisoner volunteers—as well as the prison warden, who had found himself without card partners.

In the early afternoon, the Commando Battalion started south toward Ben Shemen, with a captured armored car, christened "The Terrible Tiger," leading about 30 jeeps and several half-tracks, each equipped with two machine guns. Perhaps, it occurred to Dayan, he should consult with Yitzhak Sadeh first. After all, he was in charge of his brigade. But that would only take up valuable time—and Yitzhak would understand. He was the same breed of fighter as Dayan, a man who would give no quarter to the enemy—or even sometimes to his commander. That was why Sadeh (founder of the Palmach in 1941) had named him to lead the Commando Battalion after years of staff duty, even though Dayan had resigned from the Palmach because he didn't believe in the kibbutz ideology.* Now he was back in the field again, fighting the way he liked best. It was the only way to fight an enemy with superior force. Take him by surprise—ruthlessly. That was what Wingate—and Yitzhak Sadeh—had taught him . . .

IT HAD BEEN A LONG TIME SINCE DAYAN'S LAST BATTLE UNDER Sadeh that pleasant June morning in 1941 when he had led a squad of Palmach scouts into Lebanon (while Yigal Allon, who also served under Sadeh then but later became his superior, led troops into Syria) to clear a path for Australian forces invading the Levant. The Mediterranean had looked like glazed glass that summer dawn as Dayan's detachment made its way along the western ledge of the Lebanese mountains.

Then shots from a police station had broken the calm, and in a bitter fire fight Dayan knocked out a machine gunner with a grenade while his fighters stormed the building. He climbed to the roof and raised a pair of binoculars to his eyes. A moment later he lay barely conscious, his left eye socket a blood-filled cavity. A bullet had struck the lens of the binoculars on the left side, smashing it into his eye.

"How do you feel?" a horrified soldier asked.

"Not bad. If I can get to the hospital within three hours, I'll certainly live!"[1] . . .

Dayan's spirit had not deserted him. And now, as his column ground into Ben Shemen to a roaring welcome by the village population, he climbed out of his jeep, acknowledged the cheers with a smile, and delivered a final pep talk to his men.

"You are not to stop for any reason," he ordered. "If one of our vehicles is hit, bypass it and go on. No one, aside from me, may halt the column . . . Get on top of the enemy and trample him down in body and spirit!"

The men waved goodbye to the inhabitants of Ben Shemen, then, with Dayan commanding from a jeep in the center of the column, stormed through Lydda with all guns ablaze, leaving Arab corpses strewn in their wake. They came to a fork in the road, and the "Tiger" turned left as ordered. But in his excitement, the commander of the half-track company, Akiva, who sat in the second vehicle, mistakenly ordered his driver to turn

---

* Moshe Dayan's father, Shmuel, though having helped to found the first kibbutz, Degania, soon became disenchanted with the totally collective life and thereupon helped to found the first *moshav*, a semi-collective farm in which privacy is valued. His son developed similar views—in conflict with the kibbutz-minded Palmach.

right and the other vehicles followed. The "Tiger" was thus left to conduct its own private rampage.

Akiva finally realized his error and his driver tried to stop, but the brakes wouldn't work and within minutes the column was well on the way to Ramle. As it approached a police station located between the two cities, Dayan saw an Arab soldier standing in front of it, casually watching as if at a parade. The man suddenly dashed into the station and in a moment the Israelis were advancing, with heavy casualties, through a hail of bullets and grenades.

When, at the edge of Ramle, the depleted column at last came to a halt, Dayan stamped up to the first half-track and asked Akiva: "Do you know where we are?"

"No, where are we?"

"We're in Ramle!"

Akiva grinned sheepishly "Gee, the wrong city!"

The shattered force raced back to Lydda, suffering further casualties as it passed the police station again, and then into Ben Shemen, where Dayan radioed Yitzhak Sadeh.

"Who told you to leave Deir Tarif and attack Lydda?" asked Sadeh furiously.

"Well, you see . . ."

But Sadeh cut him off with the news that as soon as the commando force had abandoned Deir Tarif, the Arabs had recaptured it (though the Israelis, without Dayan's help, seized it again the following day).

Well, thought Dayan philosophically when the conversation had come to a swift conclusion, he couldn't win them all.

To Sadeh, it was not even clear that the bungled spree through Lydda had had more than a peripheral effect on the battle for the town. Dayan, he felt, was not likely to advance very far in the army with such performances.

Mukhtar Hafez Abu Kuwaik sat with his face buried in his hands while his wife and children huddled on the floor in a corner. It was all over. The Jews had taken the city. How easy it had been for them; how simple to defeat a betrayed people. Where was the Arab Legion? Where were the armored cars Glubb had promised to send if the town were attacked?

"What will we do?" his wife asked pathetically.

"We shall go to the Big Mosque. It is safer there."

"What will they do to us?"

"We are but leaves in the wind," Kuwaik replied. "Does a leaf know where the wind will carry it?"

*

In the early evening darkness, Simon Garfeh, the Greek Orthodox Archimandrite of Lydda, stood solemnly by the door of his apartment house, a study in black-bearded, black-robed dignity.[2]

"I would like to speak to your commander," he said in strongly accented English to a group of Israeli soldiers as they drove up in a jeep.

"I am the commander," Moshe Kelman replied, jumping down.

Garfeh surveyed the blond Israeli indifferently.

"I am the Archimandrite of Lydda," he announced. "I hope you have come to seek peace."

"If it is the desire of the people of this town to live with us in peace," Kelman assured him, "we shall be very happy. They may open their shops and resume normal life. Can you arrange for the surrender?"

"I shall try," the prelate answered, his full lips curving in a smile for the first time. "I shall ask the leaders of the Moslem and Christian communities to meet with us immediately in my apartment upstairs."

He then instructed an aide to run to the Big Mosque to fetch the Moslem leaders, and sent another to his own church to bring the Christian leaders taking refuge there.

About an hour later, a dozen Arab notables were sitting in Garfeh's living room sipping coffee and chatting with the clergyman, Kelman, and other Israeli officers. Finally, Kelman, putting down his coffee, addressed them:

"Gentlemen, the city has been conquered, and we want your cooperation. We suggest that you find the citizens who have been operating the utilities so that your people can have water and electricity without delay. But first, you must accept our terms for peace: Surrender of all fighting personnel and of all arms within twenty-four hours. If these conditions are not met, we shall have to take action."

"We agree," one of the Arabs said with quiet resignation. "May the inhabitants stay here if they wish?"

"Yes, they may," Kelman replied, "if they live here peacefully."

When the Arabs had left, Yigal Allon came to see Kelman and, beaming, kissed him on the cheek.

"Congratulations, Moshe," he said.

"Thanks, Yigal," came the reply. "Would you like to continue the argument we started this morning?"

Allon only laughed.

Toward noon the next day, July 11, Glubb sent a patrol consisting of one tank and two armored cars through the western unoccupied part of the town to determine Israeli strength. When the patrol found itself trapped, it blasted its way through the streets with the same gall Moshe Dayan had displayed the day before and managed to escape.

One of the last buildings the vehicles passed during their angry exit was the small Dahmash Mosque. Hardly had they roared past when a boy emerged from the mosque, which was packed with refugees, and threw a grenade into a group of five Israeli guards stationed outside. This was the signal for an Arab mob, rushing from the mosque and from nearby houses, to materialize within seconds. They killed the surviving Israelis and mutilated the bodies.

The Arabs were certain that the patrol was the spearhead of the long-awaited Legion effort to save them. And as this rumor spread throughout the city, Arabs began firing from almost every window and door in a massive flash revolt against their conquerors . . .

After helplessly watching the Legion patrol smash through the town, Moshe Kelman descended to his office from the roof of his headquarters building and opened a creaking shutter. The world seemed to be exploding before his eyes. His great victory was apparently about to disintegrate. Aside from the 7,000 Arabs jammed into the Big Mosque and its compound, about 30,000 were still in their houses, each of which, it seemed, had been turned into a fortress. And he had only about 500 men, scattered in patrols throughout the city, to put down the revolt.

"This is all against all," he said to an aide as he turned away from the window. "Get the word to our men somehow. Order them to shoot at any target that moves! Any target that moves, understand?"

"That's about the severest order an army can give."

"I know, but we're finished unless we take this action. This is not a conventional battle. This is a revolt by people who have already surrendered."

Within the next hour, some 200 Arabs were killed, according to Israeli estimates (far more according to the Arabs), as Israelis, crawling stealthily from doorway to doorway, tossed grenades into windows and broke into houses to silence snipers. The severity of the Israeli counteraction turned threatened defeat into final victory as firing began to cease throughout the city—except around Dahmash Mosque, which, according to the Israelis, had been converted into an armed stronghold.

About 70 armed men, firing from the windows and the tower, continued to hold out there, apparently fearful of retribution for the killing of the Israeli guards and encouraged by the sight of Legion armored cars approaching along the road from Beit Nabala. The cars were in fact halted by intense Israeli fire outside the town and forced to retreat, but the defenders in the mosque were able to keep the Israelis at a distance.

"There's only one thing we can do," said Kelman, discussing the situation with his officers. "We've got to pierce those walls."

"But they're a yard or a yard and a half thick," an officer pointed out. "And we haven't got any artillery."

"We've got a Piat."

Within half an hour, two Israeli soldiers made their way through the bullet-swept approaches to the mosque, entered a building adjacent to it, and ran upstairs to a window facing the side wall of the stronghold. One of the men aimed the Piat and fired.

An Israeli platoon immediately rushed the mosque and smashed through the front door with guns blazing. But they soon saw that they were wasting bullets and stopped firing, contemplating in silence what an explosion could do in a small enclosed space. The Persian rugs covering the floor were soaked with blood from bodies strewn everywhere, and some corpses and bits of flesh were stuck to the crimson-streaked walls from the force of the blast. Even hardened Israeli veterans quickly looked away and some felt like vomiting.

Moshe Kelman then drove up to inspect the scene.

"Get fifteen or twenty Arabs from the other mosque to carry the bodies to the cemetery," he ordered an aide. "And have them clean up in here."

Within two or three hours, all the remains had been transported on horse-driven carts to the cemetery about a mile away and buried in a long trench dug by the bearers. The interior of Dahmash Mosque was as clean as it had ever been . . .

"The inhabitants must leave for Transjordan within three hours," an Israeli officer informed the Moslem leaders and Simon Garfeh in the prelate's apartment.

"But you said the people could stay if they wanted to," Garfeh protested.

"We said they could stay if they showed they wanted to live with us in peace. But they revolted against us after they had surrendered, and many of our men have been killed."

"Well, then, will you let everybody go, including all the men? Do not take them prisoner. It shall be punishment enough for them to leave their homes."

"Yes," the Israeli responded, "they may go. If the old and the sick wish to stay, they may do so."

"And what about the Christians?" the cleric asked anxiously.

"All who wish may stay."

(Allon had issued orders that the Christian Arabs, who were known to be less anti-Israel than the Moslems, should be treated especially well.)

Mukhtar Kuwaik was frightened as the Israeli officer and the clergyman entered the Big Mosque, which suddenly grew as silent as a tomb. The fighting was over, he knew. The Legion, which he had thought was attacking, had not come. Now it looked as if the leaves in the wind would fall into the fire. The Jews would certainly take revenge; they would kill everyone in the town. And he expected the officer who had just entered to announce their death sentence. He wondered with aching heart what had happened to his wife and children, who had returned home from the mosque the night before.

In the hush, Garfeh began to speak: "O people of Lydda, I have persuaded the occupying authorities to let you all leave peacefully. But you must go immediately."

The Israeli officer beside him then elaborated: "The revolt of your people has failed and, except for those who are too old or sick to walk, all of you must leave Lydda at once. You must go to Abdullah. One road will be open to you—the road leading to Ramallah. You may take only that road. This is an order."

As the visitors left, animated conversation resumed and everyone started to get up. Kuwaik's first reaction to the order, like that of many other listeners, was one of tremendous relief and joy. Before the revolt, they had wanted to stay, hopeful of their early salvation. But the failure of the revolt had changed everything. They had thought they would be killed. Now it seemed they were not even being taken prisoner. What if they did have to leave Lydda for a while? Soon the Legion would chase the Jews out, and then the people of Lydda could return.

Outside, individual Arabs, under Israeli orders, were slowly moving down the street shouting out: "O people of Lydda, you must leave the town immediately on the road to Ramallah!"

And Israelis themselves banged on doors and repeated the order to emphasize that they meant business.

In nearby Ramle, Hamed Kashash, a wealthy citrus exporter, woke from a brief nap that morning of July 12 with a severe headache. He and his family had sat sleepless throughout the night on the cement floor of his stone-walled garage, which was used not only to shelter his truck and car but to store oranges from his lucrative groves. It was the safest place to be when shells were falling, and they had fallen all night—so close that the dust from explosions had seeped under the door.

Why were the Jews still shelling, he wondered. Why didn't they just come in and take the city? There would be no resistance. How could Ramle resist, surrounded by the enemy and with even Lydda captured? Legion troops had been evacuated from the police station on the road to Lydda that night—as had the Legionnaires in Lydda itself—and the local fighters had left Ramle a little later. The people were now at the mercy of the Jews. It had been inevitable; not only had the Arab Legion refused to defend the city, but the inhabitants themselves had done little to organize a defense system. Some local leaders had even misused funds collected officially to purchase arms.

The shelling finally halted, and Kashash opened the garage door. He glanced up at the clear summer sky and saw tiny white specks. An Israeli plane was dropping leaflets this time instead of bombs. He ran to pick one up amid the ruins of his neighbor's house. The Israelis were demanding that representatives from the city go to the Jewish settlement of Na'an nearby to surrender. Kashash walked slowly back to the garage, throwing the leaflet away. At least the shelling would stop and he would get rid of his terrible headache.

After a mission of five notables had gone to Na'an to formalize a surrender, the Israelis entered Ramle without a fight. Kashash then went to see the mayor and suggested that he ask permission for the inhabitants to stay in Ramle. Neither of the men was aware yet that the Israelis had already promised such permission in the surrender talks, although men of military age were to be taken prisoner.

"The people will demand that the Arab Legion liberate us in a few days anyway," Kashash said confidently.

The mayor agreed and appointed him and two other notables to go to the Israeli commander and make the request.

"I'm sorry," an Israeli officer told the delegation later that morning. "I cannot give you a reply. Only the commander can, and he is not here now. Come back at about two o'clock."

Kashash was on his way home when he heard a loudspeaker from a truck announcing: "O citizens of Ramle, all of you who wish to leave for Transjordan may do so within the next three days. Buses will take you to the village of Kubab on the road to Ramallah, starting tomorrow morning."

Kashash froze. "All of you who wish to leave . . . " He had just begged that the people be allowed to stay, and now apparently they could do so without trouble if they wished. But maybe it was a trick! Maybe the Israelis would kill everyone who stayed! He would not stay; he would not risk the lives of his family. He hurried home and shouted to his wife: "Quick, pack some things! We're leaving for Ramallah!"

"How long did they give us to leave?" his wife stammered, her round face gray with alarm.

"Three days."

"Then why must we hurry so?"

"We must get out of the house immediately or they will come and kill us all!"

Within half an hour, Kashash and his wife, two sons, and five daughters were sitting on the side of the main road beside a blanketful of clothing and other light belongings. Along both shoulders of the road, thousands of people with similar bundles had already gathered, and soon Kashash could not see to the ends of the long lines of humanity that stretched from one edge of town to the other. Women wailed and moaned, children cried, old men were on their knees mumbling prayers.

"When will the first buses come?" his wife asked late in the afternoon after sitting for several hours under the merciless sun.

"The Jews said in the morning."

The same broiling sun beat down on the citizens of Lydda as they marched like a column of ants down the dirt road leading through wild hill country, stony fallow covered with thorn bushes, to Ramallah in Transjordanian-controlled territory. Mukhtar Kuwaik was luckier than most as he hobbled along beside his wife, six sons, three daughters, and two grandchildren. He had a donkey to carry his bundles. But he hadn't taken much with him as he was sure that he would be back home in a few days after the Legion had killed the Jews. So certain was he of returning that he had hidden almost all his money in the ground behind his house. (He and other Arab refugees from Lydda claim that the Israelis systematically divested them of all money, jewels, and other valuables as they left town. Israelis who were present deny that any possessions were taken from the refugees.)

He was thankful that they could move more slowly now that they were out of range of the Israeli guns fired over their heads from the edge of town to keep them moving. How far had they walked since leaving town at about noon? Would the cool night never come? It was so difficult to keep track of time in the open field under a relentless sun.

He thirsted for water, but the jug he had brought along for the family had long since been emptied. And he hardly had the strength to stop and comfort—or even to care about—those who had fallen by the roadside. Some were panting convulsively, some grimacing grotesquely, their tongues protruding.

The mukhtar had picked up one woman and put her on top of the baggage heaped on his donkey, but what could he do about all the others? He passed a little girl lying prostrate on the road and tried not to look. Where were her parents? It was their responsibility. He pushed back his *khaffiya* slightly and wiped the sweat from his forehead. He saw a spider crawling in the dirt and suddenly wished he were this insect, without a mind and with many legs. How many hours till darkness? . . .

Finally the depleted file of refugees reached the village of Budros, where they were greeted by a group of Arab Legionnaires.

"O soldiers of King Abdullah, the Jews are in Lydda," Kuwaik said hoarsely. "What are you doing here? Why don't you chase them out?"

A Legion officer, whose face reflected both guilt and pity, explained: "We have no orders to do that. We can't attack without orders."

Kawaik spat and demanded: "Where can we find some water?"

When the officer pointed toward a well in the village, the refugees, summoning all their remaining strength, ran to it screaming, "Water! Water!" and cursed each drinker as they awaited turns to drink from the cup attached to a rope.

The people then gathered around the Legionnaires.

"You are dogs and traitors!" they yelled. "Even worse than the Jews!"

They moved off again toward Ramallah, sleeping under fig and olive trees on the way and leaving their dead behind.

From Ramle, an exodus to Ramallah was also in progress along another more southern road, though this one was voluntary and conducted under more comfortable conditions. Hamed Kashash and his family got down from a packed bus in Kubab and began their trek, reaching the evacuated village of Silbit a few hours later, along with thousands of others. Nearby Legionnaires notified their headquarters of the refugees' arrival, and a convoy of Arab Legion trucks appeared. Again the people angrily crowded around the soldiers, accusing them of betrayal and cowardice, the women doing most of the shouting and throwing sand in their faces, since everybody knew that the soldiers would not harm them.

The refugees were then driven in the trucks to Ramallah, where they were put up in schools, mosques, churches, and vineyards.

"Thank God we've arrived safely," Kashash said to his wife as they sprawled for the night under a fig tree.

The next day he hired a truck and drove his family to Gaza, where he owned some orange groves. Two months later, in September, his wife was killed there during an Israeli air raid.

Late on the night of July 12, Glubb Pasha was asleep in his hotel room in the Old City when the telephone rang by his bedside. It was Brigadier Lash calling from Ramallah.

The Israelis had occupied Lydda and Ramle, Lash confirmed, and tens of thousands of refugees were pouring into Ramallah. The effect had been catastrophic. Legion officers and soldiers were being stoned in the streets, hissed, cursed; they were being called "traitors."

"What condition are the refugees in?" Glubb asked.

"Many of them have nothing to eat. There is not enough bread . . . "

Glubb immediately rang the supply depot at Ramallah and ordered the bread designated for the troops to be distributed to the refugees. Then he arranged for truckloads of bread to be shipped from Amman to Ramallah at once.

He lay back in bed but was unable to sleep. What could he have done? Should he have rushed forces to the two towns when this might have meant an even greater disaster, perhaps the loss of all Palestine? He thought of his loyal troops; they had saved Jerusalem; they had fought everywhere with courage. And now they were being called traitors! But what could he have done?

In Amman the next morning, King Abdullah was discussing the latest developments with Sir Alec Kirkbride and other advisers when shouts echoed ominously in the distance. The King sprang from his chair and hurried to the window.

"They're coming, thousands of them!" he said, as he watched the tide already pouring toward the palace, about 3,000 youths crying: "Treason! Treason!"

"What can they understand of war?" Abdullah muttered. "How can they know how lucky they are?"

As he started toward the stairway, one of his aides cried: "Your Majesty, where are you going?"

"I am going to speak to them."

"But, Your Majesty, it is too dangerous!"

The King kept walking to the palace entrance, advanced alone into the crowd, and slapped one of the ringleaders on the face. The crowd was instantly shocked into silence.

"You say you want to fight the Jews," Abdullah raged, looking icily at the demonstrators. "Very well, those who do can enlist in the Arab Legion. The office is just around the corner. The rest of you leave these grounds immediately!"

He then strode back into the palace, while the crowd quietly dispersed.

The fall of Lydda and Ramle also had repercussions at Lake Success. Britain's Sir Alexander Cadogan, who had seen no reason to rush through a United Nations cease-fire resolution during the initial days of the renewed fighting, when Israel appeared to be losing, now announced that "recent developments" required speedy action by the Security Council to bring the fighting to a halt. Any party who refused to obey such an order, he said, should be subject to sanctions.

But the Council was now in less of a hurry to act than Britain, and two days of debate passed before it finally voted a cease-fire resolution on July 15. The truce, of an indefinite duration, was to take effect at 5:45 A.M., July 17, for the Jerusalem area, and 36 hours later for the rest of the country.

MEANWHILE, the Israelis thwarted a determined Egyptian attack. Egypt struck eastward from the coast toward Israeli strongholds at 6 A.M. on July 8, 24 hours before the first truce officially ended, hoping by this surprise attack to enlarge and secure the "isolation belt" that separated the Negev from the rest of the country. The principal Egyptian objective was Negba, the nerve center of the whole Israeli defense system in the northern Negev and the kibbutz that had held out against enormous odds before the truce. The strategy was to isolate Negba by capturing a number of fortified positions in the surrounding hills.

The initial attack failed when Egyptian artillerymen, acting on an erroneous flare signal from infantrymen assaulting the Israeli-held village of Beit Daras, nearly wiped out their own force. The following day, July 9, Gamal Abdel Nasser, adjutant of the 6th Battalion, who had become a major, received orders to attack the more powerfully defended enemy village of Julis immediately. Discussing the role of the artillery and air force in the operation, Nasser suggested to his battalion commander that "we should have a carefully planned, precisely timed action."

The commander, however, insisted that the "role of the artillery and air force should be determined during the fighting in accordance with battle exigencies on the spot."

When Nasser continued to argue, the commander cut in impatiently: "For God's sake, let us have no more of this Staff Academy trash!"

When the time came for the Egyptian infantry to charge toward Julis at dawn on July 10, the commander said to Nasser as they sat in headquarters: "What are we doing here? Let's go down and see what our men are doing."

"But sir," Nasser exclaimed, "who will control the operation if headquarters is abandoned?"

The commander merely laughed. "Don't worry," he said. "I'll keep full control."

When the officers arrived at the fringe of the battle zone, the commander looked around and cried out: "The men are being killed!"

Then, as he came upon a mortar team: "What are these guns doing here? Advance with them and start shelling Julis!"

And he turned to Nasser and snapped: "Go with them!"

Nasser stared at him dumfounded. His job as adjutant required him to remain with the commander to assist in carrying out the battle plan. This, he felt, was a thousand times more important than what amounted to a demonstration of bravado. But the situation was delicate; he did not wish to contradict his commanding officer and risk being accused of cowardice.

"Very well, sir," he replied stiffly.

Nasser and the mortar men then dashed through a cornfield until they were within range of Julis, and fired. As shells popped from the tube toward their target, Nasser was almost unaware of the thunder around him. His mind was consumed by the catastrophe that would inevitably envelop the battalion, a battalion without control. His whole being rebelled against the commander. He must return to headquarters, he decided. He had to return—before it was too late.

Sprinting back through the cornfield, he finally reached headquarters, which was empty. Quickly he shuffled through a pile of messages lying on the commander's desk. One of them read: "Have achieved objective. Await your orders."

Another requested ammunition, while a third asked for ambulances to carry the wounded to first aid stations.

Noting with a chill that these messages had been sent hours before, Nasser could imagine the desperate plight of the men whose leaders had asked for assistance.

The next day, the battalion commander was replaced (after he had issued withdrawal orders that resulted in enormous casualties) and the new commander was immediately ordered to attack Julis again. Nasser was convinced this was impossible, and said so, but the new commander, though he agreed with him, was afraid to complain to his superiors.

"You really have no alternative," urged Nasser. "And in any case, you cannot lose anything. If you object, you might be transferred from your command, but this is a mere possibility. If you obey the order, your inevitable failure will also lead to your transfer, in disgrace. And this is almost a certainty."

Finally convinced, the commander asked: "Will you come with me to general headquarters?"

"Of course."

As the two men entered general headquarters, Nasser stopped off in the air operations room to gather information on Julis and found a set of aerial photographs. He examined them and discovered what he considered an extraordinary fact. The village of Julis itself was of no importance. What was really important was a camp erected at the top of a hill overlooking the village. He then realized that if his troops managed to storm the village, the enemy at the top of the hill could easily trap them. When he stressed this point to general headquarters, the attack was finally called off.

But Nasser was infuriated at the thought that his battalion had been saved from catastrophe by the merest chance and that the photographs had not been automatically sent to him. Those miserable clean-shaven officers sitting at comfortable desks—they were the real enemy, he thought.

He returned to his own headquarters, and later that day received news that Egyptian units had failed in new attempts to capture positions around Negba. Nevertheless, though Negba had not been encircled yet, a message from brigade headquarters ordered him to prepare his troops for an all-out direct attack on that colony.

General Mawawi, the Egyptian supreme commander, was confident that his new plan for capturing Negba without isolating it would work. Six infantry companies, supported by tanks and artillery, would attack Negba simultaneously from four sides, cutting off all Israeli supply routes.

However, Nasser and other officers, including Brigadier Mohammed Neguib, commander of the 9th Brigade that was to lead the attack, strongly opposed the plan, feeling that the Israelis still had control of too many outposts around Negba. The Egyptian forces could thus be too easily cut off or outflanked, they thought.

"This is madness!" Neguib roared. "A direct attack like this without the proper preparation will be disastrous."

"You did a good job at Nitzanim, Mohammed," replied Mawawi, "but that doesn't entitle you to question my orders. You will lead the attack on Negba!"

Neguib reflected for a moment, then said firmly: "I'm sorry, sir, but I cannot carry out that order."

Mawawi stared at him. "Then I relieve you of your command!" he said.

"May I go now, sir?"

"Yes, go!"

The company commander blurted to Major Nasser in 6th Battalion headquarters: "This operation borders on sheer folly. It's suicide!"

"Maybe, but those are our orders," Nasser replied coldly. "Your company is to capture that road position and cut off communications between Negba and the other Jewish colonies. I'll go with you."

At about 3 A.M. on July 12, as the Egyptian artillery barrage on Negba began, Nasser and the company set out toward the exposed road position, and by dawn had occupied it under heavy Israeli fire. Nasser then went off to inspect other positions around Negba, hitching a ride with the brigade major when he drove past in an armored car. Suddenly they heard shots coming from a nearby cornfield.

"There's a sniper around here," the brigade major said. "Let's get him."

He then drove through the field but they could see no one.

"We'd better get out of here," Nasser advised. "We're losing time."

As the vehicle bounced out of the field, a volley of shots crackled in the dry air and Nasser felt a strange sensation. His chest began to ache, and when he looked down he saw his khaki shirt covered with blood.

"I've been hit," he gasped, pressing a handkerchief to the wound.

"I'll get you to Magdal Hospital as fast as possible," the brigade major said. "Is there anything I can do?"

"Light a cigarette for me, will you?" Nasser replied calmly, his face pale.

He experienced an odd serenity, almost a buoyant feeling. He thought that he would die, but surprised himself by not really caring. He recalled how as a child of six he and a companion the same age had swallowed lumps of wax in the hope of dying and thereby avoiding the fires of Hell promised by the Koran to all sinners over six. But this effort to beat God's deadline failed when the wax had simply produced two severe stomach aches. Now he would die a sinner like all men. What mainly concerned him, he says, was the effect his death would have on others.

He wondered how effectively his men would fight without him. And who would lead the Free Officers now in the crusade for a new Egypt? He then pictured his two daughters, Hoda and Mona, playing at home, and his wife anxiously awaiting his return. How would they react when they received a telegram announcing his death? . . .

WOULD THE CRIES NEVER CEASE? IT WAS ALMOST MORNING AND HE hadn't slept . . . He had acted for the sake of his country . . . To have a revolution, it was necessary to kill.

Everything had gone so smoothly earlier that night. The plan had been to shoot a certain key government official, known for his pro-British leanings, on his way home from work. The Free Officers had studied his movements and habits carefully and nothing had been left to chance.

As planned, when the intended victim came out of his office

building and started to get into his car, the executioners fired. Nasser, in his own car, had begun to drive away, content that the man was dead, when he heard a woman crying and a child wailing. He put his foot on the accelerator, but the further he got from the scene, the louder the cries seemed. And he heard them throughout the night.

At dawn, he got out of bed and went to the front door. He picked up the morning paper and glanced quickly over the front page. There it was. He smiled, and went back to get some sleep at last. The man he had intended to kill had survived . . .

Nasser, whose wound had not in fact been serious, found himself the only patient in Magdal Hospital on the afternoon of July 12. But toward evening he was joined by scores of wounded from the battle of Negba, which had again beaten back a determined Egyptian attack.

Nasser walked from bed to bed, sickened by the bleeding, mutilated bodies of the wounded. He heard a youth he had trained from the day he had joined the army screaming in delirium, a victim of nervous shock. Was this what he had trained him for? He went back to his own bed and lay down with his hands over his face. Then, he claims, he made a solemn vow to himself:

"If ever I should occupy an official position, I shall think a thousand times before dragging my men into war. I would only do so when the honor of the Fatherland was threatened and its future at stake; when nothing but the fire of battle could save the situation."

The next morning his battalion commander visited him.

"What happened to the advance company that was supposed to cut off Negba from the other colonies?" Nasser asked immediately.

"It's still in a very dangerous position," the commander replied. "The enemy's fire is concentrated on it. But the company is continuing to put up a splendid resistance."

"And what about the main battle at Negba?"

The commander said broodingly: "The 9th Battalion charged only with infantry. Wave after wave was mowed down. They lost almost half their officers and men. The rest had to retreat."

Nasser was horrified at the thought that the enemy could now concentrate on wiping out his company on the road.

"Did you order the withdrawal of the company from its advanced position?" he asked.

"No," the commander said sadly, shaking his head.

"What do you mean, you haven't?" Nasser demanded, raising himself on one elbow. "Do you intend to leave it until it is wiped out?"

"What am I to do? I contacted brigade headquarters asking for permission to withdraw the company, but they told me I actually belonged to the 4th Brigade and therefore should ask them."

"Well, have you contacted the 4th Brigade?"

"I have, but they told me that I belong to the 2nd Brigade and should get orders from them."

Nasser jumped out of bed and put on his uniform.

"Let's go," he said. "These people have lost their minds!"

The two officers finally found someone who gave them permission to withdraw the company, and Nasser went personally in an armored car to join the nearly surrounded unit and guide it to safety.

The withdrawal of the main Egyptian force from Negba was carried out under the command of Brigadier Neguib, whom General Mawawi had asked to assume the task despite his previous decision to relieve him of his command. A few days after the battle, Neguib entered Mawawi's office and said: "Sir, I wish to request reinforcements to make up for the heavy casualties that we suffered at Negba."

Mawawi looked at him sourly. Neguib, he was sure, was simply trying to rub in the fact that the troops had been defeated under his (Mawawi's) plan. And he was particularly incensed since several staff officers were present.

"Our losses were not as great as you say," he replied coldly. "You are trying to blame me quite unjustly for the defeat. There was nothing wrong with the plan of attack. It was simply carried out poorly."

The supreme commander then berated Neguib bitterly for his refusal to lead the attack. Neguib, usually calm, now grew ashen with rage.

"I demand an apology!" he shouted.

"I shall never apologize to you," Mawawi stormed back.

In violent terms, Neguib questioned Mawawi's ability as a commander, then saluted and marched out of the office, slamming the door behind him. He immediately drew up a report of what had happened and sent it to Mawawi with the request that he apologize in writing. Mawawi replied succinctly in a note:

"You are to report to GHQ in Cairo. I have recommended that you be tried for insubordination."

Neguib smiled caustically. Mawawi was making a fool of himself. After all, only a few weeks before he had recommended that Neguib receive either an exceptional promotion or the Fuad Star, the highest Egyptian military honor.[3]

FRUSTRATED by their renewed failure to take Negba, the Egyptians decided, if only to impress the people at home, to attack another far more isolated Israeli settlement, Kibbutz Beerot Yitzhak, which lay exposed just southeast of Gaza.

Mohammed Abdel Aref, a member of the assault force, moved forward awkwardly—and reluctantly—on his short, stumpy legs. He saw no sense in attacking people who, in turn, might kill him. Nor was he quite sure why he was expected to kill them. His officers had told him that these people had stolen the land from the Arabs. He felt sorry for the Arabs who lost their land, but if he had to kill somebody, why not the landlords at home, the friends of King Farouk, who had stolen land from poor Egyptians like himself? Why die to win back land for distant cousins when his own family could barely grow enough to eat—especially now that he was in the army? When he got the chance, he would certainly run home again. Maybe he could get back in time to harvest the vegetables. Maybe the army would forget about him and not drag him off to prison again. Anyway, being beaten in prison was better than being killed or wounded in a place he had never heard of.

But Aref kept advancing robot-like, afraid that his commander would shoot him in the back if he did not. He was distressed that the tanks stayed *behind* the infantry, though relieved that at least there were other infantry units in front of his own, some of which consisted of Saudi Arabians. Most of the Jews should have been killed in the ferocious bombardment before the infantry attack. Still, he didn't want to risk getting hit and missing the harvest season . . .

Suddenly, there was firing from Beerot Yitzhak, and Aref dived to earth. He would not move forward any further unless he had to. Maybe the Saudi Arabians ahead of him wouldn't need his help after all. An explosion then shook the area and Aref saw a pillbox just inside the fence disappear in a geyser of dust. The Saudis ran to the fence and poured through the hole. Aref then watched in shocked fascination as the invaders dropped their rifles, removed Bedouin knives from their belts, and stabbed several Jews in a trench behind the smoking ruins of the pillbox . . .

"Shimon! Shimon!" a youth screamed as he dashed into the headquarters shelter. "The Egyptians are inside the kibbutz!"

Shimon Forscher, commander of this religious kibbutz, ran out of the shelter and through a trench toward the point of breakthrough, and was immediately wounded as enemy soldiers fired from roofs and windows. Within 45 minutes, 17 of the 90 men and women in the settlement had been killed and more than 15 injured.

Dov Schanzer, who then took over the command, radioed Palmach headquarters in Ruhama: "The enemy has broken in from three sides. The situation is desperate. We use hand grenades."

A little later, a second message went out that unless reinforcements arrived immediately, the kibbutz would have to surrender. Then the radio stopped functioning . . .

"Any luck?"

"No," the operator at Negev Brigade headquarters in Ruhama answered Israel Carmi somberly. "The radio's still out."

"The kibbutz must have fallen," Carmi said. "Have you been able to intercept any enemy messages?"

"Yes, one Egyptian officer just reported to his headquarters that he was watching two of his fellow officers shaking hands under the kibbutz's water tower."

Carmi dashed outside and jumped into the lead jeep in a heavily armed column of light vehicles, which rolled into the desert in a storm of sand clouds.

A few hours later, the column approached the kibbutz just as a fresh battalion of Egyptians was about to overwhelm it.

"Fire five hundred rounds at the concentration of enemy troops west of Beerot Yitzhak," Carmi ordered his artillerymen.

Israeli shells crashed into the enemy's midst, and the survivors began running toward Gaza, leaving behind some 120 dead. When the invading forces inside the kibbutz saw their comrades fleeing, they too began retreating, dashing past Mohammed Abdel Aref, who had not moved from the spot where he had taken refuge that morning when the attack began. Aref was confused. He didn't know what was happening. But people were running away, and that meant it was too dangerous to stay. He quickly removed his heavy army boots and ran barefoot as fast as his short legs would carry him, desperately trying to keep up with his comrades.

WITH a new truce about to freeze boundaries again, the Israeli High Command launched a last-minute campaign to puncture the Egyptian east-west "isolation belt." The principal objective of Operation Mavet Lapolesh (Death to the Invader) was to capture the Arab village of Karatiya along the east-west road. Its occupation would sever the link between Egyptian forces in the coastal and the Hebron areas, and, at the same time, would permit the Israelis to move southward over a dirt road leading to Beersheba. The High Command assigned the task to Moshe Dayan's 89th Commando Battalion, despite its still tattered condition after its assault on Lydda.

With "The Terrible Tiger" in the lead again, Dayan's fortified column moved swiftly toward Karatiya until it was brought to an abrupt halt before a broad wadi.

Dayan jumped out of his jeep and in the light of the headlamps examined the soft, sandy cavity. His heart sank. The vehicles could not cross that wadi unless the banks were shored up, which would take at least an hour. Meanwhile, an infantry unit was waiting to follow his column into the village. Well, it would just have to wait.

"Take over the battalion until we're able to advance," he ordered a young officer. Dayan then strolled some distance away, wound a *khaffiya* round his head, and lay down to sleep.

He woke about an hour later, at 3:30 A.M., feeling refreshed. Now he could make intelligent decisions. As he rose and stretched, someone grabbed him from behind and yelled: "What are you doing on this side of the wadi? Let's move!"

And Dayan found himself being dragged to the other side.

When he scrambled loose, he looked around and cried angrily: "What the hell do you think you're doing?"

The young commander who had temporarily taken over stared at his superior.

"Oh, I'm sorry! I didn't know it was you! We were looking for you. We're ready to go."

The column thundered into Karatiya and found it abandoned. The Egyptians soon counterattacked with tanks and reached the outskirts of the village, but retreated when an Israeli Piat man, Ron Feller, fired from only 25 yards away and knocked out the first tank.

An irate officer of the infantry company that arrived to take over from the Commando Battalion asked one of Dayan's officers why the unit had come so late. "It was almost dawn," he said indignantly, "and we were about to go in alone."

"Well, you see, there was that wadi. And then Moshe fell asleep . . . "

WHILE Israeli forces advanced dramatically in the center Lydda-Ramle region and held their own in the Negev, other forces in the north moved against Fawzi el-Kaoukji's Arab Liberation Army in Central Galilee.

Israel's mission in that area was mainly to secure her precarious grasp on the Vale of Zebulon—which extended from Haifa northward along the coastal plain to Rosh Hanikra on the Lebanese border—and to capture Nazareth. The Arab Liberation Army, the Israelis believed, would be easier to deal with than the Syrian army that was tying down some of their forces in Eastern Galilee.

"We've got to end the enemy attacks on the coastal strip from the eastern hills," Moshe Carmel, the northern front commander, had told Chaim Laskov shortly before the end of the first truce. "Then, once we clean up our flank, we can push southward to Nazareth. We must hit Kaoukji fast, before he knows what's happening."

Carmel and Laskov, who were to command the action—Operation Dekel (Palm Tree)—then met with Yadin at northern army headquarters and laid plans for a lightning strike.

"Kaoukji," Yadin said, "might expect an attack from the corridor we hold south of Nazareth, but probably not from the north through Arab-held territory."

Carmel agreed. He pointed out a further advantage in the concentration of Kaoukji's troops around Sejera, the Israeli colony strategically located northeast of Nazareth near the only road connecting Nazareth with eastern Galilee and Lebanon.

"If Sejera can hold out for a while," Carmel asserted enthusiastically, "we'll be able to take Nazareth while Kaoukji is preoccupied there, and then be in a position to come to Sejera's assistance."

On the evening of July 9, Kaoukji sat in his headquarters in Nazareth, his face redder than usual and his eyes burning.

"What happened at Sejera?" he yelled at an officer.

"We hit them with several waves and took two hills overlooking the village, but just when it looked as if the place would fall, they counter-attacked and drove us off."

"We have Sejera surrounded," Kaoukji thundered. "Why can't we capture it?"

He would have to get rid of that settlement, or it would continue to harass his communications with eastern Galilee. No other Jewish colony was in a more vulnerable position and it was essential to capture at least one as a matter of prestige.

"Attack again tonight. Attack in the morning. Keep attacking until it falls!" he ordered.

In his preoccupation with Sejera, Kaoukji took little note of a message on his desk indicating that the Israelis had assaulted a hill, Tel Kissan, about two and half miles east of Acre . . .

*

Laskov's force, consisting mainly of Carmeli Brigade units, captured Tel Kissan and swung southward toward Nazareth while a diversionary Golani unit moved northward toward the same objective, managing to convince Kaoukji that this thrust was the main one. The Golani force bypassed Nazareth and made its way to the main road north of the town, where it linked up with Laskov's men pushing south. At 5:40 P.M., July 16, Nazareth fell with little resistance. The troops were warned that any soldier found desecrating the Holy Places would be executed immediately.

Kaoukji and his staff, who had been caught completely by surprise, lay hidden all that night, planning a counterattack. But with Israelis pouring into the town, the plan did not materialize, and before dawn on July 17 he and his troops slipped northward over mountain tracks. Even as he withdrew in defeat, Kaoukji ordered continued attacks on Sejera. His objective now was not to scrounge for prestige, but simply to keep the colony from slowing down his retreating troops. From his manner, however, some of his aides had the impression that he still believed he was on the offensive.

"Keep attacking!" he ordered his men confidently over the jeep radio as he fled. "Keep attacking!"

By the morning of July 17, the remnants of the Arab Liberation Army had vanished into the rugged mountain redoubts of eastern Galilee, leaving most of central Galilee to the Israelis.

As THE RATE of Israeli advance accelerated each day, no one was more relieved by the United Nations cease-fire order than Glubb Pasha. His greatest fear was that the Arabs would irrationally refuse to accept a new truce as they had refused to extend the old one.

On July 15, he sat down at his desk and hurriedly scribbled a note to Prime Minister Tawfiq Pasha advising him to agree to a new truce. The Arab Legion, he said, was not in a critical situation and had never planned to hold Lydda and Ramle. He expressed the view that the Legion could halt the Israeli attacks on its front, but said he feared that other Arab armies would be in deep trouble unless the fighting ended soon.

Two hours after he had sent this letter to the Prime Minister, he was summoned by telephone to the palace. As Glubb entered King Abdullah's office, he was startled to see all members of the cabinet sitting round the conference table, their faces grim as they acknowledged him silently. When Glubb had sat down, Tawfiq Pasha turned to the King:

"Your Majesty, may I have permission to read the letter from Glubb Pasha?"

The King, as stern-faced as the others, nodded, and the Prime Minister began to read out the letter in a voice choking with anger.

" ' . . . I am sorry to trouble Your Excellency at such a moment . . . ' "

Tawfiq Pasha paused, raised his eyes slightly, and said with a smirk: "Very kind of him to be so considerate."

As he read on, all eyes turned to Glubb. But the General looked only at the King, feeling a sinking sensation as he saw in his face an expression he had never observed before. For the first time, the King seemed to doubt him.

"If you don't want to serve us loyally," Abdullah said, his usually warm, lively eyes as cold as steel, "there is no need for you to stay."

And a minister added: "Very remarkable that we never heard anything about a shortage of ammunition until Mr. Bevin wanted the fighting to stop."

"They say the stores are full of ammunition," commented another.

Then there was silence. Glubb suddenly felt exhausted. Somehow, their accusations didn't seem to matter; what good would it do to explain the situation rationally, or to tell the ministers that they were well aware of the ammunition shortage? Someone had to be the scapegoat. He turned to the King and asked: "May I go now, sir?"

"Very well," Abdullah replied.

Glubb walked to the door, saluted, and left.

On the central front, after the fall of Lydda and Ramle, Israeli units captured Majdal Yaba and other Iraqi-held flank positions. Meanwhile larger forces blazed a bloody trail through the hill villages surrounding Latrun, gradually closing in on that long-elusive target. By July 17, only two miles separated Israeli posts west of Latrun from other Israeli strongholds east of it, and some of these positions overlooked the road to Ramallah, the main Latrun supply route. But with the truce scheduled to take effect at 5:45 P.M. the following day, there wasn't time to force a Legion evacuation as planned, or to cut completely the road link with Ramallah.

The only answer lay in a new direct attack on the Latrun police fortress, the Israeli High Command decided on the night of July 17.

"You know the international pressures B.G. is under," Yadin explained to Allon at GHQ. "We just can't delay the truce. It's got to be a direct attack."

"A frontal attack in daylight against their best-defended position!" Allon exclaimed. "Well, if we have no choice . . . "

"Maybe now that the supply lines of the Legion are almost cut," said Yadin hopefully, "they won't put up a very obstinate defense."

"With the truce about to save them?" Allon said, and he recalled with a chill how many corpses he had already seen at Latrun.

Glubb Pasha sat nervously in his office, his chair facing the window. He kept glancing at his wristwatch and then at the sleepy, sun-baked streets. The world he saw was at peace. Yet a few miles away the climactic battle of the war was about to be fought. He turned back to his desk and, toying with his amber beads, reread the latest messages.

They worried him deeply. An enemy column of 5 tanks, 10 Bren carriers, and some half-tracks was moving toward Latrun, and infantry forces were forming on nearby hills, apparently preparing to storm the police fortress. He got up and paced the floor, then sat down again and picked up the phone.

"Any signals through from division headquarters?"

"No sir. Nothing yet."

Well, there was no use waiting in the office. He couldn't do anything now anyway. He had no reserves that he could throw in to help sway the battle. The troops on the spot would have to fight it out. Besides, it was teatime. At 3:30 P.M. therefore, he went home, sat under the vine pergola in his tiny garden, and, glancing idly at the pattern of branches against the azure sky, sipped the tea his wife had brought out to him.

Haydar Mustafa, the Latrun fortress commander, was desperate. Most of his men were not around. Indeed, scarcely half an hour ago he himself had been fast asleep on his cot, certain that no further important action would take place before the truce started at 5:45 P.M.—only 2 hours and 45 minutes away.

He slipped on a shirt and rushed outside, looking up at the roof where a 6-pounder had been installed and zeroed in on the approach road. He yelled up to the two men behind the gun: "Don't fire until the tanks are within range of the gun!"

The roof was hardly the best place to put a gun, he thought. Although the weapon had an excellent field of fire, it was in full view of the enemy. Moreover, the gunner could sight such a gun downward only with great difficulty. He had told his British superiors this, but in vain. Well, it was too late now.

He went inside and grimly awaited the clash.

*

Tex, the British sergeant who had been persuaded by Desmond Rutledge to desert to the Israelis, whistled as he sat at the controls of the first tank in the attacking column while his gunner blasted away at the police fortress. Only two more hours or so and the fighting would be over, and then he'd be able to see his girl and maybe get drunk . . . The damn artillery was getting close. Well, what the hell; he couldn't remember a shell that didn't come close. An explosion suddenly rocked his Cromwell tank. The gun on the roof had almost scored a direct hit.

"Knock that gun out!" Tex ordered his gunner.

"I can't!" the gunner replied. "Our gun's jammed. A shell casing must be stuck in the barrel. Have we got an extractor tool?"

An extractor tool! The whole armored brigade had only one and it happened to be in Rutledge's tank at Lydda Airport. As this critical fact dawned on him, he saw enemy soldiers running from the station. All the column had to do now was roll in and take over the place! He ordered a halt, crawled out of the tank, and ran to the one behind him.

"My gun is jammed," he shouted to the operator. "I'm going back to the airport to get it fixed. I'll come back later. You go on in and capture the police station. Understand?"

The operator smiled and waved.

Tex waved back and returned to his own tank, turned it around, and hurried down the road.

Little more than half an hour later, he rolled into Lydda Airport and leaped out. He was about to dash off to find the extractor tool when he looked behind him and felt faint. The whole Israeli column of armor! He ran to the first tank and shouted hysterically: "What are you doing here, you stupid bastard, you son of a bitch? Why didn't you take over the police station?"

The tank operator looked puzzled.

"What's the matter with that bastard?" he yelled to some soldiers who came running up.

One of the men spoke in Hebrew with the operator, then said: "He doesn't understand English. He thought you ordered him to follow you."

Tex's weatherbeaten face whitened.

"You fool!" he cried. "You bloomin' idiot! The Arabs evacuated the station. It's unoccupied. We've got to go back! Quick, we've got to go back!"

"Look at the time," an officer said. "There's only a few minutes until the truce starts. And we have strict orders to stop all operations at five forty-five."

"Then what about the infantry? Let them take it alone. There's still time."

"The enemy must have seen your column leaving. And the place is probably occupied again. We can't risk an unsupported infantry assault."

"Oh no!"

As soon as the telephone began to ring, Glubb Pasha sprang from his chair in the garden and ran into the house.

"Glubb Pasha here . . ."

"This is Lash here, sir."

"Well, what's the news?"

"This Jewish attack has been repulsed. Our six-pounder knocked out all their tanks. We've just sent two infantry sections out with Piats to see if they can finish off the tanks. I'm afraid the ground's too open and they won't be able to get near enough."

"But what about the infantry attack?"

"Their infantry haven't attacked at all. They don't seem to like the look of us. Fire is slackening off now. Looks as if the show's over!"

"Well done, old man! That's grand. Give all the troops my love."

Glubb ran out of the house screaming "Hurrah! Hurrah!" and did a Scottish reel on the garden path. Looking up from her tea, his wife exclaimed: "My dear! What on earth is the matter?"

"We've done it!" Glubb shouted. "Five tanks knocked out by one six-pounder! Can you beat it? Infantry never came over at all! The whole thing was a fiasco!"

"How wonderful! But meanwhile your tea is getting cold. And I made these potted meat sandwiches all specially. I don't believe you've had anything to eat all day . . ."

T HREE days before the first truce ended, Mordechai Raanan had gone to the office of David Shaltiel, his Haganah counterpart in Jerusalem, and said: "Shaltiel, we'll be ready to attack the Old City in four days, the day after the truce ends."

Shaltiel had been eagerly preparing for Operation Kedem, or Antiquity, a name marking the 2,500th anniversary of the successful attack on the Jerusalem wall by Nebuchadnezzar's Babylonian army. The Haganah commander was convinced that he could duplicate the Babylonian feat, and had stated publicly that he was now in a position to take the Old City in four days. But he felt that it was not essential to rush the "four-day" campaign since he expected, as did most Israelis, a fairly long period of fighting after the truce.

"I'm sorry," he replied now, "but the Haganah is not yet ready for our joint attack. We'll be ready in about a week."

"But you promised we'd attack as soon as the truce ended!"

"I know, but the special bombs to blow up the wall are still not ready.* Also, I have clear orders from headquarters to attack Ein Karim and Maldha first. Lehi has already agreed to attack Ein Karim. Would you send your men to attack Maldha?"

"But what about our agreement to attack the Old City?" Raanan asked incredulously.

"I give you my word," Shaltiel said, "that as soon as the bombs are ready we'll attack, and that won't be later than Sunday or Monday night— only a week away."

Raanan didn't like the proposal at all. Not only would an attack on a peripheral target possibly delay the assault on the Old City longer than necessary, but he couldn't afford many casualties in such side battles. As it was, he had hardly 300 men in all. But the Stern Group had agreed, and he needed the Haganah's cooperation in the Old City venture.

"All right, we'll attack Maldha. When should we do it?"

"On Saturday night."

But Shaltiel postponed the attack on Maldha, as well as on the Old City, offering technical reasons. Raanan, enraged, finally put a proposition to Faglin and Samuel Katz, who had come from Tel Aviv.

"I think we should be ready to attack the Old City on Wednesday with or without Shaltiel's help."

His two colleagues agreed, but Faglin pointed out that without Haganah the Irgun would have to attack not from Mount Zion through Zion Gate as it was now scheduled to do, but through the New Gate, the entry assigned to Haganah.

"If the fighting continues after daybreak," he said, "we'll be too exposed to enemy fire along the walls at Zion Gate. So we must go through New Gate if we go it alone."

"But to attack through New Gate, we'd have to start out from Notre Dame," Raanan said. "And it's occupied by Haganah."

"We'll just have to take control of Notre Dame," Faglin replied.

This decision solidified when, on Monday night, July 12, a company of Irgunists, hoping to match an earlier Sternist victory at Ein Karim, occupied Maldha, only to be cut to ribbons in a counterattack. The Irgunist leaders were convinced that Shaltiel had betrayed them by withdrawing his artillery support too soon.

* One bomb was to be supplied each of the three attacking forces—Haganah, Irgun, and the Stern Group.

Raanan charged into Shaltiel's office for a showdown and found him sitting with several officers.

"I've been trying to find you," Shaltiel said. "I am aware of your preparations to occupy Notre Dame tonight. However, I can assure you that the combined operation of the three forces will be carried out by Friday night. The bombs will be ready by then. If you try to carry out your operation tonight, a fratricidal battle will ensue and we'll lose our big chance to capture the Old City. Will you wait?"

"I'll give you my answer in an hour," Raanan said.

He then rushed to his headquarters and conferred with his colleagues. They agreed to play along with Shaltiel, but decided to make several demands: 50 Irgun soldiers would enter Notre Dame immediately so that they would be in a position to attack alone if necessary; any group that penetrated the Old City would continue fighting even after a cease-fire started until the whole area was captured; the first group to enter the Old City would facilitate the entry of the other two groups; and supplies would flow into the Old City without interruption.

According to Raanan, Shaltiel had offered to give guarantees and agreed to these conditions. According to Shaltiel, he refused to commit himself to any conditions and had never offered to do so at any point.

On July 15, Shaltiel, who had withheld his plans from the High Command while the timing was in doubt, sent his adjutant, Yeshurin Schiff, to Tel Aviv with the details. Ben-Gurion and Yadin, after listening carefully, approved the plan.

But when Schiff had left, Yadin began to worry. Too many men had already died in frontal attacks on the Old City gates. If there was to be an attack on the Old City, it should be initiated from the rear, from Sheikh Jarrah. He expressed this view to Ben-Gurion, who agreed with him.

Thus, early on Friday, July 16, Shaltiel entered his office and found a message from Yadin awaiting him:

> . . . You are to decide what you will be able to carry out during this night. The evident possibilities: Sheikh Jarrah or a bridgehead in the Old City. In case only one possibility is feasible before the truce, you are to carry out Sheikh Jarrah.

Shaltiel was furious. Didn't they realize he did not have enough men to capture and occupy Sheikh Jarrah? In any case, everything was finally set for Operation Kedem. They had demanded so often that he attack the Old City, and now they were trying to stop him. He couldn't change plans at the last minute. Nor could he back out of his commitment to the "terrorist gangs," however much he despised them. He had to honor it, if only to stop the Irgunists from attacking alone. He could use force against them, but this would mean Jewish bloodshed.

As he studied Yadin's cable, it seemed to him that it did leave some room for final choice of action. And his choice was to go through with Operation Kedem.[4]

Ezra Elnakam was overcome with joy as he stood, together with his fellow Sternist fighters, listening to Yehoshua Zetler proclaiming the start of a miracle. It had all been worthwhile—Deir Yassin, his killing of a British policeman, other necessary actions. . . .

"Every generation of Jews since the destruction of the Second Temple," Zetler said with evident emotion, "has looked forward to this night. For tonight, all of Jerusalem will be ours. And you are the men who are privileged to make the dream come true."

As the group of about 50 Sternist fighters began to jump into trucks that were to take them to Barclays Bank, near the section of the Old City wall they were to penetrate, children's voices rose incongruously against a background of explosions and machine-gun fire.

"Good luck! Good luck!"

Ezra could barely keep back tears as he watched about a dozen children waving goodbye on the veranda of an orphans' home overlooking the camp. They had heard Zetler's talk. As Ezra sat down on the floor of a crowded truck, he confided to Menashe Eichler: "I have only one fear. That I'll go mad from happiness and won't be able to fight."

Eichler stroked his thick brown beard and smiled. "If you lived the Bible as I do," he said, "you would not have to worry about going mad."

"What do you mean?" Ezra asked.

"Well, you are happy about the prospect of winning back Jerusalem. But Jerusalem has always been mine—in my heart. Physical possession is like the frosting on the cake."

Heightening Ezra's joy was a secret Sternist plan (unknown to Shaltiel or even to Friedman-Yellin) to blow up the magnificent mosaic-walled Mosque of Omar, or Dome of the Rock, which marked the site of the Prophet Mohammed's ascension into Heaven. Just as the mosque had been built on the ruins of the First and Second Temples, the Sternists decided, so would the Third Temple be built on the ruins of the mosque.[5]

Faglin and Yehuda Lapidot—the latter, field commander of the Irgun operation—surveyed the area around New Gate from a window in Notre Dame, taking turns with the binoculars. At the last minute Shaltiel had decided that the Irgun would attack through New Gate and the Haganah through Zion Gate—a switch of positions. The two men had heard from Raanan that the Haganah force on Mount Zion was finding it extremely difficult to climb the hill with their new bomb, which weighed about 350 pounds. (The second bomb—the Irgun's—was to be brought by truck to Notre Dame at any moment.)

"I don't think we should use the bomb," Lapidot said. "It's impractical. With that concentrated fire from the wall, we'd probably never even get it across the street to the gate."

Faglin agreed. "The damn thing might not even work," he said. "Who can trust Shaltiel? It may be just another of his tricks."

Faglin then called Raanan, who also agreed that the Irgun attackers should use not the bomb but ordinary explosives to blow up the gate. Shaltiel had little choice at this point but to accede.

Menashe Eichler, dressed incongruously in khaki instead of the traditional long black topcoat, stood with other bearded, ultra-Orthodox members of the Stern Group in an abandoned house near Barclays Bank and mumbled prayers, his eyes closed, his skull-capped head nodding slightly. On a table in a corner lay a Torah. It was Friday night, the Sabbath Eve, and services must go on, war or no war.

Suddenly, someone rushed into the room and cried: "Menashe, come quickly! The bomb has arrived!"

Eichler grabbed his rifle and put on a helmet over his skullcap, his two long side curls protruding like corkscrew-shaped earrings. Then he rushed out into the street to gather some of his men to help carry the bomb to the wall. This was an "emergency" bomb. Shortly before, the first had exploded when a shell hit the truck carrying it to the Sternists.

The truck bringing this second V-shaped, yard-high weapon had stopped by the barbed wire barrier near the new post office about 200 yards from the wall. The bomb would have to be carried the rest of the way because of the piles of debris that blocked any further motorized advance.

When it had been lowered to earth, Eichler and a comrade, each grabbing a handle, lifted it a few inches off the ground and began edging toward the wall. A tall, broad-shouldered man, Eichler moaned and gasped as he advanced inch by inch straining every muscle. His heart pounded, his back began to throb with pain, and his burning palms seemed to be gripping hot coals. He hardly heard the bullets flying past or even the cries of wounded men. He realized that the other man helping to carry the bomb had been hit only when it fell to earth and became immovable. Calling others to aid him, Eichler stumbled on over piles of rubbish, rolls of barbed wire, and mounds of jagged masonry until his agonized body finally gave way and the burden dropped ponderously to earth again.

"Someone relieve me," he cried. "And may God be with him!"

Raanan paced the floor of GHQ chain-smoking and swearing to himself. It was 10 P.M. already and the Israeli bombardment that was to precede the attack still had not started.

"Well, what's the excuse now?" he shouted to Shaltiel. "Why aren't we shelling yet?"

"We still can't make contact with the artillery."

"Then send someone there by motorcycle or go yourself and tell them to start firing!"

Contact was finally made, and the bombardment began about midnight. But then communications failed again, and the guns kept pounding the Arabs for almost three hours, preventing an infantry assault. Raanan now threatened Shaltiel: "Unless you stop shelling in fifteen minutes, I'm going to issue orders to my boys to advance into the bombardment and I'll place the responsibility on you for what happens to them."

But Shaltiel ignored the threat.

Eventually, shortly after 3 A.M., the shelling stopped and Shaltiel gave the order for the three infantry forces to advance.

Harold Kraushar, the Brooklynite who had come to Israel on the *Altalena,* sat on the damp floor of Notre Dame against a wall trying to read Mark Twain's *Innocents Abroad* by moonlight. After a few hours of sniping at Arabs on the Old City wall, he had come down to rest for a while and had found the book on the floor. But after struggling for several pages, he closed the book and threw it across the room. What a time for satirical reading, with bullets flying everywhere and explosions constantly making him lose his place!

It was almost 3 A.M. and the attack had still not started. He had left the comforts of the United States to risk his life for Israel, but the Haganah wouldn't let him fight. When he had arrived on the *Altalena,* they had taken him prisoner. And now they expected him to do nothing but read . . .

Finally, the word came from Raanan: "Attack New Gate!"

About 50 Irgunists jumped up and strode swiftly out of Notre Dame and through some empty buildings that separated the church from the wall. From the building facing the wall, Lapidot saw Israeli shells still streaking into the Old City. And to make matters worse, one shell suddenly ignited a roadblock of wood and shavings in front of the gate so that a great blaze blocked the approach.

"Stop the shelling!" Lapidot shouted over the radio. "We can't move ahead."

When, about half an hour later, the shelling finally halted and the fire was extinguished, Lapidot sent several sappers across the road to New Gate and they blew it open. Then they blew a hole through an inner wall just inside the gate.

David Smith, an American volunteer, shouted: *"Yalleh!* Let's go!" and the first assault group of 10 men dashed across the street under heavy fire and entered the Old City while Arabs, after hurling grenades, leaped off the wall in hasty retreat.

Harold Kraushar, one of the first, felt strangely exhilarated as he found himself inside the heartland of Judaism. All his previous frustrations vanished in a flash. He was now taking part in an action that he was sure would be remembered for thousands of years. He felt deeply relaxed as he blasted his way forward with his Sten gun toward the line of shops along the wall to the left of the gate. The Irgun plan was to advance through the shops by blowing up their walls, the technique that had proved so successful in Jaffa.

Meanwhile, Lapidot, still in the building outside the wall, radioed GHQ asking whether the Stern fighters were inside the Old City and was told: "Yes, Haganah and Lehi are both inside."

But five minutes later, he received a contradictory message that it was not known whether either group was inside yet.

"Hold up your attack!" the message ordered . . .

In Bible House, near Barclays Bank, Ezra Elnakam sat on the floor in silence beside other Sternist fighters. Shortly after three o'clock, someone rushed in and cried: "Get ready! The bomb's in place! We're moving toward the wall!"

But Ezra was skeptical. After so many disappointments, he refused to let himself be wound up to his earlier emotional pitch. He and his comrades slowly made their way to a building only about 30 yards from the Old City wall so that they would be in a better position to attack when the order came. They sat down on the sidewalk with their back against the building, facing the open area that separated them from the wall.

Ezra watched with grim fascination as Arab tracers burrowed through the black sky into the New City, followed by whistling shells. Gradually, the tracers and shells swung toward the Barclays Bank zone, but Ezra and his fellows refused to budge, as if fearing to admit weakness. When a tracer struck about four yards in front of them, Ezra called to his companions: "Put your helmets over your faces!"

Hardly had he spoken when he heard a vicious screech that ended in an explosion a few feet away. He felt as if someone had struck him in the eye. He removed his helmet from his face and saw blood pouring into his lap; a piece of shrapnel had penetrated under his helmet and entered one eye. Putting a handkerchief to the wound, he got to his feet and felt pain throughout his body. He then realized he had also been hit by slivers in the hand, legs, and chest.

A Sternist nurse came by, helped him to his feet, and silently led him to a first aid station in the Ottoman Bank. As he entered, some of his friends could not recognize him because of the blood that had turned his face into a grotesque mask.

At that moment, a tremendous blast rocked the area, and the building shook to its foundations. As the nurse guided Ezra to a cot, a Sternist rushed in shouting: "That was our bomb!"

Ezra collapsed on the cot. At last the Old City would be in Jewish hands! He was brimming over with such joy that he forgot entirely about his pierced eye and his other wounds. At last, at last! . . . Could any man continue to live a normal life on earth, he wondered, when his every nerve throbbed with such ecstasy?

He started to sing a Sternist song while, outside, men wept bitter tears at the barely scratched wall . . .

At about 5 A.M., Shaltiel's chief of operations, Zion Eldad, radioed an order for a general retreat. Raanan, standing nearby, rushed over and yelled: "What do you mean, retreat? Didn't we agree that if any force entered the Old City, all would continue to fight?"

He was fully aware that both the Haganah and Sternist forces had failed in their attempts to blow holes in the wall with their secret bombs, which had proved completely ineffectual. But he was determined that the Irgun troops, which had broken through with conventional explosives, should advance— alone if necessary.

"I am not a politician," Eldad retorted, "I'm a field commander. I have received orders to retreat and that is what I am going to do!"

"Listen, Eldad," Raanan warned, "my boys are not going to retreat. Do you understand?"

"If you don't retreat, we shall cut off all supplies to your forces in the Old City and we won't evacuate any of your wounded. And if you still continue to disobey orders, we'll cut off New Gate from Notre Dame."

"This is betrayal!" Raanan raged. "The behavior of a whore! After our agreement, you would let them die?"

"I am a soldier, not a politician. Speak to Shaltiel about that."

Raanan then rushed out of the room and began looking for Shaltiel, opening one door after another along the corridor; but he could not find him. He returned to the communications room and radioed Faglin, who said that without help it would be hopeless to continue the attack.

Raanan was momentarily silent. Then he replied: "All right, retreat."

He sat down and clasped his hands to his head. Not satisfied with its crackdown on the Irgun elsewhere, the Haganah now wanted to destroy his force in Jerusalem; to destroy him as a man, just as they had tried to do in the "Hunting Season" of 1945, after the murder in Cairo of Lord Moyne (the British Minister in charge of Middle Eastern Affairs) . . .

> Sternists had killed Moyne, yet Ben-Gurion and the Haganah had declared war on the Irgun, cooperating with the British in tracking members down.
>
> "We want to know," a Haganah officer said to Raanan after he had been picked up at a bus stop, "who your commanders are, where you keep your weapons, and who finances you."
>
> "Do you think I'm going to tell you that?" Raanan replied.
>
> The following day he found himself in a cave, chained to an iron-slatted bed by wrists and ankles while drops of rainwater dripped maddeningly on his face. When after six icy days and nights he still refused to talk, they finally let him go—a numbed, hungry animal, covered with filth and barely able to walk . . .

Now, it seemed, they were still working on him.

Near Barclays Bank, Menashe Eichler, his beard wet with sweat, put his Sten into a truck and started withdrawing, along with other Orthodox Sternists, toward his home in the religious Mea Shearim Quarter. It was all right to ride to battle on the Sabbath, but not *away* from battle, nor even to walk carrying weapons. Those who were only slightly wounded or, like himself, dazed from fatigue, were prepared to crawl if necessary rather than ride.

Eichler glanced back at the wall as he trudged over rocks and debris. The ancient stones of the great barrier looked almost pink in the light of a summer dawn; a misty pinkness oddly out of place in a gray, shattered world. Then he glanced at his watch. He would still get to the synagogue in time for morning prayers.

At about 2:30 P.M. on Saturday, with all quiet on the Jerusalem front, military governor Dov Joseph telephoned Shaltiel.

"I checked with Nieuwenhuys, and he says the Truce Commission has not yet received an official statement from the Arabs agreeing to the cease-fire. Were you notified before midnight of any such agreement?"

"No," Shaltiel replied.

"Then why did our forces cease firing at five forty-five?"

"My instructions were not to fire if the Arabs stopped firing, and they had stopped firing."

Joseph was silent for a moment, then rejoined: "My understanding . . . was that we would cease fire only if the Arabs had, at a fixed time, notified the commission that they would do likewise. If we had gone on fighting, the Security Council could not justifiably have held us at fault . . . "

14

The Deadly Truce

IF they'd only stop firing long enough for you to have the baby!"
Mohammed Gharbieh, who had just recovered from the buttocks wound
sustained in the Old City Jewish Quarter, stood panic-stricken by his
German wife's bed in their home on the Mount of Olives as the doctor examined her. He had risked his life dozens of times in battle with the British
and the Jews, but had never felt so helpless. Greta, about to give birth to
her second child, had been shocked into near paralysis by an Israeli barrage
as firing in Jerusalem continued sporadically—even though a truce was
supposed to be in effect.

"Push! Push!" urged the doctor.

"No, leave it inside," Greta groaned, her blond hair fanning over a
pillow soaked in perspiration. "I can't any more. Let me die!"

"You mustn't give up! Do your best!"

"No, I can't. I have no more strength!"

Mohammed pleaded in desperation: "Do something, doctor. What
about a Caesarean?"

"I haven't got the proper instruments with me."

The doctor then took the father aside and muttered: "I'm sorry, Mohammed. It looks hopeless."

Mohammed knelt by the bed and began to wail a prayer.

Suddenly the house trembled as a shell exploded just outside, shattering
the windows and bouncing Greta about three feet into the air.

"My God, look!" cried the doctor.

"The Jews!" sobbed Mohammed joyously. "They bombed the baby
out!"

*

546

On the morning of August 10, above the noise of firing nearby, Moshe Dayan, the new commander in the New City, heard the excited voice of Dov Joseph over the phone shouting: "Moshe, Bernadotte just arrived at the Belgian Consulate and some Lehi people are demonstrating against him in front of the building. Get down there, will you, and try to disperse them. It's embarrassing us!"

"Okay," said Dayan. "I'll go right away." He hastened out to his armored car.

He hoped that he would not have to use force against the Sternists; fighting other Jews would hardly be an auspicious way to begin his new job. Ben-Gurion had recently selected him to replace David Shaltiel (who had infuriated the Prime Minister by attacking the Old City "against orders") despite his relatively undistinguished record in the war so far. He had disobeyed orders in Lydda and smashed into Karatiya with possibly undue difficulty. Still, he was one of the best and most aggressive non-Palmach commanders, and Ben-Gurion didn't want Allon or some other Palmach leader in command of so important an area.

Dayan admired many of the Sternists, even though he abhorred some of their methods, particularly assassination. They were tough, fearless, idealistic; which was why he had incorporated a platoon of Sternists into his Commando Battalion that had raided Lydda and other Arab strong-holds. Yet, well aware of the difficulties the extremists had posed for Shaltiel, Dayan was determined to use a firm hand if necessary to keep them under control—until they were forced to dissolve in Jerusalem as in the rest of the country. And that would probably be soon, for the government had declared on July 26 that the New City was Israeli-occupied territory, foreshadowing a claim to permanent possession. The dissidents could not much longer argue that they had a right to exist in Jerusalem on the grounds that it was not yet part of Israel.

Dayan's armored car pulled up behind a number of jeeps crammed with men and women holding posters with such slogans as: "Your Work Is in Vain; We Are Here!" and "Stockholm Is Yours; Jerusalem Is Ours!"

He stepped out and watched for several moments as the demonstrators, led by Israel Sheib, yelled and sang underground songs, completely ignoring him. Then he shouted authoritatively: "All right, that's enough! Get going!"

The noise tapered off and, after some protest, the demonstrators agreed to leave. They didn't want a brush with the army, and Dayan looked and talked tough.

As the jeeps moved off, Dayan climbed back into his armored car and soon dismissed the incident from his mind—even the sign that read: "Remember Lord Moyne!"

Dov Joseph was very relieved when Dayan informed him that the demonstration had ended peacefully. He had regarded the incident as undiplomatic and annoying, yet he could well understand the hostility that moderate as well as extremist Israelis felt toward Bernadotte. He had met with the mediator and the three Truce Commission consuls on August 3 to discuss means of ending the shelling and shooting and Bernadotte had pressed for the demilitarization of Jerusalem. Joseph had argued that that would be taking a very grave risk.

"At the moment," he had added, noting the cold stares of the visitors, "in view of the constant violation of the truce by the Arabs, the atmosphere is not yet ripe for discussing demilitarization."

"According to the report sent in by my observers," Bernadotte had responded with obvious agitation, "it is the Jews who are the most aggressive party in Jerusalem, though, owing to lack of personnel, I have not been able to confirm this definitely."

Joseph looked at him resentfully. It seemed rather too much to have Bernadotte calling the Jews the aggressors when, only the day before, the Arabs had marked Bernadotte's own arrival in the New City with a hail of bullets and mortar shells. His observers, Joseph felt, had only to say that this was done by "irregulars" and not by the Arab Legion, and Bernadotte was perfectly willing to overlook such attacks as unimportant. But when the Jews were forced to retaliate in self-defense, that was a serious truce violation.[1]

Despite the deepening friction between Bernadotte and the Israelis, however, the mediator was not overly concerned about his personal safety; he didn't even refer to the Sternist demonstration in his discussions with Israeli officials. He was still optimistic enough to believe that he could persuade the Jews to accept a modified version of his original "Bernadotte Plan."

FEAR THAT Bernadotte could generate irresistible pressures on Israel to accept a truncated state drove the Israelis to intensify preparations for the new drive that might be necessary to present the world with a *fait accompli*.

The High Command hastened to complete the reorganization of the army begun during the first truce, establishing four clear-cut commands: in the north, center, south, and Jerusalem and its corridor. Ranks were finally established. The chief of staff became a brigadier; the front commanders, colonels; brigade commanders, lieutenant colonels. Full-time soldiers, numbering about 50,000 when the first truce began, totaled 90,000 by mid-October with the arrival of new immigrants from camps in Europe and Cyprus and of volunteers from abroad.

But to Ben-Gurion, no reorganization measure was more important than the final elimination of the Palmach as a semi-independent organization. Confident that his victory over Yadin and the Palmach leaders during the first truce had cleared the way for this drastic step, he demanded that the High Command order the Palmach's abolition. And Yadin, after arguing that such a step at this time might dangerously lower the army's morale, finally agreed as the only means of avoiding another command crisis. The Palmach was dissolved.

Meanwhile, the Israelis expanded their arsenal . . .

Ada Sereni, Israel's chief underground agent in Italy, smiled in anticipation when she heard the voice of a high Italian official on the telephone. He seldom called unless he had important information for her.

"Signora, I have some news which may interest you," he began. "Major Fuad Mardam Bey has arrived here from Syria. He has been sent here officially by the Syrian government to salvage the arms from the *Lino*. He's trying to hire divers now."

So the business was still unfinished. In April, the Jews had sunk the *Lino* in Bari Harbor—together with the Czech arms destined for Syria. Now there was a chance to grab the arms for Israel—with the Syrians paying the salvaging expenses! Ada immediately put her staff to work keeping tabs on the quantity and conditions of the rifles in the crates brought up by divers from the bottom of the sea.

"Mardam Bey needs a new ship to carry the arms," she said to an assistant. "I think we should help him find one."

Through a trusted Italian ship captain, she then contacted a shipping agent who, for a suitable fee, agreed to help Mardam (a close relative of Syrian Prime Minister Jamil Mardam Bey) "find" a ship, and to supply him with a crew that would include two men chosen by Ada.

Mardam chartered the boat—a small wooden craft called the *Argiro*—and loaded her with the salvaged arms, about 80 per cent of the original shipment of 10,000 rifles. On the morning of August 19, Mardam watched happily from the pier of Bari as the *Argiro* pulled out to sea. Then he flew to Alexandria to wait for her to dock en route for Syria.

About half an hour after the *Argiro* had departed, a fishing boat left the port carrying two men dressed in Syrian army uniforms. Some 20 miles out, they caught up with the *Argiro*, which had come to a halt. As the fishing boat slid up alongside, the *Argiro*'s Italian captain looked over the railing.

"We were sent by Mardam Bey," one of the men yelled up to him. "He says he has news that your ship is in danger and that we should escort you to Alexandria. We've brought some communications equipment so that you can keep in contact with the Egyptians."

Operation Pirate was working perfectly. The two members of the Italian crew carefully chosen by Ada had tampered with the ship's engine and brought the vessel to a halt; and now two more agents were aboard. The captain courteously gave them his cabin and listened with a smile as they spoke over their radio in a foreign language he did not understand. In a short while, two Israeli corvettes met the *Argiro* at sea, and it finally dawned on him that the language was Hebrew and that his guests had called their headquarters in Israel. The Israelis relieved the *Argiro* of her cargo and crew, and then scuttled her.[2]

Mardam, after waiting for hours in Alexandria, called every port in the region seeking news of the *Argiro*. A broken man, he finally went home to Damascus where politicians accused him of treason, claiming that he had Jewish business associates and that he had, in the words of one accuser, fallen in love with a "devil in the shape of an extremely beautiful Yugoslav woman named Palmas, a Zionist and a Communist." Imprisoned and sentenced to death, he was eventually permitted to flee Syria, possibly as the result of indirect Israeli intervention. Ada Sereni had persuaded Ben-Gurion to inform the Syrians via the United Nations that the accused had nothing to do with the plot.

I F SYRIA was dealt a severe blow by this loss of precious weapons, Transjordan was still suffering from the blow she had sustained when Egyptian forces had hijacked a British Aqaba-bound supply ship during the first truce. And Britain, now afraid of further Israeli victories, was no longer willing to encourage a resumption of war by shipping new arms to Amman.

When the Arab League also refused to provide further assistance, Glubb stormed into the Defense Minister's office and demanded: "How can money belonging to the Arab League and subscribed by all its members be withheld from us, especially since we've done nearly all the fighting? We must have more funds!"

Together they went to see Prime Minister Tawfiq Pasha, and the Defense Minister explained the problem.

"Didn't I tell you that we had no money?" was Tawfiq Pasha's irritable reply. "I warned you not to exceed your budget heads. Don't you know finance regulations? Where am I to get the money to pay for what you have overspent?"

Glubb, in his frustration, replied huffily: "I suggest you deduct it from my pay."

There was a startled silence. Then the Defense Minister grabbed Glubb by the shoulder and hustled him out of the office.

"I never knew you had a temper like that," he said.

Meanwhile, Tawfiq Pasha viciously pressed the buzzer on his desk, ordered his car, and drove immediately to the palace to see the King. Abdullah later called for Glubb and greeted him pleasantly, if somewhat coldly.

"I think you should take a month's leave," he said. "You deserve a rest . . . "

One reason for the Arab disarray was that each state blamed the others for the Israeli victories and tried to convince its people that it, virtually alone, wanted to resume the fighting. But for all their public belligerence, the invasion leaders had no intention of doing so.

Transjordan did not have the ammunition to fight, nor was King Abdullah dissatisfied with the status quo. His aim now was to devour what remained of Arab Palestine, and to reach an agreement with Israel confirming this union. Israel, in fact, might possibly even further his aim by chasing the Egyptians from the Negev and permitting him to use a port in the Gaza Strip. Egypt, for her part, was content to keep what she had won— virtually the whole Negev except for surrounded Jewish colonies, which she felt she could harass without undue provocation. Syria was politically unstable and short of weapons, particularly after the Czech arms fiasco. Iraq was also politically shaky, and subject to Abdullah's moderating pressure. From the start, Lebanon had had no stomach for the war.

The question most worrying the Arabs now was whether Israel would strike, and if so, where, since no Arab State expected to come to the aid of others if it were not itself attacked. Though the commanders of most Arab armies ignored Abdullah's orders or wishes as "commander-in-chief," the King decided to call a meeting in Amman of Arab Prime Ministers to discuss the protection of Jerusalem. Nokrashy Pasha came from Egypt, Jamil Mardam from Syria, Riadh es-Solh from Lebanon, and Fadhil Jamali from Iraq. Transjordan's Tawfiq Pasha acted as host.

Over cups of sweet tea the group listened quietly as the King opened the meeting with a graphic and gloomy account of the Arab military position, at the end of which he said: "It is especially urgent that we consider ways of reinforcing Jerusalem or of removing the pressure on our forces there."

All but Nokrashy Pasha, who remained silent, confirmed that the protection of Jerusalem was the sacred task of the Arab countries. Abdullah looked toward Nokrashy mockingly.

"What is the matter, Your Excellency? Do you not feel well?" he asked.

"I feel quite well," the Egyptian replied. "I have come here to listen, not to talk."

"There will be plenty to listen to," Abdullah countered, adding acidly: "In my view, the action of the Egyptian government in seizing at Suez a consignment of twenty-five-pounder artillery ammunition destined for Transjordan was not an act of Arab cooperation."

The King then took his leave, and Tawfiq Pasha asked Nokrashy Pasha whether it would be possible for his forces to attack the Israelis south of Jerusalem in order to relieve the pressure on the Arab Legion. Nokrashy's military adviser, looking grim, replied that such an attack would be unwise since it might provoke strong Israeli counteraction.

But was not attacking and being attacked "an inevitable and normal part of the activities of an army engaged in warfare?" the Iraqi Prime Minister asked.

Syria's Jamil Mardam then stood up and said dramatically: "Gentlemen, I have an important announcement to make. We Syrians cannot stand by and see the city holy to both Moslems and Christians fall into the hands of the Zionists. Therefore, despite the practical difficulties and the material sacrifices involved, we are prepared to send immediately a whole infantry division to fight in Jerusalem."

There was a burst of applause, though everyone wondered where Syria would get an infantry division, the only one she was known to possess being committed in Galilee. But Tawfiq Pasha, fearing to express doubt in the face of such enthusiasm, asked when the first troops would be sent.

"In a matter of days, my dear, if God wills," the Syrian replied, beaming.

The Arab leaders then verbally blueprinted the "final offensive" that would crush the Jewish State once and for all, and quibbled over ways in which Jewish property might be split up among the conquering states when the time came.

The Prime Ministers, impressed with their progress, joined King Abdullah for dinner, which consisted of huge steaming plates of mutton and rice, to be rolled dexterously with thumb and forefinger into little balls and popped into eager mouths[3]. . .

Meanwhile, Bernadotte finally managed to bring Israeli and Arab representatives together (on August 22) to discuss truce problems, a step he hoped would lead toward agreement on general demilitarization of the city. The meeting took place after Israeli forces had attacked Colonel Aziz's volunteers, who occupied the area south of the Red Cross–administered no-man's-land between Arab and Jewish Jerusalem. The Israelis claimed that their attack had forestalled an anticipated Egyptian assault on the Jewish Agricultural School in the neutral zone. They would leave the disputed area if the Egyptians promised not to return.

"I shall have to consult with my headquarters," Aziz said. When the meeting ended at about 7 P.M., he jumped into his jeep with two other officers and ordered his driver to head for Gaza where he would discuss the situation with General Mawawi. He would not make the decision alone. Mawawi already resented him, he knew, for having attacked Ramat Rachel without orders and then losing the battle in the bargain.

Aziz was silent as he sped toward Bethlehem. Only a few days before, he had recorded in his diary his deep feelings about the splendor of this area, describing the flowers, the fields, the hills . . .

"WHAT WILL HAPPEN IF THE JEWS ADVANCE UP TO HERE?" HE had scribbled.

He decided then that he would fight to the last bullet in his pistol, keeping that last one for himself.

"If I am killed, will my men still obey my orders?" he had written, answering with another question: "How could I give orders if I were dead and in another world?"

Still, he wondered whether there wasn't some way he could keep in contact, even after death. How dreadful to think that he might not know how the war was progressing, that he could not influence its outcome . . .

He recorded how he had walked up a hill with his thoughts, passing a large stone bench beside the road, a bench on which people in peacetime could sit and feast their eyes on the wondrous world at sunset.

"What a splendid place Fate has chosen for a climax to the play of my life. Those who will visit my tomb in the future will sit here to rest after climbing the mountain and gaze at my statue . . ."

A statue? Yes, they would build a statue for him. Or maybe just a simple headstone with his name and date of death inscribed on it. Actually, a simple one would be enough; a statue was unnecessary. In any event, many people would come, including, of course, his son Khaled. He would be a man then, and the hill would not tire him. He would stand and bow his head and say proudly: "Here my father died and entered history as a hero." But he would not weep.

Aziz had quoted Nietzsche: "The hero is a man who knows how to die at the right moment in the right place."

"Yes," Aziz concluded, "Nietzsche would have approved this place . . ."

Shortly after Aziz's jeep had passed through this region, shots rang out in the night and the Colonel slumped over dead, a bullet in his side. The driver and the other passengers were uninjured.

The Egyptian government announced that he had been killed in error by an Egyptian sentry near Iraq el-Manshiya. The sentry was said to have fired a warning shot and then, when the jeep failed to stop, the fatal bullet— a report reminiscent of Colonel Marcus's death on the Israel side.

The Egyptians eventually accepted Israeli terms for withdrawal from the area in question, but Bernadotte was unable to push demilitarization any further. Aside from Israel's intransigence, he did not have enough observers to police a demilitarized Jerusalem. He began to concede that demilitarization might be possible only within the framework of an overall political solution to the Palestine problem, and the revised "Bernadotte Plan" on which he was working now took on new urgency.

He thus sent his dynamic deputy, Dr. Ralph Bunche, to Lake Success to seek, on the one hand, a larger United Nations police force, and on the other, American and British support for his political plan. Actually Bunche, a Harvard graduate and former sports star at the University of California at Los Angeles, had drawn up this plan himself, fervently believing it to be the best possible blueprint for partition. Though it called for boundaries similar to those Bernadotte had suggested in June, no mention was now made of a "Greater Palestine" union embracing Jewish and Arab states and Transjordan. And Jerusalem, instead of going to the Arabs, would now be internationalized. But the whole Negev as well as Ramle and Lydda would still be absorbed by the Arabs, with the Jews getting all of Galilee as before. The United Nations would confirm the right of the Arab refugees to return immediately to their homes, and, "because of historical connection and common interest," Transjordan would annex Arab Palestine.

The Jews did not resent Bunche as they did Bernadotte, even though the views of the two men largely coincided, for while they felt that the mediator was little more than a British agent, they regarded Bunche as fair and friendly, if sometimes mistaken. Unlike Bernadotte, they sensed, he readily adjusted his views to facts, instead of the other way around.

On his return to the United States early in September, Bunche initially asked Washington to send 5,000 troops to protect Jerusalem; but Secretary Marshall rejected this request categorically. Disappointed, if not surprised, Bunche then secretly brought together Britain's Sir Alexander Cadogan and America's Philip Jessup at a meeting at Lake Success. Arguing that the Soviets would profit from further fighting, he vigorously called for Anglo-American agreement on a compromise partition formula, and then revealed the outlines of the new Bernadotte Plan.

The scheme was greeted with approval in the State Department. And at one meeting, Robert McClintock, Rusk's assistant, suggested to Lovett and Rusk: "I know Bernadotte very well from the time I was stationed as second secretary in Stockholm. Maybe I should go to Rhodes and see exactly what they propose?"[4]

A few days later McClintock, with Sir John Troutbeck of Britain's Middle Eastern Office in Cairo, arrived secretly in Rhodes to confer with Bernadotte and Bunche, who were in the process of drawing up a final draft of the plan (with Bunche still doing the actual writing).

"It's a good plan," McClintock said, after reading the draft through carefully. "I'm going to advise my government to support it. Maybe it will help to avert new fighting." (McClintock denies reports that he and Troutbeck helped to prepare the final draft.)

Troutbeck agreed. The plan, he was sure, would meet with Bevin's approval—particularly the recommendations that the Negev go to the Arab sector and that this sector, in turn, go to Transjordan. This was exactly what the Foreign Secretary had wanted all along.

O N the muggy afternoon of Friday, September 10, a car sped from Jerusalem to Tel Aviv carrying two men on a fateful mission. Yehoshua Zetler was driving Israel Sheib to a conference with Nathan Friedman-Yellin and Yitzhak Yizernitzky, the two other members of the Stern Group's Central Committee. And Sheib was determined to leave the meeting with unanimous agreement on a "solution" to the Bernadotte threat—a solution that he had had in mind ever since the Sternist demonstration against the mediator a month before.

As the car halted before a rundown apartment building on Ben Yehuda

Street in Tel Aviv, Sheib told Zetler to wait for word from him. Then he climbed the stairs to Friedman-Yellin's apartment, where his two colleagues were waiting for him. In the simply furnished living room, the three men began to discuss the expected new Bernadotte Plan.

"If the world listens to Bernadotte and pressures our weakling government into making compromises, we will have lost our state," Sheib said. "We can't let this happen. We must show the world that it is just as futile for the United Nations to interfere in our affairs as it was for the British. Demonstrations are not enough."

Yizernitzky agreed. His view had always been, as he had explained to Stern members, that "a man who goes forth to kill another whom he does not know must believe one thing only—that by his act he will change the course of history."

The three men (according to Sheib and Yizernitzky) then discussed Count Bernadotte in the light of this philosophy. And as they exchanged ideas over wine and fruit, it seemed that the clock had been set back four years—to that day in spring, 1944, when the same three men had met in another dingy room to consider assassinating Sir Harold MacMichael, the British High Commissioner in Palestine, and Lord Moyne, the British Minister of State in the Middle East.

Within months, MacMichael had been wounded in an assassination attempt, and Lord Moyne murdered . . .

Now the Sternists would have to shake the world again, and clearly the assassination of Bernadotte would do that even more convulsively than had Moyne's killing. For the Count represented no single imperialist power, but the United Nations itself. The act would therefore mean a decisive blow to all foreign elements hoping to dictate Israel's boundaries. And it might give the government, the Sternists calculated, the "guts" it had not displayed so far in asserting Israel's rights.

After a long discussion (as Sheib and Yizernitzky relate it) the three men agreed to order Bernadotte's assassination. Friedman-Yellin, while not contradicting this assertion, says that he recalls general discussion of the Bernadotte problem but not an agreement on a particular solution. If he did agree, he may have had little choice since he had already lost almost all control over the only activist arm remaining, the Jerusalem operation, which Sheib guided politically and ideologically, with Zetler directing operations.

Sheib maintains that Friedman-Yellin then proposed that the identity of the responsible group should be disguised, the problem being to control the storm that was certain to engulf the Sternists, while simultaneously making clear to the world that Jewish patriots had killed the man—not as an individual but as a symbol of foreign interference. The answer, Friedman-Yellin allegedly pointed out, was to have a phantom nationalist organization publicly assume responsibility. People might surmise that the Stern Group was the real "executioner," but no one would be able to prove it. Also, such a claim might give Ben-Gurion an excuse not to crack down too hard on the Sternists.

It was decided, in any event, that an organization to be called the "Fatherland Front" would take the blame. Friedman-Yellin, says Sheib, suggested the name—after the wartime Bulgarian underground organization —and offered to draw up the proclamation announcing its "guilt."

According to Sheib, word was immediately sent to Zetler (who had returned to Jerusalem) that a decision had been reached to kill Bernadotte. Zetler promptly called a meeting of his top lieutenants at the Sternist camp headquarters. Aside from Zetler himself, who was to exercise overall command of the operation, the two key men, it was decided, were to be his new deputy, Joshua Cohen, and his intelligence officer, Stanley Goldfoot.

Goldfoot, lanky and distinguished-looking, had immigrated to Palestine about 10 years earlier from the Union of South Africa, where he had fervently advocated (and still does today) rigid application of *apartheid* as the only means of warding off a black slaughter of whites. With the same passion, he now started gathering every detail of information about Bernadotte's habits and traveling schedule that might be useful; as a contributor to Israeli and overseas publications, he had the access to people and places that only a journalist can gain.

Utterly contrary to him in both looks and manner was Joshua Cohen, a wiry, good-natured Sabra with fiery dark eyes set in a thin, tough, bronzed face. Experienced and efficient in such operations, Cohen had recently returned from four years in a British detention camp in Eritrea and was eager for action. He was one of the best, and best-liked, men in the Stern Group. In 1942, when almost all the Sternists had been jailed by the British, Cohen had managed, at the age of nineteen, to hold the organization together singlehandedly, using as his headquarters an orange grove where he remained day and night, pistol in hand, while his girlfriend (whom he later married) carried messages for him and brought back stale bread and water to supplement his citrus diet.

Later, when the principal Sternist leaders escaped from jail and again took over the group, Cohen trained recruits (including the two men who killed Lord Moyne), instilling in them his fierce nationalist drive.[5] Cohen did not hate, or need to hate, his enemies in order to "execute" them in cold blood and in good conscience. Yet, unlike some of his colleagues, he was reluctant to kill unless he regarded such action as absolutely essential. His idealism was undiluted and unsophisticated, with roots deep in the earth he had plowed as a farmer's son. He had been taught early that it was necessary to destroy the insects that threatened the crop.

*

James G. McDonald, the tall, slender United States Special Representative to Israel, who had arrived in Tel Aviv on August 12, was alarmed at rumors that something sinister was about to happen. The American Consul-General in Jerusalem, John J. Macdonald, had visited his namesake in Tel Aviv (the two men were not related) and reported nervously that a group of terrorists had approached him in a Jerusalem café and bluntly threatened him. The Consul-General, whom the Jews regarded as firmly pro-Arab, had also reported that open threats had been made in Jerusalem against Bernadotte for allegedly being a British agent.

The Special Representative expressed his anxiety about such reports to Sharett, who indicated that he was also worried. McDonald then repeated his warning to the chief inspector of police, Yehezkial Sachar. Sachar did not seem impressed.

"When terrorists talk most," he replied casually, "they are least dangerous. We know what they are doing. There is nothing to fear."

But McDonald's fear persisted, and was aggravated by the delicateness of his own position. He felt that many people in the State Department were eagerly waiting for him to make one bad mistake, one ill-founded prediction. The Department, he was sure, would never forgive him for having been selected by President Truman for the Israeli post without even the normal consultation with the Secretary of State. Truman, after the "trusteeship" episode, had been determined to have his own man in Israel regardless of State Department recommendations. And Marshall had, in fact, frankly indicated to McDonald before he left for Israel that he had opposed the appointment because of the President's failure to consult with him about it.

McDonald did not doubt that the Department would have opposed his selection in any event, considering his open identification with the Jewish cause since 1933 when, as a professor of history and political science, he had been appointed High Commissioner for Refugees by the League of Nations. He had supported the Zionists fervently again after the war, when he was appointed a member of the Anglo-American Committee of Inquiry on Palestine.

Now McDonald was on the spot. Just before he had left Washington, Undersecretary Lovett, whose pragmatism dictated caution at this point concerning Israel's future, had stressed to him that the Israeli government must prove that it was not a junta before *de jure* diplomatic recognition could be granted. He had pointed out that the terrorists still challenged the government with their own proclamations and military actions.

Furthermore, McDonald felt, some officials, in particular Dean Rusk, feared unduly that the Communists would profit from this situation, a concern enhanced by the flow of Czech arms into the country and by the expected arrival of boatloads of immigrants from Communist nations. Nor was the Pentagon any less suspicious. It constantly asked his military attaché, Lieutenant Colonel Robert W. Van de Velde, for evidence of Communist influence—even after the attaché had reported that such influence was minimal.

Thus, if the terrorists did commit some terrible act—possibly comparable to the assassination of Lord Moyne—the State Department, supported by the Pentagon and the CIA, might be able to destroy McDonald's influence in the White House and bring the State of Israel tumbling down.[6]

Count Folke Bernadotte looked unusually grave as he stepped from his white Dakota at Beirut Airport at about 10 A.M. on September 16. Still, there was a glint of satisfaction in his eyes. The new Bernadotte Plan was at last on its way to Paris, where it would be submitted to the United Nations General Assembly meeting in the Palais de Chaillot.

"Nice to see you alive," he said with a wan smile as he shook hands with General Aage Lundstrom, his Swedish chief of staff.

Lundstrom raised his eyebrows slightly.

"You haven't heard?" Bernadotte asked.

Then he explained that the Rhodes radio station had picked up a report that—according to a statement issued by his staff in Haifa—a policeman had found Lundstrom murdered. The chief of staff laughed.

After brief talks with Arab leaders in Beirut and Damascus, Bernadotte and his party took off at 9:30 A.M. the next day from Damascus for Kalandia Airport north of Jerusalem. As the plane approached its destination, the radio operator handed the mediator a telegram, purportedly sent by his staff in Haifa, warning that all aircraft landing in Kalandia would be fired on and advising that his plane land elsewhere. But as General Lundstrom had received no response when he had personally sent advance notice of landing, it was decided that the report was probably as false as the one about his "murder" and that the plane should land regardless.

When the aircraft touched down at 10:15 A.M., Lundstrom began to worry that perhaps the mediator really was in danger. He was particularly concerned about the scheduled crossing from Arab to Jewish territory at Mandelbaum Gate. Snipers firing from ruined houses in no-man's-land near the gate had only recently killed a Jewish liaison officer accompanying the American Consul-General in Jerusalem, as well as an observer who left his car to open a road barrier.

But Bernadotte would not agree to arm United Nations personnel or to accept armed escorts from either side. The possession of a gun, he felt, offered no protection against snipers, the principal danger, and might actually provoke more killings. And armed escorts would limit the freedom of United Nations personnel to go when and where they wished.

The mediator and his party drove first to Ramallah for discussions with Brigadier Lash, who provided an armored car for the trip to United Nations headquarters in the Old City. As the car approached Jerusalem from Ramallah, shots rang out and one bullet hit a hubcap, but no one was hurt. Then several "irregular" soldiers, whom the passengers suspected were actually bandits, waved the vehicle through a checkpoint, possibly because they did not want to argue with an armored car.

This experience added to the apprehension of the party as it prepared to leave from headquarters for Mandelbaum Gate under a clear, sunny sky.

But the convoy crossed into the New City without mishap and sped to the towering Y.M.C.A., observer headquarters in the Jewish sector, where the group was to lunch and spend the night of the 17th. Everyone breathed more easily. It looked as if the mediator was out of danger.

During lunch, the party, which had already scheduled a meeting with Dov Joseph for 4:30 P.M., decided to visit the British-evacuated Government House in the neutral Red Cross zone earlier that afternoon. Bernadotte thought that this mansion might be more suitable than the Hôtel des Roses in Rhodes for his headquarters, despite Lundstrom's insistence that a transfer would be unfeasible because of the danger.

Accompanied by Captain Hillman, an Israeli liaison officer, the group drove in two cars through the neutral zone to Government House, where Bernadotte explored the palatial maze of reception rooms, banquet halls, and luxuriously furnished bedrooms. He climbed the tower and, as if watching a panoramic movie, witnessed a group of armed Arabs in the neutral area busily blowing up a road. Lundstrom then pointed to the Jewish Agricultural School nearby and suggested to the Count that he should visit it on the way back. United Nations headquarters had just radioed the party, in any case, that Dov Joseph had requested a postponement of their meeting (to take place at his house) from 4:30 to 6:30 P.M., so there would be sufficient time for the detour. The Israelis had apparently defied truce regulations by refusing to evacuate the school, Lundstrom said.

"All right," Bernadotte agreed, looking at his watch. "Let's stop off there . . . "

At the Sternist camp in the New City, Zetler, too, glanced at his watch and pursed his lips in agitation. Things were not going as planned. Goldfoot had just reported that the Bernadotte party would remain in the Old City longer than expected. Did that mean that the meeting with Dov Joseph had been cancelled? Perhaps Bernadotte wouldn't return to the New City after all. And the longer the delay, the greater the chance that the plot would leak out.

He and his aides had planned and replanned every detail for a week. They had, for example, piled up stones and barrels on the roadside at a number of points along routes the party was likely to take through the New City. Thus, a partial roadblock could be constructed at any one point at a moment's notice. But after all the careful preparation, everything seemed uncertain now.

As the tension rose among the few Sternists aware of the plan, violent arguments broke out between Goldfoot and Zetler. Goldfoot made it clear that he considered Zetler a panicky bungler, and Zetler raged that Goldfoot was pretentious and insubordinate.

Late in the afternoon, Goldfoot angrily jumped into a jeep and drove to the government press office in the center of the city, hoping to pick up some hint of Bernadotte's plans. He found the reporters' room deserted, as it usually was on Friday afternoons just before the Sabbath. But he heard the crackle of a radio in the office of the press information officer. He pressed his ear to the door and listened to an amplifier feeding official information to the press officer for screening and distribution to newsmen.

Count Bernadotte, he learned, would enter the New City about 5 P.M. and pass over the road that ran near the Sternist camp.

Goldfoot dashed out and sped back to the camp. Within minutes (just before 4 P.M.) another jeep with four men raced from the camp to a point hardly 500 yards away along the road. The khaki-uniformed passengers quickly constructed a stone and barrel roadblock that protruded into the road enough to allow one vehicle to block it completely but not enough to disturb normal traffic meanwhile. Then the driver parked the jeep behind the makeshift "wall" and the four men slouched in their seats, pulled their visored caps over their faces so that passers-by could not identify them, and tried to look like bored and indifferent soldiers relaxing in the sun on a quiet autumn afternoon.

About 100 yards away, at the crest of the grade the Bernadotte party would climb, two other men stood on the roadside in anxious silence. Zetler and Goldfoot, interrupting their feud, did not want to miss the show that was to shake the world.

When the Bernadotte party arrived at the Jewish Agricultural School, an Israeli said that not only would he and his fellow "caretakers" remain there, but that others would soon join them. Bernadotte discussed the

situation with his subordinates, and though everyone agreed that he could
not permit such "violations" of the truce regulations, no one was sure how
these regulations were worded. The group, therefore, decided to return
to the Y.M.C.A. to get a copy of the regulations so that a complaint could
be properly drawn up and submitted to Dov Joseph. It was now not quite
5 P.M., and an hour and a half still remained before the meeting with
Joseph.

A convoy of three cars then started out for the New City. Five people
sat in the first car, including Captain Hillman, who was to facilitate passage
through the Jewish lines. A white Red Cross car carrying Dr. Facel, the
Swiss director of a clinic that had been set up in Government House, was
second in line. In the front seat of the third car, which flew a United Nations
flag on one fender and a white flag on the other, sat American commander
Cox, chief observer in the Israeli sector, and Colonel Begley, the United
Nations security chief. In the rear, Bernadotte sat by the window on the
right; Lundstrom in the center; and French Colonel Serot, chief observer
in Jerusalem, on the left. By chance, Lundstrom and Serot had switched
the positions they had occupied when they had left the Y.M.C.A. for Government House.

The convoy moved swiftly through the neutral zone to avoid possible
sniper fire, slowing down only as it neared the Israeli checkpoint. The
guard, apparently confused about how to deal with United Nations personnel, partially lowered the barrier, then lifted it again, and finally let it
drop all the way down, forcing the cars to halt. Captain Hillman shouted
in Hebrew to let the convoy pass, and the guard immediately lifted the
barrier again.

The vehicles then hastened through the Katamon Quarter, passing
another checkpoint without having to stop, and overtaking a lorry crowded
with Israeli soldiers before coming to a fairly steep hill. About halfway
up, as the convoy passed a shantytown of sheds, shacks, and piles of rubble,
the occupants of the first car noticed a khaki-painted jeep clumsily trying,
it seemed, to turn around in the middle of the road. The cars gradually
slowed down and, at 5:03 P.M. precisely, drew to a halt.

Three of the four men in the jeep blocking the way then jumped out
and casually sauntered toward the convoy, two of them on the right side
and the third on the left. Another inspection! Captain Hillman again put
his head out of the first car and yelled in Hebrew to the two men on the
right: "It's all right. This is a United Nations convoy. Let us pass!"

While the two men on the right approached more slowly, the third
man ran past the first two vehicles and stopped at the last car. When the
passengers in the rear seat saw the thin, dark, clean-shaven face of a young
man of about thirty peering through the open rear window, they mechanically began to reach for their passes.

Suddenly, the man, Joshua Cohen, stuck the barrel of his weapon through the window and fired a burst of shots. The mediator lurched forward to the right and for a moment, Lundstrom, sitting next to him, thought he was trying to shield himself against the fire.

"Are you wounded, Folke?" he gasped.

Bernadotte seemed to nod and mumble something, then raised himself to a sitting position and sank back in the seat, dead.

Serot, whom the assassins claim was shot by mistake, had crumpled up, also dead, with several bullet wounds in the head and body.

As Cohen moved back, firing more shots at the radiator to disable the engine, Colonel Begley in the front seat jumped out and tried to grab him, but was severely burned in the face by a gunflash.

Simultaneously, the two men on the right side of the convoy fired at the tires of the first two vehicles and dashed back to their jeep, which raced off to the refuge of the Sternist camp. Cohen, left behind, fled into the surrounding countryside. He had riddled Bernadotte with bullets, though the mediator, afflicted with hemophilia, might have bled to death from a scratch.[7]

Prime Minister Ben-Gurion was in his sparsely furnished office in GHQ looking over intelligence reports about the still secret Bernadotte Plan—McClintock maintains that an American Jew on Bernadotte's staff had revealed everything in advance to the Zionist leadership—when an aide rushed in at 5:45 P.M. with a wire from Dov Joseph. He read it with sinking heart. The whole world he had helped to build suddenly seemed to be tottering.

For 42 years he had done his best to build that world, ever since 1906 . . .

AN OLD RUSSIAN CARGO BOAT WITH A CREW OF RATHER SHADY reputation had brought him, bundle under arm, to the shores of Palestine after a voyage begun in the ghetto of Plonsk. How bitter was his disappointment when he saw the rundown port of Jaffa, seething with other disappointed Jews, gaunt of face and bereft of spirit, who had come to live well and were now barely living at all in a land that brutally mocked their material ambitions. But how deep was the fulfillment of that first night at the Jewish colony of Petah Tikvah, two hours' walking distance from Jaffa, where he would live and work and help to disinter the Jewish soul from the desert.

"It was sealed in my heart with the joy of victory," he had written of that night. "I did not sleep. I was amid the rich smell of corn.

I heard the braying of donkeys and the rustle of leaves in the orchards. Above were massed clusters of stars clear against the deep blue firmament. My heart overflowed with happiness, as if I had entered the realm of legend. My dream had become a reality!"

But now Ben-Gurion asked himself how real the smell of corn and the rustle of leaves had been to victims of the pogroms after a Jewish watchmaker had shot Petliura, butcher of the Ukraine, in 1926; to victims of the Nazi reprisals after a Nazi diplomat had died at the hands of another Jew in 1938; to victims of the terrible vengeance for the killing of Reinhard Heydrich, Nazi hangman of Moravia, in 1942. The Jews of Israel might be the new victims. How cruel and senseless to jeopardize the work of 42 years; the promise of 2,000 years! It was Lord Moyne all over again . . . Then the Jews had been lucky: the British had been too busy with World War II to wreak full revenge and the world could at least sympathize with a nationalist cause, if not with a despicable act. But the murder of a man sent by the world to make peace! . . .

Israel, it was clear, did not yet qualify as a nation. She was still in a condition of semi-anarchy. He would now make her into a nation in order to save her. He would eliminate, with blood and steel if necessary, the last remnants of all armed groups not integrated into the army. And he would arrest the whole Stern Group, which he was sure had committed the crime . . .

At 5:25 P.M., about 20 minutes after the killings, Moshe Barzily, the Sternist communications officer, answered the telephone at the camp. A policeman friend urgently warned: "Jewish soldiers have killed Bernadotte."

"You're sure he's dead?"

"Yes, and we're looking for the murderers."

"Good luck!"

Barzily then called together the officers among the 150 men remaining in the camp to decide on a course of action. No provisions had been made for sending them away or hiding them. Zetler had gone into hiding, Sheib and Yizernitzky had sat out the affair in secret Tel Aviv apartments, and Friedman-Yellin, who apparently had had no idea when the assassination would take place, was casually preparing to leave for Eastern Europe. Goldfoot in particular was furious about the lack of planning for the aftermath of the killing, and blamed Zetler for this. As it turned out, even provisions for whisking the killers out of Jerusalem were to go awry. Two of the men managed to make their way to Tel Aviv the night of the murders, but the other two had to hide in a truck until the following morning before they could leave Jerusalem.

When Barzily informed the men of the assassination, they smiled; most had not been brought into the plot, but they knew who was responsible. They regarded Bernadotte as fair game, and felt quite impersonally about the whole affair.

"Everybody can do what they wish," Barzily said. "The government will probably surround the camp and arrest all of us."

The meeting broke up and the men scattered, some taking refuge at Irgun headquarters, others dispersing to their homes. About 40 men, including the wounded and the homeless, remained, some not minding the prospect of arrest.

At dawn, units of the Palmach Harel Brigade under the command of Major Shmuel Glinka surrounded the camp. Ben-Gurion had called him to Tel Aviv several hours before and told him: "I have a special trust in you. Go and liquidate the Lehi camp in Jerusalem."

"But what if they resist?" Glinka had asked.

"That's why I'm sending you and your men."

Glinka was uncomfortable. Unknown to Ben-Gurion, he had participated, with other Harel officers, in secret meetings with the Sternists held before and after the British left Palestine at which plans were discussed, but never implemented, of course, for the two groups to oust Shaltiel from the Jerusalem command and to take over the Old City and the whole area between Ramallah and Hebron without consulting Ben-Gurion. Now Ben-Gurion had assigned him the task of liquidating the Sternist organization with which he had been conspiring.

Hoping he would not have to shoot his friends, Glinka bided his time while his men first fraternized and joked with the Sternists in the camp. Then they all sauntered off to jail[8] . . .

Shortly before 8 P.M. on the night of the murders, Friedman-Yellin sat with his wife and his Irgunist friend, Sam Merlin, in a café atop Mount Carmel in Haifa. He had come from Tel Aviv earlier that day to await the departure of the ship that was to take him to Europe on Sunday.

He planned to spend most of his visit in Czechoslovakia, where he hoped to obtain arms and political support for the Stern Group. He was no Communist, he claimed, only a "non-Marxist leftist." After all the help that Russia and Eastern Europe, particularly Czechoslovakia, had given Israel in the war against the Arabs, certainly the Israelis should be friendly to those countries when the war was over. And since he would try to convert what part of the Stern Group he could into a legitimate political movement, it would be helpful to tighten his ties with the Communist leaders.*

As Friedman-Yellin sipped a lemon squash, a radio in the café stopped playing music and an announcer issued a news bulletin in Hebrew: "Count Folke Bernadotte, the United Nations mediator, was assassinated in Jerusalem today . . . "

The Stern Group leader put down his lemon squash and calmly listened to the details. The killers were being sought, the broadcast said, and no one would be permitted to leave the country. Apparently, his timing had been wrong.

"I suppose they'll be looking for me," he said calmly. "Let's go."

James McDonald and his daughter Barbara were in an exalted mood as they drove through the silent streets of Tel Aviv on their way home from the Bilu School Orthodox Synagogue, where they had attended Sabbath Eve services. They could still hear the vibrant voices of the teen-aged choir-boys, and the cheers that had followed them as their car had pulled away.

Then they arrived home and learned the news, and McDonald's reverie dissolved into a living nightmare.

At about 11 P.M., he went with several aides to Foreign Minister Sharett's house, only about 100 yards away.

Ashen gray, his voice choked with emotion, Sharett expressed his own horror and that of his government at the assassination.

"We have ordered immediate arrest of all Sternists, with instructions to shoot in case of resistance," he said. "We are setting up the most rigid search for the assassins and their accomplices, and we shall execute justice at the moment guilt is proved."

McDonald replied grimly that he was not satisfied. Special action of an even more drastic nature was necessary. In his dispatches to Washington, he had denied that Israel was unstable, insisting that her government was a functioning institution capable of maintaining internal security.

"I don't want to be proved a liar," he said, "but more than that, I want the provisional government to realize how important it now is for it to demonstrate its own authority."

Then he remembered Lovett's words before he had left Washington: They must prove they are not a junta.

That night, the American Consulate in Jerusalem, like all others in the New City, received a note from an organization calling itself the Fatherland Front, which had taken responsibility for the murders, warning that other

---

* Despite his right-wing leanings, Sheib also met with the Russians in the hope of winning their support.

foreign officials would be killed if they did not stop interfering "with the interests of Jewish nationalism."

With deepening concern, McDonald went to GHQ in the morning to see Ben-Gurion, who told him that he would present to the cabinet that evening an ordinance outlawing all terrorist organizations once and for all.

After informing Washington of Israel's "tough" attitude toward the terrorists, McDonald wrote a personal letter to President Truman which he sent with Congressman Abraham Multer of Brooklyn, who had been visiting Israel and was about to return home. The Special Representative pleaded with Truman: " . . . no matter what happens in the next days or weeks, I do hope that you will discourage any possible move to weaken this Mission or to withdraw its head as a form of sanctions or as evidence of U.S. displeasure."

Truman replied that he would abide by McDonald's recommendations, saying: "I heartily approve the course you have pursued and are pursuing . . . "

McDonald smiled with relief as he read this message. Israel, it now seemed, would survive the tragedy intact after all, despite efforts by her non-Arab enemies to use it as a weapon to push through the United Nations the victim's controversial legacy—the Bernadotte Plan.

Minister of the Interior Yitzhak Gruenbaum greeted his guest, Yehoshua Zetler, with a somewhat troubled *"Shalom."* Some weeks had passed since Bernadotte's murder, and scores of Sternists had been arrested, including Nathan Friedman-Yellin, who had been found in a Haifa hideout. Charged with involvement in the crime, the Sternist leader and a subordinate were now on trial. Sheib, Yizernitzky, and Cohen, however, had escaped the police net. And so had Zetler.

"I would just like to pass on a message to Ben-Gurion," Zetler said casually as he put down the wine he had been offered. "If our people were sentenced, it wouldn't be good. We don't want to take action against Jews if we don't have to . . . "

Gruenbaum choked slightly on his wine. A political foe of Ben-Gurion despite his presence in the cabinet, he had often sympathized with the dissidents, typically having pressed for a government compromise with the Irgun during the *Altalena* episode.

"Don't worry," he said now. "They'll be sentenced to a few years in prison. Then we'll release them quite soon."

After a moment's silence, Zetler rose.

"That's fair enough," he grinned. "Anything to satisfy world opinion."[9]

*

Following a protracted trial, Friedman-Yellin and his colleagues were found guilty of "terrorist activities" and sentenced to prison terms, though evidence was lacking to convict them of the crime that had brought them to court. Nor was there any great public outcry in Israel for the apprehension and punishment of the killers; after the first few days of shock, fear that the world would demand terrible retribution had receded. Ben-Gurion reflected the mood of his people; having achieved his goal of completely eliminating the dissident groups and appeasing world opinion in the process, he offered the two convicted men a pardon if they showed willingness to mend their ways. But they refused.

Far more embarrassing to the government was the comic-opera situation in the old Turkish-built prison fortress in Jaffa, where about 200 Sternists, including the 40 arrested in the Jerusalem camp, were having the time of their lives. While police guards looked on from a safe distance, the prisoners ripped out the steel bars of their windows, broke down steel doors, and smashed through walls separating the cells. Boys and girls sat laughing and chatting together on windowsills, happily "locked in" with each other.

One sunny Saturday, the warden cancelled family visits after the Sternists had beaten up a police officer. When the women outside the front gate screamed in protest, the prisoners threw mattresses on the barbed wire surrounding the jail and walked casually across—while the police fired lackadaisically over their heads. The Sternists, piqued, then attacked the guards who, with nervous smiles, agreed to hand over their arms in exchange for a promise that they would get them back in the evening.

While Stanley Goldfoot held an impromptu press conference in a cell and other Sternists rolled in a barrel of beer to put the reporters in the proper mood, other prisoners streamed into Jaffa's cafés for a Turkish coffee or relaxed on the beach nearby.

In the evening, everybody flocked back to jail and respectfully returned the arms to the grateful guards, who guzzled down the remaining beer as the Sternists, worn out from a day of revelry, finally went to sleep.

Ben-Gurion, furious, fired the police staff at the jail and transferred the Sternists in packed prison vans to Acre Prison, where they were segregated in cell blocks. But he soon released them—and Friedman-Yellin as well, after the latter had been elected to the first Israeli *Knesset* in early 1949.[10]

Gradually, the other Sternists leaders came out of hiding. Zetler even strayed into police stations to stare with injured vanity at the baleful photographs of himself that had been plastered on the walls announcing that he was "Wanted, Dead or Alive!"

MR. President, our flight report."

Chaim Weizmann looked up with a smile at the pretty stewardess, took the report, studied it briefly, and wrote on the bottom:

> It is a great privilege to travel for the first time in an Israeli aircraft so beautifully turned out and with such an amiable crew.

"Oh, thank you, Mr. President!"

Mr. President! The first President of Israel! He remembered how three months before in New York—while the first Egyptian bombs were falling on Tel Aviv—his wife Vera had dashed into his room and breathlessly exclaimed as he lay in bed: "Congratulations Chaim'chik. You are now the President!"

He had stared at her and gasped: "What nonsense are you talking?"

But she had insisted: "It's true! The newspapers just called and told us that you have been elected. They want to know how you feel about it . . . "

He glanced around the plane. Yes, beautifully turned out. A sofa and armchairs had been nailed to a carpeted floor. Curtains had been hung. Hotel waiters—dressed in hastily tailored uniforms decorated with winged Stars of David and flying camel symbols—had been recruited as stewards. The fuselage had been repainted, and the words "Israel National Airways Company" inscribed in the center, the word "Rehovoth" (his home town) by the cockpit, and the marking "4X-ACA"—whatever that meant—on the tail fin above the national colors.

Who could have guessed that no Israeli body was authorized to declare the airworthiness of an aircraft or to license civil pilots or crews? That this "airliner," Israel's first, was really an oil-leaky DC-4 that had been flying supplies to the front lines and had been repaired and converted for the one-day mission of flying the first President home from Geneva on the last leg of his journey from New York?

"They want to know how you feel about it . . ."

How could a man answer that question? After all the years of striving and struggling, now to return home as President. He would be a good President. Of course, he would not have the power of, say, the President of the United States. And in any event, he was perfectly willing to let younger men like Ben-Gurion have a dominant voice on government policy. But, of course, they would consult him on everything. After all, had he not helped to spawn the Zionist movement? Had he not led it through its most critical stages and dealt with the world's great figures? One of the first things

he would do was sign the Declaration of Independence. Certainly they had
left space for his signature. Yes, he would like future generations of Jews
to see his name scrawled on one of the most important documents in their
history . . . He looked fondly at his wife sitting next to him. She had once
been so skeptical about his Zionism . . .

IN 1907, WHEN HE HAD RETURNED TO HIS HOME IN MANCHESTER,
England, from his first trip to the Holy Land, he had said ecstatically:
"What a wonderful country it is!"
"What's so wonderful about it?" she had asked.
"It's just, well, wonderful."
"Well, what makes it so wonderful—the flowers, perhaps?"
"I hardly saw any flowers. It's hard to explain, but the air there
is so wonderful—it's so transparent that you can see thousands of
years back . . ."

His wife nudged him as the shore of Israel loomed into view: "Look,
Chaim'chik. How transparent the air is!"
Thousands of years back! It seemed that long since those hopeless,
happy days in the ugly little town of Motol, isolated in a forest-bordered
swamp near Pinsk . . .

"YOU KEEP QUIET," THE BLACK-BEARDED RABBI BARKED. "YOU'LL
never bring the Messiah any nearer. One has to do much, learn
much, know much, and suffer much before one is worthy of that."
The child thereafter kept his dream to himself. The rabbi was
right, of course; it was pretentious to speak of a dream as if fulfillment were within reach. And what sane member of the *shtetl,* the
Jewish community, really believed that one day he would be going
home? Even his father was not yet a Zionist. Still, the longing persisted, implicit in every breath, every fragment of daily life.
His large wooden house, chaotically alive with the cries of innumerable brothers and sisters, was steeped in rich Jewish tradition.
Passover was the best season of all—if his hardworking father was
able to make it home. A timber merchant, he had to supervise the
floating of logs down to Danzig at about that time, a difficult job
that often depended on the elements. But when he returned, though
haggard and exhausted, he brought the festival with him. And also
the yearly income—about $250—a sum that marked the family
as wealthy in Motol social circles.
And how happy were the days he spent with his grandfather, a
wise, white-bearded old gentleman, in the house next door. The old
man would get up early every morning while it was still pitch-dark,
but somehow the house was always warm, even during the cold,
frosty winters. First they would recite together the long morning
prayers. Then the grandfather, after preparing a delicious breakfast

with his trembling hands, would tell the boy stories about the heroic deeds of great Jewish figures in history, and of the strength-giving sufferings of his people.

Cheder was part of the child's life, too, the squalid, one-room religious school in which the teacher's whole family lived, together with a goat. Carried there by an elder brother in the spring and autumn when the *cheder* almost vanished in swamp, and in the winter when it was nearly buried in snow, Chaim would study his Hebrew and Talmudic philosophy while the teacher's wife hung her washing, and their many children rolled boisterously on the floor.

He was hardly conscious that a non-Jewish world existed, perhaps because the Gentiles in Motol, particularly the peasants, were friendly to the Jews—except during the Christmas and Easter holidays when their priests would stir them to a high pitch of religious excitement. In many other Russian communities, Gentiles killed their Jewish neighbors, encouraged by the Czarist government, which made sure that police were not around to interfere with such natural outlets of popular emotion. Whole villages emptied of Jews after pogroms in which hundreds died and the rest fled. But Chaim rather liked the Gentiles of Motol, to the extent that he was aware of them. They did not murder a single Jew.

Certainly, fear and hatred did not feed the dream that the ill-tempered rabbi had forbidden him to mention. Zionism meant more than finding a refuge for the persecuted. That was why he had fought Herzl's plan to establish a Jewish home in Uganda. Though, during his decades-long flight to Zion, he saw constantly before him the image of smashed bodies in a gutter, he was driven far more passionately by the memory of a shadowy but familiar figure splashing homeward through the mud on Passover Eve; of an ancient sage stroking his long beard in the glow of a warm house on a wintry morning; of a goat dumbly contemplating a boy mumbling words of wisdom borrowed from the timeless script of the Torah.

And now that he had done much, learned much, and suffered much, the Messiah had come nearer at last . . .

Flashbulbs popped. Hands clasped while others clapped. A bouquet of flowers was thrust into the arms of the President's wife. A band played. A guard of honor stood at attention. Customs officials and passport control officers, recruited for the occasion, politely declined to open baggage or check passports.

"Mr. President, now you shall review the troops."

Weizmann, seeming not to hear, glanced at the faces around him. Finally, he saw his old friend and assistant.

"Well, Joshua, it has come," he said with tear-filled eyes, grasping an outstretched hand. "The day has come, hasn't it? And now give me some earth."

"Yes, Professor."

Joshua bent down, scooped up a handful of black soil, and poured it into Weizmann's withered palm. Then the President touched the earth with his lips and went to review the troops.

He was still clutching the handful of earth when he stepped into a limousine.

"There's plenty of earth around, Professor," commented Joshua. "It's the same earth."

Weizmann murmured: "The same earth. Only the times are different. Some of them were great, very great . . . "

Then off to his large, comfortable house in Rehovoth, where he would reminisce about those great times and, in restless anguish, wonder why no one ever consulted him any more about anything, or even asked him to sign the Declaration of Independence.*

As for the "airliner," crewmen repainted it and removed its fine furnishings so that it could return to the battlefront.

The show was over.[11]

---

* Ben-Gurion decided that no Zionist leader who was not in Palestine at the time of Israel's founding would sign the Declaration of Independence. Weizmann was thus left out even though he had gone to the United States reluctantly at the urgent request of the Jewish Agency so that he might influence Truman to support a state. Ben-Gurion had always regarded Weizmann as too "soft" and too "pro-British," and this feeling was apparently reflected in his decision, which many Zionist leaders regarded as "petty."

15

Operation
Ten Plagues

MAJOR Gamal Abdel Nasser felt depressed and bitter as he glimpsed scenes of Cairo from the taxi taking him home for a short leave. Nothing seemed to have changed since prewar days. People strolled in leisurely fashion along the sun-scorched streets savoring their indolence and aimlessness. White-gowned vendors squatted on the sidewalks hawking pots and pans, brooms, toys, and other wares to hordes of happy shoppers. Wealthy cigar-smoking men in black suits and red tarbooshes drove by in huge chauffeured limousines. Black-shawled women sat gossiping in the park squares while their children played barefoot in the gutters.

All was peaceful and calm. Life went on as before, while Egyptian boys sat rotting in the trenches of Palestine, their lives dependent upon capricious government whim. After paying so terrible a price for the gains they had made, Egypt's soldiers had now been told to hold their fire, to obey truce regulations, while the Jews, Nasser was sure, were plotting to win back everything at a time of their choosing. And no one seemed to care, least of all the fat men in the limousines who were profiting from every drop of spilt Egyptian blood.

His depression was relieved only on arrival when he got out his money to pay the taxi driver.

"No, sir, I cannot accept any money from you," the cabbie said. "You are returning from the battlefield. It would not be right to charge you a fare."

Nasser was also pleased when employees in neighboring shops recognized him and came up to greet him with smiles and handshakes and cries

573

of "Welcome home, Gamal!" And, for a while, he forgot his misery as he entered his house to be embraced by his wife and daughters. He tried his best to enjoy his leave, taking Hoda to the zoo and seeing his old friends, including Abdel Hakim Amer, who was in the hospital for treatment of the wound he had sustained at Nitzanim.

But what was there to talk about—or think about—except the war, the horror and the deceit, the rottenness of the command, the vulnerability of men sent to die and not to fight?

"I've heard," Amer said, as Nasser sat by his bedside, "that arms and equipment are on their way to the front."

"I pray that you're right," Nasser said drearily. "The Jews will attack at any time, and the way our forces are spread out, a breakthrough any-where could mean disaster."

This was exactly what the Israeli High Command was thinking. It was convinced that the Arabs, having failed to attack immediately after Bernadotte's assassination when the United Nations might have simply looked on, were neither in the condition nor the mood to renew the fighting. It also now calculated that Israel could shock world opinion without invit-ing dangerous diplomatic counterstrokes—particularly before the American election—since the murder had brought no strong demands for such action.

At the same time, experience had demonstrated that if a nation did not solidly control a piece of territory, it might well lose it by political decree. Therefore, as the Bernadotte Plan was receiving considerable support at the United Nations General Assembly, even from the United States, it was clearly necessary to provide the world with a *fait accompli.*

On arriving in Paris with a report on the Bernadotte Plan, Robert McClintock advised Dean Rusk, already there, to urge Secretary Marshall to press for acceptance of the plan while the assassination was still fresh in the delegates' minds.

Rusk immediately conferred with the Secretary of State, who was lead-ing the American delegation, and suggested that he deliver a speech approv-ing the Bernadotte Plan. The full delegation then met at the American Embassy to discuss the matter, and Rusk, McClintock, and others argued strongly in favor of such action. Marshall, whose mind was largely occupied by such world-shaking problems as Berlin and the Chinese civil war, was in no mood at this time to question the wisdom of his Palestine experts. In-deed, their arguments did not seem to him to lack substance.

Thus, on September 21, four days after the mediator's death, Marshall stood before the General Assembly and stated that "the United States considers that the conclusions contained in the final report of Count Bernadotte offer a generally fair basis for settlement of the Palestine question and . . . strongly urges the parties and the General Assembly to accept them in their entirety as the best possible basis for bringing peace to a distracted land."

The White House was shocked when news of Marshall's speech broke in New York, where Truman was campaigning. Lovett had sent a memorandum about the speech to Clifford only a few hours before delivery and there had been no time to do anything about it. Approval of the text had not been requested.

"How could they do this without consulting with me?" Truman barked in fury to Clark Clifford in their New York hotel suite. He was reminded of the "unauthorized" speech requesting trusteeship that had caused him so much trouble.

The President's anger was rooted not only in a feeling that Marshall had defied him, but in the growing possibility that he might lose the state of New York in the election. Clifford thereupon drew up a cable at the request of the President and sent it to the Secretary.

"Your statement that the Bernadotte report should be used as a basis for negotiation," it read, " . . . requires clarification . . . I shall have to state that my position as to boundaries has not changed . . . "

Desperately seeking a way to retreat gracefully from the Marshall position, Truman finally agreed to a new, more vaguely worded pronouncement drawn up by his advisers and the State Department. This read in part: "The Bernadotte Plan provides a sound basis for the adjustment of [Arab-Israel] differences . . . "

Rusk cabled Lovett in Washington that some members of the American delegation "feel unhappy about the new language, fearing it may cause new confusion." And Marshall cabled him that "[American delegate Charles] Bohlen, Rusk and I feel that if President himself makes statement it will inevitably carry issue direct into political campaign as Dewey will certainly respond."

But Truman issued the statement and, as expected, Dewey responded— initially through John Foster Dulles, a member of the American delegation who, though having previously supported the Bernadotte Plan, now flatly announced his opposition to it.

Clifford then quickly penned a statement on the stationery of New York's Biltmore Hotel for insertion into a presidential speech:

> No matter what you read in the papers, the United States will never vote to take away any land from the State of Israel . . . without consent of the people of Israel.[1]

*

Ben-Gurion and his military strategists, though having decided to attack again, could not agree on the target. The Prime Minister spent hours poring over the wall map in his office, and his eye always came back to rest on Jerusalem. He called a meeting of the general staff and suggested that the Israelis attack the whole area from the Judaean hills in the north to the Negev border south of Jerusalem.

His officers initially backed this idea, and immediately began working on a plan—assisted by the Arabs, who provided a pretext for the attack by blowing up the water pumps at Latrun in violation of the truce agreement.

On September 26, nine days after the assassination of Bernadotte, Ben-Gurion presented the plan to his cabinet, and was stunned when a large majority of ministers, including members of his own party, opposed it, fearing international repercussions. The Prime Minister, regarding this as one of his greatest setbacks, angrily went home and wrote in his diary:

> The plan has been dropped. Fortunately for us, most of the offensives we've launched this year were not put to the vote of that lot!

But he would not give up. He still felt the cabinet could be persuaded to approve some military effort that would at least open the road to Jerusalem. By now, however, Yadin and some other members of the High Command had come to favor an attack in the Negev.

"Egypt, not Transjordan, is our principal enemy," Yadin argued. "She controls the Negev, which is vital to the existence of the state, and the Bernadotte Plan, if approved by the United Nations, would confirm this control."

He pointed out further that Egypt had already set up a shadow Palestine government in Gaza under the Mufti, which might gain international recognition if the military situation were not immediately changed.

Ben-Gurion indicated interest, but was still not convinced.

Even so, Yadin, Allon, and other commanders began planning the campaign, which they called Operation Yoav, or Ten Plagues (referring to God's plagues on the Pharaoh before Moses led the Jews out of Egypt). They were hopeful that the Prime Minister would eventually approve it. In calculating the forces they would need for a breakthrough, they carefully considered the latest intelligence estimates of Egyptian strength. The Egyptians were deployed mainly in defensive strips that ran along the main roads in the Negev: a coastal strip reached from Rafa in the south to Ashdod in the north; an inland strip ran northeastward from El Auja in the south

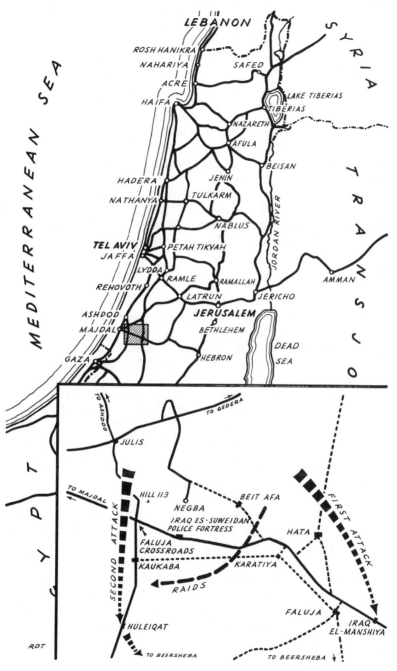

THE FALUJA CROSSROADS

through Beersheba and Hebron to Bethlehem on the outskirts of Jerusalem; and an "isolation belt," sealing off the Negev from northern Palestine, extended west to east from Majdal on the coast through Faluja to Beit Gubrin, west of Hebron.

These entrenched, immobile ribbons of fortification, only two to five miles wide, were highly vulnerable to concentrated attack, especially because of the Egyptians' extended lines of communication. But they were defended by about 15,000 men, who made up two regular infantry brigades, nine volunteer battalions, a reinforced brigade, two regiments of artillery, an armored battalion, and air units.

The Israeli campaign plan called for several diversionary assaults along the extended east-west front, and then a full-scale attack at one point. A breakthrough would cut off Egyptian supplies and communications, block lines of retreat, and permit the liquidation of enemy bases in the rear—and finally of the Egyptian army.

On September 9, Major Nasser, having returned to the front from leave in Cairo, was summoned to a conference at Egyptian general headquarters in Gaza. He was told that his 6th Battalion was to take up positions along the east-west line between Iraq el-Manshiya and Beit Gubrin, in anticipation of an Israeli attempt to break through to the south. On the morning of September 30, Nasser, on learning that enemy forces had occupied Hirbet-Mahaz and neighboring hills just north of the east-west road, attacked and drove them out after two hours of fierce fighting. He was then ordered to hand over the conquered positions to a unit of Egyptian volunteers.

The next day, he received a message that the enemy had counter-attacked and that the volunteers had withdrawn at dawn.

"Recapture the position," the message said laconically, driving Nasser almost to despair. But later in the day the order to attack was cancelled and Nasser learned that the 1st Battalion was to recover the hills, with Captain Zakaraya Muhieddin leading the assault.

Nasser accompanied his friend Muhieddin to the battle scene on October 4 and watched while Bren gun carriers and armored cars attacked the Israelis. As he lay on the grass with bullets flying overhead, the battle blurred into thoughts of home and he remembered the laughter of his daughter Hoda as she had watched the antics of a monkey at the zoo. A strange fear overtook him—that he might die in a fruitless battle that need never have taken place.

When the smoke of battle had cleared, the Egyptians were in firm control of the territory. But they lost it again when the Jews, who needed the hills to protect a new airfield just to the north, immediately counterattacked. In the next few days, the Egyptians were to attack abortively five more times, losing almost a whole armored battalion in the effort.

The furious Egyptian attack, even though frustrated, alarmed Ben-Gurion and finally won him over completely to the idea of an all-out assault on the Negev. At a meeting of the High Command on October 6, he said firmly, as if he had never questioned the Negev plan: "We must determine what forces to send to the Negev to ensure success in as short a time as possible."

The High Command then decided that three infantry brigades, the Givati, Negev, and Yiftach, plus a battalion of the 8th Armored Brigade—a total of 15,000 men, about equal to the Egyptian manpower—would join in the drive, supported by artillery and planes that had recently arrived from Czechoslovakia. The cabinet this time voted its approval, and the Prime Minister, with mixed feelings of anxiety and satisfaction, wrote in his diary that night:

> We have just made the gravest decision since the proclamation of the State.

The Israelis did not have difficulty finding a pretext for their offensive. Under the truce accord, they were to permit the Egyptians to use the east-west road to supply their forces for six hours each day, while the Egyptians were to let the Israelis use the inland north-south road to supply their settlements for the same amount of time. The Egyptians, however, claiming that the Jews were smuggling arms, refused to let Israeli convoys travel southward. Actually, none of the southern settlements critically lacked food or other supplies, which were transported to them at night by air; but the Egyptian blockade gave the Israelis the excuse they needed to launch their campaign.

A 16-truck convoy set out for the Negev at about noon on October 15, and, as expected, was fired upon while nearing Egyptian positions south of Karatiya. One vehicle burst into flames, dramatizing the incident, though it was not clear that it was *Egyptian* explosive power that caused the damage.

There was satisfaction and gratitude at Israeli headquarters. The Egyptians had not failed Israel. The government immediately announced that it was free to act, and the signal was given for Operation Ten Plagues to begin. It would continue until the Negev was Israeli—provided that Israel had correctly calculated President Truman's determination to win New York and the time it would take for the United Nations to clamp down.

At about 6 P.M. the same day (October 15), the Israeli air force bombed the Egyptian air base at El Arish, and other enemy bases at Gaza, Majdal, Rafa, and Beit Hanun. Then units of the Yiftach Brigade blew up communication and supply lines, including the railroad line near the Egyptian border, and by dawn had driven a wedge to within 600 yards of the coastal road at Beit Hanun. Givati forces, in the same period, drove other wedges into the east-west line between Faluja and Beit Gubrin.

All these operations were intended to divert the Egyptian forces from the main target, Iraq el-Manshiya, from where Israeli forces could speed south over a dirt road leading to Beersheba.

WHEN Nasser, in his Iraq el-Manshiya headquarters, learned from scouts of the Israeli advance, he immediately ordered his battalion to prepare for a counterattack. At 3 A.M., October 16, he rang the control tower situated on a hill.

"How is everything?"

"All quiet here," came the answer.

With the coming of dawn, Nasser knew, the attack would start. And then the fate of the whole Egyptian army could depend on the orders he might give.

Suddenly, at about 6 A.M., Nasser was almost thrown to the floor by a tremendous explosion, which was followed by a series of others that blended into a thunderous drumbeat. A few minutes later, the radiophone rang, and an officer shouted: "The enemy is attacking with tanks!"

"With what?" Nasser yelled back, thinking he had misheard in the ear-splitting chaos.

"Tanks!"

"You must be mistaken."

"But I can see them!"

Nasser excitedly reported the news to the battalion commander, who had just entered.

"I don't believe it," the commander said. "They've never used tanks before. Besides, the terrain around here makes them useless."

As Nasser was about to leave for the scene of attack, he asked: "But, sir, shouldn't I take our anti-tank guns just in case?"

"No, you won't need them."

"Very well, sir."

But Nasser ordered a sergeant to take two anti-tank guns anyway . . .

*

Desmond and Miriam Rutledge craned their necks to watch two flares burst in the murky dawn sky like exploding stars. The flares were the signal for Rutledge and his fellow British deserters to leave Kibbutz Gat in their two Cromwell tanks and catch up with infantry units which were to attack a school at the foot of a hill north of the road, as well as the village of Iraq el-Manshiya itself south of the road. Several smaller tanks were to follow.

Rutledge, who with the other British deserters had formed the nucleus of Israel's new armored corps, embraced his exquisite Yemenite wife. He was silent, and she knew he was worried about the infantry's lack of experience in coordinating its actions with armor. Her own concern was mixed with a sense of guilt. He had stayed to fight for Israel because of her, when he might have returned safely to England to resume his teaching. If something happened to him, it would be her fault, and he would not even have the glory of having died for his own country. She was thankful, at least, that the army permitted the British fighters to take their Israeli wives with them to the battlefront as a kind of partial payment for their services.

When they had kissed once more, Rutledge jumped onto the Cromwell, on the side of which was painted the word "Miriam."

"Cheerio, honey, see you later," he called out cheerfully as he climbed into the turret. Then he followed the other Cromwell toward Iraq el-Manshiya.

In the first tank were Michael Flanagan and Harry MacDonald, the two who had stolen the Cromwells from the British army just before it withdrew from Palestine. As their vehicle, driven by Flanagan, rumbled forward, MacDonald, commander of the operation, stood in the turret looking ahead with binoculars.

With his foot pressed hard on the accelerator, Flanagan experienced a strange excitement such as he had never felt while fighting with the British army during World War II. If this country represented to him a tremendous challenge, so did this war to save it. Somehow, he was fighting for something personal, something his own, and after the war, if he lived through it, he would settle in a kibbutz with his Israeli wife Ruth and pick cotton and raise cattle. His name was Flanagan, but this seemed the right place for a bored Irish motor mechanic who would rather repair tractors than Citroens.

Men of the 7th Battalion of the Negev Brigade had started to advance from improvised trenches about 800 yards from the village, with two com-

panies moving toward the school at the foot of the hill. The troops were
nervous as they advanced. The short home leave they had enjoyed during
the planning for Operation Ten Plagues, though permitting them to rest
after several months of continuous service in the Negev, had somehow
dulled the fine edge of their killer instinct. Nor did they feel comfortable
with their new leaders, the battalion having been put under the command
of the 8th Armored Brigade. And some of the battalion officers, at least,
were aware that Colonel Nahum Sarig (commander of the Negev Brigade)
had lent this battalion for the operation with the greatest reluctance, fearing
that a daytime attack on such a stronghold was doomed to failure.

The first infantry company had just been pinned down by heavy fire
from the school area when the Cromwells, followed by four Hotchkiss
tanks, passed it en route for the village itself. The company was forced to
withdraw after some moments and in retreat met the second company that
was advancing to reinforce it. Utterly confused by the withdrawal of the
first company, the commander of the second radioed rear headquarters for
orders. Just then, Egyptian shells fired from guns in Faluja rained down on
his men, who were spread out across the plain north of the hill. Within
minutes, about a third of the unit had been killed or wounded.

While the shelling was still going on, the commander screamed into
the radiophone: "What should we do? We're taking heavy casualties."

"Continue the attack at any cost," came the reply . . .

Desmond Rutledge's tank lumbered through the exploding battlefield
as he tried to keep up with the first Cromwell. He hoped the operation
wouldn't keep him too long from his wife. Somehow, he felt immune to
the destructive forces reaching out for him. This was better, anyway, than
being a smalltown teacher in a stuffy, stratified English society that judged
a man by his class and imprisoned him in a stifling social niche.

Suddenly, the tank ground to a halt. "God damn it!" he yelled, desperately pushing the gearstick in all directions.

"It's the gearbox," he said to his co-driver, a recent immigrant from
Czechoslovakia. "We're stuck in the middle of this hell!" . . .

Michael Flanagan raced ahead, oblivious of what was happening around
him. His tank, called "Ruth" after his wife, had lost contact with the infantry and it was almost impossible for MacDonald to look out of the turret
with the shell fire so heavy. He assumed that the other armor and the infantry were following.

A shell suddenly exploded directly in front of his tank, and the vehicle
skidded to an abrupt halt.

"I'm hit!" Flanagan cried.

Shrapnel had entered the small front window and struck him in the chest and head. The co-driver beside him shouted into the intercom micro-phone to MacDonald in the rear: "Driver's hit! Driver's hit!"

Then he stopped the blood and bandaged the wounds, while Flanagan started up the tank again and kept advancing.

"Can you keep going?" MacDonald asked over the phone.

Flanagan, despite serious wounds, did not feel great pain at the moment, only a throbbing headache. And his co-driver, a Czech refugee like the one in Rutledge's tank, had little experience in operating a tank.

"Yes, it's okay," he said, as he approached the village.

"Then ram through the barbed wire," MacDonald shouted back . . .

"An enemy tank has crossed our barbed wire and is heading toward the village itself!"

When he received this radio report from a front-line observer, Major Nasser shouted back in distress: "Where are the anti-tank guns?"

"Two shells have fallen on them and they're both useless."

"What?" screamed Nasser, and he raced out of his field headquarters toward the village nearby. Plans and maps had now become useless. With the enemy inside the defense line, he had to examine the positions himself and improvise accordingly. It looked as if only a miracle could save Iraq el-Manshiya now, especially after reports just received that the Israelis had taken the school.

As Nasser ran into the village, Sten gun in hand, he was horrified by the scenes of chaos and carnage. Shells exploded everywhere, and refugees were dashing from building to building trying to reach the open fields, where they might have a chance to survive. He saw a soldier cut down by bullets while trying to repair a telephone wire, and his replacement shot immedi-ately afterwards. Corpses and pieces of human flesh were strewn on the pitted streets, and the smell of devastation saturated the nostrils.

Nasser suddenly heard a sound that seemed different from the others, almost like the flutter of a wounded bird, heading right toward him. He threw himself to the ground by a crumbling wall just as the earth trembled under a massive explosion, then got up and stumbled through a storm of dust, wondering if he was still alive. Then he rounded up every man he could find, including cooks and drivers, to rush to the area where the tanks were breaking through, shouting to Lieutenant Abdel el-Khalek Shawaky, who was to lead them: "Block the opening in the fence and cut off the forces that have entered!"

Shawaky and his men then ran toward the armor and waited behind sandbag barriers along the path of approach. When a tank came to within 10 yards of his position, Shawaky, leaning on a pile of sandbags to aim, fired his Sten gun. Gradually, the monster started to slow down and the Lieutenant was sure that he had damaged a tread . . .

In the tank, Flanagan was aware that small arms fire was hitting the vehicle, but he knew such fire was ineffective against its armor. He had slowed down to permit the tanks behind to catch up.

"Mac," he yelled into the phone, "take a look and see where the others are!"

MacDonald cautiously lifted his head out of the turret and looked to the rear. A moment later he cried out: "Jesus Christ, we're alone! What the hell is holding up those bastards?"

As the tank jerked to a halt, MacDonald added brusquely: "Let's get the hell out of here!"

Flanagan turned the vehicle around while the Egyptians continued to bounce bullets off it with small arms, and withdrew.

Less than a mile to the rear, the second Cromwell remained crippled; and slightly further back, a Hotchkiss rested on its side in an anti-tank ditch. The second infantry company, meanwhile, was forced to retreat despite the orders to continue fighting, with only about 50 men managing to escape alive.

Rutledge, whose tank was besieged by infantrymen seeking cover behind it, ran under fire to meet the retreating Cromwell, which managed to tow his own disabled vehicle to safety even though the barrel of his tank's gun split open while keeping the enemy at bay.

Miriam silently greeted the two Cromwells as they pulled into Kibbutz Gat at about 9 A.M. Taking her husband by the hand, she walked beside him, wordlessly, to their room. Rutledge collapsed on his cot and immediately fell asleep, and his wife lay down beside him and gently brushed away the sand that covered his fair English face like a death mask. Then she closed her eyes and lay with her head against his shoulder.

LATER, while the Israelis were still evacuating their wounded under fire at Iraq el-Manshiya, Allon, the southern front commander, Rabin, his deputy, and two other officers drove from the battle area to GHQ where Yadin had been waiting for them. The Israeli commanders were morose as they sat down to discuss means of overcoming the failure at Iraq el-Manshiya. They were haunted by the thought that the United Nations might call a cease-fire before they could crack the Egyptian line.

"I think we should attack now at the crossroads," Allon affirmed, referring to the vitally strategic junction of the east-west and inland north-south highways. "If we succeed, we'll be able to move southward along the main road, splitting and destroying the Egyptian army."

Yadin shook his head. The chance of failure, he felt, was much greater than it had been at Iraq el-Manshiya. A battle at the crossroads would mean attacking three deeply entrenched groups of outposts: Hills 100 and 113 north of the crossroads; two "junction strongholds" to the southwest; and the strongholds of Kaukaba and Huleiqat to the south. And even if all these positions were taken, about a mile east of the crossroads there would still be the most formidable bastion of all—the old British police fortress of Iraq es-Suweidan, called by the Israelis, who had already attacked it several times in vain, "the Monster on the Hill."

"Your plan will simply dissipate the little time we have left," Yadin argued. "With a truce about to be called, we must choose the easiest way to put ourselves in a position to be able to claim at least part of the Negev."

He then presented his own plan. An infantry force would smash across the east-west road east of Iraq el-Manshiya and thread its way southwest through the Hebron hills along a dirt track leading to the desert settlement of Ruhama, north of Beersheba. Simultaneously, another force would swing southeastward from a point west of the crossroads, and link up with the eastern unit in Ruhama. The Israelis would thus have hemmed in the Egyptian troops entrenched along the east-west road and be able to claim a large part of the Negev north of Beersheba.

Allon listened skeptically, and responded: "Our aim should be to break the Egyptian defense line, crush the enemy forces, and open the main road to the Negev. Your plans will not achieve that. Anyway, the force that would be needed to protect the dirt road would be large enough to plow through the crossroads strongholds."

The discussion grew more heated until finally Allon, collecting himself, said in a calm, low voice: "Yigal, you have the right, of course, to give me orders. I will carry out your decisions."

There was a tense silence, and Rabin stepped on Allon's toe under the table, staring at him in shocked disapproval.

After a long moment, Yadin replied: "You have heard my arguments. Now you must decide, as you are in charge of the front."

The tension broke and Yadin ordered a soldier to bring coffee for everyone.

When Yadin had left, Rabin asked Allon: "How could you have risked being given an order without leaving yourself the possibility of appealing to the chief of staff [Yaacov Dori]?"

Allon smiled. "I knew that Yadin trusts me," he replied. "I was sure that he would leave the decision to me. Anyway, I'm not sure whether the chief of staff or the Defense Minister [Ben-Gurion] would be easier to convince."

The officers then went to prepare for an attack on the crossroads that night, possibly Israel's last chance to win the Negev.[2]

*

At about 10 P.M. October 16, in the Israeli headquarters village of Julis north of the crossroads, Mattityahu Peled stood silhouetted against the moonlit sky and addressed the men of B Company of the Givati Brigade's 51st Battalion crowded around him.

"Soldiers—rise and conquer! The nation has thrust upon your shoulders the job of regaining the homeland that was stolen, and of avenging the blood of our brothers and comrades in arms who have fallen in battle. Revenge and death to the invader!"

In the pale moonlight Matti Peled then strained to see the expression on each face, seeking some hint of reaction, some evidence that he had been right, that his hard-driving methods, his preaching, his fairness, and his compassion had cured them of a grave illness, an illness that had almost destroyed them both as men and as soldiers.

These were the men of Company "Hill 69," who had fled their positions in panic early in the war, to be regarded with disdain by their fellows. Bitterly blaming their company commander, defensively offering excuses and alibis, and seething inwardly with self-reproach, they had lived for months in festering torment. Peled, who had taken over as company commander after the retreat, knew that the men hated him for refusing to let them forget their disgrace, for relentlessly urging them to "wipe out the stain." Yet he also knew that the hatred they felt for him was really a reflection of their own sense of shame, and that it would linger as long as the shame, as long as they were burdened by their massive self-doubt.

Now as his eyes moved from face to face, Peled could see nothing but masks, the gray masks of men who had long submerged their feelings. Nobody moved or said a word. They just stood there like statues.

B Company, because of its checkered past, had been assigned what was regarded as a relatively easy task—to attack the two "junction strongholds" west of the crossroads. Intelligence reports indicated that each of the two heights was defended only by a single platoon of Egyptians. C Company, with a better record, was to assault Hills 113 and 100 north of the crossroads. Hill 113 was considered the real Egyptian stronghold in the area, and was believed to be held by at least a company.

At 10:30 P.M., while Israeli mortar and artillery fire poured into the hills to be attacked, the two companies set off for their objectives. Last thing before moving off they were given the password: "Only a goat goes back."

It was warmer than that icy night five years before, and the stars were brighter. But as Chaim Basok advanced toward Hill 113, he felt he might have been marching again with that platoon of frightened, hunted, silent men, amid crackling twigs, chirping grasshoppers, and deep-throated frogs . . .

> HE HAD FLED INTO THE LITHUANIAN FOREST AFTER BATTLING desperately in Vilna's ghetto from roof to roof—one of only five survivors out of the hundred who had fought with him. He had escaped through the sewers and, in the forest, which the Germans were afraid to enter at night, had joined some 30,000 partisans—Jews, Russians, and others who had evaded the Nazi dragnet. He soon learned how to blow up houses, sabotage railroads, and scrounge for food . . .
>
> "Milk and cheese?" asked the Lithuanian farmer, shaking his head. "We have none, but I'll send my daughter to get some."
>
> And the farmer whispered to his teen-aged daughter to run to the next farm . . . "and tell them to send the army to save us from the partisans!"
>
> But Chaim Basok had overheard him, and when the girl had gone, he and his comrades bound the farmer and his wife, threw them to the floor, and took up positions by the road leading to the house. They watched the daughter running back toward the house, followed by several Germans. They shot the Nazis one by one as they filed by, and set fire to the house.
>
> On a nearby tree Basok pinned up a wrinkled sheet of paper that warned: A DOG DIES LIKE A DOG! and, with his friends, went off in renewed search of milk and cheese. No meat, for it wouldn't be kosher, and they were religious men . . .

After another platoon of Basok's C Company had easily captured Hill 100, his own platoon reached Hill 113 from the west and, with bayonets fixed, advanced up it, firing from the hip and tossing hand grenades.

Basok jumped down into a trench and joined his companions in hand-to-hand fighting with the Egyptian occupants . . .

At midnight, Yehuda Vallach, the battalion commander, listened in base headquarters with delight as a voice from Hill 113 reported over the radio: "We have completed mopping up Hills 100 and 113."

Vallach then asked an aide: "What's new on B Company?"

"I don't know," the officer replied. "Communications with them are cut off. They seem to have disappeared."

Shortly before midnight, B Company crossed the east-west road, with one platoon, under the command of Zvi Kravitzky, an American, heading for the northern junction hill and a second, under Dan Frankel, advancing to the south of the southern hill for an attack on it from the rear. A third platoon remained at a position south of this second hill to guard the rear.

"Advise headquarters we've crossed the road," Peled, accompanying Frankel's platoon, ordered his communications officer.

The officer tried to make contact, but reported: "It isn't working. Something's wrong. I can't get headquarters."

"Well, keep trying," said Peled. "We've got to know what's happening on the other hills."

Then he murmured to Frankel: "Let's hope the reports are right about the token resistance we're supposed to meet. With one platoon attacking each hill, we'd be in a hell of a fix if the reports are wrong—especially being cut off from headquarters."

As Frankel's men began to climb the slope of the southern hill from the southeast, they suddenly found their way blocked by thick tangles of rolled barbed wire and, before they could cut through, machine-gun bullets peppered them from fortifications at the crest of the hill.

"We're caught in a crossfire!" Peled muttered, flattening himself to the ground. He sent a soldier to knock out one of the two enemy machine guns pinning down the unit, and the man—a modest, bespectacled tailor— succeeded in a daring grenade attack.

The second Egyptian machine gun, apparently hidden in a fortification at the eastern side of the hill, then also ceased firing. Peled was puzzled. No one, as far as he knew, had gotten close enough to that gun to knock it out too.

Just before Frankel's platoon had come under fire, Kravitzky and his men were making their way through the narrow valley between the northern and southern hills, intending to attack the northern height from the rear. Then, as they neared their takeoff point for the ascension, heavy firing broke out to the south.

Kratvitzky realized Peled had started his attack and prayed that the fire was coming mainly from Israeli guns. But he began to worry as the shooting grew heavier. For a moment, he wished he were back in Los Angeles, back with his family and his car and those carefree weekends at the beach with his girlfriends.

What was he doing here, in fact? Hadn't he done his share of fighting as a Marine officer in the Pacific during World War II? His men had to fight to survive but he, an American, needed only to coast along, benefiting from a well-entrenched, if rather smog-soiled, civilization until he was old enough to cash in on his social security . . . He looked back and glanced briefly at the men strung out behind him, men like Milek Slonsky who had faltered before and could never falter again and still remain men. Then he began to wonder if he were really much more secure than they and hazily perceived why he was there . . .

Bullets sliced through the platoon suddenly from the southern hill, where the Egyptians had observed the approaching force in the valley. The men raced to the slope of the northern hill, but heavy fire started coming from there, too. With the platoon pinned down, Kravitzky quickly appraised the situation. Both heights were obviously better defended than expected: how could a single platoon take either alone? The only answer was to switch tactics—to attack the southern instead of the northern hill and help out Frankel's platoon on the other side of the same hill.

Kravitzky gave the forward signal and led his men across the valley under fire to the slope of the southern hill. Like tenacious ants, they advanced behind him, some crouched over, some on their hands and knees, all throwing grenades and blazing away with rifles and Stens. Then the rattle of a heavy Egyptian machine gun from the eastern side of the hill abruptly ended in a grenade blast.

The fury subsided fully as the platoon's survivors reached the crest of the hill. Peering into the dark, Kravitzky saw something moving at the opposite edge of the crest and, as he lay on his stomach breathing rapidly, dazed with exhaustion, he wondered whether to shoot. Was he seeing Egyptians or members of the other platoon who had climbed up from the opposite side?

"Kravitzky here!" he yelled, taking a chance on drawing enemy fire. "Don't shoot!"

A shadowy figure moved toward him, gun in hand.

"Kravitzky!" Matti Peled yelled. "You stupid Yankee! What the hell are you doing here? You should be over on the other hill!"

Kravitzky got up and the two men embraced.

"I just wanted to save your skin," the American said.

Peled, Kravitzky, and Frankel immediately laid plans for an attack on the still unconquered northern hill, to be led by the third reserve platoon. It was clear the job would be far more difficult than originally foreseen, like the attack on the southern stronghold. The Egyptians had apparently based a full company on each hill, rather than a platoon.

"A few of them got away," Peled said, as he surveyed the pattern of corpses littering the hillside.

A burst of shells and bullets split the air.

"Some of them are sure as hell alive!" Kravitzky cried. "There's a two-pounder right nearby!"

A scout then yelled: "They're coming up the northern side! A counterattack!"

With artillery and mortar shells bursting everywhere, the Israelis ran to the abandoned Egyptian fortifications. The men of the reserve platoon raced up the hill from the south to help in its defense but, silhouetted against the flashing skyline, were caught in a small arms barrage and suffered about a dozen casualties within a minute.

As Kravitzky crawled around trying to organize the defense of the hill, he put his hands convulsively to his face. Someone dragged him into a pillbox and an overworked medic treated him. He had been struck in the eye by a piece of shrapnel.

After two Egyptian counterattacks had failed, Peled, who had been wounded less seriously close to the eyes but could still see, stumbled into Kravitzky's shelter and said: "The third platoon's pretty shattered, but maybe we can still attack the other hill."

Kravitzky, lying on the ground with his head bandaged, disagreed.

"About thirty of our men are dead or wounded, including ourselves. Our communications with headquarters are cut off and we can't even coordinate an attack with other units. I think we should retreat while we're still able to. We've done all we can."

Peled was silent.

Finally, at about 3 A.M., radio contact was made with headquarters, and Peled described the situation to Yehuda Vallach, who said after brief consultation: "Avidan thinks you've contributed enough and that you should retreat and evacuate the wounded. We'll send out a formation to help you in."

But Peled replied: "This company retreated once before. We're not going to do it again!"

During that day—October 17—the survivors of B Company repulsed four Egyptian counterattacks, mainly using abandoned Egyptian guns, which captured Sudanese soldiers showed them how to operate.

In one of the Egyptian attacks, Milek Slonsky was hit by a piece of shrapnel in the stomach and fell screaming to the ground. As he lay on the hillside gasping with pain, he looked around but saw no one; only the corpse of an Egyptian soldier lying like a stiff wax doll a few feet away. It was strange; he would die side by side with an enemy soldier, perhaps someone like himself who had been more afraid of being a coward than of being a hero. As he stared at the torn body, he wondered why death had to be so grotesque; why honor had to be measured by the amount of blood spilt; why the panic of a moment should mean disgrace for a lifetime. "Wipe out the stain, wipe out the stain," they had told him. Now he and his comrades, most of them dead or wounded, had done so. Yet he did not feel any braver or more of a man than he had before. In suppressing his fear, he had simply been more careful to be less human. If life was but a show for others, was it not logical to die if need be in order to prove one's capacity for dehumanization?

After a while, Milek's pain subsided into a dull ache, but he grew almost too weak to move. He stared at a patch of grass a few inches away and watched an ant laboriously make its way toward the tip of a reed, advancing, slipping, moving again. It seemed so futile . . . What would it find at the end of the reed? . . .

At dawn, an Israeli unit crawled to the foothills of the northern stronghold, threw grenades, and charged up the slope. After meeting little resistance, they found 20 startled Egyptians on top and wiped them out. The rest had fled.

With the northern hill in its hands, the unit headed for the southern height and filed its way over a scramble of Israeli and Egyptian bodies to find the bloody remnants of B Company waiting in pain and dazed silence on the hillside and in the fortifications. Many of the wounded lay dying for lack of medical aid, and others were too exhausted even to reach for the water offered them by the relieving unit, though no one had drunk—or eaten—for more than 24 hours. Milek Slonsky was among the survivors.

"Nice to see you," Peled greeted the commander of the force. "Welcome to Company 'Hill 69.' "

Later, Abba Kovner, educational officer of the Givati Brigade, wrote in his battle report:

> In the course of fighting to capture the "Gateway to the Negev," one of our units elevated itself to a level of fighting above which there is none. This unit, which has carried with it the memory of bitter days, tore a page from a stained past with a single rip and reached the summit of glory. It conquered itself. It turned weakness into heroism. As a sign of indebtedness and to mark a new start, the unit will be known from now on as the "Crossroads Company."

The Egyptians of the defending 9th Battalion, at least the Sudanese, had also fought with great courage at the crossroads; but they had been severely handicapped by a rather important factor: they lacked a battalion commander. The one officially in charge when the fighting started was on leave in Cairo. The officer who replaced him was killed by a mortar shell. His successor jumped into a car and drove southward at full speed, not slowing down until he reached Ismailia in the Suez Canal Zone. And the fourth commander found it prudent to leave the battalion and direct the battle from brigade headquarters in Majdal.

T HE FALL of the crossroads denied the east-west road to the Egyptians and cut off Egyptian forces in the coastal area from those situated east of the inland north-south road, but this latter road was not yet open to the

Israelis. Still to be conquered further south were the strongholds of
Kaukaba and, most important of all, the hills of Huleiqat. The Iraq es-
Suweidan police fortress, the "Monster on the Hill," also had to be elim-
inated to prevent harassment at the crossroads.

On the night of October 17, only a few hours after the crossroads had
fallen, advancing Givati forces occupied the Kaukaba area, which they
found abandoned. Now everything depended on an attack on Huleiqat, a
task assigned to the Yiftach Brigade. That night, units of the brigade assaulted Hill 138, the highest and best fortified of the Huleiqat hills.

The leading platoon breached the first barbed wire fence, but was forced
to withdraw at dawn. Huleiqat continued to block the road to the Negev.

With the news that the United Nations Security Council was about to
call for a cease-fire and a return of both sides to positions held before the
Negev fighting started, the Israeli High Command, steeped in gloom, met
the following morning, October 18, to decide on the next move.

"We've got to plan operations," Allon said, "on the basis that only two
more nights remain for action. We must hit them again where they're
strongest—at Huleiqat. It's the only way to push southward and crush
the Egyptian army at the same time. Then we'll have time to advance
either to Gaza or to Beersheba."

"Which is the more feasible?" a staff officer asked.

Allon said he favored Beersheba. Gaza, he pointed out, was jammed
with enemy forces withdrawing from the north, while Beersheba would be
relatively easy to take, being located to the rear of the Egyptian forces
and occupied by an inferior battalion. Also, severance of the Beersheba-
Hebron-Jerusalem road, he stressed, would isolate the Egyptian forces
in the east.

After considerable discussion and heartsearching, Allon's proposals
were approved. Gloom gave way to nervous exhaustion as the meeting broke
up. The future geography of Israel, it seemed, would be determined that
night at Huleiqat[3] . . .

Yaacov Prulov, commander of the Givati Brigade's 52nd Battalion, was
just being told in his headquarters by Avidan, the brigade leader, that his
battalion was to lead the attack when Allon telephoned.

"You're to attack tonight," Allon said, "and remember, Yaacov,
Huleiqat must be taken *at any cost.*"

When he put down the receiver, Prulov looked tense. After having
barely escaped court-martial for failing to attack aggressively enough at
Latrun—Mickey Marcus had been killed before he could investigate his
performance—he could not afford to be charged with another failure.

"Frankly, I'm worried," he told Avidan. "We have to attack tonight, yet we know almost nothing about the area. Our intelligence says it knows of four hills, but that there may be more. How can we attack without even such basic information? We need more time for reconnaissance."

Avidan shrugged. "Yaacov," he said, "we only have two days to take the whole Negev. But I'll ask Allon anyway . . . "

"Okay, we'll attack tomorrow night instead," Allon agreed reluctantly. "Meanwhile, we'll try to take the Karatiya road tonight and start pushing toward Beersheba."

Allon was referring to an Egyptian-built dirt track that began just south of Karatiya and led to the path plunging to Beersheba from the Iraq el-Manshiya area. Moshe Dayan's commandos had captured Karatiya, which lay astride the east-west paved road, just before the second truce. But the Egyptians had since sealed off the dirt road with a semicircle of strongpoints in the hills south of the village, while building around these strongpoints a new road which permitted them to bypass Karatiya and thus continue using the east-west highway.

The High Command brought down the Oded Brigade from the north, further denuding the already flimsy northern defenses on the assumption that other Arab countries would not attack in support of Egypt. And without preparation, these troops were flung into battle as soon as they arrived.

Lieutenant Saad el-Gammal (who had led an occupying force into Yad Mordechai) peered unhappily through the small window of his tin-roofed, heavily camouflaged dugout and scanned the swoop of foothills stretching northward to Karatiya. Intelligence reports indicated the Israelis might attack his stronghold in the Karatiya hills that night, and heavy shelling seemed to confirm this prediction, yet he wasn't sure that he was ready, or for that matter that he ever would be ready under existing conditions.

The Israelis—by capturing the crossroads—had cut off his position, as well as all others along the east-west road, from supply centers on the coast. Then they had routed a platoon he had sent to reopen a supply path. He reproached himself for having agreed to this attempt, which a German Nazi soldier had volunteered to lead.

"Don't worry, I'll smash right through those Jews!" he had said. How was Gammal to know that the Nazi was an undependable braggart and an alcoholic, whatever his military experience might have been under Hitler.

Gammal wasn't sure of his other men, either. When he took over command of the position, he found himself leading troops he had never fought with before. There was no longer the *esprit de corps* that had welded his own unit into the tight, hard-fighting group that had shown such courage at Yad Mordechai and elsewhere. He was particularly worried about his top sergeant, who sometimes hung back during attacks. Some of his men, of course, had shown extraordinary courage; Sergeant Meligi Aziz Rashid, for example. A weaver by profession, Rashid had begged to be sent to the front after being based for weeks in Egypt, and once he was caught trying to sneak onto a train headed for Palestine. He was finally sent into combat, and now Gammal viewed him as one of the few men on whom he could depend.

But even soldiers like Rashid could hardly be very effective without good weapons. The Bren guns had firing pins that were too short, and would not operate after three or four bullets were fired. And some of the hand grenades also had faulty pins. Someone back in Cairo, he was sure, was profiting handsomely from the bloodshed . . .

Gammal's bitter thoughts were interrupted at this point by shots sounding in the distance.

"They're attacking from the village!" he yelled to an aide. "Send up flares and order the artillery to fire!"

Immediately the sky turned silver, casting a deadly glare over rocky foothills speckled with toylike soldiers. Seconds later, the tiny figures vanished in swirling fountains of dust that rose, dark and foreboding, into the heavens like huge genies released from a magic bottle.

As the Jews approached, Gammal crawled from his dugout into a trench nearby and threw a grenade as far as he could. As it exploded, he hurled several large rocks to convey the impression to the Israelis that they were being deluged with grenades. He was delighted to see that a number of attackers then halted or retreated.

Sergeant Rashid was sitting in a trench firing a machine gun into the billowing gray clouds in front of him. He couldn't see the advancing soldiers clearly, but as he raked the whole hillside he was convinced the enemy could never advance through such fire. Suddenly, the curtain of gray burst into red, then dazzling orange, and Rashid's screams rose in the clamorous night.

"My God, he's on fire!" Gammal exclaimed, from his dugout. He dashed to the trench and wrapped Rashid in his tunic, smothering the flames. It was the first time he had seen the Israelis fight with flamethrowers.

"I can't see! I can't see!" Rashid cried, as he put his hands to his charred face.

"Don't worry," Gammal said, consoling him. "It's only shock." But from the look of the wound, he was sure that Rashid was blind.

"They're retreating!" someone yelled, and through a lifting fog of dust and smoke the toy soldiers could be seen running back toward the village.

"Look, Rashid, look!" Gammal urged. "They're . . . "

He stopped abruptly, biting his lip. Then he went to get medication to ease Rashid's pain—and to find his top sergeant who, as usual when bullets and shells were flying, had disappeared.

The failure at Karatiya added to the burden of Prulov's concern as he tried to base tactical plans for his attack on Huleiqat, which was infinitely better defended, on the limited information he was able to obtain in the extra time allotted to him by Allon. Had he had more time and information, he might have been able to bypass the northern Huleiqat hills and capture the southernmost heights alone, forcing the enemy to withdraw from the others without battle. But under the circumstances he would have to make frontal assaults on each hill. He dared attack only what he could actually see in front of him.

Mohammed Abdel Aref wiped the sweat from his scrawny face and leaned against the wall of the trench, his bare, flat feet buried in the dirt, as he paused in his efforts to dig a little deeper. His officers had said that the Jews might attack Hill 120, west of the road, that night. Aref was determined to give the Jews a fight. No longer was he thinking of ways to escape from the army and make his way back to his little farm near Cairo, even though his ancient parents needed him to help with the harvest. Things had changed. Before, he had not wanted to fight. Why should he risk his life fighting for strangers, even if they were Arabs? And he had been sure that God would understand if he did not want to fight people who did not attack him.

But God would certainly be furious if he did not fight back when people did attack him. The Jews were attacking now, and so he would have to stay for a while until he had killed some of them. Besides, after seeing them kill so many of his friends, it seemed only right that he should take revenge. So he dug his rusty shovel into the hard earth again in further preparation for killing the Jews when they came to kill him . . .

At about 11 P.M., Prulov's leading platoon charged up Hill 123, one of the northernmost hills, and broke through the defenses with flamethrowers to find not Egyptians, but rangy, fierce-looking Saudi Arabians wearing *khaffiyas.* Though apparently caught by surprise, the Saudis counter-attacked immediately and wiped out virtually the whole platoon before the few survivors could retreat northward.

But another platoon fought its way up Hill 120A just across the road against equally stiff Saudi Arabian resistance and found an arsenal of machine guns which, it was decided, would be used to support a new attack on Hill 123. Commander Benjamin Kraus of the victorious platoon called in Arabic to a prisoner: "Come here, Egyptian!"

"I'm not an Egyptian!" the prisoner protested. "We're your Saudi Arabian friends who have been forced to defend this position by the accursed Egyptians."

"If you're really a friend," Kraus replied, "and you want to finish this war alive, you'll show us how to use this machine gun."

"I shall be glad to," the Saudi said.

And within minutes, several Vickers were firing in the direction of the hill across the road, while Israelis, mainly "green" immigrants, made another attempt to capture it and this time succeeded.

On Hill 120 to the west, Mohammed Abdel Aref knelt in his trench as shells exploded nearby. Under the flare-lit sky he watched the Jews as they advanced from an olive grove, like animals running from rock to rock, under heavy fire from his fellow Egyptians. He rested the muzzle of his rifle on the edge of the trench and aimed, but decided to wait until they got closer; there was no use shooting at somebody he could hardly see. He worked the bolt several times. It was a new rifle, issued to him that day, but somehow it didn't work right, like many of the guns the men were using. The bolt kept getting stuck. Well, maybe that was the way it was supposed to be. He squinted through the sight. Too bad it wasn't daytime. Why didn't the Jews attack in daylight like the Egyptians? It was easier to fight a war that way. They were afraid of being hit, that was the reason . . . He wondered once more what would happen to the tomatoes back home . . .

Then, peering through his sight again, he saw something crawling up the hill; a shadowy thing. That must be a Jew. Now he would shoot and make God proud of him. He pulled the trigger slowly, as he had been taught to do—and fell with a scream of agony. The rifle had backfired.

The Israelis, breaking through the barbed wire, leaped into the trenches and took position after position, mainly with grenades, finally capturing the hill. But many Egyptians escaped—among them, Mohammed Abdel Aref, who was carried to safety by comrades.

The same Israeli company then raced south to take the last remaining enemy stronghold, supposedly the most powerful one—Hill 138. But all the men had to do was stroll up the hill and plant a flag. With the northern heights now taken, the Egyptians in the south had fled.

When Prulov heard the news, he glanced at his watch: 3 A.M. The operation had taken four hours.

He telephoned Avidan at brigade headquarters. Avidan had been calling every half-hour asking for news, and all Prulov would say was: "When I know, I'll tell you."

"Now I know," Prulov said.

"You know what?"

"That the way to the Negev is open!"

T HE concrete monster, square and black against the moonlit sky, squatted ominously on the hill, sporadic fire spouting from the four earlike corner towers. Israeli crossroads traffic would still be menaced as long as the Iraq es-Suweidan police fortress, located about a mile to the east along the east-west road, remained in enemy hands. And so, while Israeli troops had prepared to assault Huleiqat, others got ready to attack the fortress for the fifth time, hitting it during October 19 with the most intensive artillery barrage yet laid down in the war.

Inside the partially shattered structure, soot-smeared officers and men scurried like ants from one place to another, carrying sandbags to cover shell holes, putting out fires, rushing ammunition to key positions.

"I've found some unexploded shells!" yelled Sergeant Mahmoud Ibrahim Awad.

But as he started to pull one of them from the earth, Captain Abdel Halem, the artillery commander, said: "Sergeant, leave them there. You'll blow yourself up!"

The sergeant replied almost casually: "If God so wills."

Then he carried the shells, one by one, through the fire and wreckage and debris, to a ditch outside and buried them. Having done this, he wiped his hands, blackened with dust, on his ripped trousers and returned to the fortress trembling slightly from the ordeal.

That night, the Israelis attacked and breached two of the five surrounding barbed wire fences with hardly a shot being fired by either side. Then suddenly, the monster awakened and began flashing light from dozens of guns along the roof, in the towers, and behind slits in the wall. The Israelis retreated.

The next night, October 20, they attacked again. This time they reached the fortress wall and set off explosives which blew the western door off its hinges. But most were hit in the process, and once more the fortress held.

While the Egyptian soldiers embraced one another, Major Salah Badr, the fortress commander, said: "They almost made it that time. One more shell and I think this place would have caved in."

He looked up at gaping holes in the ceiling through which he could see the glittering star-strewn heavens. It seemed almost as if God, too, were celebrating his victory.

KEEP your eyes open," said Captain Ibrahim Shahib after inspecting the defense position at the northern edge of Beersheba and leaving a case of ammunition. "The Jews may attack tonight. God be with you."

Hamdi Hirzallah, the assistant postmaster of Beersheba, sat back against a pile of sandbags and checked his Bren gun. He wondered how he and the three men with him, and those in other defense positions around the town, would ever be able to stop a determined assault, especially by tanks. Though an anti-tank ditch encircled the city, the defenders had only two 6-pound guns, in addition to small arms. Why were the Egyptians virtually abandoning so vital a place as Beersheba to the Jews? Not only had they rejected every desperate request for more arms, but they had taken almost all the existing artillery to defend other areas. For four days, Israeli planes had bombed the town, but not one anti-aircraft weapon was available.

He calculated that his northern post would not have to bear the brunt of a Jewish attack, since the Jews were bottled up north of Huleiqat. More likely the assault would come from Beit Eshel, the kibbutz about three miles to the east, where he guessed (wrongly) many Israeli troops were based. But then he heard the sound of vehicles maneuvering on a nearby hill to the north, and shells started bursting along the whole northern front. The Jews must have broken through at Huleiqat! But why had nobody in the town received or announced the news? There was no time now even to juggle the necessary defense forces to mount a counterattack.

The artillery barrage stopped abruptly and Hamdi peered over the sandbags, laying the barrel of his Bren on top. He heard a grinding noise, then the ghostlike monsters appeared, gray and squat, only about 300 yards away. Before he could cry out to his comrades, the rattle of machine guns pierced the night and Egyptian Captain Yussef Affifi, commander of the post, fell dead.

Hamdi fired with his Bren at what he thought were tanks (in fact, they were half-tracks), and when he ran low on ammunition called out to an Egyptian soldier in the post: "Ammunition! Give me more!"

Receiving no answer, he looked around and saw the Egyptian dead beside him. Then he heard a moan. The fourth man in the post, a Palestinian, lay with a bullet in his leg.

"I'm alone against all those tanks!" gasped Hamdi . . .

The men in "those tanks" were almost as nervous and distraught as Hamdi as they waited in the darkness 300 yards from the Arab lines, exposed to a hail of Arab fire.

"Goddam! What are we waiting for?" demanded Dov Segall, squirming in the front seat of the first half-track.

As commander of the first platoon of the French-speaking Commando Company scheduled to storm into Beersheba, he sat next to the driver behind thick bullet-proof glass helplessly watching bullets smash on the vehicle. What a place to sit on one's ass—within spitting distance of the enemy!

Segall wanted to go down in history as the first Israeli to enter Beersheba, and every minute of delay now seemed intended deliberately to forestall that honor. What was holding Teddy up? Why didn't he give the order? Well, knowing Teddy, he probably had a good reason. Teddy Eytan, his company commander, was one of the best soldiers in the Israeli army. And also one of the most enigmatic. Segall, a French-speaking native of Rumania, had first met Eytan in France after World War II while helping as a Palmach agent to transport Jewish refugees to Palestine . . .

Strange—a French Christian playboy risking his life in the Israeli desert. A major in the French army who had fought with General LeClerc's Free French Army in World War II from Chad to Anzio, Teddy (whose real name was Thadée Difre) had volunteered to fight for Israel without explanation. He seemed too cold and pragmatic to be an idealist. Yet he also seemed too willing to kill Arabs to be, as some Israelis suspected, a French intelligence agent. Nor was he fighting to make money or to enliven a dull life; he came from one of the richest families in Lyon and was married to a top-flight Dior model. And he certainly wasn't the physical prototype of the soldier of fortune. He was tall and slim, with a slight stoop, and had a sensitive, aristocratic face. Only his piercing dark eyes hinted at ruthlessness.

Yet Segall, who rather fancied himself as a kind of Israeli Teddy Eytan, was convinced that he had never served under a tougher officer since he had joined the Palmach in 1944. And an officer had to be tough to control the men in the Commando Company. Its officers included many Jewish veterans of the French Foreign Legion and wartime maquis; most of the men were semi-educated North African Jews who loved to fight, but were generally undisciplined and sometimes savage when they occupied enemy areas . . .

At last a messenger came running up with the long-awaited order.

"Forward!" Segall shouted to his driver. But the driver hesitated, his hands trembling as they gripped the steering wheel.

"Can't you hear? Forward!"

The half-track suddenly lurched ahead with the driver's foot jamming the accelerator to the floorboard.

"Take it easy!" Segall shouted, as the vehicle roared heedlessly toward enemy lines with visibility almost zero.

The next moment, Segall found himself on the floor against the dashboard as the half-track came to a violent halt, wedged in an anti-tank ditch. He put his hand to his nose. Blood was dripping onto his beard, but miraculously he had suffered only a minor injury, while neither the nervous driver nor the dozen men in the rear of the vehicle were hurt.

"What a hell of a way to attack!" Segall muttered as he stumbled out of the half-track.

Then, dividing his men in three groups for a frontal assault, he led the dash through the first line of enemy defense, the blood still spurting from his nose. He attained his objective: He was apparently the first Israeli into Beersheba.

As the Israelis attacked, Hamdi listened for signs of heavy resistance from other nearby posts, but heard only light, scattered fire. What the hell good was his Bren against those tanks? Supporting his wounded Palestinian comrade, he retreated into town and, in desperation, lowered his companion and himself into a manhole leading to a sewage ditch. He found the ditch populated by a dozen other people, including the head schoolmaster, Abdullah Khatib, and the mukhtar, Haj Ali Jaradeh.

"What's happening out there?" someone asked in the evil-smelling darkness.

"The Jews are coming in. There's no way to stop them," Hamdi said.

There were groans of fear and dismay. One of the men gave Hamdi a civilian coat and he removed his military jacket.

"Remember, we're all civilians if they find us," Hamdi said.

They waited in silence. Then, as dawn broke they heard strange voices, and Hamdi saw a pair of military leggings by the opening to the ditch.

"Come on out," a voice ordered in Arabic.

The group climbed out of the hole with the help of an Israeli soldier, who guided them to a wall.

"All right, turn your faces to the wall and raise your hands," he ordered.

The soldier and two companions searched them for arms, then walked off toward a half-track some distance away. There was a sudden burst of fire, and the Arabs collapsed to earth.

Hamdi lay motionless on his stomach, wondering if he was still alive. He whispered the names of the people beside him, but received no reply. Could they all be dead? After several moments of silent agony, he became aware of heavy firing at the other end of town. They must be resisting at the police station; somehow he would join them. A desperate plan took shape in his dazed mind. He listened carefully. Not a sound nearby. He counted to three, then jumped up and dashed down the street toward the corner about 20 yards away. If he could make it, he would be out of the line of fire of the Israeli guns. His mind was an utter blank as he ran, and he moaned as if in anticipation of the bullet that would cut him down. Just as he turned the corner, bullets struck the wall right over his head. He would never again regret his shortness of stature, to which he owed his life . . .

Shortly after Hamdi had fled out of sight, several commandos—they had shot the Arab prisoners despite strict orders issued by Eytan and Segall against such atrocities—walked up to the victims and began checking whether all were dead. Abdullah Khatib, the schoolmaster, looked up and groaned: "I'm wounded. Please help me."

One of the soldiers helped him up, saying: "Come with me to headquarters."

Khatib, supporting himself on the soldier, hobbled along a few blocks until two commandos blocked the way.

"We're going to kill him," one of them said, raising his Sten gun.

Khatib, without thinking, grabbed the Israeli who was guiding him and clamped his arms around his chest, trying to use him as a shield.

One of the other soldiers then slashed at Khatib's arm with his bayonet to break his grip. Just as the schoolmaster let go of his human shield, expecting to die that second, he heard a voice shouting in Hebrew: "What's going on here?"

Khatib looked around and, seeing an Israeli officer in a jeep, cried: "They're trying to kill me!"

The officer got out of the jeep and walked over to the group of men. He looked at each of the soldiers in turn, his eyes blazing with fury.

"Are you soldiers or murderers?" he asked scornfully. "Get back to your units."

Then he guided Khatib by the arm toward the jeep. "I'll drive you to the first aid post," he said. "I apologize for them. You find a few like that in every army . . . "[4]

The commandos continued to advance, crossing the open ground of the town cemetery under heavy fire and scrambling to a large square, bounded on one side by the police station and on another by the railway station, both of which had been converted into forts. They then entrenched themselves in houses around the square. But with reinforcements delayed (having entered a minefield), the commandos soon found themselves in a critical situation as the Egyptians counterattacked at dawn. Eytan walked from building to building snapping out orders, heedless of the danger. When one of his men shouted a warning as he was about to cross a fire-swept passage between two houses, he yelled back without changing his stride: "Those bastards won't make a French major run!"

"What do we do now?" a soldier asked him as he sauntered into a doorway.

"Simple. We fight till we're dead . . . "

As the Egyptian counterattack progressed, Hamdi Hirzallah stumbled to a defense post nearby, exhausted and out of breath.

"What happened?" the Moslem Brotherhood commander asked.

"The Jews!" he gasped. "Reinforcements are breaking in from the north. I saw them."

Having run out of ammunition, the commander ordered a retreat. Within minutes about 60 men had gathered by the barbed wire in the south, and a sergeant volunteered to lead the way across a minefield just outside the fence, saying: "I'll go first, and if a mine explodes, the rest of you step over my body."

The group watched transfixed as the sergeant, step by step, made his way to safety. But as the others followed shots broke out, and several of the Egyptians fell dead or wounded, though most escaped into the desert.

While the bulk of the survivors continued west to join the Egyptian army in El Auja, nine others—including Hamdi, whose parents had earlier fled to Hebron—headed northwest toward that town. Hamdi, looking up into the morning sun, braced himself for the long trek through the desert without food or water.

With about half the town in Israeli hands, Colonel Carmi, commander of the Negev Brigade's 9th Battalion, drove from his command post outside the city, followed by two artillery-equipped half-tracks, to direct the capture of the Arab-controlled police station personally. On the way, he stopped when he saw an Arab dressed in a white hospital smock.

"I'm a nurse," the man claimed fearfully. "I'm not a soldier."

"If you want to save lives," Carmi said, "you'll go to the commander in the police station and tell him to surrender within fifteen minutes. If he doesn't, I'll blow it sky-high."

"Yes, I'll go, I'll go," the Arab said.

Carmi then gave him a white flag, and ordered his own men to cease fire.

Inside the besieged station, where most Arab defenders had gathered, the Israeli ultimatum produced a sharp split among the officers sitting on the floor in an upstairs room.

"We've almost run out of ammunition," one officer said. "How can we fight if we can't shoot? We have no choice. We must surrender."

"I shall never surrender," replied another. "We must fight until our last bullet is fired and then fight them with our hands if necessary. Maybe reinforcements will come in time."

Ibrahim Shahib, the Egyptian commander, interrupted: "I've sent scores of messages begging for help, but General Mawawi has answered only one—the last one."

He pulled a crumpled piece of paper from his breast pocket and read:

> Forces are busy. There is fighting everywhere. Cannot send help. Do not believe that those who die for God are dead. They are alive in the presence of God.

Silence prevailed for a moment, then Shahib said: "I don't think we should surrender, but there's no use trying to fight, either. We should try to escape so that we can fight elsewhere."

At that point the building shook with the force of a heavy explosion, and water began flooding into the station.

"They've hit the water tank!" someone yelled (referring to the reservoir on the roof of the station).

Immediately, Shahib and some 100 men—one-third of the Egyptian force—ran up to the flat-topped roof, jumped down to the ground, and raced blindly southward through a barrage of fire. Shahib and about 60 of the men made it through the barbed wire and disappeared into the desert. The remainder were found dead or wounded along the way.[5] . . .

Almost simultaneously, officers who decided to surrender opened the front door of the station and emerged carrying a white flag. They were nearly knocked down by members of the Commando Company who were rushing in to fire at those trying to escape via the roof.

Carmi then came running to the entrance. "Where is your commander?" he asked.

An officer stepped forward. "We've got many wounded," he said.

"Have you any doctors?" Carmi asked.

"No."

Carmi then ordered an officer to see that the wounded were taken to a nearby hospital.

Shooting broke out inside and Carmi dashed in just as a commando was raking the interior with a Sten gun, running up the stairs toward the second floor. Other commandos were also firing at random. Carmi pulled out his pistol and pointed it at the soldier on the staircase just as the man was about to shoot an Egyptian officer.

"Stop shooting, or I'll fire!" Carmi yelled.

The commando looked around and slowly walked down the stairs.

In a few minutes, all was quiet. The wounded were evacuated to the hospital and over 200 people taken prisoner.

At 9:15 A.M., Sarig sent a message to Allon: "Beersheba is in our hands . . . "

Many of the victorious Israeli soldiers interpreted this terse announcement in a very personal sense, looting every shop in town and setting fire to some. As men walked through the dusty, shell-pocked streets bent under the weight of indiscriminately snatched booty—dishes, radios, cutlery, sheep furs, mattresses—Eytan looked on in livid fury.

"Nobody is going to keep any of that junk," he snarled to Dov Segall. "I'm going to teach them a lesson!"

He then gathered his men in formation, most of them still clinging to their bulky acquisitions.

"We're going on a march," he announced succinctly. "Follow me!"

And the company headed into the withering desert, loot and all. Every so often Eytan and Segall, with quiet smiles, looked back at their perspiring men and saw the burdens grow lighter. Finally, after a four-mile hike, the column dizzily perceived trucks in the distance.

"Okay, into the trucks," Eytan commanded when his men had reached the vehicles.

"Where are we going?" one soldier asked.

"Back to Beersheba!"

As the trucks sped off, members of the Commando Company sighed bitterly as they saw strewn in the desert all the wealth they had so frantically accumulated.*

*

* Leonard Bernstein, the American conductor and composer, conducted a symphony orchestra in the Beersheba desert for the entertainment of Israeli troops several days after the city's fall—while fighting was going on nearby.

Hamdi and his party, after surviving for three days on grass, weeds, and the little water they were able to force stray Bedouins to give them, finally found a sheikh whom Hamdi knew, who provided them with three donkeys, two camels, two horses, and a guide. As soon as the group entered Hebron, a friend of Hamdi's rushed to him crying out: "Oh Hamdi, are you still alive?"

"Of course, why do you ask?" said Hamdi, perched on his camel.

"I've just come from your father's house. Many people are there to offer condolences."

"What do you mean?"

"They think you are dead. I'll run ahead and tell them. Otherwise, if they see you they'll die of shock!"

As the menagerie plodded toward the house where Hamdi's family was staying, his mother nearly fell off the roof waving to him. Then she ran out and embraced him for several moments, while his father stood by trying to hold back tears.

"Father, why did you think I was dead?" asked Hamdi at last.

"A male nurse arrived here yesterday from Beersheba after the Jews let him go. He said he had met Abdullah Khatib in the hospital and that Abdullah had told him that you had been killed."

The father then said: "You must be starved. Come in and eat. The table is full, though I must say you are the last guest we expected!"

WITH the fall of Beersheba, units of the Yiftach Brigade tried desperately to deepen their wedge toward the sea south of Huleiqat in order to cut the coastal road and trap Egyptian forces in the northern coastal area before the cease-fire. But as the Israelis drove toward Beit Hanun, west of the road, heavy Egyptian mortar fire directed into the wedge permitted convoys of troops to stream southward from Majdal to Gaza under cover of thick smoke screens.

The small Israeli navy, under the command of the American, Paul Shulman, joined in the effort to halt this traffic, shelling the road from the sea. When the Egyptians sent the *King Farouk,* flagship of their navy, and a minesweeper to disrupt this effort, the Israelis sank the flagship with explosives delivered in unpiloted motorboats.

But though the Israeli navy continued to shell the coast virtually unchallenged, neither it nor the army could plug the Egyptian escape gap. Even when, on October 22—a few hours before the cease-fire was to take effect—Yiftach units captured Beit Hanun and blocked the coastal road, the Egyptians kept coming. Their engineers, working feverishly all night, had managed to open a road, ingeniously composed of logs and boards bound with wire netting, over the sand dunes of the beach itself.

The trap never closed.

With the cease-fire closing in, Israeli troops also made a supreme effort to grab what they could at the eastern end of the Negev. They met with little resistance, as Egyptian forces in the Judaean and Hebron hills, cut off from their bases in the west, retreated in panic. But they were sharply challenged by another foe: time. Not only did they have to beat the United Nations cease-fire, but also one imposed by political circumstances. King Abdullah, who had not been particularly displeased by the Israeli operations against the Egyptians in the west, now regarded with alarm the threat posed for Jerusalem by the Israeli drive toward Hebron. He was convinced that he did not have the physical force to stop the Israelis, but he knew that they wanted to avoid at all costs a clash with the Arab Legion that could restart the war with Transjordan; and that they were, moreover, hopeful that he would negotiate peace with them. He therefore sent word to the Israelis that he might indeed negotiate if they would halt their attack.

When the Israelis showed no sign of relenting, Abdullah consulted with Glubb Pasha.

Two courses were open, Glubb told him. The Legion could carry out diversionary attacks in the Jerusalem or Latrun areas to draw Israeli forces away from the south, though such action probably wouldn't be very effective at this point. Or it could send a force to Hebron.

The King, who had long wanted to take control of Hebron from the Egyptians in any case, heartily agreed that the second alternative was preferable. A small force would be sent, not necessarily to fight the Israelis but to make it impossible for them to take Hebron without fighting and thereby risking renewed war with Transjordan. And so, on October 22, just before the cease-fire, Glubb sent south an improvised token column of two infantry companies and a squadron of armored cars, in all, a total of about 350 soldiers or, more accurately, political pawns.[6]

Although mainly military and political factors shaped the decisions of both Arab and Jew on action in the Hebron area, a powerful psychological factor also played a role. Both sides remembered the 1929 Arab massacre of Jews, mainly in Hebron. To some Jews, Israeli control of Hebron would represent a measure of vengeance; to some Arabs, such control would mean, they were sure, vengeance in the form of a reverse massacre. In any case, nowhere in Palestine was mutual hatred so deeply rooted as in the city where Abraham, a prophet to the Moslems as well as the Jews, is thought to lie at rest. . . .

> THE MASSACRE IN HEBRON HAD BEGUN WHEN ARABS IN THE COUN-tryside who were in debt to the Jewish merchants decided to wipe out the Jews and the debts simultaneously. A mob chased a group of Jews to an inn, broke down an upstairs door and, finding 23 men, women, and children cowering inside, stabbed them all with daggers and then chopped them to pieces with axes. When British police arrived, they saw blood flowing down the stairs to form a large pool on the ground floor, and more dripping from the dining room ceiling onto a table below like rainwater after a storm. Mingled with the blood in many houses and offices were the ashes of promis-sory notes[7] . . .

Now, 20 years later, the Jews were fighting for control of Hebron, and every drop of sweat shed in the effort seemed to avenge a drop of that blood.

On the night of October 19, while the decisive drive on Huleiqat was being launched, Moshe Dayan led an Etzioni unit from Jerusalem through the Judaean hills toward Bethlehem and Hebron, but only after three long delays that gave the enemy more than enough time to discover his intentions. The forward company commander then proved timid when a machine-gun position held up his leading platoon and thus the whole brigade. Finally, the force took the fortified village of Walaga, west of Jerusalem, but Dayan halted the attack at that point for fear of being caught in daylight in the open hills.

Because of the mishaps, he lost the race with time. The Legion had not yet moved, but Ben-Gurion, reluctant to chance a confrontation with Glubb's troops along a road frequented by them, ordered Dayan to stand fast despite contrary advice from most members of the High Command. This just wasn't Dayan's war, it seemed.

By October 22, other Israeli forces confronting the Egyptians had stormed to within a few miles north and west of Bethlehem and were planning a final all-out push toward Hebron when the commanders received orders to stop all military operations. Pleas from Yosef Tabenkin, the

Harel commander (he had replaced Yitzhak Rabin, who had become Allon's deputy), for "just a few more hours" had no effect. The 3 P.M. cease-fire deadline had passed and the Arab Legion detachment sent by Glubb had reached Bethlehem on its way to Hebron. Operation Ten Plagues had formally ended.

AT a meeting of Arab leaders in Amman on October 23, the day after the cease-fire, Abdullah, his eyes gleaming with satisfaction, greeted his guests with the cheerful, self-confident air of a victor. It would, after all, be much easier to deal with a Jewish State than with an Egyptian puppet State headed by the Mufti. Moreover, the Negev debacle served Cairo right for not even informing him, as Arab commander-in-chief, of the progress of the fighting.

As the Arab leaders—the Prime Ministers of Egypt and Syria, the Regent of Iraq, and the Iraqi chief of staff—sat down that evening in the royal salon, more than five minutes passed without anyone saying a word. The Regent finally motioned to Abdullah to begin the conversation, but the King was enjoying the silent torment of Egyptian Prime Minister Nokrashy Pasha. It helped to make up for the many Egyptian insults and plots, and he only wished that King Farouk himself were present.

Looking at Nokrashy Pasha, Abdullah said at last: "Let us hear what His Excellency has to say. I think that Your Excellency should do the talking under the present cirmumstances, in view of the fact that Beersheba has been lost and Faluja is besieged."

"Who said so?" Nokrashy stormed. "The Egyptian forces are still holding their positions."

"Perhaps," the King countered, "the news has not yet reached the ears of Your Excellency? I had thought that you would point out the necessity of military help . . . in order to save the situation."

"No, the Egyptian government has no need of anyone's assistance. But where are the royal Transjordanian and Iraqi forces? And we all know that the Syrian forces are useless."

Syrian Prime Minister Jamil Mardam Bey turned pale but before he could speak, the King said: "I take it then that Your Excellency has come here to accuse us . . . Are you heaping scorn on the Arabs in their own house—the house in which Transjordan, Iraq, and Syria are gathered?"

"I seek forgiveness of God," the Egyptian leader retorted. "I have not come to accuse anyone."

Rising, Abdullah then said: "I am going to perform my evening prayers while you talk."

The meeting broke up and reconvened later at the Egyptian Legation, where Nokrashy Pasha admitted: "I have just heard the news. Yes, it is true. Beersheba has fallen."

The King smiled. Ways of helping Egypt were then discussed; but, at another meeting the next day, when it appeared that the cease-fire would favor Egypt, Nokrashy Pasha rejected any assistance.

"The need has passed," he said.[8]

In the Augoza Hospital in Cairo, Mohammed Abdel Aref lay silently in bed, the pain wracking his body from the wounds inflected at Huleiqat exceeded only by the torment of apprehension about the fate of his family. Who had harvested the tomatoes and the other crops? How were his sickly mother and father able to keep alive without his help? And what would happen when he died? For no man suffering as much pain as he could possibly go on living. It was just a matter of time now. God would have to care for his family . . .

He heard voices outside the ward, as if many people were approaching. More wounded to fill more beds, men perhaps like himself, who had been shot with their own guns and who would die without knowing why.

The door burst open, and in walked a fat man in a uniform glittering with medals and surrounded by nervous-looking people. The man's red-tasseled tarboosh crowned a round, puffy face that broadened into a mechanical grin. Aref could hardly believe his eyes: King Farouk himself!

As the King went from bed to bed offering a word of comfort to each startled "hero" of the war, Aref's heartbeat quickened. So this was the man who had had him dragged from his hut into the army and ordered him beaten whenever he escaped to go home and help his family in the fields. The man who was forcing girls to go to bed with him while their husbands were at the front. The man who gave him a gun that would only shoot backward!

Farouk finally reached Aref's bed and, smiling unctuously, said: "You've done a fine job. How do you feel?"

Aref stared into a pair of round black lenses. He saw the shadows again. They were coming closer and closer. He could see them in the sight of his rifle . . . then the terrible pain . . .

The peasant said calmly to the King: "I'd feel a lot better if you stopped fucking every girl in Cairo while your soldiers are getting killed with their own guns."

Farouk's face turned pasty. Then he muttered to an aide behind him: "Arrest that man!"

Aref lingered in jail until 1952, when he was freed after the revolution led by Gamal Abdel Nasser.

16

The Bracelet of Faluja

Now is the time to strike," urged Fawzi el-Kaoukji, meeting with Lebanese army leaders in Beirut.

"Do you think the ALA (Arab Liberation Army) can beat them?" a Lebanese officer asked.

"Of course. The Jews are busy down south, and will continue to be even after the cease-fire."

"Hitting them during the cease-fire might be delicate."

"Why? I'm the leader of an international army of volunteers. What have I got to do with the United Nations?"

Kaoukji was encouraged by the improved condition of his army, which had been reorganized and reequipped by Lebanon. That country had assumed control of it, though leaving Kaoukji as the real leader. If he defeated the Israelis, Lebanon could claim some territory in northern Palestine; if he lost, it could disclaim responsibility for the setback.

Thus, on October 22, the day the truce with Egypt took effect, Kaoukji's army, in a surprise move, captured the hill of Sheikh Abd, north of Manara and east of the Lebanese frontier. An attempt to dislodge him failed, and he now had a tight grip on this border area.

The Israelis did not believe that Kaoukji was capable of launching a major offensive by himself, but they were concerned that if he acted in conjunction with one of the regular Arab armies, he could endanger the narrow strips of Israeli territory surrounding his mountainous stronghold.

The Israeli commanders initially discussed the possibility of a counter-attack in the area where Kaoukji had advanced, but after calculating the likely casualties they started considering another objective.

"I think we should use this opportunity to liberate the whole of Galilee," said Moshe Carmel, commander of the northern front, at a meeting of the High Command. "We can probably do that with hardly more casualties than we'd have if we simply counterattacked in a limited area."

He was overjoyed when the others agreed. He had regretted having had so little to do while most Israeli commanders had been fighting in the Negev—a campaign he had originally opposed in favor of an attack on the Triangle. Now he, too, would have a chance to help determine Israel's future boundaries as commander of Operation Hiram, named after the King of Tyre, the ally of David and Solomon, who had sent cedars from Lebanon to build the Temple in Jerusalem.

Four Israeli brigades, the most ever used by Israel in a single battle, were to hit the Arab bulge (extending southward from the Lebanese border to the Valley of Beit Netofa) in a two-phased, tank-led *blitzkrieg* attack.

While Israeli units launched diversionary attacks in the south, one main force further north would march eastward to Tarshiha and Sasa, and a second would advance westward through Jish and link up with the first in Sasa, closing the trap on the Arabs before they could escape into Lebanon. Then the Israelis would move northward up the Huleh Valley to the Lebanese border.

On October 28, planes attacked Arab bases in the area throughout the day while artillery mounted on trucks attacked sporadically in various places to spread confusion . . .

That night, Kaoukji was in his headquarters in a mountain village. As he sat talking to some officers, he was confident that his three Yarmuk Brigades, named after the famous Arab Army of the Yarmuk that had captured Palestine from the Byzantines, could handle any Israeli attack. One brigade was based in Tarshiha, guarding the west; a second in Sasa and Jish; and the third to the south.

"The Jews seem to be firing all over the place," Kaoukji said, "but I've received reports from the south of considerable military activity in the area. They'll probably attack from there."

Some time later, his telephone rang.

"How large are the forces?" his officers heard him ask.

Then, after several moments, he said: "I'll call you back. Meanwhile, hold them off."

He informed his officers: "Just as I thought. They're attacking from the south . . . "

*

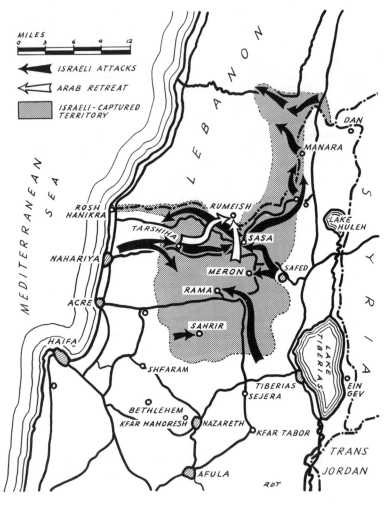

OPERATION HIRAM

Wasfi Tel, the Transjordanian volunteer commander of the ALA brigade in the south (and a relative of Abdullah Tel, the Arab Legion commander in Jerusalem) was confident he could handle the attack. The Israelis were firing sporadically, but he would wait to throw his full power at them when they attacked in force.

An intelligence officer ran into the dugout and reported: "They're trying to encircle us, sir!"

Wasfi Tel promptly informed headquarters of this development, and Kaoukji ordered him to withdraw northward to a new defense line, being still convinced that the main attack was coming from the south, as the Israelis had hoped he would be.[1] But he reacted to this calculation contrary to their expectations. Instead of engaging the attackers while the trap closed further north, Kaoukji unwittingly, in his timidity, pulled them out of the trap by ordering them to regroup in the very area where the Israelis planned to snap it shut.

Meanwhile, at the western edge of the bulge, troops of the Oded Brigade found themselves bogged down near Tarshiha. To add to Israeli troubles there was the misfortune of a Druze company which had been sent to gain control of Yanuach, a large Druze village south of Tarshiha. The company took the village with the help of the Druze residents, but when the Arab forces counterattacked, these inhabitants, fearing retaliation, joined in the attack on the Druze company to "prove" their loyalty to Kaoukji, and the company fled with many casualties.

But the other main Israeli force, the 7th Brigade, which had been born at Latrun, surged ahead from the east toward Sasa, where the trap was to be closed. When it reached Jish, an ancient Jewish fortress that had held out against the Romans, it found itself face to face with an ALA battalion of Syrians that had arrived a few hours before in buses which had been painted brilliant colors and covered with victory inscriptions. Under Israeli fire, the Syrians fled down the narrow lanes of the village into surrounding orchards, leaving some 200 bodies, about half the battalion, strewn along the way.

That night, Oded troops finally captured Tarshiha and continued on toward Sasa, while Wasfi Tel's troops fled northward across their path. The following day, October 30, the Oded Brigade linked up with the 7th. As Carmel and the commanders of the two brigades met on a road just outside Sasa, they embraced, speechless.

"We've done it!" said Carmel finally, his professorial face aglow. "Now let's get moving to Lebanon!"

While the 7th Brigade was starting northward toward Lebanon, Carmel received a message from the Carmeli Brigade, which had just gone into action at Sheikh Abd (the hill further north which Kaoukji had originally grabbed, setting off the Israeli offensive).

"We've reached the border," the message said. "Request permission to advance into Lebanon. Little resistance expected."

Carmel immediately called Yadin at High Command headquarters and relayed the request.

"I think they should advance," Carmel said. "Do you agree?"

Yadin hesitated, wondering what repercussions an invasion of Lebanon, even in "hot pursuit" of enemy forces, would have at the United Nations. After consulting with Ben-Gurion, he said to Carmel: "Very well, you may advance, but not further than the Litani River."

Carmel then gave the order for both the Carmeli and 7th Brigades to advance, and they promptly passed through more than 20 Lebanese hillside villages, where they were molested less by Kaoukji's men than by aggressive Levantine salesmen armed with fountain pens, nylons, and souvenir trinkets from the markets of Beirut and Tyre. But Carmel was disappointed that his troops could not move west of the Litani River. That would mean they would occupy only a small slice of Lebanon, about 20 miles deep, along the eastern border. Why stop there? He wanted to sample the cuisine in Beirut.

And so did Carmeli commander Makleff, who had planned Operation Hiram. With Carmel's blessing, Makleff drove to Tiberias and went to see Ben-Gurion at the Galei Kinneret Hotel.

"Just give us twelve hours more to reach Beirut," he pleaded.

"No," Ben-Gurion replied firmly, "I've got enough trouble with the United Nations over the Negev."

"But if we want peace, the best way to get it is to knock out the weakest link completely and force it to make peace. Then the stronger ones will follow."

The Prime Minister disagreed, arguing that Israel's power should, on the contrary, be concentrated against the strongest link.

Makleff, in desperation, then appealed to Ben-Gurion's strong political instincts, saying: "If we take Beirut, we can establish a Mapai government there."

Ben-Gurion smiled at this reference to his party, but remained adamant.

He did, however, agree to let the Israeli troops remain in the occupied border area until an armistice agreement was reached.

"Cheer up," he remarked with twinkling eyes. "After all, we've captured the whole Galilee."[2]

Fawzi el-Kaoukji had only one consolation. Most of his troops had escaped the Israeli trap, fighting their way to the Lebanese border before the pincers could close. As Kaoukji himself rode in a jeep from his mountain headquarters toward the frontier, weaving between his ragged, retreating forces, he was a broken man. How could he fight without trained soldiers, without the support of the regular Arab armies? Was it his fault that the Mufti had sabotaged him, or that the Jews had obtained modern arms illegally?

As the jeep wound through the mountains, he gazed down upon villages which he had once entered in triumph to hysterical cheers. Then he lit a cigarette and watched the unruly remnants of his Arab Liberation Army stumble along the dusty road into military oblivion.

> If you just looked at the map you would see that the Israelis surround you as a bracelet does a wrist. You have to choose; if you prefer life, you must yield and surrender. . . . Your leaders . . . expect medals and rewards and never think of hundreds and thousands of their soldiers dying. They get medals and you death. . . . Everyone that comes with this leaflet in hand will get security and we promise him a safe return home. . . . Keep in mind that this is an ultimatum.

MAJOR NASSER was enraged as he read one of the leaflets dropped from an Israeli plane over Egyptian positions in the Faluja pocket —partly because he felt the Jews had correctly estimated the Egyptian leaders, partly because he was sure they vastly underestimated the tenacity of the Egyptian fighters. The Egyptian soldier, he conceded, might not be sufficiently aggressive in attack, lacking military training, confidence in his weapons, education, and, because of social conditions in Egypt, a personal stake in victory. But in defense he could be very stubborn—if his leaders supported him—fighting as if for his own home.

As the leaflets continued to float down, however, Nasser and his fellows began to enjoy them, even waiting for them as they might for the evening newspaper—though they were never sure when bombs might fall instead. For fighting in the Negev continued despite the "truce" ending Operation Ten Plagues, each side still trying to improve its positions.

"How can I surrender when I still have ammunition, equipment, and soldiers?" Colonel Taha, the commander of the pocket, asked his officers with a smile, referring to the leaflets.

A stocky man with a black face and a gentle manner, Taha (whose mother was Sudanese, and father Arab) was a tough, courageous soldier like most of the fighters of Sudanese descent in the Egyptian army. And he was more understandable to his men, who proudly called him the "Black Panther," than were most Egyptian officers. He had little in common with upper-class officers who had joined the army to attain prestige and comfort, or with the politically and ideologically motivated younger officers like Gamal Abdel Nasser. He was fighting simply as a soldier who had been ordered into battle, and to fight his best was a matter of intense personal and national pride. Though of lower-middle-class origin, he had the peasant's instinct for standing his ground in the face of challenge.

The question of food worried him more than the Israeli bombs, to which he had become accustomed. Often, he helped his men plant onions in the earth near his headquarters dugout in Faluja. They were eating only two skimpy meals a day, enough to keep them going. But the food would not last long. Even the small mill in Faluja had been destroyed by the bombs, and his men were grinding wheat themselves with stone implements. Otherwise, they had only beans and *khobeza,* a green plant picked in the hills by a "children's brigade" organized in the village. Of course, if necessary he could buy almost inedible food from local Arabs—at excessive prices. But the thought infuriated him. His men had come to save these Arabs, and were now being exploited by them.

"Look out, run!" someone yelled during one planting effort. Taha and the other planters jumped into a trench as a plane flew overhead. There was the usual singing sound and then a great blast nearby. Taha looked up from the trench as dust billowed skyward.

"Well," he said. "No more onions!"

As for Nasser, the food problem reinforced his conviction that he had grievously erred in supporting the war in the first place. He was haunted by the image of a little girl dressed in rags, about the age of his daughter Hoda. He had watched as she scrounged in the weeds for roots while bullets whistled by, her cheeks sunken and her eyes strangely expressionless. And suddenly the questions of government and high politics, conspiracy and Arab unity, had become fanciful and irrelevant. He was fighting to defend his home and children, nothing more. He was fighting so that his little girls would never have to search for roots to eat. But was the real battle in Palestine?[3]

Lieutenant Saad el-Gammal's post south of Karatiya and east of the Iraq es-Suweidan fortress was one of the most persistently attacked and doggedly defended strongholds in the Faluja pocket. But Gammal remained deeply concerned about the problem of morale, partly because of his top sergeant's timidity under fire, but also because more and more of his weapons were proving defective.

Finally he persuaded his battalion commander to replace the sergeant and to give him a heavy machine gun, one of only four in the pocket.

A few hours after he had obtained the gun an Israeli artillery barrage heralded another attack, and Gammal personally visited every position to encourage his men.

"Don't shoot until they try to get through the last wire," he said.

Gammal had a surprise for the attackers. He had strung a fifth barbed wire fence around his post, though they expected, from past experience, to cut through only four. This would permit his men to let the Jews advance closer to the post so that they would be easier prey for the machine gun. At the same time, the Jews might find themselves without sufficient demolition material to cut through the fifth fence.

The Israeli artillery barrage stopped, and the Egyptians waited. Soon they saw shadowy figures crawling toward them, cutting through the first fence, then the second, third, and fourth. As they reached the fifth fence and lay quietly waiting while someone tried to cut it, Gammal yelled from his dugout:

"Come on, Jews, come on! We're waiting for you! Come and catch us!"

A heavy silence paralyzed them all for a moment; then an Israeli shouted back in Arabic: "Surrender, Egyptians!"

At that moment, a machine gun spat into the darkness, killing many of the attackers and forcing the rest to flee.

But the Israelis continued to attack on succeeding nights, though they were unable to knock out the machine gun, which Gammal moved from place to place. One night, the gunner was finally hit by a bullet, but within minutes the gun was firing again. Gammal was shocked to see who was manning it: Sergeant Meligi Aziz Rashid.

Rashid had been permanently blinded during the Israeli attack of October 17 and had been sent to a rear hospital, but after a few days had asked to be returned to his post even though he could not see. Gammal, thinking that his presence could help the morale of the other men, had agreed despite the man's uselessness as a fighter. But there he was firing at an enemy he couldn't see! Gammal finally had to remove him from the gun position by force.

Only in the mornings was there peace. Early in the fighting, an Israeli carrying a white flag had proposed to the Egyptians an hour's truce each morning, during which the Jews would be permitted to carry away their dead and the Egyptians allowed to obtain water from a nearby well in an Israeli-controlled area. The Egyptians had agreed, and Israelis came to collect the bodies after each battle.

One morning Gammal stood by the outermost barbed wire fence and watched the usual Israeli truck wind its way up a steep path toward him. Some distance away, it stopped and three Israelis jumped out, an officer and two soldiers. Gammal watched the officer curiously, squinting to get a clearer image. His lips parted slightly and his eyes gradually widened as the three men halted a few yards from him. He and the officer exchanged stares for a long, silent moment . . . Sasson?

Suddenly, he was a student again, back in the lazy, luxurious days when no one dreamed of war or thought about Palestine. He had lived in an apartment building inhabited by 10 Jewish families, and Sasson had been his next-door neighbor.

He remembered the delicious summer days when Sasson had taken him swimming at the Jewish Maccabee Club in Ein el-Sira, near Cairo. Why hadn't Sasson stayed in Egypt? Why had he forced him to suppress a remnant of memory that somehow seemed important?

"So we meet again," Gammal said now with a faint smile.

"Yes. Among the dead."

"There are no dead today. Come back tomorrow. Maybe there will be some."

How peaceful the world was. Not a shot to be heard. Only the shrill cries of desert birds floating in the cloudless sky. What a day for a swim, or maybe a picnic in the park . . .

"Perhaps we shall meet again," said Sasson. "Under different circumstances."

And the Israelis turned and left.

As scattered fighting continued during the truce, with both sides accusing the other of provoking battle, Taha radioed GHQ in Rafa on November 3 a desperate plea for help.

> Our situation requires special attention now so that a swift and successful solution can be achieved. . . . Our supplies have diminished to the lowest, and almost to an unbearable level. . . . The enemy is occupy-

ing new positions daily. . . . We have decided to hold out to the last
bullet, and the end seems near, I place my hopes in your hands.

When General Mawawi replied that the besieged forces should try to
break through the Israeli lines, Taha angrily radioed back:

> Your suggestion . . . cannot be followed. The positions on both sides
> of the road are infested with enemy forces. We have already notified
> you about the condition of our vehicles after the air attacks. The usable
> vehicles lack gasoline. Our ammunition is not sufficient even for defense.
> The gun tows are not working. Therefore, either you must break through
> the lines with your own forces, or we shall have to solve the situation
> through negotiations. Let us know!

On November 6, Mawawi replied:

> Don't rely on a political solution. Call a meeting and decide on a
> retreat of your forces . . . and we will help you to withdraw. . . . Do
> your best and move swiftly. Give us your decision and the date.

To which Taha responded bluntly:

> . . . Our position in Faluja dictates that you find an immediate polit-
> ical and military solution that will save us.

DESMOND RUTLEDGE awakened early on November 9 and, trying
not to disturb his wife lying on the damp ground beside him, rose and
looked out of his pup tent. Over the edge of the wadi in which the Commando Battalion of the 8th Armored Brigade was camped, he could make
out the crown of the "monster." In a few hours the Israelis, in conjunction
with artillery assaults on other posts, would attack the fortress of Iraq es-
Suweidan for the sixth time, but the first time with tanks in daylight.
Once the fortress fell, he was confident, the whole Faluja pocket would
collapse.

Miriam woke up as the Israeli artillery began ranging in on the fortress
in preparation for the attack that afternoon. She joined her husband outside
the tent.

"The monster is dying," Miriam said, as she watched smoke rising
in the gray dawn sky.

"Maybe," Rutledge said, putting his arm around her. "But does the
monster know it?" . . .

At noon, Major Salah Badr, the station commander, sitting in the communications room amidst smoking wreckage, radioed Taha in Faluja village that his situation was critical. Taha then reported to GHQ:

> The enemy is cutting off all of our positions and is shelling Iraq es-Suweidan with artillery fire without cease. The station is being destroyed. I'll probably have to evacuate the units that are here. This would be a very dangerous move. A quick move by you might save the day.

Forty-five minutes later, after failing to receive a reply, Taha reported further:

> I am forced to remove the forces from the Iraq es-Suweidan police station because enemy shelling is destroying it entirely. This is a critical situation. Notify what to do.

Meanwhile, with growing apprehension, Major Badr watched through a slit in the fortress wall as the Israelis seemed to be organizing for an attack in the wadi just barely in sight. He thought he could make out tanks. This was the end, he was certain. The fortress could never hold out against tanks.

A sergeant ran up and reported: "Sir, there are several big holes in the wall facing the enemy, and we've run out of sandbags."

Badr looked at him with hard eyes and replied: "Then fill up the holes with dead bodies. We've got plenty of them."

He then ran from room to shattered room shouting to his men: "Everybody will withdraw to Iraq el-Manshiya except the commando unit and myself."

After assigning a lieutenant to lead his men, he dashed back to the communications room and reported the retreat to Taha, who immediately informed Gaza: "The situation is very bad. We are retreating . . . "

A few minutes later, Taha pleaded: "Heavy attacks on all of our positions. Save us with planes!"

And then again: "I request immediate airpower to help us."

In five minutes, he received a response: "We'll do our best to send air support . . . "

At 4 P.M., after the greatest artillery bombardment of the war, Rutledge's Cromwell, together with a second Cromwell driven by another British deserter, started grinding toward the fortress followed by half-tracks crowded with infantrymen. As the force advanced firing relentlessly, the flagpole on the roof of the fortress, from which fluttered the Egyptian flag, suddenly began to tremble and then toppled to earth. Above the boom of the artillery, cries of *Bool!* ("Bull's eye!") sounded from every vehicle, and men embraced each other. The fall of the flag symbolized to them the end of the rule of the invader in Israel.

As the tanks neared the barbed wire, they stopped and covered the flanks while infantrymen tumbled down from the half-tracks and blew up the fences. A half-track raced toward the building and sappers jumped out to lay explosives.

Inside the fortress, Major Badr, watching through the slit, shouted: "They've broken through the fences!"

At that moment, an explosion blew a huge hole in the wall, and Badr yelled: "Quick, plug the hole with the truck!"

His commandos ran outside and pushed a rock-loaded lorry in front of the opening. But a moment later another shell blew the vehicle to pieces.

Through the massive hole, Badr could see half-tracks racing toward them. He waited calmly, almost smiling. The first half-track plowed through the shattered wall, and as the Israelis jumped out they found bathed in smoke and blood a small group of dazed men, mostly wounded, sitting on corpse-strewn heaps of wreckage.

Some minutes later, Allon, Rabin, and Yeroham Cohen, Allon's personal aide, drew up in a jeep, having watched the battle from a nearby hill. Cohen, as he examined the wreckage, noticed two Israeli soldiers guarding an officer who sat on the ground with his hands raised. He took charge of the officer and brought him to Yitzhak Sadeh, who had entered the fortress with his 8th Armored Brigade troops.

"I am the commander of this post," Major Badr announced.

Sadeh stared at him and said: "Major, I congratulate you on your courageous stand."[4]

Colonel Taha sat at his desk agonizingly contemplating the defeat, which had reduced the pocket by almost half—to an area about three miles in width and a mile in depth. He radioed Gaza:

> From the pocket to the command. The entire force at Iraq es-Suweidan has been destroyed. Casualies on all parts of the front are heavy. Iraq es-Suweidan [village] and Beit Affa have been evacuated, as have the positions opposite Karatiya. The forces have been concentrated at Iraq el-Manshiya. Supply situation is very bad, and we can't depend on air or land supply routes because of the tight siege both on land and in the air.

Taha leaned on his elbows, his face in his hands. He had planned to plant more onions, but now he wondered who would be around to eat them.

"Yeroham, I think it's time to speak with the Egyptians," Yigal Allon said to his aide, Yeroham Cohen, a short, swarthy man. "The messages we've intercepted indicate their commander might want to negotiate. Have you found the right man to go to them yet?"

"Yes, Yigal."

"Who is it?"

"Me," Cohen replied with a smile.

"Yeroham, how many times have I told you No? I want to have dinner again in your mother's kitchen."

"But Yigal, who is better qualified than I? I know the Arabs. I've lived among them. I speak their language. My mother's kitchen will be open to you no matter what happens."

Allon was silent for a moment. Yeroham was certainly qualified, and there was no man in the world he trusted more. A Yemenite Jew, Cohen had served in Orde Wingate's "night squads" in the late 1930's, in the Allied intelligence service disguised as an Arab during World War II, and as the Palmach's chief intelligence officer after the war. Perhaps it wasn't right to protect Yeroham's life more than he might some other man's.

"All right, you win," Allon said, trying to withhold a smile. "Go to see them tomorrow. We'll cease fire at eight in the morning. With the fortress captured, who knows, maybe they'll be in the mood to talk business."

About 10 A.M. on November 10, the morning after the fall of the fortress, Major Nasser was in his headquarters in Iraq el-Manshiya glumly reading reports of the disaster when a sergeant burst in and cried:

"Sir, an enemy armored car with a white flag is waiting outside our lines. The loudspeaker is saying 'An Israeli officer wants to meet an Egyptian officer.' "

Nasser dashed outside and heard the call repeated in Arabic and English. What had he to lose? Maybe he could learn something of Israeli intentions. He found two junior officers and a sergeant who was armed with a Sten gun, and all jumped into a jeep. As the engine started, it occurred to him that he was dressed in khaki shorts and a pullover of the same color. Should he dress more formally for a meeting with the enemy? The hell with it.

"Okay, driver, let's go!" he ordered.

Cohen's armored car had stopped about 800 yards from the barbed wire fence, just out of range of anti-tank artillery in case the Egyptians wanted to give him a hot welcome. He repeated his call every few moments while watching for some kind of response through his binoculars. Finally, after about 20 minutes, he saw a distant speck on the asphalt road. They were coming! As he climbed out of the car to meet the approaching vehicle, the armed soldier with him started to get out too.

"Stay where you are," Cohen ordered. "I'll go alone. There'll be less chance of trouble then."

"But you aren't even armed."

"I know," Cohen replied. "Keep me covered."

And he started to walk down the road toward Iraq el-Manshiya where scores of Israelis had been slaughtered a few weeks before . . .

Sitting in the front seat next to the driver, Nasser experienced strange emotions as his jeep sped toward a rendezvous with an officer he had been trying his best to kill and who had been trying to kill him. The situation of the Egyptian forces was critical and enemy attacks were ceaseless, with planes, tanks, artillery. Yet everything was so peaceful at this moment. Not a sound except for the whir of the jeep's motor. He might have been traveling down a quiet country road outside Cairo. Yet, there was the enemy. It suddenly occurred to him that perhaps this was a trap. The thought only served to enhance his excitement and curiosity.

The jeep stopped when it reached a barbed wire barrier across the road. The three officers got out and walked around the barrier while the sergeant covered them with his submachine gun . . .

Cohen advanced on rubbery legs. He looked around and saw scores of Israelis watching from the surrounding hills. It was good to know he wasn't alone. But he wondered how much protection they could offer. It would take only one bullet or shell, and he was certain that the enemy had the road zeroed in. Yet he would not dare move off it since there were probably mines everywhere. He strained to hear the whine of an approaching shell so that he could fall in time, but all he heard was the sound of his own boots clicking on asphalt. He tried to drown his fear in the pride of performing so important a task, but only when the three figures drew closer did he begin to relax. They must certainly have realized that if anything happened to him they would be ripe targets for the Israelis.

About 15 yards from the Egyptians, Cohen suddenly became flustered. It was normal to salute in a situation like this, but he had never saluted before. It wasn't the custom in Israel's infant army. He tried to remember from the movies how to do it, and when he was about two yards from them he stopped and attempted a salute that made him look as if he were shading his eyes from the sun.

As the three Egyptians halted and smartly returned the salute, Cohen said in Arabic: "Good morning, gentlemen. I am Captain Cohen."

He shook hands with them, and they identified themselves. "I'm Major Nasser," the man in the middle said coldly. "Why have you come here?"

"I have come as the personal representative of the commander of the front," Cohen replied. "I wish to arrange a meeting between our two sides."

After a brief silence, Nasser asked: "You wish to demand our surrender?"

"At this meeting," Cohen responded, "each side would try to clarify the military situation and to reach some agreement for an end to the fighting. As you know, you are completely encircled."

Nasser stared at him with disdain. What arrogance, he thought. "As for the situation," he replied calmly, "we fully realize its gravity. But we will never surrender. We are here to defend the honor of our army."

Cohen realized that he was up against a stone wall of Arab pride, which he well understood after years of dealing with the Arabs. He would have to chip away at the wall.

"By the way," he said with a smile, "the commander of Iraq es-Suweidan sends his best regards."

Nasser looked startled. "Is he alive?"

"Could I speak to dead people?" Cohen replied. "I promised him to ask you to cable his family that he is alive and that they shouldn't worry."

Nasser's face brightened for the first time.

"Yes," he said, "tell him we'll inform his family immediately."

"You people fought very well," Cohen observed, "but that is the luck of war."

The wall was breached, it seemed. Nasser instructed one of his colleagues: "Go and ask Colonel Taha if he will agree to a meeting with the Israelis. We can work out details later."

The three remaining men then sat down on the grass by the side of the road—after Nasser had assured Cohen that there were no mines there—to wait for the reply.

"Nice day, isn't it?" Cohen remarked.

Before long, the conversation had turned to the economic and social problems of Egypt, and Nasser was astonished by Cohen's knowledge of that country.

"When I was a student, my specialty was Egypt," Cohen said as he lay back, his hands under his head, staring up at the sky. "At Oxford I wrote a thesis on the origin of the Egyptian nationalist movement and the British occupation of Egypt."

"You did?" Nasser exclaimed with a smile. "I have a special interest in those subjects myself." And he spoke bitterly of the "politicians," who, he claimed, were exploiting the Egyptian people.

"We need social reform and an end to feudalism," he asserted.

"This isn't your war," Cohen said. "Why should your best men die here when they are needed to make such changes in their own country? The British pushed you into this war."

"I agree," Nasser replied. "They pushed us into a war we were not ready for—they and the politicians. And though I feel it is our sacred duty to help our Palestinian brothers, they are shiftless and are giving us no help. Meanwhile, Abdullah is sitting on the sidelines laughing at us."

"Have you done much fighting?" Cohen asked, feeling that Nasser had probably exaggerated his attitude to emphasize a sportsmanlike stance toward a friendly enemy.

Nasser then described some of his battle experiences and, mentioning the struggle for Hirbet-Mahaz, said: "Your soldiers fought magnificently."

Then he returned to the subject of the British and, expressing his admiration for the way the Israelis had got rid of them, asked Cohen: "How did you do it? Maybe we can learn something from you."

Finally, after about three hours of conversation ranging from Haganah tactics against the British to the kibbutz philosophy, the jeep drove up with the returning captain.

"Colonel Taha said that he wouldn't object to a meeting, but he has to ask permission from general headquarters," he reported.

The three men got up and Nasser said to Cohen: "Let us meet here tomorrow morning at the same time and we'll have an answer. All right?"

The Egyptians shook hands and exchanged salutes with the Israeli. Then all walked to their respective vehicles under the incredulous eyes of hundreds of soldiers on both sides. . . .

The next morning, Cohen returned alone in a jeep and met Nasser and another officer. There were salutes and warm handshakes again, and Nasser said: "Colonel Taha agrees to the meeting."

"Wonderful," Cohen replied with a smile. "Now we've got to decide on the time and place. Of course, you understand the meeting must take place on our side of the line."

"Wherever you wish."

"Well, I suggest either Beersheba or Beit Gubrin [which had defined the eastern tip of the Faluja pocket until it fell to the Israelis just after Beersheba's capture]."

Nasser looked puzzled. "But they're in our hands," he said. "We have taken them back."

Cohen suddenly realized that the Faluja officers had been completely misled by Cairo propaganda.

"Sir," he said, "since October 21, Beit Gubrin and Beersheba have been in our hands. And I'm telling you this from personal knowledge since I have been in both places since their capture."

"Impossible!" Nasser persisted. "They are in *our* hands!"

"Well, there's no use arguing if you don't want to be convinced. How about Kibbutz Gat? You *know* that's in our hands. Say, at three o'clock this afternoon?"

The Egyptians agreed.

"Clean up the one room that hasn't been destroyed or damaged," Cohen ordered the settlement commander on arrival at Kibbutz Gat. "Also, clear the area of debris. The whole Egyptian command is coming . . . And dig up cold drinks and fruit, and tell the cook to bake some cookies. We've got to be hospitable."

The commander stared oddly at Cohen. "Are you mad?" he said. "This war's been too much for you. The whole Egyptian command . . . fruit and cookies . . . you need a furlough!"

"I'm telling you they're coming!" Cohen replied impatiently. Then he telephoned Allon.

"Yigal, be here at Kibbutz Gat at three-thirty this afternoon."

"Why?"

"They're coming."

"Who's coming?"

"The Egyptian commander and other officers."

"Are you crazy?"

"Come and find out for yourself."

"Then *they* must be crazy, risking a trap like that!"

Cohen drove to the agreed meeting place on the road, where he found three Egyptian jeeps, each with a white flag, waiting for him. Nasser introduced him to Taha and four other officers, and the party followed him to the kibbutz.

As the guests approached, they saw what the Israelis wanted them to see—tractors plowing the fields, people working in the vegetable garden, life going on normally. They were greeted at the gate by two saluting military policemen, and further on by Rabin and other officers of the southern command, whom Cohen introduced without giving their names. (It was Israeli policy to keep secret the names of commanders and their units to prevent an analysis of any particular unit's military behavior.) One of the officers quietly asked Taha if he would speak privately with the Israeli commander, but he refused, apparently not wishing to arouse any suspicion among his subordinates of involvement in any secret agreement.

Entering the conference room, the visitors found Allon at the head of the table, on which stood a vase of flowers. Allon, after being introduced by Cohen as "General Yesha'ya Bergstein" (his underground name during the British mandate), welcomed his guests in Arabic.

"We would prefer," Taha said as he sat down, "to speak in English."

Allon agreed, but unhappily, since he and some of the other Israeli officers knew little or no English. He would have to speak Hebrew, using Cohen as an interpreter, though the latter was not confident he could communicate every nuance. Arabic in Egypt was spoken mainly by the *fellahin,* not by members of the middle or upper classes, who usually conversed in English or French among themselves, regarding Arabic as a peasant language.

"Colonel," Allon began, "allow me to extend to you my compliments on your soldiers' courage. The capture of Iraq es-Suweidan and other places was costly . . . "

Taha: "Thank you, sir, and I must say that the tenacity of your forces astonished me and put me in a very difficult position."

Allon: "Is it not tragic for two sides, who actually have no reason to fight, to set upon each other mercilessly?"

Taha: "A real tragedy, but that is the way of the world. Fate is fate, and there is no avoiding it."

Allon: "I hope that you have noted that this war was imposed on us by force. It is being fought here in our country, not in Egypt. It is clear that we are winning and it would be better to put an end to the fighting."

Taha: "Perhaps. But I, as an officer, can only carry out my government's commands."

Allon: "It would be worth your while to realize that you are fighting a war without any hope of winning, and that all your efforts will be in vain. In your own country, the British army is in control. We have just gotten rid of them."

Taha: "You have astonished us with your success in ousting the British. It will not be long before we throw them out of our country, too."

Allon: "But how will you get rid of them if your whole army is stuck here, after a great defeat . . . ? Do you not feel that it would be best for you to go home to Egypt and look after your own problems, instead of getting mixed up in troubles in a land which is not your own?"

Taha: "As long as my government orders me to fight here, I will do so. When I am told to make peace, I will do so. When I am told to go back to Egypt and fight the British, I will do it with pleasure and as ordered."

Allon: "I have a high regard for your obedience, Colonel; that is the way of a soldier. I also must obey my government's orders without question. All the same, it seems to me that you should inform your commander, or prove to him, that there is no hope for you in this war. I do not try to hide my thoughts, my problems, and my worries, or my demands for the right to fight from my government. But this does not mean that I am defying the law of the land. Only through such frankness can there be an alliance between statesmanship and military strategy."

Taha: "There is no doubt that the position on the front and in Egypt is clear to my government, and I am sure that they will do everything that is necessary."

Allon: "This was surely your belief when you invaded Palestine, and see how wrong your leaders were. If not for the intervention of the United Nations, the Egyptian army would have been completely crushed by now, including your brave and courageous brigade. You must understand, Colonel, that the situation at the front has been settled. Your brigade is now besieged on all sides, and has no hope of breaking out. It is my duty to avail myself of any opportunity to destroy your formation. What purpose would be served by your desperate stand? The fate of the second half of the pocket will not differ from that of the first . . . "

Taha was silent for a moment, then replied: "Yes, sir, I see. But as long as I have soldiers and ammunition there is no reason why I should stop fighting."

Allon realized that he was confronting an obstinate fighter. Nevertheless, he resorted to diplomacy again.

"I greatly admire your courage, Colonel, but do you not agree that the lives of men are precious, and that there is no logic in sacrificing your men fighting a nation that does not consider itself your enemy, and which has only good intentions toward you? I am not advising you to surrender dishonorably, but with full respect and military honor, with the possibility of an immediate return home. Think about it. Let us save the blood of our soldiers and cease fighting. I cannot cease firing as long as foreign armies are on our soil. But you do not fight on your soil. Try to understand that I am right."

A tense silence gripped the gathering as Taha hesitated. Allon and the other Israelis looked at him expectantly, seeing in his dark eyes the torment of a man torn between logic and pride. Nasser and the other Egyptians watched him anxiously, wondering why he hesitated when only one reply was possible. Finally, Taha gave it. In a quiet voice charged with suppressed emotion, he said, staring directly at Allon:

"Sir, there is no doubt that your position is much better than mine. The planning of your operation and the performance of your soldiers have been admirable. You have broken through our strongest lines, and you have put to shame the Egyptian army, which had never before tasted defeat. I do not flatter myself by thinking that I can possibly change the existing situation to our advantage. But there is one thing that I can save— the honor of the Egyptian army. And that is why I shall fight until the last bullet and the last soldier, unless I receive different orders from my government."

There was another brief silence, and the Israelis looked as moved as the Egyptians.

"As a soldier," Allon then responded, "I can understand your sentiments well, but you must know that under extraordinary circumstances a local commander must take responsibility for decisions, as Von Paulus did at Stalingrad. Believe me, Colonel, your government would have little reason to criticize a soldier of your caliber. Consider your men and your country, and lay down your arms."

Taha replied without hesitation this time: "No, sir, I have no alternative but to continue fighting. It is clear that I must preserve the honor of the Egyptian army."

Allon then urged with a smile: "May I ask you to give your government and your commanders a description of the real situation and to request their consent to your surrender?"

"I will send a full report of our talks to them."

With the tension eased, Allon said: "Gentlemen, help yourselves to refreshments."

As they all took sandwiches and cookies from the table, as if at a meeting of Rotary Club officers, Nasser said to Taha: "May I ask a question of the Israeli commander?"

Taha glanced at Allon and replied: "Please ask, and I'm sure that if your question does not deal with military secrets you will receive an answer."

Nasser then inquired with a smile: "Is the emblem on your lapel showing two sheaves of wheat and a sword that of the Palmach?"

Allon debated for a moment how to answer, realizing that the identity of Israeli fighting organizations was supposed to be a secret. But he guessed that Nasser probably knew anyway.

"Yes," he said. "I see that you are a good intelligence officer."

"How do you know that I am an intelligence officer?"

"Because I have good intelligence."

"Now I understand our difficulties," said Nasser, smiling. "We've been fighting the Palmach!"

After an hour and a half, the meeting ended and the Israelis accompanied the Egyptians to their jeeps. As Taha climbed into his vehicle, Allon said: "I am pleased to have met you, Colonel. If you should wish to see me again, you can always send a messenger. May we meet in better times."

"May we meet in peacetime," Taha replied, saluting.

Cohen then escorted the party back to Faluja, and as he bid goodbye to Taha, inquired: "Sir, may I ask why you took such a chance in coming to speak with us, when we are your enemy? Weren't you afraid of a trap?"

The Colonel replied casually: "Major Nasser told me about you, and I was convinced that he trusted you completely. So I didn't hesitate to go. And now we see that I was not mistaken."

As Cohen drove off he was exhilarated by a feeling of deep respect, and even affection, for the Faluja leaders. Then suddenly he felt depressed. He would now have to try once more to kill them if he could.[5]

And as Taha stepped into his jeep, he said to Nasser: "Gamal, we were guests at that settlement. Let's not shell it any more."

On his return to Faluja, Taha immediately radioed a message to GHQ about the meeting:

> Having negotiated with the Jews, we found that they insist upon unconditional surrender. They will not let us withdraw until the whole Egyptian army leaves Palestine. If you do not find a solution within 24 hours, I regret to say that I shall no longer be able to control the situation. Aircraft would not help. The enemy's air force has complete control over the whole front. Let me know your decision by tonight.[6]

Taha then went to visit the wounded in the hospital, a makeshift mud structure, as he did almost daily to keep up morale. While he chatted with his men, a sergeant walked up with a radio message. Taha read it and smiled. It was from King Farouk, announcing that Taha had been promoted to Brigadier.

Taha was convinced that he had to continue fighting, but also that supplies had to get through to the pocket at any cost, and he pleaded with general headquarters to infiltrate Israeli lines with a convoy. The request was sympathetically received by the new Egyptian supreme commander, General Fuad Sadek. He had arrived in Gaza on November 11 to replace General Mawawi (who had become a symbol of the Egyptian catastrophe in the Negev) and gave first priority to boosting the morale of his dispirited troops. Sadek had already taken one step by recommending an immediate promotion for Taha; a daring breach of the blockade, he felt, would now do more than anything else to raise their spirits. The 2,000 or so Israelis surrounding the pocket were concentrated at scattered approaches and infiltration was by no means impossible.

Three days after his arrival in Gaza, Sadek called in Zakaraya Muhieddin, who had recently been promoted to Major.

"I have good news for you, Zakaraya," he said. "I want you to lead a supply convoy to Faluja. You'll be accompanied by Major Salah Salem and two local Bedouins. It's a dangerous mission, I know, but I'm sure you want to lead it."

Muhieddin beamed. "I welcome this mission," he said eagerly. "And I know the Faluja area well."

At 6 P.M. that evening, Muhieddin and Salem, wearing Bedouin robes over their uniforms, started out on the 35-mile trek to Faluja, with two Bedouin guides leading two mules and a horse. They marched across sand dunes through a driving rain, until they finally reached a valley that led into Faluja, now only about half a mile away.

The problem was to get through the valley, about 200 yards wide, without being noticed by Israeli forces on the two hills flanking it. They waited until the moon disappeared behind a small cloud, then dashed ahead —until one of the mules lay down and refused to budge. After several minutes of desperate pulling, they heard vehicles approaching, followed by shots. The Bedouins promptly ran off in panic, and so did the animals, including the now frightened reluctant mule. The two officers then dashed through the mud, slipping, falling, stumbling, hiding behind rocks and in shallow pits.

At dawn, Lieutenant Saad el-Gammal, recovering from wounds received shortly after his stand near Karatiya, was just awakening in his trench on the outer edge of the Faluja pocket when he heard a shot. He picked up his radiophone and demanded: "What's happened?"

"We saw some people moving near the post," came the answer.

Gammal rushed to the outpost and heard a voice in the weeds moaning: "Don't shoot. It's Muhieddin and Salem."

As the two men (who had been expected earlier by another route) crawled to the post, their faces gaunt and pale, Gammal asked: "What happened? Where are the mules?"

"I'd say they're probably in Tel Aviv by now," Muhiedden gasped as he collapsed in the mud.

The mere arrival of the two men, even without the supplies, considerably raised morale in Faluja, for it showed that the Israeli siege could, if with difficulty, be breached. Indeed, Egypt and the Arab League began considering means of cracking the blockade completely. The trouble was that Egypt could never be sure whether the would-be helper intended to help Egypt or itself at the expense of Egypt. Nor did the would-be helpers trust each other.

After several tentative plans had fallen through, Glubb Pasha suggested what he called the "Damascus Plan."

The plan was simple, he told Arab military leaders in Amman. On a night agreed upon, the Egyptians would walk out of Faluja to the east guided by an Arab Legion officer who knew a secret road. Two Iraqi battalions and one Arab Legion battalion would advance in the Beit Gubrin area to meet them and engage from the rear any Jewish forces attempting to bar the way.

"What about the heavy equipment in Faluja?" an Egyptian officer asked.

"It would have to be abandoned or destroyed."

"And who is the officer who would guide us?"

"Major Lockett."

Geoffrey Lockett, in Glubb's view, was just the man for the job. In peacetime, he appeared to be a nervous wreck and could often calm himself only with alcohol. But give him a war—he had wandered from one war to another over the years—and he needed no other tonic, particularly if the risks were great. Now Lockett had volunteered to infiltrate the Israeli lines, and Glubb felt confident that he could do it.

The Egyptian High Command in Cairo considered the plan—and found itself in a dilemma.

A successful breakout from Faluja to Hebron could change the course of the war, General Osman el-Mahady said at one meeting. The Jews would then find themselves facing strong forces on the western coast, in the east, and in the south, and might be forced to withdraw from Beersheba.

But the fate of the forces in Faluja would be in the hands of Abdullah and Glubb, another officer argued. Why should they want to facilitate the occupation of Hebron by strong Egyptian forces; or to put these troops in a position possibly to reoccupy Beersheba? Did they not want to control these places themselves?

The question on everybody's mind was: Would Major Lockett lure them into a trap?

While Cairo considered the plan, Glubb sent Lockett on a test-run trip to Faluja on November 20 over the "secret road," accompanied by an Arab corporal, and the two men arrived there safely. Taha greeted Lockett warmly, and Lockett outlined the details of the Damascus Plan. Taha said skeptically as he took Lockett on an inspection of positions: "It sounds risky to me. The Jews could annihilate us."

"You've got to take the risk."

"Let's go to my headquarters. I'll call General Sadek."

Taha radioed Sadek and explained Lockett's proposal.

"I don't like the idea," was Sadek's response. "But don't let him know yet. We might as well get something out of this. Tell him to prove to us that he can infiltrate the enemy lines with a large caravan by bringing you forty-five or fifty camels loaded with food and supplies. Say that if he succeeds in doing that, we'll see about the plan."

Taha did as instructed and Lockett said: "Very well, I hope to be back here in a few days—with forty-five camels!"

When Lockett had left, Taha received orders directly from Cairo to prepare to execute the Damascus Plan, the High Command having finally

decided that the rewards were great enough to warrant the gamble. Taha
was deeply concerned. He was responsible for the lives of his men; for all
he knew, there might be collusion between Abdullah and the Israelis. He
immediately radioed Sadek and informed him of the order.

"What?" Sadek exclaimed, his thin, black face taut with fury. "They
gave you orders without consulting me? My answer is No. And if Cairo
insists, I'm going to resign!"

Sadek, like Taha, was a proud, tough soldier. Also half Sudanese and
half Arab, he had fought bravely under the British against the Abyssinians
and Sudanese during World War I and had received a spear wound in the
Sudan. At this late stage in his career, he would not play what he regarded
as the pawn's role of his malleable predecessor, General Mawawi, who
had permitted himself, in his view, to be ordered around and humiliated.
He immediately cabled the High Command in Cairo that he opposed acceptance of the Damascus Plan, and that if it continued to bypass him with
orders to the Faluja command he would resign. Receiving no reply, he
assumed that he had won his point.

Before dawn one morning, a sergeant dashed into Taha's headquarters
and shouted: "Sir, sir, they've arrived!"

Taha, who had been sleeping on a blanket on the floor, sat up and asked:
"Who's arrived?"

"The camels! There must be a hundred!"

Taha rushed out to meet Major Lockett who, accompanied by a British
demolition expert and a Moslem Brotherhood officer, had infiltrated the
Israeli lines with 45 camels piled high with supplies.

"Well, here I am," Lockett said, smiling. "Just like I said."

Taha grinned broadly. He couldn't help but admire the man for what he
regarded as an incredible feat. On second thought, however, he began to
wonder whether the feat had not been a little too incredible. Was it possible
that the Israelis had not seen the long, lumbering caravan? Could there
have been some kind of deal . . . ?

"The sergeant here," said Lockett, "will help you destroy all your big
equipment before we break out of here."

Taha radioed Sadek that Lockett had arrived with the camels and
requested instructions.

"It is impossible to rely on a plan initiated by Glubb Pasha," Sadek
replied, "and it is impossible to keep the details of the plan from the Jews
if it originated in Amman. The evacuation of the troops by foot through
areas held by Jews means a massacre of these troops. Reject the plan and
expel the drunkard Lockett. It will not bring honor to our army but will

be a grave disaster. Defend your positions to the last bullet and to the last man."

Sadek then suggested that Taha should keep most of the camels for meat and send the walking wounded back with Lockett "so you won't have so many mouths to feed."

Lockett was enraged when he heard the news. "Didn't I bring the camels as you asked?" he cried. "Do you all want to die here?"

"I'm sorry, Major," Taha said coolly, "but orders are orders."

The same night, Lockett's party, including several wounded men, started out for Hebron again, but they had gone only a few miles when they found themselves surrounded by car headlights.

Lieutenant Saad el-Gammal, one of the wounded men, shouted: "Scatter and run for your life!"

As the group dashed off in all directions, Israeli police dogs howled in the night, hungry for a catch. Gammal and five others jumped into a deep ditch; then, when all was clear, they continued their trek.

Three days later, they straggled into an Arab village near Hebron, and collapsed by a dirty pond to gulp down worm-infested water. Gammal, as he sat up and wiped his mouth, muttered: "That was a trap. What they wouldn't have done to our forces if they had broken out!"

In Faluja, Taha sat with his men around a fire supervising the roasting of a camel. "If I weren't so hungry I'd like to see Major Lockett rather than that camel roasting over the fire!" he said, smacking his lips.

And in Israeli general headquarters, a soldier rushed to deliver a message to Yadin that Taha's forces had not tried to break out of Faluja after all—despite all the radio talk about the Damascus Plan that had been intercepted.

A̶T the United Nations conference in Paris, Britain—still counting on the Bernadotte Plan to give her Negev bases—feverishly pushed for a resolution that would slap sanctions on Israel if she did not withdraw from the newly conquered areas. American delegates agreed with Britain that pressure for a cease-fire should be exerted on Israel, but felt that the application of sanctions was entirely unrealistic, not only because of domestic politics but because sanctions could not be implemented and, in any event, could be rendered useless by Russian unilateral aid to Israel.

The State Department therefore suggested to Truman that the United States should propose amendments to the British resolution, calling on both sides to return, not necessarily to the old cease-fire boundaries, but to "provisional" ones to be determined by acting United Nations mediator Ralph Bunche. A belligerent who refused to obey such an order would be subject not specifically to sanctions, but to "appropriate action" under Article 42, Chapter VII of the United Nations Charter, which could mean sanctions, but would more likely take the form of wrist-tapping.

The White House agreed that these suggestions might produce language strong enough to prevent a serious Anglo-American split at a time when unity was essential in the cold war crisis, but obscure enough to permit Israel to emerge unscathed, or almost so, if she disobeyed the resolution.

"The President approves the draft resolution incorporating the suggestions indicated by the State Department," Clark Clifford informed Lovett in a memorandum on October 27.

And on November 4, immediately after Truman's stunning reelection, the Security Council, with American support, passed the resolution—calling on both sides in the conflict to withdraw to the boundaries they had held before the Israeli Negev offensive started.

As Bunche negotiated with Israel for a withdrawal, Britain increased her pressure to apply sanctions if Israel did not cooperate.

On November 15, Prime Minister Attlee invited American Ambassador Douglas to Chequers for tea and told him with considerable emotion that his government thought the situation in Palestine presented dangers as great and immediate to world peace and to Anglo-American cooperation as Berlin.

Britain, he said, regarded enforcement of the November 4 resolution as crucial. In this matter, he went on—employing with unintentional irony the argument so often used by those who had accused Britain of trying to sabotage the original partition resolution—the British government believed that the future of the United Nations itself was at stake. If Israel flouted the authority of the United Nations, the organization should lift the embargo on the Arabs, isolate Israel economically, and possibly even blockade her. Attlee then warned that if the Jews attacked Transjordan or Egyptian territory, the British government would, in any event, give armed aid to the Arabs. And in the case of Transjordan, Britain might even feel it necessary to attack the Israelis within Palestine.

Attlee sipped his tea while Douglas absorbed these words.

Two days later, on November 17, Douglas cabled Lovett in part:

... WHILE THE BRITISH JCS [Joint Chiefs of Staff] HOPES [Israel] WILL BE FRIENDLY, IT HAS CONCLUDED THAT IT WOULD BE UNSAFE TO RELY UPON [Israel] TO GIVE BRITISH AIR INSTALLATIONS IN NEGEV WITH FREE ACCESS THERETO ...

Douglas suggested that President Truman, in order to avoid a major British-American crisis, should reevaluate his statement that the United

States would refuse to support modifications in the partition resolution unless they were "fully acceptable to the State of Israel."[7]

But Attlee and Douglas were unaware at the time that Israel, with Bunche's help, had already won the diplomatic battle. Bunche at first proposed to the Israelis the establishment of a neutralized zone in the Negev south of the east-west road, and the appointment of an Egyptian civil governor in Beersheba. Ben-Gurion dismissed this proposal as a "penalization of Israel for an attempt to recover the Negev, which was assigned to the Jewish State by the partition resolution," and a "reward to Egypt for its contemptuous violation" of that resolution.

Bunche realized that Israel would risk sanctions rather than give an inch. And he also took note of a secret report by General William Riley, the United Nations chief military representative in Palestine, that "if the Jews so desire, they could undoubtedly clear all of Palestine of Arab forces in a relatively short time." That was exactly what the Israelis would do, Bunche felt, if some kind of agreement was not reached.

Thus, on November 17, 24 hours before the time limit for obeying the November 4 resolution, Bunche told Abba Eban at a tense meeting: "I think I can suggest an arrangement that we can both agree on."

Early the next morning, the Security Council received a cable from Tel Aviv that Israel had withdrawn her mobile forces in the Negev—but retained her garrisons in the settlements. As for Beersheba, the cable said, security considerations required the retention of troops there. Israel thereby continued to occupy the Negev, if in a less obvious way.

"This satisfies the terms of the November 4 resolution," Bunche, the realist, blandly told the Security Council.

"We've been tricked!" a British delegate growled.

Then came more bad news for Britain. She had hoped to delay a vote by the United Nations Political Committee on the Bernadotte Plan until the "withdrawal" resolution had cleared the Negev of Israelis. But now she attempted to bull the plan through the committee—only to have it flatly rejected. Ironically, even the Arab bloc voted against the plan, though General Fuad Sadek, seeing it as a way out of his impossible military situation, had pleaded with Arab League secretary-general Azzam Pasha in Cairo to support it.

"Do you think I want to get killed?" was Azzam's reaction.[8]

After the vote, Harold Beeley, the suave chief architect of Britain's pro-Arab policy, rushed out of the committee room and met Minister of State Hector NcNeil in the corridor.

"This is a complete disaster!" Beeley shouted.[9]

The decision thus ended all effective diplomatic efforts to deprive Israel of territory won in war. After a national election in January, 1949, which produced Israel's first permanent government, the United States granted the country *de jure* diplomatic recognition and arranged a large export-import bank loan. And on May 11, 1949, the United Nations voted to admit into its ranks the state it had helped to spawn.

17

The Road to El Arish

KING Abdullah, wearing regal robes and a tightly wound, snow-white turban, sat upright in a thronelike chair as the notables waited their turn to greet him with a kiss on the hand. They had just come from Jericho where, earlier that day, December 1, they had attended a historic conference that voted to fuse Transjordan and the Arab-controlled sector of Palestine into a unified nation—to be called "Jordan." With the Arab Legion in control of Arab Palestine, there were few audible protests in that area.

Egypt and Syria immediately denounced the decision and Iraq would not support it; these states all backed the Mufti-dominated shadow Palestine government that had been set up under Egyptian auspices in Gaza a month before. But Abdullah was willing to face the jealous wrath of the other Arab States. He only regretted that they had forced him into war with the Jews when Israel would have permitted him to absorb Arab Palestine without fighting. For, as a result of battle, he had lost at least temporarily certain areas, such as Ramle and Lydda, which would have been his under the partition plan. Still, the war permitted him to absorb the Old City of Jerusalem, which was to have been internationalized under the plan. He had achieved a long-cherished goal. He was King of Jerusalem, the hallowed city where his father was buried. And this was a vital step toward the creation of the Greater Syria that he envisaged as his future empire.

As the delegates knelt around him, describing the "enthusiasm" evoked by the fusion resolution, Abdullah smiled and pulled at his small brown beard in satisfaction.

638

"I consider your resolution a gift from God," he said magnanimously.[1]

A gift he had sought ever since the train had pulled into a desert station near Amman that steamy day in 1921 . . .

SIR ALEC KIRKBRIDE MUMBLED TO HIMSELF AS HE AND MEMbers of his ruling council waited restlessly at the station. This was ridiculous! He was the administrator of this part of British-controlled Transjordan (called Moab) and yet he was standing, hat in hand, awaiting a trainful of "invaders" who were to take over his territory! When Kirkbride had heard that Emir Abdullah was about to invade Transjordan with a private army of some 2,000 men, he had sent a message to the High Commissioner in Jerusalem asking for instructions.

He had only 50 policemen who might resist if ordered to do so, he had written. Should he just say to Abdullah: "Sir, welcome to Transjordan!"

The High Commissioner, dreadfully unhelpful, had cabled back:

IT IS CONSIDERED MOST UNLIKELY THAT THE EMIR ABDULLAH WILL ADVANCE INTO TERRITORY WHICH IS UNDER BRITISH CONTROL FULL STOP!

The day after this cable arrived, Kirkbride learned that the Emir was on his way to Amman.

So here he was waiting for the train, his dark pompadour ruffled in the desert breeze. He wondered what kind of man he was meeting. An angry, ambitious man, certainly. With the Arab lands freed from Turkish rule in World War I, his father, King Hussein of the Hejaz (later Saudi Arabia), had envisaged a great Arab empire led by himself. If he died before this project materialized, his eldest son Ali was to succeed him, while his second son Abdullah was to be King of Iraq, and his third son Faisal, King of Syria. Faisal had managed to talk the Syrians into accepting him as King in 1918, but Abdullah, finding it hard to win Iraqi support, served, while waiting for his royal domain, as his father's Minister for Foreign Affairs.

Then, suddenly, this whole British-backed family plan began to fall through. Faisal, ejected by the French from his new kingdom in 1920, was about to be accepted by the Iraqis as their King. This left Abdullah out in the royal cold. And now he was hungry for at least the crumb of Transjordan, undeveloped and landlocked though it was. And his hunger was enhanced by the feeling that the British (who had supported the plan in return for his father's agreement to fight the Turks) owed it to him.

Kirkbride hoped that Lawrence had misjudged Abdullah, whom the great British desert fighter, during the struggle against the Turks, had considered to be less a leader than a capricious, indolent poet and prankster. When Abdullah, in Lawrence's view, should have

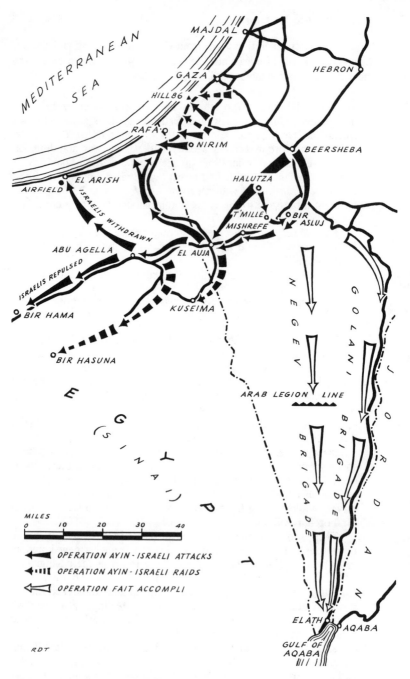

MEDITERRANEAN SEA

MAJDAL

HEBRON

GAZA

HILL 86

RAFA

NIRIM

BEERSHEBA

EL ARISH
AIRFIELD

HALUTZA

ISRAELIS WITHDRAWN

T'MILLE
MISHREFE

BIR
ASLUJ

ABU AGELLA

EL AUJA

ISRAELIS REPULSED

N E G E V

G O L A N I

J O R D A N

BIR HAMA

KUSEIMA

ARAB   LEGION   LINE

BIR HASUNA

B R I G A D E

B R I G A D E

E G Y P T
(S I N A I)

MILES

0   10   20   30   40

⬅◀ OPERATION AYIN - ISRAELI ATTACKS

◀•III OPERATION AYIN - ISRAELI RAIDS

◁ OPERATION FAIT ACCOMPLI

RDT

ELATH
AQABA

GULF OF
AQABA

OPERATIONS AYIN AND FAIT ACCOMPLI

been fighting, he remained in his big cool tent reading newspapers, eating sumptuously, sleeping, or playing games—usually chess or practical jokes. He had stabbed one particular aide with thorns, stoned him, dropped sun-heated pebbles down his back, set him on fire, and shot a coffeepot off his head from 20 yards away, finally giving him three months' wages as payment for his sporting cooperation.

Such thoughts only confirmed in Kirkbride's mind the wisdom of holding his hat in his hand.

The train pulled in at last and Emir Abdullah, followed by his aides, descended, wrapped in Bedouin robes. After the British officials and the "invasion" leaders had shaken hands and inquired after each other's health, Kirkbride, towering over the Emir, said: "We have come to welcome Your Highness officially to the territory under our control."

Abdullah replied: "Thank you, thank you. I come here with the friendliest sentiments toward the people of this country, whom I regard as my brothers, and toward Great Britain, by whose side we fought to liberate the beloved homeland from its oppressors."

"Am I correct," Abdullah then asked Kirkbride, "in assuming that you are here to welcome me on behalf of the government of Great Britain?"

"Hmm," Kirkbride responded, seeking a diplomatic answer as he observed Abdullah's troops pouring out of the train. "Well, as a matter of fact, I came with my colleagues here to meet Your Highness as the council of the national government of Moab. I expect that His Majesty's government will send a representative, in due course, who is more senior than myself."

Abdullah smiled and said politely: "I could not wish to be welcomed by anyone more acceptable than yourself . . . I trust that you will remain to give me your support and advice in the difficult days which are to come. By the way, has the national government of Moab ever been recognized internationally?"

"I feel," Kirkbride said carefully, "that the question is largely of an academic nature now that Your Highness is here."

"Ah, I was sure that we understood each other!"[2]

Shortly thereafter, Moab and the other administrative districts of Transjordan passed away painlessly as Abdullah consolidated his hold on the area. By May, 1921, a few months after his arrival, even Winston Churchill, the British Colonial Minister, was ready to recognize the *fait accompli.*

Abdullah and Churchill charmed each other from the moment they met at dinner in Jerusalem's Government House during a visit by Churchill to Palestine. When the meal was over, the Emir took some snuff from a green and gold enameled box, and Churchill, his curiosity aroused, also took some and sneezed violently. Everyone laughed, and Abdullah found the occasion almost as stimulating as when he had dropped hot pebbles down his aide's back.

At a meeting the next morning, Churchill agreed to support Abdullah's claim to Transjordan, which had until then been administered as a part of Palestine and intended to serve as a reserve of land for the resettlement of Arabs when the Jewish national home became an accomplished fact.

"I propose," Abdullah said, hoping to win control of the rest of Palestine as well, "the formation of a single Arab State out of Palestine and Transjordan."

"We cannot agree," Churchill demurred. "Such a state could not be reconciled with the British government's promises to the Jews."

"The people of Palestine," Abdullah responded, "reject the Balfour Declaration and insist on the retention of the Arab character of Palestine . . . The Arabs are not like trees, which, when cut, grow again . . ."[3]

Now, almost 30 years later, Abdullah, as he sat surrounded by his supporters, was realizing at least part of his dream—the union of Transjordan and a section of Palestine. And while he still believed that the Arabs were not like trees, as a politician he had developed certain treelike qualities. He was ready to bend with the fierce Zionist wind.*

Israel, meanwhile, reveled in her victory at the United Nations, which cleared the way for a final campaign to drive the Egyptians out of Palestine once and for all. Israeli leaders felt that such a campaign was necessary to force Egypt to the peace table and to make sure that when she came she would be faced with a *fait accompli:* an Israeli Negev from one end to the other. Israel, therefore, was not at all disappointed when rumors of immediate Egyptian willingness to talk peace proved hollow. For the Jewish State, the time was not quite ripe, either.

Nor did the Israelis lack an excuse for a new offensive, one that they had unwittingly helped to create by refusing to let supplies enter the Faluja pocket. With the besieged troops there facing starvation, Egyptian forces in the south felt compelled to launch attacks that would relieve the pressure on Faluja. In late November and early December, 1948, Egyptian units thus advanced eastward from the coast into the Israel-controlled desert and managed to establish a series of positions.

* Glubb Pasha told me that King Abdullah once explained his attitude to him by quoting an old Turkish proverb: "If you meet a bear while crossing a shaky bridge, call to her: 'Dear Auntie!'"

The Israeli High Command met on December 10 to discuss plans for taking advantage of the Egyptian initiative. Members agreed to eliminate the bulge into the desert first, and then to launch a big offensive.

Yadin immediately issued a directive for Operation Ayin (meaning the Hebrew letter *A,* which appeared in the names of the major targets— El Auja, Bir Asluj, and Aza, the Israeli name for Gaza). He declared its objective to be the "defeat of the invading enemy force and its expulsion from the boundaries of the country."

Ben-Gurion then set about making sure that King Abdullah would not interfere with the operation, dangling the prospect of a peace accord before his eyes.

The day the directive was issued (December 10), Colonel Abdullah Tel, who some weeks before had been "kicked upstairs" from the command of the Arab Legion's 6th Regiment to the military governorship of Jerusalem, received a telephone call at his headquarters from the chief United Nations observer.

"Colonel Dayan," the observer said, "would like to meet you in the de-militarized zone about an important matter. Would you come right away to Mandelbaum Gate?"

Tel immediately left for the rendezvous and found Dayan waiting for him. The two men saluted and greeted each other cordially, Tel's aristocratic bearing clashing somewhat with Dayan's blunter manner. (Since late November, they had met several times and had agreed on a "sincere" cease-fire for Jerusalem on December 1.)

"I have a very urgent message for His Majesty from an important Israeli official," Dayan announced, handing Tel an envelope. "Nobody should open it except the King."

"Of course," Tel assured him.

As Tel left, he was tantalized. What important person was contacting the King? And what was he proposing? Was this part of the conspiracy? Curiosity aggravated his torment, bringing into sharp relief the struggle raging in his mind. How long could he, an ardent Arab nationalist, play a role in what he was certain was a British imperialistic plot? How long could he take orders from Glubb Pasha, who had relieved him of his military command and was using the King for his own ends?

It would be so much easier if he didn't feel so strongly bound to the King. His Majesty had plucked him from obscurity and promoted him over officers senior to him despite Glubb's objections, treating him like a son. The King trusted him, and he was grateful. But the King's desire for personal power, he felt, had blinded him to the pan-Arab nationalism that was burning in every Arab's soul. He himself strongly supported the King's cherished aim—an Amman-led Greater Syria embracing Transjordan, Syria, and at least a part of Palestine. But in striving for this goal, it should be seen in the context of Arab unity, not as a matter of personal power.

Which was the more binding loyalty, Tel dared to ask himself as he wound his way through the Old City. Did his debt to the King supersede that to his country and the Arab world? Of course, he could go on serving the King—falsely, using His Majesty's trust to keep abreast of his, and Glubb's, plans in order to be able to thwart them. Or he could simply resign and give up his access to the palace. But then he would be serving neither the King nor Arab nationalism. No, he would cling to his present position for a while. At least he might be able to modify the disastrous course Jordan was pursuing.

With darkness setting in, Tel stopped at an army control post, opened the envelope Dayan had given him, and held the message under a dim light. Handwritten in Arabic, it read:

> Your Majesty, respected and esteemed. I hope that you enjoy the best of health. I hope that God will continue to grant you good health. Sir, I arrived today in Jerusalem from Paris for a short visit to ask Your Majesty if you would grant me the honor of an audience so that we might cooperate in solving complex matters, and in achieving what all of us wish—the restoration of peace in this land that is so dear to you and to us.
>
> I hope that Your Majesty, in the prevailing situation, will send some person in whom you have trust to meet me in Jerusalem for negotiations, and I hope this person will be accompanied by our friend, Dr. Shawkat Pasha, and that this person will sincerely support the common cause. I further hope that he will be able to see me without delay—tomorrow, Saturday, if possible, since my time is very limited and I must return to Paris immediately.
>
> I hope that circumstances will permit me the honor of meeting Your Majesty at some favorable opportunity, if God permits. And I hope that the person who comes to meet me will carry your Majesty's comments concerning all matters that might guide us during our conversations.
>
> May God prolong the life of Your Majesty. Amen.
>   Sincerely, Eliahu Sasson*
>   Jerusalem, Friday, 10 Dec., 1948.

A further sentence at the end of the message added: "I met, before I left Paris, our friend Prince Abdel el-Megid Hayder, and we spoke for a long time about many things."

Hayder, the Jordanian Minister to London! So the King was secretly talking peace with the Israelis through him, Tel deduced. Yes, Abdullah Tel felt a sense of loyalty to the King; but was the King being loyal to his

---

* Eliahu Sasson should not be confused with the Israeli officer, Sasson, who met Lieutenant Gammal, his boyhood friend, on the battlefield at Karatiya.

people and to his Palestinian brethren?

Tel slipped the message into a fresh envelope, sealed it, and returned to his office. Early the next morning he drove to Amman and went to see the King at Shuneh Palace. On reading Sasson's message, the Sovereign smiled broadly and color came to his wrinkled cheeks.

"Here, read it," he said, holding it out to Tel, who took it rather self-consciously and pretended to read.

The King then shuffled out of the room, returning a short time later with Dr. Shawkat el-Satte Pasha, his personal physician.

"Read this message," he said, as Tel handed it to the doctor.

The King instructed Shawkat: "I want you to go to Jerusalem and meet Sasson to negotiate pending matters with him. Abdullah Bey will help you on technical matters."

He ordered a servant to bring him some paper, and started to dictate the subjects he wanted discussed with Sasson, while Shawkat took notes.

"Point out to him," the King emphasized, "that I am taking a great risk by negotiating, and my political opponents will make the most of it if they find out."

The King then broke off to say to Tel: "Go and show Sasson's message to Tawfiq Pasha."

Tel went to see the Prime Minister, expecting him to voice reservations about secret armistice meetings with the Israelis, but Tawfiq's response was: "The government has no objection, and His Majesty always informs us of the outcome of his personal contacts with the Jews in London and Paris. As for us, we could not negotiate openly with the Jews, of course, or we would be criticized by the other Arab States. The attitude of the government is sensitive, though we accept the outcome of any agreement His Majesty reaches with the Jews."

Tel returned to Jerusalem on noon that day, December 11, and saw Moshe Dayan, with whom he set up another meeting between the Jordanians and the Israelis for 6:30 that evening at a house in the demilitarized zone.

"Would you press these uniforms please, dear, and make sure you put a good crease in the pants."

Eliahu Sasson's wife took the crumpled United Nations uniforms. "What's this?" she asked. "You've joined the United Nations now? And what do you need two uniforms for?"

"One is for me and one is for Moshe Dayan."

"What's the matter? Moshe Dayan hasn't got a wife to press his pants for him?"

Sasson smiled. "It's for a secret mission."

"For the United Nations?"

"No, never mind. And if we come home late tonight, don't worry."

Shawkat Pasha arrived at Tel's headquarters shortly before the meeting.

"May I please see the list of topics the King wants to have discussed with the Jews?" Tel asked. He read through it: acceptance of the Jericho Conference resolution on the absorption of Arab Palestine; the return of Lydda and Ramle; the questions of Jaffa, the Negev, Galilee, Jerusalem, and Arab refugees. The King, it seemed, was simply suggesting discussion of various topics without taking positive stands.

"May I suggest, Shawkat Pasha, that you ignore the list," Tel then said, "and concentrate on three questions: the need to return Lydda and Ramle as a gesture of good will; the need to let the Arab refugees return to their homes before the planting season starts; and the need to permit the Arabs to return to their quarters in the New City."

Shawkat stared at Tel, startled. "You want me to disobey His Majesty's orders?" he asked.

Tel and Shawkat found Sasson and Dayan waiting for them at the designated house. Sasson greeted Shawkat, whom he knew well, with an embrace, and the doctor said: "His Majesty sends you his greetings. He was very pleased when your tender letter reached him."

Sasson, a heavy-set man with a quiet, gentle manner, smiled in appreciation. He had a genuinely tender feeling toward the King, as he had had toward his late brother Faisal. A newspaper editor in Syria after World War I, Sasson had become close friends with Faisal during the latter's brief reign as King of that country. In fact, Faisal had donated money to Sasson's newspaper to show his good will toward the Jews and Zionists— though it was never clear whether he was ready to accept a fully independent Jewish State or simply an autonomous national home within an Arab State. When the French threw Faisal out of Syria, they had threatened to imprison his staunch supporter, Sasson, who was forced to flee to Turkey.

In the early 1930's, after Faisal died, Sasson, who had joined the Jewish Agency, maintained contact with the Hashemite family through frequent meetings with Abdullah, and the two men came to trust each other implicitly, though Abdullah was never pro-Zionist as Faisal apparently had been.

"It is unfortunate," Shawkat lamented, "that a misunderstanding has led to armed conflict between our two countries. Mrs. Myerson did not seem to show much understanding when she visited His Majesty just before the war started. I'm sure if you had come instead there would have been greater understanding."

The men then sat down at a table, and Shawkat read out the suggested topics of conversation.

"His Majesty," he said, "would like to hear your views on these subjects."

"I can't say anything definite until I consult Tel Aviv," Sasson replied. "I suggest we hold another meeting in two days, and we shall study the topics meanwhile."

The meeting thus ended, and the two Arab representatives drove back to Amman, where they arrived close to midnight. To their surprise, the King was still up waiting for them, though he usually retired at about 9 P.M.

"Tell me, what happened?" he asked anxiously, as they walked into his lamplit study. "Were they reasonable? I want to know every detail."

His enthusiasm lapsed into disappointment when he heard that nothing of substance had been discussed.

"Well, perhaps at the next meeting," he murmured as he went off to bed, his head down.

At the next meeting, on December 13, Tel and Shawkat decided not to express their views until Sasson and Dayan had indicated theirs. Sasson removed some papers from a briefcase and dictated suggestions to Shawkat, who took hasty notes:

Israel, preferring Jordanian to local Palestinian rule, did not oppose the Jericho resolution calling for a Jordan-Arab Palestine union and indeed advised its immediate implementation to create a *fait accompli.*

The question of old and new Jerusalem should be left to future negotiations, Sasson said, adding: "And we believe that there is a solution which he and we will accept"—apparently meaning that the Jews and the Arabs would remain where they were, each in possession of a part of the city.

The King should declare a permanent armistice which would permit him to withdraw his army from all fronts, Sasson went on. "If present circumstances prevent him from declaring such a truce, a secret agreement could be reached between us. And in this case, we can assure him that we would not attack any of his posts."

The King, furthermore, should encourage the Egyptian forces south of Jerusalem and in Hebron to withdraw, in order to reduce political frictions with Israel.

Finally, Jordan should seek the withdrawal of Iraqi forces from the Israeli border. (According to Tel, Sasson advised that they be replaced by Jordanian forces that would be used for preserving internal security only. Sasson, however, denies having made such a suggestion. The question was to be of vital importance in later talks.)

After receiving these Israeli terms, Shawkat hurried back to Amman, arriving again close to midnight.

"Why are you late this time?" the King demanded, even more tense than on the previous occasion.

The two men then discussed the Israeli proposals, and the King generally approved them, being especially delighted with the Israeli attitude toward the Jericho resolution.

The next day, Shawkat went to see Sasson alone and presented the King's reactions. A new meeting at which negotiations would begin was set for December 30.

The whole Egyptian army, Israel felt, would have been driven out of the Negev by then, and the victors could press their bargaining points with Jordan more effectively since they would be free to attack along other fronts if necessary.

IMMEDIATELY after their December 10 decision to launch Operation Ayin, the Israelis hit the southern Egyptian bulge all along the line and soon broke through it, driving the enemy back to the positions it had held before its limited offensive. The Jews then relented in their attacks in order to plan for the big offensive that would presumably clear the Negev completely of Egyptian forces.

The Egyptians were deployed slightly to the north of the Sinai frontier, with two prongs reaching northward along main roads from the village of El Auja, just north of the border. The western prong curved through Rafa to Gaza, and the eastern prong swooped in a semicircle from El Auja through a chain of fortified hills to Bir Asluj, about halfway along the road leading to Beersheba. Southwest of the western curve, on the coast, lay El Arish, the principal Egyptian staging base. Southwest of El Auja, along the Sinai extension of the Beersheba–El Auja road, was Abu Agella, from where a road led west directly to El Arish.

Two Egyptian brigades were dug in along each prong, with few if any troops deployed in the desert between the two powerfully fortified lines. If the Israelis attacked, the Egyptians assumed, they would advance along the main roads since it seemed militarily out of the question that tanks and other motorized equipment could move through the sand-swept wastelands.

And this was the heart of the problem holding up the Israelis as they planned Operation Ayin; the Egyptians were waiting for them along the main roads.

"What choice have we?" Allon asked. "If we don't attack the road strongholds, we may lose our last chance to conquer the whole Negev."

"But think of the casualties," Yadin demurred.

For almost a week, the two young commanders and their aides grappled with the problem, agonizingly searching their minds and their consciences, sometimes lying awake at night and exploring imaginary maps. Was there an alternative to certain, and possibly fruitless, mass slaughter?

Then, one day, a patrol of the Negev Brigade filed a report that it had discovered a track under the shifting desert sands south of Beersheba. When Yadin received the report, he scrutinized every map he could find, but not one indicated the existence of any such road. Suddenly, it struck him—of course the road wouldn't show on a *modern* map . . .

He rushed to the archeological files in his study at home (files which his father, Dr. Yussef Sukenik, Israel's most famous archeologist, had accumulated) and pulled out a dust-covered folio containing a map of Greco-Roman Palestine. As he pored over the ancient, wrinkled document spread across his desk, his finger came to rest at a point just south of Beersheba. An expert archeologist himself, he felt a sudden surge of joy.

There it was—the old Roman road! For a moment he could envisage the long files of Roman soldiers clanking over a narrow, stone-paved path in their breastplates and arrow-crested helmets. Then he rushed back to discuss with Allon and other commanders the possibility of using that forgotten road for the attack on El Auja, showing that it in fact connected Beersheba and El Auja in an almost straight line through the ruins of the ancient Nabatean cities of Ruheiba and Halutza.

"We'd be bypassing Bir Asluj," Yadin pointed out, "and the Egyptians wouldn't know we were attacking El Auja until we were there!"

"But it's little more than a desert track," one officer commented dubiously. "Can we move all our equipment and armament along such a road?"

"We're sending out engineers to determine its feasibility for tanks. We should know by dawn."

In a few hours, the engineers reported back that they did not believe the track could be used for motorized traffic. Allon then sent Rabin with other experts to survey the road. The next day Rabin gave the High Command his assessment.

"It is difficult, but possible—after a certain amount of repair."

The commanders were elated. The main problem now was to make the repairs without the knowledge of the Egyptians.

"Our best chance," suggested one commander, "would lie in a diversionary attack on their coastal strip perhaps forty-eight hours before the main attack in the east. Most of the track probably could be made passable in the interval while the enemy's attention was focused on the coast. We could work on the last few miles during the last night."

That night, December 17, dozens of engineers set out from Beersheba into the desert to lay planks along the most difficult stretches of the old Roman road. They worked swiftly and silently, hardly daring to whisper for fear of being heard by the Egyptians manning outposts less than two miles away at some points.

Meanwhile five brigades, matching Egyptian strength in the area, prepared to launch Operation Ayin. The Golani Brigade, which had been brought down from the north, was to begin the operation with an attack on Hill 86 along the coast. In order to split the main enemy forces in a diversionary move that was to be followed up 48 hours later by the main assault from the desert track on El Auja to the east.

"The enemy braces himself, and his aim is to strike a blow at us in order to wipe out his disgrace . . . We will, therefore, nullify his plot with a crushing blow . . . "

The Golani battalion commander read the Order of the Day to his men in the late afternoon of December 22. It was almost zero hour, when the battalion would leave the abandoned Arab village of Shu'ut and head for Hill 86 south of Gaza near the coastal road. Isak Dora listened impatiently as he stood with his comrades in the village square. He didn't feel he needed a pep talk.

Finally, after Israeli planes had heavily raided Egyptian airfields and troop concentrations along the coast from Gaza to Rafa, the troops clambered into trucks with only the most essential equipment and drove without incident to a point some five miles from Hill 86. Then they slogged through the mud and by 11 P.M. had climbed to the peak.

"I can't believe it," Isak Dora marveled to a comrade as he began digging a foxhole. "We're on top of the hill, and no infantry has tried to stop us!"

"Wait. We only just got here," his companion replied.

"They've caught us by surprise!" stormed Brigadier Mohammed Neguib (who was now in charge of the newly formed Egyptian 10th Infantry Brigade group) in his headquarters about a mile from Hill 86. "We've got to throw them off at any cost. If we don't, they'll isolate and destroy our garrison in Gaza and we'll have another Faluja."

Neguib was especially determined to succeed since General Sadek had insisted that he be appointed to his new post despite efforts by General Mawawi, when supreme commander, to discredit the brigadier after the second Egyptian defeat at Negba.

"At dawn we can encircle them," said Mahmud Ra'afat, the sector commander.

"Yes. We'll use three companies and perhaps five tanks in the first assault . . . Have we got five tanks that will work?"

"We can only hope," sighed Ra'afat. "The automobile batteries with which they are equipped are not strong enough to start their engines more than a few times on a single charge."

"How can we fight a war with toys?" Neguib said bitterly. "By the time each tank recharges its battery we'll lose the advantage of surprise. We also need more mortars and artillery."

"Yes, sir. There is a problem, though. We've got to bring the guns in those four-cylinder Fiat trucks, and they keep getting stuck in the mud!"

"Oh, my God! Well, prepare to attack anyway."

"May God send you a bullet," Ra'afat jested, smiling, "if you get us into any more trouble than we're in already."

At dawn, the silence was rudely shattered as five Egyptian tanks, blasting away, slithered northward toward Hill 86, and bullets raked the Israelis from an Egyptian position atop a neighboring hill only 200 yards to the south.

Neguib sat watching in a jeep from a distance as the first tank stalled near the hill. Two men emerged and ran for cover, but one was cut down by machine-gun fire.

"There's a man still in the tank!" Neguib exclaimed to the staff officer beside him, his scholarly face taut. "Look, he seems to be wounded! He's trying to get out but he can't because of the heavy fire!"

Neguib felt that he was personally responsible for the plight of the trapped soldier. Had he not ordered the soldier to attack? The whole war seemed suddenly reduced to what would happen to that youth.

"I've got to help him!" he muttered, and he leaped from the jeep and began to crawl under heavy fire the 500 yards separating him from the tank.

He sweated and groaned as he wormed his way along. If only he were younger and stronger!

With mortar shells bursting all around him, Neguib finally reached the tank, climbed in, and started to pull the wounded man out of the hatch. Then, as a machine gun rattled, the soldier slumped to the floor and Neguib jumped to the ground to take cover behind the vehicle. Lying on his back, he felt a burning pain in his right side. He looked at his watch and could just discern the time in the strangely descending darkness—7 A.M. He unbuttoned his jacket, loosened his shirt collar, and lay semi-conscious while blood flowed from a chest wound . . .

"All right, let's carry him back to the jeep," Captain Gamal Sahber ordered two soldiers.

As the three men began to lift Neguib, he gasped: "No, let me put my arms around your shoulders. I don't want anybody to see me being carried."

At the company command post, Neguib, struggling to remain conscious, urged Ra'afat: "Continue the battle at all costs!"

"Of course," Ra'afat replied, adding hesitantly: "Please forgive me for asking God to send you a bullet. I had no idea . . . "

"Never mind," Neguib interrupted with a pale smile. "I'll forgive you on one condition. You must write down my testament and make sure that it reaches my sons."

Ra'afat took out a small notebook from his jacket pocket and wrote in it as Neguib dictated:

> Remember that your father died honorably and that his last desire was that you should avenge our defeat in Palestine and work for the unity and independence of the Nile Valley.

When Neguib had been driven to a field hospital near Rafa, a doctor felt his pulse, shook his head, and said solemnly: "No pulse. This man is dead."

An orderly then pulled a blanket over Neguib's face.

When Captain Salal el-Din Sherif, commander of the medical transportation service, heard the news he rushed over to pay his last respects. He lifted the blanket and was shocked to see the eyes blink. Then the corpse said: "How can I breathe with that thing over my head?"

By afternoon the Israelis, though having thwarted a counterattack by the tanks and infantry, were surrounded on all sides and badly shaken by the intensive enemy fire. A second counterattack started, and four enemy half-tracks spouted fire—from the first flamethrowers Egypt had used in the war.

While some defenders began to retreat, Isak Dora, whose rifle had been jammed by sand and dust, rose from his prone position and was about to throw a grenade at one of the half-tracks when he was struck by a ball of fire. Screaming, he rolled on the muddy earth to smother the flames. Then he looked up, surprised to find that he was only slightly burned, and saw the half-track on fire, the victim of its own flames.

Isak ran toward the vehicle, only some yards away, and, without thinking, leaped into it. An Egyptian, still strapped in his seat, aimed his gun but a split second later slumped back gasping with Isak's knife in his chest. A second Egyptian, the driver, was already dead. Isak grabbed a submachine gun and jumped out of the vehicle just before flames engulfed it completely. He ran back to his position to spray other Egyptians with their own weapon. As a result of such individual Israeli actions, the Egyptians retreated—except for those left hanging on the barbed wire rigid in death.

"No, I cannot do it!" General Sadek shouted over the telephone to Egyptian Defense Minister Haydar Pasha. "How can I withdraw from Gaza and leave a quarter of a million of my brothers to be slaughtered like chickens by the Jews? If we retreated to Rafa, could we hold out any better there? No, I will not withdraw no matter what happens!"

And Sadek banged down the receiver. What kind of allies did Egypt have? His government had appealed for help from the other Arab States, but all it had received were promises! Nevertheless, he would not give in. He called Ra'afat and ordered: "Hit them with everything you've got! The existence of the whole Egyptian army is at stake!"

With the Egyptians thus unaware that the attack on the coast was only diversionary, they concentrated heavy forces at Hill 86 and counterattacked again, only to be turned back, flamethrowers and all, a second time. The Israeli deputy battalion commander, Emmanuel Barache (left in command after his superior had been called to another hill), then reorganized his troops holding the northern side of the height for a desperate assault that he hoped would decide the battle.

"We only have one round of Piat ammunition left," an officer reported.

"Never mind," Barache replied. "We'll attack anyway."

But while advancing toward the Egyptian positions, the forward units halted abruptly when they saw in the distance a reserve of Egyptian armor which had not yet been committed to action.

Barache reported this discovery to brigade headquarters by radio.

"We think you should retreat," he was told.

But he continued to fight—until a bullet killed him.

According to General Sadek, captured copies of messages Barache had written indicated that the Israeli had replied to headquarters: "It would be suicide to retreat in daylight. I prefer to fight until we die."

"He was quite correct," Sadek told the author. "And he was also one of the bravest officers I've ever encountered. He knew that a retreat would permit us to shoot at his back and that from a military point of view it would be wiser to stay and fight."

At any rate, after Barache's death his replacement ordered a retreat.

An Egyptian jeep halted before a military post in Rafa and within minutes Isak Dora, who had been wounded and captured, found himself being interrogated by Egyptian officers. To every question, he gave an answer— whatever came into his half-delirious mind.

"I don't feel well," he complained after a while. "Please give me dry clothes and medical treatment."

He was surprised when the Egyptians complied immediately.

The next day, an Egyptian interrogating officer began to lose patience.

"In all this time," he shouted, "you have not given us one important bit of information."

"How can I?" Isak said almost sympathetically. "I don't know anything."

"Then we'll have to use other methods to tear the truth from you!"

Torture! But they didn't know the Jews. They didn't know that the Jews were immune to torture.

"You want to frighten me," Isak said calmly. "But you won't succeed, sir. I spent five years in a concentration camp in Germany. Do you know what that means? Are you able to do things more terrible than they did? I'm a single man without a family and I shall not leave great sorrow behind when I die."

The Egyptian officer was silent. He walked over to a window and stared at a barren scene of desert and sky stretching to infinity. What an ugly country this was! He turned and ordered a soldier: "Take him away and see that he gets proper medical care."

Shortly after the Israeli retreat, General Sadek visited Brigadier Neguib in the field hospital where he had "risen from the dead." The patient looked up and asked, almost in a whisper: "Did we win any sort of victory?"

Sadek, tears in his eyes, replied: "Yes, we forced the Jews to retreat from Hill 86. The Egyptian army is saved."

"Now I can die happily," Neguib murmured, smiling faintly.

But Neguib did not die and the Egyptian army had not been saved.

Wtext HILE Israeli units held down a large part of Sadek's forces at Hill 86 and other less important positions on the coastal strip, Allon made final plans for moving the main weight of his attack against the eastern Egyptian defense line. With their lights dimmed, convoys of the 8th Armored and Negev Brigades crawled southward from Beersheba over the old Roman road to their takeoff point at the ruins of Halutza while engineers feverishly repaired the next extension of the road to Ruheiba. The 8th Brigade was to continue along this path at about 9 A.M., December 24, to El Auja and, in the main attack, storm it on Christmas morning. Meanwhile, on Christmas Eve, a Negev unit was to turn west at Halutza and hit the T'mille Hills along the Beersheba–El Auja road to keep as much of the enemy force as possible away from El Auja. At the same time, another Negev unit would swing directly from Beersheba in a semicircle through the desert east of the road, cutting the Egyptian line at a second point further south—at Mishrefe Hill—between the T'mille Hills and El Auja.

This last unit arrived at Mishrefe Hill at about midnight.

"Hey, look, a telephone line!" an Israeli exclaimed as his patrol reconnoitered the area.

The Israelis tapped the line, and at about 3 A.M. one of them who knew Arabic heard an Egyptian commander at T'mille ask a commander at El Auja for reinforcements. The El Auja commander promised to send them. This meant the Israeli unit attacking from Halutza was apparently succeeding in its flank attack on the T'mille Hills. And once those positions fell, the highly fortified stretch of road between them and Mishrefe would be cut off from the north and the south.

"If only the El Auja commander knew," an officer commented, "that we are here in the middle to meet his reinforcements—and that in a few hours he'll need plenty of them himself!" . . .

It was just like the attack on Beersheba, Dov Segall griped to himself as he jumped out of a truck. The 9th Battalion's French-speaking Commando Company was supposed to have captured the T'mille Hills by about midnight, but here it was after 1 A.M. (December 25) and the company had only just arrived at the takeoff point for the attack. This time the guide had lost his way.

When all the men had emerged from the trucks, Teddy Eytan led them through the scrubby desert toward the hills, about two miles to the east, while the wolves howled an eerie welcome. And shortly, the company attacked the enemy holding the main hill, and finally captured it after savage fighting. At the same time, the Egyptians, in their fright, evacuated two other neighboring hills.

"Frankly, I thought it would be rougher," Eytan said—before learning that one of his three platoons had been wiped out to the last man.

He glanced at his watch. It was about 3 A.M. The rest of the 9th Battalion under commander Chaim Bar-Lev was due any minute to relieve the company.* Firing suddenly started again and Eytan ran to his headquarters bunker and radioed Bar-Lev: "We're being counterattacked! Come urgently!"

"Hold on!" a voice replied. "We're coming!"

But even as the words died, wave after wave of enemy soldiers stormed the hill . . .

A few miles west, the rest of Bar-Lev's motorized 9th Battalion was stalled on a dirt road while sappers slowly removed mines blocking the way. Because of the rugged terrain, it was impossible to go off the road. Bar-Lev's deputy, Micha Peri, urged: "Hurry! Hurry! Every second counts!"

But he knew it was hopeless to prod the men. They were working as fast as they could. Too fast for their own good. He wondered if Eytan's unit would be able to hold out—a shattered company against possibly a whole battalion . . .

"We've almost run out of ammunition," Dov Segall reported. "And there's only fourteen of us still unwounded."

Teddy Eytan remained silent as he lay on the pebbly earth peering down the hill only several feet away from an Egyptian he had just smashed to death with the butt of his Sten. The enemy at the base of the hill was regrouping for another attack.

"All right," he said finally, glancing at his watch. "It's six-thirty and those sons of bitches haven't come yet. I'm ordering a retreat."

Within minutes, the 14 able-bodied men had carried 18 wounded down the western slope and placed them in a water drainage tunnel in the desert nearby. Eytan decided that it would be impossible to retreat over flat, open ground carrying more than 10 wounded; 8 men would have to remain behind.

"Don't worry, we'll be back for you soon," the Frenchman assured them, swallowing hard.

As the able men started running with their burdens, they saw the silhouettes of the enemy against the dawn sky atop the hill they had just

* Shortly after the Six Day War in 1967, Bar-Lev replaced Yitzhak Rabin as chief of staff of the Israeli armed forces.

evacuated. But hardly had they gotten out of range of Egyptian guns when they heard a battle raging on the hill.

"The reinforcements have finally come!" Segall yelled with mixed delight and frustration.

The men rushed back toward the hill but stopped in horror when they reached the water tunnel. The Egyptians, in their few minutes of glory, had killed and ripped open the bellies of all the wounded.

Eytan and his men waited in shocked silence as a file of grimy Israelis approached them after reconquering the hill.

"Sorry we're late," Micha Peri muttered.

Eytan glared at him with seething contempt. Yes, five minutes too late.

Then he glanced down at his crepe-soled shoes as if aware for the first time that he had been shot in the toe.

"*Merde!*" he snarled to Segall beside him. "A perfectly good pair of shoes. Made to order, too."[4]

WHILE diversionary fighting raged along the main road, the chief attack force, the 8th Armored Brigade, found itself stalled on the Roman road north of El Auja, which it was supposed to capture at dawn December 25, waiting for engineers to repair the last link of the road leading to that town. So secret was its mission that carrier pigeons rather than radio were used to communicate with Allon's headquarters; but as Christmas Day stretched into night, fear grew that a surprise attack might be impossible.

"What the hell's the matter with those engineers?" demanded Desmond Rutledge, who was to lead a column of tanks, half-tracks, and armored troop carriers into El Auja. "The way they're going, we'll be greeted by the whole Egyptian army by the time we arrive!"

"It's taking longer than expected," an Israeli officer replied calmly.

"What a Christmas this was!" Rutledge said grimly, folding his arms tightly around his body to reduce the chill of the night. "Stuck in the desert, freezing, miserable, and waiting for a road to be built under the enemy's nose!"

"Never mind," the officer sympathized. "Maybe you'll enjoy a nice quiet Purim at home with your wife. Merry Christmas, anyway!"

As dawn (December 26) approached, it was decided to hitch the tanks to tractors and tow them toward El Auja. However, when these tanks were finally ready to attack an outpost south of the town, the Egyptians were fully alerted to Israeli plans—though, the Israeli commanders hoped, too late. But just in case it was the Israelis who were too late, Allon telephoned

Negev Brigade commander Sarig at the brigade's field headquarters after the Negev units had captured the T'mille Hills and other strongpoints:

"Nahum, the 8th Armored is a little behind time. We can't take any chances. I know you're supposed to be engaged in diversionary action, but push through to El Auja over the main road as rapidly as you can."

Sarig, however, had his own plans for supporting the 8th Armored Brigade in the attack on El Auja, hoping to bypass remaining strongpoints on the main road and strike from the desert.

"But, Yigal," he protested, "a direct attack over the road could be disastrous. The enemy has strongpoints along the way. Let me do it my way and I promise that by two tomorrow afternoon [December 27] I'll start firing on El Auja."

"All right," Allon agreed after a pause. "Let's hope you or somebody gets there in time."

General Sadek sat at his desk in his Gaza headquarters just before dawn on December 27 smoking nervously. What was happening at El Auja? Shortly after the Israelis had bombed the town the previous morning, he had sent a combined tank and infantry force from Rafa to El Auja but it had been stopped by a roadblock near the town and had lost much armor. Then, during the night, he had dispatched other forces from Rafa and Abu Agella. If they failed to get through at dawn—and he glanced at his watch— El Auja would almost certainly be lost. Already enemy tanks, the previous evening, had taken a desert outpost. How in the name of God had tanks ever reached El Auja when the road from Beersheba was so well fortified? Across the desert? Why, a camel could hardly make it!

Finally, at about 7:20 A.M., the telephone rang. As Sadek listened, he took the cigarette from his mouth and ground it into an ashtray. His troops had failed to get through the roadblocks, and enemy tanks and armored cars were attacking El Auja from the rear. It was funny . . . Mohammed Neguib "dying" happily . . .

"Fire at the police station on top of the hill!" Rutledge ordered his gunner, who could barely see the building through the smoke screen laid down by the Israelis to cover their advance toward the strategic hill just south of El Auja. Then Rutledge moved ahead through the smoke, leading his armored column over a carpet of wreckage toward the crest of the hill. He smiled. If all went well from now on, he might still be able to join his wife for New Year's.

While the armor smashed into the enemy rear, an infantry battalion advanced slowly toward the village itself and, after an initial repulsion, swept through the Egyptian line into the town square.

At 7:40 A.M., the commander of El Auja radioed Egyptian headquarters at Rafa: "Enemy tanks have breached positions. Urgently request reinforcements, particularly fighter planes."

At 8:05 A.M., he reported: "Enemy has captured positions."

Even so, the police station, in which the commander and most of his troops were now entrenched, continued to hold out. Having swung their guns round to the south after the initial surprise, the Egyptians fired at the Israeli armor at point-blank range and the Jews suffered many casualties. Finally, at 12:36 P.M., the Egyptians raised a white flag and their commander walked out of the heavily barricaded building to surrender, still dressed in his pajamas.

Shortly before 2 P.M., Sarig, as he had promised Allon, signalled 8th Armored Brigade headquarters: "I am ready to attack El Auja."

The reply came back: "Thanks, but don't need your help. We've taken El Auja . . . "

WHEN Allon learned that El Auja had fallen, he elatedly planned his next step. He would invade the Sinai, storm El Arish on the coast, then move northward to Rafa and Gaza, trapping almost the entire Egyptian army. The High Command had not given him orders to do this, having simply told him to take El Auja and destroy enemy forces in the Negev. But it hadn't forbidden such a move, either. Why not exploit this opportunity? For the time being, it was necessary only to inform general headquarters that he was heading toward the Sinai village of Abu Agella, a perfectly acceptable case of "hot pursuit." Besides, if he asked for approval of his plan, the High Command might say No. There would be time enough to explain everything when he got to El Arish.

When Sarig requested further orders, Allon therefore said: "There's no time for a rest, Nahum. I'm putting the tanks of the 8th Armored under your command. Link up with them at El Auja and advance as swiftly as possible to Abu Agella and El Arish."

"I was just about to suggest that," Sarig responded in delight.

Allon then cabled GHQ that the Negev Brigade and armored units "are starting toward Abu Agella today at 1400 hours [2 P.M.]," calculating that a reply could not be received before the advance started. He was right. That evening he sent another cable, reporting: "Today at 1330 hours [1:30

P.M.] our forces crossed the border on their way to Abu Agella. En route they encountered enemy forces. Additional information is not at hand."

Finally, at 9 P.M. (December 27), more than seven hours after the Israelis had crossed the border, Allon, still in his Beersheba headquarters, received a cable from Yadin: "Refrain from advancing toward Abu Agella until you see me. If you are already moving, you should attack and return to base."

Allon, smiling to himself, immediately dictated to Yeroham Cohen: "There is no possibility of stopping movement. After occupying the area we will be able to leave if this is the order. In my opinion we should hold the place for several reasons."

There were times, Allon thought, when slow communications could work to a commander's advantage.

A doctor knelt down by the road leading to Abu Agella and listened to the heart of Colonel Fuad Thabet, the commander of Egypt's lost eastern strip of territory. Then he said caustically: "He's all right. He's just fainted."

Two Egyptian soldiers lifted the unconscious man into a jeep and drove off toward Abu Agella.

Their leader's fainting spell was not guaranteed to improve the morale of the retreating troops. In panic, they fled through the desert from posts all along the eastern defense strip, bypassing captured El Auja and then continuing on toward Abu Agella and El Arish, many leaving their bulky shoes behind so they could run faster. Interrupting their flight only during strafing attacks, they hurtled over bullet-riddled corpses and moaning wounded, past hundreds of vehicles—some abandoned, others overturned in ditches, many smoking, burning, and crackling with the sound of exploding gunpowder.

Only the Moslem Brothers, who had fought most fiercely in the battle for the eastern strip, thought seriously of setting up a new defense line to stop the Israelis before they reached El Arish. On arriving in Abu Agella after most of the retreating forces had already passed through, the Brotherhood leader, Kamal Ismael al-Sharif, suggested to an Egyptian army colonel that the Brothers should establish such a line at the entrance to the town.

"Do as you think best," the colonel stammered in confusion. "I'll send you reinforcements and arms as soon as I get to El Arish . . ."

A few hours later, when darkness had fallen, Sharif and his men, who had taken up positions along the road, saw trucks with dimmed lights approaching from the direction of El Arish.

"At last!" Sharif exclaimed, as he ran toward the vehicles.

When he reached them, he cried out to the first driver: "What have you brought us? Mortars and machine guns?"

"Why no," the driver replied, rather startled. "They told us you were hungry. The back is chock full of biscuits!"[5]

"Quick, radio them or they'll kill us all!" Nahum Sarig shouted to his communications man as he jumped out of his jeep about half an hour after his troops had crossed the Sinai border.

But it was too late. The Israeli planes swooped down over the convoy, strafing it and killing four men.

"My God!" exclaimed Sarig as he extracted himself from a ditch. "We've advanced so swiftly our own planes can't believe we're here!" (He didn't realize that some of the captured enemy trucks being used still had Egyptian markings.)

As the planes circled for a second attack, one of the soldiers remembered the good luck souvenir he carried in his pack—the flag of the Jewish Brigade that had fought with the British during World War II. He immediately hoisted it on his rifle and swung it in the breeze as the planes approached. While everyone held their breath, the aircraft swung over the convoy without firing.

With Rutledge's Cromwell in the lead, the convoy then moved on, meeting anti-tank resistance at an Egyptian outpost about six miles from Abu Agella, which held up the Israelis until about 3 A.M. the following day, December 29, when the outpost was finally eliminated. At 6 A.M., Rutledge's tank nosed its way to the center of a cluster of clay houses.

"Well, here we are!" Rutledge whooped as he came to a halt by an ancient well. "The metropolis of Abu Agella!"

Barely visible on the horizon were puffs of dust swirling in the wake of rearguard trucks crammed with Moslem Brothers bitterly gnawing on stale biscuits.

General Sadek shuffled the reports on his desk and said gravely to the commanders sitting in his office; "I still don't think they're serious about taking El Arish. There'd be too much international pressure on them. It's only a feint. They want us to pull our troops southward out of Rafa. I think they really intend to hit us in Rafa."

"But can we afford to take the chance?" a staff officer asked. "What if they do attack El Arish? Our forces on the coast will be trapped."

"We'll send down some units to El Arish just in case. But most of our forces must stay in the Rafa area."

When the meeting ended, Sadek clenched his fists on the desk and quietly prayed: "May God see that I am right!"

On the morning of December 29, the Israeli High Command met in an atmosphere compounded of joy, anger, and uncertainty. Allon had taken El Auja, but had not even waited to ask permission to head into the Sinai toward Abu Agella. That could perhaps be excused on the grounds of "hot pursuit." But the question on everybody's mind was: What would he do now? And knowing Allon, some did not doubt that he would drive toward El Arish, perhaps conveniently forgetting to inform GHQ about it. But aside from his disturbing attitude, was an attack on El Arish desirable? There was no unanimity on this question.

Ben-Gurion, who was ill in Tiberias, telephoned his opinion to the command that such action, while perhaps militarily justifiable, would be politically dangerous and could cause serious international repercussions for Israel. Ailing chief of staff Dori let it be known that he regarded such an advance as militarily inadvisable. He felt, as did some other staff officers, that to attack El Arish and push northward would stretch Israeli forces too thin in the Negev and expose Beersheba to possible enemy assault from the coast and the Hebron area. Allon's forces should move from Abu Agella toward Elath, rather than toward El Arish and Gaza. Gaza, he believed, was of secondary importance to Israel. He was, moreover, highly doubtful whether Allon could destroy the Egyptian forces on the coast even if he trapped them, believing that there would be a second Faluja.

Yadin was noncommittal. He admired the audacity of Allon's plan, but sensed that Ben-Gurion was right in his political appraisal.

With most of its members thus either cool or opposed to Allon's still unannounced plan, the High Command decided against pushing on to El Arish.

Shortly after the capture of Abu Agella, a jeep rolled into the village carrying Allon, Rabin, and Yeroham Cohen.

"Congratulations, Nahum," Allon grinned as he stepped out. And putting his arm around Sarig's shoulder, he added: "El Arish is our next stop."

The commanders promptly set up a headquarters tent and planned the attack. One infantry company would assault the newly constructed Bir Hama airstrip about 55 miles southwest in the direction of Ismailia in the

Suez Canal Zone, while the tank battalion and some infantry units would advance westward to capture El Arish Airport and the town itself.

At about noon, December 29, the two attack forces headed for their objectives, with Allon, Rabin, and Cohen joining the convoy to El Arish. Some two hours later, after an uneventful drive through the desert, their force captured deserted El Arish Airport, about 12 miles from the town.

A jeep then sped up from the rear and a soldier jumped out with a message for Allon. Cohen took it and handed it to Allon, who was sitting in his jeep on the side of the road. Allon smiled as he put the cable down.

"GHQ says they've heard from the Egyptian radio and our pilots that we're heading for El Arish . . . Send back a message, Yeroham. This is not an operation. We're simply chasing the enemy in self-defense. They won't stop firing at us!"

The convoy, with Rutledge's tank in the lead, then continued to advance in the face of sporadic fire to within about three miles of El Arish, when Rutledge's earphones echoed to the shout: "Halt the advance!"

"Halt the advance?" he cried, "When there's nothing between us and El Arish?" . . .

A few minutes earlier, a jeep coming from the direction of Abu Agella had roared to a stop and, as before, a soldier ran to deliver a message to Cohen for Allon who, with his officers, had been watching the action from a sand dune off the road. The tight flesh on Allon's youthful face quivered slightly as he read and reread the message, which was from Yadin:

1. I have been informed that our units are moving toward El Arish.
2. You are hereby ordered to halt any movement without my previous consent.

"Yeroham," Allon said, "we're driving back to Abu Agella immediately. Call for a Piper Cub as soon as we arrive. I'm flying to Tel Aviv tonight to see B.G."

As he strode to his jeep, Allon snapped to Sarig: "Keep your men here. If you don't hear from me by tomorrow morning, attack El Arish and head north to Rafa . . . How could they order a retreat when the Egyptian army is practically in our pocket?"

He was further depressed by the news he received in Abu Agella as he was about to board the Piper Cub parked on the road. The attack on the Bir Hama airstrip had failed . . .

"Where's the airport?" Allon asked the pilot.

"That's a good question," the pilot said. "In this blackout it's impossible to tell. They're supposed to turn on the lights for a few minutes while we land."

"There they are," Allon said, pointing to two rows of lights in the distance. "Let's get down quickly before the Egyptians start shelling from the sea."

The plane landed on an airstrip in north Tel Aviv, and Allon walked swiftly to a waiting car and was whisked off to general headquarters.

"I'm sorry," said the junior officer on duty, "but General Dori is ill and Brigadier Yadin went home some time ago."

Allon got back in the car and ordered the driver to take him to Yadin's residence.

"I thought you were in Egypt," Yadin greeted him with a surprised smile as he opened the door. "You're just in time to share an omelet with me."

"I've come to ask you to let us stay in Egypt until we take El Arish," Allon explained as he followed Yadin into the kitchen. "Yigal, we can take it in half a day and then move north to Gaza too swiftly for any international complications to develop."

Holding a frying pan over a small stove, Yadin remarked calmly: "There's a feeling it would be safer to take Gaza directly from Beersheba."

"If we're going to move into Gaza," Allon retorted, "let's take a place not already in our hands."

"From a military point of view, I agree," Yadin said sliding the omelet onto a plate, "but it's a political decision. B.G. made it."

"Where is he now?"

"In Tiberias."

"Well, who can I talk to?"

"Maybe Shertok [Sharett]."

Allon considered the possible value of seeing Foreign Minister Sharett. He, of all people, was sensitive to international reaction, and would probably be the last person to push his view. Perhaps he should go directly to Tiberias to see Ben-Gurion. But there was nothing to lose by trying Sharett first.

"I'll see Moshe," he said.

"Okay, but first taste my cooking."

"Sorry. It looks delicious, but I'm not hungry at the moment."

Allon drove directly to Sharett's house in Ramat Gan, arriving at about 2:30 A.M. The Foreign Minister came to the door in his pajamas, bleary-eyed and barefooted.

"It's a brilliant plan," he responded to Allon's surprise when the latter had argued his case again, "but it might provoke a British reaction that could have grave results."

Allon then countered: "Well, I have an alternative plan."

"Yes?"

"Tell the Americans and British we'll withdraw our forces from the Sinai, but that we need four days to do it. If there are any international repercussions, blame me. Say that it simply takes that long to effect a withdrawal. In fact, I think any American general would agree. Then, we can at least pretend we're attacking El Arish and the Egyptians will feel it necessary to bring their forces south from Gaza. Meanwhile, we'll concentrate fresh forces opposite Gaza and see where they take their reserves from. Then, when we discover their weak points, we'll attack and drive a wedge to the sea."

Sharett's eyes reflected excitement. "It sounds interesting," he commented. "I'll phone B.G. and ask him about it."

Sharett found that his telephone was out of order, so he dressed and the two men drove swiftly to general headquarters where the duty officer called Ben-Gurion.

"Hello, B.G.?" Sharett said, "Sorry to awaken you, but Allon just flew in to Tel Aviv and has suggested a new plan for attacking the Egyptians. I personally feel it deserves careful consideration . . ."

After explaining the plan, Sharett was silent for several moments as he listened to Ben-Gurion's reaction while Allon nervously paced the floor nearby. For him, the whole future of Israel would be decided in the next moments.

"I see," Sharett said finally, "All right, I'll tell him."

He put down the telephone and turned to Allon. The commander knew the answer the moment he looked into the Foreign Minister's eyes.

"I'm sorry," Sharett reported, "but B.G. said you must start withdrawing your troops from the Sinai within twenty-four hours. He said it was an order."

Allon was silent. Only a few more hours until dawn (December 30). And he had ordered Sarig to attack El Arish in the morning if he hadn't heard from him. Maybe, if communications were bad enough, Sarig would not receive word from him until the assault was under way . . .

Allon arrived back in Beersheba a few hours later and immediately asked his officers: "Has Sarig started attacking El Arish yet?"

To his disappointment, he learned that the attack had been delayed because the two last operative tanks had bogged down in the sand. Turning to Rabin, he said: "Yitzhak, drive to Abu Agella tonight and give Nahum the bad news. He's got to start retreating by tomorrow. Meanwhile, I'll send Ben-Gurion a personal cable asking him to revise his order. We can only pray for a miracle."

A few hours later, Ben-Gurion wired back that he would not change his mind, but that he was returning to Tel Aviv on January 2, and would be glad to discuss the situation with him then. By that time, Allon raged, the withdrawal would be completed. He cabled GHQ, which had ordered that the withdrawal be completed by January 1, asking for more time. Yadin agreed, but extended the deadline only to 5 A.M., January 2, a few hours before Ben-Gurion was to return to Tel Aviv.

J AMES McDonald (the American envoy to Israel) was not paying much attention to what he was eating as he sat at the table with his family discussing the New Year's Day party they were to give the following afternoon.

"Is everything ready?" he asked his wife.

She was in the middle of explaining that everything was when the telephone rang.

"Yes, Charley," McDonald said when he had picked up the receiver.

"This is something very important," Charles Knox, his assistant, said. "May I see you right away?"

"Of course. Come right over."

McDonald finished his meal just as Knox and Sam Klaus, a mission "legal adviser" whose main task was to report on Communist infiltration, arrived.

"Glad to see you," said McDonald.

"You may not be when you read this," Knox replied gravely, looking down at the document he was carrying.

The three men retired to the study, locked the door, and sat silently while McDonald read the paper. It was a top secret message from Washington, sent in the name of the President, instructing him to deliver immediately to the Israel authorities the substance of a cable from Britain. This cable threatened to invoke British obligations under a 1936 defense treaty with Egypt to come to her aid in the war against Israel unless Israeli troops withdrew from Egyptian soil. If Israel refused, the United States, for her part, Washington warned, would reexamine the character of her relations with that country, including her support of Israeli admission to the United Nations. The note also emphasized that Washington was disturbed by reports from American Consul-General Stabler in Amman that the Israelis had "threatened" Jordan in secret talks that were in progress.

McDonald then said to his two colleagues, who, like him, supported Israel: "I know how you feel, but your interpretation of this may be a bit pessimistic. In any case, we must get a reply from the Israelis as soon as possible."

McDonald sent his daughter Barbara to Sharett's home and she returned with the Foreign Minister promptly.

"I have received from Washington a cable of the greatest importance," McDonald told him. "You might like to take it down as I read it to you." Sharett, sitting down, removed a pad and pen from his pocket and wrote in shorthand as his host slowly read a paraphrase that Knox and Klaus had prepared. His fingers tightened around his pen and he turned pale as McDonald dictated.

Sharett then conceded that Israeli troops had crossed the Egyptian border, but said their advance was only tactical. Such action, he added, was inevitable when the military situation reached a point where its own logic took command.

McDonald, however, did not feel that Sharett's answer satisfied Washington's demand or that it was completely authoritative.

"I must see the Prime Minister as quickly as possible," he insisted. "I must have a definitive reply from him."

"He is in Tiberias undergoing bath treatments."

"Very well," McDonald replied, "either he can come to me or I can go to him. Whatever happens, we must meet at once."

"I'll telephone him and let you know the moment I have word," Sharett said.

When the Americans had seen him to his car, they sat down and, reinforced by military attaches, pondered the wisdom of a trip to Tiberias through war-torn territory if Ben-Gurion could not come to Tel Aviv.

"I think you should go," Knox advised.

Everyone agreed, and the meeting ended.

At 8:20 P.M. on New Year's Eve, McDonald, Knox, and Rubin Shiloah of the Foreign Ministry set out for Tiberias, speeding at 60 to 70 miles an hour over the coastal road, through the Galilean hills, and finally into Tiberias, arriving at the Galei Kinneret Hotel at about 10:30 P.M. Shiloah led the Americans through the hotel lobby up a short flight of steps to an alcove room that was curtained off from the lobby. Then he pulled the curtain and there sat Ben-Gurion and his wife Paula.

"I'm delighted to see you," Ben-Gurion said, "but you shouldn't have taken the risk of coming all the way here."

"I felt it was necessary," McDonald replied. "Do you think we could order tea and later an escort for the return trip?"

"You're not going back tonight, are you?"

"I'm afraid I must."

Then the party got down to business and the Prime Minister politely offered the same reply as had Sharett, but added that all Israeli troops would be out of the Sinai by January 2.

"Was it necessary," he asked, "for a great power to address a small and weak state in such a manner?"

McDonald glanced at Knox and replied: "Frankly, I was somewhat surprised myself. The British apparently applied considerable pressure on Washington."[6]

On January 2, Ben-Gurion returned to Tel Aviv from Beersheba and found Allon waiting for him at GHQ.

"All of our troops are out of Egypt," the commander reported, "but I wish to implore you once more to let us go back and attack El Arish."

"Offer any alternative plan you want," Ben-Gurion replied, "but I promised the Americans we would withdraw from Egypt by today and the stakes are too high to go back on that promise."

"All right," Allon said, "I have an alternative plan. We can drive a wedge south of Rafa and cut off the enemy forces in Gaza from El Arish."

He explained that he would attack down the El Auja–Rafa road, which ran mainly in Egyptian territory. Rafa itself was in Israel, he pointed out, though some hills south of the village might be just over the border.

Allon detected a glimmer of interest in Ben-Gurion's heavy-lidded eyes. "But Rafa," the Prime Minister said, "would be much more difficult to capture than El Arish. The enemy could reinforce it from north and south."

"That's true," Allon persisted, "but its capture would have the same effect of trapping the Egyptian army without incurring as great a risk of British intervention."

Ben-Gurion, silent again, looked away as if to hide the agony of indecision. It sounded logical. But what if Britain interpreted its threat as covering the border area? And what if the United States supported that interpretation? Would Jews 1,000 years into the future, perhaps the survivors of new pogroms and gas chambers, ever forgive him if he should gamble everything away? Was Gaza really that important? He flicked at a fly that had settled on his desk and scratched his neck. Then he stared at Allon, unable to suppress his admiration for this steel-willed young man, however politically innocent; this magnificent product of Zionism, strong, dedicated, confident—and uncomfortably persuasive.

"Very well, Yigal," he said in a quiet voice. "When do you think you can start the attack? The Security Council may order a truce at any moment."

"By tomorrow night," Allon replied, his face flushed with joy and surprise.[7]

Ａs zero hour neared on the night of January 3, Philip Bock, a stout, high-spirited American volunteer prone to extraordinary mishaps, sat impatiently in the driver's seat of his armored car at Kibbutz Gevulot, east of Rafa, a base for the Golani Brigade attack on that town. His company was to capture Hill 102, one of the key sand dunes towering to the east and south of Rafa designated for attack by Golani, Harel, and 8th Armored units that night. Once they were taken, the road and railroad to the south would be cut off and the Egyptian army would be hemmed into the Gaza area.

Even at this late hour, Bock was worried that his sergeant might leave him behind. The sergeant had already tried to keep him out of the action, calling him a "dangerous" driver who would get them all killed. Only after the American had fired a burst into the air and faked an attempted suicide had the sergeant finally relented.

Now he was ready to drive into battle again, confident that he would not lose the car key as he had during a previous skirmish.

Shortly before midnight, Bock's company of armored cars attacked Hill 102. As curtains of sand and smoke swirled around him, cutting off his vision and virtually isolating him from the rest of the company, Bock ground his car to a halt and stood up to get his bearings. Hardly had a companion beside him pulled him down when a shell fragment scraped his scalp and beheaded a soldier in the seat behind him.

He started off again, hopelessly lost, but the car now struck a mine, and he and the other passengers jumped out and joined the hard-hit company in flight. As he leaped onto the runningboard of a fleeing car, an officer kicked him off, shouting: "We're too crowded already!"

Indignant but undaunted, Bock desperately dived into the rear of the vehicle, landing on a number of heads.

"Sorry, fellows," he said. "But my goddam car broke down!"

And just when he was about to storm the hill, too . . .

While Bock's company retreated from Hill 102, another company assaulted a cemetery on a nearby hill, captured it, and held out against two Egyptian tank-led counterattacks.

As General Sadek received reports of these failures, he was grateful that he had had the foresight to bring back the troops he had sent to El

Arish the night before as soon as he learned that the Israelis were pulling out of the Sinai. His first instinct had proved correct, he was convinced. The enemy had never really intended to attack El Arish, but had threatened an attack only to divert troops from Rafa, its real objective. But being right would not necessarily save Rafa. History would not commend him for knowing what the enemy planned if he could not frustrate the plan.

"Counterattack again immediately!" he ordered his commanders. "Give the infantry artillery support and use at least two half-tracks equipped with flamethrowers!"

And he added solemnly: "The fate of the Egyptian army may depend on this battle . . . "

"The anti-tank guns have been damaged by artillery," the Israeli officer informed the company commander on the crest of the cemetery hill.

"Won't anything work?" the commander shouted, having already learned that many of the small arms would not operate because of the clinging sand.

He watched with a feeling of helplessness as the enemy force advanced toward the hill. The half-tracks were about 100 yards away and some infantry units only 30 yards away. One of his men then fired a Piat at the first half-track, and it disappeared behind a cloud of brown dust.

"You've hit it!" someone yelled.

As the cloud dissolved, the half-track could be seen withdrawing, and the others following. The infantry, now without close support, turned and ran under heavy fire, leaving about 150 dead.

The Egyptians then began to evacuate a neighboring army camp. The Israelis had driven a vital stake into the Egyptian escape route.

Meanwhile, on the night of January 3, the Harel Brigade had arrived in the area from El Auja, reaching a point just south of Rafa on the Egyptian side of the border.

"All we have to do," Colonel Yosef Tabenkin told his officers with a smile as they stood on a sand dune near the road, "is to capture six strongpoints and we'll be in Rafa. Since we don't have much information, our plan must be simple. We'll move along the main road and capture each outpost in succession by direct assault."

A Harel battalion under Morris Ben Dror set out that night toward the first strongpoint, but soon Ben Dror radioed to Tabenkin in headquarters: "We're lost. We can't see a thing in the darkness."

"Radio man!" Tabenkin shouted. "Contact Freddy!"

In a moment, Tabenkin was asking Freddy Eiron, his artillery commander: "Are your guns aimed at the strongpoints?"

"Of course. Ever since morning."

"Morris is advancing toward the first strongpoint but can't find his way in the darkness. Can you shell it every five minutes to guide him to his target?"

"Sure."

Tabenkin then notified Ben Dror of the plan, and in a short while the first strongpoint fell. The next morning, January 4, the Israelis captured the second one, and then found the third deserted. The fourth and fifth fell by evening. An attack on the last strongpoint before Rafa failed that night. Even so, the Egyptian forces were now effectively sealed off from Egypt.

"The situation is extremely grave," General Sadek lamented to his aides on the morning of January 5 as they sat in Egyptian headquarters in Rafa. "Cairo might as well know the hard truth."

And he radioed a message to Cairo expressing his opinion that "there is no way of solving the Israeli problem by force, and therefore, a political solution should be found."

Sadek's message confirmed the belief in Cairo that diplomatic action was the only alternative to military disaster—and possible political upheaval. With almost the whole Egyptian army in Palestine, there were few troops at home to protect the government against street mobs that were already being whipped into frenzy by the Moslem Brotherhood. On December 25, Prime Minister Nokrashy Pasha had ordered the dissolution of the organization on the grounds that it was preaching revolt. Three days later, he was assassinated in the elevator of an office building by Moslem Brothers posing as policemen.

The new Prime Minister, Ibrahim Abd el-Hadi Pasha, feeling, in the light of his predecessor's fate, that his survival depended at this point more on peace with Israel than on a fear-inspired refusal to make peace, persuaded Farouk and fellow cabinet members of the need to end the war and bring the army back home.

"After all," he pointed out to them, "our delegates are already negotiating with official representatives of Israel at the Security Council and other United Nations organizations without this implying recognition, direct or indirect."

Thus, on January 4, 1949, even before Sadek independently reached the same conclusion, the Defense Minister sent two Egyptian officers to tell Ralph Bunche's representative in Cairo that if the acting mediator were able to procure an immediate suspension of hostilities, Egypt would send a delegation to Rhodes with powers to negotiate and implement an armistice.

*

"We've got to finish this job while there's still time," Allon insisted to his commanders the next morning in his Beersheba headquarters. "The Egyptians are pushing for a cease-fire by tomorrow. We must be in Rafa before it takes effect so there can be no question about who occupies the place."

That night, it was decided, Golani forces would make a renewed effort to take Hill 102 from the east, while Harel units attacked the single still uncaptured strongpoint south of Rafa. The 8th Armored Brigade would then break into Rafa from the south.

This time, Phil Bock vowed, he would not get lost. He would capture Hill 102 with the help of his buddies if he had to push his armored car by himself all the way up the hill. As he approached the slope, shells began exploding all around, even more thickly, it seemed, than in the previous battle. Suddenly, a tremendous blast shook the vehicle, shattering the windshield.

"My eyes! I can't see!" Bock cried, slamming on the brakes with such force that the car nearly turned around.

As he covered his blood-streaked face with his hands, the man beside him looked back and shouted to the squad of soldiers in the rear: "Who can drive, quick? We've got to get out of here!"

But no one else in the car knew how to drive.

"I can get you back to the kibbutz," Bock moaned, mopping the blood from his face with his sleeve. "You direct me."

His eyes closed, he began driving toward Kibbutz Gevulot while his buddy next to him guided the steering wheel. Then, without warning, a fierce wind swept in from the sea, filling the chill night air with tornados of sand that attacked the flesh brutally like a million pinpricks.

The sandstorm blew relentlessly through the broken windshield, seeking out, it seemed to Bock, the two bloody, tightly closed slits from which he was sure he would never see again. Already in agony from innumerable glass and shrapnel splinters embedded in his eyes, the sand aggravated the excruciating pain and made him wish he had really shot himself that day when he had feigned a suicide attempt . . .

While the Golani Brigade failed once more to occupy Hill 102, Harel units took the last hill south of Rafa just before the sandstorm struck.

"Now the Armored Brigade has only to roll into Rafa," Tabenkin rejoiced when an aide rushed into his field headquarters with news of the victory.

Then the storm began and visibility was reduced to 70 or 80 yards.

Although this untimely phenomenon worried the Harel commanders, they were cheered when, in the early morning, they heard the engines of an armored column approaching the hill.

"The 8th Armored—they're coming!" an officer shouted gleefully as dozens of men left their positions and raced toward the tanks, cheering and waving, though they could not see through the thick wall of dust.

Finally, emerging ghostlike through the wispy cloud, the first tanks came into view along the road adjacent to the hill.

"Oh, no!" exclaimed Morris Ben Dror from his vantage point at the top of the hill. "It can't be!"

"But it is!" another officer groaned in dismay. "Those are enemy tanks!"

At that moment, the tanks opened fire on the surprised Israelis, who withdrew in disorder from the hill, the first time that Harel Brigade troops, reputed as among the best in the Israeli army, ever retreated.

Later that afternoon, Miriam Rutledge was listening to the radio in her quarters at Kibbutz Tsehilim near Rafa when she heard the announcer report that her husband had been killed on the outskirts of Rafa. Dashing to the signal office, she demanded hysterically that he check the report.

Then, as she waited half in tears, she heard the radio announce that Israel and Egypt had agreed to a cease-fire starting the next day, January 7. He had missed by one day, she sobbed. And she was responsible. She had asked him to stay and fight a war that was not his own.

"Miss," the radio operator called, "I've checked and have news for you. It was a mistake. He isn't dead. He was only wounded in the hand."

The girl stared at him silently. Then she said, "Thank you," and walked out.

On the morning of January 6, Allon was sipping coffee in his headquarters when Cohen entered his office with a cable from Yadin:

WE MIGHT HAVE TO FINISH TODAY STOP MAXIMUM EFFORTS SHOULD BE EMPLOYED NEAR RAFA STOP DETAILS AS SOON AS POSSIBLE.

"We've got to recapture the hill south of Rafa," Allon asserted. "Tell Yitzhak [Sadeh] to attack as soon as possible."

"It'll be rough attacking in this sandstorm."

"I know, but we have no choice."

The 8th Armored Brigade thus made a last desperate effort a few hours later to recapture the hill, but was forced to withdraw after suffering severe casualties in the midst of the sandstorm. Allon then received another message from Yadin:

ALL SIGNS ARE THIS MIGHT BE LAST NIGHT OF FIGHTING STOP I'LL INFORM YOU LATER FINAL DECISION STOP TAKE THIS INTO CONSIDERATION.

Allon laughed bitterly to himself as he looked out of the window at the raging brown blizzard that engulfed the world like a plague from heaven. It seemed almost hilarious in a way, Tel Aviv pressing *him* to attack. Rafa, it seemed, was beyond his reach.

The last important fighting before the cease-fire took place that morning as the sandstorm subsided. But Israel's adversary was not Egypt. It was Britain.

Bevin, wishing to make sure that the cease-fire would not find the Israelis on Egyptian soil, asked the British Air Ministry to order RAF planes to fly over the battlefield and determine the exact location of the fighting, take photographs of the respective positions of the armies, and bring back as much information as possible on the progress of the battle. Thus, on the morning of January 7, the aircraft took off on their special mission.

A few hours later, Charles Knox burst into McDonald's home with the news that the Israelis had shot down five British planes, and that one pilot had been killed and two taken prisoner while flying over Israeli territory. McDonald was shocked, and his shock turned to fear when the British reacted by landing reinforcements in Aqaba, apparently to underscore the possibility of British retaliation in the Negev. He sent an urgent cable to Washington emphasizing the "danger" of Britain's opposition to Israeli occupation of the Negev, and urged that pressure be exerted on the British to work in good faith for peace.

To McDonald's pleasant surprise, the State Department replied that it hoped "the United Kingdom–Israel air incident would not be allowed to exacerbate the Middle East situation."

"Well, it seems that our friends in Washington have grown wiser," McDonald told Knox with grim satisfaction. "This means that the United States won't be stampeded."

Nor, apparently, would the British press and Parliament, which reacted with indignation not toward Israel as Bevin had hoped, but toward Bevin himself for having risked British lives by flying over the area in the first place.

Adding to Bevin's embarrassment was the revelation that Egypt had rejected a British request that the reconnaissance operation should be launched under the 1936 defense treaty between the two countries. Invocation of this agreement would have lent fuel to the anti-government campaign by ultra-nationalists, who hated Britain for her colonialist policies almost as much as they hated Israel.

The Farouk regime, however, felt its hand strengthened by British public disclosures that the Israelis still occupied Egyptian territory. And though the Israelis had accepted a cease-fire on the understanding that armistice negotiations with Egypt would start promptly, Egypt now said that she would honor this arrangement only if the Jews withdrew from the border areas, including the occupied points around Rafa.

"Ben-Gurion, it's your turn to wash the dishes."

"I know, Paula," the Prime Minister said as he sat hunched over the kitchen table after having picked at his supper of cheese, bread, sour cream, and salad.

Paula looked at him from across the table. Her husband's eyes peered from dark sockets and the lines in his face seemed deeper than usual. He hadn't even finished his cheese and sour cream. Maybe they should have stayed longer at the hot springs in Tiberias. But no, she realized, he was needed in Tel Aviv. Why did he have to be such a great man that nobody could do anything without his approval?

"Never mind, Ben-Gurion," Paula said, getting up, "I'll wash the dishes tonight. You can wash them the next two nights. Now go and take a rest."

The Prime Minister seemed relieved. He rose slowly and walked upstairs to his study, where he glanced at the books lining the walls. Plato . . . Aristotle . . . Indian philosophy . . . He wished he had time to browse through them again. Maybe he could find something in those books to help him see the way clearly. He sat down at his desk and started thumbing through reports.

Yigal Allon had done almost exactly what he had said he would do. He had not captured the city of Rafa, but he had taken most of the heights around it, and the Egyptian army on the coast was cut off. But what should Israel do now? Keep the Egyptians penned up and under constant attack—at the risk of British intervention? Or agree to the Egyptian condition for immediate armistice talks: the withdrawal of Israeli troops from the Rafa area? A true leader had to know how far to push his adversaries and when to fire the last shot. The question now was: Had he pushed them far enough?

Late into the night, Ben-Gurion pondered over his reports and gradually what may have been the most important decision of the war crystallized in his mind.

Finally, he heard Paula calling: "Ben-Gurion, it's after midnight. Come to bed! And don't forget to turn out the light!"

The Prime Minister rose. Yes, it was time for bed. He had made up his mind and no one could change it now. Not even Yigal Allon.

On the morning of January 9, Yeroham Cohen, with a distraught expression, handed Allon a radio message. "Yigal," he said, "a cable from Yadin. You won't like it."

Allon raged inwardly as he read:

ALL OUR FORCES SHOULD BE EVACUATED FROM BEYOND THE BORDER IN-CLUDING THE POSITION ON THE AUJA-AGELLA ROAD   STOP   COMPLETE EVACU-ATION BY MONDAY JANUARY 10   STOP   CARRY OUT WITHOUT RESERVATION STOP   A MESSENGER HAS BEEN SENT TO YOU WITH A LETTER   STOP   START EVACUATION IMMEDIATELY

"Oh, no!" Allon exclaimed as he dropped the cable on his desk. "How can they ask us to retreat from Rafa when we've got the Egyptian army bottled up, when we can call the tune in peace negotiations? It means voluntarily giving up the Gaza Strip."

"Well, we've got to answer right away," Cohen said.

"I'll answer all right! Address this message to Yadin, Dori, and Ben-Gurion, and send it immediately!"

Cohen sat down to take notes and Allon, pacing the floor, dictated:

I CONFIRM RECEIPT OF ORDER TO EVACUATE POSITIONS BEYOND BORDER STOP   SHALL EXECUTE ACCORDINGLY   STOP   I AM SHOCKED BY THIS ORDER AS WE ARE LOSING ONE OF OUR TACTICAL ADVANTAGES AGAINST THE ENEMY   STOP THIS SECOND TIME IN THIS OPERATION THAT WE LETTING OPPORTUNITY GO BY AND LOSING DEFINITE POSSIBILITY OF INFLICTING FINAL DEFEAT ON EGYPTIAN ENEMY

Allon paused for a moment while Cohen scribbled the final words, then said: "Yeroham, get me a Piper Cub. I'm leaving for Tel Aviv to see B.G. again."

"Yigal Allon?" Ben-Gurion barked to an aide. "I knew he'd be coming. Did you see this cable he sent?"

Allon entered and saluted with a cold formality foreign to his character.

The Prime Minister walked over to him with a smile, embraced him, and said: "Yigal, when will you learn to be a good soldier?"

"Am I not? I'm doing my best."

"Yes, you're good when you're advancing, but bad in retreat. You must obey orders."

"Didn't my cable say that I was obeying?"

"Yes, you cable that you're obeying, and then you protest."

As Ben-Gurion sat down, he pulled a letter from a drawer and declared: "I sent this letter to General Dori about an hour ago. Here, read it."

Allon took the letter and read: "General Dori: Please explain to the commanding officer of the southern command that he must obey orders without offering political arguments."

Allon grinned reluctantly and handed the document back.

"I see it as my duty," he said, "to give my superior my estimate of the likely results of an action."

"Tell me what you're so angry about. Don't you understand the importance of the first official conference with an Arab country? Pulling out the wedge is a cheap price to pay for this."

"But even more important are the results of such a conference."

"But they won't talk at all if we don't pull out the wedge!"

"On the contrary, if we let them know we intend to maintain the wedge, they will talk. The same factors that forced them to consider negotiating in the first place will force them to talk if we keep the wedge. Then, if negotiations start and fail, we will be in a good position to take over Gaza."

"Yigal, I will present you Gaza on a silver platter."

"Mr. Ben-Gurion, you're older than I am. But I know the Arabs better than you do. You mustn't pull out the wedge or we will lose Gaza."

"Yigal, you're a brilliant commander, maybe the greatest in this war, but you are not yet a mature politician."

"Maybe that is to my advantage."

Ben-Gurion rose, strode over to Allon and, laying a hand on his shoulder, said like a father admonishing his child: "Commanders must obey orders even if they don't like them."

Allon knew then that Ben-Gurion would not change his mind. He walked to the door, saluted, and left.

With heavy heart, he returned to Beersheba and ordered a withdrawal from the Rafa area.[8]

> "There is no room for any appeal or delay in carrying out the order, however harsh it may be," read the radio message to his commanders.

As Miriam Rutledge walked through the desert camp, she heard men grumbling on every side. Some seemed to be weeping as they pulled down their tents and packed their equipment.

"Why are we fleeing in the middle of the night?" one man asked. "Is the Pharaoh chasing us with his Egyptians?"

"After we clobber them," his buddy commented, "we're told to sneak out like thieves. You'd think we made a mistake by winning."

Miriam approached a bonfire around which some shadowy figures were squatting, and suddenly in the flickering glare saw her husband's rugged profile. She walked over to him and stood silently beside him for a moment.

He looked up and stared at her in mute astonishment. In a moment she was in his arms, and an hour later curled up next to him on the flat body of his Cromwell as it crawled off toward Beersheba.

18

End of an
Unfinished War

MAJOR Nasser's hawklike face brightened as he stood on the road near Iraq el-Manshiya watching the jeep approach.

"Hello, Yeroham," he called, waving.

Yeroham Cohen waved back. He jumped out, followed by his driver—a pretty blond girl with green eyes who somehow looked smart even in khaki.

Nasser was glad that Cohen, who had visited him many times since their first meeting, had come with the girl. It was refreshing to observe such beauty amid the depressing drabness of the brown Faluja landscape. When the reporter of the brigade magazine had asked a number of officers and soldiers what they thought was the most pleasant sight in Faluja, Nasser had replied: "Cohen's beautiful driver."

While the girl waited by the jeep, Nasser and Cohen sat down as usual on the grass beside the road and spoke, as they had so many times, of "dirty" Egyptian politics, of British imperialism, and of the bravery of Egyptian and Israeli soldiers who had been slaughtering each other almost daily. Then they compared notes on a bloody battle that the Egyptians had won at Iraq el-Manshiya—the second big Egyptian victory in that village—on the night of December 28.

"It was one of the most horrible nights I have ever experienced," Nasser grimaced.

"It was horrible for us, too."

"We have five prisoners."

"You people will be held responsible for them, Gamal."

"Don't worry, Yeroham, I will be personally responsible for them. Two of them were wounded and we're giving them medical attention. Please tell your commander of my pledge."

"May I bring food and clothing for them?"

"Of course."

Nasser then reached into his shirt pocket and drew out several envelopes.

"Here are some messages from your men," he said, handing them to Cohen.

"Thanks, Gamal. We took nine bodies back with us when we withdrew. That means you should have seventy-four."

"You're wrong, Yeroham. I was expecting you right after the battle to come for your dead, but when you didn't we buried them—seventy-five in all. We gave them a military burial and marked their graves."

"Would you let a military rabbi come and perform services by the graves?"

"I'll ask Brigadier Taha."

The two men were silent for several moments as they sat gazing into the cold blue sky trying, it seemed, to cleanse their minds of the obscenities of war.

"You know, Yeroham," Nasser mused, "it's a pity that I shall never see my wife and daughters again. I feel that something is going to happen to me."

"Are you crazy, Gamal? For you the war is over. I don't know of any man who is more certain than you of going home alive."

"Well, I have a feeling . . . "

"Gamal, I am willing to bet that you'll not only see your wife and daughters again but that you'll have a son!"

Nasser smiled as he plucked a weed from the earth, rolling the stem between his thumb and forefinger.

A few days later, Cohen returned with Colonel Shlomo Goren, chief rabbi of the Israeli army. Nasser led them to the four mass graves of Israeli dead through rows of soldiers standing on either side of the road at present arms. At the graves, a guard unit also presented arms and a group of officers saluted.

Rabbi Goren then stood by each of the graves, marked with freshly whitewashed stone slabs, and performed services while Nasser and his men stood at attention.

IN THE sedately luxurious Hôtel des Roses in Rhodes, Egyptian and Israeli representatives arrived for the start of armistice talks on January 13. Ralph Bunche and his staff had established their headquarters and living quarters in one wing of the hotel and had reserved the other for the two delegations, the Israelis occupying most of one floor and the Egyptians the floor just above. The proximity of the antagonists led to awkward situations at first. An Egyptian, on seeing an Israeli approaching in the corridor, eyed him contemptuously and then looked away, though sometimes, unable to quell his curiosity, glancing back.

When the Egyptians initially refused to meet with the Israelis at all, Bunche told them brusquely but diplomatically: "It was my understanding that we had come here to negotiate, and to do this, gentlemen, one side must talk to the other."

Finally, the Egyptians agreed to a meeting in Bunche's sitting room, with the acting mediator himself presiding from the sofa and the two delegations grouped on either side of him.

Egyptian efforts to address all their remarks to Bunche, as if the Israelis were not present, soon broke down, and the two contending parties began arguing with each other in English and French. Argument led to understanding, at least on the personal level, and eventually to friendliness as the days stretched into weeks. Members of the two delegations even competed in billiard contests, complete with cheering sections. And when Abdul Moheim Mustafa, the chief Egyptian political adviser, fell ill, Walter Eytan, director-general of the Foreign Ministry, and Eliahu Sasson sat at his bedside and comforted him.

But the arguments were heated, and they were complicated by the pressure on the Egyptian delegates to save face before the Egyptian public, which was still unaware of the enormity of its army's defeat and did not even know that Beersheba had fallen.

"You must return Beersheba to us," one delegate insisted to the Israelis. "Otherwise the Egyptian public will think that we permitted you to take it."

Israeli fury was aroused at this logic, and Yadin, a top Israeli delegate, burst out: "Before we give Beersheba back to you, we'll give back the sun and the stars!"

As Yadin shouted angrily, he banged on the conference table and the pencil in his hand flew into the air, hitting the chief Egyptian delegate, General Sif el-Din, squarely on the forehead.

There was an appalled silence. The flight of the wayward pencil, it seemed, could put an end to the armistice talks. Then an Egyptian delegate looked at Yadin and asked: "Why don't you give us back the moon also?" The tension broke as everybody laughed.

But the Egyptians clung to their demand for a concession on Beersheba and finally argued that the Israelis should at least permit the appointment of an Egyptian governor in that town.

"But that is absurd," Eytan replied. "Israel controls Beersheba!"

An Egyptian delegate came up with a new idea. "Will you agree to the appointment of an Egyptian military governor at Bir Asluj?"

The Israelis were astonished, and somewhat amused, by this suggestion, since Bir Asluj was little more than a cluster of mud huts on the road from Beersheba to El Auja and hardly warranted the presence of a military governor.

"Of course we cannot agree," Eytan said, his usually puckish face now deadly serious. "And it is surprising that you should make this request since such an appointment would simply make Egypt a laughingstock in the eyes of people who know what Bir Asluj is."

The Egyptians then asked for the appointment of an Egyptian military governor in El Auja. The Israelis again refused.

Bunche, feeling that the Egyptian need to save face was genuine, however awkward, then suggested: "Well, perhaps both sides would agree simply not to keep troops in El Auja, which would then become a demilitarized area."

The Israelis protested but finally agreed to this compromise. When other questions proved even more insurmountable, Bunche, sensing when to be gentle and when firm, used another tactic. He ordered two sets of decorated ceramic plates from a local manufacturer and had inscribed on them "Rhodes Armistice Talks 1949." Then he called the delegates into his room, and opened a chest of drawers.

"Have a look at these lovely plates!" he said, his face alight. "If you reach agreement, each of you will get one to take home. If you don't, I'll break them over your heads!"

Shortly afterward, Israel agreed that the Egyptian brigade in the Faluja pocket could depart for Egypt when an armistice was signed, and that it could be supplied meanwhile with food and drugs. Both sides then agreed that they would hold the areas they occupied at the time of the cease-fire. Egypt would thus retain the coastal area, which was to be known as the Gaza Strip—at least until a more permanent peace arrangement was reached.

On February 24, the two delegations signed an armistice agreement and attended a gay party in the evening. But conspicuously absent was Yitzhak Rabin, a military member of the Israeli delegation, who had argued heatedly against giving the Gaza area to Egypt.

"Why should Egypt get a slice of Palestine?" he asked his colleagues. "Why are we giving it up so meekly after we fought so hard at Rafa?"

"An armistice with Egypt is worth the Gaza area," Eytan replied, reflecting Ben-Gurion's decision. "And besides, this is only a temporary military armistice. When we have full-scale peace talks, then we can press for better boundaries."

Speechless with fury, Rabin then flew home to Israel, having gone to Rhodes reluctantly anyway.

Allon was equally enraged (he had refused even to attend the talks, sending Rabin in his place), remembering with a sense of betrayal that Ben-Gurion had promised him the Gaza zone "on a silver platter." And he was by no means consoled when the Prime Minister further rejected a proposal he made for taking over the whole west bank of the Jordan, including the Old City of Jerusalem, within three days. The government, to his chagrin, wanted an immediate armistice agreement with Jordan as well as with Egypt.

Yigal Allon, who had probably done more than any other soldier to bring Israel to life again after 2,000 years, felt crushed and humiliated.

Yeroham Cohen arrived in Faluja just after his friend, Gamal Abdel Nasser, had already departed for Gaza with his troops en route for Cairo.

"He is very fond of you and had hoped to see you before he left," Taha told him when the Israeli drove up to his headquarters. "But I'm sure you'll meet again somewhere."

The two men then drove to the ruins of the Iraq es-Suweidan police fortress, where Rabin had set up a temporary headquarters to help in the evacuation of the Egyptians. After a friendly last conversation with the Israelis, Taha got up to leave.

"All the best," he said.

Then, looking at Cohen, he added with a smile: "You've done an excellent job. I hope you'll be appointed the first Israeli Ambassador to Egypt."

The Black Panther saluted, climbed into his jeep, and said to his driver: "Let's go."

As they drove off, he looked down at his mud-encrusted shoes. He wished there were a way to preserve the mud—the mud that had provided his men with shelter; the mud that had absorbed so much Egyptian blood and in which so many Egyptians had been buried; the mud in which grew the roots that had helped to keep other men alive . . . He wondered what the people would say when he got home. Though his own forces had never surrendered and were marching home with their arms, their colors flying, these forces were, after all, part of a defeated army. And who could comprehend the value of a bit of mud?

But on his arrival in Cairo at the head of his troops, he received a tumultuous public welcome. Obviously, his fellow Egyptians considered him one of the greatest heroes in Egyptian history.[1]

Moshe dayan and Rubin Shiloah, who had replaced Eliahu Sasson when the latter was assigned to the Rhodes armistice talks with Egypt, had met on December 30 as scheduled with Abdullah Tel and Shawkat Pasha. Their aim at this meeting, however, was to delay peace negotiations until the final crushing defeat of Egypt, and nothing substantive emerged from it. The Israelis wanted to impress on the Jordanians that the whole Israeli army was free to strike elsewhere if they did not prove "reasonable." They also desired an interval between the conclusion of armistice agreements with Egypt and with Jordan so that they could establish themselves without Egyptian interference in the southern Negev, which the Arab Legion had infiltrated with British encouragement (the area that had been awarded to Israel under the partition resolution after Chaim Weizmann's dramatic talk with President Truman).

On January 15 the two delegations met again, and this time—to the surprise of the Israelis—Abdullah Tel did most of the talking for Jordan, the King having felt that he might be a more effective negotiator than Shawkat.

"The bases on which His Majesty can accept negotiations," Tel announced, "are: First, you must restore Lydda and Ramle to Jordanian control. Second, you must permit Arab refugees to return to their cities and villages immediately. Third, you must permit Arabs who had been living in new Jerusalem before the departure of the British to return to their homes."

A stunned silence settled over the conference. Shawkat was as startled as the Israelis, since these conditions were hardly conducive to the swift agreement that everyone had thought the King wanted. Indeed, they had not even been brought up at the earlier conferences.

Tel enjoyed watching the shocked expressions of the others, though he was a bit concerned about how he would explain his performance to the King. Well, hadn't the King asked him to determine the enemy's intentions? What better way was there to force them to show their hand than by hitting them with unanticipated conditions? But the Jordanians had the impression by the time they departed that the Israelis had presented them with a kind of ultimatum to start negotiations on Israel's terms—or suffer the consequences.

Tel then went to the palace and found Sir Alec Kirkbride, the British Minister, sitting with the King.

"Explain to us," demanded Abdullah, "what happened at the conference."

"The Jews," Tel began, "spoke in the language of the victor . . . "

The King cut him off, snapping: "That's enough. Just tell us what happened."

When Tel revealed the conditions for peace he had presented, the King, trembling, demanded: "Who told you to present those conditions?"

"I simply wanted to find out their real views as Your Majesty ordered," Tel replied.

When Tel left the palace, after detailing his talks with the Israelis, he was sure he would no longer be asked to participate in the negotiations.

The King's concern about Israel's intentions was not relieved by the news that Britain, Jordan's protector, was to extend *de facto* recognition to Israel. What irony, he thought. The flight of British planes over the Sinai, intended to frighten Israel, had instead aroused Parliament to force a "normalization" of relations with that country—and at the very moment when Jordan most needed international pressure on the Israelis.

"I KNOW it's the Sabbath tomorrow, but come in early, and wear a dark suit and a black hat."

Joseph Linton, who had been acting as Israel's unofficial representative in London, spoke to his press attaché with a glint in his eye. The following day, he would become Israel's first diplomatic envoy to Great Britain. Though the Foreign Office had simply said that Bevin wanted to see him, a source had revealed that the Foreign Secretary intended to inform him that Britain had decided to recognize Israel.

"But I haven't got a black hat," the press attaché said.

"Then buy one. It isn't every day that an Israeli gets to shake hands with Mr. Bevin."

He couldn't suppress a guffaw.

"And don't forget to bring some wine and cake for the celebration afterwards."

At about 8 A.M. on Saturday, January 29, Linton duly arrived at his office dressed in black jacket, striped trousers, and black homburg, and sat at his desk nervously reading the morning newspapers. He was to see Bevin that morning, but no time had been fixed. Finally, the phone rang and a voice said: "The Foreign Secretary is running behind schedule. Could he call you at noon?"

"Fine, but would you please advise me of the time of my appointment one hour in advance, since it will take that long to walk from my office to the Foreign Office."

"But why must you walk?"

"It's the Sabbath, and as a representative of Israel I feel I should keep to our tradition of not riding on this day."

A few minutes later, the official called again and said: "The Foreign Secretary would not like to inconvenience you and would be prepared to postpone the meeting until Monday."

"Oh no," Linton hastily replied. "I like walking. In any case, it's not raining."

"Very well, then can you be here by noon?"

Linton and his assistant walked happily through the streets of London, arriving at the Foreign Office just before noon. An inner door opened and Bevin came in, beaming. When he had escorted Linton into his office, Bevin sat down, adjusted his glasses, and read aloud a formal document stating that Britain had decided to grant Israel *de facto* recognition.

Linton then removed a slip of paper from his breast pocket and formally expressed his government's appreciation and its desire for good relations between the two countries—though his government did not even know yet of Britain's decision.

"How is it that you have a formal reply ready?" Bevin asked with a puzzled smile. "Who told you we would recognize Israel?"

"A little bird told me," Linton said.

Bevin laughed.

The two men then discussed British policy toward Israel, and Bevin solemnly explained: "I have been misjudged. I am not anti-Zionist. I did not hold up recognition out of ill will. I had simply hoped to be able to recognize Israel simultaneously with other members of the Commonwealth. Now that Australia and Canada have recognized you, we think it is time for us to do so, too."

The Foreign Secretary's thin lips then stretched in a tight, melancholy smile. He knew his visitor didn't believe his denial that he was anti-Zionist; that he probably regarded him as anti-Semitic. Yet, in 1930, as a trade union leader, had he not pressured the government to withdraw restrictions on Jewish immigration into Palestine? And during World War II, had he not influenced the authorities to cancel the deportation order against refugees who had landed illegally in Palestine? He had even advised Weizmann to push for a Jewish State before the war was over—before the Zionists themselves thought the time ripe for such a move!

True, he had changed his views after the war when he became Foreign Secretary. But certainly, he felt, his earlier record proved that the change was rooted not in anti-Semitism but in considerations of the British national interest.

Linton returned Bevin's smile. Here was the man who had cynically told the press shortly after World War II, when he had refused to open the doors of Palestine, that "if the Jews, with all their suffering, want to get too much at the head of the queue, you have the danger of another anti-Semitic reaction." The man who had proclaimed that "the British Government does not accept that the Jews should be driven out of Europe, or that they shall not be permitted to live again in these countries without discrimination . . . " The countries that had been turned into Jewish cemeteries!

He wondered what the Foreign Secretary must be thinking at this moment of utter defeat. He himself felt no rancor or resentment, but a touch of sympathy. After all, who had done more to bring Lord Balfour's promise to final fruition?

"I will be available to you at any time you find it necessary to discuss matters of interest to both countries," Bevin then assured his visitor. "Have you any special point you wish to raise now?"

"Not at the moment, Your Excellency, as I have no instructions, but I would like to bring up one personal matter."

"Yes, what is it?"

"Well, this is my first diplomatic post and I have no experience in diplomatic protocol. Israel's protocol stems from the time of King David and might be out of date. So I would appreciate it if the Foreign Office would offer me guidance when needed."

Bevin leaned back in his chair and roared with laughter.

Iɴ ᴠɪᴇᴡ of Tel's frequent contact with the Israelis, the King, who retained an underlying faith in his loyalty, continued to rely on him as his liaison with the enemy in efforts to negotiate an armistice accord. He thus called Tel on the morning of January 30 and said pleasantly: "Hello Abdullah, I hope you are well."

"Yes, of course, Your Majesty," Tel replied, utterly mystified by the King's sudden warmth.

"Listen, Abdullah, I want you to bring Sasson and the one-eyed man to the palace so that we can speak frankly."

The phone nearly fell from Tel's hand. He could not conceive of the King stooping so low as to invite two Zionist leaders to his palace.

"Your Majesty," he answered in cold anger, "I would appreciate the honor of discussing this matter with you personally in detail."

The King agreed, but Tel did not go to see him, calculating that the Monarch would understand from this that he strongly opposed the suggestion and might simply leave him out of further negotiations.

But Defense Minister Fawzi el-Mulki soon summoned him to his office in Amman.

"His Majesty is angry with you."

"He is?" Tel said innocently. "Why?"

"His Majesty thinks that you disobeyed his orders."

"I don't recall. When?"

"His Majesty says that you are deliberately trying to delay a meeting between him and the Jews and that you did not keep your promise to go to the palace to discuss the question with him."

"Well, it is improper for His Majesty to meet the Jews at his palace. What would happen if this became known to the public? It would be a scandal."

"That's not your business, Abdullah. His Majesty does things in his own way. We do not all approve of many of his deeds and views, but we obey him as long as he assumes responsibility for everything."

"But I am still the commander who defeated the Jews in the Old City. His Majesty's action will reflect on all of us."

"Never mind that. Your deeds are well known. Policy changes, and we have to go along with the current."

"I prefer to resign than to serve under those conditions."

The minister gaped. "Are you mad? I don't want to hear such talk again. Abdullah, be strong."

"As you wish. I will stop at the palace on the way to Jerusalem to discuss the situation with His Majesty in detail."

Fawzi stood up and smiled. "That's more like it," he said, shaking hands. "I wish you success, Abdullah."

As Tel entered the palace reception room, the King welcomed him. Certainly, thought Tel, the minister must have called and told him what had transpired.

"In the name of God," the King said as the two men sat down, "I am fond of you, so don't oppose me. I don't depend much on the government. I could change it with a stroke of the pen. Nor do I depend on the bureaucratic way the government has of solving problems. On the other hand, I see the need to meet the Jews, particularly Sasson, who is an old friend and a fair man. And I am ready to go to Jerusalem to meet him secretly. But it is better to bring him here, together with Dayan."

"As you wish, Your Majesty. I will inform them of your desire. I only hope that the army will protect them while they are coming and going."

"I will speak to Glubb Pasha about that. Perhaps you could bring them for dinner at eight this evening."

Abdullah Tel returned infuriated to Jerusalem and asked several Palestinian leaders their advice as to what he should do.

They insisted that he obey the King, since he was needed in Jerusalem to serve the Palestinian cause. His resignation, they pointed out, would not prevent the King from meeting with the Jews. He would simply find some other officer to help him. Moreover, Tel's presence at the talks would keep him, and the Palestinians, informed of the King's plans.

Tel then made contact with Dayan in the demilitarized zone through a United Nations observer and said: "His Majesty invites you and Mr. Sasson to have dinner at eight o'clock tonight at his table [meaning "home"]."

Dayan looked surprised. "Give me one hour to reply so that I can request permission from Tel Aviv and find Sasson."

One hour later, a messenger delivered a message to Tel: "Tel Aviv approves idea of meeting with His Majesty . . ."

Sasson and Dayan found an armored car waiting for them at Mandelbaum Gate, and shortly afterward they were sitting in the palace salon in Amman. A servant shouted, "His Majesty, the King!" and everyone stood up as the Monarch entered with a serene smile. He greeted Dayan, then shuffled over to Sasson and embraced him, saying: "Brother, why did you not come to the last meeting?"

Sasson grinned. "Unfortunately, I was in Rhodes, Your Majesty."

The King retained his friend's hand in his own and sat down beside him.

Abdullah Tel was silent as he watched the King talk with animation to his two guests. He felt a sense of shame. His Majesty was treating them not with the cool and dignified correctness that was normal in intercourse with the enemy, but as if they were his sons. The conversation soon turned from the weather and social inquiries to the business at hand.

"I am an Arab King," the sovereign said. "I never break a pledge. And I never betray anybody with whom I reach an agreement. You know exactly what my intentions are. And I make sure that nobody mediates between us. The battle has subsided and your forces have occupied the Negev."

Tel was certain that the King was rejoicing as he said this.

After a pause, the King looked at Sasson and continued: "You know, Sasson, we didn't fight you. And we didn't make any incursions into any part of your land [referring to the partition scheme]. As you know, brother, we had an agreement before, and you have just demands, and we also have just demands. In my opinion, old Jerusalem should stay in our hands, with the condition that your people are permitted to pass freely to your holy places. And in return for this, we will not dispute any of the areas you now have."

Tel turned pale as he listened. He found himself interrupting:

"Please forgive me, Your Majesty. But when you say old Jerusalem, I'm sure you mean to include the Arab quarters in new Jerusalem."

The King glared at Tel for an awkward moment and snorted: "Yes, yes." But he added: "We should leave such details to official negotiation between the two governments."

Tel feverishly went over other things the King had said. So he admitted that he had an agreement on the division of Palestine with the Jews. (Sasson says that the King apparently referred simply to an agreement in principle on Israel's right to live, not to any particular geographical division.) And he had suggested a status quo accord with the Jews even before they themselves presented such a proposal. The King was doing all the talking, all the giving away, while the Jews just sat there without having to offer anything.

Finally, the King stood up and said to his guests: "Now let us go to dinner."

Everyone followed him into the spacious dining room and the Israelis were seated on either side of him. Political talk now stopped and the King set the tone of the conversation when he remarked, referring to the Jewish contractors who had built the palace: "Where are the engineers today? I hope I shall see them again. They did an excellent job."

Several days after this palace gathering, the King asked Tel to arrange another. Tel went to see Prime Minister Tawfiq Pasha in the hope of getting him to persuade the King to change his mind. But Tawfiq merely said: "I advise you, Abdullah, to carry out the wish of His Majesty. Do not fear, I will be with him this time and perhaps I can hold the reins on him."

But though Tawfiq was indeed present at the meeting, which took place on January 30, he did not dare interrupt the King, even when the monarch told Sasson and Dayan: "In the name of God, I was hoping that you would take Gaza for us! It is our door to the sea, and we must have a port! Could you not take Majdal?"

Sasson's face reddened with laughter and Tel's with anger at this reference to an apparent Israeli promise to let Abdullah have a port in the Gaza zone if Israel won control of the area.

"May God help us to carry out the wish of His Majesty," Sasson responded, according to Tel.

"May your mission be crowned with success," the King said.

*

A few days later, another meeting was scheduled in the palace. This time, Sasson and Dayan hoped to persuade King Abdullah, since he was in a peacemaking mood, to release the 700-odd Israeli prisoners of war held by Jordan, most of them from the Etzion Bloc and the Old City Jewish Quarter. On the way to Amman in Abdullah Tel's car, Sasson concentrated on trying to win the Colonel over to the idea in view of his strong influence on the King.

"O Abdullah Tel, what do you need the prisoners for?" he asked Tel. "It's costing you a lot of money to feed them. Anyway, many of them are women, children, and old people. Why not put them in twenty or thirty buses during the night and let them go? Nobody will know, and you shall be blessed."

Tel, after reflecting for several moments, replied: "Where would I get the buses? Who would pay for them?"

Sasson smiled. He was sure he had won his case.

"That's no problem," he said. "We'll pay for them."

"Do you have Palestine pounds?"

"Yes, we do. We'll pay twenty, thirty, fifty, even a hundred pounds per prisoner. You name the price and you'll get it."

Tel remained silent.

When the party reached the palace, the King received his guests graciously as usual and hours were spent on a discussion of Arabic poetry, the splendors of nature, and other matters unrelated to serious business. Then, for entertainment, Abdullah asked his advisers riddles; all knew the answers but pretended not to so that the King could show his wisdom by answering himself. Finally, Dayan, who had been largely silent throughout the conversation, nudged Sasson and whispered: *"Nu?"* But Sasson, an Arabist who realized that nothing would loosen up the King more than a long discussion of delightful irrelevancies, ignored Dayan's elbow.

Then, after negotiations having nothing to do with prisoners, the King stood up, and it seemed the meeting was over. Dayan's face blazed with anger at Sasson's failure to broach the subject they had intended to press. But at that moment, Sasson walked over to the King and slid his hand under his Bedouin sash. The King gasped, realizing the significance of this action: Bedouin custom dictated that if a man put his hand under the sash of a sheikh, the sheikh was bound to grant any wish the man might make.

"In the name of God, Eliahu," he exclaimed quickly, raising his hands in subjection, "please ask what is possible! Don't embarrass me!"

Dayan, who did not understand the custom, stood by incredulously, wondering if Sasson had gone mad.

"Your Majesty," Sasson said, "you have seven hundred Israeli prisoners, including women and children. Please release them and they will bless you and God will bless you."

Abdullah turned to Tel and asked: "Is it true, Abdullah? Have we seven hundred prisoners?"

"Yes, Your Majesty," Tel replied.

"Can we release them?"

"If that is your wish, Your Majesty, we can."

"And what will our British friends say?"

"This does not concern them. Anyway, many of the prisoners are not soldiers in the formal sense."

"Taib!" ("Good!") said the King. "Let them go and may they be blessed."

Sasson removed his hand from the King's sash and the two men embraced. The Monarch then hooked Sasson's little finger in his own and walked with his guests to the door. Most of the prisoners were released the next day, and the remainder shortly thereafter.

On February 21, Shawkat telephoned Tel in Jerusalem with the news that the King wanted to invite members of the Israeli delegation that was to negotiate in Rhodes to the palace in order to decide on peace terms in advance.

Tel reluctantly called Dayan, who told him that, to his regret, the Israelis could not come. Tel happily reported the rejection back to the King, who was furious and implied doubt that Tel had even delivered the invitation to the Israelis. He could not understand why they should refuse to reach a final armistice agreement in advance of the official talks.

Then, on February 25, Glubb Pasha informed him that an Israeli patrol had been seen the previous day deep in the southern Negev about 10 miles northwest of Aqaba. And the King began to suspect why his invitation had been refused.

"**Y**IGAL, they've agreed!" Yeroham Cohen cried as he entered Allon's office waving a message from Chief of Staff Dori.

Allon read the message and smiled. Dori had approved a proposal suggesting that a reconnaissance patrol be sent to the southern Negev to find undefended paths that would permit the Israelis to occupy these areas without confronting enemy forces.

"Well, it's a start anyway," he said. "But we've got to work fast. The armistice talks with Jordan start in a few days."

The occupation of the area, Allon knew, would not be simple. For one thing, the only known usable road leading to Elath on the Gulf of Aqaba wound through the Sinai, and with the Egyptian armistice agreement providing that no Israeli troops could cross the border into that region, use of this road seemed out of the question. A new path would have to be found through the narrow cone-shaped corridor separating the Sinai border on the west from the Jordan border along Wadi el Araba on the east.

On February 24, Nahum Sarig sent a specially picked patrol into the southern Negev with orders to find such a path and to obtain information on the distribution of Arab Legion troops. (It was this patrol, seen by Glubb's soldiers, that offered King Abdullah a clue to the sudden aloofness of his Israeli friends.)

After more than a week in the desert, the patrol returned to Beersheba on March 2 exhausted from its adventure but brimming over with just the information that was needed.

"Yes, we can get down there," one member reported to Allon and Sarig.

Now the main problem, Allon was sure, would be Ben-Gurion and the High Command, who were afraid of violating the Egyptian armistice agreement, afraid of sabotaging the peace talks with Jordan, afraid of provoking action by the British in Aqaba.

Jordan, meanwhile, protested the Israeli patrol movement to Bunche, but Israeli officials denied knowledge of any such advance. Then they created endless delays at the conference table in Rhodes with unexpected demands, baffling the mediocre group of Jordanian delegates who had been ordered by the King simply to sign a preliminary cease-fire agreement based on existing military frontiers. The Jordanians could not understand why Israel was not playing the game.

On the night of March 4, Yigal Allon had finally fallen into a restless sleep in his Tel Aviv apartment when he was awakened by the persistent ringing of his doorbell. He stumbled out of bed, half-asleep, and opened the door.

"Yes, what is it?" he asked an army messenger.

"A message from General Dori, sir."

Allon took an envelope, removed the note, and read it. His eyes opened wide. The letter contained a statement that troops moving toward Elath would not fight the enemy, but would halt their advance at the

first sign of resistance. Nor, said the statement, would the troops cross
the Sinai border in view of the recently signed armistice agreement with
Egypt.

"What am I supposed to do with this?" Allon demanded.

"General Dori wants you to sign it, sir."

"What . . .?"

Mumbling curses to himself, Allon spread the document against the
wall and scrawled his signature. He could imagine what Sarig and Golan,
the Commanders of the Negev and Golani Brigades, which were to capture Elath, would say when he told them.

"Colonel Sarig and Colonel Golan," the messenger volunteered, "are
being asked to sign notes, too."

Allon was stunned. This was unprecedented. They were not only
humiliating him by demanding his written agreement, but had directly
forced his subordinates to make similar pledges. He had signed because
Operation Uvda—or *Fait Accompli*—was to begin in a few hours and he
didn't want to risk a delay. But did they really think he would halt his
troops at the first sign of resistance?

Before dawn, Allon drove to Dori's house and said stiffly: "General,
I am responsible not only for the operation but for the lives of my
soldiers. I would like you to modify the order to say that if we are
attacked we can at least defend ourselves."

Dori rubbed his chin reflectively and said: "That makes sense, Yigal.
I'll modify the order. If the enemy attacks you, you have the right to defend
yourselves. But you must not permit our troops to fire first."

Allon was triumphant. "I can assure you," he pledged, "that we will
only fire if fired upon."

He then ordered Sarig and Golan to "defend yourselves all the way
to Elath," even if it meant destroying an enemy regiment.

"But of course," he added, "you're forbidden to fire first!"

Later that morning, in Beersheba, Sarig stood before two companies,
totaling about 200 men, and read the Order of the Day:

> The Negev Brigade is ready for action. We are called upon to complete
> the job we started, to capture the whole Negev. Political limitations will give
> this operation a special character and create difficult conditions for action . . .
> But I am sure the brigade will succeed as it has in the past . . .

The Negev Brigade units were to head south through the center of
the Negev, while Golani troops curved around to the east and then
headed south along the Jordanian border to protect the Negev Brigade's

eastern flank. The two forces, regarding themselves in a kind of race, were to meet in Elath.

Sarig led an advance company over the center road, halting occasionally while engineers blew up large boulders and cleared the route. The group reached the area of a projected airfield without incident on the morning of March 7, and that night planes carrying Allon, three more companies, and an artillery unit landed by the light of two rows of bonfires.

"So far so good," Allon greeted Sarig. Then, pointing south, he added: "In the morning, we'll take a patrol and go looking for a path through those hills and see how we can avoid crossing the Egyptian border."

The next day, March 8, Allon, with Sarig beside him, stood on a mountain ridge surveying the region to the south.

"There's at least a platoon of Jordanians dug in, Nahum," Allon said, peering through binoculars. He observed a path winding through a hilly area to the Jordanian flank but was not sure whether it led through Egyptian territory or not. He spread a map on the ground and the two men, on their knees, studied it for several moments.

"It's very difficult to say," said Allon, pointing to a spot on the map. "But let's give ourselves the benefit of the doubt and assume it's in Israeli territory."

On March 7, the Golani Brigade's four-company task force set out southeastward from the Kurnub area south of Beersheba toward the Jordan border, hoping to beat the Negev Brigade to Elath. Driving one of the half-tracks in the advance column of about 20 vehicles was Philip Bock, who had miraculously recovered from the injuries sustained in the battle for Rafa after dozens of glass and shrapnel splinters had been removed from his eyes.

Bock hummed happily to himself as he drove through the desert, overwhelmed by the honor of being among the first troops assigned to enter Elath in the climactic action of the war. He was also intrigued by the adventure of this thrust into the wilderness. His column would not even be supplied by planes as was the Negev Brigade force, though a Piper Cub flew overhead to observe and report enemy positions.

When, except for some stray shots, no resistance had materialized by the second day, Bock was disappointed. But perhaps it was all for the best, he conceded. In a few hours he would be bathing in the cool waters of the Gulf of Aqaba, possibly the first soldier to dive in.

*

On March 9, the Jordanian delegation in Rhodes again protested the Israeli advance to Bunche, but the acting mediator replied: "If the Jordanian government is right in its allegation, why doesn't it resist the advance of the Israelis in order to prove there have been Israeli military movements?"

The delegation, embarrassed by the question, did not reply. Nor did members know that on March 6 Glubb had in fact ordered a withdrawal of Legion forces from the southern Negev, including Elath itself, to Aqaba. With no fighting, therefore, to report, Bunche told the Security Council that there were no fixed fighting lines and that the military positions held by both sides were not defined.

In an ancient Turkish-built dugout about 40 miles north of Elath, Captain Nigel Bromage, a handsome British youth who looked like a cinematic version of the desert soldier, was thankful that the advancing Israelis, after an exchange of fire, had halted. He wondered how one platoon could long hold off what looked like an armored brigade group. Yet, his soldierly honor forced him at least to ask himself—and Glubb—whether he should resist regardless. Could he let the Jews take the Gulf of Aqaba with hardly a bullet fired? He was torn between the desire to live and the obligation to fight. He decided finally that the decision must be left to Glubb and requested instructions on the evening of March 9 . . .

In his comfortable study at home, Glubb sat brooding. Another Israeli trick! Yet he was powerless. It was impossible to reinforce Bromage effectively. Any large-scale reinforcements would have to be withdrawn from the Jerusalem area through Amman and obliged to cover 260 miles along dirt paths, a trek that would take at least three days. And with exposed flanks, Bromage's force could not hold up the large air-supported enemy force for so long in the open desert. In any event, the Iraqis were about to withdraw in the north, and the Arab Legion, which had to hold the entire front, could not spare troops for so uncertain a venture.

Glubb hesitated before sending a reply to Bromage. How could he ask him to die without being able to appreciate his chances for a successful stand? He finally signalled the young commander to use his own discretion. Then he hurried to attend a performance by the Amman English Amateur Dramatic Society of *The Importance of Being Earnest*.[2]

*

Yigal Allon's dust-caked face reflected something close to agony as he read the radio message in his rear headquarters on the morning of March 10.

"Not again! They couldn't do this!" he muttered.

A few hours earlier, he had sent a message to GHQ explaining that the Negev Brigade force would try to slip past the Jordanian outpost that night and head straight for Elath. In fact, he had already teasingly chided Sarig: "Get moving to Elath or Golani will beat you!"

And now GHQ was prohibiting such action, though, he had to admit, not very unexpectedly. Tel Aviv still feared that he would clash with the Jordanians or pass through Egyptian territory. Actually, Allon himself strongly suspected that the path leading south did indeed cross the Sinai frontier, but he expected to claim that the map did not indicate this clearly. Yadin the archeologist, however, probably harbored little doubt about this point. And Yadin, he knew, would agree with Ben-Gurion that a drive to Elath under the circumstances would jeopardize the armistice accord with Egypt and possibly provoke British armed intervention in the Negev.

But how could GHQ, on the basis of such theoretical dangers, expect him to halt his advance now that he was only a few miles from Elath? Anyway, was it his fault that the message from GHQ arrived "too late"?

While he still held the order in his hand, an aide came in with a monitored enemy radio message indicating that the Jordanian force blocking the way to Elath had withdrawn during the night. Allon's grim expression suddenly vanished. If only the enemy had known that by resisting it might have delayed the Israelis long enough for the politicians to call off an advance to Elath! He glanced at the messages in either hand. How fragile, he thought, were the factors shaping history . . .

"On to Elath!" he ordered Sarig.

And within minutes a unit led by Sarig himself, Micha Peri, and Uzi Narkis set out in jeeps along a mountain trail and bumped across the Sinai frontier. They surrounded an Egyptian police station, and Narkis, bursting in, yelled to the startled occupants: "Put your hands up! Keep your mouths shut and sit quietly, and nothing will happen to you!"

The Israelis had no desire to use violence and thereby trigger an uproar in Cairo that would nullify the armistice accord. In fact, to placate the Egyptians, they left behind cans of kosher meat and other food. Then they continued along the hilly tracks, crossing back into the Negev where they met another Israeli unit, which had meanwhile discovered a second path leading south.

Around noon, the Israelis reached a peak from which they could see spread before them the beach of Elath, an undulating, sun-baked stretch of glittering sand, its edges licked gently by the crystal blue wavelets of the

Gulf of Aqaba. Sarig joyously led his men down the path winding to the beach and at about 4 P.M. entered the police station of Umrashrash—the Arab name for Elath—a group of adobe buildings roofed with palm tree rafters. He installed his men in defense positions and ordered Peri to meet the approaching Golani force.

Then he dashed toward the sea with some of his officers, tearing off his grimy clothing as he ran, and dived naked into the welcoming glassy bay where Solomon's ships had once sailed laden with gold from Ophir . . .

About two hours later, Peri's jeep lurched back into Elath, followed by a glum-looking advance column of the Golani Brigade, which had lost the race. At the police station, Peri carefully unfolded a white bedsheet on which he had crudely inscribed with blue ink a Star of David and two horizontal stripes, and a soldier shinnied up a pole in the police station compound and attached the makeshift flag to it.

Sarig then radioed Allon: "Inform the government of Israel: On the 'Day of Haganah,' the 11th of Adar [March 10], the Palmach Negev Brigade and Golani Brigade present the Gulf of Elath to the State of Israel."

"It's hard to believe," a Negev Brigade officer told a Golani colleague, "but we got here without a single casualty."

"We only had one," the Golani officer replied. "An American driver (Philip Bock) hit a mine and was wounded in the foot. We had to take him back."

In Aqaba Harbor, British seamen watched the Israeli campfires from their battle stations on the decks of their warships, hopeful that the Israelis would fire just one bullet or advance one foot over the Jordanian boundary. They wondered why their government was so timid, permitting them to fire only if the Jews attacked Aqaba. And the Jordanian leaders wondered, too, having invoked the British-Jordanian defense treaty and asked the British to halt the Israeli advance.

But the Israelis had waged their last campaign of the war. In Rhodes, on receiving word that Operation *Fait Accompli* was exactly that, the Israeli delegation casually informed the Jordanians that the southern Negev had been allotted to the Israelis under the United Nations partition plan and that they "planned" to occupy it. The following day, March 11, the two delegations signed a preliminary cease-fire agreement.

WITH the whole Negev finally in Israel's hands, the Israelis
now turned their attention once more to the Triangle, the Iraqi-controlled
west bank area that reached at one point to within 10 miles of the sea. With
a waist that could be so easily cut, Israel was determined to control some
strategic points atop the heights overlooking the coastal plain.

Allon's plan for taking over the whole west bank in three days had
been considered by Ben-Gurion and the High Command and finally rejected on the grounds that such an operation might bring Britain into
the war, sway world opinion against Israel, and aggravate the already
enormous Arab refugee problem. The Israeli leaders, who had been
reluctant enough to use force in the southern Negev, were even less ready
to tempt fate in the Triangle. The question again was how to gain a vital
piece of territory without having to fight for it. And this time Iraq
provided the answer.

When the Iraqis indicated that they would refuse to sign an armistice
agreement with Israel, the Israelis at first were deeply concerned, wanting
peace guarantees from all the Arab belligerents. Sasson, therefore, at the
January 30 meeting in Amman with King Abdullah, had issued a veiled
threat that Israel might attack the Iraqis unless the King persuaded Iraq
to withdraw her troops.

According to Abdullah Tel, who was present at the meeting, Sasson
suggested that Arab Legion forces, which would be bound by armistice
terms, should replace the Iraqis on their front. Ben-Gurion (Tel quotes
the Israeli diplomat as saying) promised to guarantee not to attack Legion
troops. Sasson concedes having demanded the withdrawal of the Iraqis,
but denies that he proposed their replacement by Jordanian forces. At
any rate, King Abdullah interpreted Sasson's comments to mean that
Israel wanted Legion forces to take over the Iraqi positions. And he was
delighted with this opportunity to extend his control over large additional
areas of Palestine without military effort.

As soon as Sasson—and Dayan—had left the palace that evening,
the King telephoned Prince Abdul el-Ah in Baghdad, though it was midnight, and informed him of Israel's demand.

"I would like to discuss the matter with you as soon as possible," he
told the Iraqi Regent.

Two days later, on February 2, the two leaders met at the Iraqi
Petroleum Company station, "H-3."

"Since you do not wish to sign an armistice agreement," Abdullah advised the Regent and Iraqi Prime Minister Nuri el-Said Pasha, who had accompanied him from Baghdad, "it would be wise for your troops to withdraw from Palestine and let us take over for you. Otherwise, the Jews will certainly attack your forces and create many problems for us all."

The King made an impression. The Iraqi leaders had enough problems as it was. Nuri Pasha had only some days before returned from exile in Ankara to head a new Iraqi government, the third time he had been called from abroad in his long political career to save a deteriorating situation. The Iraqi army, unpaid for months, was on the verge of revolt, while general unrest had grown under Nuri's dictatorial predecessor.

Nuri, a moderate pro-Westerner, had thus been brought back because of his close ties with Britain in the hope that the British would furnish Iraq a loan. But the situation was touch and go, and the Iraqi leaders hoped to profit politically from their refusal to sign an armistice agreement with Israel—though Nuri had silently favored acceptance of the United Nations partition plan in the first place. These leaders were in no mood now to gamble all in a new battle which Iraq would probably have to fight alone.

"Very well," the Regent answered Abdullah, "we will withdraw our forces as soon as possible."

The King was delighted and, on returning to Amman, immediately sent Shawkat to Jerusalem to deliver the results of the "H-3" meeting to the Israelis in a sealed envelope.

Abdullah was therefore shocked when, during the conference at Rhodes, the Israelis sent a note to Bunche saying:

> The Israeli government was informed that Iraqi forces stationed in the territory of the Arab Triangle will withdraw and give their posts to Jordanian forces. . . . The Israeli government considers this a violation of the armistice regulations, and is therefore unable to recognize the legality of this replacement. . . . We are of the opinion that Iraq is not carrying out and has no intention of carrying out the resolution of the Security Council concerning negotiations, and is trying to avoid its responsibilities and to secure for itself the right to allege that it is the only Arab State which has not negotiated an agreement with Israel . . .

The Israeli delegates then made it clear to the Jordanians that Israel felt she had the same right as Jordan to occupy the Iraqi-held territory. And to underscore the point, the Israeli High Command began moving troops in daylight to areas adjacent to this region.

The Israelis had decided on a gigantic bluff to gain the land they regarded as vital to their security. The bluff was based on two elements—a foolproof legal argument and a knowledge, confirmed by the Elath episode, that Abdullah and Glubb wanted to avoid battle at almost any cost.

The King, in his despondency, wrote Moshe Sharett on March 15 "reminding" him that Sasson had urged him to occupy the Iraqi front and expressing puzzlement about the Israeli change in attitude. The same day, he received a reply from Walter Eytan of the Israeli Foreign Ministry, who informed him that Sharett had gone abroad, but that the Israeli government would be glad to talk over the Iraqi question within the context of a general armistice agreement.

"We are ready," Eytan wrote, "to call Moshe Dayan [who was heading the Israeli delegation] from Rhodes to discuss with Your Majesty everything concerning an agreement acceptable to both sides."

Replying on March 19, Abdullah, after reviewing again his conversation with Sasson and Dayan, said: "We don't believe that the Israeli side is intentionally trying to create difficulties for me with either the Arabs or the Israelis. If Your Excellency can arrange a meeting between you, Dayan, and me it would be beneficial to us all. Both sides have rightful demands which can be conciliated, if God permits."

The Israelis were delighted with this response. So far, their bluff had worked to perfection.

Flying in from Rhodes, Moshe Dayan met with the King at Shuneh Palace that evening (March 19) with orders to do some plain talking. According to Abdullah Tel, who was present, the Sovereign maintained early in the conversation that he had only met with the Iraqi Regent because the Israeli side suggested that the Arab Legion should replace the Iraqi troops on the Israeli frontier. But, Tel claims, Dayan ignored this remark. In any event, Dayan explained that Israel wanted Jordan to give up some strategic heights overlooking the coastal plain and to open a wadi and a road running through her military positions. Israel would then agree to an adjustment of some positions to the advantage of Jordan and, in principle, to Jordanian replacement of Iraqi troops.

Abdullah's smile this time had more sparkle. He seemed to be surprised that the demands were not greater.

"I do not object to those terms," he said, "and will issue orders immediately to our delegation in Rhodes to accept these conditions as a basis for negotiations."

When Dayan had departed, the King called a meeting of a government negotiating team at which Glubb and Tel were present. The King said to Tel: "Bring the Jews tonight and our delegation will be waiting for them here."

Then he turned to Justice and Deputy Defense Minister Fallah Madadha Pasha, the head delegate, and said: "I want you to accept their demands, whatever the cost, to relieve me of this problem. We have many strategic posts in the mountains of Tubas and Jericho. What can we lose by giving them some hills to protect their lands?"

Abdullah Tel, trembling with anger, finally burst out: "Your Majesty, if they ask for hills we must demand something in return!"

The King looked at Tel as if about to pronounce his death sentence. But before he could reply, Education Minister Sheikh Mohammed Amin Shankity, another delegate, distracted his attention.

"The Arabs in Palestine," he stammered, "have fled their villages, left their homes to the Jews, and His Majesty—may God prolong his life—is their protector. So it is best to negotiate with the Jews, whatever the cost."

Glubb Pasha was silent. He had never favored replacing the Iraqi troops, feeling that the Arab Legion would be stretched too vulnerably thin if it had to guard the Triangle. The King, he thought, should have tried to persuade the "ungrateful" Iraqis to sign an armistice agreement and stay where they were instead of asking them to leave their positions to the Legion. Now they flatly refused to remain in their positions and sign a truce accord despite belated efforts by the King, in the face of the Israeli threat, to get them to reverse their decision.

Abdullah Tel went to Jerusalem and asked the Israelis for a new meeting but, in a token effort to avert what he regarded as the besmirching of the nation's dignity, lied: "His Majesty prefers that these negotiations take place in the demilitarized zone in Jerusalem."

When the Israelis agreed, Tel telephoned the King, who wanted to meet with them again in Amman, and said: "Your Majesty, the Jews demanded that the meeting be held in Jerusalem."

The King reluctantly approved.

To the meeting, held in a house at Mandelbaum Gate, came an Israeli team headed by Yadin, Dayan, and Eytan. After a welcoming speech by Fallah, Eytan expressed his deep admiration for the King, who, he said, was wise and had a sense of realism. Then he motioned to Yadin, and the Israeli military leader opened a large map of the Arab Triangle, spread it on the long conference table, and explained Israel's demands. As he drew a line on the map to illustrate them, Tel whispered to Fallah sitting next to him: "Our friend must have illusions." If those were Israel's maximum demands, even their minimum ones were certain to be unacceptable.

Tel, who was present as military adviser, then asked to reply and sneered: "The committee was not assigned to discuss such demands since they could not be carried out, calling as they do for fantastic territorial changes."

And Fallah added: "Don't be stubborn. We are ready to go further than any of the other Arab States since we are neighbors . . . There is an old saying: 'A neighbor is closer than a distant brother!' "

Eytan then asked Yadin to modify the line he drew, and he himself suggested some changes. But Abdullah Tel still described the line as "fantastic." He whispered to Fallah: "Ask them for their minimum demand."

Fallah did so, and Yadin, studying the map for several moments, drew another line.

"This is our minimum demand," he announced. Whereupon Tel remarked that negotiations meant give and take on both sides. "We also have some demands."

"What are your demands?" Eytan asked.

Tel called for the sharp pullback of Israeli troops from several key positions.

The Israelis just smiled and looked at each other. And so the meeting ended.

"What did you say? The talks failed?"

As he lay in bed at 3 A.M. with the telephone receiver to his ear, Fallah Pasha, who had stayed overnight in Jerusalem, wondered for a moment if this was still part of his nightmare. But as he rubbed his hand over his face, he realized he was awake; and this was worse than a nightmare. The King was on the phone, and he was in a rage.

"You and Abdullah come to the palace in the morning!" he stormed.

Fallah dressed quickly and, still in a daze, dashed to Tel's house, woke him up, and informed him of the royal order. The telephone rang. It was the King.

"What have you done?" he asked Tel in despair. "The committee and Glubb are coming here at nine o'clock. I want you to be here, too."

"As you wish, Your Majesty. We shall explain everything . . . "

Hardly had the visitors kissed the King's trembling hand and sat down when he abruptly asked Fallah: "Why did the meeting fail?"

"Your Majesty, they wanted to annex large areas to their lands, and we were afraid to agree, fearing that Your Majesty might be angry with us. I must admit that Abdullah Bey advised us to reject their suggestions."

Before Tel could reply, the King interrupted: "You all know that the Arab countries have abandoned us and that we are alone in the battlefield. The Arab Legion is small. It was set up originally to defend the borders, not to occupy Palestine, where the Jews, brought there by the British, are powerful . . . The West has given us up and we can't depend on it. If the war had started under such circumstances, we would have lost more than what the Jews are asking for now. And if war breaks out again, you will not find another leader to master the situation."

The ministers all shouted replies simultaneously. "We are all your slaves," cried one. And "We would sacrifice our souls if ordered to do so by Your Majesty," confirmed another.

When quiet again prevailed, Tel said: "The Jews asked . . . for territorial changes that were unreasonable and would not accept our demands in return. I suggest that Glubb Pasha or Lash Bey go with the committee to negotiate with the Jews, since the Jewish acting chief of staff, Yigal Yadin, is a member of the Jewish delegation."

He paused, glancing at Glubb, then added: "Your Majesty, the British have led the Arab Legion in the fighting with the Jews, and they are responsible for the present situation. If Your Majesty had organized the army by yourself, the situation would be different. But it is the responsibility of the British to negotiate with the Jews and they alone should bear that responsibility."

The atmosphere was strained, and both the King and Glubb looked embarrassed. Abdullah would not even consider suffering the indignity of having a foreigner negotiate for him, but he did not want to hurt Glubb's feelings by saying so to his face, and Glubb was aware of the awkwardness of the King's position.

"What is your opinion?" the King asked him. "Which officers do you think should be represented on the committee? Can we reject the Jewish demands?"

"You know, Your Majesty," Glubb said, "that the Arab Legion's potential in the war is very poor and that the British have not given us any ammunition since they evacuated Palestine. We were left in the battlefield alone, and it is impossible for us to fight the Jews now that they have united their forces against us. As for me joining in the negotiations, I apologize, but I could not, since I do not wish to meet with the Zionists . . . If Abdullah Tel refuses to go, I can send my chief of operations to the negotiations."

The King, relieved, then decided to invite to the conference British Chargé d'Affaires Gordon and American Chargé d'Affaires Stabler. The latter had been promoted from Consul-General after Washington's recognition of Jordan, which Britain had requested in return for her own recognition of Israel. The two men arrived at the palace at about 11 A.M. while the meeting was still in progress, and the King, after welcoming them, criticized the United States for supporting the Jews and thereby encouraging them to escalate their demands. Abdullah then explained the status of the peace talks to Stabler and asked his advice on how far Jordan should go to satisfy the Israelis.

"I cannot offer any official advice at this time, Your Majesty," Stabler said. "I must first discuss the matter with my government. I understand, however, that my government has instructed our representative in Tel Aviv to advise Israel to agree to the withdrawal of the Iraqi army from the Triangle and its replacement by the Arab Legion units."

The King then turned to Gordon and asked if he could offer any advice. But he also replied that he would have to consult his government first.

The King was satisfied. What he really wanted was not advice, but support from Britain and the United States. Perhaps after hearing of the Israeli attitude they might, with a combination of threat and persuasion, force Israel to be more "reasonable." He stood up and invited all those present to lunch with him.

During the meal, he commented: "I am ready to give up my throne before renewing battle with the Jews. But the question is, who would take power after I had gone? In the name of God, I love Jordan and its people, not from personal interest, as the country is poor. If I left Jordan, I wouldn't have enough money to pay for even a single dinner!"

After lunch, as he was about to retire for a nap, the King ordered Tel to invite the Israelis to dinner at the palace . . .

At the palace that evening, Eytan handed Abdullah a gift, a rare Old Testament, saying: "Prime Minister Ben-Gurion has the honor of presenting to Your Majesty this gift, simple in its material value but precious in its meaning; a present which can be a symbol of friendship between our two countries, which signifies the good will of the Israeli government."

But when Abdullah turned to the first page, his face flushed with shock and indignation.

"What is this?" he demanded.

Eytan, a rather short man, reached to look over his shoulder, and shuddered. On the first page was a map of Israel from the days of King Solomon, when the nation embraced areas now controlled by Jordan.

"What is this here?" the King repeated with a scowl.

"That is a map of ancient Israel," Eytan explained, nervously brushing back his thin black hair.

The King paused in thought for a moment, then smiled.

"And I have something for you," he said, handing his guest an ornamental silver dagger.

Now there were smiles on all sides, though Tel saw both gifts as carrying a significant message.

When everybody had filed into the salon and sat down, the King asked Eytan: "How is my friend Shertok?"

"Fine, fine. He sends you his regards."

"Please send him mine. And how is Mrs. Golda Myerson?"

"Mrs. Myerson is now Israel's Ambassador to Moscow."

Abdullah smiled in satisfaction. He remembered the rather cold meetings he had had with Mrs. Meir. Anyway, how could he have bargained seriously with a woman?

"Good!" he exclaimed. "Leave her there!"

Then he stood up and began making a speech, which he directed less to the Israelis, it seemed, than to his own ministers.

"The Jews belong to a united, advanced nation," he said, "and the Arabs belong to weak, backward nations. The West is against us. And I swear, by the name of God, that we did not receive a single bullet from abroad during the war . . . The Arabs hoped to win, but the contrary happened. We did not intend to fight but the Egyptians and the other Arab nations pushed us into war."

Then, glaring contemptuously at his ministers, who were sitting lined up on his left, he shouted: "I told you from the start that we had no chance to beat the Israelis, but you wouldn't listen to me!"

And, turning to the Israelis, he went on: "I am not afraid, and I am ready to bear the responsibility for what I say. The problem is to reach an agreement with you, a reconciliation . . . This is my intention, and you can be sure of my frankness . . . "

There was a shocked silence as Abdullah paused. This was not the kind of speech usually addressed to representatives of an enemy nation.

"I am a Bedouin," he continued, "and we Bedouins have a saying: 'When you're riding a mule that is overloaded with goods and your enemy chases you, you have one of two choices. You either fall prisoner with your goods or you run away, ridding yourself gradually of the load.' I have invited the Israelis here in order to get rid of the load!"

The King then reminded his guests of the alleged suggestion made by Sasson that the Jordanians should take over the Iraqi-held areas, and pleaded with them to make reasonable compromises so that his position would not be weakened in the Arab world.

When the King had finished speaking, he turned to Prime Minister Tawfiq Pasha and said: "Now it is your turn to speak."

Tawfiq stood up, trembling slightly, and coughed. "I request your permission to be excused, Your Majesty," he mumbled. "I don't feel well."

Abdullah waved his arm in a gesture of disgust and shouted at him: "Then get out of here!"

As the Prime Minister left almost in tears, the Israelis silently squirmed with embarrassment at the discomfort of the Jordanians. Then Walter Eytan, a cheerfully cynical man, replied in English to the King's address, saying that he carried "the greetings of Prime Minister Ben-Gurion to His Majesty, who receives the Israeli delegation generously and with an open heart." He asserted that he shared the King's wish to reach a final settlement between the two countries as soon as possible, but emphasized that Jordan had to agree to territorial changes in the Triangle.

"Israel," he went on, "has undergone much suffering as a result of the narrow width of its territory along the Triangle. Every day men and women are killed in clashes due to the unnatural situation there. This territory exposes Israel to danger. If the government of His Majesty the King refuses to accept Israel's demands, I advise the government of Jordan not to interfere between the Iraqis and ourselves and to let us settle the situation in our own way."

A further cold silence pervaded the room in the wake of this clear new threat to attack the Iraqi positions if the Jordanians did not agree to Israel's terms.

Everyone then went into the dining room and sat down to consume a sumptuous meal served on gold and silver plates. Abdullah pointed to various items of tableware, announcing proudly: "I received this from King George, this from Roosevelt, and you see that candelabra over there? Pincas Ruttenberg gave me that." (Ruttenberg, one of the first Zionist industrialists, established the first electric power plants in Palestine.)

Abdullah turned to Yadin, seated beside him, and jovially remarked: "Do you know what I like to do in my leisure time? Listen to old Arab poems."

Yadin swiftly thought back to his schooldays when his teacher had forced him to learn long Arabic poems by heart. How he had cursed his teacher. Little had he realized that one day he would have an occasion to use this knowledge in the service of his country.

"I know an Arabic poem," he told Abdullah.

Then he recited: "Here is the weeping mother, weeping over her sons on the battlefield. And so she says: 'O, I weaned you, I fed you, I raised you . . . ' "

The King embraced Yadin and exclaimed: "By my head, that's my favorite poem! Tell me, where did you learn it?"

Everyone thought it was a shame that the discussion should have to revert again to politics . . .

After dinner, at about 11 P.M., the guests followed the King into a long conference room decorated with an oil painting of the Battle of Trafalgar, a gift from King George V. Abdullah sat at one end on a dais, flanked on the right by his ministers and on the left by the Israelis, with some of the conferees sitting on stools, others on mats. After a few minutes, Abdullah rose, declaring:

"I shall leave now to enable the two delegations to negotiate an agreement, but I swear that I shall not sleep until you bring me the news that your talks have succeeded."

The discussion was immediately deadlocked when the Israelis repeated the demands they had made in Jerusalem. But as the bartering gradually proceeded, the King reappeared from time to time dressed in a white nightshirt and assured everyone: "Don't despair. Everything will work out. We shall reach an agreement."

But no agreement was reached that night, and before dawn, Abdullah Tel, who chose not to be present at the meeting because of his reluctance to share in the responsibility for an accord strongly favoring Israel, drove the Israelis to Jerusalem.

Another was held a few days later at which the Israelis reached an agreement in principle with the Jordanians, led by Brigadier Coaker, Glubb's chief of operations, for satisfaction of most Israeli demands. But the conferees, to the King's disappointment, still could achieve no final accord.

In desperation, the King called a ministerial meeting in his palace on the morning of March 26 and explained once again how limited was the Arab Legion's war potential. He then read out Bevin's reply to the message of British Chargé d'Affaires Gordon relaying Abdullah's request for "advice." Bevin simply advised him to ask for President Truman's advice. The King said he had, in fact, cabled a special message to Truman that day asking him to induce the Jews to be more reasonable, though he did not expect this approach to be fruitful. And he turned to Tawfiq.

"Do you advise us to depend on foreigners? In the name of God, I prefer not to fight!"

"I do not, Your Majesty," Tawfiq responded.

The Prime Minister then announced that a final meeting with the Israelis would be held on March 29.

"The government," he said with an air of bitter resignation, "will accept all of their demands, but will endeavor to amend some articles."

The King smiled and told his ministers: "You are all honorable sons of Jordan."

The Jordanians asked that Ben-Gurion himself head the Israeli delegation this time, but this request was politely rejected. Dayan and Shiloah joined Yadin and Eytan for the showdown meeting, while Abdullah Tel decided to participate this time, hoping to force last-minute concessions from the Israelis.

The King, his depression deepened by a cable from President Truman saying, in effect, that all the United States could do was to try to influence the Jews not to increase their current demands, again served a grandiose meal, and even Tel seemed more resigned than previously to an Israeli diplomatic victory. Yadin was shocked to hear him say between courses: "I recently returned from Damascus and I swear all of Damascus is protected by just one company. You would be able to conquer Syria very easily. My friends there told me I could conquer all of Syria with one battalion."

Yadin smiled, well aware of Tel's enthusiasm for the establishment of a Greater Syria under Jordan's leadership.

Tel then asked, grinning: "If we launched a campaign against Syria, would you be prepared to lend us a few planes?"

Yadin wondered whether Tel was joking. "What? How could you even imagine such a thing?"

"It's very simple," Tel answered calmly. "You lend us a few planes for one night. We'll paint them with Jordanian colors, just to impress the Syrians, and we'll return the planes right away."

Yadin stared at Tel, and the two men laughed.

When dinner was over, the King rose and declared: "This is it! Tonight we sign!"

Then he left for his quarters while the others went to the conference hall again and sat on mats around a large map.

Suddenly, after studying the previously reached agreement in principle, Defense Minister Fawzi el-Mulki, who had not been present at the earlier meetings, exclaimed: "What is this? You've tricked the King! You've got Wadi Ara, the crest, everything! The King won't be able to keep his throne even one day if you get all this!"

The King then entered in his nightshirt, and said angrily to his delegates: "I said that tonight we finish—so finish!"

And he departed, slamming the door behind him.

The delegates, who had risen, sat down on their mats again and Mulki, somewhat embarrassed, continued: "The agreement in principle gives you too many Arab villages. Move the line a bit on the map."

"I'm ready to move it," Yadin said, "if the lands of those villages remain in our territory."

"I don't care about land," Mulki replied. "Who cares about land in this world? Only the names of towns appear on maps, and the less names there are in your territory, the better for us. Anyway, this is just a temporary armistice agreement until we agree on a permanent peace arrangement."

Yadin smiled and drew a new line with a colored crayon.

Abdullah Tel entered the room, sat down, and said to Yadin: "The King asks that you do one personal favor for him. Since we're giving up so much to you, he asks that you give him Beit Gubrin so that we will be able to leave the negotiations honorably."

"We came here to discuss the area under Iraqi control," Yadin rejoined.

The King himself then entered and, as everybody rose, put his hand on Yadin's shoulder, hugged him, and pleaded: "Mr. Yadin, give me Beit Gubrin. Tomorrow is my birthday. Give me Beit Gubrin as a birthday present."

Yadin had never felt uneasier. An old King was virtually begging him, a young man of thirty-two, for a "favor." He sympathized with him, but there would be hell to pay back home if he gave up a strategic point like

Beit Gubrin—even if he were personally prepared to do so. He would relinquish other pieces of territory along the Hebron Hills, but no more. After all, Abdullah was getting almost the whole of Arab Palestine.

"Who am I and what am I?" Yadin asked dramatically, "You are a King and I am a dog. Even if I gave you Beit Gubrin, they would kick me out tomorrow and wouldn't give you anything!"

The King stroked his beard and said merrily: "*Taib!* [Good!] Let's go and sign!"

Israeli and Jordanian delegates flew with the approved maps to the peace talks and informed Ralph Bunche that their two countries were ready to sign an armistice agreement. Bunche examined the maps and was amazed to see that so many important changes had been agreed upon, with Israel gaining the strategic hills she wanted and Jordan some areas in the Hebron mountains.

"You both argued for weeks about every centimeter of ground and suddenly you come to me with a new map and say you're ready to sign today. I just don't understand . . . But I'm delighted."

And on April 3, the Israelis and Jordanians signed the agreement a second time for the benefit of the public.

Some time later, Sasson met with the King in Shuneh to suggest the transformation of the armistice agreement into a permanent peace accord, but Abdullah replied: "Eliahu, my friend, I must tell you that I am unable to negotiate a permanent peace settlement with you. Our friends, the British, have told me: 'Stop!' They think that the time isn't ripe yet, that we should wait a while. They think that peace between us will result in a new deterioration in their relations with Egypt."

The King paused and his smile dissolved in agitation. "Only the British are to blame, only the British!"[3]

O N MARCH 23, an armistice accord was concluded with Lebanon under which Israel agreed to withdraw from Lebanese territory unconditionally. Colonel Salem, the Lebanese chief of staff, assured Mordechai Makleff, the Israeli delegate, that Lebanon had "no reason to be at war with you." He added: "As we are a weak country, we will not be the first to make permanent peace with you. Make peace with another Arab State first, and we'll be number two . . ."

Syria, more fanatically anti-Israel than any other Arab nation, was reluctant to negotiate at all, at least in part because any agreement would inevitably call for a withdrawal of Syrian forces from the Israeli territory of Mishmar Hayarden.

When the talks started on April 5, Syrian delegate Selo would not even shake hands with Makleff. The second day, he shook hands and said stiffly: "We demand Haifa!"

Makleff smiled and replied: "We demand Damascus!"

For the next three days, Makleff kept promising that he would stop demanding Damascus if his Syrian counterpart would drop his claim on Haifa.

Finally, when the Syrian agreed, Makleff asked: "Why should we have wasted three days discussing such stupid proposals?"

"Is it a sin to want?" Selo asked.

This broke the ice, and the two men became very friendly; but Selo still felt it was politically impossible for him to make any concession. Nonetheless, they talked. One evening, over coffee, Selo said: "You know, I've worked it out. Your army and mine, if we joined together, would be the most powerful in the Middle East."

"Join together against whom?" Makleff asked in puzzlement.

"I haven't thought of that yet," Selo replied.

Nor had he thought yet about negotiating. But as the political and economic chaos in Syria increased, so did Syrian fear of an Israeli attack; and Makleff did not relieve this fear when he threatened an attack if Syria did not come to terms soon.

As in Iraq, trade had collapsed and living costs had skyrocketed, aggravating popular feeling against the 100 or so oligarchal families who owned most of the land and ran a corrupt government that cared little about the needs of the impoverished peasantry. The political temperature had risen almost to the boiling point when the Premier's brother had been arrested for involvement in a great financial scandal, when funds intended for Palestine refugees had vanished, and when the Israelis had grabbed the shipload of Czech arms purchased by Syria.

After defeat in the Palestine war, the frustration had finally erupted, as crowds demonstrated in the streets and, in an orgy of violence, forced the Prime Minister to flee the country. Then two other coups shook Syria, one after the other, and it appeared that King Abdullah might, after all, in the confusion of this anarchy, move in to realize his dream of an Amman-dominated Greater Syria.

So, gradually, Selo gave way. He agreed to withdraw Syrian forces from Israel, though stipulating that Israeli forces could not replace them in the evacuated areas. A demilitarized zone was thus established, and an agreement was signed on July 20, 1949.[4]

The First Arab-Israel War was officially over.

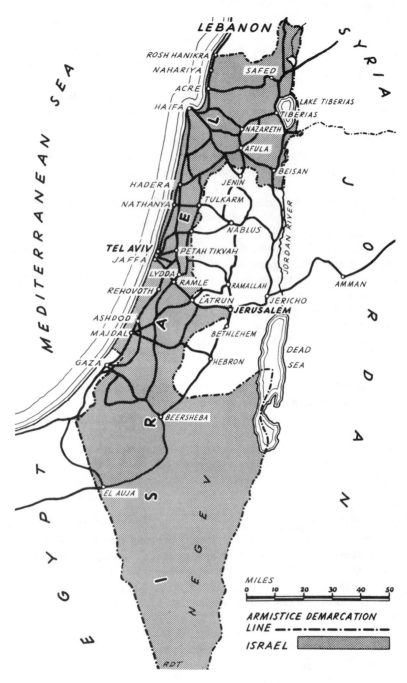

THE FINAL ARMISTICE PARTITION

A's THE last shots were being fired, Salem Jarufi and surviving members of his family packed their meager belongings and climbed into the truck waiting in the British-operated refugee camp. The camp in the Sheikh Othman suburb of Aden had become so overcrowded with Jews streaming in from Yemen on their way to the Promised Land that, to make room for newcomers, the British had agreed to let the Israelis inaugurate Operation Magic Carpet—a refugee airlift from Aden to Israel.

Within an hour, the Jarufis were tramping along a hard-surfaced clearing and up a stairway into the body of a huge metal bird. The cushioned seats were so uncomfortably soft that most of them chose to squat in the aisle. Everything was happening with such little ceremony and fanfare that Salem found it hard to believe that he was on the last leg of his long journey. Even when the giant bird took off into space, everything seemed so natural. He was more astonished by his own matter-of-fact reaction than by the adventure itself.

"Father, Father, are we really riding to Jerusalem on the wings of an eagle?"

Salem smiled as he looked at his blind son Yihyeh sitting on the floor of the plane beside him. Now he knew why he did not feel overawed in this hour of deliverance.

"Certainly, my son. It's just like the Bible says . . . "

I'N February, 1950, Gamal Abdel Nasser and Yeroham Cohen met in El Auja and drove together to Faluja so that Nasser could point out the location of Israeli graves. As they walked among the graves, Nasser asked: "Do you remember, Yeroham, when we sat on the grass and I told you I didn't think I would ever see my wife and daughters again?"

"Yes, Gamal. And I told you that you would not only see your daughters but would have a son as well."

"Well, I've got a son."

That night, Cohen, on returning to Tel Aviv, sent a package of baby clothes to his Egyptian friend.

It was too bad, he reflected, that a man like Gamal Abdel Nasser was not running Egypt.

Epilogue

THREE years after the war, Gamal Abdel Nasser, now a colonel, was running Egypt. And soon afterwards, he became Israel's most dangerous foe in the Middle East.

When a group of "Free Officers," in mid-1952, ousted King Farouk and took over the government, Israel had had high hopes for a permanent peace accord with Egypt. For the Israelis regarded General Mohammed Neguib, who ostensibly led the revolt, as a moderate who would be willing to negotiate with them. They were even more hopeful when they learned that the real leader of the *coup d'état* was Nasser—who placed Neguib under house arrest for seeking real power.

But to shore up wavering popular support after setbacks in his program for social revolution, Nasser launched a campaign for the unification of the Arab world under his leadership, and found two policies helpful to his cause: the exploitation of a general Arab hatred of Israel through terrorist attacks, and the purchase of Soviet arms, largely (at that time) as a matter of prestige.

The terrorism led to the Israeli capture of the Gaza Strip and the Sinai during the Suez War of 1956—though Israeli forces, under American pressure, withdrew from these areas after the fighting, to be replaced by United Nations troops. In 1967, Nasser ordered these troops out and closed the Red Sea strait at Sharm el-Sheikh to Israeli traffic, thereby triggering the Six Day War.

Abdel Hakim Amer, Nasser's closest friend, served as first Vice-President in the Nasser government until after the Six Day War, when he was accused of negligence in failing to prepare the armed forces for the struggle. While awaiting trial, he died mysteriously. The government claims he committed suicide.

Zakaraya Muhieddin, too, became a Vice-President under Nasser and won a reputation for pro-West tendencies. Immediately after the Six Day War, Nasser announced that he was resigning and that Muhieddin would replace him, but "changed his mind" when the public demonstrated in his support. Later, Muhieddin, apparently at odds with Nasser over the question of relations with the West, resigned his vice-presidential post. Mohammed Hassenin Heikal, the Egyptian journalist, has long been editor of the Cairo newspaper *Al Ahram,* and was Nasser's chief spokesman.

The first war also had an explosive aftermath in Jordan. Following the armistice, King Abdullah continued to negotiate secretly with the Israelis for new, permanent boundaries between Israel and Jordan and for a corridor through Israel to the port of Haifa, Gaza, or Ashkalon. In the midst of these talks, on July 20, 1951, the King was shot to death at point-blank range as he was entering the Mosque of Omar in the Old City of Jerusalem for Friday services.

The assassin, who was killed on the spot by Abdullah's bodyguard, was reported to have been an agent of the Mufti, Haj Amin el-Husseini. The Mufti and his Arab Higher Committee firmly denied complicity in the murder, and two of the Mufti's brothers were acquitted for lack of evidence. But a cousin, Mousa Abdullah el-Husseini, was sentenced to death.

Given the same sentence, *in absentia,* with the vigorous approval of Glubb Pasha, was Colonel Abdullah Tel. He had fled to Cairo, where he denied charges of involvement but claimed that King Abdullah, in league with Glubb, had betrayed the Arabs. More than a decade later, the slain monarch's grandson, King Hussein, pardoned Tel and permitted him to return to Jordan a free man. The Mufti would live in Beirut until his death. Most of his supporters had become refugees and gave their allegiance to modern fighting and terrorist groups, which would eventually be integrated into the Palestine Liberation Organization led by Yasser Arafat.

As for Glubb, he and other British commanders in the Arab Legion were summarily dismissed in 1955 during a nationalist upsurge in Jordan and replaced by Jordanian officers.

In Syria, Colonel Adib Shishekli, who had led the Arab Liberation Army contingent in the battle for Safed, took over the government in a new coup shortly after the first war. Then he himself was ousted by other officers and later assassinated by political enemies while living in exile in Brazil.

In Iraq, Prime Minister Nahas Pasha was assassinated during the Iraqi revolution of 1958 which overthrew the monarchy in that country. And in Lebanon, the army commander-in-chief, General Fuad Shehab, assumed the presidency as a compromise leader when pro-Nasser rebels ousted President Camille Chamoun in 1958—an act that prompted the landing of American troops in Beirut.

Fawzi el-Kaoukji lived in Beirut until his death. Mohammed and Greta Gharbieh lived in Jericho, where he worked as a Jordan government official, until they fled during the Six Day War. Bahjat Gharbieh was a businessman in the Old City of Jerusalem until he, too, fled during this war.

In Israel, Prime Minister David Ben-Gurion remained in power until 1953, when Moshe Sharett replaced him. He returned to the post in 1955 but resigned again in 1963 after a bitter political dispute with other leaders of his Mapai Party. He formed the Rafi Party with the support of Moshe Dayan, who had served as chief of staff during the Suez War and had then switched to politics. In the days before the Six Day War, Dayan was swept by popular demand into the position of Defense Minister in the expanded war cabinet of Prime Minister Levi Eshkol, who had succeeded Ben-Gurion.

Yigal Allon resigned from the army after the first war because of his tenuous relations with Ben-Gurion and also entered politics. He was eventually appointed Minister of Labor in the Eshkol government and, after the Six Day War, deputy Prime Minister. On Eshkol's death in February, 1969, he took over as acting Prime Minister—until Golda Meir, who had served for ten years as Foreign Minister after the first war, emerged from retirement to become a compromise Prime Minister. In late 1969, she solidified her position when her party won a national election.

Yigal Yadin resigned from the army shortly after the first war and, following in his father's path, became Israel's leading archeologist. He later entered politics and joined the government of Menachem Beigin in 1977. Yitzhak Rabin was chief of staff during the Six Day War, and is credited with having done the most to forge the victorious fighting machine. After that war, he was appointed Ambassador to Washington, and later became Prime Minister, then Defense Minister. Moshe Carmel would serve as Minister of Transportation, Israel Galili as Minister of Information; and Eliahu Sasson, who negotiated with King Abdullah, Minister of Police.

Menachem Beigin converted his Irgun Zvai Leumi into the Herut (Freedom) Party after the first war. His party joined with other right-wing parties to form Likud, which came to power in 1977, with himself as Prime Minister. He resigned the post in 1982 and became a recluse.

Mordechai Raanan, who had been the Irgun chief in Jerusalem, became a leading book and magazine publisher, and Nathan Friedman-Yellin (later Yellin Mor), the former Sternist leader, an editor of a small left-wing newspaper that advocated a dovish attitude toward the Arabs. Yitzhak

Yizernitsky (later Shamir), moved from the Stern Group to Mossad, the Israeli intelligence service, and eventually became Prime Minister, succeeding Beigin in that post. He would vigorously oppose giving up any occupied lands. Yehoshua Zetler, formerly the Sternist leader in Jerusalem, became a businessman in Tel Aviv.

Joshua Cohen, Zetler's deputy in Jerusalem, returned to his Negev kibbutz and has become the personal bodyguard of Ben-Gurion, a member of the same settlement. David Shaltiel, the Haganah commander in Jerusalem, served for a while as Ambassador to Brazil, then as an official in the Foreign Ministry. Yeroham Cohen, who had become a close friend of Nasser, served as Ambassador to Ethiopia and then entered business.

Moshe Rousnak, commander of the Old City Jewish Quarter, was appointed an official in Jerusalem's Hadassah Hospital. Judith Jaharan, heroine of the Jewish Quarter battle, also found work in a hospital. Monroe Fein and his wife Topsy, who met on the Altalena, made their home in a suburb of Chicago.

Mathilda Muhtaseb, who, after the first war lived in Jewish Jerusalem, was reunited with her daughters when the Israelis captured the Old City in the Six Day War. She and her daughters, all married to Moslems, for years had been within sight of each other's homes on either side of a no-man's-land separating the two sections of Jerusalem.

Notes

CHAPTER I

[1] Sharif el-Shanti wrote the story of the Mufti's attempt to negotiate with the Jews in the July 27, 1950, issue of *Al Youm,* a daily Arabic-language newspaper published in Jaffa. The Israelis do not deny the story.

CHAPTER II

[1] From interview with Emile al-Ghouri.

[2] A conversation between the Mufti and I. A. Abbady, a Palestinian Jew, is quoted in *The Mufti and the Fuehrer* by Joseph B. Schechtman, New York, Yoseloff, 1965.

[3] *Documents of German Foreign Policy,* Series D, Vol. V, June, 1937–March, 1939; Doc. 569, pp. 758–760.

[4] See *The Cat and the Mice* by Leonard Mosley, London, A. Barker, 1958.

[5] Quoted in Quentin Reynolds, Ephraim Katz, and Zwy Aldouby, *Minister of Death: The Adolf Eichmann Story,* New York, Viking, 1960.

[6] "The Arab Higher Committee"—*Nation Associates* (May, 1947).

[7] From interview with Ahmad Shannak.

[8] For details of Sheib's background, see his book *The First Tithe* (*Maaser Rishon*), Tel Aviv, Hamatmid (Hebrew).

[9] For details of Abraham Stern's death, see *The Deed* by Gerold Frank, New York, Simon and Schuster, 1963.

[10] For details of the Acre Prison break from the Irgun point of view, see *The Revolt by* Menahem Begin (Menachem Beigin), Tel Aviv, Hadar, 1964.

[11] See *Arabian Jubilee* by Harry St. John Philby, New York, Day, 1953.

[12] See *Trial and Error* by Chaim Weizmann, New York, Harper, 1949.

[13] See *Roosevelt and Hopkins* by Robert Sherwood, New York, Harper, 1948.

[14] See *Years of Trial and Hope* by Harry S Truman, Garden City, N. Y., Doubleday, 1956.

[15] The story of the Arab Liberation Army's arrival in Palestine was obtained from interviews with Fawzi el-Kaoukji, Sir Alec Kirkbride, General McMillan, Glubb Pasha, and Abdullah Tel; and from Tel's *The Tragedy of Palestine,* Cairo, Dar al Kalam, 1959 (Arabic).

CHAPTER III

[1] See *The Forrestal Diaries,* Walter Millis (ed.), New York, Viking, 1951.

[2] From the papers of Clark Clifford, who was kind enough to let me go through his White House files on Palestine.

[3] From State Department sources and Eliahu Elath, who told me White House officials related this story to him.

[4] From Clark Clifford's papers.

[5] Diez de Medina emphasized this point in interview.

[6] See *A Soldier with the Arabs* by Sir John Glubb (Pasha), New York, Harper & Brothers, 1957.

[7] See *Seven Fallen Pillars* by Jon Kimche, New York, Praeger, 1953.

[8] From interview with Joseph Linton.

[9] See *Years of Trial and Hope* by Harry S Truman.

[10] See *In the Cause of Peace* by Trygve Lie, New York, Macmillan, 1954.

[11] See *We Need Not Fail* by Sumner Welles, Boston, Houghton Mifflin, 1948.

[12] See *In the Cause of Peace.*

CHAPTER IV

[1] Details related in Robert St. John's *Ben Gurion: The Biography of an Extraordinary Man,* Garden City, N.Y., Doubleday, 1959.

[2] See *Orde Wingate* by Christopher Sykes, London, Collins, 1959; also *Gideon Goes to War* by Leonard Mosley, London, A. Barker, 1955.

[3] From interview with Julius Jarche.

[4] Details of Al Schwimmer's activities were learned from interviews with Schwimmer himself and with Nahum Bernstein; also from Benjamin Kagan's *The Secret Battle for Israel,* New York and Cleveland, World Publishing, 1966.

[5] See *Where I Stand* by Herman Milton (Hank) Greenspun, New York, McKay, 1966.

[6] See *Haganah* by Munya Mardor, New York, New American Library, 1966.

[7] From interview with Ehud Avriel.

[8] The story of the *Lino* was obtained from interviews with Ada Sereni and from Munya Mardor's *Haganah.*

[9] Details in *The Tragedy of Palestine* by Aref el-Aref, Beirut (Arabic) (not to be confused with Abdullah Tel's book of the same name). Information was also obtained from interviews with aides of Abd el-Kader el-Husseini.

[10] Sir Henry Gurney's unpublished diary was made available to the author by Dr. Elizabeth Monroe of Oxford University.

CHAPTER V

[1]See *À Jerusalem un drapeau flottait sur la ligne de feu* by Jacques de Reynier, Geneva, Histoire et Société d'Aujourd'hui, 1950.

[2] See Glubb's *A Soldier with the Arabs.*

[3] The story of Deir Yassin is reconstructed mainly from interviews with Arab survivors and the following Israelis: Menache Eichler, Ezra Elnakam, Nathan Friedman-Yellin, David Gottlieb, Yehuda Lapidot, Mordechai Raanan, Yeshurun Schiff, David Shaltiel, Israel Sheib, and Yehoshua Zetler.

[4] For Arab view of the flight of refugees from Haifa, see the article "The Fall of Haifa" by Walid Khalidi in *Middle East Forum,* Beirut (December, 1959). For a view supporting the Israeli contentions, see *A Clash of Destinies* by Jon and David Kimche, New York, Praeger, 1960.

[5] See *Memoirs* by Bernard Law Montgomery, New York and Cleveland, World Publishing, 1958.

[6] See *Aliyah: The Peoples of Israel* by Howard M. Sachar, New York and Cleveland, World Publishing, 1961.

[7] For details of the efforts by Safed's leaders to obtain help, see Aref's *The Tragedy of Palestine.*

[8] See Aref's *The Tragedy of Palestine.*

[9] From interviews with Amihai Faglin.

[10] See Aref's *The Tragedy of Palestine* for details of Jaffa's fall from the Arab point of view. Aref sharply criticizes the local Arab leaders for indulging in corrupt practices and terrorizing their own people in the chaos of battle and flight. For the Irgun view of the battle, see Begin's (Beigin) *The Revolt.* Much of the above material was obtained in interviews with Amihai Faglin and Menachem Beigin. Former Haganah leaders did not deny their contentions, though they were not eager to offer their own versions of the battle.

CHAPTER VI

[1] For a detailed account of conditions in the besieged New City, see Bernard (Dov) Joseph's *The Faithful City,* London, Hogarth, 1962.

[2] From interviews with Colonel Goldie and Haganah officers, and from an American diplomatic report in Clark Clifford's papers.

[3] From interviews with Golda Meir and Ezra Danin, and from *Three Days* by Zeev Sharef, London, W. H. Allen, 1962, and *Golda Meir: Woman with a Cause* by Marie Syrkin, New York, Putnam, 1961.

[4] From Clark Clifford's papers.

[5] For details of this meeting, see Moshe Sharett's *The Gates of the Nations* (*Beshar Haoumot*), Tel Aviv, Am Oved, 1958 (Hebrew), and Zeev Sharef's *Three Days.*

[6] From interview with Ben-Gurion.

[7] Details of this key White House conference were obtained from interviews with Clark Clifford and Robert McClintock, from Clifford's papers, and from *Man of Independence: A Biography of Harry S Truman* by Jonathan Daniels, Philadelphia, Lippincott, 1950.

[8] From interview with Clark Clifford.

[9] Much of the material in this book about Nasser is based on his memoirs of the war published in Cairo in newspapers and in a pamphlet, *The Truth About the Palestine War.* Also significant were interviews with former United Arab Republic Vice-President Zakaraya Muhieddin and with Yeroham Cohen, an Israeli officer (introduced later in this book) who got to know Nasser well

during informal truce talks. Several books were also useful: *Egypt's Liberation: The Philosophy of the Revolution* by Gamal Abdel Nasser, Washington, D.C., Public Affairs Press, 1955; *The Boss: The Story of Gamal Abdel Nasser* by Robert St. John, New York, McGraw-Hill, 1960; and *Nasser of Egypt: The Search for Dignity* by Wilton Wynn, Cambridge, Mass., Arlington Books, 1959.

[10] Material in this book on Aziz is based mainly on his diary and on articles written about him during the war by Mohammed Hassenin Heikal in the Cairo newspaper *Akhbar el Youm.*

[11] See Abdullah Tel's *The Tragedy of Palestine.*

[12] Lieutenant Effendi's monitored report on the attack is reproduced in *Siege in the Hills of Hebron,* edited by Dov Knohl, New York, Yoseloff, 1958. This books offers many day-to-day details of the fighting at the Etzion Bloc.

[13] Information about the struggle between Ben-Gurion and Galili was obtained in interviews with the two men, and with Yigal Yadin, Yigal Allon, and Yitzhak Gruenbaum. The Kimches' *A Clash of Destinies* was also helpful.

[14] Information about the events leading up to this decision was obtained from interviews with Ben-Gurion, Israel Galili, Golda Meir, and Yigal Yadin; from Ben-Gurion's diary; and from two books in particular: Michael Bar-Zohar's *The Armed Prophet,* London, A. Barker, 1967, and Zeev Sharef's *Three Days.*

[15] The British reporter was John Kimche, who quotes this remark by Ben-Gurion in his book *A Clash of Destinies.*

[16] Information about Washington's recognition of Israel was obtained from interviews with Clark Clifford and Eliahu Elath, from David B. Sachar's Harvard University doctoral thesis, *David K. Niles and U.S. Policy Toward Palestine,* and from Jonathan Daniels' *Man of Independence.*

[17] Material on this General Assembly meeting was obtained in interviews with a number of delegates, including John Ross and Raymond Hare of the American delegation, and Enrique Rodriquez Fabregat of the Uruguayan delegation; and from the Official Records of the 2nd Special Session of the (United Nations) General Assembly, Vol. 1, Plenary Meetings of the General Assembly, April 16–May 14, 1948; Summary Record of Meetings (Lake Success, N.Y.).

[18] David B. Sachar's thesis, *David K. Niles and U.S. Policy Toward Palestine.*

CHAPTER VII

[1] This meeting between Aziz and Heikal was reported by Heikal in the Cairo newspaper *Akhbar el Youm.*

CHAPTER IX

[1] See *A Village on the Jordan* by Joseph Baratz, Tel Aviv.

[2] See *Pioneers in Israel* by Shmuel Dayan, New York and Cleveland, World Publishing, 1961.

[3] See Howard M. Sachar's *Aliyah: The Peoples of Israel.*

CHAPTER X

[1] Based on interview with Chaim Herzog and information in *Mission in Palestine* by Pablo de Azcarate y Flores, Washington, D.C., Middle East Institute, 1966, and *Promise and Fulfilment* by Arthur Koestler, New York, Macmillan, 1949.

[2] From interviews with Ben-Gurion and Shaltiel.

[3] See Glubb's *A Soldier with the Arabs.*

[4] From interview with Azzam Pasha.

[5] From interview with Kaoukji.

[6] See Glubb's *A Soldier with the Arabs.*

[7] See Aref el-Aref's *The Tragedy of Palestine.*

[8] See Abdullah Tel's *The Tragedy of Palestine.*

[9] From interviews with Rousnak and Nathanson.

[10] For details of this meeting, see *Mission in Palestine* by Pablo de Azcarate y Flores.

[11] For a dramatic account of this attack on Jaffa Gate, see Daniel Spicehandler's *Let My Right Hand Wither,* New York, Beechhurst Press, 1950.

[12] Narkis gave me this version of the confrontation. Shaltiel said that he did not recall the details but that the meeting was stormy.

[13] Details of the surrender talks were obtained from interviews with Issar Nathanson, Moshe Rousnak, Shaul Tawil, Abdullah Tel, and Yehudit Weingarten. Also helpful were Dov Joseph's *The Faithful City;* Netanel Lorch's *The Edge of the Sword,* New York, Putnam, 1961; John Roy Carlson's *Cairo to Damascus,* New York, Knopf, 1951; and Pablo de Azcarate's *Mission in Palestine.*

CHAPTER XI

[1] Details of the Israeli conflict over strategy at Latrun emerged from interviews with Yigal Allon, Shimon Avidan, David Ben-Gurion, Yaacov Dori, Israel Galili, Zvi Gilat, Chaim Laskov, Yaacov Prulov, Shlomo Shamir, and Yigal Yadin. Also helpful were the Kimches' *A Clash of Destinies* and Israel Baer's *Battles of Latrun (Carvot Latrun)*, Tel Aviv, 1953 (Hebrew).

[2] From interviews with Rousan and other Arabs. See also Rousan's book, *Battles of Bab el-Wad,* Amman (Arabic).

[3] Several Arab Legion officers told me they were ordered to the Jordan side of Allenby Bridge for the duration of Bevin's speech. When it was over, they were ordered back into Palestine.

[4] This is Raanan's version of what happened at the meeting of the three men. Shaltiel does not deny these details, but says that he doesn't recall them.

[5] See Howard M. Sachar's *Aliyah: The Peoples of Israel.*

[6] I was able to obtain access to the official investigation report from the Israeli military archives only after the greatest difficulty. The report has never been made public or been seen before by anyone except top military officials and some persons directly involved. For a colorful story of Marcus's life, see *Cast a Giant Shadow* by Ted Berkman, Garden City, N.Y., Doubleday, 1962.

CHAPTER XII

[1] From Clark Clifford's papers.

[2] For Bernadotte's view of his role in the Himmler talks, see his book *The Curtain Falls,* New York, Knopf, 1945. For a less friendly view, see *Bernadotte* by Baruch Nadel, Tel Aviv, 1968 (Hebrew). (Nadel was a member of the Stern Group.) The Bernadotte role is also discussed in *The Last Days of Hitler* by H. R. Trevor-Roper, New York, Macmillan, 1947.

[3] See Glubb's *A Soldier with the Arabs.*

⁴ From interview with Raanan.
⁵ From interview with Faglin.
⁶ From interview with Kelman.
⁷ See Sheib's *The First Tithe (Masser Rishon).*

⁸ Information on the *Altalena* incident was obtained from interviews with Yigal Allon, Samuel Ariel, Menachem Begin, David Ben-Gurion, Mulah Cohen, Amihai Faglin, Richard Fallon, Monroe and Malka (Topsy) Fein, Israel Galili, Shmuel Katz, Moshe Kelman, Zvi Kraushar, Yaacov Meridor, Sam Merlin, and Israel Sheib. Source books include Eliahu Lankin's *The Story of the Commander of the Altalena (Sipuru shel Mefaked Altalena),* Tel Aviv, Herut, 1954 (Hebrew); Begin's *The Revolt;* Samuel Katz's *Days of Fire,* Garden City, N. Y., Doubleday, 1968; Sheib's *The First Tithe;* Allon's *Battles of the Palmach,* Tel Aviv, Hakibbutz Hameochad, 1965, (Hebrew); and Arthur Koestler's *Promise and Fulfilment.*
⁹ See Greenspun's *Where I Stand.*
¹⁰ See *To Jerusalem* by Folke Bernadotte, London, Hodder, 1951.

CHAPTER XIII

¹ See Naphtalie Lau-Lavie's *Moshe Dayan,* London, Vallentine Mitchell, 1968.
² All scenes involving Simon Garfeh were described by him in an interview. Israelis interviewed did not contradict his remarks.
³ See *Egypt's Destiny* by Mohammed Neguib, London, Gollancz, 1955.
⁴ From interview with David Shaltiel.
⁵ The existence of this plan was revealed to me by several Sternist leaders.

CHAPTER XIV

¹ See Bernadotte's *To Jerusalem* and Bernard (Dov) Joseph's *The Faithful City.*
² From interview with Ada Sereni and from Munya Mardor's *Haganah.*
³ See *A Crackle of Thorns* by Sir Alec Kirkbride, London, Murray, 1956.
⁴ From interview with Robert McClintock.
⁵ See Gerold Frank's *The Deed.*
⁶ See *My Mission to Israel* by James G. McDonald, New York, Simon and Schuster, 1951.
⁷ See Bernadotte's *To Jerusalem.* The epilogue deals with his assassination.
⁸ See Baruch Nadel's *Bernadotte.*
⁹ From interview with Yehoshua Zetler.
¹⁰ See Arthur Koestler's *Promise and Fulfilment* and Kenneth W. Bilby's *New Star in the Near East,* Garden City, N. Y., Doubleday, 1950.
¹¹ The story of Weizmann's return to Israel is based on material from Mardor's *Haganah;* Weizmann's *Trial and Error,* New York, Harper, 1949; Vera Weizmann's *The Impossible Takes Longer,* New York, Harper, 1967; and Schmuel Shihor's *Hollow Glory,* New York, Yoseloff, 1960.

CHAPTER XV

¹ From Clark Clifford's papers.
² Details of this meeting were obtained from interview with Yeroham Cohen and from his book *By Daylight and in Darkness (Leor Ubamachshach),* Tel Aviv, Maarachot, 1969 (Hebrew).

[3] From interviews with Yigal Allon and Yeroham Cohen.

[4] From separate interviews with Hamdi Hirzallah and the brother of Abdullah Khatib. Israelis who were in Beersheba at the time did not recall the particular episodes described here, but said they were possible since some members of the Commando Company felt they had a right "to do to the Arabs what they would have done to us." Dov Segall says he threatened to shoot one of his own men for acting on this basis.

[5] See Aref's *The Tragedy of Palestine.*

[6] See Glubb's *A Soldier with the Arabs.*

[7] For an excellent account of the 1929 massacre, see D. V. Duff's *Sword for Hire,* London, J. Murray, 1934.

[8] See King Abdullah's (Abd Allah Ibn Husain) *My Memoirs Completed* (*al-Takmilah*), Washington, D.C., American Council of Learned Societies, 1954.

CHAPTER XVI

[1] From interview with Wasfi Tel.

[2] From interviews with Moshe Carmel and Mordechai Makleff.

[3] From Taha's diary and Nasser's *Egypt's Liberation: The Philosophy of the Revolution.*

[4] From interviews with Yeroham Cohen and Arab officers.

[5] From interviews with Yigal Allon and Yeroham Cohen.

[6] The Egyptian messages quoted were intercepted by the Israelis.

[7] From Clark Clifford's papers.

[8] From interview with General Fuad Sadek.

[9] This remark was overheard by John Kimche (*A Clash of Destinies*).

CHAPTER XVII

[1] See Abdullah Tel's *The Tragedy of Palestine.*

[2] See Sir Alec Kirkbride's *A Crackle of Thorns.*

[3] See *Memoirs of King Abdullah of Transjordan,* ed. Philip P. Graves, London, Cape, 1950.

[4] For the full story of Teddy Eytan's experiences in the 1948 war, see his book *Neguev: l'héroique naissance de l'état d'Israël,* Geneva, Éditions de la Bacconière, 1950 (French).

[5] See *The Moslem Brotherhood in the Palestine War* by Kamal Ismail Sharif, Cairo, Wahba (Arabic).

[6] See McDonald's *My Mission to Israel* and Michael Bar-Zohar's *The Armed Prophet.*

[7] Mainly from interview with Yigal Allon. Ben-Gurion offered a few details, which did not seem to contradict Allon's version.

[8] Mainly from interview with Allon, with contribution from Ben-Gurion.

CHAPTER XVIII

[1] From Taha's diary and Cairo newspaper articles on Taha when he returned home. Though he was welcomed as a hero, the Egyptian High Command apparently mistrusted him, assigning him to a relatively minor post. When

Taha died in 1952, Yigal Allon cabled condolences to his wife but did not receive a reply.

[2] From interviews with Glubb and Bromage, and from Glubb's *A Soldier with the Arabs.*

[3] Information on the armistice talks between Israel and Jordan was obtained from interviews with Eliahu Sasson, Abdullah Tel, and Yigal Yadin, and from Abdullah Tel's *The Tragedy of Palestine* and Walter Eytan's *The First Ten Years,* New York, Simon and Schuster, 1958. Israeli newspaper interviews with Yadin and Sasson were also helpful.

[4] Information on the armistice talks between Israel on the one hand and Lebanon and Syria on the other was obtained from an interview with Mordechai Makleff and from the books of Tel and Eytan.

Bibliography

In researching this book, the author consulted more than 500 books, newspapers, periodicals, pamphlets, diaries, and documents. The most important are listed below.

BOOKS

ABD ALLAH IBN HUSAIN (King Abdullah), *My Memoirs Completed* (*al-Takmilah*), Washington, D.C., American Council of Learned Societies, 1954. *See also* Graves, Philip P. (ed.).

ADIN (Edelman), BENJAMIN, *Adventure at the Wheel,* Jerusalem, Alfa Jerusalem Press, 1965.

AGAR, HERBERT, *The Saving Remnant,* New York, Viking, 1960.

ALLON, YIGAL, *Battles of the Palmach,* Tel Aviv, Hakibbutz Hameuchad, 1965 (Hebrew).

AMINA, N. (ed.), *At the Gates of Gaza* (*Be Shaarey Aza*), Tel Aviv, Hakibbutz Hadati, 1949 (Hebrew).

AMRAMI, YAAKOV, *History of the War of Independence* (*Toldot Milchemet Hakomemeut*), Tel Aviv, Shelach, 1951 (Hebrew).

ANTONIUS, GEORGE, *The Arab Awakening,* Philadelphia, Lippincott, 1939.

AREF, AREF EL-, *The Tragedy of Palestine,* 7 vols., Beirut (Arabic).

ATTLEE, EARL, *As It Happened* (autobiography), London, Heinemann, 1954.

AVINOAM, REUBEN, *Leaves of Fire,* 3 vols., Jerusalem, 1952–61 (Hebrew).

————, *The Nation Remembers* (*Misrad Habitachon*), Tel Aviv, 1954 (Hebrew).

AVNERY, URI, *Fields of Palestine* (*Bisdot Pleshet*), Tel Aviv, Tversky, 1950 (Hebrew).

AZCARATE Y FLORES, PABLO DE, *Mission in Palestine,* Washington, D.C., Middle East Institute, 1966.

BAER, ISRAEL, *Battles of Latrun* (*Carvot Latrun*), Tel Aviv, Maarachot, 1953 (Hebrew).

BARATZ, JOSEPH, *A Village on the Jordan*, Tel Aviv, Ichud Habonim.

BARODI, FAKHRI, *The Catastrophe of Palestine*, Damascus, Ibn Zaidon, 1950 (Arabic).

BAR-ZOHAR, MICHAEL, *The Armed Prophet*, London, A. Barker, 1967.

BAUER, YEHUDA, *Scripta Hicrosolymitana*, Vol. 7, Jerusalem, Publications of the Hebrew University of Jerusalem, 1961.

BEGIN, MENAHEM (Beigin, Menachem), *The Revolt: Story of the Irgun*, Tel Aviv, Hadar, 1964.

BELL, J. B., *Besieged: Seven Cities Under Siege*, Philadelphia, Chilton, 1966.

BEMIS, SAMUEL FLAGG, *The American Secretaries of State and Their Diplomacy*, New York, Pageant Book Co., 1958.

BEN-GURION, DAVID, *Israel: Years of Challenge*, New York, Holt, 1963.

BEN-JACOB, JEREMIAH, *The Rise of Israel*, New York, Grosby House, 1949.

BEN SHAUL, MOSHE (ed.), *Generals of Israel*, Tel Aviv, Hadar, 1968.

BENTWICH, NORMAN, *Israel*, London, Benn, 1952.

————, *Judah L. Magnes*, London, Horovitz, 1955.

BERKMAN, TED, *Cast a Giant Shadow*, Garden City, N.Y., Doubleday, 1962.

BERLIN, ISAIAH, *Chaim Weizmann*, New York, Farrar, Straus & Cudahy, 1958.

BERNADOTTE, FOLKE, *The Curtain Falls*, New York, Knopf, 1945.

————, *To Jerusalem*, London, Hodder, 1951.

BETCHY, MOHAMMED AL, *Our Martyrs in Palestine*, Cairo, 1949 (Arabic).

BILBY, KENNETH W., *New Star in the Near East*, Garden City, N.Y., Doubleday, 1950.

BIRDWOOD, CHRISTOPHER B., *Nuri as-Said: A Study in Arab Leadership*, London, Cassell, 1959.

BROOK, DAVID, *Preface to Peace*, Washington, D.C., Public Affairs Press, 1964.

BULLOCK, ALAN, *The Life and Times of Ernest Bevin*, London, Heinemann, 1960.

BURROWS, MILLAR, *Palestine Is Our Business*, Philadelphia, The Westminster Press, 1949.

CARLSON, JOHN ROY (Arthur Derounian), *Cairo to Damascus*, New York, Knopf, 1951.

CARMEL, MOSHE, *The Campaigns in the North* (*Maarachot Zafon*), Israel, Ein Harod, 1949 (Hebrew).

CASPER, BERNARD M., *With the Jewish Brigade*, London, Goldstone, 1947.

CELLER, EMANUEL, *You Never Leave Brooklyn*, New York, Day, 1953.

CHURCHILL, WINSTON, *The Sinews of Peace* (postwar speeches), London, Cassell, 1948.

————, *Their Finest Hour*, Boston, Houghton Mifflin, 1949.

COHEN, ISRAEL, *The Zionist Movement*, London, Muller, 1945.

COHEN, YEROHAM, *By Daylight and in Darkness* (*Leor Ubamachshach*), Tel Aviv, Maarachot, 1969 (Hebrew).

CROSSMAN, R. H. S., *A Nation Reborn*, London, H. Hamilton, 1960.

————, *Palestine Mission*, New York and London, Harper & Brothers, 1947.

CRUM, BARTLEY, *Behind the Silken Curtain*, New York, Simon and Schuster, 1947.

DANIELS, JONATHAN, *Man of Independence: A Biography of Harry S Truman*, Philadelphia, Lippincott, 1950.

DAYAN, SHMUEL, *Pioneers in Israel*, New York and Cleveland, World Publishing, 1961.

DIMONT, MAX, *Jews, God, and History,* New York, Simon and Schuster, 1962.

DUFF, D. V., *Sword for Hire,* London, J. Murray, 1934.

EDDY, WILLIAM ALFRED, *F.D.R. Meets Ibn Saud,* New York, American Friends of the Middle East, 1954.

EDELMAN, MAURICE, *David: The Story of Ben-Gurion,* New York, Putnam, 1965.

ELATH, ELIAHU, *Israel and Elath,* London, Weidenfeld, 1966.

ELSTON, ROY, *No Alternatives,* London, Hutchinson, 1960.

EYLON, AVRAHAM, *The Givati Brigade Opposite the Egyptian Invader (Hativat Givati Mul Hapoleish Ha-Mitzri),* Tel Aviv, Maarachot, 1963 (Hebrew).

————, *The Givati Brigate in the War of Independence (Hativat Givati Bemil-chemet Haatzmaut),* Tel Aviv, Maarachot, 1959 (Hebrew).

EYTAN, TEDDY, *Neguev: l'héroique naissance de l'état d'Israël,* Geneva, Éditions de la Bacconière, 1950 (French).

EYTAN, WALTER, *The First Ten Years,* New York, Simon and Schuster, 1958.

FARAG, SAYED, *Our Army in Palestine,* Cairo, Fawakol, 1949 (Arabic).

FRANK, GEROLD, *The Deed,* New York, Simon and Schuster, 1963.

GABBAY, RONY E., *A Political Study of the Arab-Jewish Conflict,* Geneva, Librairie E. Droz, 1959; Paris, Libraire Minard, 1959.

GARCÍA GRAÑADOS, JORGE, *The Birth of Israel,* New York, Knopf, 1948.

GERVASI, FRANK H., *To Whom Palestine?,* New York, Appleton-Century, 1946.

GLASS, ZRUBAVEL (ed.), *Book of the Palmach (Sefer Ha-Palmach),* 2 vols., Tel Aviv, Hakibbutz Hameuchad, 1953 (Hebrew).

GLICK, EDWARD B., *Latin America and the Palestine Problem,* New York, Theodor Herzl Foundation, 1958.

GLUBB, SIR JOHN BAGOT (Pasha), *Britain and the Arabs,* London, Hodder, 1959.

————, *A Soldier with the Arabs,* New York, Harper & Brothers, 1957.

————, *Story of the Arab Legion,* London, Hodder, 1948.

GRAVES, PHILIP P. (ed.), *Memoirs of King Abdullah of Transjordan,* London, Cape, 1950.

GRAVES, RICHARD MASSIE, *Experiment in Anarchy,* London, Gollancz, 1949.

GREENSPUN, HERMAN MILTON (Hank), *Where I Stand,* New York, McKay, 1966.

HAEZRAHI, YEHUDA, *The Living Rampart,* London, Zionist Youth Council, 1948.

HALPERN, BEN, *The Idea of the Jewish State,* Cambridge, Mass., Harvard University Press, 1961.

HARIRI, SALEH AL, *The Saudi Army in Palestine,* Cairo, Dar al Ketab, 1950 (Arabic).

HASHEMI, TAHA, *Diary of the War,* Beirut (Arabic).

HECHT, BEN, *Perfidy,* New York, Messner, 1961.

————, *A Child of the Century,* New York, Simon and Schuster, 1954.

HOROWITZ, DAVID, *State in the Making,* New York, Knopf, 1953.

HUREWITZ, J. C., *The Struggle for Palestine,* New York, Norton, 1950.

HYAMSON, H. M., *Palestine Under the Mandate,* London, Methuen, 1950.

HYRKANOS-GINZBURG, DEVORA, *Jerusalem War Diary,* Jerusalem, Wizo Zionist Education Dept., 1950.

JACOBOVITZ, MORDECHAI, *Heroes Tell Their Stories: Chapters on the War of Independence,* Tel Aviv, Niv (Hebrew).

JARVIS, CLAUDE, *Three Deserts,* London, J. Murray, 1936.

JOSEPH, BERNARD (Dov), *The Faithful City,* London, Hogarth, 1962.

JOSEPHUS, *The Jewish War,* Baltimore, Penguin, 1959.

KAGAN, BENJAMIN, *The Secret Battle for Israel,* New York and Cleveland, World Publishing, 1966.

KATZ, SAMUEL, *Days of Fire,* Garden City, N.Y., Doubleday, 1968.

KHATIB, MOHAMMED NEMR AL, *The Result of the Catastrophe,* Damascus, Matba Umomeya, 1951 (Arabic).

KIMCHE, JON, *Seven Fallen Pillars,* New York, Praeger, 1953.

KIMCHE, JON and DAVID, *A Clash of Destinies,* New York, Praeger, 1960.

————, *The Secret Roads,* London, Secker, 1954.

KIRK, GEORGE, *A Short History of the Middle East,* London, Methuen, 1961.

————, *Survey of International Affairs: 1939–46: The Middle East in the War,* London, New York, Oxford University Press, 1952.

————, *Survey of International Affairs: The Middle East 1945–50,* London, New York, Oxford University Press, 1954.

KIRKBRIDE, SIR ALEC, *A Crackle of Thorns,* London, J. Murray, 1956.

KNOHL, DOV (ed.), *Siege in the Hills of Hebron,* New York, Yoseloff, 1958.

KOESTLER, ARTHUR, *Promise and Fulfilment,* New York, Macmillan, 1949.

KURZMAN, DAN, *Subversion of the Innocents,* New York, Random House, 1963.

LANKIN, ELIAHU, *The Story of the Commander of the Altalena (Sipuru shel Mefaked Altalena),* Tel Aviv, Herut, 1954 (Hebrew).

LARKIN, MARGARET, *The Six Days of Yad Mordechai,* Tel Aviv, Maarachot, 1965.

LAU-LAVIE, NAPHTALIE, *Moshe Dayan,* London, Vallentine Mitchell, 1968.

LAWRENCE, THOMAS EDWARD, *Seven Pillars of Wisdom,* Garden City, N.Y., Doubleday, 1935.

LAZAR, HAYIM, *Acre Citadel (Mibzar Ako),* Tel Aviv, Shelach, 1953 (Hebrew).

LEVER, WALTER, *Jerusalem Is Called Liberty,* Jerusalem, Massadah Publication Co., 1951.

LEVIN, HARRY, *I Saw the Battle of Jerusalem,* New York, Schocken Books, 1950.

LIAS, GODFREY, *Glubb's Legion,* London, Evans, 1956.

LIDDELL HART, BASIL HENRY, *Strategy: The Indirect Approach,* London, Faber, 1954.

LIE, TRYGVE, *In the Cause of Peace,* New York, Macmillan, 1954.

LILIENTHAL, ALFRED M., *What Price Israel?,* Chicago, Regnery, 1953.

LIRON, AARON, *Old Jerusalem: Under Siege and in Battle (Yerushalayim Haatika Bematzor Be-Bakrav),* Tel Aviv, Maarachot, 1957 (Hebrew).

LITVINOFF, BARNET, *The Story of David Ben-Gurion,* New York, Oceana Publications, 1959.

LORCH, NETANEL, *The Edge of the Sword,* New York, Putnam, 1961.

LOWDERMILK, WALTER C., *Palestine Land of Promise,* New York and London, Harper & Brothers, 1944.

————, *The Untried Approach to the Palestine Problem,* New York, American Christian Palestine Committee Publications, 1948.

LUKAN, KADRI, *After the Catastrophe,* Beirut, Dar el Elm, 1950 (Arabic).

MANUEL, FRANK E., *The Realities of American-Palestine Relations,* Washington, D.C., Public Affairs Press, 1949.

MARDOR, MUNYA (Meir), *Haganah,* New York, New American Library, 1966.

MARLOWE, JOHN, *Rebellion in Palestine,* London, Cresset Press, 1946.

————, *The Seat of Pilate,* London, Cresset Press, 1959.

MCDONALD, JAMES G., *My Mission in Israel,* New York, Simon and Schuster, 1951.

MEINERTZHAGEN, RICHARD, *Middle East Diary,* London, Cresset Press, 1959.

MILLIS, WALTER, in collaboration with E. S. Duffield (ed.), *The Forrestal Diaries,* New York, Viking, 1951.

MONROE, ELIZABETH, *Britain's Moment in the Middle East, 1914–1956,* London, Chatto, 1963.

MONTGOMERY, BERNARD LAW, *Memoirs,* New York and Cleveland, World Publishing, 1958.

MOSLEY, LEONARD, *The Cat and the Mice,* London, A. Barker, 1958.

———, *Gideon Goes to War,* London, A. Barker, 1955.

NADEL, BARUCH, *Bernadotte,* Tel Aviv, 1968 (Hebrew).

NASSER, GAMAL ABDEL, *Egypt's Liberation: The Philosophy of the Revolution,* Washington, D.C., Public Affairs Press, 1955.

NEGUIB, MOHAMMED, *Egypt's Destiny,* London, Gollancz, 1955.

NOFAL, SAYED, *Ben-Gurion's Version of History,* Cairo, Arab League, 1962.

O'BALLANCE, EDGAR, *The Arab-Israeli War, 1948,* London, Faber, 1956.

PARKES, J. W., *A History of Palestine from 135 A.D. to Modern Times,* London, Gollancz, 1949.

PEARLMAN, MAURICE, *The Army of Israel,* New York, Philosophical Library, 1950.

———, *Mufti of Jerusalem,* London, Gollancz, 1947.

PERETZ, DON, *Israel and the Palestine Arabs,* Washington, D.C., Middle East Institute, 1958.

PHILBY, HARRY ST. JOHN BRIDGER, *Arabian Jubilee,* New York, Day, 1953.

POLK, WILLIAM R., DAVID M. STAMLER, and EDMUND ASFOUR, *Backdrop to Tragedy,* Boston, Beacon Press, 1957.

RABINOWICZ, OSKAR K., *Vladimir Jabotinsky's Conception of a Nation.* New York, Beechhurst Press, 1946.

———, *Fifty Years of Zionism,* London, Anscombe, 1952.

REYNIER, JACQUES DE, *À Jérusalem un drapeau flottait sur la ligne de feu,* Geneva, Histoire et Société d'Aujourd'hui, 1950 (French).

REYNOLDS, QUENTIN, *Leave It to the People,* New York, Random House, 1949.

RIBALOW, HAROLD (ed.), *Fighting Heroes of Israel,* New York, New American Library, 1967.

RIVLIN, GERSHON (ed.), *The Alexandroni Brigade in the War of Independence (Hatavet Alexandroni Be-Milchemet Hakomemeut),* Tel Aviv, Maarachot, 1964 (Hebrew).

ROOSEVELT, ELEANOR, and WILLIAM DE WITT, *U.N.: Today and Tomorrow,* New York, Harper & Brothers, 1953.

ROOSEVELT, KERMIT, *Arabs, Oil, and History,* New York, Harper & Brothers, 1949.

ROUSAN, MAHMOUD AL, *Battles of Bab el-Wad,* Amman (Arabic).

SACHAR, HOWARD M., *Aliyah: The Peoples of Israel,* New York and Cleveland, World Publishing, 1961.

———, *From the Ends of the Earth: The Peoples of Israel,* New York and Cleveland, World Publishing, 1964.

SACHER, HARRY, *Israel: The Establishment of a State,* London, Weidenfeld, 1952.

SADAT, ANWAR EL, *Revolt on the Nile,* London, Wingate, 1957.

ST. JOHN, ROBERT, *Ben-Gurion: The Biography of an Extraordinary Man,* Garden City, N.Y., Doubleday, 1959.

———, *The Boss: The Story of Gamal Abdel Nasser,* New York, McGraw-Hill, 1960.

———, *Shalom Means Peace,* Garden City, N.Y., Doubleday, 1949.

SCHECHTMAN, JOSEPH B., *The Mufti and the Fuehrer,* New York, Yoseloff, 1965.

SCHWARTZ, LEO WALDER, *The Redeemers,* New York, Farrar, Straus & Young, 1953.

SHAHAN, AVIGDOR, *The Wings of Victory (Kanfer Hanizachon),* Tel Aviv, Am Hasafer, 1966 (Hebrew).

SHAREF, ZEEV, *Three Days,* London, W. H. Allen, 1962.

SHARETT, MOSHE, *The Gates of the Nations (Beshar Haoumot),* Tel Aviv, Am Oved, 1958 (Hebrew).

SHARIF, KAMAL ISMAIL, *The Moslem Brotherhood in the Palestine War,* Cairo, Wahba (Arabic).

SHEIB, ISRAEL, *The First Tithe (Maaser Rishon),* Tel Aviv, Hamatmid (Hebrew).

SHERWOOD, ROBERT, *Roosevelt and Hopkins,* New York, Harper & Brothers, 1948.

SHIHOR, SCHMUEL, *Hollow Glory,* New York, Yoseloff, 1960.

SHWADRAN, BENJAMIN, *Jordan, A State of Tension,* New York, Council for Middle Eastern Affairs Press, 1959.

————, *The Middle East, Oil, and the Great Powers,* New York, Council for Middle Eastern Affairs Press, 1959.

SPICEHANDLER, DANIEL, *Let My Right Hand Wither,* New York, Beechhurst Press, 1950.

STARK, FREYA, *Dust in the Lion's Paw,* London, J. Murray, 1961.

STEIN, LEONARD, *The Balfour Declaration,* London, Vallentine Mitchell, 1961.

STEINBERG, ALFRED, *The Man from Missouri,* New York, Putnam, 1962.

STONE, ISIDOR, *This Is Israel,* New York, Boni, 1948.

STORRS, SIR RONALD, *Lawrence of Arabia; Zionism and Palestine,* Middlesex and New York, Penguin Books, 1943.

SYKES, CHRISTOPHER, *Crossroads to Israel,* New York and Cleveland, World Publishing, 1965.

————, *Orde Wingate,* London, Collins, 1959.

SYRKIN, MARIE, *Blessed Is the Match,* Philadelphia, Jewish Publication Society of America, 1947.

————, *Golda Meir: Woman with a Cause,* New York, Putnam, 1961.

TALMAI, EPHRAIM, *Book of the Negev (Safer Hanegev),* Tel Aviv, Amihai, 1953 (Hebrew).

————, *Israel in Battle (Israel Be-Maareicha),* Tel Aviv, Amihai, 1952 (Hebrew).

TALMAI, MENAHEM, *Convoys Under Fire (Shayarot Baesh),* Tel Aviv, Amihai, 1957 (Hebrew).

TANAI, SHLOMO, *Three Arrows and a Spade (Shlosha Chezim Ve'et),* Tel Aviv, Gadish, 1955 (Hebrew).

TEL, ABDULLAH, *The Tragedy of Palestine,* Cairo, Dar al Kalam, 1959 (Arabic).

TREVOR, DAPHNE, *Under the White Paper,* Jerusalem, The Jerusalem Press, 1948.

TREVOR-ROPER, H. R., *The Last Days of Hitler,* New York, Macmillan, 1947.

TRUMAN, HARRY S, *Years of Trial and Hope,* Vol. 2: *Memoirs,* Garden City, N.Y., Doubleday, 1956.

VAZE, PINHAS, *Objective: To Acquire Arms (Ha-Mesima: Rechesh),* Tel Aviv, Maarachot, 1966 (Hebrew).

VESTER, BERTHA, *Our Jerusalem,* Garden City, N.Y., Doubleday, 1950.

VILNOY, ZEV, *The Battle to Liberate Israel (Hamaaracha Leshichrur Israel),* Jerusalem, Tor-Israel, 1953 (Hebrew).

WEISGAL, MEYER W., and JOEL CARMICHAEL (eds.), *Chaim Weizmann: A Biography by Several Hands,* New York, Atheneum, 1963.

WEIZMANN, CHAIM, *Trial and Error,* New York, Harper & Brothers, 1949.

WEIZMANN, VERA, *The Impossible Takes Longer,* New York, Harper, 1967.

WELLES, SUMNER, *We Need Not Fail,* Boston, Houghton Mifflin, 1948.

WILLIAMS, FRANCIS, *Ernest Bevin: Portrait of a Great Englishman,* London, Hutchinson, 1952.

———, *A Prime Minister Remembers,* London, Heinemann, 1961.

WILSON, R. D., *Cordon and Search,* Aldershot, England, Gale and Polden, 1949.

WISCHNITZER, MARK, *To Dwell in Safety,* Philadelphia, Jewish Publications Society of America, 1948.

WYNN, WILTON, *Nasser of Egypt: The Search for Dignity,* Cambridge, Mass., Arlington Books, 1959.

YARDENI, GALIA, *The First in Battle (Rishonim Lakrov),* Tel Aviv, Hakibbutz Hameuchad, 1967 (Hebrew).

ZASLOFF, JOSEPH JEREMIAH, *Great Britain and Palestine,* Geneva, Librairie E. Droz, 1952.

ZEINE, Z. N., *The Struggle for Arab Independence,* Beirut, 1960.

ZURAYK, CONSTANTINE R., *The Meaning of the Disaster,* Beirut, 1956.

The following are additional source books in Hebrew. Names of authors and, in some cases, names of publishers and dates of publication were often unavailable. Most of these books were published only for distribution to members of the settlement concerned.

Battles of 1948: 23 Stories of the War of Independence (Maarachot 1948: Sipurim Me-Milchemet Hakomemeut), Tel Aviv, Maarachot, 1955.

Day of Gesher (Yom shel Gesher), Kibbutz Gesher, Israel, 1958.

History of the War of Independence (Toldot Milchemet Hakomemeut), Tel Aviv, Maarachot, 1959.

In the Eyes of the Enemy (Be-Einay ha-Oyev), Tel Aviv, Maarachot, 1954.

In Front of the Gate: Degania B in Battle (Bishaar Degania B Bikravot), Degania B, 1949.

Misgav, Zionist Organization Religious Section, Jerusalem, 1950.

Mishmar Haemek, Tel Aviv, Sifriat Hapoalim, Shomer Hatzair, 1950.

Mishmar Hayarden, Tel Aviv.

Negba, Tel Aviv.

Nitzanim, Tel Aviv.

Shulamit, Tel Aviv, 1961.

PAMPHLETS, DOCUMENTS, AND SPEECHES

Abba Hillel Silver, Moshe Shertok (Sharett), Chaim Weizmann before the United Nations, October, 1947, New York; American Zionist Emergency Council, 1947.

Arab Higher Committee, The Great Betrayal in the United Nations (memorandum to the United Nations delegations), New York, 1948.

"The Arab Higher Committee, Its Origins, Personnel, and Purposes"—*Nation Associates* (May, 1947).

A Collection of Official Documents Relating to Palestine Question, 1917–1947, submitted to the General Assembly, U.N., by delegation of Arab Higher Committee, New York, 1947.

David K. Niles and U. S. Policy Toward Palestine, unpublished thesis by David B. Sachar, Harvard University, Cambridge, Mass.

Documents of German Foreign Policy, Series D, Vol. V, June 1937–March, 1939; Doc. 569, pp. 758–760, Department of State, Washington, D.C.

Iraq Parliamentary Investigation Committee Report on the Palestine War, Baghdad, 1948.

Iraq's Point of View on the Palestine Question, statement by M. Fadhel Jamali to UNSCOP, Washington, D.C., Arab Office, 1947.

Israel Before the Security Council, May 15–July 15, 1948; A Record of Fidelity to the U.N., New York, Israel Mission to the United Nations, 1948.

Israel and the United Nations, Carnegie Endowment for International Peace, New York, 1956.

The Jewish People and Palestine, a speech delivered by Chaim Weizmann before the Palestine Royal Commission in Jerusalem, November 25, 1936; London, Zionist Organization.

The Jewish Plan for Palestine, Jewish Agency for Palestine, Jerusalem, 1947.

"The Lesson of Palestine," *Middle East Journal,* Washington, D.C., October 2, 1949.

The Mandate for Palestine, memorandum submitted to Council of League of Nations by Zionist Organization, July, 1922; London, The Whitefriars Press, 1922.

Nazi-Soviet Relations, 1939–1941, documents from the archives of the German Foreign Office, Department of State, European and British Commonwealth, Series VI, "Department of State Publication 3023," ed. by Raymond James Sontag and James Stuart Beddie, Washington, D.C., Department of State.

Official Records of the 2nd Regular Session of the (United Nations) General Assembly, September 6–November 29, 1947.

Official Records of the 2nd Special Session of the (United Nations) General Assembly, Vol. 1, Plenary Meetings of the General Assembly, April 16–May 14, 1948.

Official Records of the United Nations Security Council—253rd, 254th, 255th, and 258th meetings, February and March, 1948.

The Palestine Arab Case, a statement by the Arab Higher Committee, April, 1947; Cairo, Costa Tsoumas.

Palestine in the UNO by Sir Muhammad Zafrulla Khan, Karachi, Pakistan Institute of International Affairs, 1948.

A Palestine Solution, speech delivered at the U.N. General Assembly, Flushing Meadows, New York, May 14, 1947, by Andrei A. Gromyko, New York; Morning Freiheit Assn., 1947.

Palestine: Termination of the Mandate 15th May, 1948, London, H.M.S.O., 1948.

The Political History of Palestine Under British Administration, reprinted by British Information Services, New York, 1947.

Report from Arab Delegation in Haifa to Arab Higher Committee in Damascus, Haifa, April 30, 1948.

Report to the General Assembly by the UNSCOP, Geneva, August 31, 1947; London, H.M.S.O., 1947.

The Truth About the Palestine War (memoirs of the 1948 war) by Gamal Ab-
    del Nasser, Cairo (pamphlet).

NEWSPAPERS AND PERIODICALS, ETC.

American: *Christian Science Monitor, Middle East Journal, Nation Associates,*
    New York *Herald-Tribune, New York Times*
British: *Jewish Observer and Middle East Review, The Spectator, The Times;*
    also the BBC
Egyptian: *Akhbar el Youm, Akher Saa, Al Ahram, Rose el Yussef*
Israeli: *Al Youm, Davar, Haboker, Maarachot, Maariv, Palestine Post* (now
    Jerusalem Post), *Yidyot Achronot;* also Kol Israel (Voice of Israel—radio)
Jordanian: *Al-Dafa, Falestin, Palestine News*
Lebanese: *Daily Star, Hayat, Middle East Forum, Mukarrir Supplement*

DIARIES

Colonel Ahmed Abdel Aziz (Egypt)
Major Salah Badr (Egypt)
Prime Minister David Ben-Gurion
Sir Henry Gurney (deputy to British High Commissioner)
Haj Amin el-Husseini (Grand Mufti)
Brigadier Sayed Taha (Egypt)

PAPERS AND CORRESPONDENCE

Clark Clifford (White House files on Palestine)
Abd el-Kader el-Husseini (papers found on his person when killed)
Dr. Elizabeth Monroe (research papers for Oxford University)
David Shaltiel (file of military correspondence)

LIBRARIES AND ARCHIVES USED

American University Library, Beirut
Arab Information Center, New York
Arab League Library, Cairo
Government Press Department Library, Tel Aviv
Israel Army Archives, Tel Aviv
Library of Congress, Washington, D.C.
Middle East Institute Library, Washington, D.C.
New York Public Library (including Jewish and Oriental sections), New
    York
Vladimir Jabotinsky Archives, Tel Aviv
Zionist Archives, New York and Jerusalem

Index

Arab Higher Committee, 4, 19, 35, 71, 72, 157, 715. *See also* Husseini, Haj Amin el-

Arab League, 58, 59, 70, 71, 137, 170, 206, 208, 222, 243, 262, 444, 448–49, 493–94 496, 506, 550, 551–52, 576, 608, 638. *See also* individual Arab countries

Arab Legion, 24, 32, 58, 60, 61, 90, 167, 170, 184, 205, 207, 208, 223–25, 234, 235, 247, 250, 262, 289, 294, 334, 348–49, 350, 354–58, *map* 359, 360–62, 365, 372, 382–83, 386–405 passim, *map* 408, 409, 411–16 passim, *map* 417, 420–21, 422, 425, 426, 430–31, 433, 436, 438, 451, 494, 508, 509, 510, 511, 514–15, 517–18, 520–21, 532, 533–34, 550–51, 606, 607, 608, 631–34, 638, 684, 692, 693, 696, 702, 703, 704, 708, 715. *See also* Glubb, John Bagot

Arab Liberation Army (ALA), 60, 61, 68, 69, 70, 144, 161, 166, 167, 170, 181, 183, 204, 243, 326, 330–31, 332, 355, 404, 405, 530–32, 610–11, 613–14. *See also* Kaoukji, Fawzi el-; military forces under individual countries

Aranha, Oswaldo, 19, 25

Arazi, Yehuda, 109, 110, 121, 488

Arce, José, 253, 255

Aref, Mohammed Abdel, 221–22, 528, 529, 595, 596, 609

Argiro (ship), 549–50

Argov, Nechemia, 118

Ariel, Samuel, 457, 458, 460, 461

Arielly, Nahum, 134–35

Arlosoroff, Chaim, 471–72

Ashdod, 295, 296, 298–99, 300, 308, 448, 576

Astrakan, Sonya, 197

Attieh, Haj Ismail, 141

Attieh, Mohammed, 141

Attlee, Clement, 5, 6, 7, 159–60, 635, 636. *See also* Great Britain

Austin, Warren, 84, 87, 97, 98, 99–100, 254

Avidan, Simon, 129, 295, 296–97, 298, 315, 418–19, 424, 590, 592–93, 597

Avidar, Yossef, 496

Avriel, Ehud, 118–20

Avrunin, Benjamin, 124, 127

Awad, Mahmoud Ibrahim, 597

Ayalon, Zvi, 496, 497

Aza. *See* Gaza

Azcarate, Pablo de, 343, 372, 395

Aziz, Ahmed Abd el-, 219–20, 222, 262, 264–65, 288–89, 291, 292–93, 294, 553–54

Azzam Pasha, Abdul Rahman, 8–9, 223, 354, 496, 636

Bab el-Wad, 200, 426, 434

Back, Arie, 298

Badr, Salah, 598, 619, 620–21

Baer, Israel, 334–35, 339

Bakry, Yassin el-, 144

Baleshnikov, Abraham, 333

Balfour, Arthur James, Earl of, 11

Balfour Declaration, 11–12, 14, 16, 31, 642

Barache, Emmanuel, 653–54

Baratz, Joseph, 320, 324

Barelko, Arie, 301, 303, 307

Bari, Abdel, 169–70, 171–72, 176, 181, 183, 185–86

Barkay, Naomi, 125

Bar-Lev, Chaim, 656

Baron, Moshe, 271

Barsky, Moshe, 322

Barzily, Moshe, 564, 565

Basok, Chaim, 586–87

Batar, 459

Bechhoeffer, Bernhard, 83–84

Bedouins, 208, 691

Beeley, Harold, 6, 9–10, 25, 636

Beerot Yitzhak, 528–29

Beersheba, 262, 288, 578, 592, 598–604, 609, 625, 632, 636, 648, 649, 655, 658, 662, 681

Beginsky, Moshe, 225–26, 232–33, 234

Begley, Col., 562, 563

Beigin, Menachem, 56, 173–77 passim, 182, 185, 345, 454–70 passim, 474–77, 482–85, 716

Beilin, Harry, 152

Beit Affa, 621

Beit Daras, 308–13 passim, 522

Beit Dejen, 478

Beit Eshel, 288–89, 598

Beit Gubrin, 578, 625, 631, 709–10

Beit Hanun, 580, 605, 606

Beit Jiz, 409, 414, 415, 426

Beit Nabala, 508, 510, 511, 515

Beit Netofa, Valley of, 611

Beit Nuba, 411

Beit Susin, 409, 413, 418, 419, 426–27, 428

Bek, Madlul Abbas, 67

Bek, Safr, 61

Belgium, 18

Belkind, Chanan, 319, 323–24

Bellows, Hank, 112

Ben-Ari, Mira, 301–02, 303, 305, 306

Ben-David, Moshe, 190, 198

Ben Dror, Morris, 670, 671, 673

Ben-Gal, Michael, 188, 474–75, 478

About the Author

Dan Kurzman, a former correspondent for *The Washington Post,* has reported from almost every country in Europe, Asia, the Middle East, Africa, and Latin America. He has covered more than two dozen wars, revolutions, and riots.

In 1960, his first book, *Kishi and Japan,* was described by the *New York Times* as "one of the most important biographies of the year" and by the *San Francisco Chronicle* as "probably the best book on the Japanese point of view yet written in English."

In 1963, Mr. Kurzman won the Overseas Press Club Award for the year's best book on foreign affairs, *Subversion of the Innocents,* a searching, country-by-country study of Communist strategy in the underdeveloped world.

In 1964, he won the Washington-Baltimore Newspaper Guild's Front Page Award for a series of articles he wrote for *The Washington Post* based on a visit to Cuba.

In 1965, he won Long Island University's George Polk Memoria Award for "insight, resourcefulness, and courage" in coverage of the Dominican revolution for the *Post.* His third book, *Santo Domingo: Revolt of the Damned,* was based on his articles.

In 1966, Boston University established a Dan Kurzman Collection to preserve his papers and correspondence in recognition of his "important contribution to twentieth-century journalism and historical literature."

Mr. Kurzman has served as a correspondent in Paris for the International News Service and in the Middle East for the National Broadcasting

About the Author

Dan Kurzman, a former foreign correspondent for *The Washington Post*, is the author of eleven books on current affairs and contemporary history, and the winner of five major literary and journalism awards. He won the George Polk Memorial Award for articles that formed the basis for his book *Santo Domingo: Revolt of the Damned*; the Overseas Press Club's Cornelius Ryan Award for the best book on foreign affairs for both *Miracle of November: Madrid's Epic Stand, 1936* and *Subversion of the Innocents*; the National Jewish Book Award for *Ben-Gurion: Prophet of Fire*; and the Newspaper Guild's Front Page Award for dispatches he wrote from Cuba.

    Mr. Kurzman has written or broadcast from almost every country in Europe, Asia, the Middle East, and Latin America. Before joining *The Washington Post*, he served as Paris correspondent for the International News Service, as Jerusalem correspondent for NBC News, and as Tokyo Bureau Chief for the McGraw-Hill News Service. He is a native of San Francisco.

Other DACAPO titles of interest